PUBLICATIONS OF THE NEW CHAUCER SOCIETY

THE NEW CHAUCER SOCIETY

President 2014–2016 SUSAN CRANE, Columbia University

Executive Director RUTH EVANS, Saint Louis University

Trustees 2012–2016 ARDIS BUTTERFIELD, Yale University
THOMAS HAHN, University of Rochester
LYNN STALEY, Colgate University
SARAH STANBURY, College of the Holy Cross

Trustees 2014–2018 CANDACE BARRINGTON, Central Connecticut State University
ALEXANDRA GILLESPIE, University of Toronto
DAVID MATTHEWS, University of Manchester

Editor, Studies in the Age of Chaucer SARAH SALIH, King's College London

Book Review Editor SHAYNE LEGASSIE, University of North Carolina at Chapel Hill

Editorial Assistant SOPHIA WILSON, King's College London

Advisory Board ALASTAIR MINNIS, Yale University
DAVID WALLACE, University of Pennsylvania
JOHN GANIM, University of California, Riverside
RICHARD FIRTH GREEN, Ohio State University
CAROLYN DINSHAW, New York University

Graduate Assistant JESSICA REZUNYK, Washington University

Bibliographer STEPHANIE AMSEL, University of Texas, San Antonio

Studies in the Age of Chaucer, the yearbook of The New Chaucer Society, is published annually. Each issue contains substantial articles on all aspects of Chaucer and his age, book reviews, and an annotated Chaucer bibliography. Manuscripts should follow the *Chicago Manual of Style*, 16th edition. Unsolicited reviews are not accepted. Authors receive twenty free offprints of articles and ten of reviews. All correspondence regarding manuscript submissions should be directed to the Editor, Sarah Salih, Department of English, King's College London, Virginia Woolf Building, 22 Kingsway, London WC2B 6LE, United Kingdom; e-mail ageofchaucer@kcl.ac.uk. Subscriptions to The New Chaucer Society and information about the Society's activities should be directed to Ruth Evans, Department of English, Saint Louis University, Adorjan Hall 231, 3800 Lindell Blvd., St. Louis, MO 63108–3414. Back issues of the journal may be ordered from University of Notre Dame Press, Chicago Distribution Center, 11030 South Langley Avenue, Chicago, IL 60628; phone: 800-621-2736; fax: 800-621-8476; from outside the United States, phone: 773-702-7000; fax: 773-702-7212.

Studies in the Age of Chaucer

Studies in the Age of Chaucer

Volume 37
2015

EDITOR

SARAH SALIH

PUBLISHED ANNUALLY BY THE NEW CHAUCER SOCIETY
SAINT LOUIS UNIVERSITY IN ST. LOUIS

The frontispiece design, showing the Pilgrims at the Tabard Inn, is adapted from the woodcut in Caxton's second edition of the *Canterbury Tales*.

Copyright © 2015 by The New Chaucer Society, Saint Louis University. First edition. Published by University of Notre Dame Press for The New Chaucer Society.

ISBN-10 0-933784-39-2
ISBN-13 978-0-933784-39-0
ISSN 0190-2407

CONTENTS

THE PRESIDENTIAL ADDRESS

Fragmentations of Medieval Religion: Thomas More, Chaucer, and the Volcano Lover
    Alastair Minnis   3

THE BIENNIAL CHAUCER LECTURE

Not Yet: Chaucer and Anagogy
    James Simpson   31

ARTICLES

Scribes, Misattributed: Hoccleve and Pinkhurst
    Lawrence Warner   55

Fugitive Poetics in Chaucer's *House of Fame*
    Rebecca Davis   101

The Place of the Bedchamber in Chaucer's *Book of the Duchess*
    Sarah Stanbury   133

Beaten for a Book: Domestic and Pedagogic Violence in *The Wife of Bath's Prologue*
    Ben Parsons   163

"Now y lowve God": The Process of Conversion in *Sir Gowther*
    Alan S. Ambrisco   195

The Poetics of Time Management from the *Metamorphoses* to *Il filocolo* and *The Franklin's Tale*
    Kara Gaston   227

"The writyng of this tretys": Margery Kempe's Son and the Authorship of Her Book
    Sebastian Sobecki   257

REVIEWS

Dallas D. Denery II, Kantik Ghosh, and Nicolette Zeeman, eds., *Uncertain Knowledge: Scepticism, Relativism, and Doubt in the Middle Ages* (Jordan Kirk)   285

CONTENTS

Elizabeth Elliott, *Remembering Boethius: Writing Aristocratic Identity in Late Medieval French and English Literatures* (Marco Nievergelt)   289

Matthew Fisher, *Scribal Authorship and the Writing of History in Medieval England* (Michael Johnston)   293

Eleanor Johnson, *Practicing Literary Theory in the Middle Ages: Ethics and the Mixed Form in Chaucer, Gower, Usk, and Hoccleve* (Ryan McDermott)   296

David Matthews, *Medievalism: A Critical History* (Louise D'Arcens)   301

Alastair Minnis, *The Cambridge Introduction to Chaucer* (Corey Sparks)   305

Tison Pugh, *Chaucer's (Anti-)Eroticisms and the Queer Middle Ages* (Wan-Chuan Kao)   307

Nicole Rice, ed., *Middle English Religious Writing in Practice: Texts, Readers, and Transformations* (Sean Otto)   311

Wolfgang Riehle, *The Secret Within: Hermits, Recluses and Spiritual Outsiders in Medieval England* (Laura Saetveit Miles)   314

Wendy Scase, ed., *The Making of the Vernon Manuscript: The Production and Contexts of Oxford, Bodleian Library, MS Eng. poet. a. 1* (Aditi Nafde)   317

Fiona Somerset and Nicholas Watson, eds., *Truth and Tales: Cultural Mobility and Medieval Media* (Joel Fredell)   321

Paul Strohm, *Chaucer's Tale: 1386 and the Road to Canterbury* (Sebastian Sobecki)   325

Conrad van Dijk, *John Gower and the Limits of the Law* (Jonathan M. Newman)   328

Daniel Wakelin, *Scribal Correction and Literary Craft: English Manuscripts 1375–1510* (Rory G. Critten)   332

Jon Whitman, ed., *Romance and History: Imagining Time from the Medieval to the Early Modern Period* (Kara Gaston)   335

Stephen M. Yeager, *From Lawmen to Plowmen: Anglo-Saxon Legal Tradition and the School of Langland* (Eric Weiskott)   338

BOOKS RECEIVED   343

AN ANNOTATED CHAUCER BIBLIOGRAPHY, 2013   347

Stephanie Amsel
    Classifications   349
    Abbreviations of Chaucer's Works   351
    Periodical Abbreviations   355
    Bibliographical Citations and Annotations   361
    Author Index—Bibliography   401

Program, Nineteenth International Congress   405

INDEX   439

Studies in the Age of Chaucer

THE PRESIDENTIAL ADDRESS
The New Chaucer Society
Nineteenth International Congress
July 16–20, 2014
University of Iceland, Reykjavík

The Presidential Address

Fragmentations of Medieval Religion: Thomas More, Chaucer, and the Volcano Lover

Alastair Minnis
Yale University

R OOSEVELT STREET, NEW YORK, 1929–30. Outside a store that is advertising the sale of soda, candy, and ice cream hang various objects made of wax. Some of them are, quite obviously, candles. Others defy easy categorization. Basically, they are effigies of, respectively, an adult arm, a child's arm, and a heart. Here I am describing a photograph taken by Walker Evans (1903–75), as included in an exhibition held at The Metropolitan Museum of Art, New York, during the period February 1–May 14, 2000, and published in the accompanying catalogue.[1] The caption simply reads "Votive Candles." But the wax depictions of human body parts, evidently not designed to function as lightsources, can hardly be called "candles." "Votives" these fragmented

---

I chose this topic for my presidential address because, among the many possible futures of Chaucer Studies, its interrelation with the study of medievalisms both past and present strikes me as being particularly fruitful. Thus my essay seeks to explore how demotic religious practices from Chaucer's time, as attested by surviving fragmented objects and narratives of fragmentation, have been subjected to an ever-changing process of interpretation and appropriation, a process vividly exemplified by texts ranging from *The Pardoner's Tale* to Sir William Hamilton's account of strange events in a (once) remote town in the Kingdom of Naples. It is also offered as a small contribution to the history of humor and its sociopolitical uses. Humor—by turns an instrument of thought, a subversive device, and a means of enforcing insider and outsider status—is one of the most elusive of subjects, though its dynamics are of central importance for appreciation of a writer who was so concerned with its performance. I am grateful to Carolyn Dinshaw, Richard Firth Green, Nicola McDonald, and Stephanie Trigg for comments on earlier versions of the following.

[1] Maria Morris Hambourg, Jeff L. Rosenheim, Douglas Eklund, and Mia Fineman, *Walker Evans* (New York: The Metropolitan Museum of Art, 2000), Plate 18.

images certainly are, however. Taken collectively, they constitute a cultural fragment, challenging to the twenty-first-century cataloguer, that once was given meaning by religious practices that go back to the Middle Ages. And even earlier.

Votive offerings were a common feature of medieval shrines—effigies of complete bodies or of body parts, such as a foot, leg, arm, eye, teeth, heart, or breast, together with the crutches or bandages left by the faithful. The afflicted part of the human body was modeled in plastic form, to identify the location of the corporeal disorder that was to be cured or that had been cured. Images of animals (particularly cows and horses) were also made, indicating the anxieties of men and women who depended on such creatures for their livelihood. Such objects bedecked medieval pilgrimage destinations, which had as their main focus of worship the relics of saints—whether the complete corpse of some holy man (as at Thomas Becket's shrine at Canterbury) or some part thereof (such as the head of Saint James at Compostela), here being another type of fragmentation characteristic of medieval Christianity. Usually ex-votos were made of wax, but sometimes wood was used, or even silver or gold, depending on the wealth of the supplicant.

Their use, however, was exclusively neither Christian nor medieval. Anatomical ex-votos made of terracotta were a regular feature of pagan religious practices in the era of the Roman Republic (i.e., from 509 BCE until Augustus assumed power in 27 BCE), though it should be noted that the rites performed at sacred places were quite different, not least because the veneration of relics was abhorrent to Roman sensibilities. Many fine examples have been unearthed in archeological excavations. To quote from Catherine Johns's useful summary of the evidence:

> Parts of the body frequently figured are the eyes, head, hands, breasts, male genitals, legs and feet. Some internal organs are also found, particularly wombs, while complete statuettes of animals presumably indicate an appeal for help with the illnesses of domestic beasts. The precise interpretation of the parts of the body in terms of what diseases were common is very difficult. . . . The prevalence of a particular part of the body at any given sanctuary could indicate that the shrine had a good reputation in the healing of diseases afflicting that part, so that sufferers attended it from a wide radius. On the other hand, it could also indicate that disorders of that part of the body were especially common in that area, or were an especially serious disability in that particular community.[2]

[2] Catherine Johns, *Sex or Symbol: Erotic Images of Greece and Rome* (London: British Museum Publications, 1982), 57–58.

For instance, votives in the form of feet were in common use at the healing shrine at Ponte di Nona, in Rome, and it has been speculated that, in a rural community such as the one that once existed around that bridge, "injuries or afflictions of the feet and legs would be particularly serious."[3]

Many instances of shrines that sought to heal serious disabilities not just of a "particular community" but "from a wide radius" may be cited from medieval evidence—which brings us to one of the most challenging documents to be discussed in this paper. And the challenge consists in the fact that the account is humorous, and clearly intended to be so. Laughter at body parts and their representation in painting and the plastic arts is a human practice of long standing that requires no documentary evidence or archeological excavation, but when the objects in question bear some religious significance—or, at least, when the serious analogue of some dubious object bears some religious significance—then the identification and comprehension of humor are hard indeed. It is difficult if not impossible to know when to laugh, and what exactly we should be laughing at.

The document in question is the *Dialogue Concerning Heresies*, which Sir/Saint Thomas More published in 1529. Herein the More-persona converses with a messenger sent by a friend who is seeking advice on certain matters of faith, including the problems caused by false relics, going on pilgrimage for the wrong reasons, and asking inappropriate petitions of the saints. This treatise is remarkable for many reasons, not least the fact that, over and over again, we see the discussants telling, and laughing at, "mery tales."[4] (Indeed, More's reputation as a "merry man" long survived him, being memorialized in popular culture.[5]) The most important one for our purposes concerns a strange shrine in Picardy that is dedicated to Saint Valéry, who is especially sought out "for the stone" (i.e., for his ability to relieve the pain of kidney stones).

---

[3] Ibid., 58.

[4] Thomas More, *A Dialogue Concerning Heresies*, II.11, ed. T. M. C. Lawler, G. Marc'Hadour and R. C. Marius, in *The Yale Edition of the Complete Works of St. Thomas More*, Vol. VI, Part 1 (New Haven: Yale University Press, 1981), 234.

[5] For example, it features strongly in the Elizabethan play *Sir Thomas More*, together with his championship of poetry. See *Sir Thomas More: Original text by Anthony Munday and Henry Chettle; censored by Edmund Tilney; revisions co-ordinated by Hand C; revised by Henry Chettle, Thomas Dekker, Thomas Heywood and William Shakespeare*, ed. John Jowett (London: Arden Shakespeare, 2011), 161, 231, 232–33, 241–42, 245–46, 280–81; "In life and death, still merry Sir Thomas More" (309).

A young English gentleman, who has traveled here with his wife, finds it far stranger than expected. Whereas at other pilgrimage sites one may see wax votives of arms and other such body parts, here they represent the "gere" (genitalia) of men and women. "For lyke as in other pylgrymages ye se hanged vp legges of waxe or armes or suche other partes/ so was in that chapell all theyr offrynges yt honge aboute the walles/ none other thynge but mennes gere & womens gere made in waxe."[6] The particular form of suffering in which Saint Valéry specializes concerns the urogenital tract; therefore the genital votives hanging on the chapel walls are fit testimonies to his special healing powers.

William Tyndale (to be martyred for his Protestant beliefs in 1536) was not amused. In his long-winded refutation of More's *Dialogue*, he brushes this anecdote aside with disdain. "The tenth chapter, of St Walery, is meet for the author and his worshipful doctrine."[7] In other words, this particularly offensive account is representative of More's abhorrent teaching in general, and justifies the vigor with which it must be rejected. Tyndale's nineteenth-century editor, the Revd. Henry Walter, was more explicit: "The tale which More has told, of a pilgrimage to the chapel of St. Valeri, in Picardy, . . . is too grossly indecent to admit of any allusion to its subject."[8] But how did More himself intend his tale to be taken? He offers no judgment concerning the goings-on described therein. Indeed he refuses to comment, given that this shrine is in France, and so it is up to the University of Paris to pronounce on the situation. I read this as jocular in (at least) two ways. No Englishman should dare to comment on what the French get up to. And the merry matters of Saint Valéry are beneath the notice of distinguished Parisian scholars.

Here we encounter one of the major problems that troubles scholarly research into demotic or, as I prefer to call it, "vernacular" religion. Certain religious practices, although often of long standing and enjoying considerable popularity throughout medieval Europe, functioned "under the radar" of academic and other forms of institutional discourse (though, of course, certain cults could be rendered official, receive formal authorization and considerable support, when that was deemed in

---

[6] More, *Dialogue Concerning Heresies*, II.10 (228).
[7] William Tyndale, *An Answer to Sir Thomas More's "Dialogue,"* ed. Henry Walter (Cambridge: Cambridge University Press, 1850), 124.
[8] Ibid., 124 n. 2.

the best interests of the establishment).⁹ Hence their documentation is partial, refracted, fragmented. When humor is added to the cultural mix, a further layer of complexity is added—or, rather, a filter that can occlude rather than sharpen. Does the marking of his tale as "mery" imply that More is rejecting its account of Saint Valéry out of hand? Or can we find therein, however distorted for the purpose of humor, *some* intimations of actual practice?

I believe that we can. The first interpretive step, however, involves a radical cultural leap, whereby the relevant fragments of medieval (and indeed of Roman) religion are desexualized: seen not in terms of erotic stimulus or sexual arousal but rather as evidence of an eagerness to find cures for some of the most distressing and deadly diseases known to man, including kidney stones, breast cancer, heart disease (which explains the large wax heart in Walker Evans's photograph), and impotence. Further: issues relating to male impotence in particular and human fertility in general should not be trivialized (or, not simply be trivialized) as the stuff of dirty jokes, but recognized as matters of immense political and social import, encompassing on the one hand a farming family's desperate desire for offspring to help work the land and provide care for the elderly, and on the other the eagerness of high-ranking aristocrats to beget male heirs. This explains the appeal of the shrine of Our Lady of Walsingham, one of England's most popular pilgrimage destinations—which had as its most precious relic some of the Virgin Mary's breast milk, kept in a crystal container on the high altar, and supposed to be highly efficacious in matters concerning fertility, childbirth, and the nurture of children. Richard II and Anne of Bohemia seem to have gone there twice in 1383.[10] Even King Henry VIII paid a visit in the days when he was still "Defender of the Faith." His first wife, Catherine of Aragon, also went on pilgrimage there.[11] Had the Virgin of Walsingham responded differently to their plight, the course of English history might have been very different.

Catherine Johns has addressed such matters particularly well in writing about the terracotta models of male genitalia that commonly were

---

[9] For this use of the term "vernacular" see Alastair Minnis, *Translations of Authority in Medieval English Literature: Valuing the Vernacular* (Cambridge: Cambridge University Press, 2009), 12–16. The present paper develops some of the ideas that feature in Chapter 6 of this book, "Chaucer and the Relics of Vernacular Religion."

[10] Susan Signe Morrison, *Women Pilgrims in Late Medieval England: Private Piety and Public Performance* (London and New York: Routledge, 2000), 16.

[11] J. C. Dickinson, *The Shrine of Our Lady of Walsingham* (Cambridge: Cambridge University Press, 1956), 42–44.

used as votives during the time of the Roman Republic, objects that in the past have often been categorized—quite erroneously and inappropriately—as "obscene." Their purpose "is no more obscene than is that of a diagram in a medical textbook," Johns argues; "they are intended simply to draw the attention of the deity to the part requiring help."[12] Indecency should not be read into the representation of breasts and wombs; "the gynecological problems for which help was most often invoked" seem to have "concerned fertility, birth and the nourishment of infants," rather than diseases specifically relating to sexual intercourse, such as gonorrhea. Johns speculates further that some of the terracotta male genitals found at Ponte di Nona "may show evidence of the condition called phimosis, a tightness of the foreskin which can lead to painful and unpleasant consequences," one (just one) of which is impotence. Others may indicate "troubles of the urinary system, a very common type of affliction among older men." And, as Thomas More would no doubt wish us to add to this list, kidney stones may have been another ailment—which, lacking the interventions of modern medicine, could prove fatal.

The historical relationship between the terracotta votives of the Roman Republic and the wax votives, real or humorously imagined, of late medieval Europe is far beyond the scope of the present paper, and in any case the matter is not susceptible to any comprehensive solution, perhaps to any satisfactory and generally acceptable explanation at all. However, it seems reasonable to postulate a process of assimilation rather than total destruction, reconfiguration rather than erasure, revaluation rather than devaluation. To cite the position advanced by Aron Gurevich, "the transition from paganism to Christianity involved a reorganization of existing beliefs rather than a clean sweep."[13] A much more partial view was taken by Protestant propagandists who sought to accentuate the comparisons between pagan religion and Catholicism in order to pillory the superstitions of Rome. Thomas More's humor, as found in his account of the suspicious shrine of Saint Valéry and throughout the *Dialogue Concerning Heresies* generally, is, quite intriguingly, of a supportive kind; he expresses warm human sympathy for the

---

[12] Johns, *Sex or Symbol*, 58.
[13] Peter Burke, "Editorial Preface" to Aron Gurevich, *Medieval Popular Culture: Problems of Belief and Perception* (1988; repr., Cambridge: Cambridge University Press, 1997), ix.

common mass of people who find comfort and support in demotic practices that their social betters might well sneer at (until their own suffering brings them down a peg or two). Although, as already noted, William Tyndale refused to meddle with such merriness, several of his fellow Reformers were more than willing to do so. In their hands, however, the humor is sharp and satiric, a means of ridicule and an instrument of propaganda. Similar tales may be told but their significance is very different.

A good example from Reformation England is afforded by the way in which John Bale (1495–1563) attacked the cult of Saint Walstan of Bawburgh (near Norwich). "Both Men and Beastes which had lost their Prevy partes, had newe members again restored to them, by this Walstane," Bale remarks contemptuously, likening this saint, as the "god of their feldes in Northfolke and Gyde of their Harvestes," to the pagan god Priapus.[14] Similar attacks on alleged Priapic throwbacks feature in the polemic of continental Protestants. In his *Confession du Sieur de Sancy* (1597–1617), the staunch Calvinist Agrippa d'Aubigné describes the shrine of a certain "Saint Foutin" in Provence, which is adorned with wax effigies of male and female sexual organs, suspended from the ceiling of his chapel and blown against each other by the wind.[15] (There is an obvious etymological—perhaps folk-etymological—connection between the saint's name and the French verb *foutre*, "to fuck.") The resemblance to Thomas More's description of the shrine of Saint Valéry is striking. Agrippa also claims that, when the Huguenots took the town of Embrun in the lower Alps, they found among the relics in the main church an ancient wooden phallus, its head turned red owing to the amount of wine that had been poured over it. Thus women made "holy vinegar"—which they put to some (unspecified) strange use, Agrippa coyly remarks. An even bigger wooden phallus, he claims, was discovered and burned by the troops who destroyed the temple of Saint Eutropius at Orange.

It is a matter of historical record that Huguenot soldiers sacked churches at Orange in 1562 and at Embrun in 1585, but their discovery

---

[14] See Eamon Duffy, *The Stripping of the Altars: Traditional Religion in England, 1400–1580* (New Haven: Yale University Press, 1994), 204; cf. F. Blomefield and C. Parkin, *An Essay towards a Topographical History of the County of Norfolk*, 2nd ed., 2 vols. (London: printed for W. Miller, 1805–10), II.389.

[15] Agrippa d'Aubigné, *Confession du Sieur de Sancy*, II.2, in *Agrippa d'Aubigné: Oeuvres*, ed. H. Weber, J. Bailbé, and M. Soulié (Paris: Champion, 1969), 633.

of large wooden phalli may well be a tall tale. What does seem quite obvious, however, is that a corpus of anecdotes concerning the fecundating powers of certain saints, shrines, and relics was in circulation by the end of the Middle Ages, a source of merry tales among the faithful that later became grist to the mill of Protestants who used them for propaganda purposes. Now the evidence is heavily sexualized, all the better to heap derision on their opponents, in a trenchant version of the biased hermeneutics that we have heard Johns warning against. And yet: we seem to be dealing not with caricature of a kind so extreme that the imitation is far distanced from the genuine article, but rather with exaggerations of actual practices. Perhaps this is how the humor works, or was meant to work. On the same argument, it is impossible to deny the possibility that wax models of male and female genitalia once adorned the roofs or walls of certain shrines: how unfortunate that More ducked the issue. Sometimes an artifact turns up that provides some support for that possibility, such as the late medieval wooden phallus dug up on the Norwegian coast near Bergen.[16] Could it have been a votive offering? Could practices of the type described (however inaccurately, however distorted by humorous or satiric intent) by the likes of Thomas More and Agrippa d'Aubigné have occurred after all?

Supporting evidence for this claim may be found in the existence (whether through continuity or conscious revival, and however fragmentary or garbled) of such practices into more recent times. The Museo Raffaele Corso at Palmi has in its possession wax votives in the form of male genitalia that were in ritual use in the area as late as 1950, and in the 1960s models of "male and female genital organs" were being offered at the shrine of San Rocco at Stellitanone.[17] Here, however, I want to concentrate on the phallic votives deposited by Sir William Hamilton (1730–1803) in the British Museum in early June 1784, along with his account of the festival in which they were used, at Isernia in Abruzzo. Perhaps best known nowadays as one of history's most prominent cuckolds (his wife Emma having been the mistress of Horatio Nelson, the hero of Trafalgar), in his own day William Hamilton was British envoy to the royal court of Naples, an antiquarian and archeologist of some distinction, and a volcanologist whose pioneering study of

[16] A. M. Koldeweij, "Lifting the Veil on Pilgrim Badges," in *Pilgrimage Explored*, ed. J. Stopford (Woodbridge: Boydell and Brewer, 1999), 161–88 (187).
[17] Giancarlo Carabelli, *In the Image of Priapus* (London: Duckworth, 1996), 16.

Mount Vesuvius won him the accolade "The Modern Pliny."[18] This partially explains why Susan Sontag dubbed him "the volcano lover" in her 1992 novel.[19] I say "partially" because of the ironic import of Sontag's title. To judge from Emma Hamilton's long-term extra-marital liaison, Sir William's loving did not make the earth move for her. She preferred the embraces of a man who in combat had lost an arm and the sight in one eye—raising issues concerning the social (and sexual) valence of bodily fragmentation and lack that are beyond the parameters of the present discussion.[20]

On July 17, 1781 Sir William wrote to Joseph Banks, president of the Royal Society, claiming that "in a Province of this Kingdom, and not fifty miles from its Capital, a sort of devotion is still paid to Priapus, the obscene Divinity of the Ancients (though under another denomination)."[21] This he thought "a circumstance worth recording; particularly, as it offers a fresh proof of the similitude of the Popish and Pagan Religion, as well observed by Dr. Middleton, in his celebrated Letter from

---

[18] On which see John Thackray, "'The Modern Pliny': William Hamilton and Vesuvius," in *Vases and Volcanoes: Sir William Hamilton and His Collection*, ed. Ian Jenkins and Kim Sloan (London: British Museum Press, 1996), 65–92. The recent research that has focused on Hamilton's scholarly achievements tends to treat him kindly. For instance, Jonathan Scott has praised him as "the first British collector of antiquities to make a significant impact on national taste through the influence of his collections and the publications devoted to them," particularly his pioneering collection of Greek vases. He certainly did much to make the fortune of the English potter Josiah Wedgwood. See Jonathan Scott, *The Pleasures of Antiquity: British Collectors of Greece and Rome* (New Haven: Yale University Press, 2003), 172–85.

[19] Susan Sontag, *The Volcano Lover: A Romance* (New York: Farrar, Straus, and Giroux, 1992).

[20] Shortly before his death, Nelson said, "I leave Emma Lady Hamilton . . . as a legacy to my King and Country." That same king and country allowed her to drink herself to death in Calais. Yet subsequently Lady Hamilton became a national treasure, a memento of England's imperial glories—and the legitimated subject of prurient regard. The 1941 movie *That Hamilton Woman*, starring Vivien Leigh as Emma and Laurence Olivier as Nelson, boosted morale in wartime Britain; Winston Churchill pronounced it his favorite film. Vivien Leigh was ridiculously miscast, her cut-glass vowels being linguistically distant from Emma's lower-class Cheshire accent (she was the daughter of an illiterate blacksmith), which snobbish detractors frequently mocked as vulgar. Cf. David Constantine, *Fields of Fire: A Life of Sir William Hamilton* (London: Weidenfeld and Nicolson, 2001), 163, 209–10, 250–51, 253. A recent biography, published by Kate Williams in 2006 (New York: Ballantine Books), is entitled *England's Mistress: The Infamous Life of Emma Hamilton*—quite a spin on the notion of love of one's country.

[21] Richard Payne Knight and Thomas Wright, *Sexual Symbolism: A History of Phallic Worship*, introduced by Ashley Montagu, 2 vols. (New York: Bell, 1957), I.13. This reprints Hamilton's letter and Knight's *The Worship of Priapus*, along with Thomas Wright's essay (on which see below).

Rome." The reference is to the *Letter from Rome, shewing an exact conformity between popery and paganism*, which the deist writer Conyers Middleton published in 1729. One of Middleton's proofs was the evidence of continuity afforded by the ancient Roman antecedents of Catholic votive offerings.[22]

What had excited Hamilton was the apparent survival of "the ancient Cult of the God of the Gardens" in "the Fête of St. Cosmo and Damiano, as it actually was celebrated at Isernia . . . so late as in the year of our Lord 1780."[23] Hamilton did not witness the spectacle himself, but was alerted to it by an engineer—"a person of liberal education" employed in building a new road from Naples to the Province of Abruzzo, who "chanced to be at Isernia just at the time of the celebration of the Feast of the modern Priapus, St. Cosmo."[24] Hamilton planned to be present at the feast the following year, but, as he explained the situation, "the indecency of this ceremony having probably transpired, from the country's having been more frequented since the new road was made, orders have been given, that the *Great Toe* of the Saint should no longer be exposed."[25] A "great toe" was a local euphemism for a phallus, Hamilton tells us. But what exactly was "exposed" is far from clear, as is noted by Ian Jenkins and Kim Sloan in the catalogue they compiled to accompany the 1996 Hamilton Exhibition in the British Museum, *Vases and Volcanoes: Sir William Hamilton and His Collection*. Perhaps "it was a relic of the saint, or another term for the wax models of male genitalia that were sold at the festival for dedication in the shrine." [26]

With this problem in mind, we may turn to the account that Hamilton pieced together from his informants. On "one of the days of the Fair," he explains, "the relicks of the Saints"—perhaps including Saint

---

[22] Carabelli, *Image of Priapus*, 6.
[23] Knight and Wright, *Sexual Symbolism*, I.18. Cosmas and Damian were twin Syrian saints, martyred in the third century during the Diocletian persecutions and renowned for their healing powers, their most spectacular feat being the replacement of a patient's diseased leg with one from a recently deceased Ethiopian. The miraculous nature of this surgery is emphasized in the common depiction of a black leg engrafted on a white body, an instance of integration calling attention to previous fragmentation. See Carabelli, *Image of Priapus*, 15–16. Relics of Cosmas and Damian were acquired by Isernia Cathedral in 1602 (though other churches also claimed possession of such items), and their cult has survived to the present day—though in a less sensational form than that recorded by Sir William.
[24] Knight and Wright, *Sexual Symbolism*, I.17–18.
[25] Ibid., I.18.
[26] Jenkins and Sloan, *Vases and Volcanoes*, 238–39.

Cosmas's "great toe"?—"are exposed . . . and afterwards carried in procession from the cathedral of the city to this church, attended by a prodigious concourse of people. In the city, and at the fair, *ex-voti* of wax, representing the male parts of generation, of various dimensions, some even of the length of the palm, are publickly offered to sale."[27] Waxen votives of other body parts were also on offer, mixed up with the phallic ones, "but of these there are few in comparison of the number of the Priapi." "The devout distributers of these vows"—the hint of sarcasm is obvious—"carry a basket full of them in one hand, and hold a plate in the other to receive the money, crying aloud, 'St. Cosmo and Damiano!'" If the price of one of them is asked, the answer is, "più ci metti, più meriti": "the more you give, the more's the merit."[28] It is mainly women who present such ex-votos, Hamilton notes, and the ones they most commonly present "are seldom such as represent legs, arms, etc." but rather "the male parts of generation." One woman who presented a votive is quoted as saying, "Blessed St. Cosmo, let it be like this": i.e., may her husband have a phallus of like size and potency.[29] Another thanked Saint Cosmas, presumably for having answered such a prayer. The votives were always presented with money, Hamilton adds, and "kissed by the devotee at the moment of presentation."

Another even more intimate rite is then described, involving the use of "the oil of St. Cosmo," believed to have exceptional healing properties and made (Hamilton is convinced) according to a recipe that goes back to Roman antiquity. Sufferers expose their afflicted body parts at the great altar ("not even excepting that [member] which is most frequently represented by the *ex-voti*"),[30] and the reverend canon then anoints

---

[27] Knight and Wright, *Sexual Symbolism*, I.21. This account is paralleled by the testimony of another eighteenth-century English traveler to Italy, Richard Colt Hoare, who described the use of votives made of "red wax by the natives of Isernia" in the shapes of "feet, legs, arms, eyes, heads, hands, *membri genitali*, and even whole figures." Their use was banned at the fair of Saints Cosmas and Damian by the civil (rather than by the religious) authorities, Hoare claimed, though he managed to obtain specimens. Carabelli, *Image of Priapus*, 14, 79. In 1828 Craufurd Tait Ramage reported that the walls of the church at Isernia were adorned with ex-votos of red wax, and that "in former times" they had included representations of "membra genitalia," though now those were "discontinued." Ibid., 82.

[28] Here "meriti" may bear the technical sense of those spiritual "merits" that, following a successful petition, are bestowed upon the needy sinner from the inexhaustible heavenly treasury of merit. However, Carabelli suggests a more demotic reading: "the more you pay, the better it works." Ibid., 13.

[29] Knight and Wright, *Sexual Symbolism*, I.22.

[30] Ibid., I.23.

them, invoking the aid of Saint Cosmas. Hamilton emphasizes that the oil in question "is in high repute for its invigorating quality, when the loins, and parts adjacent, are anointed with it." Here one may recall how, according to Agrippa d'Aubigné, the women of Embrun made "holy vinegar" by pouring wine over a wooden phallus, a concoction subsequently put to some tantalizingly unspecified use. The oil of Saint Cosmas seems to have been produced in great qualities, "no less than 1,400 flasks" of the liquid having either been "expended at the altar in unctions, or charitably distributed, during this fête in the year 1780." A "very lucrative" business for the canons of the church, in Hamilton's cynical view.

Hamilton's letter has something of the merry tale about it, for he expresses the hope that it will "amuse" Joseph Banks "for the present"; in the future "authentic proofs" of his "assertion" will be "deposited in the British Museum" (as indeed they were).[31] Further, Hamilton ended this same letter to Banks with the wish that his friend's "Great Toe and his purse" would never fail him.[32] And in a later letter to Banks (dated June 7, 1784) Hamilton remarked that he had "recommended to Maty" (Paul Henry Maty, Keeper of Natural and Artificial Productions at the British Museum) that he should keep his "hands off" the votives.[33] But beyond this male banter there is a serious intent of complex proportions, which is clarified by the company kept by Hamilton's account of the Isernia festival. It was published in 1786 alongside an essay on "The Worship of Priapus" by Richard Payne Knight (1750–1824),[34] in an edition of eighty copies, by the Society of Dilettanti for private distribution among its membership, which included Hamilton and Knight.[35]

---

[31] Ibid., I.13.

[32] Carabelli, *Image of Priapus*, 2. "Purse" has long functioned as a metaphor for the scrotum, and may be thus used at *PardT*, VI.943–45, where the Pardoner invites Harry Bailly to unbuckle his purse and make an offering to his relics (all Chaucer references are to *The Riverside Chaucer*, gen. ed. Larry D. Benson, 3rd ed. [Oxford: Oxford University Press, 1988]). If interpreted in this way, these lines can be read as having prompted Harry's jocular treatment of the Pardoner's *coillons* as a relic (VI.951–55), on which much more below. Cf. *MED*, s.v. *purs(e)* (n.), def. 4.

[33] Carabelli, *Image of Priapus*, 3–4.

[34] On whom see especially Michael Clarke and Nicholas Penny, eds., *The Arrogant Connoisseur: Richard Payne Knight, 1751–1824; Essays on Richard Payne Knight Together with a Catalogue of Works Exhibited at the Whitworth Art Gallery, 1982* (Manchester: Manchester University Press, 1982).

[35] *An Account of the remains of the worship of Priapus: lately existing at Isernia, in the kingdom of Naples; in two letters: one from Sir William Hamilton . . . to Sir Joseph Banks . . . : and the other from a person residing at Isernia: to which is added, A discourse on the worship of Priapus: and its connexion with the mystic theology of the ancients*, by R. P. Knight (London: T. Spilsbury, 1786). An excellent analysis of Knight's style is provided by Bruce Redford, *Dilettanti: The Antic and the Antique in Eighteenth-Century England* (Los Angeles: J. Paul

This society included young men of privileged birth whose attitudes had been formed through the cultural and corporeal experiences of the Grand Tour. They were (or fancied themselves to be) connoisseurs of art and arbiters of taste, free spirits with a desire for the foreign, the exotic, and the erotic.[36] To dismiss the Dilettanti as self-centered rakes with more money than sense would be quite simplistic, however, for many of them were playing, or would play, important roles in British political life.[37] Their society's vaunted libertinism was as sociopolitical as it was sexual. Drink and debauchery were certainly on the agenda (though the relationship between homosocial words and hedonistic deeds is impossible to gauge, after all this time; the waves of scandalized comment go back to the mid-eighteenth century). Yet this was interwoven with the assertion of republican ideals, support for enterprises of social reform, and the funding of archeological excavations. Here we are dealing with "assertions of exceptionalism available only to élite males who had little fear of social repercussions."[38] Jason M. Kelly, whose words I have quoted here, goes on to speak of the Dilettanti's distinctive version of libertinism "as a modern update of medieval codes of chivalric honor in that it emphasized social status, masculine fortitude, and virility."[39] All of which was shot through with an anti-Catholicism piqued by their contacts with Italian religion and religious art, and fostered by the assumptions of cultural superiority inbred in the power elite of their imperial Protestant nation.

Some of the Dilettanti were members of clubs with even more dubious reputations, the most notorious example being Francis Dashwood, fifteenth Baron le Despencer (1765–81), a charter member of the Dilettanti who went on to form a society known variously as the Brotherhood of Saint Francis of Wycombe, the Knights of Saint Francis, the

---

Getty Museum and Getty Research Institute, 2008), 113. The text is a "hybrid," he suggests: "on the one hand, a coterie product that speaks a private, libertine language; on the other, a learned exercise in comparative religion." It "combines the earnest and the ironic, the scholarly and the subversive."

[36] In this period "dilettante" referred to a connoisseur or "virtuoso," a person with genuine knowledge of, and a passion for, antiquities. It did not bear the negative connotation of amateurish dabbling in an area wherein one lacked real expertise or commitment; that came with the subsequent professionalization of scholarship. See Redford, *Dilettanti*, 1–2; and Jason M. Kelly, *The Society of Dilettanti: Archaeology and Identity in the British Enlightenment* (New Haven: Yale University Press, 2009), 8–12.

[37] See Shearer West, "Libertinism and the Ideology of Male Friendship in the Portraits of the Society Dilettanti," *Eighteenth-Century Life* 16 n.s. 2 (1992): 76–102 (84).

[38] Kelly, *The Society of Dilettanti*, 36.

[39] Ibid., 39.

Monks of Medmenham, and, simply, as the Hell-Fire Club. At its meetings, if the sensationalist gossip can be believed, the "Bona Dea (the ancient goddess of fertility) was worshipped with parodies of Christian ritual and acts of sexual intercourse."[40] In a more verifiable performance of irreverent burlesque Dashwood had himself painted (by George Knapton, also one of the Dilettanti) in the costume of a Franciscan friar, raising aloft a chalice inscribed "matri sanctorum" (to the mother of the saints) whilst gazing at the exposed pudendal area of a classical nude statue (reminiscent of the Medici Venus), her decorously protective hand having been broken off.[41] Rarely has the relationship between corporeal fragmentation and sexual voyeurism been made more obvious.

Such, then, was the audience to which the Hamilton/Wright volume appealed, with its argument for the "similitude of the Popish and Pagan Religion" and speculation "that the secret of all religions was worship of vital forces—the four elements, sexual energy—and that the cross itself was probably a stylized phallus" (as Susan Sontag puts it).[42] This view of the relationship between paganism and Christianity—a marked reconfiguration of the attitudes found in Reformation attacks on popery of the kind illustrated above—is a reflex characteristic of the so-called "Age of Enlightenment." Some of its *philosophes* saw religion as a realm of backwardness and error, and suspected that all the major world religions derived from common sources, perhaps indeed from a primitive sexual pantheism. "The farther back we go in the history of every country, the deeper we explore into all religions, ancient as well as modern, we stumble the more frequently upon the incessantly intensifying distinct traces of this supposedly indecent, mystic worship [i.e., phallic worship]." Thus wrote Hargrave Jennings, an authority on Rosicrucianism, occultism, and esotericism, in the preface to his 1883 version of "The Worship of Priapus" (printed in a limited edition, of course). "Vulgarly apprehended" as "obscene" but "in reality" a "grand and profound religion," phallic worship survives "in the rites, and the ceremonial of all

---

[40] Randolph Trumbach, *Sex and the Gender Revolution*, Vol. I, *Heterosexuality and the Third Gender in Enlightenment London* (Chicago: University of Chicago Press, 1998), 86. As Trumbach says, "It has ever since been difficult to separate fact from fiction in the history of the monks of Medmenham Abbey."

[41] Reproduced as Fig. 1.23 in Redford, *Dilettanti*, 34. See further Kelly, *The Society of Dilettanti*, 42, 44; and West, "Libertinism and the Ideology of Male Friendship," 86. Redford notes that this painting probably predated the founding of "the Monks of Medmenham" by a decade, and suggests that "it influenced rather than imitated their rituals" (33).

[42] Sontag, *The Volcano Lover*, 120.

faiths (more or less successfully disguised), and in the domestic, quaint usages, and superstitious practices of all peoples."[43] Here are the consequences of belief in an historical progression from the "primitive" to the "refined," wherein, as Giancarlo Carabelli remarks, "islands of retarded evolution" may be discovered "in the present" and compared with the practices of "contemporary primitives" like the "savages" who lived "outside European society and the 'common people' within it."[44] Such principles were believed to unite "all faiths," and in particular to connect the ancient worshipers of Priapus with the "domestic, quaint usages" of the common people of Isernia.

Attacked as "one of the most unbecoming and indecent treatises which ever disgraced the pen of a man,"[45] the Hamilton/Knight treatise enjoyed considerable success as a pornographic book, fetching fancy prices within a highly select and secretive market.[46] Readers who were willing to admit they knew it included James G. Frazer, author of *The Golden Bough* (1890), which in turn exercised considerable influence on that foundational text in the history of criticism of medieval romance, Jessie Weston's *From Ritual to Romance* (1920), together with a galaxy of twentieth-century writers, including W. B. Yeats, Robert Graves, T. S. Eliot, D. H. Lawrence, and James Joyce.[47] Another avid reader was Sigmund Freud, whose conviction that neurotic adult behavior is rooted in childhood repression of sexual fantasy and desire afforded the processes of sexualizing interpretation a new role within the emerging science of psychoanalysis.[48]

Yet another was a medievalist whose contribution to scholarship on

---

[43] Richard Payne Knight, *The Worship of Priapus*, ed. Hargrave Jennings (London: George Redway, 1883), ix–x.

[44] Carabelli, *Image of Priapus*, 8–9.

[45] Ibid., 88.

[46] Ibid., 72.

[47] Filmmakers too fell under its spell, such as Francis Ford Coppola (*Apocalypse Now*, 1979) and John Boorman (*Excalibur*, 1981).

[48] Carabelli, *Image of Priapus*, 111–12, 116. Freud's collection of antiquities included phallic amulets, probably purchased during his travels in Italy. For discussion see Whitney Davis, "Wax Tokens of Libido," in *Ephemeral Bodies: Wax Sculpture and the Human Figure*, ed. Roberta Panzanelli (Los Angeles: Getty Research Institute, 2008), 107–29. On his collection more generally, see Juliet Flower MacCannell, "Signs of the Fathers: Freud's Collection of Antiquities," in *Excavations and Their Objects: Freud's Collection of Antiquity*, ed. Stephen Barker (Albany: State University of New York Press, 1996), 33–56; and Lynn Gamwell and Richard Wells, eds., *Sigmund Freud and Art: His Personal Collection of Antiquities* (London: Freud Museum, in association with Abrams, New York, 1989).

Old and Middle English literature was immense: Thomas Wright (1810–77). Indeed, in 1866 the texts of Hamilton and Knight were republished together with Wright's essay on "The Worship of the Generative Powers during the Middle Ages of Western Europe." "Antiquity had made Priapus a god, the middle ages raised him into a saint, and that under several names," asserts Wright,[49] launching into an account of Saint Foutin, whose acquaintance we have already made in Agrippa d'Aubigné's account. But Wright tells the tale for a reason rather different from the one that motivated the French Calvinist. There is no satire in "The Worship of the Generative Powers," and little if any humor; we also miss that "irony of skeptical intellectual superiority" that, in Bruce Redford's view, Knight learned from Edward Gibbon.[50] Instead we have a rather earnest demonstration of what Wright regards as an historical fact (though he does not find it "an agreeable subject"), i.e., that the "superstition" of Priapic worship "prevailed throughout Southern and Western Europe largely during the Middle Ages, and that in some parts it is hardly extinct at the present day."[51]

Vestiges of ancient worship of the generative powers are sought in the Irish *Shelah-na-Gigs* (for Wright devotes considerable attention to representations of female sexual organs), genital amulets supposed to ward off "the evil eye," the heresies of the Waldensians and Cathars, the dubious ceremonies of the Knights Templar, and the Satanic deviancies associated with witchcraft. Maypole dancing inevitably is scrutinized, as is the Feast of Asses ("the ass was an animal sacred to Priapus")[52] and even the hot cross bun, which Wright suspects was originally marked with the phallus. Scholarly obsession interweaves with sexual voyeurism, investigative punctiliousness with a willingness to make generalizations of a staggering kind. This is the same person who published, *inter alia*, pioneering editions of *The Owl and the Nightingale*, the Chester Plays, *The History of Fulk FitzWarine*, *The Seven Sages of Rome*, Thomas Hoccleve's *De regimine principum*, Giraldus Cambrensis, the political songs of England, Robin Hood ballads, Geoffrey Gaimar's Anglo-Norman metrical chronicle, Alexander Neckam's *De naturis rerum*, *The Book of the Knight of La Tour-Landry*, *Piers Plowman*, Malory's *Morte d'Arthur*, and of course

---

[49] Knight and Wright, *Sexual Symbolism*, II.49.
[50] Redford has chapters 15 and 16 of *The Decline and Fall of the Roman Empire* specifically in mind; *Dilettanti*, 123.
[51] Knight and Wright, *Sexual Symbolism*, II.8.
[52] Ibid., II.104.

Chaucer's *Canterbury Tales*. At least some of these editions are still in use today. Wright's editorial achievements have long outlasted his views on the worship of the generative powers during the Middle Ages.

The collected endeavors of Hamilton, Knight, and Wright fell easily within the category of books that were kept from general consumption by librarians and other protectors of public morals, and appealed to a shadowy community of "rich pornophiles," as Carabelli has termed them.[53] A very different interpretive context surrounds the last outing of Sir William's wax genitalia to be considered here, their presentation as an exhibit in the 1996 Hamilton Exhibition in the British Museum.

Hamilton himself worried about the fragile nature of the Isernian votives he had collected, which is why he himself undertook to deliver them to the museum.[54] His fears were well founded, for subsequently all of the items were broken into fragments. Fortunately their original appearance may be inferred from the frontispiece to the 1786 Hamilton/Knight treatise (see Fig. 1), an engraving that shows four of the votives presented in a bizarre yet artful tableau, which, as Redford has well said, "combines to unite documentation with provocation: the wax phalluses are arranged in such a way as to suggest both an anatomical illustration and an outré still life."[55] This engraving enabled two votives to be "reconstructed by Frank Minney of the Museum's Department of Conservation."[56] Replicas of the two others were made, and all four objects showcased in an arrangement that imitated the one shown in the 1786 frontispiece. A color photograph is included in the exhibition catalogue, opposite a reproduction of the frontispiece, so the images may be compared—and the restorers' skill appreciated. The two darker-colored phalli in the picture are Mr. Minney's reconstructions from the fragmented originals; the other two, much lighter in color, are the replicas.

Beautifully lit and photographed to the highest technical standards, these objects attain a strange, exotic presence, at once engaging and repulsive. Here is a spectacle prepared for the consumption of the British Museum's nationally and ethnically diverse clientele, who (I presume) were meant to find in this unusual display a welcome distraction from the more traditional artistic and archeological items on show, all those vases and images of volcanoes. The great toes certainly got a lot of

---

[53] Carabelli, *Image of Priapus*, 112.
[54] Ibid., 2–3.
[55] Redford, *Dilettanti*, 13. Cf. Fig. 5.1, on 114.
[56] Jenkins and Sloan, *Vases and Volcanoes*, 239.

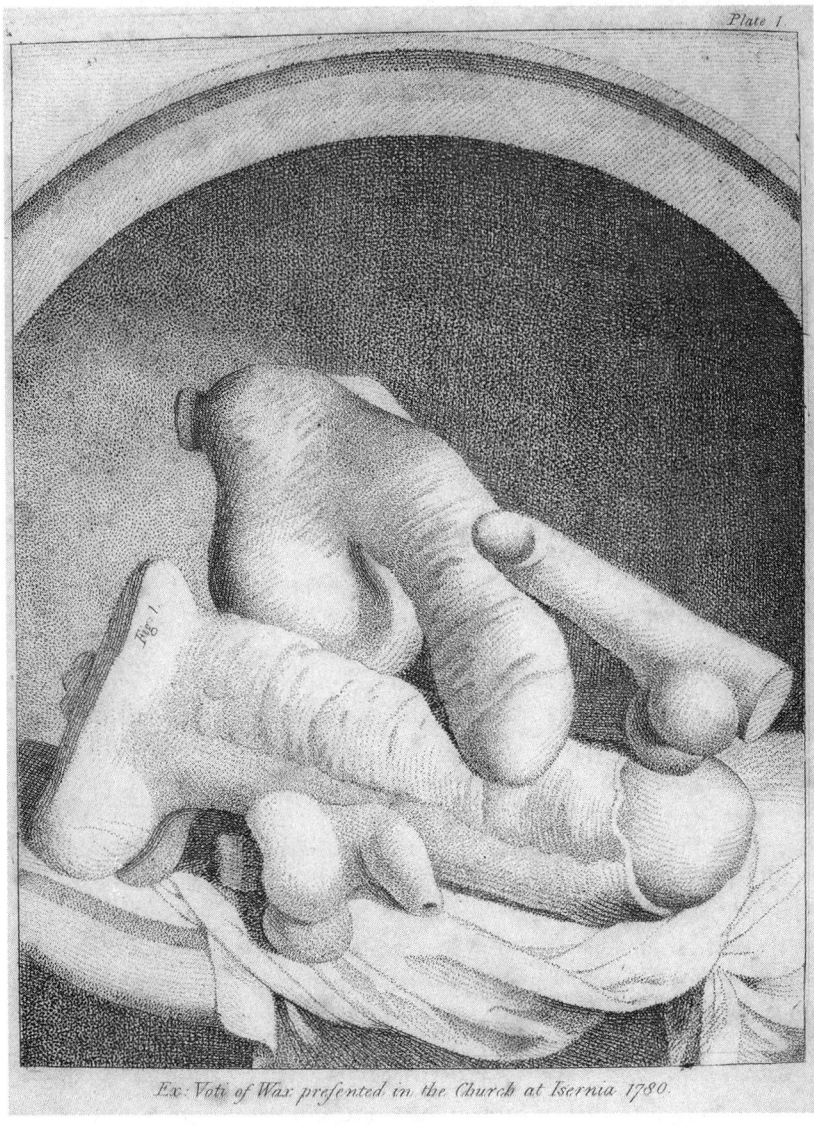

Fig. 1. Frontispiece to Knight and Wright, *Sexual Symbolism*, reproduced courtesy of the Beinecke Rare Book and Manuscript Library, Yale University.

attention, and laughter was a quite common reaction. Which is hardly surprising, and no doubt the curators were well aware of the consequences of risqué and/or ridiculous objects being presented with the respect and reverence that tacitly surround the exhibition of *objets d'art*. Sir William's fragmented originals have been resurrected, made whole thanks to the expertise of contemporary curators, and enshrined in accord with the cultural and commercial values of today's museum industry.

It has been suggested that either Hamilton's sources or Hamilton himself may have garbled somewhat his account of the Isernian festival, in large measure because of preexisting assumptions concerning pagan Priapic survivals in popery. Thus what may actually have involved men seeking relief from the problems (including erectile dysfunction) caused by phimosis was misread as female devotion to Priapus.[57] (We may compare Johns's speculation concerning the purpose of the terracotta genital votives found at Ponte di Nona, as already quoted.) This is an eminently reasonable suggestion, and similar bias-induced garbling may underlie Agrippa d'Aubigné's salacious allusions to dubious Catholic practices involving wooden phalli. The sexualization of those representations of genitalia renders them "obscene" in interpretive acts at once historically anachronistic and inappropriately judgmental in moral terms, the very process that Johns has warned against. But other priorities drive the transmutations we are dealing with here, whether the intent is to enclose within an accepting Catholicism, to expose to patronizing Protestant ridicule, or to appropriate in the service of some totalizing theory of the worship of Priapus. And in each case some measure of sexualization is in play.

Given the dynamics of that process, perhaps the fragments of medieval religion that Hamilton so carefully sought to preserve, and the humor he sought to weave around them, can help us contextualize one of Chaucer's most complex and controversial jokes. For here issues of fragmentation and veneration are again moot. At the end of *The Pardoner's Tale*, Harry Bailly first responds to the Pardoner by exclaiming, why, you would swear that your shit-smeared "breech" was "a relyk of a seint" and have me kiss it (VI.948–50). Then he changes tack, jocularly proposing that the Pardoner's "coillons" should be cut off and treated like a relic—and what a fine relic they would make!

[57] Davis, "Wax Tokens of Libido," 124–26.

> But, by the croys which that Seint Eleyne fond,
> I wolde I hadde thy coillons in myn hond
> In stide of relikes or of seintuarie.
> Lat kutte hem of, I wol thee helpe hem carie;
> They shal be shryned in an hogges toord!
>
> (VI.951–55)[58]

What might it cure? A range of urogenital disorders, presumably, including kidney stones, and phimosis or some other cause of male impotence. But it is reasonable to assume a strategy of sexualization that goes far beyond that, particularly since the Pardoner may be regarded as a lover of volcanic proportions—if we give credence to his claim that he has a jolly wench in every town (VI.453), even as he contemplates marriage (III.163–68). Such a sex machine would surely produce a potent relic, which eager worshipers would flock to visit, for reasons rather more dubious than those mentioned above. Little wonder that Harry Bailly would prefer to have this new relic in his hand, in place of any existing relic or reliquary. Sex is, after all, one of this character's main topics of conversation; witness his loud praise for the virility of the Monk and the Nun's Priest, a natural potency unfortunately curbed by their vows of chastity (VII.1929–64 and 3447–60).

To continue in this vein: the fact that the Pardoner would need help in carrying that object (which Harry generously offers to provide) seems to indicate an item of substantial proportions, perhaps even greater than the great toe of Saint Cosmas, which attracted "a prodigious concourse of people," particularly women, when it was borne in procession. Alternatively, the Pardoner's prize relic deserves to be carried in a large and sumptuous reliquary or *seintuarie*; again, he would need help in carrying it and, again, size and weight imply high value. In either case (to develop Harry's fantasy) a lucrative trade might well develop in wax phallic votives at the shrine of this English Saint Foutin. The Isernian votives could be as big as the palm of a hand; no doubt the Pardoner's would be bigger and better. And what amazing amounts of "holy vinegar" or oil would issue, far exceeding the "1,400 flasks" produced at Isernia. We know that the Pardoner already has some experience of such

---

[58] On the crucial importance of relics in Chaucer's characterization of the Pardoner see Robyn Malo, "The Pardoner's Relics (and Why They Matter the Most)," *ChauR* 43, no. 1 (2008): 82–102; and also her book, *Relics and Writing in Late Medieval England* (Toronto: University of Toronto Press, 2013), 125–47.

concoctions, because (he claims) the well-water in which his shoulder-bone from a holy Jew's sheep is dipped miraculously cures livestock, and—an even more wondrous feat!—if the farmer himself drinks from that same well, "His beestes and his stoor shal multiplie" (VI.350–56). But the fecundating powers of that relic would pale into insignificance in comparison with those of the one proposed by Harry Bailly.

Evidently Thomas More really liked Chaucer's joke about the "hooly Jewes sheep," for he made good use of it, on two occasions, in his *Dialogue Concerning Heresies*.[59] (More's treatise is replete with Chaucerian allusions.) Unsurprisingly, Tyndale avoids engaging with Chaucerian humor in his reply to the *Dialogue*. Indeed, here the term "poet" is an insult to be hurled at More, the author of *Utopia* and occasional verse, and the translator of Lucian from Greek into Latin. For Tyndale this is a means of accusing his opponent of practicing sophisticated forms of deception, dressing up lies in which he himself believes. "M. More hath so long used his figures of poetry that (I suppose) when he erreth most, he now, by the reason of a long custom, believeth himself that he saith most true."[60] In Tyndale's view, those sayings are "as true as his story of Utopia, and all his other poetry."[61] Addressing More's belief in purgatory and the pope's role in its governance, Tyndale decries his opponent for "captivating his wits to believe phantasies," for supposing that "every poet's fable is a true story."[62] More's views on free will, good works, and grace prompt the exclamation, "O poet, without shame!"[63]

---

[59] More, *Dialogue Concerning Heresies*, I.17 (98, 217).
[60] Tyndale, *An Answer to Sir Thomas More's "Dialogue,"* 15.
[61] Ibid., 193.
[62] Ibid., 143–44.
[63] Ibid., 188. Elsewhere Tyndale alludes to Chaucer's *Troilus and Criseyde*, in an attack on a "thousand histories and the doctrines fables of love and wantonness and of ribaldry as filthy as heart can think," to corrupt the minds of youth, "clean contrary to the doctrine of Christ and his apostles." William Tyndale, "W. T. unto the Reader," in *The Obedience of a Christian Man*, ed. David Daniell (London: Penguin Books, 2000), 24–25. The attitude of More's daughter Margaret to *Troilus* could hardly have been more different. When she visited him in the Tower under instructions to persuade him to conform to the Act of Succession, she quoted Criseyde's exclamation: "In good faith, Father, . . . I can no ferther goe, but am (as I trow Cresede saith in Chauser) comen to Dulcarnon, euen at my wittes ende." This is from a letter Margaret wrote to Lady Alice Alington (in which More's own involvement is suspected); *The Correspondence of Sir Thomas More*, ed. Elizabeth Frances Rogers (Princeton: Princeton University Press, 1947), 529. The reference is to *TC*, III.929–31, where Criseyde complains about the pressure Pandarus is putting her under to consent to the nocturnal meeting with Troilus at which their love will be consummated. "Dulcarnoun" was the name given to a specific Euclidian proposition, so the point is that Criseyde is in a state of some perplexity, like a person confronted with such a difficult geometrical problem. The fit is a good one: one con-

Doubtless Tyndale regarded More's virtuoso foolery—in which Erasmus took great delight[64]—as yet another means of couching "his errors . . . so subtilly" that "no man can espy [detect] them."[65]

But let us—shamelessly—take even further the possibility that the Pardoner's cullions are being imagined as a fecundating relic. Behind *The Pardoner's Tale*, VI.951–55 may lie Jean de Meun's joke at the end of the *Roman de la rose*, where Amant adores his beloved's genitalia as if they were relics, his own members being allegorized as a pilgrim's staff and scrip. The rose is duly impregnated. But Chaucer did not need to take any lessons from the French text in humor relating to risible relics and suspicious saints; such jokes were ubiquitous throughout medieval Europe. John Heywood (d. c. 1580), who married Thomas More's niece,

---

flicted woman, persuaded (perhaps even coerced) to act in a way at least partly against her own wishes, uses the words of another. This testifies to a remarkable knowledge of Chaucer in the More circle, which is manifest even more prominently by the rich tapestry of Chaucerian phrases (some of which may well be unconscious echoes) in More's own writings, which far exceed the number of specific, and obviously deliberate, quotations. On which see Alistair Fox's two articles, "Chaucer, More, and English Humanism," in *Rulers, Religion and Rhetoric in Early Modern England: A Festschrift for Geoffrey Elton from His Australasian Friends*, ed. J. C. Davis, *Parergon*, special issue n.s. 6 (1988): 63–75; and "Thomas More's *Dialogue* and the *Book of the Tales of Caunterbury*: 'Good Mother Wit' and Creative Imitation," in *Familiar Colloquy: Essays Presented to Arthur Edward Barker*, ed. P. Brückmann (Ottawa: Oberon Press, 1978), 15–24; along with Francis X. Ryan, "Sir Thomas More's Use of Chaucer," *SEL* 35 (1995): 1–17.

[64] As expressed in his *Encomium moriae*, a "praise of folly" that is also a praise of More. For both men, humor was a powerful rhetorical device, and could function as an instrument of thought. If a frivolous subject is properly handled, Erasmus declared, a sensible reader "can profit by it a good deal more than he can from the forbidding and showy subjects undertaken by some writers," though he admitted that some might find his *Encomium* "too light and frivolous for a theologian" (2, 4). The Leuvenese professor Martin Dorp (d. 1525) was one such. In responding to Dorp's claim that he had "bitterly" assailed "the whole theological profession," Erasmus cited the practice of "the wisest men of ancient times" who "preferred to deliver the most wholesome rules of conduct in humorous and (to all appearances) childish fables[,] because the truth . . . penetrates more readily into the minds of mortals when it comes recommended by the allurement of pleasure." Desiderius Erasmus, *The Praise of Folly*, trans. Clarence H. Miller, 2nd ed. (New Haven: Yale University Press, 2003), 2, 4, 143, 149. The satiric style of Lucian profoundly influenced Erasmus and More; see David Marsh, *Lucian and the Latins: Humor and Humanism in the Early Renaissance* (Ann Arbor: University of Michigan Press, 1998), 9–13, 167–76, 193–97; and Alexander Welsh, *The Humanist Comedy* (New Haven: Yale University Press, 2014), 55–63, 70–87. See further Walter Jacob Kaiser, *Praisers of Folly: Erasmus, Rabelais, Shakespeare* (Cambridge, Mass.: Harvard University Press, 1963), 35–100; Alistair Fox, *Thomas More, History and Providence* (New Haven: Yale University Press, 1983), 10–11, 23–27, 35–44, 124–25; and Arthur F. Kinney, *Continental Humanist Poetics* (Amherst: University of Massachusetts Press, 1989), 80–86.

[65] Tyndale, *An Answer to Sir Thomas More's "Dialogue,"* 15.

added several of them to what Chaucer had written.⁶⁶ In his farce *The Pardoner and the Frere*, after re-describing the miraculous multiplication allegedly wrought by the shoulder-bone from the holy Jew's sheep, Heywood introduces a fresh relic, "The great too of the Holy Trynyte." Put it in your mouth, says this play's pardoner, and you'll have no problem with toothache, ulcers, or pustules (139–44).⁶⁷ The pardoner in another Heywood play, *The Foure PP*, also displays the "great toe of the Trinite," and once again it is supposed to cure toothache (508–13). Here the detail is added that this relic is shaped in such a way that it looks like "thre toes in one" (516), quite appropriate for an image of the Trinity but obviously evocative of men's "gere," to return to More's euphemism. Heywood's editors suspect he may have invented this impossible object, and relate the humor here to that associated with certain "phallic saints," such as the "Sainct Couillbault" who appears in the French farce *Le pardonneur, le triacleur et la tavernière*⁶⁸—evidently a *confrère* of Saints Valéry and Foutin. The parallel with the "great toe" of Saint Cosmas is obvious, though its sphere of operation, like that of the relic of Harry Bailly's sexualizing imagination,⁶⁹ extends far beyond the cure of toothache. Many medieval relics were capable of multitasking.

On this reading, the Host is paying the Pardoner's virility a compliment—for the purpose of his satiric jest, of course. And the (mock-) reverence of this discourse is shattered when Harry suggests that his victim's "coillons" be enshrined in pig dung. However, if we believe

---

⁶⁶ Quotations are from *The Plays of John Heywood*, ed. Richard Axton and Peter Happé (Cambridge: D. S. Brewer, 1991).

⁶⁷ Then Heywood offers his version of Chaucer's "veyl" of "Oure Lady" (*GP*, I.695), Mary's "bongrace," or the shade that protects her from sunburn; if pregnant women kiss it, they will soon be eased of their burden, which presumably means that they will have a prompt and safe delivery (*The Pardoner and the Frere*, 145–52).

⁶⁸ Heywood, *Plays*, 239, note to *The Pardoner and the Frere*, line 134. In the French text a pardoner carries relics of this "Saint Balls" together with those of his sister, Saint Pubes ("Velue," meaning "hairy" or "furry"; lines 10–12). At lines 206–7 we encounter another male and female pairing, in the form of Saint Sausage ("Boudin") and Saint Slit ("Fente"). André Tissier, ed., *Recueil de farces, 1450–1550*, 13 vols. (Geneva: Droz, 1987–2000), V.244–45, 264.

⁶⁹ In contrast, the Scottish courtier Sir David Lindsay (c. 1486–1555) exercises what might be called a desexualizing imagination, when describing the equally absurd but less smutty relics carried by yet another unscrupulous pardoner; see Sir David Lindsay, *Ane Satyre of the Thrie Estaitis*, ed. Roderick Lyall (Edinburgh: Canongate, 1989), lines 2087–111. The point is well made by William Calin, *The Lily and the Thistle: The French Tradition and the Older Literature of Scotland* (Toronto: University of Toronto Press, 2014), 130–32. However, Lindsay does include a grotesque *arsse*-kissing incident (lines 2174–82).

that the Pardoner is all talk and no action (like his equivalent in the fifteenth-century *Canterbury Interlude* which prefaces the *Tale of Beryn*),[70] then the humor works rather differently. Harry Bailly is ironically praising something that has little or no actual value. As a relic, the Pardoner's cullions would fail to satisfy, in accord with their lack of potency when joined to their owner. Thus the Pardoner's relic becomes the prize fake in a large collection of fakes (as described in *GP*, I.695–700; cf. VI.350–51).

Yet another possibility: if Chaucer's character is judged to be some sort of eunuch in material (as opposed to metaphorical) terms, i.e., if he suffers from a genital deformity or deficiency, then it is the Pardoner himself who should be visiting the relevant shrine and reverently kissing the appropriate relic, rather than setting up in the business of curing others. Finally, what of the "queer" Pardoner of recent criticism, whose proclivities include same-sex desire, and whose references to townswomen of lax morals and to a possible marriage may therefore be a cover-up or camp humor or a bit of both?[71] In that case, we could understand Chaucer's joke thus: kiss this relic at your own risk! It is so powerful that one cannot predict, or be held responsible for, the consequences.

All of these interpretive possibilities are just that, mere possibilities. I am not offering any of them as a definitive explanation, but rather seeking to access the dynamics of the humor surrounding the Pardoner's fragmentation—by telling some of my own "mery tales," perhaps, yet tales that stand in line with those offered by Thomas More, various Protestant polemicists, and William Hamilton. Tales of the fragments of medieval religion. Fragments of saints real and imagined, of relics true and false, of votives plausible and impossible. Fragments subject to historical contingency, their value determined in and for the moment by the shifting sands of creed, class, and power. Fragments that, in their more recent interpretive contexts, may reveal religion itself as fragmented, "a province of loss and memorabilia," a museum cabinet of "images and texts that testify to someone else's encounter with the divine"[72]—whether that "someone else" is a woman of Isernia or a volcano lover, and whatever view of the divine is involved. A crucial part

---

[70] On which see Alastair Minnis, *Fallible Authors: Chaucer's Pardoner and Wife of Bath* (Philadelphia: University of Pennsylvania Press, 2007), 150–51.

[71] For discussion and bibliography see ibid., Chapter 2, section 4.

[72] Here I borrow phrases from Susan L. Mizruchi, "Introduction," in *Religion and Cultural Studies*, ed. Mizruchi (Princeton: Princeton University Press, 2001), ix–xxv (xv). See further Jenny Franchot's essay in this collection, "Unseemly Commemoration: Reli-

of that loss and lapse into vague memory is the transition of humor into pastness, when we listen—uneasily and excluded—to someone else engaging in mockery that either affirms holiness or seeks to reduce holiness to humor. Having failed to get the joke, we are left to make our own.

---

gion, Fragments, and the Icon" (38–55). Franchot writes: "the status of religion in intellectual culture is that of a loss, a collection of images and texts that are now irrevocably a recollection, a memorial of past faith, or, depending on one's perspective, of past illusion. . . . [R]eligion now dwells in front of us as a visual and textual fragment to be remembered precisely as that which is not us: a subject not only *for* memory but deeply constitutive of Western memory" (38, 40).

THE BIENNIAL CHAUCER LECTURE
The New Chaucer Society
Nineteenth International Congress
July 16–20, 2014
University of Iceland, Reykjavík, Iceland

The Biennial Chaucer Lecture

Not Yet: Chaucer and Anagogy

James Simpson
Harvard University

Chapter 22 of Harriet Beecher Stowe's *Uncle Tom's Cabin* (1852) adumbrates the child Evangeline's Bible reading to the adult slave Tom. Evangeline, we learn, prefers "Revelations and . . . Prophecies." These biblical books are not wholly intelligible either to Evangeline or to Tom, but both characters are drawn to these genres in particular, since they "spoke of a glory to be revealed,—a wondrous something yet to come, wherein their soul rejoiced, yet knew not why":

> For the soul awakes, a trembling stranger, between two dim eternities,—the eternal past, the eternal future. The light shines only on a small space around her; therefore, she needs must yearn towards the unknown; and the voices and shadowy movings which come to her from out the cloudy pillar of inspiration have each one echoes and answers in her own expecting nature. Its mystic imagery are so many talismans and gems inscribed with unknown hieroglyphics; she folds them in her bosom, and expects to read them when she passes beyond the veil.[1]

Stowe imagines a scene of biblical reading in the here and now of the novel, but that reading is for the moment unintelligible to both Evangeline and Tom. Only when the soul "passes beyond the veil" will the text become clear. For the moment, the souls of our readers are alert and aroused between two eternities, yearning for futurity.

I warmly acknowledge the many responses I received in Reykjavík to the New Chaucer Society Biennial Lecture 2014 from which this essay was developed; Penelope Buckley, Stephen Clingman, and Jeffrey Robinson also each offered astute and welcome comment.

[1] Harriet Beecher Stowe, *Uncle Tom's Cabin*, ed. Elizabeth Ammons, 2nd ed. (New York: Norton, 2010), Chap. 22, 236–38.

Stowe is working from within a tradition of biblical reading here, whereby the biblical narrative points not only to the past event (the literal sense); not only to the fulfillment of that past event in the intermediate past (the allegorical sense); and not only to the applicability of those senses to the present (the moral, or tropological sense).[2] Evangeline and Tom are also, however uncertainly, imagining their way into the future here, where the future is a higher version of the broken present. They inhabit an interim state, suspended between implicit rejection of the present and uncertain perception of a future that drives that rejection. Dogma of any kind is in flux: that of the present is losing its legitimacy, even as the dogma of the new dispensation remains unclear. Tom and Evangeline are, in short, practicing an anagogical reading, or a "leading up."

The novel, however, is not merely representing anagogical reading, but enacting it. Stowe pitches her own book, that is, into the future, from a present that confronts only "unknown hieroglyphics," and is itself the locus of "voices and shadowy movings."

That anagogical posture simultaneously underlines two key aspects of this novel. On the one hand, Stowe implicitly recognizes the novel's present as wounded, a provisional and damaged shadow of better things to come, from which one can only desire a different future. That a novel occupying such a wounded present should have had such very mixed reception history is perhaps unsurprising, from President Lincoln's famous and admiring (though possibly apocryphal) comment about it in 1862 ("the little woman who wrote the book that started this great war") to the fiercely negative response that, from 1910 or so, produced the phrase "an Uncle Tom."[3]

On the other hand, more positively, Stowe uses her *own book* as a reading prophecy of sorts. Even if the present from which her novel derives is provisional and wounded, it prophesies a future in which its

---

[2] For which terms, see especially Henri de Lubac, *Exégèse médiévale: Les quatre sens de l'Écriture*, vols. 41, 42, and 59 of *Théologie*, 2 vols. in 4 (Paris: Aubier, 1959–64), translated as *Medieval Exegesis*, trans. Marc Sebanc and E. M. Macierowski, 2 vols. (Grand Rapids: Eerdmans, 1998); Beryl Smalley, *The Study of the Bible in the Middle Ages* (Notre Dame: University of Notre Dame Press, 1964); and Gilbert Dahan, *L'Exégèse chrétienne de la Bible en Occident médiéval, XIIe–XIVe siècle* (Paris: Cerf, 1999).

[3] For the reception history of *Uncle Tom's Cabin*, see Adena Spingarn, "Uncle Tom in the American Imagination: A Cultural Biography," Ph.D. diss. (Harvard University, 2012), esp. Chap. 4. I am extremely grateful to Adena Spingarn for her guidance in this matter.

own intelligibility will become clearer through readers' responses to it. Biblical prophecy leans into a messianic future of the New Jerusalem; Stowe's own novel leans into an uncertain, but imagined, secular future in which Evangeline and Tom's relations will no longer be underwritten by slavery. This future is activated by the novel itself: by reading it, we ourselves participate in the construction of that future—a massively incomplete future, which is, as yet, not yet.[4]

Stowe's mighty novel implicitly recognizes, then, that it will remain incompletely intelligible until the conditions that have brought it into being are resolved. Such a "not yet" temporal posture in fact characterizes many novels and movies. E. M. Forster's *A Passage to India* (1924) ends by underlining the impossibility of a romance ending, an ending in which futurity is satisfactorily absorbed "happily ever after." Instead, Aziz and Mrs. Moore's son recognize that they cannot yet themselves be friends, because, as Aziz says, "the two nations cannot be friends." To this Moore replies "I know. Not yet."[5] Like *Uncle Tom's Cabin*, *A Passage to India* has been a lightning rod for widely differing judgments across time.[6] If, however, we fully understand the provisionality of what I am calling an anagogical posture, then we also understand how these novels recognize their own inadequacy, their own wounded, lapsarian and provisional state in time. They are, it might be said, martyrs of sorts, suffering history even as they help bring an alternative future into being.

I'm sure that we can all think of other "not yet" narratives. These narratives are not tragic: they do not disallow a future (e.g., *King Lear*); neither are they elegiac: they do not express the irredeemable victimhood of the narrator in someone else's possibly triumphant history (e.g., the letter of Dido in Ovid's *Heroides*). These are, instead, usually unfulfilled romances, where the yearning for just community is somewhere in

---

[4] I say this, even if Stowe cannot herself imagine "an integrated future nation. . . . *Uncle Tom's Cabin* participates in the construction of a national future that remains shadowy even to Stowe, who in some sense is writing from behind a veil." Adena Spingarn, private communication, September 3, 2014.

[5] E. M. Forster, *A Passage to India* (1924; New York: Harcourt, Brace, 1952), 311.

[6] Compare, for example, the liberal account of Lionel Trilling ("Great as the Problem of India is, Forster's book is not about India alone; it is about all of human life"), with that of the anti-imperialist Edward Said ("Forster's India is so affectionately personal and so remorselessly metaphysical that his view of Indians as a nation contending for sovereignty with Britain is not politically very serious, or even respectful"). See, respectively, Lionel Trilling, "*A Passage to India*" (1944), in *E. M. Forster's "A Passage to India,"* ed. Harold Bloom (New York: Chelsea House, 1987), 11–27 (27); and Edward Said, *Culture and Imperialism* (New York: Knopf, 1993), 204.

the future, as in Barry Levinson's *Good Morning Vietnam*, or Ridley Scott's *Gladiator*, whose final scene has the black slave citing Forster with another "not yet."[7] Each of these narratives not only predicts, or desires, a future in which that which has been lost will be found, that which has been divided united. Additionally, they help *bring that transformed community into being*, by changing the consciousness of their own readers. Such texts say to us "not yet," where the incompletion is double: not only is the ideal city state outside the work, whether Jerusalem or Rome, incomplete.[8] So too is the reader's consciousness, which will help bring that state into being, incomplete.

In this essay I look to Chaucer as an anagogical writer, a writer who leans into the future and who challenges us as readers to see ourselves in time, participating in the shaping of the future. The future I have in mind is constituted by the central issue of the European Reformation, which is how humans are justified before God. Chaucer, I argue, foresees that terrible challenges lie not far ahead. Despite his skepticism about prophecy, Chaucer leans into the future with foreboding, less confidently foreseeing a future resolution than uncertainly seeking alternatives to a dark future prophesied.

Reading that is attentive to a work's projection into the future is necessarily diachronic and possibly improper. Diachrony permits us to see texts as processual rather than end-stopped, as part of a movie rather than as a still photograph. It is certainly a historicist reading practice, but the historicism is diachronic. As such, reading of this kind runs against the grain of our deep-set, synchronic philological and historicist persuasions. To understand anagogy, we need to think diachronically.

Such reading is also prepared to ask an unusual, possibly improper, question within the protocols of synchronic historicism: was Chaucer *really* a prophet of sorts? The last decade has seen a powerful set of Chaucer *Nachleben* studies.[9] These studies have looked at Chaucer's

---

[7] http://www.youtube.com/watch?v=OFVk5xVK7vs (accessed October 7, 2014).

[8] As my friend Jeffrey Robinson astutely pointed out after the oral version of this essay, the status of a work as "not yet" is in part determined by the radically fallen state of its extra-literary, "real world" environment.

[9] See, for example (in chronological order), Paul G. Ruggiers, ed., *Editing Chaucer: The Great Tradition* (Norman: Pilgrim Books, 1984); Ruth Morse and Barry Windeatt, eds., *Chaucer Traditions: Studies in Honour of Derek Brewer* (Cambridge: Cambridge University Press, 1990); Seth Lerer, *Chaucer and His Readers: Imagining the Author in Late-Medieval England* (Princeton: Princeton University Press, 1993); Theresa M. Krier, ed., *Refiguring Chaucer in the Renaissance* (Gainesville: University Press of Florida, 1998); Daniel J. Pinti, ed., *Writing after Chaucer: Essential Readings in Chaucer and the Fifteenth Century* (New York: Garland, 1998); James Simpson, "Chaucer's Presence and Absence, 1400–

future as from our present; in this essay I attempt to turn the telescope around, and look as from Chaucer's present to his future. Are Chaucer's works prophetic? To ask the question is to imply a sense of history that synchronic historicism has tended to avoid, if not proscribe.

I

First, though, let me adumbrate anagogy. I begin with an account of why I found myself wanting to talk about it.

As a graduate student in the early 1980s I fell upon Beryl Smalley's *Study of the Bible in the Middle Ages* and Henri de Lubac's *Exégèse médiévale*, just as I was gripped by the debate in Middle English studies about how exegesis played out in vernacular literature.[10] I could understand how three of the four senses of Scripture dynamically informed medieval English writing: the literal; the allegorical; and the tropological, or moral. What, though, of the fourth sense, the anagogical? It left me either puzzled or bored. I was told, by reading Aquinas for example, that when the biblical text points to "things that lie ahead in eternal glory," that is called the anagogical sense.[11] I could very well see the literal, allegorical, and moral meanings of the story of Abraham and Isaac, for example, but how was I to understand that narrative as pointing to the Heavenly Jerusalem? That was the puzzle. Perhaps the salvation of Isaac was to be understood as pointing thematically to salvation, but that universally applied theme struck me as simplistic and uninteresting. The standard mnemonic was, at that stage, of no more help: "Litera gesta docet, quid credas allegoria, moralis quid agas, quo tendas anagogia" (The letter teaches history; allegory, what you should believe;

1550," in *A Chaucer Companion*, ed. Jill Mann and Piero Boitani, 2nd ed. (Cambridge: Cambridge University Press, 2003), 251–69; Alexandra Gillespie, *Print Culture and the Medieval Author: Chaucer, Lydgate and Their Books 1473–1557* (Oxford: Oxford University Press, 2006); and Helen Cooper, "Fame, Chaucer and English Poetry," in *Cultural Reformations: Medieval and Renaissance in Literary History*, ed. Brian Cummings and James Simpson (Oxford: Oxford University Press, 2010), 361–78.

[10] Beryl Smalley, *The Study of the Bible in the Middle Ages* (Oxford: Clarendon Press, 1941); Lubac, *Exégèse médiévale*; and in particular the essays by E. Talbot Donaldson and R. E. Kaske in "Patristic Exegesis in the Criticism of Medieval Literature," in *Critical Approaches to Medieval Literature: Selected Papers from the English Institute 1958–59*, ed. Dorothy Bethurum (New York: Columbia University Press, 1960).

[11] Thomas Aquinas, *Summa theologiae*, ed. Thomas Gilby, 61 vols. (London: Blackfriars, 1964), 1a.1.10, 1:39.

the moral sense, what you should do; the anagogical, your future destination).[12] I just didn't get anagogy, or didn't get excited by it. So I actively pursued each of the first three senses in my texts, and left the fourth, anagogy, discreetly aside.

In my work over the last fifteen years or so, however, I have gradually become aware that I need to revisit anagogy. For, despite my earlier commitment to synchronic historicism, I increasingly found myself working, along with many other scholars, diachronically, persuaded as I was that interpretation had to take its own history, and its own place in history, into account. We are preoccupied by history precisely because we are ourselves in history, necessarily part of history's problem and therefore part of its solution.[13] And so I increasingly found myself reading Middle English works as a premature Reformation, prophetic of the convulsions of early modernity to come.[14]

The very fact that our periodic divisions wish to block and neutralize narratives of this projective kind provoked me to question "medieval studies," and any other tightly policed periodic schema.[15] The fact, too, that the classical practice of philology aims to fix and still texts synchronically also prompted me to question that practice.[16] For, understanding texts wholly in their own terms, wholly in their own place and

---

[12] The distich is attributed to Augustine of Dacia; see A. J. Minnis and A. B. Scott, eds., *Medieval Literary Theory and Criticism, c. 1100–c. 1375* (Oxford: Clarendon Press, 1988), 267 n. 194.

[13] For which see Hans Georg Gadamer, *Truth and Method*, trans. Joel Weinsheimer and Donald G. Marshall, 2nd ed. (London: Sheed and Ward, 1989; first published in German in 1960); and the recent, profound reflection on Gadamerian hermeneutics by Thomas Pfau, *Minding the Modern: Human Agency, Intellectual Tradition and Responsible Knowledge* (Notre Dame: University of Notre Dame Press, 2013), 9–34. See also James Simpson, "Cognition Is Recognition: Literary Knowledge and Textual 'Face,'" *NLH* 44 (2013): 25–44.

[14] I am of course mindful of the example of Anne Hudson, *The Premature Reformation: Wycliffite Texts and Lollard History* (Oxford: Clarendon Press, 1988).

[15] James Simpson, "Diachronic History and the Shortcomings of Medieval Studies," in *Reading the Medieval in Early Modern England*, ed. David Matthews and Gordon McMullan (Cambridge: Cambridge University Press, 2007), 17–30.

[16] For which see Anthony Grafton, *Defenders of the Text: The Traditions of Scholarship in an Age of Science, 1450–1800* (Cambridge, Mass.: Harvard University Press, 1991): some early modern humanists, he says, "put the ancient texts back into their own time, admitting . . . that success may reveal the irrelevance of ancient experience and precept to modern problems" (26–27). For the classic example of philology putting artifacts back into their precise temporal context, see Lorenzo Valla's 1440 *On the Donation of Constantine*, trans. G. W. Bowersock (Cambridge, Mass.: Harvard University Press, 2007). For a revisionist account of Valla scholarship, see Margreta de Grazia, "A Story of Anachronism," in Cummings and Simpson, *Cultural Reformations*, 13–32.

time, and wholly in their radical alterity forbids understanding of how texts lean into their futures, and so lean toward us. And, furthermore, the very fact that the historicism dominant since the 1980s was intensely synchronic provoked me to question that historiographical mode, however immensely productive New Historicism had been. Like classical philology, and possibly for the same revolutionary reasons (both wish to seal off one period from another as tightly as possible), New Historicism aimed to understand texts in their own, tightly bounded chronological context. That fertile movement was wonderfully promiscuous in its *discursive* purview, but severe in its refusal to challenge chronological periodization.[17] On the contrary, New Historicism was driven in part by Foucauldian, French revolutionary historiographical persuasions, the premise of which is that history can be stopped, and started afresh. For Foucault, historical periods were hermetically sealed, and so participated in a larger project of *denying* the intelligibility of one period to another.[18] I found myself wishing to pursue a different philology, where the comparator texts are less synchronic and more diachronic, and where the accent was less on absolute alterity and more on connectedness. I did not want to identify wholly with texts from the past, in a loving embrace, but I did want to befriend them.[19] I certainly did not want to treat them as complete strangers.

For all these reasons, I found myself thinking about the way in which texts lean passionately into the future, whether the passion be of hope or fear. Great works of literature are prophetic as they manifest what have been called symptoms of culture, and symptoms of where a culture is going. As I made these reflections, it occurred to me that medieval biblical exegesis had a concept already prepared for me—the very concept I had rejected in the 1980s—the concept of anagogy.

---

[17] For an account of the shape and force of New Historicism, see Louis Montrose, "New Historicisms," in *Redrawing the Boundaries: The Transformation of English and American Literary Studies*, ed. Stephen Greenblatt and Giles Gunn (New York: Modern Language Association of America, 1992), 392–418.

[18] For Michel Foucault's understanding of historical periods as utterly distinct "epistemes," see his *The Order of Things: An Archaeology of the Human Sciences* (London: Tavistock, 1970; first published in French in 1966). At least one broadly New Historicist medievalist himself wrote an anagogical text about the ways texts point beyond their present: see Paul Strohm, "Chaucer's *Troilus* as Temporal Archive," in his *Theory and the Premodern Text* (Minneapolis: University of Minnesota Press, 2000), 80–96.

[19] See Nicholas Watson, "Desire for the Past," *SAC* 21 (1999): 59–97; and, for an alternative account of friendly, not erotic relations with texts of the past, see James Simpson, "Confessing Literature," *ELN* 44 (2006): 121–26.

I therefore revisited anagogy. For I think I now understand this fourth sense better, and understand how profoundly fertile it might be in cultural understanding. Anagogy, that is, is less a kind of meaning to be extracted from a text, and primarily a process toward a future place or time, through which that meaning will be understood in time. Anagogy does not so much point to the *theme* of the Heavenly Jerusalem, as point to a modality and a temporality of reading. It points to the Heavenly Jerusalem as a utopian, future communitarian intelligibility, led up to by a process of understanding in time. The end of anagogy is the timeless place in which the reading community will be ready to read fully, and so fully understand a text as it has unfolded across history.

To be sure, high medieval exegetes do rehearse the standard, and rather unilluminating, thematic definition of anagogy, as heavenly reward. Thus Richard of Saint Victor in his *Benjamin Minor* (written before 1162) says this about anagogical understanding:

Quid enim dicimus anagogen nisi mysticam et sursum ductivam supercoelestium intelligentiam? In praedictis duobus quaeritur doctrina morum et mysteriorum. Ad anagogen spectat sperandorum praevidentia praemiorum.

[For what do we call *anagoge* but the mystical and upward directive understanding? In the two previously mentioned [senses: i.e., allegory and tropology] there is sought a teaching of customs and of the mysteries. To *anagoge* belongs an advance insight into the rewards to be hoped for.][20]

Richard points, then (like any number of exegetes), to anagogical thematics of a simple kind. His teacher Hugh of Saint Victor, however, adumbrates the much richer psychological and temporal modalities of anagogical reading:

Anagoge enim, sicut dictum est, ascensio mentis, sive elevatio vocatur in contemplationem supernorum. Anagogice igitur circumvelatur, quia ad hoc velatur ut amplius clarescat; ob hoc tegitur ut magis appareat. Ejus igitur obumbratio nostri est illuminatio; et ejus circumvelatio nostri elevatio.

[For the ascension or lifting up of the mind to the contemplation of things above is called *anagoge*. Such contemplation is anagogically veiled, in order that

---

[20] Richard of Saint Victor, *Benjamin Major*, in *Patrologia latina*, ed. J.-P. Migne, 221 vols. (Paris: Migne, 1844–64), Vol. 196, col. 200D. Cited in, and translation drawn from, Lubac, *Medieval Exegesis*, 2:181.

it shine all the more strongly; it is thus covered that it appear all the more clearly. The shadowing of this truth is our illumination, its wrapping our elevation.]²¹

Hugh's account of anagogy, that is, is a way of reading. It is psychological and processual: the mind is certainly illuminated and raised, but the illumination is gradual. It happens in time ("*amplius* clarescat . . . *magis appareat*"). So powerfully is the ignorant beginning of the process related to its illumined end, that the dark beginning is itself transformed: "obumbratio nostri est illuminatio."

This kind of reading experience is premised on the idea that the utopian futurity of reading is to dispense with the need for reading altogether. Not only will the lapsarian conditions of present reading be transformed, but reading itself will be rendered otiose. Augustine imagines this surpassing of reading in his commentary on the Gospel of John:

Sed . . . fidei fructus intellectus, ut perveniamus ad vitam aeternam, ubi non nobis legatur Evangelium; sed ille qui nobis modo Evangelium dispensavit, remotis omnibus lectionis paginis, et voce lectoris et tractatoris, appareat.

[But the fruit of faith is understanding, so that we may arrive at eternal life, where the Gospel would not be read to us, but he who has given us the Gospel would now appear with all the pages of the reading and the voice of the reader and commentator removed.]²²

This utopian position of reading is, of course, premised on the historicist persuasions of Christian eschatology, in which events in time also point to the end of time itself. Within this scheme we can have no access to, or example of, anagogical reading, since it's possible only in the eschaton.

That said, might we have access to more moderate and secular forms of the temporal unfolding of meaning and meaning-making in humanly

---

²¹ Hugh of Saint Victor, *Commentariorum in hierarchiam coelestem . . . libri x*, in *Patrologia latina*, Vol. 175, col. 946B (my translation), discussed in Lubac, *Medieval Exegesis*, 2:183. Lubac himself distinguishes between the ways in which anagogy prompts abstract theorization about final ends on the one hand, and the ways in which anagogy transports its subject into a contemplative state not reliant on signs. See *Medieval Exegesis*, 2:188–97.

²² Augustine of Hippo, *In Joannis evangelium*, Tractatus 22, in *Patrologia latina*, Vol. 35, col. 1575, discussed and translated in Lubac, *Medieval Exegesis*, 2:188–89.

made books, "quo tend[imus]"? And might anagogy also apply to vernacular literature, to the reading of "old books" from which we expect "new science" to appear?[23]

Dante, in one of his most intense poetic claims, affirms that he writes not only for present readers, but also for "coloro / Che questo tempo chiameranno antico" (those who will call this time antique).[24] Reading of this kind necessarily leaves contemporary readers with a sense of *not* having fully grasped a text. In Middle English writing, the most profound and explicit statement of such anagogical reading is made by Julian of Norwich. Thus, in the final chapter of her *Revelation of Love*, Julian declares that her text is "begonne by Goddes gifte and his grace, but it is not yet performed, as to my sight."[25] For, she goes on, "truly I saw and understode in our lords mening that he shewde it for he will have it known more than it is." The text as we have it is only a start: Julian surprisingly declares in her *final* chapter that her text is . . . "*begonne*" (my emphasis). The gradual fulfillment of visionary meaning is activated in Julian's own two versions (anagogical texts will likely have more than one version), but there is more to come.

More profoundly, the text's completion, or "performance," involves us as readers. Julian wants us to receive this text as "common and general." It will become applicable to all of us commonly and generally only, however, insofar as each of us is potentially and ideally unified with each other. For, says Julian, her visions are "common and general even as we are all one."[26] The existential state of the readership, that is, determines the ongoing reception and understanding of the text—its performance and its eventual obsolescence—through time. The manuscript of the longer version declares the text to have ended: "Explicit liber revelationum Juliane anacorite Norwiche"; Julian herself would take issue with that standard formula: on the contrary, her text has

---

[23] The reference is, of course, to *PF*, 22–25. The passage points itself to the ways in which books will be renewed in future readings. This is, aptly, used as the epigram to the second imprint of Thomas Speght's 1598 edition of Chaucer's works: *The workes of our antient and learned English poet, Geffrey Chaucer, newly printed* (London, 1598), STC, 5079, image 1.

[24] Dante Alighieri, *La divina commedia*, ed. Natalino Sapegno (Florence: Nuova Italia, 1979), *Paradiso*, XVII.119–20.

[25] Julian of Norwich, *A Revelation of Love*, in *The Writings of Julian of Norwich*, ed. Nicholas Watson and Jacqueline Jenkins (University Park: Pennsylvania State University Press, 2006), Chap. 86, p. 379.

[26] *A Vision Showed to a Devout Woman*, in Julian, *Writings*, section 6, p. 73.

hardly started its hermeneutic and ethical unfolding—its performance—in time.[27]

II

Is, however, Julian's exact contemporary Chaucer an anagogical and prophetic writer? We can define Chaucer as an anagogic author more precisely by looking to the exaggerated ways in which Protestant readers received him as a prophet.

Protestant polemicists in the sixteenth and seventeenth centuries did indeed see Chaucer as a prophet, and as part of a small group of clear-sighted pre-Reformation figures who understood the truth. Thus John Bale, in his *Laboryouse Journey* (1549), declares that, although the majority of pre-Reformation writers were "wholly given to serve Antichristes affectes in the parelouse ages of the Churche,"

Yet were there som amonge them, whiche refusynge that office, sought the onlye glorye of their Lorde God. In the middest of al darkenesse, have some men by all ages, had the livynge sprete of Goddes chyldren, what though they have in some thynges erred. Gal.iiii. Never yet were the spelunkes of Abdias wythoute the true Prophetes of God.[28]

That perspective generates post-Reformation literary history, as when, for example, Bale says that Langland "on account of various and happy similitudes . . . prophetically foresaw many things, which we have seen come to pass in our own days."[29]

Chaucer was crucial to this self-confirming Protestant story, and Chaucer had to be remade to serve that crucial need. Thus the stridently antipapal *Ploughman's Tale*, first printed separately in 1535, was by 1542 incorporated in editions of Chaucer, and, by 1550, inserted in the *Canterbury Tales*, just before *The Parson's Tale*.[30] It was also in 1542 that a

---

[27] Julian, *Revelation*, Chap. 86, p. 381.
[28] John Bale, *The laboryouse Journey and serche of Johan Leylande for Englandes Antiquitees* (London, 1549), *RSTC*, 15445, C1v.
[29] John Bale, *Scriptorum illustrium maioris brytannie, quam nunc angliam et scotiam uocant, catalogus* (John Oporinus, 1559), repr. in facsimile, 2 vols. (Farnsworth: Gregg, 1971), 474; my translation. See also the edition of *Piers Plowman* published in 1550, with a second edition, and reprinted in 1561: e.g., *The vision of pierce Plowman nowe the second time imprinted by Roberte Crowlye* (London, 1550), *STC*, 19907, image 2.
[30] For the history of Thynne's inclusion of *The Ploughman's Tale* in *CT*, see Anne Hudson, "John Stow (1525?–1605)," in Ruggiers, *Editing Chaucer*, 53–70 (59).

statute banned, and ordered the destruction of, all books published before 1540 except the Bibles in English not translated by Tyndale, and the following: the king's "proclamations, injunctions, translations of [some religious matter], Chronicles, Canterbury Tales, Chaucers bokes, Gower's bokes, and stories of mennes lieves."[31] Post-1550 readers were, then, almost certain to have read Chaucer in editions that presented him as a true prophet of the Protestant present.

Some post-1600 evangelical readers were no less concerned to see Chaucer as a prophet of the Puritan present. In the second and third decades of seventeenth-century England, revolutionary modernity started to take irreversible shapes in response to issues of how Christians might achieve pardon. This was the period when Puritanism became locked into the status of both party and sect. This was the moment at which the uneasy but just manageable coalition of higher and lower in the English Calvinist Church, which had held since the Elizabethan Settlement of 1563, broke apart.[32] The Puritanism that came into programmatic opposition to the English Church and monarch in this period produced, on the one hand, Presbyterian parliaments and the English Revolution, and, on the other, the flight of Independents to America.

These mighty revolutionary forces, which would reshape English Constitutionalism and, no less, world history, were united above all, paradoxically, by predestinarian, Calvinist repudiation of free will in the matter of achieving divine pardon. What brought such active and intransigent concentration of Calvinist force into more programmatic shape was the arrival, from the Netherlands, of doctrines defending a moderated exercise of free will, in the form of Arminianism. With that defense of free will suddenly available, particularly with the publication of Richard Montagu's *New Gag* in 1624, the new King Charles I effectively broke the Calvinist consensus: he proscribed any discussion of predestination after the York Conference of 1626. Oddly, we have a situation in which the reactionary, absolutist king defends free will, while his new-world, revolutionary opponents deny it.

---

[31] T. E. Tomlins, A. Luders, J. France, W. E. Taunton, J. Raithby, J. Caley, and W. Elliott, eds., *Statutes of the Realm*, 11 vols. (1963; London: Dawsons, 1810–28), 34 Henry VIII, Chap. I.I, 3:895.

[32] See Nicholas Tyacke, "Puritanism, Arminianism and Counter-Revolution," in *The Origins of the English Civil War*, ed. Conrad Russell (London: Macmillan, 1973), 119–43, and his *Anti-Calvinists: The Rise of English Arminianism, c. 1590–1640* (Oxford: Clarendon Press, 1987); and Dewey D. Wallace, *Puritans and Predestination: Grace in English Protestant Theology, 1525–1695* (Chapel Hill: University of North Carolina Press, 1982).

In this extraordinary and pre-Revolutionary seventeenth-century moment, Chaucer was there, and thought to be prophesying all that came to pass. Chaucer's works, duly Protestantized, had of course been published by Thomas Speght in 1598 (three editions) and 1602 (two editions).[33] The Calvinist George Abbot, who was archbishop of Canterbury from 1611 to 1633, cited Chaucer emphatically at least twice. Abbot isolates Chaucer as one of his own, a fellow evangelical. Thus he says, in his *Treatise of the perpetuall visibilitie, and succession of the true church in all ages* (1624), that Chaucer "did at large paint out the pride, lascivious, vicious and intolerable behaviour of the Pope, Cardinals, and Clergy, even applying the name of Antichrist diverse times vnto the Romane Bishop," for evidence of which he cites *The Ploughman's Tale*.[34] More extensively, in another text, Abbot enlists Chaucer as ahead of his time in promoting the key evangelical doctrine of predestination. For in 1618 Abbot reissued an edition of the fourteenth-century *De causa Dei contra Pelagium*, by predestinarian Thomas Bradwardine, himself also briefly archbishop of Canterbury in 1349.[35] In the preface Abbot cites Chaucer as a committed predestinarian, with citation of Chaucer's putative approbation, "more suo iocis seria intertexens" (mixing, in his way, serious with playful matters) of Bradwardine in *The Nun's Priest's Tale*.[36]

One could also cite Simon Birckbek's treatise *The Protestants evidence taken out of good records* (1634).[37] The aim of the text is to prove that the True (evangelical) Church had always existed. Birckbek's evidence is taken from a wide chronological range, but his intent is to affirm the continuous, visible existence of the True Church. When he comes to

---

[33] For 1598: *The workes of our antient and learned English poet*, printed three times: RSTC, 5077, 5078, 5079. For 1602: *The workes of our ancient and lerned English poet, Geffrey Chaucer, newly printed* (London, 1602), printed twice: RSTC, 5080, 5081. Both editions include *The Ploughman's Tale*; the 1602 edition adds *Jack Upland*. See Derek Pearsall, "Thomas Speght (ca. 1550–?)," in Ruggiers, *Editing Chaucer*, 71–92.

[34] George Abbot, *A treatise of the perpetuall visibilitie, and succession of the true church in all ages* (London, 1624), STC, 39.3, image 40.

[35] *Thomae Bradwardini Archiepiscopi olim Cantuariensis, De causa Dei, contra Pelagium . . . : iussu reverendiss. Georgii Abbot Cantuariensis Archiepiscopi* (London, 1618), STC, 3534.

[36] Ibid., image 4.

[37] Simon Birckbek, *The Protestants evidence taken out of good records; shewing that for fifteene hundred yeares next after Christ, divers worthy guides of Gods Church, have in sundry weightie poynts of religion, taught as the Church of England now doth* (London, 1635; first published 1634), STC, 3083. Neither Abbot nor Birckbek is mentioned by Caroline F. E. Spurgeon, *Five Hundred Years of Chaucer Criticism and Allusion 1357–1900*, 3 vols. (Cambridge: Cambridge University Press, 1925); or in Derek Brewer, ed., *Chaucer: The Critical Heritage*, 2 vols. (London: Routledge, 1978).

the fourteenth century, Birckbek cites what he takes to be Chaucer's *Ploughman's Tale* and the anti-fraternal *Jack Upland* (also attributed to Chaucer in the edition printed in 1536).[38] The weight of his citations falls, however, upon the authentically Chaucerian *Pardoner's Tale*. Birckbek summarizes his comments about the Pardoner with this citation from False Seeming's speech in Chaucer's *Romance of the Rose* translation, revealing in the process a wide reading of Chaucer's oeuvre, and a well-informed reading of Chaucer's sources for *The Pardoner's Prologue*:

> Of Antichrist's men am I,
> Of which that Christ sayth openly;
> They have habite of holinesse,
> And living in such wickednesse.[39]

Chaucer, that is, by this account, perfectly understood the total hypocrisy of the Catholic Church, as a harbinger of last days, via the hypocrisy of the Pardoner.

To sign Chaucer up as a member of the True Church, and as a prophet in his own dark days, is to describe Chaucer as a prophet almost fully possessed of the truth, "what though," as Bale says, "[he has] in some thynges erred." For evangelical readers, God's interventionist action in the world is immanent and legible to the Elect in each moment, pre- or post-Christ. That produces less an account of historical unfolding and progressive revelation, and more a sequence of moments, each of which legibly replays the same intense drama. Thus the reading habits of Lutherans and, later, Calvinists effectively abolished anagogy proper, not only because they abolished fourfold exegesis, but also because they abolished futurity. They did so by their insistence that the fullness of scriptural meaning is permanently and fully available to the Elect at any given moment in history.[40]

---

[38] *Jack vp Lande compyled by the famous Geoffrey Chaucer* (London, 1536), *STC*, 5098. The title page clearly signals the Chaucerian text as prophetic, with a quotation from Ezekiel: "Woe be unto you that dishonor me to the people for an handful of barley and for a piece of bread" (Ez 13:19).

[39] Birckbek, *The Protestants evidence*, image 177. The citation is drawn from Chaucer's translation, *The Romaunt of the Rose*, in *The Riverside Chaucer*, gen. ed. Larry D. Benson, 3rd ed. (Boston: Houghton Mifflin, 1987), 7009–12 (the text as cited by Birckbek differs slightly from the *Riverside* text). All further citations from the works of Chaucer will be drawn from this edition.

[40] For which see James Simpson, *Burning to Read: English Fundamentalism and Its Reformation Opponents* (Cambridge, Mass.: Belknap Press, 2007), Chap. 6.

Evangelicals thus read from the vantage point of the eschaton, and so render the unfolding of anagogical reading obsolete. They already know absolutely what the text means, as if from the end of time. They can enjoy certain knowledge because they already inhabit that totally visible future. That position legitimates their own assumption of the prophet's mantle, as, for example, when William Tyndale encourages his clerical readers to model themselves on Old Testament prophets. Just as "many holy prophetes . . . in the olde testamente dyd call the people backe and brought them agayne in tyme of aduersyte," so too the "kynge in Goddes stede . . . toke an oth of them, to be the lordes people and to turne agayn to the lordes couenaunte."[41]

Such an evangelical account of permanent visibility contrasts with a more truly anagogic account of scriptural unfolding as given, for example, by Thomas More, in his *Confutation of Tyndale's Answer* (1532–33):

For God doth reveal his truths not always in one manner, but sometime he sheweth out at once . . . Sometime he sheweth it leisurely, suffering his flock to come and dispute thereupon, and in their treating of the matter, suffereth them with good mind and scripture and natural wisdom, with invocation of his spiritual help, to search and seek for the truth, and to vary for the while in their opinions, till that he reward their virtuous diligence with leading them secretly in to the consent and concord and belief of the truth by his Holy Spirit. . . . So that in the mean while the variance is without sin.[42]

Evangelicals, then, saw Chaucer as a prophet, but a prophet in their own image, as fully in possession of the truth. His texts do not unfold, but, like Scripture as read by evangelicals, declare their incontrovertible and salutary truth literally. For evangelicals, the reader's soul cannot be said to awake as a "trembling stranger, between two dim eternities," since the reader's soul is already in full and confident possession of the saving truth and a brightly lit eternity. The reader's soul already reads as from the eschaton.

Chaucer was clearly *not* the kind of prophet Protestant readers would have had him be. For the most part, on the contrary, Chaucer expresses

---

[41] William Tyndale, *An exposycyon vpon the v.vi.vii. chapters of Mathewe* (London[?], 1536), STC, 24441.3, image 92.
[42] Thomas More, *The Complete Works of St. Thomas More*, Vol. 8, *The Confutation of Tyndale's Answer*, ed. Louis A. Schuster, Richard Marius, James P. Lusardi, and Richard J. Schoeck, 3 parts (New Haven: Yale University Press, 1973), 1:248.

skepticism about prophecy, and avoids utopianism. In comic mode, Pertelote counsels the would-be visionary prophet Chaunticleer to dismiss his visionary dreams as merely the product of humoral imbalance, and to "taak som laxatyf" (*CT*, VII.2943). In tragic mode, Chaucer also underlines the sheer difficulty of rising above the complex opacity of earthly existence to see beyond or above it. Thus in Book II of *Troilus and Criseyde*, Pandarus finds Criseyde reading a book with her women companions. "Is it of love?," Pandarus asks (II.97), to which Criseyde replies that it is in fact the narrative of the siege of Thebes, and that they have just got to the point where Amphiorax, the one figure who does foresee the destruction of the multiple catastrophes that await all the Theban players, "fil thurgh the ground to helle" (II.105). Chaucer's follower Lydgate gives full voice to prudential prophets in his narratives of both Thebes and Troy. These figures from within the text (e.g., Helenus, Amphiorax) courageously articulate the destruction that will ensue on going to war.[43] But in *Troilus and Criseyde* this hair-raising narrative of a prudential figure dying in spectacular horror is evoked only to be displaced by the edgy social comedy of Pandarus's amatory manipulations. Chaucer's classical-epic forebears (Virgil and Statius), no less than England's great epic poet Milton, all, in their different ways, shape poetic structures that point history forward into a future, and all write poems with explicitly prophetic passages. For Chaucer, by contrast, history appears to be one damn thing after another, whose only constant is the inconstancy of Fortune. Chaucer writes by natural order; unlike the epic poets he knows well, and unlike Milton, he does not enter the dynamic of history by starting in the middle of things.

Except for its self-interested prophet Calchas, its rhetorically brutal prophet Cassandra, and its far-sighted if mocking Epilogue, *Troilus and Criseyde* is embedded in the opacities of history. So embedded is it in history as lived that it can gain no secure foothold from which to mount clear-eyed prophecy. The poem instead occupies the lapsarian space of "fals and sooth compouned,"[44] of experience as lived, whether the unpredictable lived experience be that of brutal war or of painful personal experience within Troy. Not only Criseyde, but the poem itself,

---

[43] For which see James Simpson, "'Dysemol daies and Fatal houres': Lydgate's *Destruction of Thebes* and Chaucer's *Knight's Tale*," in *The Long Fifteenth Century: Essays in Honour of Douglas Gray*, ed. Helen Cooper and Sally Mapstone (Oxford: Oxford University Press, 1997), 15–33.
[44] *HF*, 2108.

with its ever-shifting, earth-bound temporal perspectives, has only two of Prudence's three eyes—it can see past and especially present with exceptional clarity, but, as Criseyde says, "future tyme, er I was in the snare, / Kould I nat sen."[45]

III

Evangelicals, then, were clearly mistaken about the kind of prophecy Chaucer made, and the commitment to prophecy he entertained. In making such an argument, I operate like a paid-up synchronic historicist. For the synchronic historicist, that is, all texts are only intelligible within their own terms and their own time. So, for such a historicist, *any* claim that a text is prophetic is by default wrong; synchronic historicist *Nachleben* studies are histories of mistaken presentism, of self interest, and of error. Before we leave the matter there, however, what if we were to pause and ask whether or not evangelical readers like Abbot and Birckbek might be *right* in describing Chaucer as a prophet, of sorts?

Does Chaucer draw on anagogy as I have defined it? Does Chaucer, that is, practice a form of prophetic writing, from a wounded present, that calls on its readership to contribute collaboratively to its resolution in time?

That Chaucer was writing prophetically is not at all historically implausible, for he was surrounded by vernacular religious texts that did precisely this, even if none participates in Joachite millenarian traditions.[46] In addition to Julian of Norwich, whose anagogy we have already considered, one could point to *Piers Plowman*, another anagogic text with many versions. This is a poem whose narrative through biblical time, from past into present and then into prophetic future, cannot in my view be resolved as a text until all its readers identify with its narrator to become one will, the will of the long land.[47] The greatest obstacle

---

[45] *TC*, V.748–49. For a brilliant account of the delusions of prophetic hope as invested in the prophecies of Apollo in *TC*, see Jamie C. Fumo, *The Legacy of Apollo: Antiquity, Authority, and Chaucerian Poetics* (Toronto: University of Toronto Press, 2010), esp. Chap. 3.

[46] For which see David Aers, *Beyond Reformation? An Essay on Langland and the End of Constantinian Christianity* (Notre Dame: University of Notre Dame Press, forthcoming), section 12; and Kathryn Kerby-Fulton, *Reformist Apocalypticism and "Piers Plowman"* (Cambridge: Cambridge University Press, 1990).

[47] James Simpson, "The Power of Impropriety: Authorial Naming in *Piers Plowman*," in *William Langland's "Piers Plowman": A Book of Essays*, ed. Kathleen M. Hewett-Smith (New York: Routledge, 2001), 145–65.

to that collaborative ethical effort is the damage being done to the sacrament of penance. That damage is so grave as fundamentally to weaken the Barn of Unity, so much so that the poem ends, prophetically in my view, with an isolated Conscience figure leaving the institution and crying tragically after grace, all sacramental resources having failed.

Perhaps the readiest case for anagogical writing contemporary with Chaucer can be made for the "verray avision" of *Pearl*.[48] In that poem the dreamer witnesses the Heavenly Jerusalem, but his premature yearning for incorporation in that timeless and utopian city sends him painfully back into the *saeculum* and into history. The painfully abrupt ending of the poem is not, however, without its promise of "quo tend[imus]," since we are implicitly called upon as readers to make the utopian city possible. The poem's first line is echoed yet altered by the pluralized last: "Perle, pleasaunte to prynces paye" (1), "And precious perlez unto his paye" (1212). The first line expresses devotion to a single pearl, possessed by the father, whereas the last marks the narrator's acceptance of his identity with every other Christian soul. The referent of the pearl shifts across the poem, from the earthly to metaphorical to spiritual. In so doing, those referents imitate the constant upward and forward move in scriptural exegesis, from "carnal," literal readings to ultimately anagogic meanings. The critical turning point is made by reference to the parable of the pearl of great price (Mt 13:45–46) "the joueler gef fore alle hys god":

> For it is wemlez, clene, and clere,
> And endelez rounde, and blythe of mode,
> And commune to alle that ryghtwys were.
>
> (737–39)

This is the pearl of salvation that must be "bought" by the dreamer himself. The poem has, however, now made it clear that all readers are part of this utopian project, since the pearl is, like Julian's vision, "commune to alle that ryghtwys were."[49]

What, though, of the texts chosen by our early seventeenth-century

---

[48] *The Poems of the "Pearl" Manuscript*, ed. Malcolm Andrew and Ronald Waldron, rev. ed. (Exeter: University of Exeter Press, 1987), 1184. Letter forms have been modernized.

[49] I warmly acknowledge the work of Michelle de Groot, whose Ph.D. dissertation persuasively develops this aspect of *Pearl*.

evangelical to exemplify Chaucer as prophet? Abbot's choice of *The Nun's Priest's Tale* as evidence of Chaucer's belief in predestination is clearly vulnerable. But Abbot might, however, prompt us to start with that opaque and amusing passage as a symptom of culture; once we do that we also turn to a passage in which Chaucer clearly does take predestination very seriously indeed. In Book IV of *Troilus and Criseyde*, Troilus's dark, nineteen-stanza, unabsorbed meditation on divine "predestine" (IV.953–1082), when he was "so fallen in despeyr . . . That outrely he shop him for to deye" (IV.954–55), is a pre-play of the psychic drama of any number of evangelicals in the sixteenth and seventeenth centuries.[50] Second, we might reflect that when we as scholars explicate this philosophical passage, we tend, not unreasonably, to turn backward, to the authors Chaucer himself mentions, particularly Augustine, Boethius, and Bradwardine.[51] We tend not to look forward, to the fact that the issue of predestination is, in evangelical culture, twinned with the dismissal of the sacrament of penance. Both these issues, which energize each other, will exert mighty, world-changing pressure within just over a century of this passage's composition.[52] Chaucer's despairing Troilus, no less than his suffering Criseyde, might be looking forward as much as backward as he endures both emotional and theological pain.

Birckbek's choice is *The Pardoner's Tale*. Is it prophetic? Is it anagogic? Does Chaucer imagine the "anagoge," or "leading up," of a utopian reading?

The *Canterbury Tales* does offer at least one clear example of an anagogical narrator. Thus the Parson encourages us, by citation of the prophet Jeremiah, to "stand upon the weyes"; he commands us thus: "seeth and axeth of olde pathes," so as to make out the future of "Jerusalem celestial," where "ye shal fynde refresshynge for youre soules." As Chaucer's pilgrimage nears Canterbury Cathedral in the *saeculum*, the Parson encourages the pilgrims to a raised, spiritual, anagogic journey to the Celestial Jerusalem. That upward journey can be undertaken only by the ethical collaboration of the pilgrims, however, since "This wey is cleped penitence" (X.77–81).

---

[50] For which see the brilliant book by John Stachniewski, *The Persecutory Imagination: English Puritanism and the Literature of Religious Despair* (Oxford: Clarendon Press, 1991).

[51] As, for example, Ida L. Gordon, *The Double Sorrow of Troilus: A Study of Ambiguity in "Troilus and Criseyde"* (Oxford: Clarendon Press, 1970), Chap. 2.

[52] See Wallace, *Puritans and Predestination*.

Penitence, however, is precisely the sacrament that is fundamentally damaged in the *Canterbury Tales*, as it is in *Piers Plowman*. The Friar and Summoner abuse it, but no one more so than the Pardoner. In his tale and its surrounds, pardon and therefore penitence are impossible, since, inside and outside the tale itself, the vortex of sin is so aggressive, so rapid, so decided as to disallow the reflective intervention of repentance and restitution.

The Pardoner himself derives, of course, from a powerfully prophetic, ecclesiological conception. William of Saint-Amour's self-consciously prophetic *De periculis novissimorum temporum* (1256) is the ultimate source for the figure of the hypocrite ecclesiast as expressed by Chaucer. William directed his moral attack on the friars as "pseudo" preachers, but, as the title of his work suggests, his larger scheme is ecclesiological and temporal. The friars are signs of the last times, forerunners of Antichrist, who "are false; it even appears that through such men the dangers of the last times will threaten or already are threatening the entire church."[53] When, then, the Pardoner begins his tale by declaring that the revelers "doon the devel sacrifise / Withinne that develes temple in cursed wise" (VI.469–70), he evokes a very much wider attack, not so much on tavern doings, as on the Church itself, the very Church that is populated not only by rapacious friars (and we have already seen one of these in the *Tales*), but also by Pardoners bearing their authorization of "bulles of popes and of cardynales" (VI.342). This is the Church described 130 years later by evangelicals as essentially and lethally hypocritical, and a Church whose relics were never anything but fraudulent bric-a-brac, with nothing but a broken and irreparable connection to a dynamic past.

The "devil's temple" of the tale threateningly predicts what some readers nearly contemporary with Chaucer were already prepared to declare—that the Church itself had become the devil's Church, populated by "sellers of sacramentis," institutionally authorized by a "special lettir of lisence, that is clepid the mark of this beest antichrist," as the Lollard, not to say Donatist, *Lantern of Light* (c. 1410) puts it.[54] In the 1390s the appalling possibility that the Church is wholly hypocritical and murderous has a large, long, and violent future ahead of it.

---

[53] William of Saint-Amour, *De periculis novissimorum temporum*, ed. G. Geltner (Paris: Leuven, 2008), 59.

[54] *The Lanterne of Liȝt*, ed. Lilian M. Swinburn, EETS o.s. 151 (London: Kegan Paul, Trench, and Trübner, 1917), 132 and 14 respectively.

Anagogical narratives will not be wholly absorbable into their own present. That inability to be absorbed is most powerfully expressed from within *The Pardoner's Tale* by the old man who, despite longing for Nature to let him die, cannot die.[55] Like Spenser's figure of Despair,[56] constantly trying and failing to kill himself, the old man can only forever diminish, "vanish[ing], flesh and blood, and skin" (VI.732). In a purely material, death-dominated world deprived of sacramental renewal of any kind, the old man articulates a searing state of existential loneliness. He must forever walk "lik a resteleees kaityf," since "Deeth, allas, ne wol nat han my lif!" (VI.726–27). The old man (Chaucer's addition to the tale) stands in searing isolation both from the scheme of generation and from sacramental renewal of any kind.[57]

That isolation evokes the Pardoner himself. For, just as the isolated old man cannot be absorbed by the tale itself, so too the Pardoner cannot be absorbed at the end of his tale-telling. He remains profoundly, prophetically isolated, in his open hypocrisy, from all his fellow, vernacular-reading pilgrims.

The Pardoner's extrusion from the pilgrimage is prophetic, but so too is the attempt to reabsorb him. For that reabsorption is itself, also prophetically, full of danger. In the first place, it's significant that only a secular figure, the Knight, is capable of intervening effectively. The ecclesiastical figures of Friar and Summoner are, for example, too imbricated in the system corrupted by the Pardoner, or too marginal, like the Parson, to exercise authority. The intervention of secular authority in the secular person of the Knight itself points to a future for the English Church, which will soon be incapable of resolving its internal dissension.

More darkly, the Knight's apparent reconciliation replicates some of the most threatening features of *The Pardoner's Tale*. Host and Pardoner draw near at the Knight's instigation, in order to reinstate the festive order of the pilgrimage, whereby they "laughe and pleye." And so "Anon they kiste, and ryden forth hir weye" (VI.967–68). The very attempt of readers to exercise an ethically restorative and communitarian act is, however, pregnant with danger. For the pardoning embrace

---

[55] See Lee Patterson, "Chaucer's Pardoner on the Couch: Psyche and Clio in Medieval Literary Studies," *Speculum* 76 (2001): 638–80 (657). Patterson's essay is an exemplary instance of synchronic historicism.

[56] Edmund Spenser, *The Faerie Queene*, ed. Thomas P. Roche (London: Penguin, 1987), Book I, Canto 9.

[57] See Robert M. Correale and Mary Hamel, eds., *Sources and Analogues of the "Canterbury Tales,"* 2 vols. (Cambridge: Brewer, 2002–5); for the sources of the old man (Elegy 1 of Maximianus), 1:312–19.

of the Pardoner, to reestablish the "pleye" of the *Canterbury Tales*, has a murderous, hypocritical exemplum within the tale. The two revelers plan to murder the third; when the third arrives back, says one reveler to another,

> Aris as though thou woldest with him pleye;
> And I shal ryve him thurgh the sydes tweye
> Whil that thou strogelest with him as in game.
> (VI.827–29)

Embracing the hypocrite is potentially to participate in his hypocrisy. To forgive and to accept a hypocrite, as in Jean de Meun's *Roman de la rose*, and as in Langland's *Piers Plowman*, is to step onto a fraught and very treacherous line.[58] By forgiving the hypocrite, we become the hypocrite's victim, as does, for example, Malebouche. But by badmouthing the hypocrite, we also become the hypocrite's victim.[59]

Chaucer's *Pardoner's Tale* is prophetic, then, in a variety of ways. It is also anagogic insofar as it adumbrates a future. The fact that this tale, like *Piers Plowman*, was drawn upon or referred to so often in the following 150 years or so itself points to its engagement with futurity (anagogical texts will often have a rich and contested *Nachleben* as they ripple forward in history).[60] *The Pardoner's Tale* is anagogical too insofar as we as readers are involved in resolving the profound failings represented by its narrator. Anagogical texts will also represent a readership in dispute about a text's meaning, precisely because the text cannot be absorbed into its own present, and requires a future for resolution. In all these ways, the tale is properly anagogic. It certainly does not adumbrate a utopian future, since the viciousness of the Host's response (VI.946–55) tells us that these issues will prompt convulsion and vicious civil war, involving many abused martyrs and secular intervention, before they are

---

[58] In the *Roman de la rose*, the God of Love accepts False Seeming into his entourage (1093), and in *Piers Plowman* Conscience admits Friar Flatterer into the Barn of Unity (B XX.356), for which last see James Simpson, *"Piers Plowman": An Introduction to the B-Text*, 2nd rev. ed. (Exeter: University of Exeter Press, 2007), 211.

[59] *Roman de la rose*, 12097–380.

[60] A very partial list of responses to the Pardoner and his Tale: Lydgate's *Siege of Thebes* (c. 1420); the pseudo-Chaucerian *Tale of Beryn* (c. 1420); John Heywood, *The Pardoner and the Frere* (published 1533); Thomas More's *Dialogue Concerning Heresies* (1529); and the seventeenth-century authors cited in this essay. For the contested afterlife of *Piers Plowman*, see James Simpson, "Grace Abounding: Evangelical Centralization and the End of *Piers Plowman*," *YLS* 14 (2000): 1–25.

properly, or at least partially, resolvable. Chaucer is an anagogical writer in all but utopianism. His passion for the future is the passion of fear.

IV

Anagogy, as defined by medieval exegetes, and as practiced by Harriet Beecher Stowe, is inexplicit and visionary. To draw on Macrobius's early fifth-century Neoplatonic genres of prophetic dream-writing with which Chaucer was certainly familiar, the anagogic writer produces *visio* rather than *oraculum*.[61]

If Chaucer disowns prophecy on the biblical model, and if he certainly does *not* write oracular prophecy, I suggest nonetheless that some of his texts are prophetic, where the "light shines only on a small space around [him]." Whereas anagogy classically expresses a profound desire for the future from a broken and wounded present, "yearn[ing] towards the unknown," Chaucer foresees, though recoils from, a sacrament-deprived future, in which the soul, "lik a restelees kaityf," faces existential loneliness and irresolution.[62]

In conclusion, we can say that many Middle English texts say, as Christ says in another great anagogical text, "Tempus meum nondum advenit" (My time is not yet come; Jn 7:6). The anagogic text will most likely exhibit some or all of these characteristics: inexplicit prophecy; an extra-literary crisis surrounding it; different versions; crises of representation; unabsorbed narrative and/or formal features that cannot be accommodated in the here and now of the text; a sense of its own woundedness; an appeal to readers to make or avoid the future predicted by the text; and a significantly divergent, contested reception history. Anagogy classically expresses a profound desire for the future from a broken and wounded present, "yearn[ing] towards the unknown." In *The Pardoner's Tale*, however, as in many other works of the late fourteenth-century premature Reformation, Chaucer both foresees and retreats from a given future.

Anagogical texts, then, are in some ways prophetic of things to come, even if they sometimes prophesy unwanted futures. They are premised

---

[61] For which terms, see A. C. Spearing, *Medieval Dream Poetry* (Cambridge: Cambridge University Press, 1976), Chap. 1.
[62] For a parallel argument with regard to Langland, see Simpson, "Grace Abounding."

on history *not* having stopped. Instead they capture and channel historical currents so as to produce a rippling effect across history. The job of the diachronic philologist is to trace the shape and intensity of those ripples, and thereby to reactivate many of the narratives neutralized and prohibited by the periodic strictures of our disciplinary categories.

Scribes, Misattributed: Hoccleve and Pinkhurst

Lawrence Warner
King's College London

A HISTORY OF MIDDLE ENGLISH LITERARY PRODUCTION in London c. 1380–1420 remarkable for its richness, elegance, and detail has taken shape over the last decade or so, thanks to a series of stunning studies by Linne Mooney and her collaborators Simon Horobin and Estelle Stubbs.[1] In the 1370s, so we learn, one Adam Pinkhurst, king's archer, became acquainted with Geoffrey Chaucer, fellow member of Edward III's household. This Adam eventually retired to his family's home region of Surrey–Sussex, but in the meantime his son or nephew, and namesake, came to be Chaucer's scribe, copying *Boece* and *Troilus* (perhaps in copies fragments of which are still extant) for the poet in the 1380s and earning a notorious place as addressee of a light-hearted stanza bemoaning his copying errors. He also did bureaucratic work for some guilds and John of Northampton and produced a beautiful *Piers*

Linne Mooney, Estelle Stubbs, and especially Simon Horobin, who graciously commented on an earlier draft of some of this essay, have been supportive from my earliest interest in the manuscripts of Chaucer and Langland. I am grateful for extensive feedback from and discussion with Tony Edwards, Alexandra Gillespie, Michael Johnston, Sheila Lindenbaum, Jane Roberts, and Sebastian Sobecki, and for advice, bibliographical and otherwise, from Julia Crick, Kathleen Kennedy, Ethan Knapp, Elon Lang, Bobby Meyer-Lee, Aditi Nafde, Andrew Prescott, Pamela Robinson, Jacob Thaisen, David Watt, and Rivkah Zim. Thanks as well to *SAC*'s editor, my colleague Sarah Salih, and to both readers for the journal, of whom Ralph Hanna identified himself. These acknowledgments imply neither endorsement of my arguments nor responsibility for any of my errors.

[1] These first three paragraphs for the most part present the conclusions reached, sometimes tentatively, by Simon Horobin and Linne R. Mooney, "A *Piers Plowman* Manuscript by the Hengwrt/Ellesmere Scribe and Its Implications for London Standard English," *SAC* 26 (2004): 65–112; Linne R. Mooney, "Chaucer's Scribe," *Speculum* 81 (2006): 97–138; Linne R. Mooney, "A Holograph Copy of Thomas Hoccleve's *Regiment of Princes*," *SAC* 33 (2011): 263–96; and Linne R. Mooney and Estelle Stubbs, *Scribes and the City: London Guildhall Clerks and the Dissemination of Middle English Literature, 1375–1425* (York: York Medieval Press, 2013).

Plowman, thus altering our understanding of Chaucer's political affiliations and knowledge of Langland's work, and even of the development of standard English.

For it is as "Chaucer's own scrivener" that Pinkhurst is so important: the Hengwrt *Canterbury Tales*, Aberystwyth, National Library of Wales, MS Peniarth 392D, was produced just before the poet's death and possibly under his supervision, and over the following decade he copied the lavish Ellesmere *Canterbury Tales*, San Marino, Huntington Library, MS EL 26 C.9, his greatest production. During this period, and perhaps earlier, Adam Pinkhurst held a clerkly position in the Guildhall, recording a handful of entries in Letter Book I and working alongside the only other copyist of vernacular literature who could approach his own importance and ambition in the dissemination of vernacular English poetry, one John Marchaunt, Common Clerk. Pinkhurst was "Scribe B," and Marchaunt "Scribe D," of Cambridge, Trinity College, MS R.3.2, the *Confessio Amantis*, dated after 1408.[2]

At this point the other major figure of the story, notable as scribe, poet, and civil servant, comes into the picture of the Guildhall's central role in Middle English literary production. For "Scribe E" of the Trinity Gower, and possibly its supervisor, was Thomas Hoccleve, clerk at the Privy Seal, in which capacity he came to know Marchaunt, his apprentice John Carpenter, and, most remarkably, Chaucer himself, on whose behalf he wrote a petition in 1399, as Pinkhurst had done as well. Hoccleve remained active, if beset by frequent psychological and financial hardships, in the 1410s and 1420s. A major new addition to this history is the claim that London, British Library, MS Royal 17 D.XVIII, an ordinary-looking *Regiment of Princes*, is in fact a holograph copy, with new readings reflecting the changed circumstances of both country and poet in the year since this poem was first issued. Any discovery of a holograph by a Middle English poet is a major event, and this one has implications for his career, our editorial practices, and our understanding of how scribal behavior could change over long periods of time.

This is a thrilling account, and it is no wonder that the Pinkhurst

---

[2] On the production of Trinity R.3.2, and these appellations, see A. I. Doyle and M. B. Parkes, "The Production of Copies of the *Canterbury Tales* and the *Confessio Amantis* in the Early Fifteenth Century," in *Medieval Scribes, Manuscripts and Libraries: Essays Presented to N. R. Ker*, ed. Parkes and Andrew G. Watson (London: Scolar Press, 1978), 163–210. I use "Scribe B," "Hengwrt-Ellesmere scribe," and "Hg-El scribe" interchangeably.

identification in particular has captured so many imaginations. Less than a decade after Linne Mooney's "Chaucer's Scribe," Adam Pinkhurst has received an entry in the *Oxford Dictionary of National Biography*,[3] featured prominently in the latest biography of Chaucer,[4] and become a mainstay of criticism on his poetry and career and on medieval manuscript production. What I most admire about this history, which grows from Mooney, Stubbs, and Horobin's project seeking to identify the scribes of Middle English literature,[5] is the way it demonstrates paleography's centrality to the interpretation of medieval English culture at large and not just of a poet's meaning. These scribes, like Chaucer and Langland, had names, relations, and political affiliations.

All the same, the alacrity with which the story has been embraced should give us pause. Jane Roberts's has been a lonely voice in attempting, in some detail, "to indicate how the Adam Pynkhurst canon has elaborated quickly and perhaps ill-advisedly," concluding: "Convincing evidence that Adam Pynkhurst was Scribe B remains uncertain."[6] But she does not go so far as to say that Pinkhurst could not have been Scribe B; and critics weighing this against Mooney and her colleagues' claims that their identifications are in "no doubt," can be asserted "conclusively," are "too weighty for any other conclusion," and are "without question,"[7] might be forgiven for preferring to follow Kathryn Kerby-Fulton's lead: "Roberts's challenge, then, is inconclusive, but it deserves

---

[3] Linne R. Mooney, "Pinkhurst, Adam (*fl*. 1385–1410)," in *Oxford Dictionary of National Biography*, online ed., ed. Lawrence Goldman (Oxford: Oxford University Press, 2012), http://www.oxforddnb.com/index/101101080/ (accessed July 2, 2015). Inclusion in the *ODNB* is reserved for "people who have left their mark on an aspect of national life"; http://global.oup.com/oxforddnb/info/faqs/#biographies1 (accessed July 2, 2015).

[4] Paul Strohm, *The Poet's Tale: Chaucer and the Year that Made the "Canterbury Tales"* (London: Profile, 2014), 242–43, remarking: "Although elements of [Mooney's] analysis have been questioned, none have seriously doubted that Pinkhurst enjoyed privileged access to Chaucer's papers after his death, and that his hand is present in these two crucial early manuscripts," that is, Hengwrt and Ellesmere (276). This slightly reworks Alexandra Gillespie, "Reading Chaucer's Words to Adam," *ChauR* 42 (2008): 269–83 (270), to which Strohm's following sentence directs readers. But this is an overstatement: see note 6 below, and Ralph Hanna's remark that "[t]he Hengwrt editor cannot have had any access whatever to Chaucer's papers"; *Pursuing History: Middle English Manuscripts and Their Texts* (Stanford: Stanford University Press, 1996), 147.

[5] See *Late Medieval English Scribes*, http://www.medievalscribes.com/ > "About the Project" (accessed July 1, 2015).

[6] Jane Roberts, "On Giving Scribe B a Name and a Clutch of London Manuscripts from c. 1400," *MÆ* 80 (2011): 247–70 (263).

[7] Respectively, Horobin and Mooney, "A *Piers Plowman* Manuscript," 72; Mooney, "Chaucer's Scribe," 138; Mooney, "Holograph Copy," 280; Mooney and Stubbs, *Scribes and the City*, 85. Mooney and Stubbs's penultimate sentence acknowledges, for the first time, that its authors "are not as certain of some identifications as of others" (141), yet,

attention . . . In the absence, however, of a broader-based challenge to Mooney's identification (one that includes all the historical, codicological, literary and dialect analysis that Mooney engagingly brought to the problem), we will persevere here with the Pinkhurst identification at least for Hengwrt and Ellesmere."[8]

This essay provides that broader-based challenge, by showing in part that even such caution as Kerby-Fulton's does not serve as protection from too strong a trust in Mooney's methodologies. For the case is so overwhelming that Adam Pinkhurst copied Cambridge, Trinity College, MS B.15.17—the *Piers Plowman* B mentioned above—I will argue, that it becomes impossible to believe that he had anything to do with Hengwrt and Ellesmere. This local claim marks one of my differences from Roberts's more measured conclusion—she rejects the attributions of the *Piers* to Scribe B and of the Chaucer manuscripts to Pinkhurst, without noticing the evidence that the former manuscript is by the latter scribe—which otherwise, however, together with many conversations in which she has generously shared her thoughts, has provided a benchmark for the critical analysis of the issues at hand. What enabled me to unravel the Pinkhurst case, though, was an earlier engagement with Mooney's more straightforward and recent claim that MS Royal 17 D.XVIII is a holograph copy of the *Regiment of Princes*; this essay tracks my own development in beginning there. If my arguments are accepted, the narrative presented above will be in need of revision or reversal in both detail and arc. But perhaps more urgent is the need for a serious conversation concerning the methodologies of scribal attribution, and the desires and imperatives that lead to those methodologies' employment even where no obvious need or reason presents itself.

Ry3

The announcement that Royal 17 D.XVIII is a new Hoccleve holograph in some ways participates in a larger project whereby Stubbs, Mooney,

---

as A. S. G. Edwards remarks, "The general tone throughout does not indicate such levels of uncertainty, nor are specific areas of doubt clearly signalled"; review of *Scribes and the City*, *The Library* 15, no. 1 (March 2014): 79–81 (81).

[8] Kathryn Kerby-Fulton, Maidie Hilmo, and Linda Olson, *Opening up Middle English Manuscripts: Literary and Visual Approaches* (Ithaca, N.Y.: Cornell University Press, 2012), 81. The small impact of Roberts's challenge is clear from, e.g., note 4 above and Michael Calabrese, review of *Scribes and the City*, *TMR* 14.08.06 (accessed August 20, 2015), https://scholarworks.iu.edu/journals/index.php/tmr/article/view/18640/24753: "Study of medieval English literature has experienced a Copernican revolution since Linne Mooney gave her dramatic paper at Glasgow identifying Adam Pinkhurst as Chaucer's

and Helen Killick discovered over 1,000 documents from the Privy Seal in his hand, including a record identifying his father, a document with his seal, and another that "may be taken as confirmation that Hoccleve knew Chaucer personally."[9] This new attribution is set apart, though, in concerning his poetry, which enables the testing of it against his language, his meter, and the stemma of the poem's manuscripts. Such tests are of a different order from that of the more subjective, paleographical, and historical ones lying behind the most pressing question: "at what point do we start believing in a scribal identity mooted between hands in different manuscripts?"[10]

In Mooney's account Royal 17 D.XVIII was neither the authorial original of the *Regiment of Princes* nor merely an unexceptional copy far down the stemma that Hoccleve happened to copy. It was instead the presentation copy for John of Lancaster, later duke of Bedford, whose text "represents a revised version of the poem written in 1412–13, in which the author had made alterations reflecting the changed circumstances of himself, of his dedicatee, Henry of Derby, and of the country a year or two after the completion and first dissemination of the poem."[11] Marcia Smith Marzec had characterized Ry3, as the manuscript's text is called in this field of endeavor, as representing "a distinct

---

Scribe. The applause, as I recall, went on for quite a while and can still, justly, be heard today," and so forth, with no substantive criticisms.

[9] Linne R. Mooney, "Some New Light on Thomas Hoccleve," *SAC* 29 (2007): 293–340 (312); Helen Katherine Spencer Killick, "Thomas Hoccleve as Poet and Clerk," Ph.D. diss. (University of York, 2010), which adds over 900 new items from The National Archives in Hoccleve's hand to the c. 150 listed in Appendix B of Mooney's essay; and Estelle Stubbs and Linne R. Mooney, "A Record Identifying Thomas Hoccleve's Father," *JEBS* 14 (2011): 233–37. For a correction of Mooney's reading of Hoccleve's seal, which she is careful to say is provisional because "the imprint of the seal is not absolutely sharp and the lettering is somewhat stylized" ("Some New Light," 317 n. 64), see Richard Firth Green and Ethan Knapp, "Thomas Hoccleve's Seal," *MÆ* 77 (2008): 319–21. Killick, "Thomas Hoccleve," 94–95, defends Mooney's reading but without addressing most of Green and Knapp's linguistic objections.

[10] Alan J. Fletcher, "The Criteria for Scribal Attribution: Dublin, Trinity College, MS 244, Some Early Copies of the Works of Geoffrey Chaucer, and the Canon of Adam Pynkhurst Manuscripts," *RES* n.s. 58 (2007): 597–632 (598). Fletcher's perspective is that of one seeking to extend the corpus of manuscripts ascribed to Pinkhurst; from the other side, Edwards asks how extensive such variations within one identified hand "have to be to call into question their reliability as the primary criterion for scribal identification" (review of *Scribes and the City*, 80). See also Roberts, "On Giving Scribe B a Name"; and the bulk of Alan J. Fletcher, "What Did Adam Pynkhurst (Not) Write? A Reply to Dr. Horobin," *RES* n.s. 61 (2010): 690–710, directed against Simon Horobin, "The Criteria for Scribal Attribution: Dublin, Trinity College MS 244 Reconsidered," *RES* n.s. 60 (2009): 371–81.

[11] Mooney, "Holograph Copy," 263.

and quite early stage in the transmission of the *Regiment* texts";[12] Mooney pushes this still further by rejecting Marzec's own conclusion that Ry3 is genetic partner with Oxford, Bodleian Library, MS Dugdale 45 (Du), seeing it instead as the latter's exemplar. She thus positions Ry3 as Hoccleve's revision of the original, it and Du in its wake attesting "a separate branch of the stemma."[13]

On the assumption that she has established this manuscript's hand as Hoccleve's, and its text as set apart from all others (save Du), Mooney cites "significant changes to the text that are distinct from all other extant copies of the *Regiment*," which, so she says, have it that Hoccleve worked at the Privy Seal "twenti yeer / And foure" and "three and twenti yeer and more," but in this revision as represented by Ry3 he puts the figures at twenty-five years (804–5, fol. 16r) and twenty-four years and more (1023, fol. 20r). Likewise, the Old Man's suggestion that, "Syn **thow maist nat** be payed in th'eschequer," Hoccleve should request that the Prince "make instance / That thy patente into the hanaper / May chaunged be" (1877–80), "has been changed" in Ry3 to "Syn **it is hard** be payed in th'eschequer" (fol. 35v), which reflects "the better times," since he had been paid in the meantime.[14] This account is mistaken. First, Ry3 and Du, which together constitute the epsilon family, do not here record anything distinct from all other extant copies:[15] at both lines 805 and 1023 seven of the eight extant copies of the

---

[12] Marcia Smith Marzec, "The Latin Marginalia of Hoccleve's *Regiment of Princes* as an Aid to Stemmatic Analysis," *TEXT* 3 (1987): 269–84 (271).

[13] Mooney, "Holograph Copy," 280. Marzec had identified DuRy3 as a genetic group in "Thomas Hoccleve's 'De regimine principum,' Sections 12 and 13: A Critical Edition," Ph.D. diss. (Northern Illinois University, 1980), cxxxiii, citing these errors in common (**bold** DuRy3, in Ry3's spelling): lines 4659–60, Ry3, fol. 85v, "a kyng **needes muste** flee / A chynches herte" (correct *moot algates*); 4781, fol. 87v, "Vertu gyeth hir **occupacioun**" (*operacioun*); 4785–86, fol. 87v, "love is the armure / Of **siker-nesse**" (*seuretee*). Line numbers and punctuation are from Thomas Hoccleve, *The Regiment of Princes*, ed. Charles R. Blyth (Kalamazoo: Medieval Institute, 1999), as are subsequent quotations not taken from a manuscript.

[14] Mooney, "Holograph Copy," 280–81.

[15] As there is no critical edition of *Regiment of Princes*, I rely below mainly on Charles Blyth's collation sheets, which are being made available at http://repositories.lib.utexas.edu/handle/2152/24688; my thanks to Elon Lang for providing me with those regarding certain lines not yet posted to that site. For Marzec's stemma see David Greetham, "Phylum-Tree-Rhizome," in *Reading from the Margins: Textual Studies, Chaucer, and Medieval Literature*, ed. Seth Lerer (San Marino: Huntington Library, 1996), 99–126 (124). The version of the stemma in Marzec, "Latin Marginalia," 279, is identical in its fundamentals, except that it presents alpha as I, beta as II, gamma as alpha, delta as beta, and epsilon as gamma. Thus Mooney's references to Marzec's gamma are to the epsilon manuscript on my Figure 1, which presents a précis of Marzec's stemma.

delta group plus one conflated text agree, as do a few other manuscripts, for one or the other reading,[16] and at line 1877 the number is still higher, with nearly all witnesses to the beta family, almost thirty of which are extant, sharing the reading.[17] Marzec's stemma, a précis of which is Figure 1, indicates these groups' interrelationships, and shows that she does not see the epsilon branch as "separate" from everything else. It is sibling to delta and gamma, all of which descend from beta. It is not impossible that these readings represent Hoccleve's revisions, but the only reason for thinking so to date, the belief that they originated in Ry3, is unfounded.

Mooney has also misunderstood the evidence for the necessity of the DuRy3 exemplar, her rejection of which leaves open, so she believes,

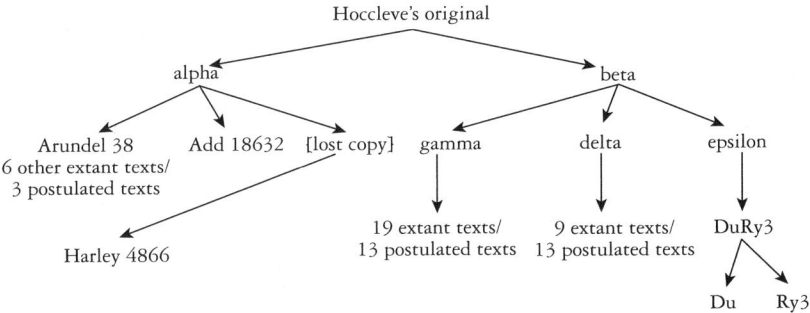

Fig. 1. Précis of Marcia Smith Marzec's stemma of *Regiment of Princes* manuscripts.

[16] The seven delta manuscripts that agree for both 805 and 1023 are: British Library, MSS Arundel 59 (Ar), Harley 116 (Ha1), Sloane 1212 (Sl1), and Royal 17 C.XIV (Ry1); Oxford, Bodleian Library, MS Douce 158 (Do); Chicago, Newberry MS f.33.7 (Ne; I assume this is MS 6); Philadelphia, Rosenbach MS 1083/30 (Ro). The final manuscript in this family extant for these readings, San Marino, Huntington, MS Hm 135 (Hn2), agrees for 805 only. The conflated text, Cambridge, St. John's College, MS 223 (Sj), too, agrees for both readings, while another conflated text, Bodleian, MS Rawlinson poet. 10 (Ra1), agrees at 805 only. The sibling to the celebrated BL, MS Arundel 38 (A)—BL, Additional MS 18632 (Ad)—agrees at 1023 only.

[17] What Mooney takes to be the reading of all manuscripts save Du and Ry3 at 1877, "thow maist nat be payed," is in fact that of only the alpha group, as the twenty-plus manuscripts of gamma, delta (all manuscripts as cited in previous note save Hn2, not extant here), and epsilon read some form of "it is hard to be payed" (*to* sometimes omitted, *be payed* sometimes transposed). The gamma manuscripts highest up the stemma with this reading are Cambridge, Queens' College, MS 12 (Qu) and Corpus Christi College, MS 496 (Cc); and University of Edinburgh Library, MS 202 (Ed). Two gamma manuscripts, BL, MS Royal 17 D.XIX (Ry4, sibling to Qu) and its descendant Cambridge, Magdalene College, MS Pepys 2101 (Ma), agree with alpha.

"the possibility that Royal 17 D.XVIII itself is the holograph presentation copy and that Dugdale was copied from it."[18] Marzec, she says, "argued for the existence of a common exemplar, rather than the manuscripts being copied one from the other, because of a substantial passage" comprising five stanzas on Chaucer "that appears in Royal and not in Dugdale," which, Marzec believed, was removed from that exemplar between Ry3's and Du's copying of it.[19] Yet it is not Du's lack of these stanzas that led to the conclusion that "it is doubtful that one is copied from the other; rather, the two are copies of a common exemplar," but the existence of "numerous unique readings in each manuscript."[20] Ry3 alone reads, among others, "**That** thow were **falle**" for "Thow were yfalle" (line 1059, fol. 20v); "And tokne in it shalt thow **noun** fynde or se" (*noon*; 1082, 21r); "By thre causes he halt **is** gretter vice" (*it*; 4609, 84r); "Lightly now, for vertu is kynges **pay**" (*pray*; 4631, 85r); "Welthe in the lordes **soil** blowith ful merie, / But the needy berith his **soule** so lowe" (*sail* both; 4716–17, 86v); "And if **you** conseil whiche þat yee han take" (*your*; 4922, 90r). If Du descended from Ry3 one would expect it to feature at least some, and probably most or even all, of the latter's unique variants. Ry3 was thus neither Du's exemplar nor, that means, a presentation copy.

The body of data that Marzec had collected and analyzed years earlier disproves this and the notion that Ry3 was a revision copied from the authorial original, two of Mooney's three claims about the manuscript. While it is not particularly easy to track down that data, it is difficult to account for this material's absence from Mooney's list of reasons why critics have not embraced the notion that Royal 17 D.XVIII is in Hoccleve's hand.[21]

---

[18] Mooney, "Holograph Copy," 292.

[19] Ibid., 290, "because" repeated 292, responding to Marzec, "Latin Marginalia," 271. Since only five stanzas are missing, Mooney replies, "one would have to assume a three-quarter-page miniature as the portrait of Chaucer, since Dugdale, like most manuscripts of the *Regiment*, contains four stanzas per page." That these five missing stanzas "exactly cover the references to the portrait of Chaucer, discussion of images, and prayers for his soul" supports her alternative: "a scribe might deliberately omit them from a manuscript to which the portrait of Chaucer would not be added, so as not to draw attention to the omission of the portrait itself" (291). While not supporting her own thesis, Mooney's point is apt, showing that their common exemplar, DuRy3, lacked the portrait.

[20] Marzec, "Thomas Hoccleve's *De regimine principum*, cxxxiii.

[21] Mooney says that critics have been diverted by the "sumptuously prepared" BL, MSS Arundel 38 and Harley 4866, and by John Burrow's dating of Royal 17 D.XVIII to 1425–50 (*Thomas Hoccleve* [Aldershot: Variorum, 1994], 51), as well as the fact that "the hand of this manuscript differs somewhat in general aspect from that of the

How Did Hoccleve Spell YOU and HEART?

The previous section shows not that Royal 17 D.XVIII is not a holograph, but simply that it lacks the features one would expect to find in one: textual proximity to the original version and unique signs of tinkering or even substantial changes. Even if it seems unlikely, in theory Hoccleve could still have copied a manuscript far down the stemma, as must be the case if Mooney's remaining argument, about its hand, is correct. Mooney suggests that there is one other body of evidence, "the language of the *Regiment* in Royal 17 D.XVIII," which, she says, "also matches Hoccleve's usage in the known holographs,"[22] but even if this claim were accurate it would constitute not evidence in favor of her argument but only the absence of evidence against it. In any case, she immediately acknowledges that 94 of the 101 appearances of the term YOU in Royal 17 D.XVIII are spelled *you*, with only the remaining seven spelled *yow*, even though, as Charles Blyth observes, in his holographs Hoccleve uniformly spelled this term "with a **w**, never a **u**" exemplifying the fact that the "great majority of words in his lexicon have a single spelling" in the holographs.[23] Mooney instead proposes this to be a "spelling that Hoccleve appears to have changed over his career."[24]

A still more pervasive indication that Ry3's language is unHocclevean is found in its substantial number of unmetrical lines. At 4520 (fol. 83r), Ry3 reads "But if so be, or thow go thy beere," omitting *to* after *go*, resulting in nine metrical syllables. Judith Jefferson shows that, of those lines in the holographs, Durham University Library, MS Cosin V.III.9 and San Marino, Huntington Library, MSS Hm 111 and 744, in which there is no question of whether to pronounce final *-e*, 98 percent have ten syllables (not counting extra-metrical unstressed syllables at line end), and of those where final *-e* is to be pronounced where it would not

---

accepted Hoccleve holographs" (Mooney, "Holograph Copy," 265). Blyth writes that his completion of a full collation "convinced me that there was no justification for recording such a mass of trivial data, even in a critical edition (which the present edition plainly is not)"; *Regiment of Princes*, ed. Blyth,16.

[22] Mooney, "Holograph Copy," 278, citing Blyth's remark that "it preserves some of Hoccleve's characteristic spellings"; *Regiment of Princes*, ed. Blyth, 16–17.

[23] *Regiment of Princes*, ed. Blyth, 18; the figures here are from Mooney, "Holograph Copy," 278.

[24] Mooney, "Holograph Copy," 278.

naturally elide, 96 percent are decasyllabic.²⁵ Thomas Hoccleve would have been the scribe least likely to omit a word, not just because he wrote it but also simply to preserve its decasyllabic metrical character.

This discovery also reveals, as John Burrow remarks, that "there can be no doubt that wherever Hoccleve writes <e> in unstressed position," whether medial or final, "it is to be pronounced as a syllabic /ə/," and that he always included that letter when necessary for meter.²⁶ Thus "But weleaway so is myn **hert** wo" (1958, fol. 36v) has nine syllables for lacking metrically necessary *-e* on *herte*, which is also how "Hoccleve always spells that word" in the holographs, "reserving the spelling without *-e* for 'hart' (deer)."²⁷ In "Write to him a goodely tale or two / On which he may desport him by nyght" (1902–3, fol. 35v), the first line is eleven syllables thanks to *goodely*'s extraneous medial <e>, which in Ry3's genetic partner Du is correct, *goodly*, while the second is nine, on account of the scribe's failure to notice that where Hoccleve's "syllable count required that the *-e* should not be elided, he usually resorts to the fuller form *-en*," thus: *desporten*.²⁸ Ry3 even has some twelve-syllable lines.²⁹

Despite his special attention to this issue, Hoccleve could have erred thus on occasion, but the rate of non-decasyllabic lines in this copy— 143 instances over the 1,114 lines from the beginning and end portions of the Prologue (fols. 2r–16r, 33v–37v), just over 12 percent—is about four times the rate of that of the known holographs. There can be no attributing the fastidiousness about unstressed <e> and the decasyllable to Hoccleve's later years, as the two best texts get many of these lines right, such as, among dozens of examples, both terms in 1902–3:

---

²⁵ Judith A. Jefferson, "The Hoccleve Holographs and Hoccleve's Metrical Practice," in *Manuscripts and Texts: Editorial Problems in Later Middle English Literature*, ed. Derek Pearsall (Cambridge: D. S. Brewer, 1987), 95–109.

²⁶ *Thomas Hoccleve's Complaint and Dialogue*, ed. J. A. Burrow, EETS 313 (Oxford: Oxford University Press, 1999), xxix; see also John Burrow, "Some Final *-e*'s in the Hoccleve Holographs," in *Yee? Baw for Bokes: Essays on Medieval Manuscripts and Poetics in Honor of Hoyt N. Duggan*, ed. Michael Calabrese and Stephen H. A. Shepherd (Los Angeles: Marymount Institute Press, 2013), 45–53 (46).

²⁷ *Regiment of Princes*, ed. Blyth, 23; noted also by Burrow, "Some Final -e's," 50.

²⁸ Burrow, "Some Final *-e*'s," 47 (Du reads *desporte* in 1903); *Write* is two syllables as per note 26. Other typical eleven-syllable lines in the Royal MS are 5 (see *Regiment of Princes*, ed. Blyth, 22), 7, 20, 29, 37, 49, 61, 64, 74, 78, 163, 249, 290, 305. Other nine-syllable lines on these folios are 1 (see below, note 30), 72, 164, 177, 193, 199, 201, 232, 265, 289.

²⁹ E.g., "A poore olde hoore man cam walkynge by me" (122, fol. 4r; corr. *hoor, walkyng*; Blyth retains *walkynge*), and "And ful seelde is þat yonge folke wyse been" (147, fol. 4v; corr. *yong folk*); Du is correct for both readings. See also lines 131, 136.

"Wryte to hym a **goodly** tale or two / On whyche he may **desporten** hym by nyght" (Arundel 38, fol. 34v; also Harley 4866, fol. 34v).[30] The idea that Hoccleve introduced or removed these syllables for whatever reason would not explain how Ry3 alone attests so many of them. Nor would it be convincing to attribute to the Harley and Arundel scribes a more fine-tuned approach to the syllabic character of Hoccleve's line than his own at this early date, or to suggest that the poet introduced these alterations to a text that was already correct.

Thomas Hoccleve, Scribe

If the hand of Royal 17 D.XVIII were identical to those of the accepted holographs, the formulary Hoccleve gathered in his capacity as clerk of the Privy Seal, BL, Additional MS 24062, or his stint as Scribe E in the Trinity Gower, then the fundamentals of the editing of Middle English poetry—the grouping of witnesses according to agreed errors and the assumption that poets operated according to metrical principles—might be due for substantial revision.[31] But the burden of Mooney's argument on its own terms is to explain why Ry3's hand "differs somewhat in general aspect from that of the accepted Hoccleve holographs," which is the most important of her reasons for its neglect by critics (see above, note 21). I will here argue that, whatever the status of Ry3's textual affiliations and linguistic character, its paleographical features are not Hoccleve's.

H. C. Schulz's landmark 1937 essay, "Thomas Hoccleve, Scribe," elaborated and supplemented by A. I. Doyle's introduction to the Early English Text Society's facsimile of the three Hoccleve holographs, identified what all of his scribal works exclusively have in common, regardless of their level of formality.[32] First, all the items are very similar in both *aspect*—that is, "the general impression on the page made by a

---

[30] Similarly, Blyth observes that Arundel 38's line 1 has correct *restlees* (as does Harley 4866; *restelees* in Ry3), which he prints thus not for that reason, though, but because the holographs show it to be correct by analogy (*Regiment of Princes*, ed. Blyth, 19).

[31] On Hoccleve's stint as Scribe E of Trinity R.3.2, copying fols. 82r–84r, see Doyle and Parkes, "Production of Copies," 182–85. See also Mooney and Stubbs, *Scribes and the City*, 123–26, who propose that Hoccleve supervised the manuscript's production.

[32] H. C. Schulz, "Thomas Hoccleve, Scribe," *Speculum* 12 (1937): 71–81; *Thomas Hocceleve: A Facsimile of the Autograph Verse Manuscripts*, intro. J. A. Burrow and A. I. Doyle, EETS s.s. 19 (Oxford: Oxford University Press, 2002), xxxiv–xl.

specimen of handwriting at first sight" or "a unique ensemble of common elements which is only recognized after some (though not necessarily a long) extent of acquaintance, in comparison with others of the same genetic group"—and *duct*, "the act of tracing strokes on the writing surface."[33] These features "do not form sufficient criteria to identify the manuscripts as the work of a single scribe," Doyle and M. B. Parkes explain: "However, once we suspect that we recognize the handwriting of a scribe in another manuscript, further detailed analysis may reveal idiosyncrasies in the formation of individual letters and the presence of other distinctive habits which would enable us to establish that the same scribe was responsible for the different manuscripts."[34]

It is their common attestation of aspect, duct, and a distinctive combination of letter forms, identified by Schulz and here described by Doyle, that confirms a common hand at work on these manuscripts of Hoccleve's poetry, Scribe E's stint in Trinity R.3.2, and the formulary:

an expansive **A** with a sweeping deep downwards stroke turning upwards counter-clockwise across itself as it turns clockwise either to a flattened head with an angular junction on the right with a straight broken downstroke or else continuing with a simple curve, in each with a more or less strongly seriffed foot; a flat-topped **g** with variant tails, turning either tightly or in a wide sweep on the left to its head or else turning back more or less sharply to the right; a round or oval **w** made usually with only two strokes, the second like a 2 within the circle; and **y** with its tail turning right up alongside or often back through the head as a hair stroke to make a dot or tick above.[35]

Schulz observes that "no one of these four"—or five, including "the letter **h** in which the stem, shoulder and limb drop below the level of the other letters" that Doyle and Parkes add to his list—"can be said to be unique with Hoccleve, but as a group (and with identical slope, size, shading, position of pen, and degree of curvature) they have not been found to occur in any of the numerous Middle English hands so far

---

[33] M. B. Parkes, *Their Hands before Our Eyes: A Closer Look at Scribes* (Aldershot: Ashgate, 2008), 149 ("general impression"), 151 (*duct*); and A. I. Doyle and M. B. Parkes, "A Paleographical Introduction," in *The Canterbury Tales: A Facsimile and Transcription of the Hengwrt Manuscript, with Variants from the Ellesmere Manuscript*, ed. Paul G. Ruggiers (Norman: University of Oklahoma Press, 1979), xxxv ("unique ensemble").

[34] Doyle and Parkes, "Production of Copies," 168; see also Schulz, "Thomas Hoccleve, Scribe," 72.

[35] Burrow and Doyle, *Facsimile*, xxxiv.

examined."³⁶ All five feature in Figure 2, two excerpts from Hoccleve's formulary, written in a fluent "well-formed court hand" that "is unusually cursive."³⁷ See "Ancestres" (line 1), "gen*e*ral" (3); "witnesse," "which" (6, 7); "y," "yeer" (5); "which sholde" (7). Figure 3, an excerpt from the Durham manuscript's final page, features instances in both his standard poetic hand—line 4, "to which god of his grace brynge us all Amen"—and his most formal hand, in the dedication at page bottom: "And" (9, 11), "thow" (11), "thy might" (12).

Mooney's claim for Royal 17 D.XVIII is part of a series of new attributions to Hoccleve: fols. 105r–108v and at least one other folio of the formulary, both in a more formal hand,³⁸ the second of which is on a page that Doyle says is "perhaps by his under-clerk John Welde," whose hand matches that of the first such attribution,³⁹ and whose description

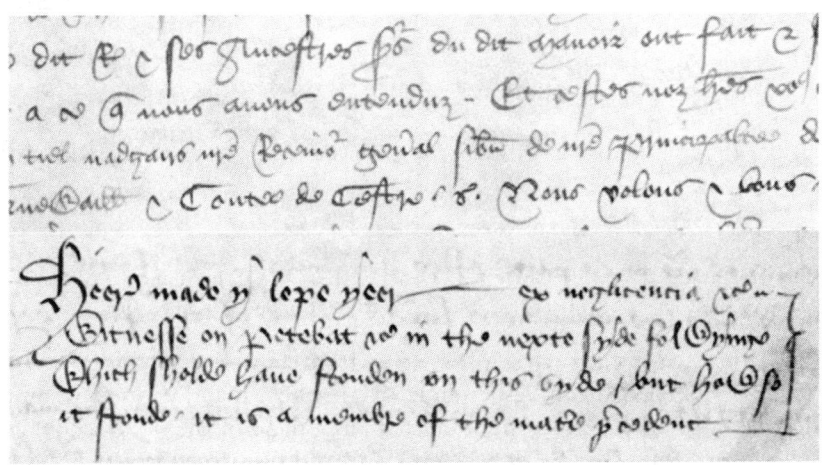

Fig. 2. © The British Library Board, Additional MS 24062, fols. 101v and 194v (excerpts).

³⁶ Schulz, "Thomas Hoccleve, Scribe," 72; Doyle and Parkes, "Production of Copies," 185.
³⁷ Schulz, "Thomas Hoccleve, Scribe," 72, using these excerpts as his examples.
³⁸ Mooney, "Holograph Copy," 267–68, and the page from Additional 24062, fol. 161v illustrating Hoccleve's hand at http://www.medievalscribes.com/ > "Scribes" > "Thomas Hoccleve" > "London, British Library, MS Additional 24062." Nearly 80 percent of the "Hocclevean" letter forms in the latter are taken not from the lines that are unquestionably his that occupy the bottom third of that page but from the formal hand of the upper two-thirds, never before attributed to him.
³⁹ Burrow and Doyle, *Facsimile*, xxxvi n. 1. Doyle finds this hand at work in fols. 145r–154r, 160v–163v, 187v–188r, and 189v–190v; I think it is also the hand of fols.

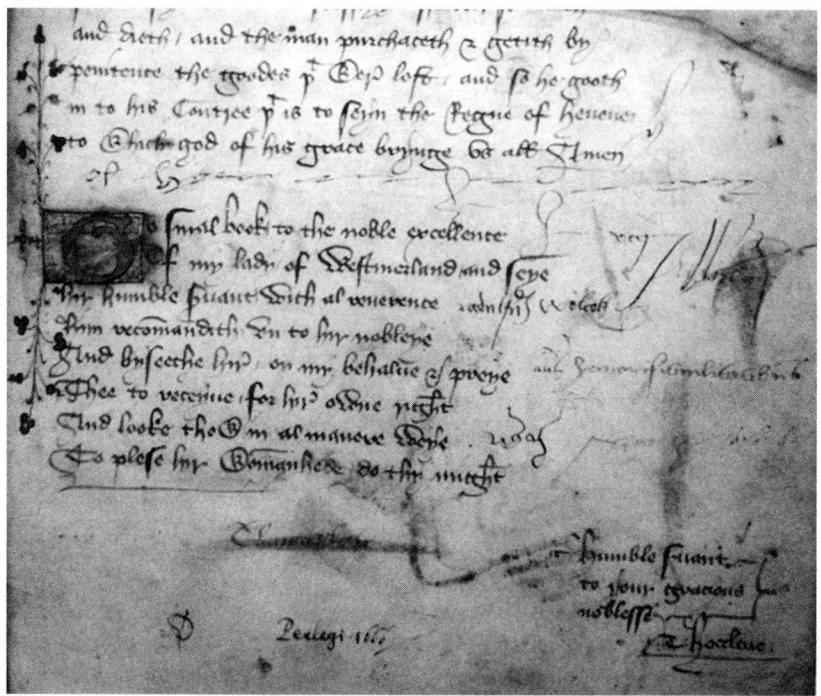

Fig. 3. Durham University Library, MS Cosin V.III.9, fol. 95r, bottom half. With kind permission of Durham University Library Department of Special Collections.

by Mooney emphasizes its differences from Hoccleve's hand;[40] some folios of BL, MS Cotton Vespasian B.XXII, whose h and y forms prompt Doyle and Parkes to say only that it is "in a hand of the same school as Hoccleve's and other Privy Seal clerks";[41] and possibly thirty-two folios of the *Confessio Amantis* in BL, MS Egerton 913, which, as Doyle says,

---

105r–108v, among others. Mooney does not mention that Hoccleve both annotates and corrects this text in his informal hand.

[40] Of the relevant letter forms, "the tendency for Hoccleve to drop the shoulder of h below the level of surrounding graphs . . . is not so noticeable on the folios examined"; the tail of one of the sample y forms, unlike all accepted instances, "is not carried back up over the graph"; and, also unlike all other accepted Hoccleveean items longer than a few lines, "Unfortunately there are no examples of Hoccleve's circular w which is such a distinctive feature in some of his manuscripts" (citation in note 38). In addition, neither the g nor the A from the formal text looks anything like any definitely Hoccleveean ones, and the A that she calls a "variation" on his one I have not encountered in his texts.

[41] Doyle and Parkes, "Paleographical Introduction," xlvi n. 32. Mooney put forth this attribution in "Thomas Hoccleve in His Working Clothes, or the Variability of Scribal Handwriting in the Fifteenth Century," presented at the Early Book Society

feature "flat-topped **g** with elegant tail to the left and long overhanging s like Hoccleve's," but are "certainly not by him."[42]

Mooney has argued positively only for the Royal 17 D.XVIII attribution, in a manner in which those just cited are implicated in any case. The paleographical evidence against the attribution comprises this hand's dissimilarity to Hoccleve's, both in aspect and in those three of the five distinctive letter forms it does feature; its complete lack of the other two; and its featuring in their places ones in turn found only very rarely in the accepted items. Mooney explains the difference in aspect just as she had the different spelling of *you*, by treating it as evidence for the change of his hand over time rather than against her identification in the first place. It shows, she claims, that Hoccleve employed "a script somewhere between that of the Trinity College MS R.3.2 of Gower's *Confessio Amantis*," which demonstrates the neater, smaller script he used "in his younger days," "and the later holographs."[43] The idea is reasonable: Daniel Wakelin judges Royal 17 D.XVIII's general aspect to be similar to Hoccleve's, even as he notes the "more jagged movement" of its duct, "with points in letters such as **g** and even in the descender of **y** on occasion (e.g. fol. 26v/21, 'yong')."[44] Yet Mooney would not have appealed to otherwise unattested stages in the development of Hoccleve's hand if Royal 17 D.XVIII's aspect and duct, which in most situations would provide the foundation for further paleographical analysis, did not constitute an embarrassment to her argument.

One might expect, then, to find at least that the graphs of Royal 17 D.XVIII "match exactly Hoccleve's idiosyncratic letter forms," but this statement is instantly qualified rather severely as well, on account of the text's "most striking differences . . . from the later holographs," which include "the forms of **w** and **g**."[45] Instead of the characteristic round **w** whose second stroke looks like a "2" within the circle, Royal MS's 5,400-plus lines feature, as Wakelin says, a "lotus-flower **w** with a pointed tapering bottom and flattened loops above" that is "unlike

---

Conference in Oxford, July 2015. This item's contents, on maritime ordinances and the like, are very far from anything else in Hoccleve's hand.

[42] Respectively, http://www.medievalscribes.com/ > "Scribes" > "Hand A" > "London, British Library MS Egerton 913"; and Burrow and Doyle, *Facsimile*, xxxv–xxxvi n. 2.

[43] Mooney, "Holograph Copy," 266, 272.

[44] Daniel Wakelin, *Scribal Correction and Literary Craft: English Manuscripts 1375–1510* (Cambridge: Cambridge University Press, 2014), 283 n. 33, where he explains why he treats Royal 17 D.XVIII as a holograph.

[45] Mooney, "Holograph Copy," 272.

Hoccleve's" (Fig. 4: "swiche" [1], "war" [9]),[46] and the same goes for the flat-topped **g** found everywhere else, instead of which Royal features only a form with angular top, as Wakelin observed (note 44) ("good" [2 (twice), 4]). This alone renders the proposal that Royal 17 D.XVIII is a holograph very implausible. To account for it Mooney cites what she presents as occurrences of Royal's forms in the accepted Hocclevean items, but whatever similarities might exist—and the examples she cites look very little like those here—are not diagnostic in any case.[47] Royal's

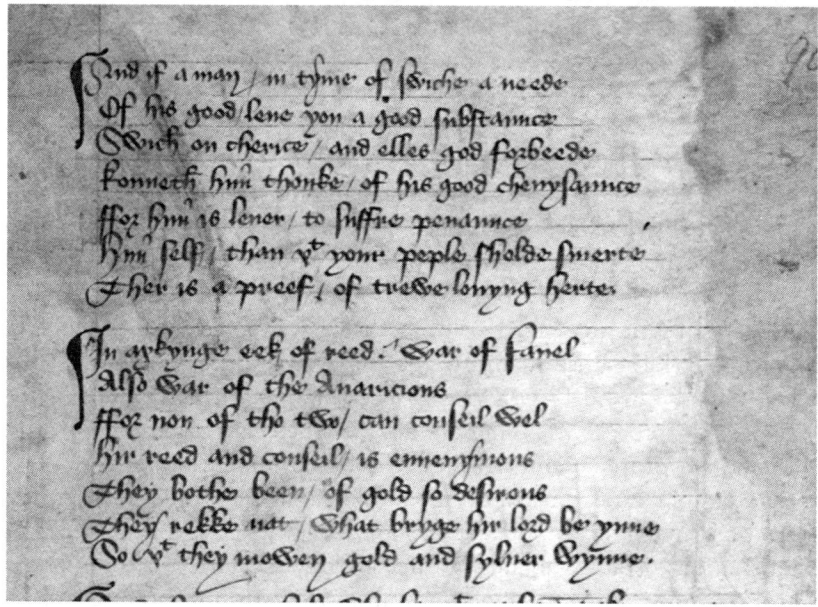

Fig. 4. © The British Library Board, Royal MS 17 D.XVIII, fol. 90r, top half.

[46] Wakelin, *Scribal Correction*, 283 n. 33.

[47] Mooney says that "such forms [of **w**] with rounded bases" as those here "can be found in his copying in the Trinity Gower" ("Holograph Copy," 272), which she exemplifies, however, with what Doyle describes as Hoccleve's "more complex three-stroke bipartite **w** with angular feet . . . employed chiefly in initial positions or for greater formality," as found in the Durham dedication and the Trinity Gower (Burrow and Doyle, *Facsimile*, xxxiv; also Schulz, "Thomas Hoccleve, Scribe," 73) rather than the lotus-flower form. Mooney likewise says that **g** with angular top appears as well in the formulary and Trinity Gower (274), but those forms do not match Royal's, as their lower lobes do not meet the stalk. Hoccleve's stint in Trinity R.3.2 features 23 **g**s with an angular head that appear very rarely in the holographs (Burrow and Doyle, *Facsimile*, xxxvi, cite 15 appearances of the angular-headed **g** in Trinity R.3.2 but I think that count is a bit conservative). Still, the flat-topped **g** dominates, with 153 appearances.

predominant **A** letter-form ("Also," "Avaricious" [9]), "an enlargement of the normal two-compartment lowercase with both upper and lower lobes closed," too, is very rare in Hoccleve's texts.[48] Other features distinctive to this manuscript include "the curling tail on the last mimim of word-final **m** or **n**" ("man" [1], "mowen" [14]) and "the broken strokes in the crossbar and tongue of **e**" ("swich**e**" [1]), as noted by Wakelin.[49]

Mooney's case thus comes down to a belief that Royal 17 D.XVIII's **h**s, **y**s, and some **A**s "match exactly Hoccleve's idiosyncratic letter forms," and, though she does not put it this way, that this match compensates for the differences in aspect, duct, language, and other letter forms.[50] Royal features a version of Hoccleve's **A** as a minority form (Fig. 4: "And" [1]), but unlike those of the Trinity Gower and holographs, its downward sweeping stroke starts too low to intersect with the line resulting from the final clockwise curve. As for **h**, she says that her sample page illustrates its appearance "with low shoulder,"[51] but most forms' shoulders (and stems and limbs, which she does not mention) are not low. In Figure 4 the first three appearances of **h** have a stem higher, not lower, than the base of the surrounding letters ("swiche," "his," "Swich" [1, 2, 3]). And while Royal does feature some self-dotting **y**s ("tyme" [1], "envenymous" [11], "They" [13]) they are very much in the minority: three in these stanzas, versus eleven non-self-dotting (from "you" [2] through "wynne" [14]), where by contrast the accepted Hocclevean texts feature almost no non-self-dotting **y**s.

"One could argue that these language matches result from a scribe copying *literatim* from a good exemplar using Hoccleve's spellings," Mooney summarizes, "but the coincidence of language, idiosyncratic letter forms, layout, and punctuation seem to me too weighty for any other conclusion than that this manuscript is another Hoccleve holograph."[52] These first two characteristics occupied us above; as there, the

---

[48] Mooney, "Chaucer's Scribe," 124, regarding Scribe B's hand; she does not mention its appearance or dominance in Royal 17 D.XVIII. I count 262 of the preferred forms versus 20 of the square-topped forms through 30v; 102 versus 25 in 70v–80v. A two-humped **A** appears four times in Trinity but nowhere else in the holographs, but there too the form with the simple curved rather than straight top still dominates, appearing 93 times.

[49] Wakelin, *Scribal Correction*, 283 n. 33; see also above at note 46 for his comments on **w**.

[50] Mooney, "Holograph Copy," 272.

[51] Ibid., 269.

[52] Ibid., 280.

third, its layout, differs substantially from the holographs via its lack of the separating lines, starting with a "2"-like curve, between stanzas.[53] Hoccleve "stubbornly prioritized" the stanza form, Aditi Nafde observes, via his ruling of the holographs' pages "so that he takes care never to split a stanza in half across two folios"; and yet Royal exemplifies those manuscripts that "accidentally spoil these carefully calculated pages and sometimes have incomplete sets of stanzas per page with a few extra lines per folio," a rubric on fol. 75v forcing the scribe to carry two lines of its last stanza over onto 76r, a problem he eventually fixes by bringing single lines over on fols. 77v, 79v, 80r, and 80v, "until the complete stanza is readjusted and the layout is fixed by folio 81r."[54]

Finally, its punctuation, while similar to that of the holographs (and of many other manuscripts) in some ways, is quite different in others.[55] As Nafde points out, "Unlike Hoccleve's autographs, the non-autograph manuscripts never have mid-line or mid-stanza paraphs; nor do they replace these with other indicators of speech or topic development. As such, the scribes of these manuscripts," in which she includes Royal 17 D.XVIII, "have changed the use of the paraph and the initial: whereas Hoccleve uses the paraph to indicate clauses, or changes in topic or speaker within each stanza, this was not the function of the paraphs and initials in the non-autograph manuscripts. Here the paraph is used solely to exaggerate the stanza form on the page," as represented by Figure 4.[56] In sum, difficulties attend the attribution of Royal 17 D.XVIII to Hoccleve from every side, while none attends the received conclusion that it is not a holograph.

Adam's Mark

While this Hoccleve attribution is too recent to have had much impact, Mooney's work on Adam Pinkhurst has fundamentally changed the character of Middle English studies. The bringing to light of Pinkhurst's

---

[53] Burrow and Doyle, *Facsimile*, xxi.

[54] Aditi Nafde, "Hoccleve's Hands: The *Mise-en-Page* of the Autograph and Non-Autograph Manuscripts," *JEBS* 16 (2013): 55–83 (61, 66, 67).

[55] Mooney's description indicates the Royal MS's minor differences from the holographs: "Virgules appear more frequently in this holograph copy of the *Regiment* than Burrow and Doyle describe for the HM 111 copy of the *Male Regle*"; one of its versions of the *punctus elevatus* is "an abbreviated and more angular form," which is "hasty" and "unusual"; "Holograph Copy," 277, 278.

[56] Nafde, "Hoccleve's Hands," 70; see also Burrow and Doyle, *Facsimile*, xxxviii–xxxix.

confirmation, also called "oath," in the Scriveners' Company Common Paper, recorded around 1395 and now part of the London Metropolitan Archives collection and kept in the Guildhall Library (Fig. 5), was extraordinarily valuable.[57] The attribution of the Hengwrt and Ellesmere manuscripts of the *Canterbury Tales* to this hand, together with the corollary belief that he must thus be the "Adam" referred to in the lyric recorded by John Shirley under the title "Chauciers Wordes, a Geffrey un to Adame his owen scryveyne," provides the basis for Mooney's characterization of Pinkhurst as "Chaucer's scribe."[58] This latter proposal has received the most attention, but it is moot if its basis is incorrect.[59] And just as the hand of Royal 17 D.XVIII "differs somewhat in general aspect from that of the accepted Hoccleve holographs" in Mooney's assessment (note 21 above), so too "the script used for [Pinkhurst's]

[57] On the term "confirmation," and for a fascinating account of the circumstances of this document's production, which shows that the confirmations respond to a rebellion by one of their members against the wardens of the company and thus dates them to c. 1395 rather than the previously assumed 1392, see Richard Firth Green, "The Early History of the Scriveners' Common Paper and Its So-Called 'Oaths,'" in *Middle English Texts in Transition: A Festschrift Dedicated to Toshiyuki Takamiya on His 70th Birthday*, ed. Simon Horobin and Linne R. Mooney (York: York Medieval Press, 2014), 1–20. These pages record "a later, and . . . somewhat sanitized, narrative of the events of the early 1390s," he writes, when Bishop Braybrooke had "sent a pastoral letter . . . to the priests of his diocese exhorting them to admonish those of their parishioners who continued to practise their trades on Sundays and religious festivals and to threaten them with legal action if they did not desist; amongst the trades he singled out for particular attention was that of the scriveners" (6, 3).

[58] J. S. P. Tatlock was to my knowledge the first to say that Hengwrt "is in the same hand throughout, as the Ellesmere is, and these hands are almost certainly the same"; "The *Canterbury Tales* in 1400," *PMLA* 50 (1935): 100–39 (133). For recent endorsement see A. I. Doyle, "The Copyist of the Ellesmere *Canterbury Tales*," in *The Ellesmere Chaucer: Essays in Interpretation*, ed. Martin Stevens and Daniel Woodward (San Marino: Huntington Library, 1997), 49–67 (49). For Mooney's claim that Adam Pinkhurst is the addressee of the lyric "Adam Scriveyn" (Cambridge, Trinity College, MS R.3.20, 367), see "Chaucer's Scribe," 101–4. "The only reasons for not accepting the identifications given here would be if one does not accept that the oath by Adam Pinkhurst in the Common Paper is in the hand of the Hengwrt/Ellesmere scribe," to which I now turn, "or if one argues that Chaucer could have had one scribe named Adam working for him in the 1380s or 1390s, copying *Boece* and *Troilus*, whereas another scribe named Adam Pinkhurst copied Hengwrt and Ellesmere and the other literary manuscripts attributed to that hand" (101 n. 16). Another reason, though, would be if one does not take "Adam Scriveyn" literally in the first place. "Knowledge that this was in fact the name of a scribe employed by Chaucer puts [such arguments] to rest," she says (102), but if this conviction accounts for the exclusion of this reason from her list, the logic is circular.

[59] On Adam Pinkhurst and "Adam Scriveyn," see, e.g., Gillespie, "Reading Chaucer's Words to Adam"; Jordi Sánchez-Martí, "Adam Pynkhurst's 'Necglygence and Rape' Reassessed," *ES* 92 (2011): 360–74; and Strohm, *The Poet's Tale*, 213–14.

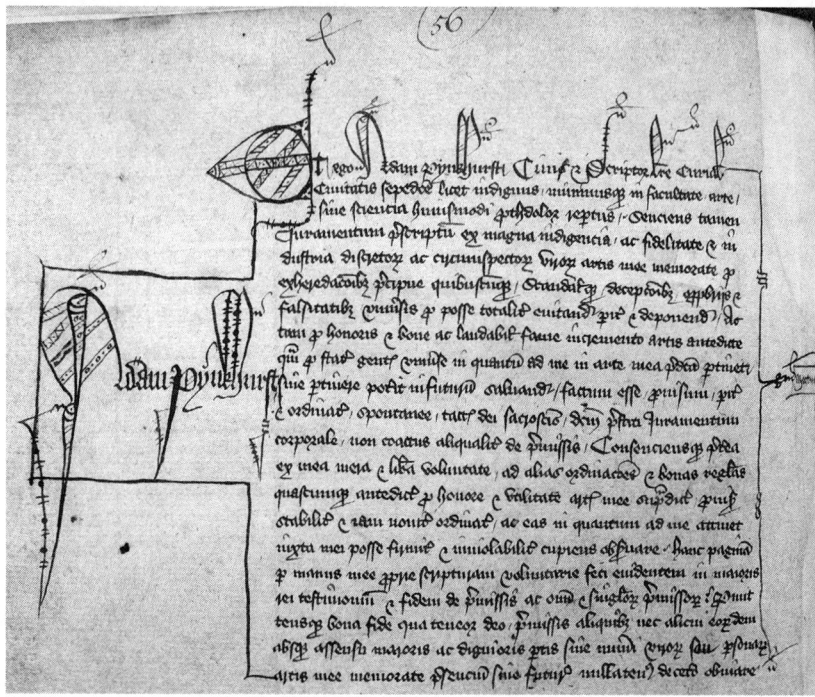

Fig. 5. London Metropolitan Archives, City of London: CLC/L/SC/A/005/MS05370, p. 56. Reproduced by the kind permission of the Scriveners' Company.

oath differs slightly from the scribe's more consistently Anglicana formata hand in Hengwrt and Ellesmere," being "a much more formal script even than these other samples of his hand and with letters more tightly packed together than in the other samples of his writing identified to date."[60]

In the Hoccleve essay Mooney attempts to circumvent the difference in aspect by citing instead perceived similarities of letter form and language; here, she has it that Pinkhurst's hand is "unmistakably that of the Hengwrt/Ellesmere scribe," despite the difference in aspect, on other grounds: "Certain decorative features reveal him immediately, and the letterforms confirm the identification," features that, having opened the

---

[60] Mooney, "Chaucer's Scribe," 100, 137–38. All quotations in the next paragraph are from these pages as well: "unmistakably," "the text being in Latin" (100); "decorative features" (137); "conclusively," "correct" (138).

case, also close it, allowing her to "say conclusively" that all these were in the same hand. The remark that "letterforms confirm the identification" might seem to point to an employment of a Schulz-like approach, in which a particular cluster of distinctive forms is found nowhere other than Pinkhurst's confirmation and those other manuscripts she attributes to him; but she had already observed that, "the text being in Latin, there are none of the characteristic w's, no thorns or yoghs, and the only y is in the scribe's surname," so that the claim is instead the weak one that certain forms are merely "correct for this hand."

The entire case rests, then, on decorative features, two of which, it is claimed, are distinctive to Pinkhurst, another way of saying that they appear in his confirmation; the *Piers Plowman* in Cambridge, Trinity College, MS B.15.17; Hengwrt; and Ellesmere. First is the "'tremolo' or 'tremolo and knot,' similar to an n or to an n with knotted finishing stroke over and to the left of it. Such a graph or feature," Mooney claims, "is used for 'nota' by other contemporary scribes, but Pinkhurst uses it also as a purely decorative feature, like a banner to the right of heightened ascenders," as seen on the top line and in the signature of the confirmation (Fig. 5).[61] The entry for a manuscript of Chaucer's *Boece* in Mooney, Stubbs, and Horobin's "Late Medieval English Scribes" database goes so far as to call this "the identifying mark of Adam Pinkhurst," yet they themselves are conflicted about his potential role in this item's production.[62] In any case the purely decorative use of this motif is not confined to Pinkhurst or those items potentially attributed to him. Very similar or identical instances appear in Kew, The National Archives, E 40/5267, letters patent copied by the chancery scribe Robert

---

[61] Ibid., 125, referring to Doyle and Parkes, "Paleographical Introduction," xxxviii.

[62] See http://www.medievalscribes.com/ > "Scribes" > "Adam Pinkhurst" > "Wales, Aberystwyth, National Library of Wales MS Peniarth 393D." Stubbs tentatively attributed this fragment of the *Boece* to Scribe B while also, given that its aspect is different and that the tremolos are in a different ink, allowing that they might be the products of a scribe copying his style, or of his work as corrector and finisher: Estelle Stubbs, "A New Manuscript by the Hengwrt/Ellesmere Scribe? Aberystwyth, National Library of Wales MS Peniarth 393D," *JEBS* 5 (2002): 161–68. Mooney first suggested the possibility that this was in Pinkhurst's hand with corrections in Chaucer's ("Chaucer's Scribe," 103 and n. 23), then that Pinkhurst merely "embellished" it (Linne R. Mooney, "Vernacular Literary Manuscripts and Their Scribes," in *The Production of Books in England 1350–1500*, ed. Alexandra Gillespie and Daniel Wakelin [Cambridge: Cambridge University Press, 2011], 192–211 [199 n. 27]), before she and Stubbs finally and unequivocally identified Pinkhurst as its scribe in *Scribes and the City*, 68. Below I present the evidence that Pinkhurst—not Scribe B—did in fact embellish, but did not copy, this manuscript.

Muskham in 1381, as Horobin and Mooney themselves note;[63] the *Piers Plowman* A–C splice that is now Cambridge, Trinity College, MS R.3.14;[64] and atop the elaborate initial Is in the Register of Wills enrolled in the Archdeaconry Court of London, 1393–1415, where, as in Pinkhurst's confirmation, they serve as fishing line (first three items in Fig. 6).[65]

"Another characteristic not previously noted," according to Mooney, "is the double-slash and dot decoration Pinkhurst uses on wide sweeping extensions to enlarged initials and as a decorative detail on heavy strokes that vertically divide lobes of enlarged ascenders"; like the decorative knotted tremolo, this "is so distinctive to Pinkhurst as to be virtually a signature in those pieces of his writing where he uses it."[66] Yet

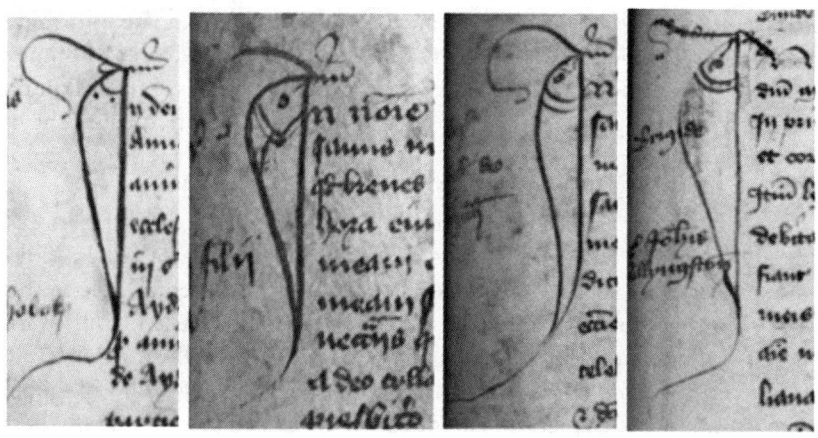

Fig. 6. London Metropolitan Archives, City of London: DL/AL/C/002/MS09051/001/001 (Diocese of London Collection), fols. 78v/124v, 86r/133r, 96Br/126r, 140r/188r (excerpts). Reproduced by kind permission of London Metropolitan Archives.

[63] Horobin and Mooney cite Muskham's "style of writing similar to Scribe B, and even similar decoration of ascenders with tremolo" ("A *Piers Plowman* Manuscript," 97 n. 66), referring to Charles Johnson and Hilary Jenkinson, eds., *English Court Hand, AD 1066 to 1500* (Oxford: Clarendon Press, 1915), Part 2, Plate XXXa, which Stubbs brought to their attention.

[64] See http://sites.trin.cam.ac.uk/manuscripts/ > "R.3.14," fols. 2r top line on final exaggerated ascender, 13v on the MS's sole extant catchword (accessed July 7, 2015). The database just cited refers to the latter of these: http://www.medievalscribes.com/ > "Manuscripts" > "Cambridge" > "Trinity College" > "R.3.14 (594)."

[65] I provide both later foliations of this volume. These entries are dated 1399, 1400, 1400, and 1414.

[66] Mooney, "Chaucer's Scribe," 125.

this had been around for over a century, allowing chancery clerks to display "their own calligraphic skills by lengthening, thickening, exaggerating and decorating certain of the ascenders and capital letters in the king's style and title on the top line of the document."[67] Roberts cites an instance from 1378, to which my superficial survey can add slashes and dots adorning the ascenders in royal charters and letters patent of much earlier years: 1291; 1316;[68] and, in an especially elaborate instance, Edward II's charter of January 21, 1326 establishing "The Hall of the Blessed Mary at Oxford," later known as Oriel College.[69]

Mooney herself, only a few pages before claiming this was Pinkhurst's "signature," had written no more than that two entries with this feature recorded c. 1409–12 in the Mercers' Account Book were "probably" Pinkhurst's (fols. 50v, 56v); she now acknowledges that they are instead most likely in the hand of the Mercers' principal clerk, Martin Kelom.[70] The final excerpt in Figure 6 varies the motif by replacing the single dot with two snowballs on either side of the line, while the usage preferred by Pinkhurst appears in the opening pages of the Scriveners' Common Paper (Fig. 7);[71] three of the livery companies' petitions of 1388 appealing Nicholas Brembre of treason (two others of which Mooney has

---

[67] Elizabeth Danbury, "The Decoration and Illumination of Royal Charters in England, 1250–1509: An Introduction," in *England and Her Neighbours, 1066–1453*, ed. Michael Jones and Malcolm Vale (London: Hambledon, 1989), 157–79 (163).

[68] Respectively, Ipswich, C/1/1/8 (Roberts, "On Giving Scribe B a Name," 260, citing David Allen, *Ipswich Borough Archives 1255–1833* [Woodbridge: Boydell, 2000], 4 and Plate 2—so far as I am aware this was the earliest instance cited in response to Mooney's claims until now); Stratford-upon-Avon, Shakespeare Birthplace Trust, DR 18/1/706 (https://shakespaedia.files.wordpress.com/2013/12/seal-of-edward-ii.jpg [accessed July 1, 2015]); letters patent of Edward II, August 4, 1316 (Kew, The National Archives, E 41/495/(a), depicted as Fig. 1c of Danbury, "Decoration and Illumination," 158). See also Fletcher, "Criteria," 611 n. 40 on another instance I have not seen myself.

[69] See http://upload.wikimedia.org/wikipedia/commons/b/b2/Oriel_College_Charter.jpg; or visit the Hans and Märit Rausing Gallery, Ashmolean Museum, Oxford.

[70] Mooney, "Chaucer's Scribe," 110 ("probably"), 111 n. 55. It appears as well on fol. A2v, which she does not cite, and in other matter in this volume, fols. 6r–10v, more securely Pinkhurst's, on which more below. See Mooney and Stubbs, *Scribes and the City*, 82–83, 83 n. 51 for the change in attribution; for full discussion see Lisa Jefferson, *The Medieval Account Books of the Mercers of London: An Edition and Translation* (Burlington: Ashgate, 2009), 10–11, who refers to the Pinkhurst possibility, but notes differences from fols. 6r–10v that seem now to have convinced Mooney. Jefferson cites as other possibilities for these folios' scribe Thomas Lincoln, Robert Kemp, and Thomas Constable (10 n. 40, 11 n. 41). Jefferson dates fol. A2v to 1404 and assigns it to the same hand responsible for fols. 11r–64r (10, 58). Folio 50v contains accounts from 1409–10; 56v, from 1411–12.

[71] So far as I know only Jane Roberts, who cites that on page 2 ("On Giving Scribe B a Name," 260), has ever mentioned any of these, but Mooney's comment to Green that these pages "may have been Adam Pinkhurst's" can only respond to this feature,

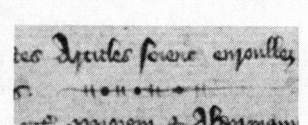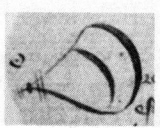

Fig. 7. London Metropolitan Archives, City of London: CLC/L/SC/A/005/MS05370, pp. 1, 2, 3, 3, and 5 (excerpts). Reproduced by kind permission of the Scriveners' Company.

attributed to Scribe B);[72] and six entries between 1406 and 1412–13 in Letter Book I, including the three depicted in Figure 8.

Mooney and Stubbs in fact attribute four of these six instances in Letter Book I to Pinkhurst, and would certainly have included a fifth, that on fol. 99r depicted in Figure 8, had they noticed it (they instead call its twin on fol. 98r his final entry).[73] None of these hands' respective aspects and letter forms is very close to that of any of the others, or

---

since his "own slight preference . . . for Martin Seman," co-master of the Scriveners in March 1392 (Green, "Early History," 5), is supported by the precise match between this hand's aspect and letter forms, and those of Seman's own confirmation (Scriveners' Common Paper, 53). Green observes that the attribution to Seman dates these pages to sometime between August 28, 1404 and April 11, 1405 (5 n. 23).

[72] These are in The National Archives; see http://www.nationalarchives.gov.uk/. The three with slash-and-dot motif are the Goldsmiths' (SC 8/198/9882), Cordwainers' (SC 8/20/998), and Embroiderers' (SC 8/20/1000). See Mooney, "Chaucer's Scribe," 106–8, 106 n. 37; and Mooney and Stubbs, *Scribes and the City*, 79–80 where they attribute to Pinkhurst the Mercers' (SC 8/20/99) and Leathersellers' and White Tawiers' petitions (SC 8/21/1001B). I consider it quite likely that Scribe B copied these as well as SC 8/21/1001A, which might "be a copy of the charter of pardon which would have been issued between 1383 and 1386 and copied out by the Leathersellers and Whittawyers in 1388"; Robert Ellis, "*Verba vana*: Empty Words in Ricardian London" (see http://www.blogs.sed.qmul.ac.uk/2015/01/17/empty-words-writing-medieval-london / [accessed July 1, 2015]), 2 vols., Ph.D. diss. (Queen Mary, University of London, 2012), 2:477. See 1:95–155 (Chap. 2), 2:367–478 (appendices).

[73] They attribute excerpts on fols. 36r, 62v, 87r, and 98r of Letter Book I to Pinkhurst, reproducing only 36r and 87r and discussing only 87r (Mooney and Stubbs, *Scribes and the City*, 75–77 and 75 n. 38), which is not so obviously in the same hand as 36r as they assume. Horobin, too, doubts the attribution of these two items to the identical hand in "Thomas Hoccleve: Chaucer's First Editor?," *ChauR* 50 (2015): 228–50. The excerpt from fol. 99r depicted in Fig. 8 is manifestly in the same hand as that on 98r which they cite as his final entry (75 n. 38). Another slash-and-dot motif, on neither an extender nor lobe and not mentioned by Mooney and Stubbs, is on 118r. Horobin and Mooney, having attributed Trinity B.15.17 to Scribe B, refer to 36r as among the items by "[o]ther City of London clerks writing book-hands," but with no indication that it too might be his ("A *Piers Plowman* Manuscript," 97 n. 66).

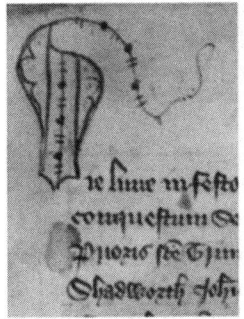  

Fig. 8. London Metropolitan Archives, City of London: COL/AD/01/009 (Letter Book I), fols. 36r, 62v, 99r (excerpts). Reproduced by kind permission of London Metropolitan Archives.

Pinkhurst's, or Scribe B's. Compare, for instance, the respective treatments of "Shadworth" on fols. 36r and 99r (Fig. 8, bottom line), which is spelled "Schadeworth" on 62v, not here shown, with each other and with Pinkhurst's version of that name in the Mercers' Accounts, fol. 6r.[74] The double-slash-and-dot motif here represents Pinkhurst's "tendency to over-elaboration" rather than his "signature," an implicit acknowledgment, perhaps, that their earlier discussion of Martin Kelom showed Mooney's earlier approach to be untenable.[75] But, whatever the reasons for these disparate texts' presence here, this shared feature, too, speaks against their attribution to a single clerk. The three dots of 36r are centered on the wavy line, the two of 62v rest above it, and the single one on each of 98r and 99r is a snowball rather than a dot.

The theories that Pinkhurst was a Guildhall clerk or, much more influentially, that he was Scribe B, never relied on aspect, as do most attributions, and Mooney herself acknowledges that the match of letter forms can do no more than not contradict them. Both cases rely wholly on the notion that Pinkhurst had two "signatures" that, we have now seen, were commonplace. But as the response to Roberts's earlier expression of this point suggests, such a conclusion might not convince readers

[74] For this Mercers' instance see Mooney, "Chaucer's Scribe," Fig. 7, first main entry, right. Regarding fol. 87r, Mooney and Stubbs say that "some features of his handwriting and some letter-forms reveal this to be written by his hand," of which features only two (y and terminal -s) are among the dozen Mooney identifies as characteristic of Pinkhurst in "Chaucer's Scribe," neither supporting this attribution in any case. They also cite two standard, non-diagnostic forms, d and e (*Scribes and the City*, 75–76).

[75] Mooney and Stubbs, *Scribes and the City*, 76.

disposed to see Adam Pinkhurst as Chaucer's scribe otherwise. The next few sections push the case against that belief still further, seeking to show not just that there is no evidence for that identification, but also that there is abundant evidence against it.

Triangles, Snowballs, and Minnows

The isolation of the double-slash and tremolo motifs was both arbitrary and circular: they were his "mark" and "signature" because they appeared in his manuscripts; these were his manuscripts because they featured his mark and signature. But as with Hoccleve's distinctive letter forms, Pinkhurst's decorative motifs are unique not in themselves but rather in their particular aspect and clustering. These are the dozen decorative features I identify in his confirmation:

1. The exaggerated descenders on **A**, **P**, and long **s** in his signature.
2. The triangles of which each of those descenders makes up one of the three sides.
3. The exaggerated ascenders of **h**, **k**, **l**, and **A** "in the top line and at any other places in the text where he has space to do so,"[76] as exemplified in the charters discussed above.
4. The tremolo, or tremolo and knot, as discussed above.
5. The "oblique double line inside the loop when followed by this tremolo."[77]
6. The patterns of triangles, dots, parallel lines, circles, zigzags, and clovers in the signature's **A** and initial line's **E**, also commonly found in such charters and elsewhere.
7. The double-slash-and-dot decoration as discussed above.
8. The use of a "formalized fish as a design element," which "appears remarkably early" in the western tradition of manuscript decoration, as Jane Stevenson writes,[78] and is very common in the fourteenth century: see Figure 6 above. Pinkhurst creates

[76] Mooney, "Chaucer's Scribe," 124.
[77] Ibid., 125.
[78] Jane Stevenson, *The "Laterculus Malalianus" and the School of Archbishop Theodore* (Cambridge: Cambridge University Press, 1995), 106; see also 103–4. Among innumerable other examples, see the first line of a letter patent of 1394 by King Richard II, Wells City Charter no. 13, http://www.wells.gov.uk/index.php?page = archive (accessed July 1, 2015).

minnows in the left legs of the two **As** and an angel fish in the left section of the **E**.

9. The two dashes without dots on the curved line connecting **d** and **a** in the bigger "Adam" and just above the foot of **A** in the first line.
10. The "three curving lines that break the straight line, which are ... found breaking the line of the brace to the right of the oath," as well as the descender of the **s** in his signature, just above the triangle.[79] Again, other scribes, such as John Shirley, employ this feature.[80]
11. The group of three circles, looking like snowballs or traffic lights, that parallel these curving lines on the other side of the brace's tremolo and knot.
12. The y adorned by a large curl in place of a dot in his signature, a feature Shirley and other scribes employed as well.[81]

It might seem inviting to see Pinkhurst's decorative flair in the confirmation as a function of its "much more formal script" on account of the text's Latinity or civic importance (see note 60). The problem is that these features abound as well in at least three other items with identical aspect and date, most extensively in a copy of an English poem. All twelve pervade the *Piers Plowman* B in Cambridge, Trinity College, MS B.15.17—all but the y with curl, absent for obvious reasons (though a similar feature is atop *-ma-*), appearing in its explicit alone (Fig. 9). This explicit is the culmination of an extensive program. At least 69 ys adorned with large curl appear through fol. 60r,[82] while of the 260 sides

---

[79] Mooney, "Chaucer's Scribe," 138, citing only the instance on the brace.

[80] See Shirley's signature in Senate House Library, University of London, MS 1, fol. 2r, the Chandos Herald's "Edward, Prince of Wales, the Black Prince," reproduced in Michelle Brown's entry on this manuscript in *Senate House Library: University of London*, ed. Christopher Pressler and Karen Attar (London: Scala, 2012).

[81] For a variation see, e.g., BL, MS Lansdowne 851 (*Canterbury Tales*), fol. 2r: search "851" at http://www.bl.uk/catalogues/illuminatedmanuscripts/welcome.htm (accessed July 1, 2015); and for a near equivalent see John Shirley's y, as in San Marino, Huntington Library, MS El 26 A.13, fol. iiv, depicted at http://www.medievalscribes.com/ >"Scribes"> "John Shirley."

[82] Thirty-six of these appear on fols. 41v–60r alone, six on fol. 38v and on each of the openings of fols. 54v–55r and 55v–56r. This feature is noted in Thorlac Turville-Petre and Hoyt N. Duggan, eds., *The Piers Plowman Electronic Archive*, Vol. 2, *Cambridge, Trinity College, MS B.15.17 (W)* (CD-ROM ed., 2000; web ed., 2014; cited from the latter, http://piers.iath.virginia.edu/exist/piers/main/B/W/, Introduction, I.6, "Handwriting" [accessed July 2, 2015]).

Fig. 9. Cambridge, Trinity College, MS B.15.17, fol. 130v, bottom third. Reproduced by kind permission of the Master and Fellows of Trinity College, Cambridge.

of this manuscript's *Piers*, no fewer than 257—99 percent—feature the soaring ascenders found in the confirmation.[83] Some 49 sides feature at least 96 instances of the double-slash-and-dot motif, many of which adorn the 11 triangles upon the descenders of ornamental initial letters, which in turn among them also feature the curved lines, zigzags, oblique lines, dashes alone, and angel fish.[84] A dozen sets of snowballs, accompanied by tremolo and knot, appear on the red lines boxing passus divisions; another half-dozen embellish the left legs of ornamental initial **A**s, usually occupied by the three wavy lines.[85]

[83] Those without are fols. 1r, which has elaborate illuminated capital with vinet across the top; 92r, top line boxed in red; and 108r, a passus division. For complete facsimiles see http://sites.trin.cam.ac.uk/manuscripts/ > "B.15.17"; and *William Langland's "The Vision of Piers Plowman": The B-Text; A Facsimile of Trinity College, Cambridge MS B.15.17*, ed. Tomonori Matsushita (Tokyo: Senshu University Press, 2010).

[84] The slash-and-dot motif appears on these folios (those in bold featuring the motif on a descending triangle, with any other motifs noted): 3v, 10v, **11v** (wavy lines), 15v, 16v, 22r, **23r** (angel fish, oblique lines), 24r, 24v, 25v, 26r, 27v, 30v, 32v, 33r, 34v, 35v, 38v, 41v, 43r, 46v, 47v, **49v** (angel fish), 50r, 52r, 53v, 55r, 55v, **56v** (zigzagging river), 62v, 63r, 66v, 73v, 74v, 81r, 83r, 86v, 90v, 93v, 99v, 101v, 103r, **104v** (angel fish), 112v, 119r, **125v** (wavy lines), and **130v** (see Fig. 9, first descending **p**; also in line 4: see Fig. 11). The remaining descending triangles are on fols. 1v, 9r (angel fish), 20v (wavy lines), and 68v (wavy lines).

[85] Those on red brackets, which never occur on boxed Latin tags or quotations within the text, are on fols. 5r, 8v, 13r, 19v, 23v, 35v, 47r, 86r, 101v, 115v, 124r, and 130v; those on **A**s are 70v, 96v, 99v, 103r, 105v, and 112v.

Mooney and Stubbs have drawn attention to two other items that can confidently be attributed to Pinkhurst on these grounds. First are fols. 6r–10v of the Mercers' Account Book, recording John Organ's receipts and expenditure for the years 1391–92 (Fig. 10).[86] A series of exact matches in distinctive letter forms and entire words supports the attribution: that of the bastard anglicana enlarged *d* with decorated topstroke, angled strokes, and broken minims in its second term, *denar(i-orum)* (fol. 6r; Mooney's Fig. 7), with the final three letters of Pinkhurst's signature *Adam*; of the term *incremento* in Organ's accounts (fol. 10v) with its equivalent in line 8 of my Fig. 5; of the initial ornamental **J** (fol. 9v; Mooney's Fig. 4) with Trinity B.15.17's many inaugural **I**s (fols. 25v, 26r, 30v, 33r, 101v); and of the distinctive capital **R** that inaugurates its fol. 8r with that which opens the Trinity *Piers*, fol. 113v. A slightly more elaborate and rounded version of this last form, **R**, appears as well on fol. 6r, and on the top line of the second item, quite likely to be in Pinkhurst's hand: a deed from March 1393 recording the transfer of property back to John of Northampton after his return from exile (BL, Additional Charter 40542).[87] Both documents feature exaggerated

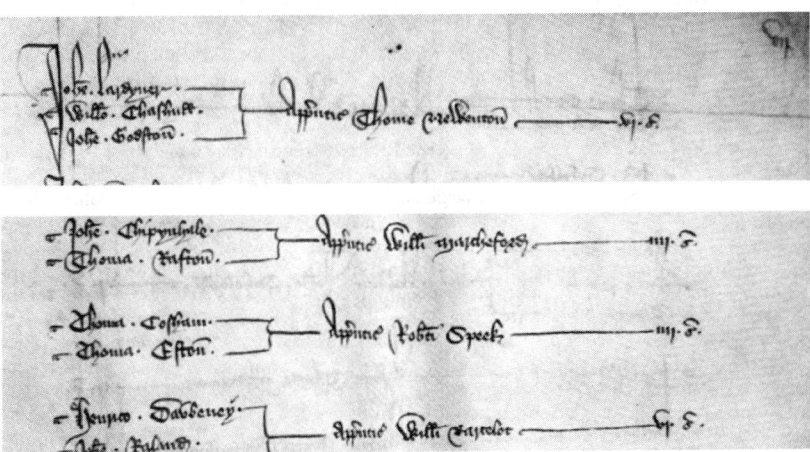

Fig. 10. Mercers' Company Account Book, fol. 7r (excerpts). Reproduced by kind permission of the Mercers' Company.

[86] See Mooney, "Chaucer's Scribe," 110–12 and figs. 4 (9v) and 7 (6r); and Jefferson, *Medieval Account Books*, 11–12. Roberts objects strongly to this attribution ("On Giving Scribe B a Name," 255–57), but the issue is confused by the conflation of Pinkhurst and Scribe B and by the initial discussion of much more than these few folios (see above, note 70). Pinkhurst's (i.e., not Scribe B's) copying of Trinity B.15.17 was also not yet apparent.

[87] Mooney and Stubbs, *Scribes and the City*, 80–82 and Fig. 4.9.

ascenders, oblique lines, tremolos (not necessarily with knot), y with large curl,[88] and double-slash-and-dot motif; the petition features an angel fish in its initial O and decoration within its vertical cross-bar; and the Mercers' Accounts have the descending triangle of the initial J of my Figure 10, the two dashes (initial J of 9v, Mooney's Fig. 4), and three curving lines interrupting the descender (middle of 6r, Mooney's Fig. 7, "Austyn"). Only the snowballs appear in neither item. Finally, it is very likely that Pinkhurst ornamented the *Boece* mentioned above (Aberystwyth, National Library of Wales, MS Peniarth 393D), fulfilling a role that Estelle Stubbs originally suggested might have been Scribe B's; if my analysis of Pinkhurst's career below is accurate, this becomes the first manuscript of any of Chaucer's works securely dateable to his lifetime.[89]

A *Piers Plowman* Manuscript by the Hengwrt-Ellesmere Scribe?

Paleography

Since 1913 readers have been able to compare the hands of Trinity *Piers* (W), Hengwrt (Hg), and Ellesmere (El) in facsimile,[90] and as Doyle and

---

[88] See Add. Charter 40542, "Kyng" middle of top line and "Risby" penultimate line (and quite large curl above the I in "Gihalde," line 1); and in the Mercers' Account Book, my Fig. 10, final line on left, "Daubeney," as well as instances on fols. 6r, 7r, and 7v.

[89] See above, note 62. In addition to the knotted tremolos on which Stubbs focused, the boxing of textual divisions looks exactly like the Trinity *Piers*'s boxing of catchwords and passus divisions. We also find a large curl above y, 9r top line, and the oblique lines in the d, 9v top line. Neither the aspect nor the dialect matches Pinkhurst's, however. I consulted the facsimile of the manuscript at https://www.llgc.org.uk/discover/digital-gallery/digitalmirror-manuscripts/the-middle-ages/peniarth-ms-393d/ (accessed September 27, 2015). "It has traditionally been agreed by scholars that none of the extant copies of Chaucer's works dates from the poet's lifetime," as Simon Horobin has observed (*The Language of the Chaucer Tradition* [Cambridge: D. S. Brewer, 2003], 36), and it seems almost certain that Pinkhurst would have embellished it before his retirement to Surrey in the year of Chaucer's death as discussed below. See below, note 107 on some scholars' recent attempts to date Hengwrt to the 1390s.

[90] Its *Piers* is W "[b]ecause Mr. Thomas Wright printed this Trinity MS. *in extenso*" in his 1843 edition; William Langland, *The Vision of William Concerning Piers the Plowman in Three Parallel Texts*, ed. Walter W. Skeat, Vol. 2 (London: Oxford University Press, 1886), lxiv n. 1. The early facsimiles were *Autotype Specimens of the Chief Chaucer MSS, Part I*, Chaucer Society, Series 1, no. 48, ed. Frederick J. Furnivall (London: Trübner, 1876), Hg, fol. 204r; National Library of Wales, *Charter of Incorporation and Report on the Progress of the Library from the Granting of the Charter to the 31st March, 1909* (Oswestry: Woodall, Minshall, Thomas, 1909), 50, Hg, fol. 56v; *The Ellesmere Chaucer Reproduced in Facsimile*, ed. Alex Egerton, 2 vols. (Manchester: Manchester University Press, 1911); and *Facsimiles of Twelve Early English Manuscripts in the Library of Trinity College, Cambridge*, ed. W. W. Greg (Oxford: Oxford University Press, 1913), Plate vii, W top three-quarters of fol. 5r.

Parkes remarked in 1979, "no one has hitherto remarked on any very close resemblance to the Hengwrt hand except that of the Ellesmere Chaucer, to which we can now add the Trinity Cambridge Gower and the Hatfield fragment of *Troilus*."[91] Doyle knew MS W well. A few years earlier he had advised George Kane and E. Talbot Donaldson on their descriptions of the *Piers Plowman* B manuscripts (W "bears a strong resemblance to the hand of the Ellesmere manuscript, and while not by the Ellesmere scribe, is pretty certainly of the same school and period");[92] on two occasions he compared W's and El's exaggerated ascenders, tremolos, and the like;[93] and in his 1986 overview of the manuscripts of *Piers Plowman* he opined that while "in certain respects" W's script resembles that of the Hg-El scribe, in others it "resembles that of a prolific Staffordshire scribe of the same period."[94] In 2004

[91] Doyle and Parkes, "Paleographical Introduction," xxxv. The Hatfield fragment is "the fragment of one leaf of Chaucer's *Troilus and Criseyde* in the library of the marquess of Salisbury at Hatfield House (Hertfordshire)" (Doyle, "Copyist," 49; see 58–59 for discussion and facsimile). Other vernacular manuscripts sometimes attributed to Scribe B are Dublin, Trinity College, MS 244 (prose tracts, some of which are Wycliffite [above, note 10]); and the fragment from *The Prioress's Prologue and Tale*, Cambridge University Library, MS Kk.I.3, Part 20, about which Doyle expresses "serious hesitation" (60). It is accepted, however, by Horobin and Mooney, "A *Piers Plowman* Manuscript," 91 n. 54; and Mooney and Stubbs, *Scribes and the City*, 69 and n. 13. Kathleen L. Scott sees it "possible to add" Oxford, Bodleian Library, MS Hatton 4—an hours and psalter written in "a liturgical Textura"—"to the company, already assembled by A. I. Doyle and M. B. Parkes, of manuscripts by the Ellesmere scribe," but does not pursue the case—she focuses on the artists of the borders—and to my knowledge no one has since mentioned it; Kathleen L. Scott, "An Hours and Psalter by Two Ellesmere Illuminators," in Stevens and Woodward, *The Ellesmere Chaucer*, 87–119 (87). And Ralph Hanna reports that Jeremy Griffiths was convinced that Scribe B copied the Holloway fragment of *Piers Plowman* C, now New Haven, Yale University, Beinecke Library, MS Osborn fa.45; *Introducing English Medieval Book History: Manuscripts, Their Producers and Their Readers* (Liverpool: Liverpool University Press, 2013), 146 n. 10). Since Hg and El provide by far the fullest record of their scribe's work and decoration I focus on them alone.

[92] William Langland, *Piers Plowman: The B Version*, ed. George Kane and E. Talbot Donaldson (London: Athlone Press, 1975), 13 n. 91. "The old notion that simply by undertaking to edit a text a man becomes a palæographer has been discredited in our time with the growth in knowledge and understanding of vernacular manuscripts, and while we think we know how to use these we make no pretence to palæographic expertise; anything in our edition which might seem to suggest it we owe to the patient instruction of these three"—that is, T. J. Brown, Doyle, and N. R. Ker: "Our particular obligation is to Dr. Doyle, who read and checked our descriptions of manuscripts" (vi).

[93] Doyle and Parkes, "Paleographical Introduction," xxxiii; and Doyle, "Copyist," 54, 67 n. 23.

[94] A. I. Doyle, "Remarks on Surviving Manuscripts of *Piers Plowman*," in *Medieval English Religious and Ethical Literature: Essays in Honour of G. H. Russell*, ed. Gregory Kratzmann and James Simpson (Cambridge: D. S. Brewer, 1986), 35–48 (39; for the manuscripts in this scribe's hand see Turville-Petre and Duggan, *Piers Plowman Electronic Archive*, Introduction, I.1, "Date," second note; and Horobin and Mooney, "A *Piers*

the situation changed, Horobin and Mooney announcing that Trinity B.15.17 did not just resemble, but was, the work of Scribe B. Its scribe's current identity as "Adam Pinkhurst" is thus the result not of the comparison of W's hand and decorative features with those of Pinkhurst's confirmation, but rather of a two-stage process whereby he first became the Hg-El scribe and was then part of the package when that scribe in turn was identified as Adam. What is now clear is that Trinity B.15.17 is not a mere nice addition to more important Chaucer attributions, but, given how overwhelming is the evidence that Pinkhurst was its scribe, the linchpin of the entire case that he copied Hengwrt and Ellesmere, not to mention that he is the referent of "Adam Scriveyn."

According to Ralph Hanna, Malcolm Parkes "responded to an early presentation of Mooney's work by saying that he thought Pynkhurst responsible for all the manuscripts Mooney had assigned to him except the two most important, his two full *Canterbury Tales*," anticipating my own argument, and Roberts has more recently rejected the attribution of Trinity B.15.17 (as well as Pinkhurst's confirmation and much else) to Scribe B.[95] At the other end of the spectrum is Hanna's characterization of Horobin and Mooney's case as "plausibly certain."[96] The most common response—caution—is represented by Kathryn Kerby-Fulton's comment that Scribe B copied Hg, El, and "perhaps also (though this is less certain)" W.[97] No one has articulated the reasons for the proposal's

---

Plowman Manuscript," 70). So far as I am aware no one else compared W with El prior to 2004.

[95] Ralph Hanna, review of *Scribes and the City, TLS* 5750 (June 14, 2013): 29; Roberts, "On Giving Scribe B a Name," 257–59. Pamela Robinson says that Mooney's argument regarding Pinkhurst "has already been challenged, the unconvinced including Malcolm Parkes"; Pamela Robinson, review of *Scribes and the City, JEBS* 17 (2014): 395–98 (396).

[96] Hanna, *Introducing Medieval Book History*, 146; he had earlier said merely that W was in "a script style, particularly in its presentation of the Latin, very reminiscent of Doyle–Parkes scribe B," referring to Horobin and Mooney "for a stronger claim that the hand is in fact scribe B's"; Ralph Hanna, *London Literature, 1300–1380* (Cambridge: Cambridge University Press, 2005), 244. The most positive response to Horobin and Mooney's claim I have seen is Stephen Kelly, "Piers Plowman," in *A Companion to Medieval English Literature and Culture c. 1350–c. 1500*, ed. Peter Brown (Oxford: Blackwell, 2009), 537–53 (551 n. 5); I accepted the attribution in my *The Lost History of "Piers Plowman": The Earliest Transmission of Langland's Work* (Philadelphia: University of Pennsylvania Press, 2011), xv.

[97] Kerby-Fulton, Hilmo, and Olson, *Opening up Middle English Manuscripts*, 39–40 (see above, note 8). Her collaborator Maidie Hilmo remarks that Scribe B (whom she does not necessarily take to be Pinkhurst) "possibly" copied W (ibid., 248); Thorlac Turville-Petre says Pinkhurst "may" have copied W ("The B Archetype of *Piers Plowman* as a Corpus for Metrical Analysis," in Calabrese and Shepherd, *Yee? Baw for Bokes*, 17–30 [28]); and Luigina Marina Domenica Caon says "he was engaged in the produc-

lukewarm reception, but I would imagine that the reasons are in line with those behind critics' silence about the possibility that Royal 17 D.XVIII is a holograph: the easy attribution of W, Hg, and El's shared features to two scribes from a similar or identical milieu, and the difference of W's aspect, letter forms, and language from those of the latter two.

"Given that almost all the characteristics by which Doyle identifies this hand are present in B.15.17, and that the aspect is different only to the extent that one would expect of a scribe writing Langland's alliterative verse as opposed to Chaucer's *Canterbury Tales*," say Horobin and Mooney, "there seems to us no doubt that this is the work of the same hand" as that of Hg and El.[98] All rests on that qualification, "only to the extent . . . ," which responds, as must Mooney's argument regarding Royal 17 D.XVIII, to the "difference . . . in the aspect of the hands" between Scribe B and the Trinity B.15.17 scribe.[99] Doyle and Parkes describe Hg and El's "most distinctive qualities" as their aspect and duct, manifested in a "vertical impetus," setting them apart from W, whose "distinct spaces left between words, together with short ascenders and descenders," as Horobin and Mooney acknowledge, "give a boxy look to the words and result in a horizontal, as opposed to a vertical, aspect to the overall appearance of the text."[100]

Their explanation, which they attribute to an unnamed colleague, is that scribes of *Piers Plowman* adopted a different aspect so as to highlight that poem's alliterative terms.[101] Roberts points out, however, that "the spacing does not seem particularly to emphasize alliterative words": it is unclear, then, how readers would recognize that the spacing was at all unusual unless they had other manuscripts known to be by this scribe at hand available for comparison.[102] One wonders how anyone who did spot the difference would know its purpose was to highlight the alliteration. A more effective means of indicating as much would have been to

---

tion of texts by Chaucer, Gower and also by Langland, if he indeed was the copyist of" W ("Authorial or Scribal? Spelling Variation in the Hengwrt and Ellesmere Manuscripts of *The Canterbury Tales*," Ph.D. diss. [University of Leiden, 2009], 26).

[98] Horobin and Mooney, "A *Piers Plowman* Manuscript," 71–72.
[99] Ibid., 69.
[100] Respectively, Doyle and Parkes, "Production of Copies," 170; and Horobin and Mooney, "A *Piers Plowman* Manuscript," 70. Roberts adds that W's minims are "sometimes backwards-tilting, and the body of the letters looks smaller in relation to the ascenders and descenders and less pleasingly assured than in the Hengwrt-Ellesmere group"; "On Giving Scribe B a Name," 259.
[101] Horobin and Mooney, "A *Piers Plowman* Manuscript," 70.
[102] Roberts, "On Giving Scribe B a Name," 259.

follow the lead of his contemporary, the copyist of the wild *Piers* in Oxford, Corpus Christi College, MS 201, who "frequently rubricates the first letters of alliterative series," as Noelle Phillips remarks.[103] All these objections aside, Horobin and Mooney's novel idea runs up against the fact that the spacing in the Rolle text on fols. 131r–147v of B.15.17, as they say about eight other features, is "the same" as its *Piers* text.[104] Yet the most fundamental problem with this new proposal is the absence of any problems with the conventional belief, articulated by Doyle, that two separate scribes were responsible for these respective productions. No reason to seek out another explanation presents itself in the first place, and the one Horobin and Mooney light upon as discussed here strikes me as very implausible. Yet the stakes are so high that it will be worth pursuing the many other categories of evidence that point away from any sense that Scribe B copied Trinity B.15.17. We will begin by turning to its other paleographical features.

The most striking feature revealed by comparison of these productions, given that the assumption otherwise provides the foundation of Mooney's subsequent argument that this scribe is Adam Pinkhurst, is the relative absence of his repertoire of decorative motifs from the Chaucer texts.[105] "Chaucer's Scribe" cites only those five motifs shared as well by the two *Canterbury Tales* manuscripts: the two "signatures" discussed above, the heightened ascenders, the oblique lines in those ascenders, and the three wavy lines. (It will help readers to consult the complete facsimiles of each manuscript for this discussion, now easily accessible online and elsewhere.)[106] Of fols. 2r–50v of the earlier of the two productions, Hg (early 1400s), only the opening one has exaggerated ascenders and oblique lines, while only six sides have a total of some

---

[103] Noelle Phillips, "Seeing Red: Reading Rubrication in Oxford, Corpus Christi College MS 201's *Piers Plowman*," *ChauR* 47 (2013): 439–64 (448). Although Mooney and Stubbs say that when Richard Osbarn "writes prose, as in the *Brut* in Lambeth 491, his letters are more closely packed into a line; when he writes verse, especially alliterative verse, they are written with greater horizontal spread," citing Horobin and Mooney's own earlier remarks as support (*Scribes and the City*, 20), their figs. 2.1 and 2.2 show the opposite to be the case.

[104] Horobin and Mooney, "A *Piers Plowman* Manuscript," 72.

[105] See ibid., 104 and n. 87 for brief discussion of decorative features in common.

[106] See https://www.llgc.org.uk/discover/digital-gallery/digitalmirror-manuscripts/the-middle-ages/thehengwrtchaucerpeniarth/ (accessed September 27, 2015); Ruggiers, *Facsimile and Transcription of the Hengwrt Manuscript*; and http://hdl.huntington.org/cdm/ref/collection/p15150coll7/id/2838; *The New Ellesmere Chaucer Monochromatic Facsimile*, ed. Daniel Woodward and Martin Stevens (San Marino: Huntington Library, 1997), and note 83.

seventeen tremolos and knots: five in the first line of the poem (2r; this however is not the top line), most of the remainder appearing to serve as indicators to the rubricator.[107] Later, things pick up a bit, though top margins remain empty.[108] El, most likely dated after Hg, abounds in exaggerated ascenders, at least—this is one of the "primary distinctions between Scribe B's work in Hg and El"—even if rarely with oblique lines or knotted tremolos, and it also features a good handful of minnows and some double-slash-and-dot motifs, if at a much smaller rate than we find in W.[109] A few of Pinkhurst's other motifs appear very rarely here as well (e.g., one double slash above the foot of an **A**, 106r), but almost always looking much different. In all of Hg and El I have found no curls above lower case ys (and only one above a capital **Y**, El 44v); no sets of three curving lines; a single descending near-triangle in El, neither completed nor decorated (137v); no zigzags or anything elaborate in the few desultory attempts at decoration (El 39r, 130v, 193r).

Neither does Horobin and Mooney's remark that "almost all the characteristics by which Doyle identifies this hand" are present in B.15.17 to my mind fairly represent Doyle, for whom these characteristics are not diagnostic apart from similarity in aspect. In any case he does not believe W to be a production of Scribe B (see note 94). Letter forms join aspect and decoration in arguing against the idea. While

---

[107] The tremolos and knots in this portion appear on fols. 2r, 13r, 25v, 36v, 41r, and 50v, all at breaks in the text rather than on top margins. See Doyle, "Copyist," 64–65, endorsing the traditional placement of Hg before El. Horobin has forcefully argued that "Chaucer had no input into the production of the Hengwrt manuscript," most likely because he was dead, putting the date in the early 1400s: Simon Horobin, "Adam Pinkhurst, Geoffrey Chaucer, and the Hengwrt Manuscript of the *Canterbury Tales*," *ChauR* 44 (2010): 351–67 (364). Scott, "Hours and Psalter," argues that El is the product of the very early 1400s and thus "that Hengwrt was made before the death of Chaucer" (119 n. 55), but I am not convinced by her premise that the El borders could only have been made within so small a chronological window. Another of many possible interpretations of the evidence is that that window is too narrow.

[108] One finds sets of snowballs on brackets on 128r, 190v, 234v; an angel fish, a few double slashes, and a patterned decoration on 112r; ascenders, oblique lines, a tremolo and knot, and the occasional double slash motif (once or twice with dot) on 68r, 79v, 86v, 88r, 89r, 153v, 204r, 213v.

[109] Daniel W. Mosser, "Manuscript Description," in *The Hengwrt Chaucer Digital Facsimile (2000)*, http://www.petermwrobinson.me.uk/canterburytalesproject.com/pubs/HGMsDesc.html (accessed July 2, 2015), paragraph on "Hands." For minnows see El, fols. 29r, 70r, 87r, 88v, 111v, 129r, 178v, 201r. I find some thirteen of the double-slash-and-dot motifs on eight sides through fol. 50v (fols. 3v, 5r, 7r, 16v, 21r, 36v, 49r, 50r); see above, note 84 for W's statistics (almost three times as many sides featuring the motif through 50v).

nearly every side of W opens with an ornamental capital, this occurs never in Hg, and rarely in El. We have already noted the distinctive **R** in Organ's accounts and the Trinity *Piers*; Hg has nothing like this, while El's nearest equivalent reverses the ratio of compartmental sizes (41v, 47v, 136v). Likewise, the ornamental **A** that opens no fewer than 49 of W's 260 pages, including fol. 130v, as shown in Figure 11, lacking cross-bar and usually adorned by three or four items from Pinkhurst's repertoire,[110] is echoed a mere three times in El (128v, 146r, 200v), its most common relative almost always differing from W's in having a double cross-bar and "sweeping strokes on the left," doubled left leg, and occasional ornamentation with double-slash-and-dot but none of the other characteristic features that adorn Pinkhurst's As (e.g., 21r).[111]

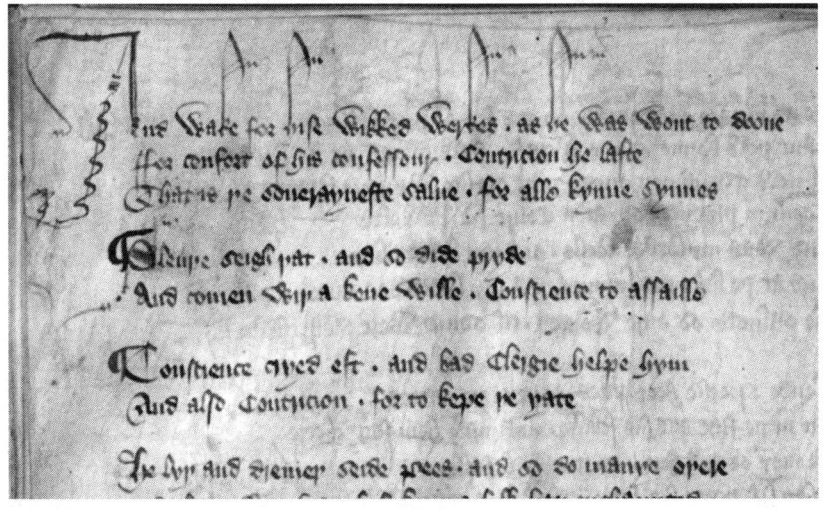

Fig. 11. Cambridge, Trinity College, MS B.15.17, fol. 130v, top third. Reproduced by kind permission of the Master and Fellows of Trinity College, Cambridge.

[110] See fols. 1v, 5v, 9r, 10v, 11v, 13r, 14v, 16v, 17r, 20v, 21v, 22r, 24r, 24v, 34v, 36r, 38v, 41r, 43r, 46v, 50r, 52v, 53v, 55v, 63v, 68v, 70v, 71v, 73v, 74v, 75v, 77v, 78r, 83r, 84r, 96v, 97r, 99v, 100r, 103r, 104v, 105v, 107r, 112v, 114r, 114v, 119r, 125v, 130v; in second place, "the normal enlargement of the minuscule closed two-story form" that dominates El and Hg (Doyle, "Copyist," 53) lags behind with nineteen appearances: fols. 4r, 16r, 20r, 32r, 39v, 44r, 50v, 57v, 62r, 64r, 65r, 80v, 84v, 90r, 98r, 104r, 124v, 127r.

[111] Ibid., saying that this form is "used only as the first tall elegant ornamented letter on a verse page, of capital form with a double cross-bar and sweeping strokes on the left," citing the top lines of fols. 18v, 20v, and 21r; it is "not to be found in Hg as far as I have noticed." Horobin and Mooney had claimed to "set forth in our Appendix

As for non-ornamental capitals, the loop of the Trinity *Piers*'s Ts "often circles back to the top stroke enclosing the whole letter" (Fig. 11, "That" [3]; also Fig. 10, "Thoma" [line 2 of second excerpt]), and its Hs have "a loop through the ascender" so as to distinguish them from h (Fig. 11, final line; also Fig. 10, lower left word).[112] Both of these features also characterize the "prolific Staffordshire scribe of the same period" with which Doyle compares W's anglicana formata,[113] but in Hg and El the T is very rarely enclosed by a loop, and the H has only a dot rather than a loop.[114] Also, the loops of capital W in the items assigned to Pinkhurst above often soar in parallel curves, and never intersect (see, e.g., Fig. 10, the two "Will*iam*"s; Fig. 11, the alliterating terms of the top line), while those in Hg and El almost always intersect (e.g., top lines Hg 8v, 13r, El 1v).[115] Likewise, only the confirmed Pinkhurstian texts feature his "doubled f for the uppercase form," in which "he connects the ascenders, forming a ligature between ascenders that sometimes extends to further ascenders in the line, as in the Mercers' account book, fol. 6r ([her} Fig. 7, 'ffressh,' in the third heading on the right), and in Trinity College B.15.17, fol. 65v ([her} Fig. 9, line 1, 'ffor hir')";[116] in El the ligature does not extend further (e.g., fols. 7v, 123v) and, again, it is absent from Hg.

Finally, in all the items assigned here to Pinkhurst, the tails of xs

---

and the accompanying illustrations" the paleographical support for their argument that W is by Scribe B ("A *Piers Plowman* Manuscript," 68), but that appendix takes their argument as already proven, presenting W's form of ornamental A as sole example not of the form with which I have aligned it, but of Scribe B's second form of the letter, "with an exaggerated, upsweeping lead stroke replacing the upper lobe and 'an angular foot on the line, with an oblique separate stroke, decorated with short cross-strokes, cutting the curve'" (102, citing Doyle, "Copyist," 53). In any case, of Doyle's own examples of this form—El, fols. 10r, line 32; 153v, line 3; and, "more ornamentally," 3v, top line (53; I find it also on, e.g., 16v, 47r, 130v, 132r, 136r, 141r)—only the last, 3v, bears a slight resemblance to Horobin and Mooney's Fig. 4.

[112] Turville-Petre and Duggan, *Piers Plowman Electronic Archive*, Introduction, I.6, "Handwriting." Cf. Fletcher, "Criteria," 613 and n. 51.

[113] Doyle, "Remarks," 39 (see above, note 94). See, for instance, Manchester, John Rylands Library, MS Engl. 50, fol. 91, available at http://enriqueta.man.ac.uk/luna/servlet/Man4MedievalVC~4~4 (accessed July 2, 2015); search "JRL0924199dc": first two lines beginning with this T and line 3 beginning with this H.

[114] Hg's T "has a considerable range of variations of the same basic form: the head stroke is flat or arched, left free or looped closely or widely back into the bowl, or underneath," say Doyle and Parkes ("Paleographical Introduction," xxxvi). Looped Ts do occasionally occur, as in Hg, fol. 23v, lines 2, 35, 36; but that side has eleven non-looped versions, while W's Ts are almost always looped.

[115] Cf. Mooney, "Chaucer's Scribe," 137.

[116] Ibid.

and ys characteristically extend under the previous letter before angling sharply at 45 or fewer degrees back to the right in a straight line, sometimes extending under the following letter: see, e.g., Fig. 5 "Pynkhurst" top line and left, "ex" line 4; Fig. 10 "Lardyner," "Chipynhale," and "Daubeney" on left and xs throughout in the tallies (not shown); Fig. 11 ys in lines 3, 4, 6, 7, 8. Scribe B's tails occasionally do this, but they more often curve up neatly under the same letter. Horobin and Mooney attempt to recruit Trinity B.15.17's ys to their characterization of Scribe B's form of the letter, "its left branch . . . usually upright rather than slanted, and the crossing of left and right branches occur[ring] below the bottom of minims or line of non-descender letters in the rest of the line," adducing a single instance (fol. 59v, line 16, *manye*).[117] To my eye, however, that y's limb slants, and its form coincides with the script baseline, as do those of the nine ys in my Fig. 11. Roberts observes as much about the Trinity *Piers*'s ys in general, also pointing to other features of Scribe B's letter forms "that are hardly matched in the [Trinity College, Cambridge] Langland hand: a flower-like shape of a rather cursively constructed w; the frequently short descenders of f and long -s."[118]

Yoghs

The remainder of Horobin and Mooney's case is that, as with letter forms, "the linguistic evidence supports the identification of the Trinity manuscript as the work of Scribe B," but "supports" here has the weak connotations that attend "confirm" in the remark that letter forms of Pinkhurst's confirmation "confirm the attribution": it simply means that the language is not different enough, from a certain perspective, to show the attribution to be incorrect.[119] Indeed, Jacob Thaisen has observed that the linguistic profile for the *Canterbury Tales* text in BL, Add. MS 35286 (Ad3), clearly not by Pinkhurst or Scribe B, "matches the profile for [W] more closely than does the profile for either Hg or El," confirming that "all that Horobin and Mooney (2004) have shown is that [W's] text is written in a variety of London-Westminster English that is close to Chaucer's own dialect."[120]

---

[117] Horobin and Mooney, "A *Piers Plowman* Manuscript," 104.
[118] Roberts, "On Giving Scribe B a Name," 260.
[119] Horobin and Mooney, "A *Piers Plowman* Manuscript," 90.
[120] Jacob Thaisen, "Adam Pinkhurst's Short and Long Forms," in *Scribes, Printers, and the Accidentals of Their Texts*, ed. Thaisen and Hanna Rutkowska (Frankfurt am Main: Peter Lang, 2011), 73–90 (84).

While these texts are linguistically close, Thorlac Turville-Petre and Hoyt Duggan nevertheless cite "considerable differences" between W's and Hg-El's spellings of diagnostic items, such as NOT, spelled *noȝt* (334 instances)/*noght* (1)/*nat* (4) in W, where Hg and El, by contrast, together attest 1877 instances of *nat* versus only 425 of *noght*; and THROUGH: *poruȝ/Thoruȝ* (156)/*porugh* (2) in W versus unanimous *thurgh* (247) in Hg/El. Horobin and Mooney explain this variety as Mooney had Royal 17 D.XVIII's spelling of YOU: "It may be that here we have evidence of changes in spelling preferences during Scribe B's copying career, and that he used Type II forms such as 'þoruȝ/Thoruȝ' early in his career and subsequently rejected these in favor of the Type III forms 'thogh,' 'though,' and 'thurgh.'"[121]

However convincing that approach might be, this instance is part of a much larger change between W and Hg necessitated by Scribe B's naming as Adam. At issue are the 490 yoghs in W's *noȝt*s and *poruȝ*s, nearly one-third of its 1,526 instances of that letter form, an average of a dozen per opening.[122] At this rate one would expect thousands of yoghs over the roughly 960 sides of Hg and El—well over 5,000 if the rate were comparable—but they instead feature only 3, of which only 2 are by Scribe B, of which only 1 is in the main text.[123] Every other early scribe of the *Canterbury Tales* used this letter, in at least some cases replacing the ys in their exemplars.[124] This near-absolute banishment of

---

[121] Horobin and Mooney, "A *Piers Plowman* Manuscript," 85–86. On Types II and III of Middle English see M. L. Samuels, "Some Applications of Middle English Dialectology," *ES* 44 (1963): 81–94, which Horobin and Mooney claim to be correcting by identifying two of Samuels's main representatives of Type III language, W and Hg/El, as products of a single scribe.

[122] A search for &yogh; in the ASCII text of W in Turville-Petre and Duggan's *Electronic Archive* edition, available from the drop-down menu on its main page, yields 1,531 hits, 5 of which are double encodings of single instances.

[123] One is a painted capital over a guide letter Y (Hg, 214v), by a flourisher who was not the main scribe; one is squeezed into the margin of Ellesmere's *Parson's Tale* for reasons of space (*thurȝ*; El, 219r; Hg is deficient here); and one in a main text (*veȝe*; Hg, 27r). See Doyle and Parkes, "Paleographical Introduction," xxxvi–xxxvii on the two in Hg, xxxix on the flourisher. I learned of El's instance from Caon, "Authorial or Scribal?," 218.

[124] I.e., the scribes of Cambridge, Corpus Christi, MS 198 (Cp) and BL, MS Harley 7334 (Ha4; both copied by Scribe D, ?Marchaunt); BL, Add. MS 35286 (Ad3) and MS Lansdowne 851 (La); and Cambridge University Library, MSS Dd.IV.24 (Dd; by "Wytton") and Gg.IV.27 (Gg). I have benefited from *The Multitext Edition: The Norman Blake Editions of "The Canterbury Tales,"* ed. Estelle Stubbs, Michael Pidd, Orietta Da Rold, Simon Horobin, and Claire Thomson with Linda Cross (2013), http://www.chaucermss.org/multitext (accessed July 2, 2015), which enables users to compare these six plus Hg and El for any line. Jacob Thaisen and Orietta Da Rold, "The Linguistic Stratification in the Cambridge Dd Copy of Chaucer's *Canterbury Tales*," *NM* 110 (2009): 283–297

yogh between W and Hg, if a single scribe copied both manuscripts, is difficult enough in its own right—especially so, in my judgment, given Turville-Petre and Duggan's observation that the W scribe had "a remarkably consistent spelling system which he must have been taught to impose upon the language of his exemplars."[125]

Horobin has identified Scribe B as the main corrector to the *Piers Plowman* B-text in BL, Additional MS 35287 (sigil M), which puts the problem into still sharper relief since this corrector's "simplest" change, notes Turville-Petre, "and the most pervasive, is to remove or alter initial yogh."[126] Noting that none of the terms from which the corrector removed the yogh is spelled with that letter in W, Turville-Petre suggests that the corrector's purpose seems to have been "to alter the language of M in the direction of London English on the model of W."[127] Getting yogh right was clearly central to this mission. And yet this did not translate into the addition of yogh, or replacement of *-gh* or other letters with that letter: W has over 200 more yoghs than M after we account for the latter's deletions. If Pinkhurst is Scribe B, these three different approaches to yogh—writing them everywhere in W as part of his graphetic system, deleting many but adding none to M in a partial attempt to render it W-like, and obliterating them from the graphetic system employed in Hg and El—are very difficult to reconcile with each other. If they are two separate scribes, though, then the problem vanishes, and Scribe B turned to M with only a local feature in mind as

---

(292–93) remark on the Dd scribe's replacement of y with yogh. See also Jacob Thaisen, "Overlooked Variants in the Orthography of British Library, Additional MS 35286," *JEBS* 11 (2008): 121–43 on the importance of including variants such as yogh/y in such analysis; he observes that "the fourteen Ad3 examples [of yogh] are all found in its General Prologue and Knight's Tale" (139 n. 40; see 133 on this scribe's preference for y over the yogh of his exemplar).

[125] Turville-Petre and Duggan, *The Piers Plowman Electronic Archive*, Introduction, III.1. See also Fletcher, "What Did Adam Pynkhurst (Not) Write?," 707 and n. 49 on the spellings of NOT and on Horobin's conflation of yogh and gh in his reporting of them.

[126] Respectively Simon Horobin, "Adam Pinkhurst and the Copying of British Library, MS Additional 35287 of the B Version of *Piers Plowman*," *YLS* 23 (2009): 61–83; and Thorlac Turville-Petre, "Putting It Right: The Corrections of Huntington Library MS Hm 128 and BL Additional MS 35287," *YLS* 16 (2002): 41–65 (55). Horobin's identification is based primarily on similarity of aspect.

[127] Turville-Petre, "Putting It Right," 63. I searched for *thorugh* in the text of M (and for *&yogh;* as mentioned next sentence) in the ASCII text available from the main page of *The Piers Plowman Electronic Archive*, Vol. 5, *London, British Library, MS Additional 35287 (M)*, ed. Eric Eliason, Hoyt N. Duggan, and Thorlac Turville-Petre (CD-ROM ed., 2005; web ed., 2014; cited from the latter, http://piers.iath.virginia.edu/exist/piers/main/B/M [accessed July 2, 2015]).

object of his corrections, one that accorded with his own approach to yogh, substantively different from Pinkhurst's in this regard.

Some readers may wonder whether the other differences catalogued above between W and Hg/El—spacing; length of ascenders and descenders; employment of wavy lines and decorated descending triangles; formation of w, y, T, and H; use of ornamental initial **A** and **R**; and the rest—may have been due to a change in the scribe's habits over time parallel to the forces of standardization that in Horobin and Mooney's scenario both changed his spelling and, they must believe, did away with his yoghs as well. Yet the aspect of the two petitions of c. 1388 that Mooney and Stubbs have to my mind more convincingly attributed to Scribe B is identical to that of Hengwrt and Ellesmere, and distant from that of Pinkhurst.[128] The claim would thus be that Pinkhurst adopted his Scribe B hand around 1388, switched to his Pinkhurst one for the years 1392–95, and then back to the Scribe B hand after the turn of the century. It is a variation on the claim that he was passionate about his decorations around 1395, all but abandoned them a decade later in Hg, and brought them back half-heartedly for El.

"It seems necessary to explain striking differences between the [Trinity College, Cambridge] Langland hand and scribe B as well as to point to similarities," writes Jane Roberts in her essay on giving Scribe B a name.[129] The list of striking differences between W and Hg-El is substantial, and their character substantive, yet Horobin and Mooney only mention a few spellings; offer a subjective, unprecedented, and unlikely explanation of the crucial category of aspect; and remain silent concerning letter forms and the biggest difference, the respective decorative programs. Neither do they explain why their approach is preferable to the alternative. Here is the corollary to Roberts's point: that no compelling reason to fit all these disparate characteristics into a single scribe's career presents itself in the first place. If the position maintained

---

[128] See above, note 72. Mooney remarks that the aspect of the Mercers' Petition "most resembles the Hengwrt manuscript of *The Canterbury Tales*, an Anglicana formata both rounded and vertical" ("Chaucer's Scribe," 125), while conversely Roberts comments that the petition's mix of anglicana and secretary letter forms is "very different" from the mix of those forms in Pinkhurst's confirmation ("On Giving Scribe B a Name," 254). The aspect of the "less formal, more hasty script" of the Leathersellers' and White Tawiers' petition, say Mooney and Stubbs, "matches other less formal examples of his writing in the Mercers' Petition" and other documents they take to be in his hand not discussed here. *Scribes and the City*, 79; see their Fig. 4.7.

[129] Roberts, "On Giving Scribe B a Name," 260.

by Doyle and Parkes themselves that Trinity B.15.17 is not by the Hengwrt-Ellesmere scribe is indeed problematic, the problems should be identified, and the reasons for preferring the extraordinarily difficult alternative explained. In the absence of any such reasons, there is no evidence that Adam Pinkhurst either knew Chaucer or had anything to do with his work apart from embellishing a manuscript of *Boece*.

The Lives and Afterlives of "Adam Penkhurst," Scribe B, and Thomas Hoccleve

Mooney speculates that the historical records regarding "Adam Pinkhurst" refer to two men: a father, born c. 1335 and married to one Joanna c. 1355, member of the king's archers, and retiree to Surrey c. 1400; and his son, our scrivener, still active in London through the first decade of the fifteenth century.[130] She grants the possibility that the records all refer to the same man, but prefers her option because otherwise he would be "a very old man by 1408, after which he is thought to have copied his share of the Gower manuscript at Trinity College" and the Ellesmere manuscript, and because it is difficult to imagine anyone wishing to journey back and forth from Surrey, where he was retired, to London to do all that copying, especially given his advanced age.[131] His disentanglement from Scribe B, however, does away with the need to create two Adams. Retirement at about age sixty-five to his home region of Surrey after a decade or two focused on his work in London presents no problems.

Whether he was the scribe's father or the scribe himself, Adam Pinkhurst was by 1380 a very rich man. This is no surprise, given his award of an annuity of 6d per day for life by Edward III in April 1370, the year Adam and his wife Joanna rented a property in Bramley, Surrey.[132] What has only just come to light is that the 1381 Poll Tax records for

---

[130] I have come upon one Pinkhurst life-record from 1393, which fills out the picture a bit: "William Changelton sued Adam Pynkhurst for the manor of Felde [in Surrey], which John Kyngesnode had given to John Marchall and Joan, his wife, and the heirs of their bodies": Plea Rolls, Michaelmas, 17 Rich. II, m. 103; see *Pedigrees from the Plea Rolls, Collected from the Pleadings in the Various Courts of Law, AD 1200 to 1500*, ed. George Wrottesley (Great Britain: Public Record Office, ?1905), 194, available at https://archive.org/details/pedigreesfromple00wrotrich (accessed July 2, 2015).

[131] Mooney, "Chaucer's Scribe," 116; my "all that copying" material paraphrases 119. She grants that the separation of these two Adams is "entirely speculative" (118).

[132] See Mooney, "Chaucer's Scribe," 117–18 on these transactions, and Mooney and Stubbs, *Scribes and the City*, 84–85 for more information on the lease.

Bramley show that the Pinkhurst couple paid 6s 8d, their two servants John Houwyk and John Colles paying 4d and 6d respectively.[133] As Gary Baker has observed, "even if he were paying only half the 6s. 8d. for himself," the other half paid by Joanna, "and potentially less if paying for other un-listed family members, this was still three times the amount the average person was expected to continue."[134] That his entry in the Common Paper "is the longest, the most rhetorically ornate, and the most elegantly copied of all," in Richard Firth Green's judgment, "speaks volumes . . . about Pinkhurst's prominent position in the pecking order of the fledgling scriveners' company,"[135] a prominence that makes good sense if this very wealthy man had been a King's Archer in earlier decades. And any sense that King's Archers were purely military men is mitigated by the fact that another royal archer, John Kenne, is listed as a weaver (*textor*) in the 1379 Poll Tax.[136]

Another Pinkhurst life-record, unmentioned by Mooney or Mooney and Stubbs, supports the notion that all these records pertain to a single Adam. Jane Roberts draws attention to The National Archives, SC 8/134/6655, a petition in French dated to 1399–1401 "by one 'Adam Penkhurst' requesting confirmation of grants made by Edward III and Richard II to the petitioner," a facsimile of which is available to download for free.[137] She says that the hand of the petition "bears comparison with the oath in the Common Paper, although a less formal piece of writing," in that it "lacks the extravagant embellishments of the oath

---

[133] Carolyn C. Fenwick, ed., *The Poll Taxes of 1377, 1379 and 1381*, Part 2, *Lincolnshire–Westmorland* (Oxford: Oxford University Press, 2001), 558, col. 1. Mooney's "Pinkhurst, Adam" entry for the *Dictionary of National Biography* cites Joanna as flourishing c. 1355–69, whose end date we can now push forward by at least a dozen years.

[134] Gary Baker, "Investigating the Socio-Economic Origins of English Archers in the Second Half of the Fourteenth Century," *Journal of Medieval Military History* 12 (2014): 173–216 (195), which eventually led me to the Poll Tax record, once I had navigated his citation of erroneous page numbers and placement of Pinkhurst in Southwark rather than Bramley. Baker does not mention anything about the scrivener.

[135] Green, "Early History," 15.

[136] Baker, "English Archers," 195. Likewise Mooney and Stubbs: "such shifts of career or position were not unheard of: consider the case of Geoffrey Chaucer, who served as soldier, then king's esquire and member of Edward III's household until around the age of thirty-four, then controller of customs for twelve years to age forty-six, and holder of other offices in the gift of the king until his death in 1400" (*Scribes and the City*, 84).

[137] Roberts, "On Giving Scribe B a Name," 263. My thanks to Andrew Prescott for advice on this issue. Mooney and Stubbs do not mention this petition, though they elsewhere cite Roberts's essay: see *Scribes and the City*, 82–85 on the other Pinkhurst life-records, and the citations of Roberts in 68 n. 4, 82 n. 49, and 83 n. 51.

and has a more restrained sprinkling of Anglicana letter forms."[138] Our ability to compare the petition with Trinity B.15.17 and the Mercers' accounts reveals similarities in aspect and letter forms close enough to say that this is most likely the hand of the famous scribe. Its initial **A**, the **I** in the following phrase "Ista billa," and the ys with extensive tails all feature the characteristics discussed above. The simplest explanation, if not an inevitable one, is that this script on behalf of "Adam Penkhurst" is so close to that of our "Adam Pynkhurst" because they are the same man, who retired to Surrey in 1400 and had nothing to do with the copying of the *Canterbury Tales* in London in subsequent years.

Adam Pinkhurst and Scribe B were not the same man, but there is good reason to believe they knew each other and perhaps even collaborated. The similarities of certain features of decoration and hand that led to their combination in the first place, the textual relationship between the W manuscript of *Piers Plowman* B that Pinkhurst copied and the M manuscript that Scribe B probably corrected against W, their affiliations with the circle surrounding John of Northampton, and their respective work for the Mercers all suggest as much. This is not to say that they were exclusive partners; it seems more likely instead that they were part of a close network of scribes, perhaps including the scribe of the *Canterbury Tales* in Cambridge University Library, MS Dd.IV.24, which like Adam's work features heightened ascenders, double slashes, zigzags, and the knotted tremolo (only as indicator for the rubricator).[139] The only indication that either Adam or Scribe B had any connection with Chaucer comes in the form of a petition on the poet's behalf requesting a deputy, which Horobin has attributed to "Pinkhurst" (that is, Scribe B).[140] It is an enticing claim, but the text is too short, and

---

[138] Roberts, "On Giving Scribe B a Name," 263.

[139] *The Dd Manuscript: A Digital Edition of Cambridge University Library MS Dd.4.24 of Chaucer's "Canterbury Tales,"* ed. Orietta Da Rold, http://www.chaucermss.org/Dd (accessed July 2, 2015), the zigzag at, e.g., fols. 39r, 151v, 186v. "It is plausible that the Dd scribe was collaborating with other scribes and that he was involved in the network of the London manuscript production which was so famously described in Doyle and Parkes' seminal work [Doyle and Parkes, "Production of Copies"]," which would explain the common use of this feature by him and Pinkhurst (Da Rold, *The Dd Manuscript*, section 5.9, "The Scribe").

[140] Kew, The National Archives, C/81/1394. See Horobin, "Adam Pinkhurst, Geoffrey Chaucer," 354–56. The petition is reproduced in color at https://whatisapetition.files.wordpress.com/2014/03/petition-chaucer-1385-text2.jpg (accessed July 2, 2015), and in large format in Mooney and Stubbs, *Scribes and the City*, 72–73. Intriguingly, it seems that the scrivener whose confirmation is immediately below Pinkhurst's owned a copy of Chaucer's *Troilus* during the poet's lifetime: Martha Carlin, "Thomas Spencer,

Scribe B's hand too indistinct, to know for sure: the letter forms Horobin cites are the same ones erroneously used to attribute Trinity B.15.17 to Scribe B, for instance, though in this case the close similarity of aspect constitutes the primary evidence. Given the collapse of any evidence that Scribe B's name was "Adam," it goes too far to see this as providing "important supporting evidence for the view that [he] was employed by Chaucer to make fair copies of his drafts of *Troilus* and *Boece* in the 1380s"; but it might well be that this points to a fuller relationship.[141]

Neither is there any evidence that Pinkhurst or Scribe B had anything to do with the Guildhall, save that the latter was involved in the production of one Gower manuscript in which a man who might have worked there was among the five scribes.[142] Pinkhurst is subject of one of *Scribes and the City*'s four chapters, the book's star attraction, and his supposed status as Guildhall clerk and as "Scribe B" of the Trinity Gower provides the sole means by which Thomas Hoccleve comes to be most prominent of the "other scribes associated with" that institution.[143] The disappearance of Pinkhurst from the site and thus of Hoccleve from that association thus weakens that book's argument that the Guildhall was "a repository for works of vernacular literature" in this era.[144]

The list of other topics in need of revisiting in light of the recognition that Pinkhurst was not the Hengwrt-Ellesmere scribe is quite long, encompassing all the conclusions Mooney and her colleagues drew regarding Chaucer's knowledge of *Piers Plowman*, his political affiliations, the status of "Type III" of standard English, the authority of the

---

Southwark Scrivener (d. 1428): Owner of a Copy of Chaucer's *Troilus* in 1394?," *ChauR* 49 (2015): 387–401; see also Strohm, *The Poet's Tale*, 215.

[141] Horobin, "Adam Pinkhurst, Geoffrey Chaucer," 356.

[142] That is, John Marchaunt as Scribe D, though Pamela Robinson cannot believe Marchaunt, as common clerk of the Guildhall, could have had time to copy so many manuscripts (review of *Scribes and the City*).

[143] Mooney and Stubbs, *Scribes and the City*, 123; see 123–31 for their discussion of Hoccleve. A connection between Hoccleve and one Guildhall clerk is apparent in his "Balade to my maister Carpenter," which Mooney and Stubbs plausibly suggest was originally addressed to his predecessor, Marchaunt (129–31). Yet Hoccleve addresses him solely in an administrative rather than any literary capacity.

[144] Ibid., 140. Most of the evidence for that claim, aside from the simple fact that the scribes identified worked at the Guildhall, inheres in the dating of Richard Osbarn's activity on San Marino, Huntington, MS Hm 114 and London, Lambeth Palace, MS 491 as plans for a library in the Guildhall were taking place. But nothing indicates either that that library was to include English texts or that these manuscripts were intended for anything but private use. On the latter point see Hanna, review of *Scribes and the City*; and Noelle Phillips, "Compilational Reading: Richard Osbarn and Huntington Library MS HM 114," *YLS* 28 (2014): 65–104, esp. 75–80.

Chaucer manuscripts, and so forth, as well as any number of subsequent arguments by others (including me) built upon such claims.[145] But the above reconsideration of claims regarding Hoccleve and Pinkhurst ought as well to give rise to a conversation concerning our methods of scribal attribution, the impulse to engage in that activity despite manifest counter-indicators, and the larger question of what constitutes evidence in such realms of inquiry. One wonders how the study of Middle English manuscript production would look if Hoccleve's metrical practices had received as much attention as his self-dotting ys, or if the descending triangles and ys with large curls of Trinity B.15.17 had attracted the same notice as did its double slashes and dots. It might have been one in which Adam Pinkhurst, Scribe B, and Thomas Hoccleve were seen as the collaborators who set the standard for their associates like Scribe D and the Dd.IV.24 scribe; or it might have been something altogether different.

---

[145] See Lawrence Warner, "Adventurous Custance: St. Thomas of Acre and Chaucer's *Man of Law's Tale*," in *Place, Space, and Landscape in Medieval Narrative*, ed. Laura L. Howes (Knoxville: University of Tennessee Press, 2007), 43–59.

Fugitive Poetics in Chaucer's *House of Fame*

Rebecca Davis
University of California, Irvine

I<small>N BOOK II OF</small> *The House of Fame*, Geffrey's eagle guide expounds the Aristotelian principle of motion that governs the poem's universe of things. All natural bodies move, he explains, because they are drawn toward the "stede" or "place" where they belong:

> . . . every kyndely thyng that is
> Hath a kyndely stede ther he
> May best in hyt conserved be;
> Unto which place every thyng
> Thorgh his kyndely enclynyng
> Moveth for to come to
> Whan that hyt is awey therfro[.][1]
> (730–36)

Scholars have previously linked the principle of "kyndely enclynyng" with Lady Philosophy's exposition of Nature's regulatory operations in *The Consolation of Philosophy*, but its impact on the underlying material dynamics of *The House of Fame*, and the consequences of those dynamics

---

My thanks to Elizabeth Allen, Jeremy Kiene, and the members of Former, a working group on form and poetics, and to Sarah Salih and the journal's anonymous readers, for encouraging this project and providing insightful feedback on previous drafts. I am grateful to J. Allan Mitchell and Tom Goodmann for organizing sessions at New Chaucer Society meetings in 2012 and 2014 that fostered my inquiries into materiality and form.

[1] All citations of *The House of Fame* and other Chaucerian texts are from Larry D. Benson, gen. ed., *The Riverside Chaucer*, 3rd ed. (Boston: Houghton Mifflin, 1987). Line numbers are given parenthetically in the text.

for Chaucer's developing poetics, has not been recognized.[2] This essay argues that natural inclination, the motion intrinsic to things, is not only responsible for the upward movement of "tydynges" to Fame's house—what Karla Taylor calls their "natural history"[3]—but serves more broadly as the basis of an *ars poetica* of material agency. Indeed, Geffrey's ascent to the House of Rumor has long been read as metapoetical, a writer's meditation on the sources, purpose, and value of his art. Some see its "tydynges" as an archive of fresh subject matter for a new vernacular tradition rooted in the affairs of the "shipmen and pilgrimes, . . . pardoners, / Currours, and eke messagers" who gather at the poem's conclusion like prototypes of their Canterbury-bound cousins (2122, 2127–28).[4] This essay, too, reads *The House of Fame* as a "theoretical General Prologue to the *Canterbury Tales*," but seeks to establish their connection on grounds of form rather than content or theme.[5] Borrowing the epithet of "Fugitif Aeneas," whose flight from Troy embodies the principle of "kyndely enclynyng" in Book I, I describe Chaucer's investigation of the relationship of motion and form in *The House of Fame* as a fugitive poetics, a way of making poetry in a world in which "every kyndely thyng that is" reveals itself in transit.[6]

[2] In *Chaucer and Ovid* (New Haven: Yale University Press, 1973), for example, John Fyler connects the eagle's speech with Boethian inclination, but dismisses the larger import of the passage: "[T]he most remarkable quality of the argument on sound is its irrelevance to the central issues of the poem" (54). But see Eleanor Johnson, *Practicing Literary Theory in the Middle Ages: Ethics and the Mixed Form in Chaucer, Gower, Usk, and Hoccleve* (Chicago: University of Chicago Press, 2013), who examines the Boethian underpinnings of Chaucer's experiments with "mixed form" in *Troilus and Criseyde* and the *Canterbury Tales*.

[3] Karla Taylor, *Chaucer Reads "The Divine Comedy"* (Stanford: Stanford University Press, 1989), 31.

[4] Reading *The House of Fame* as an *ars poetica* goes back to George Lyman Kittredge, *Chaucer and His Poetry* (Cambridge, Mass.: Harvard University Press, 1915), who suggests that in the characters gathered at the end of the poem one can "almost descry the Canterbury Tales in the distance" (102). For a recent contribution to the *ars poetica* tradition that reviews and critiques many of its previous assumptions, see Susan Schibanoff, *Chaucer's Queer Poetics: Rereading the Dream Trio* (Toronto: University of Toronto Press, 2006), esp. 1–22 and 152–96.

[5] See Helen Cooper, "The Four Last Things in Dante and Chaucer: Ugolino in the House of Rumour," *NML* 3 (1999): 39–66 (63 n. 45).

[6] In describing the poem's material world as distinctly "active," this essay engages questions raised by new materialist critiques of anthropocentric and subject-centric concepts of agency. See especially Jane Bennett, *Vibrant Matter: A Political Ecology of Things* (Durham, N.C.: Duke University Press, 2010), 2–3; and "Powers of the Hoard: Further Notes on Material Agency," in *Animal, Vegetable, Mineral: Ethics and Objects*, ed. Jeffrey Jerome Cohen (Washington, D.C.: Oliphaunt Books, 2012), 237–69. Among medievalist literary critics, Kellie Robertson has led the way in establishing the value of new materialist approaches for medieval literary, historical, and philosophical concerns. See

That material agency, what I call "fugitivity," bears consequences for *poiesis* becomes apparent near the end of *The House of Fame*, when Geffrey declines to recount the "tydynge" he overhears. He protests not only that others "kan synge hit bet," but that, finally, "al mot out, other late or rathe, / Alle the sheves in the lathe" (2139–40). This essay reads Geffrey's demurral, and the rationale behind it, as a complex claim about the methods and materials of authorship, a claim upon which Chaucer stakes out a theory of literary form that anticipates the composite and open-ended shapes of his later works, especially the *Canterbury Tales*. For as Geffrey disclaims his own skill in a manner typical of Chaucer's self-deprecating narrators, he finally subordinates the agency of *all* tale-tellers to the strange agency of poetic matter itself, the stuff that, as of its own accord, "mot out."[7] Indeed, in the motion of the poem's Boethian universe, I propose, Chaucer discovers a law of natural propensity that reveals the constitutive forces of social engagement and literary creation alike, the tendencies of all bodies to "longen . . . to goon," as *The General Prologue* to the *Canterbury Tales* famously has it (12). In this sense, following V. A. Kolve's comment in his classic study of *The Friar's Tale* that "[p]ilgrims and carters were they all," *The House of Fame* stages itself, and the literary project it inaugurates, "in the middle," amidst a busy thoroughfare, a world in which everyone is a fugitive.[8] In *The House of Fame*, Chaucer explores how to make a poem—a stable and effective formal structure—out of materials that won't stop moving. The solution

---

Kellie Robertson, "Medieval Materialism: A Manifesto," *Exemplaria* 22 (2010): 99–118; "Medieval Things: Materiality, Historicism, and the Premodern Object," *LitComp* 5 (2008): 1060–80; and "Exemplary Rocks," in Cohen, *Animal, Vegetable, Mineral*, 91–121. In adducing a Boethian context for the lively matter of Chaucer's *House of Fame*, I seek in part to redress the bracketing of medieval concepts that Robertson observes in contemporary accounts of materialism.

[7] The poem features numerous examples of "tydynges" in outgoing motion beyond the instances I discuss in this essay. See, for example, Geffrey's comparison of the petitioners of Fame to a swarm buzzing "as been don in an hive / Ayen her tyme of out-fleynge" (1522–23), and, near the end of the poem, when the embodied "tydynges" attempt to exit the House of Rumor through a "wyndowe out to goon" (2086). Schibanoff, *Chaucer's Queer Poetics*, also observes the "incessant busyness" of matter in the House of Rumor, an attribute that flips the gendered assumptions of hylomorphism in the Platonic and Aristotelian traditions (in which an active male agent gives form to passive female matter) (190–91). But while Schibanoff opposes Rumor's "queer poetics" to the "natural poetics" of the eagle's "orderly" sound waves, I argue that the eagle's account of natural inclination, an Aristotelian principle Chaucer borrowed from Boethius, is in fact the basis of a new poetics of motion.

[8] Kolve examines the theological, iconographical, and literary tradition of human middleness in V. A. Kolve, "'Man in the Middle': Art and Religion in Chaucer's Friar's Tale," *SAC* 12 (1990): 3–46 (45).

toward which *The House of Fame* points is not to "fix" matter but to invent forms that accommodate its dynamism.

The first half of this essay examines the poem's representation of the Boethian principle of natural motion and its disruption of stable forms. In the metamorphic world of *The House of Fame*, Geffrey's confidence in matter ("al mot out") seems initially to produce a corresponding pessimism with respect to form: none can hold. As John Fyler observes in tracing Ovidianism in *The House of Fame*, Chaucer "repeatedly builds systems only to undermine them, and his poem moves in a diastolic/systolic rhythm of expansion and collapse."[9] The poem's preoccupation with order manifests in its distinct architectural settings, a series of houses subdivided into "sondry habitacles" (1194).[10] Previous studies have contextualized these structures within monastic and rhetorical theories of memory, including the technologies of artificial memory devised to reify, manipulate, and preserve fleeting temporal and textual experiences.[11] But while the memory houses of medieval mnemotechnics devise *loci*, stable though virtual depositories for things to be remembered, in *The House of Fame* things rarely stay put. Juxtaposed to its fixed structures, numerous catalogues spew forth an ever-burgeoning supply of poetic matter, stuff that not only takes up space in the poem's massive archive but also *moves*, disordering its organization.[12] The poem's most iconic conflict of form and motion is in the ice foundation of Fame's castle, where the names of great literary and historical figures are memorialized, or erased, depending on their exposure to the sun.

---

[9] Fyler, *Chaucer and Ovid*, 25.

[10] With its doors open wide and its hyperbolically grand dimensions ("sixty myle of lengthe" [1979]), the House of Rumor is distinctly less "organized" than the other two structures, but it too features discrete "angles" (1959) and "corners" (2142). In *Chaucer and the Imaginary World of Fame* (Cambridge: D. S. Brewer, 1984), Piero Boitani notes that the poem's settings evoke a "precise organization" (178).

[11] See especially Mary Carruthers, *The Book of Memory: A Study of Memory in Medieval Culture* (Cambridge: Cambridge University Press, 1990); Beryl Rowland, "The Art of Memory and the Art of Poetry in the *House of Fame*," *University of Ottawa Quarterly* 51 (1981): 162–71; and Ruth Evans, "Chaucer in Cyberspace: Medieval Technologies of Memory and *The House of Fame*," *SAC* 23 (2001): 43–69.

[12] On the disordering effect of Chaucer's catalogues, see Stephen A. Barney, "Chaucer's Lists," in *The Wisdom of Poetry: Essays in Early English Literature in Honor of Morton J. Bloomfield*, ed. Larry D. Benson and Siegfried Wenzel (Kalamazoo: Medieval Institute Publications, 1982), 189–223; and Lara Ruffolo, "Literary Authority and the Lists of Chaucer's *House of Fame*: Destruction and Definition through Proliferation," *ChauR* 27 (1993): 325–41. William Jordan examines the poem's affinities with postmodern metafiction—"the writer struggling to control his material"—in "Lost in the Funhouse of Fame: Chaucer and Postmodernism," *ChauR* 18 (1983): 100–15 (110).

Here natural motion assails form as the sun striking the ice melts away the textual record. As suggested by Geffrey's image of the empty "lathe" or granary (2140), Chaucer's treatment of formal structures in *The House of Fame* debunks fantasies of perpetual storage and commemoration (such as Fame's monumental attempts) in favor of the formal possibilities of provisional, we might even say *seasonal*, collocations and confederations (like that of the Canterbury pilgrims). In *The House of Fame*, physics works against notions of form as a fixed structure, a container for matter, or an ordered arrangement of parts, but Chaucer does not give up on form. Instead the poem asks us to reconceive form's relationship to matter, and to think of poetic form not as an end point but as a conduit through which dynamic matter takes shape.

To elucidate the poem's emphasis on forms that work by channeling, not impeding, material energies, the second half of this essay focuses on two sites of formal rupture in *The House of Fame*: the juncture between Books I and II, in which Geffrey emerges onto a vast, empty field of sand; and the poem's open-ended conclusion, in which Geffrey finds himself caught up in a melee. Each passage stages a "fugitif" act, an eruption or outflow characteristic of the poem's porous forms. At both sites, moreover, watercourses facilitate and emblematize material fugitivity. The lifeless field of sand seems exempt from the world of motion that surrounds it, but to the contrary, I suggest that its littoral features—it materializes the beachhead of Dido's shores, not an inland desert—offer a singular glimpse of the forces that shape poetry in *The House of Fame*. The imagery of water courses through the poem's conclusion, too, where Geffrey compares the stamping feet of the frenzied crowd to a technique used by eel trappers. Amplifying the catalogue of lightweight, portable baskets evoked in the preceding lines—"panyers," "hottes," "dossers," "scrippes," and "boystes"—the eel trap at the end of the poem models a formal alternative to the monumental structures of Venus and Fame and becomes, I argue, the token of a new *poiesis*. In reckoning with its lively matter, *The House of Fame* destabilizes the notion of poetry as product—fixed, unified, closed—and offers instead a theory of poetry in motion.[13]

---

[13] My interests in materiality and form take directions distinct from John Fyler's linguistic focus, but my conclusion here agrees with his claim that *The House of Fame* "celebrates . . . a language that is itself the very essence of energy and ceaseless flux." See John Fyler, *Language and the Declining World in Chaucer, Dante, and Jean de Meun* (Cambridge: Cambridge University Press, 2007), 154.

"Kyndely enclynyng": Poetry and Natural Propensity

In observing the way that motion in *The House of Fame* is at odds with traditional memorial structures, I share Ruth Evans's sense of Chaucer's apparent dissatisfaction with "positivist" forms of collection and memorialization. In "Chaucer in Cyberspace," Evans describes the House of Rumor as "an image of the archive gone mad," for it is "ever receptive to sounds and meanings but unable to preserve them."[14] Here I build on Evans's insights to explore further the roles of motion and material ephemerality and their tension with conservation and form in Chaucer's developing poetics. Evans interprets Chaucer's vision of nature's order as the supreme example of a positivist archive, aptly paraphrasing the eagle's physics lesson as "Everything in its place and a place for everything."[15] For Evans, nature's positivist tyranny is what the poem's "disruptive" archives work to overthrow. By contrast, I propose a different perspective on nature that understands Chaucer's vision of the phenomenal world as a place still coming to order. In this view, the principle of "kyndely enclyning" emerges not as an impediment to improvisation, a lockstep law of conformity, but as the very engine that drives the disruptions that Evans observes, laying waste to artificial efforts to contain and to reify restless matter so that through cycles of death and rebirth new corn may rise out of old fields.

The eagle's theory that everything moves by innate inclination toward its "kyndely" or proper "stede" ultimately derives from Aristotle's *Physics*, where heavy things, like rocks, naturally "desire" to move downward and so typically remain grounded, while things that are light, such as feathers and air, rise toward their natural place in the heavens.[16] These precepts were adapted in Christian contexts to explain, by analogy with physical things, how the human soul "flies up" to God. In the *Confessions*, for example, Augustine writes that

corpus pondere suo nititur ad locum suum. pondus non ad ima tantum est, sed ad locum suum. ignis sursum tendit, deorsum lapis . . . minus ordinata inquieta sunt; ordinantur et quiescunt. pondus meum amor meus; eo feror, quocumque feror. dono tuo accendimur et sursum ferimur; inardescimus et imus.

---

[14] Evans, "Chaucer in Cyberspace," 57, 65.

[15] Ibid., 68.

[16] See Aristotle, *Physics*, VIII.4; and Fyler's note on this passage in his edition of the poem in *The Riverside Chaucer*, 983. On the sources of Chaucer's theory of sound, see J. A. W. Bennett, *Chaucer's Book of Fame* (Oxford: Clarendon Press, 1968), 76–80.

[A body by its weight tends to move towards its proper place. The weight's movement is not necessarily downwards, but to its appropriate position: fire tends to move upwards, a stone downwards ... Things which are not in their intended position are restless. Once they are in their ordered position, they are at rest. My weight is my love. Wherever I am carried, my love is carrying me. By your gift we are set on fire and carried upwards: we grow red hot and ascend.][17]

The opening canto of Dante's *Paradiso* also reflects Aristotelian laws of natural propensity, now recast via Augustine as the gravitational pull of divine love extended to govern human teleology. A purified soul's ascent is natural and irresistible, Beatrice assures Dante: "Non dei più ammirar, se bene stimo, / lo tuo salir, se non come d'un rivo / se d'alto monte scende giuso ad imo" ("You should not wonder more at your rising, if I deem aright, than at a stream that falls from a mountain top to the base").[18] Chaucer likely had Dante's ascent in mind when his own guide elaborates the rules governing the universe of *The House of Fame*.[19] Here falling water again exemplifies natural propensity, as the eagle explains to Geffrey:

> ... every ryver to the see
> Enclyned ys to goo by kynde,
> And by these skilles, as I fynde,
> Hath fyssh duellynge in flood and see,
> And treës eke in erthe bee.
> Thus every thing, by thys reson,
> Hath his propre mansyon
> To which hit seketh to repaire,
> Ther-as hit shulde not apaire.
> (748–56)

---

[17] Augustine of Hippo, *Confessions*, ed. James J. O'Donnell (Oxford: Clarendon Press, 1992), XIII.9 (187). English translation in Augustine of Hippo, *Saint Augustine: Confessions*, trans. Henry Chadwick (Oxford: Oxford University Press, 1991), 278. See also Augustine, *City of God*, IX.28.

[18] Dante Alighieri, *Paradiso*, I.136–38. The Italian text and English translation are from Dante Alighieri, *The Divine Comedy*, ed. and trans. Charles S. Singleton, 3 vols. (Princeton: Princeton University Press, 1975).

[19] On Dante's influence on *The House of Fame* (a poem that Lydgate called "Dante in Inglissh"), see Fyler's headnote in *The Riverside Chaucer*, 977. See also H. Howard Schless, *Chaucer and Dante: A Reevaluation* (Norman: Pilgrim Books, 1984), 29–76; Taylor, *Chaucer Reads "The Divine Comedy,"* 20–49; Cooper, "The Four Last Things in Dante and Chaucer"; and Fyler, *Language and the Declining World*, 101–54.

Every created thing has a "propre mansyon," a slot in the universal order, where it feels at home, so to speak; or, to use Augustine's terms, "ordinantur et quiescunt" ("in their ordered position, they are at rest"). Native motion, then, is a response to displacement. Its purpose, paradoxically, is conservation: things move because they seek "to repaire," or return, to their natural places so that they "shulde not apaire," or deteriorate.

We find the fullest elaboration of the theory of natural inclination and the providential order it supports in Boethius's *Consolation of Philosophy*, especially in the "Quantas rerum flectat," its famous hymn to Nature in Book III. The eagle's physics lesson resounds with Boethian language, an influence made apparent in Chaucer's own translation of this meter in the *Boece*. Singing of "Natura potens," Chaucer's Lady Philosophy describes a force that "enclyneth and flytteth the governementz of thynges."[20] Nature binds, "restreyneth," and "kepith the grete world" in its proper order, so that even temporary misdirection must return to its determined course.[21] Examples of tamed lions, caged birds, tethered trees, and the setting sun—imagined as Phoebus's wayward chariot[22]—describe perversions of natural inclination that Nature's power ultimately restores to normative order.[23]

But despite Chaucer's debts to Boethius, there are at least two ways in which the Boethian system seems ill-fitted to the world of *The House of Fame*, a discrepancy that has prevented critics from appreciating the serious purpose of the Boethian material in the eagle's speech. First, reading the eagle's discourse against spiritualized appropriations of Aristotelian physics, like those of Augustine, Dante, and Boethius, sets into relief the very different aspirations of matter in *The House of Fame*. As Christopher Baswell notes, the eagle "makes mechanical and mundane those explanations which Lady Philosophy presented as metaphoric and spiritual."[24] Second, the totalizing scope of Nature's sway, and the

---

[20] *Bo*, III, met. 2.3–4.
[21] Ibid., III, met. 2.5–6.
[22] Chaucer also draws on this mythology in *The House of Fame*, 941–56.
[23] The concept of natural inclination appears elsewhere in Chaucer's works, perhaps most memorably in the example of the caged bird imagined by Canacee's jilted falcon in *The Squire's Tale*. Though his keeper provides "sugre, hony, breed, and milk," the creature will flee his artificial environment "right anon as that his dore is up," hastening toward the meal of worms that his nature craves (*SqT*, 607–17).
[24] Christopher Baswell, *Virgil in Medieval England: Figuring the "Aeneid" from the Twelfth Century to Chaucer* (Cambridge: Cambridge University Press, 1995), 239–40. Fyler, *Language and the Declining World*, similarly observes that the eagle's "argument that speech, like all other sound, has its home and fitting resting place in the House of

resulting vision of a universal order in which every thing lines up in its "propre mansyon" (754), seems comically at odds with the disorder and inconclusiveness that actually characterize *The House of Fame*. Yet a closer look at Chaucer's translation of the terms of natural inclination in the *Boece* reveals that these discrepancies in fact point to significant features of Chaucer's analysis of form and motion in the poem.

In the *Consolation*, motion is governed by cyclical terms like "repetunt," "recursus," and "reditu" that limit movement to a prescribed course, a running out ("currum") that is always a running back ("vertit ad ortus").[25] Chaucer's translation observes the recursive demand of natural order: "Alle thynges seken ayen to hir propre cours, and alle thynges rejoysen hem of hir retornynge ayen to hir nature. Ne noon ordenaunce is bytaken to thynges, but that that hath joyned the endynge to the bygynnynge, and hath maked the cours of itself stable (that it chaunge nat from his propre kynde)."[26] But even as he affirms Nature's determining influence on the physical world, Chaucer's translation of Nature's regulatory function departs in subtle but significant ways from Boethius's Latin terminology, a distinction we can observe by revisiting Chaucer's claim that "Nature, myghty, enclyneth and flytteth the governementz of thynges."[27] "Enclyneth" and "flytteth" translate Boethius's "flectat" and "stringat," both verbs that indicate some manner of restriction of motion or will. "Flectat," from *flectere*, meaning "to bend,"

Fame, depends on emptying speech of meaning by reducing it to its physical properties" (147). See also Martin Irvine, "Medieval Grammatical Theory and Chaucer's *House of Fame*," *Speculum* 60 (1985): 850–76, who argues that with the eagle's proof Chaucer playfully engages the grammarians' debate about the relationship between the physical and substantive qualities of *vox*. That the eagle is by and large read as comedic, parodic, or otherwise limited in his authority does not mean that his contribution to the larger literary and philosophical concerns of the text is insignificant. For example, John Leyerle, "Chaucer's Windy Eagle," *UTQ* 40 (1971): 247–65, describes the eagle's discourse on sound as "an elaborate joke on flatulence" (255), but also understands the eagle's speech as central to the poem's purpose, which he identifies as a critique of "private love." In "Flying through Space," in *Milton and the Line of Vision*, ed. Joseph Anthony Wittreich, Jr. (Madison: University of Wisconsin Press, 1975), 3–23, Donald Howard concludes that "[t]he eagle is funny, a smug pedant and a compulsive talker. And the flight through space is absurd: it leads to a realm of hot air which has risen up by 'kyndely enclynyng' to Fame's house, something between a crazyhouse and a casino" (5). But Howard also concedes that the poem is "like all great humorous works of art profoundly serious" (5). On the eagle's symbolic and literary resonances, see A. J. Minnis, *Oxford Guides to Chaucer: The Shorter Poems* (Oxford: Clarendon, 1995), 201–3.

[25] Boethius, *Consolation of Philosophy*, III, met. 2.33–35.
[26] *Bo*, III, met. 2.39–45.
[27] Ibid., III, met. 2.2–4.

figuratively suggests persuasion or, more forcefully, coercion.[28] "Stringat," from *stringere*, meaning "to draw tight," more visibly renders the "habenas," the "straps" or "reins," that Nature uses to direct and constrain the motion of things.[29] By contrast, while Chaucer's translation of these lines retains the Boethian description of Nature's powers as "byndynge," in the *Boece* Nature works not by restraining or proscribing the movement of her charges, but rather by inspiring them to "enclyne" and to "flyte," two verbs that suggest Nature's sponsorship of active, desirous motion, as echoed in the eagle's principle of "kyndely enclynyng" (734). While *enclinen* can simply indicate the action of guiding or directing motion, it primarily connotes a slanted or bowed posture.[30] Neatly corresponding to "flectat" in its reference to bending, "enclyneth" nevertheless suggests a more subtle account of Nature's governance by evoking an image of movement toward, less constraint than tilt.

Chaucer's "flytteth," from *flitten*, is likewise a more neutral kinetic term than either "flectat" or "stringat." In its transitive sense *flitten* means "to move," "to drive," or "to thrust" something, signifying impulsion without necessarily suggesting any corresponding restriction of that motion. In its intransitive sense, not used in this instance but nevertheless activated, *flitten* indicates the action or condition of change.[31] Chaucer uses this sense of *flitten* in the *Boece* to characterize the world as understood by the wicked, who are "governyd with no ledere" but "ravyssched oonly by fleetynge errour," and later to describe the perpetual inconstancy of "flyttynge Fortune."[32] In these examples, Chaucer's translation reveals a paradox at the heart of natural propensity: Nature preserves the universe by means of its mutability. I suggest that Chaucer's recognition of this paradox—a Boethian principle, not a Chaucerian misreading of Boethius—accounts for the discrepancy between the eagle's claims of an orderly universe and the patent disorder that characterizes *The House of Fame*. That is to say, motion and apparent chaos are as fundamental to the Boethian system as the underlying and ultimately irresistible order that the *Consolation* expounds. *The House of*

---

[28] Charlton T. Lewis, *A Latin Dictionary Founded on Andrews' Edition of Freund's Latin Dictionary* (Oxford: Clarendon, 1962), s.v. *flecto*.
[29] Ibid., s.v. *stringo*.
[30] *MED*, s.v. *enclinen* (v.).
[31] Ibid., s.v. *flitten* (v.).
[32] *Bo*, I, pr. 3.69–72; II, pr. 1.78–83.

Fame's reconciliation of motion and form, or, more precisely, its assertion of form's utter dependence on motion, is for Chaucer a profoundly Boethian project.

While an idealizing interpretation of Boethian providential order might see a tidy, totalizing system at odds with the rush and whirl and frequent randomness of *The House of Fame*, in fact the *Consolation* also describes a world in motion, a world in which swerves are possible, even necessary to maintain free will. Nature holds the "bridelis" of providential design, but this order can be achieved only through movement in time as each body seeks its place of physical and spiritual rest.[33] As Lady Philosophy herself insists, human beings are pulled like the rest of creation by a "naturel entencioun" that inclines toward the good, but like the drunk man staggering home, often misses the mark: "many maner errours," she warns, "mystorneth yow therfro."[34] This is why Chaucer highlights the materiality of the world of *The House of Fame*, the "mechanical and mundane" emphasis that Baswell detects in the eagle's non-transcendent physics: the "fleeting" matter on display in *The House of Fame* is a constant reminder that poetry is made in and of a world of becoming.[35] In the following section, I examine the consequences of "misturns" in the context of Geffrey's and Aeneas's paired adventures and consider how these fugitives embody *The House of Fame*'s use of motion to interrogate ideas about form.

"Fugityf of Troy": Motion and Tradition

The field of sand at the end of Book I might well describe the antithesis of form and memorialization. Finished with the matter of Troy, Geffrey comes "out at the dores" of Venus's "chirche," staging his departure from the poetic tradition that Venus's graven edifice represents (473). Passing through the "wiket," or gateway, leading out of Venus's realm, Geffrey finds himself in a "large feld," "[w]ithouten . . . tree, / Or bush or gras," an endless dry seabed of sand, a canvas of infinite proportions, but one that is expressly barren (477, 484–85, 482). The very opposite of *Piers Plowman*'s opening conspectus of the bustling "field full of folk," Chaucer's sterile field lacks not only vegetation, but specifically the artifacts of human existence, "toun, or hous . . . or eryd lond" (484–85).

---

[33] Ibid., V, met. 1.20.
[34] Ibid., III, pr. 3.6–8.
[35] Baswell, *Virgil in Medieval England*, 239–40.

Later in the poem, when Geffrey reaches the crowded House of Rumor, he can scarcely find "a fote-brede of space" in which to stand (2042). Here, by contrast, stepping outside Venus's storied hallways in search of information—"any stiryng man / That may me telle where I am" (478–79)—Geffrey finds himself standing alone in a surplus of open space: "For al the feld nas but of sond" (486).

In his edition of the poem, Nick Havely observes that the field of sand has become a "playpit" for critics.[36] While the field's indeterminacy begs for scholarly sand-castle building, critics have generally understood the field in negative terms, reading its emptiness as a reflection of the moral or artistic sterility of the foregoing subject matter, what J. A. W. Bennett calls the "barren loves of Dido."[37] For some, however, the field's challenge results not from its emptiness, but from its excess of possibility. Sheila Delany, for example, describes it as the result of a crisis of authority generated by conflicting Virgilian and Ovidian accounts of the Trojan story,[38] and John Fyler suggests that its sandy formlessness "connotes a world of unconnected fragments."[39] Hailing it as an index of stymied creativity, these and other readers understand the field, though barren and useless in itself, as a necessary step toward poetic renewal.[40]

[36] See Geoffrey Chaucer, *The House of Fame*, in *Chaucer's Dream Poetry*, ed. Helen Phillips and Nick Havely (London: Longman, 1997), 112–218 (145).

[37] Bennett, *Chaucer's Book of Fame*, 48. Similarly, Leyerle, "Chaucer's Windy Eagle," observes that Venus's glass temple is made of the "same material that makes the barren, sterile desert" and associates both environments with a critique of "private love": "[i]ts dazzling radiance is transparent, it is set in a wasteland, and it leaves a brazen record for all to read" (258).

[38] Sheila Delany, *Chaucer's "House of Fame": The Poetics of Skeptical Fideism* (Gainesville: University of Florida Press, 1994), 59. See also Taylor, *Chaucer Reads "The Divine Comedy,"* who describes the place as "the desert of his uncertainty," and the eagle as the return of Dantean tradition (31).

[39] Fyler, *Language and the Declining World*, 41. See also Ashby Kinch, "'Mind like Wickerwork': The Neuroplastic Aesthetics of Chaucer's House of Tidings," *postmedieval: A Journal of Medieval Cultural Studies* 3 (2012): 302–14, who describes the field of sand as "a startling analogy for the dependence of the human mind on objects of attention through which mental processes are formed" (307). Here, Kinch observes, Chaucer stages "a systematic thwarting of perceptual expectations" through a series of negations wherein the "eye fails to find visual stimuli that match the templates of visual experience" (308).

[40] See, for example, Jacqueline T. Miller, "Writing on the Wall: Authority and Authorship in Chaucer's *House of Fame*," *ChauR* 17 (1982): 95–115. Miller argues that the temple's "conventional literary 'truths' could not furnish an adequate context for the narrator's voice, but the empty landscape unmarked by any prior or superior text inhibits and overwhelms the authority and autonomy of the individual mind that con-

Throughout *The House of Fame*, however, the movement between enclosure and open space, fixed form and flowing matter, tradition and improvisation, follows a dialectical course. Every turn away from authority generates a corresponding impulse to return to it. My contribution to the question of the "playpit" tends toward those readings that see the field as a sign of something new, but my reading resists the idea that its trajectory points only forward, toward future forms, while, in itself, the field of sand is simply barren. As Geffrey crosses the threshold of tradition, represented by the "mother church" or poetic cradle of Venus's temple, the featureless field seems staged precisely to impart a dramatic sense of rupture with what came before. But in stressing the function of the field as a conduit, and as such, a vital part of the poem's system of motion, I suggest that it is not a break with the past, but of a piece with it—indeed, that the field of sand is made of the pieces of the past.[41] It figures, in this sense, an archive of obliteration, but this does not mean that history ends there; to the contrary, the field is the place where the poem's mythical and material iconographies meet. Kellie Robertson has observed that "Chaucer continually dramatizes his quest for literary subject matter . . . using material metaphors . . . tropes that help him grapple with . . . questions of how the *matere* of the physical world and the *matere* of the poet were related."[42] The field of sand is one such site of grappling, where a landscape and the processes that shaped it represent the matter of poetry itself.

---

fronts it" (111). Miller thus reads the desert as depicting "a new potential for creative autonomy" (114).

[41] In an essay that refutes earlier critical assumptions about the fragility and ephemerality of glass, David K. Coley, "'Withyn a temple ymad of glas': Glazing, Glossing, and Patronage in Chaucer's *House of Fame*," *ChauR* 45 (2010): 59–84, also reads the field of sand in generative terms. Coley argues that Chaucer associated glassmaking with vernacular poetic production, and so it follows that sand is the "origin of the vernacular poetic text itself, the raw *materia* that will be translated, structured, and fixed into the vitreous narrative window" (83). "The 'desert of Lybye,' in other words, is not the end of the vernacular text," Coley writes, "but the vernacular text's beginning. It is not the rubble left over from the glass temple's collapse, but the potential germ and root of the temple's vitreous narrative medium" (83). Although I argue that the field of sand represents the material residue of the past, Coley and I both understand the field as a site of continuity, a place where endings and beginnings meet.

[42] Robertson, "Medieval Materialism," 112. Robertson describes Chaucer's and other medieval poets' appropriation of the terms of natural philosophy as a "material poetics" (110). Bennett, *Chaucer's Book of Fame* similarly hails Chaucer's "poetical physics," observing that in *The House of Fame* he "makes out of scientific theory the very stuff of his verse" (74).

As brass takes the shape of the matter of Troy in Venus's temple, the field of sand that surrounds it materializes Geffrey's encounter with that story. That is to say, this field is not just a generic place (or no-place); as many readers have noted, the wasteland refers back to the Libyan desert where the shipwrecked Aeneas "tok arryvage" (223) and wandered until Venus urged him to seek refuge in Carthage: "For al the feld nas but of sond / As smal as man may se yet lye / In the desert of Lybye" (486–88).[43] We should note, however, that the field resembles the Libyan desert not only visually—as a flashback to the story etched on the graven tablet—but also functionally: for Geffrey, as it had been for Aeneas, the desert is a conduit between two legs of a journey. In fleeing tradition to find himself standing in a field of sand, Geffrey becomes a second Aeneas, a translator of both culture and poetry yet uncertain of his own authority or where he has landed.[44]

Most crucially, by observing the field's reference back to Carthage, we can better read this image in its poetic context: it begins to take shape as a coast, a place where sand and water meet. From the opening invocation to Morpheus in his cave upon the River Lethe, to the strange final comparison of clambering bodies to men "stamping" for eels (to which I return in this essay's conclusion), the imagistic landscapes of *The House of Fame* resound with water features. The poem's waterways have tended to be overshadowed by its more spectacular architectural spaces, but their insistent, if sometimes quiet, presence mimics the ceaseless surges of time, the shifting currents of chance, and the many forms of circulation that resist memorialization but enable a living and lively engagement with past literary matter by shaping and reshaping littoral boundaries.[45] By reading this desolate landscape as a reference back to Dido's shores, we can see the desert that lies beyond Venus's temple not only as a part of these systems, but as a testament to their power to stir, to dislocate, and to make things new.

---

[43] See Howard R. Patch, "Chaucer's Desert," *MLN* 34 (1919): 321–28; John M. Steadman, "Chaucer's 'Desert of Libye', Venus, and Jove (*The Hous of Fame*, 486–87)," *MLN* 76 (1961): 196–20; and Charles P. R. Tisdale, "Virgilian Reason and Boethian Wisdom," *CL* 25 (1973): 247–61.

[44] In *Virgil in Medieval England*, Baswell also reads Geffrey as Aeneas's double in *The House of Fame*. The two figures are linked as gazers "in moments of narrative suspension" and as readers "responding to the problematic power of human artifice to draw [them] away from [their] role[s] as . . . actor[s]" (227).

[45] In "Getting a Feel for *The House of Fame*" at the 2012 New Chaucer Society meeting in Portland, Lara Farina described *The House of Fame* as an "underwater poem."

The history that the field evokes has important consequences for Chaucer's poetic dilemma, here imagined as tantamount to Aeneas's moral one. In the brass tablet's paraphrase of Virgil's opening lines, Chaucer establishes Aeneas's identity as a man in motion, a man moving inexorably toward his place of destiny:

> I wol now synge, yif I kan,
> The armes and also the man
> That first cam, thurgh his destinee,
> Fugityf of Troy contree,
> In Itayle, with ful moche pyne
> Unto the strondes of Lavyne.
> (143–48)

"Fugityf of Troy," Aeneas exemplifies the poem's system of natural inclination. His association with flight over water befits the son of Venus, whose traditional iconography Geffrey observes painted within the temple: "in portreyture / I sawgh anoon-ryght hir figure / Naked fletynge in a see" (131–33).[46] Moreover, as the story on the tablet reveals, it is Venus who first "bad hir sone Eneas flee" (165). So urged, "[f]ugityf" Aeneas takes to the water, steering a course for the "strondes of Lavyne," his intended, and ultimate, but not initial destination (148). Aeneas finds the sea not only a route of escape but also a "misturn" as tempests scatter his fleet and deposit him on a different "strond" altogether. Carthage becomes a makeshift haven, at once safe but transitory, one of *The House of Fame*'s many places that turn out to be a thoroughfare.

These connections among Aeneas, his sea-born mother Venus, and the sea as both a medium of transmission and an emblem of flight are worth tracing because in them we can begin to see the energies of the poem in their most fundamental form. That is to say, the theory of natural propensity outlined in the eagle's speech begins here to express itself at the level of narrative. The desire for conservation—poignantly etched in Venus's intervention in the destruction of Troy "[w]han that she sawgh the castel brende" (163)—impels her to action, urging Aeneas to save himself through flight. The image of burning Troy establishes the originary unreliability of human edifices, while the sea, the open channel of egress, offers immediate if not lasting relief.

---

[46] *MED*, s.v. *fleten* (v.[1]), def. 1(a), "To rest or move on the surface (of a liquid), float, drift; of a ship: sail." Venus is likewise disposed in *The Knight's Tale*: "The statue of Venus, glorious for to se, / Was naked, fletynge in the large see" (*KnT*, 1955–56).

Throughout this section, Chaucer associates "fugitif" Aeneas with the tidal transience of water; with the somewhat unreliable mobility represented by his ships; and with art, specifically the suasive art of storytelling.[47] Each of these three terms—sea, ships, stories—facilitates both physical and affective movement. The potency of their collusion in the figure of Aeneas becomes apparent in Geffrey's observation of the shipwreck that brings Aeneas and his retinue to Carthage. As Geffrey explains, "Ther saugh I such tempeste aryse / That every herte myght agryse / To see hyt peynted on the wal" (209–11). Indeed he next beholds Venus herself "[w]epynge with ful woful chere" as Eolus plays upon the sea, whipping its waters against the progress of the Trojan fleet (214). Geffrey's response is refracted, in a kind of secular *pietà*, through the pitiful mother who, locked in brass, stands as perpetual witness to the scene of her son's destruction. Eolus's tempest flows through Venus's tears, which predict Dido's own sympathetic response to this welter of sea and ships when Aeneas will later recount "every caas / That hym was tyd upon the see" (254–55). "[T]yd," here the past tense of the verb *tiden*, meaning "to happen," is linked etymologically with the noun *tide*, which chiefly means "time" or "season," but also denotes the tidal currents, the periodic ebb and flow of the sea.[48] Both of these terms are linked as well with "tydynges," the news of happenings that rise and mingle in the halfway House of Rumor before rising further to their destinies in Fame's hall. Like the fluid tides that are their semantic cousins, "tydynges" derive their potency from their motion, their instability, and their ability to canvass large distances effortlessly. Like Geffrey the reader, and Venus the woeful mother, Dido too is moved by the "tides" of contingency that buffet Aeneas and that he, in turn, harnesses to his own rhetorical purpose.

While his representation of the story of Dido and Aeneas reveals the power even of static images to move their audiences, Geffrey's ultimate desire to pass beyond Venus's realm ("now wol I goo out and see" [476]) underscores his affinity with that other fugitive. Fleeing the temple in search of a "stiryng man," Geffrey finds himself alone. In suggesting his affinity with "fugitif" Aeneas, I propose that Geffrey has become the stirring man he seeks—living, responding, circulating. Moreover, as a double of Dido's shores, the field evokes the "strond" in its basic sense:

[47] Baswell, *Virgil in Medieval England*, aptly describes Aeneas and his counterpart Geffrey as "hermeneutic heroes" (223–29).
[48] *MED*, s.v. *tiden* (v.), def. 1(a)., and s.v. *tid(e* (n.), defs. 6 and 7.

as a place between land and sea, a place of change and exchange, where the end of one story becomes the beginning of another. The field, from this view, remains a site of egress, but less a rupture than a junction. As Robert Edwards reminds us, the field is not after all truly an empty space. Chaucer fills it with a single feature: "sond," a word that evokes several Middle English homonyms, including that other ubiquitous quantity, the "sound" that rises through the atmosphere to Fame's house and reverberates through its halls, becoming the substance of the tidings that Geffrey seeks.[49] Edwards considers the sand a prediction that points forward (in fact, upward) to the sea of sound above. I suggest further that the relationship between sand and sound is more than aural—in material terms, it is also a relation of causality. It offers another of the poem's natural histories: in *The House of Fame*, "sound" and "sand" represent a vital force and its product. For the desert sand is the precipitate of all that noise above, sand, of course, being rock ground into smaller and smaller parts by wind and wave action over time, the very process to which the narrator later compares the roar that greets him upon his approach to Fame's house: there he hears a "grete soun . . . / that rumbleth up and doun" just like the "betynge of the see . . . / ayen the roches holowe, / Whan tempest doth the shippes swalowe" (1025–26, 1034–36). The "tydynges" within now fulfill their etymological promise by merging aurally with the watery tides that buffet the shore and turn rocks, over time, into piles of sand.

"A thousand holes, and wel moo": A Theory of Porous Form

I have argued that the field of sand is the material correlative of the dissolution of tradition, a liminal place that is shaped by the fluid pressures that subtend it. But it remains to consider how Chaucer envisions poetic making in the midst of these exigencies. In this section, I reflect on how the final book of *The House of Fame* reimagines poetic form in terms that are constituted by, not at odds with, the native motion of things, here again represented by the imagery of water. The House of Rumor, the poem's third, and final, architectural setting, stands in a valley beneath Fame's "castel" (1917). This "queynte" house whirls,

---

[49] Robert Edwards, *The Dream of Chaucer: Representation and Reflection in the Early Narratives* (Durham, N.C.: Duke University Press, 1989). As Edwards writes, "The sand (sonde) of the field represents what he is about to uncover in a realm of ever increasing sound" (102).

infused with the energy of the embodied "rounynges" and "jangles" that have made their way into its wickerwork (1925, 1960). During his initial ascent to Fame's house, Geffrey hears a sound like waves crashing against hollow rocks. At the House of Rumor, he compares the whirring voices to the rushing waters of the River Oise as they flow toward Rome, another reminder of natural propensity at work.[50] "Kyndely enclynyng" has brought these "tydynges" into the wicker funnel as they follow their natural inclination to rise.

However, Geffrey's likening of the House of Rumor's interlaced wicker structure to a "cage" (at line 1938 and again at 1985) seems at odds with this scene's depiction of natural motion. The purpose of a cage is to keep things penned in that would rather get out.[51] Yet though its structure resembles a cage, the twig house does not restrain or confine its charges against their natural inclinations but only temporarily marshals these "kynde" tendencies. On this same principle Harry Bailly protests that his proposed tale-telling game merely gives structure to an activity the pilgrims would engage in even if there were no game to prompt them. "And wel I woot," he says, "as ye goon by the weye, / Ye shapen yow to talen and to pleye" (771–72). An artful "governour" (813), the Host proposes that it is not he but they who "shapen" themselves to such behavior: telling stories during a journey is as natural as the desire to go out in the first place. As the title of "Host" suggests, he and his structuring game provide a site wherein the pilgrims express their instinct to tell tales and amuse themselves ("to talen and to pleye"), and, in doing so, to seek "confort" and "myrthe" as they "ride by the weye" (771–73).

The House of Rumor, like the Host's proposed contest, is a place of gathering, a way station or conduit that enables new combinations of matter en route but that does not impede its passage. The figures who meet inside the House of Rumor embody speech, which, as the eagle explains, "ys but air" (768), and so "of pure kynde, / Enclyned ys upward to meve" (824–25). But Rumor's "cage" is only a detour on the

---

[50] As Havely notes, pilgrimage routes from England to Rome would have crossed the Oise before it flowed into the Seine north of Paris; Chaucer, *The House of Fame*, ed. Havely, 204.

[51] Boitani, *Chaucer and the Imaginary World of Fame*, associates the cage with Chaucer's previous reference to the "Domus Dedaly," or labyrinth (208–10). In a Boethian context, a cage is a device that inhibits the native inclination of things and prevents them from "repairing" to their natures, as in Lady Philosophy's example of the caged bird in *The Consolation of Philosophy* (III, met. 2), a figure that reappears in Chaucer's *Squire's Tale* (606–31) and *Manciple's Tale* (163–75).

way to the House of Fame, which is itself strategically placed "in myddes of the weye" (714). Both houses, we might say, represent structures of opportunity, for both take advantage of native motion, and neither is truly an end point. The House of Rumor prepares and packages matter for submission to Fame's judgment, but its function depends on its permeability, its formal responsiveness to its environment.

In turning now to the fugitive poetics of the poem's conclusion, I draw attention to the several containers that Chaucer evokes in succession following the analogy of the cage:

> And al thys hous of which y rede
> Was mad of twigges, falwe, rede,
> And grene eke, and somme weren white,
> Swiche as men to these cages thwite,
> Or maken of these panyers,
> Or elles hottes or dossers[.]
> (1935–40)

Tools of the field, the market, and the open road, these "panyers," "hottes," and "dossers" are the common carrying cases familiar to Chaucer's audiences.[52] A few lines later, Geffrey observes still other kinds of traveling and commercial gear: the shipmen, pilgrims, pardoners, and couriers who populate the House of Rumor lug overstuffed "scrippes bret-ful of lesinges" and "boystes crammed ful of lyes" (2123, 2129). In contrast to the poem's earlier fixed models of storage, most of which take the form of grand edifices like the Temple of Venus and the House of Fame, these devices are significant because they are designed to be portable.[53] The reedy containers that are Rumor's worldly counterparts were fashioned to breathe, to travel, and finally to release their contents back into circulation to form ever new assemblages.

The small, common, and porous containers that appear in the last book of the poem offer a different way to think about the related

---

[52] *MED*, s.v. *panier(e* (n.), def. a.; s.v. *hotte* (n.), def. a.; and s.v. *doser* (n.), def. 2(a). Essentially synonyms, each term designates a type of basket used to transport foodstuffs and other goods. As the etymology of *doser*, from French *dos*, suggests, these baskets were designed to be borne upon the back, or elsewhere upon the bodies of their users.

[53] A *scrippe* is a bag or a purse, often associated with pilgrims' gear. See *MED*, s.v. *scrip(pe* (n.), def. a. A *boiste* is a jar, box, or case appropriate for carrying a variety of items, including ointments; the Eucharistic Host; ordinary bread; and, as it seems in this case, letters. See *MED*, s.v. *boist(e* (n.), defs. 1(a) and (b).

endeavors of mnemonic and poetic making at issue in *The House of Fame*. The memory was commonly conceived as a container in classical and medieval writing, as Mary Carruthers has shown, taking shape variously as a storehouse (*thesaurus*); a room or compartment (*cella*); a cage, coop, or pen; and even as a sack or traveling case (*sacculus*).[54] *The House of Fame* draws from the full range of these examples, from the large-scale, fixed architectural models to the portable accoutrement of the traveler's rucksack. I suggest that the poem's general shift toward moveable, permeable, and commonplace containers is significant because it registers Chaucer's formal response to the problem of fugitivity.

Chaucer makes explicit reference to the container model of memory in the invocation to Thought at the beginning of Book II:

> O Thought, that wrot al that I mette,
> And in the tresorye hyt shette
> Of my brayn, now shal men se
> Yf any vertu in the be
> To tellen al my drem aryght.
>
> (523–27)

Here the poet's brain becomes a "tresorye," or *thesaurus*, enclosing Thought's transcription of "al that [Geffrey] mette."[55] But the analogy makes clear that hoarding is not the goal. These lines describe a double translation of poetic matter from one form to another, from the dream to the strongbox of the poet's brain, and then again to the legible shape of words that "now shal men se" (525). Thought turns out to be a device both of collection and of dispersal, a significant feature of the flexible, porous containers to which Chaucer increasingly resorts in the poem's final book. Like the "lathe," whose doors open to release the harvest (2140), Thought's "vertu" depends on its capacity not only to contain but ultimately to "tellen" the dream. In choosing this verb to describe Thought's translational and transactional work, Chaucer playfully

---

[54] Carruthers, *Book of Memory*, 40–55. Carruthers notes that Chaucer draws on the metaphor of the money pouch in his use of the word "male," as "an English-language version (indeed the first recorded) of an author opening the organized compartments of his memory to disclose its store of riches" (49).

[55] Chaucer's invocation to Thought may be based on Dante's invocation to "mente," or memory, in *Inferno*, II.7–9. On the association of memory with a thesaurus, or treasure-house, see Carruthers, *Book of Memory*, 37–38. Evans, "Chaucer in Cyberspace," notes that while the term "tresorye" evokes an architectural space, in this period treasuries were also "portable chests, not static repositories" (60).

extends the metaphor of the brain as treasury, for *tellen* means both "to narrate" and "to enumerate," a coincidence of meaning joined in the verb "to recount."⁵⁶ The invocation to Thought, then, is a pun referring back to the eagle's gentle mockery of Geffrey's day job as a maker of "rekenynges" (653). Geffrey the tabulator continues at night as he had by day, exchanging one set of books for another, a dull life according to the eagle, but one that the invocation to Thought reveals to be vitally connected to Geffrey's ability to recount his vision (651–58). The figure of Thought as the manager of a treasury imagines the relationship between mnemonic and poetic making as a transfer of funds: a poem is a device that reckons matter "shette" in the memory (524).

Chaucer's treatment of Thought also draws an analogy between the work of the mind and the work of the House of Rumor, the wicker structure that, as Geffrey observes, spins "as swyft as thought" (1924). That Thought writes, encloses, and then tells the matter of Geffrey's dream suggests a dynamic model of the mind, one that envisions the mind not only as a lockbox for ingoing matter, but as a porous container capable of turning out what it collects and, crucially, like the House of Rumor, capable of collecting things because it is permeable.⁵⁷ In Book III, taking up ever more organic forms, Chaucer explores this permeability through a catalogue of pliant and portable containers that, as we have seen, elaborate and complicate the House of Rumor's resemblance to a cage.

I have argued throughout this essay that waterways facilitate and emblematize motion in *The House of Fame*. Its final lines evoke one last waterway and one more porous container designed to work with the native flow of its environment: an inconspicuous eel trap. Here, frenzied, the embodied "tydynges" push toward some revelation:

> And whan they were alle on an hepe,
> Tho behynde begunne up lepe,
> And clamben up on other faste,
> And up the nose and yën kaste,

---

⁵⁶ *MED*, s.v. *tellen* (v.); cf. defs. 1–2, which denote speech and storytelling, and def. 17, which denotes counting.

⁵⁷ Kinch reads Chaucer's dynamic and "physical sense of the brain" through the language of contemporary neuroplasticity in "Mind like Wickerwork" (305). Reaching a conclusion similar to my own view of the translational work of Thought, Kinch elaborates Chaucer's concern with "cognitive extension . . . how the human mind extends its mental processing capabilities into the world" (306).

> And trodden fast on others heles,
> And stampen, as men doon aftir eles.
> (2149–54)[58]

A delicacy on the medieval table, eels were typically caught with basket traps that would be affixed to a weir and weighted with small stones.[59] The flow of the river would carry unsuspecting eels into the traps. An image from the Luttrell Psalter depicts an unlucky eel drawn into such a trap, as the water flows along its course to the mill and wheel stationed just downstream (figs. 1 and 2). Chaucer alludes to a related practice used to rouse eels toward traps, perhaps in calmer waters or in daylight,

Fig. 1. Watermill, stream, and eel traps in the Luttrell Psalter, London, British Library, Add. MS 42130, fol. 181r, with detail. Courtesy of the British Library.

[58] The reference to "stomping after" eels has received little substantive commentary. In the *Riverside* edition, Fyler quotes F. N. Robinson's note on the line, which offers anecdotal evidence for the custom. See Geoffrey Chaucer, *The Complete Works of Geoffrey Chaucer*, ed. F. N. Robinson, 2nd ed. (Oxford: Oxford University Press, 1957), 788. Skeat says nothing of the actual practice of eel fishing, but adduces evidence from Plautus and the *Roman de la rose* that eels were associated with slyness and moral slipperiness. Similarly, in *Chaucer and the Tradition of Fame: Symbolism in the House of Fame* (Princeton: Princeton University Press, 1966), B. J. Koonce identifies the eels with the biblical iconography of treading down serpents and "the medieval problem of evil" (273).

[59] See J. M. Steane and M. Foreman, "Medieval Fishing Tackle," in *Medieval Fish, Fisheries, and Fishponds in England*, ed. Michael Aston, 2 vols. (Oxford: BAR, 1988), 137–81, especially on "Fish Traps and Weirs," 170–78; and Marcus Jecock, *River Fisheries and Coastal Fish Weirs*, Introductions to Heritage Assets (Swindon: English Heritage, 2011).

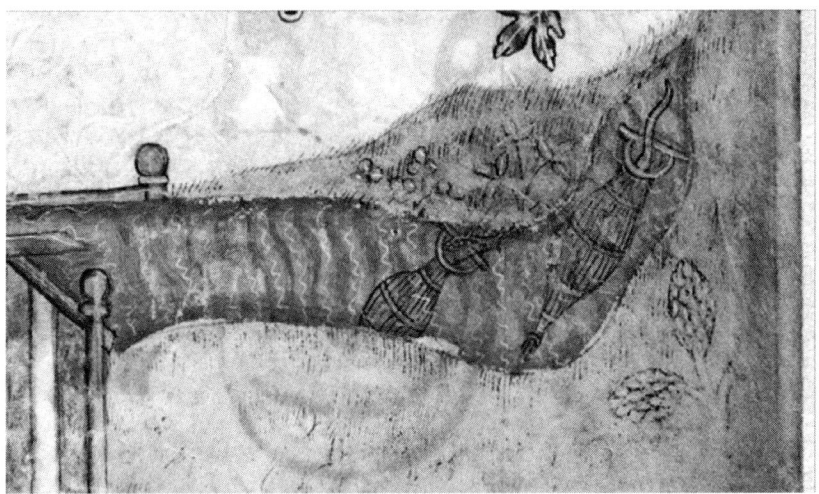

Fig. 2. Detail of eel traps from the Luttrell Psalter.

when eels were said to sleep.[60] In such circumstances, fishermen would stamp their feet along the shallows near the river's bank, prompting their quarry toward waiting traps.

Artifactual remnants and functional modern replicas of medieval basket traps (figs. 3 and 4) reveal a striking similarity to Chaucer's description of the reedy construction of the House of Rumor. With their undulating lines and intricate wickerwork, these baskets showcase an alluring aesthetic appeal at the convergence of form and function, an effective design that has remained remarkably stable over time. The baskets suggest an elegant material "source" for the House of Rumor, whose construction from "twigges" (1936) diverges from a description otherwise heavily indebted to Ovid's account of Fame's house in the *Metamorphoses*.[61] To work properly, an eel trap must be porous, which

---

[60] Mortimer J. Donavan, "Three Notes on Chaucerian Marine Life," *PQ* 31 (1952): 439–40, cites Isaak Walton's *The Compleat Angler* on the nocturnal nature of eels. To catch them during the daytime, one must stomp the banks to awaken them.

[61] Chaucer's description of the porousness of the House of Rumor borrows from Ovid's description of Fame's doorless house in *Metamorphoses*, XII.39–63, but while Ovid's edifice is made of brass, Chaucer's choice of twigs has prompted much speculation among the poem's readers. For an overview, see Fyler's note to lines 1925–85 in the *Riverside* edition, 989. Mary Flowers Braswell suggests that a birdcage was Chaucer's model for the House of Rumor in "Architectural Portraiture in Chaucer's *House of Fame*," *Journal of Medieval and Renaissance Studies* 11 (1981): 101–12 (109–12).

Fig. 3. A medieval wicker fish trap, excavated at the Hemington Quarry, Leicestershire. Courtesy of the University of Leicester.

Fig. 4. A modern, functional replica of a medieval eel trap. Courtesy of Windrush Willows, Exeter.

enables it to remain submerged and allows water and smaller objects to flow through while it strains out passing eels. The traps evoked in the poem's final analogy are easily passed over as we readers hasten with the crowd toward the payoff, the revelation of the "man of gret auctorite" (2158).

But the trap poised at the end of *The House of Fame* is not only a basket within a basket—a smaller, mundane version of its cosmic counterpart "sixty myle of lengthe" (1980). Its placement at the end of the poem also demands a reappraisal of the poem's broken form. The eel trap gathers its contents in passive fashion, designed, precisely as the House of Rumor is "shapen" (1985), to take advantage of the fugitive nature of its environment, to register what passes through. As Geffrey had observed couriers with their bags as full of lies as "ever vessel was with lyes"—that is, the lees that remain at the bottom of an emptied cup (2130)—the analogy of the eel trap leaves us thinking not, or not only, of loss—what the poem is missing, where it fails to arrive—but of what remains. At first these unlucky eels seem to contradict the poem's commitment to motion: for them, the trap *is* an end point. In arresting these eels, the basket trap is an acknowledgment that all poetry, however innovative its forms, partakes of the violence that archival structures like Fame's edifice do to the natural inclination of things. Yet because it remains only projected, we might finally read these eels' capture as the poem's deferred *telos*, like the projected journey to Canterbury, an intention or final boundary that governs form but remains contingent—what V. A. Kolve describes as the "middleness," the "rhetorical space" of the "not yet" that characterizes Chaucer's art.[62]

While I have described fugitivity as an essentially outgoing rather than recursive motion, *The House of Fame* is nevertheless studded with circles.[63] I conclude by considering the poem's use of circularity as a means to recalibrate the antagonism between motion and form. We see circles, for instance, on its many broken surfaces, a chief example being the structure of the House of Rumor itself, where "on the roof men may yet seen / A thousand holes, and wel moo" (1948–49). In the lines that

---

[62] Kolve, "Man in the Middle," 44.

[63] Despite the poem's broken form, Baswell in fact reads the conclusion as one of its several moments of circling back to beginnings. "By the end of the *House of Fame*, Geffrey . . . finds himself virtually where he began," that is, "in a fallen world," without a firm handle on authority; *Virgil in Medieval England*, 244. Baswell collapses the poem's three houses into a singular edifice through which the narrator travels three times, following a "sequence of ever more general, less reliable and simultaneously less mediated report" (245).

follow, Chaucer catalogues the contents of the woven house in a fashion that visually and aurally mimics the form of their porous container:

> And over alle the houses angles
> Ys ful of rounynges and of jangles
> Of werres, of pes, of mariages,
> Of reste, of labour, of viages,
> Of abood, of deeth, of lyf,
> Of love, of hate, acord, of stryf,
> Of loos, of lore, and of wynnynges,
> Of hele, of seknesse, of bildynges,
> Of faire wyndes, and of tempestes,
> Of qwalm of folk, and eke of bestes;
> Of dyvers transmutaciouns
> Of estats, and eke of regions;
> Of trust, of drede, of jelousye,
> Of wit, of wynnynge, of folye;
> Of plente, and of gret famyne,
> Of chepe, of derthe, and of ruyne;
> Of good or mys governement,
> Of fyr, and of dyvers accident.
> (1959–76, my emphasis)

Visually the anaphora "pokes holes" in the text. Its vertical line of capital "O"s conjures the form of Rumor's ventilated edifice upon the perforated manuscript page (Fig. 5).[64] Aurally the repetition of "O" (not only in the initial genitive "Of," but in the "O"s that proliferate along each horizontal line) echoes the assonant description of the roof's "th*ou*sand h*o*les, and wel m*oo*," rounded apertures designed to let the "*soun out goo*" (1950–51, my emphasis). As the catalogue enumerates its contents, it simultaneously disperses them. It also draws attention to the speaking mouth as orifice of outgoing sound, framing the poet's (or any reader's) own body as the material passageway of "tydynges."

Indeed, the anaphoric circles that catalogue the contents of the House of Rumor might be seen as a manifestation, or resurfacing, of an earlier paean to circular imagery in the eagle's explanation of the way sound travels in waves, like concentric circles across the broken plane of a body of water:

---

[64] Havely suggests this moment of mimesis produces "a kind of concrete poem" (Chaucer, *The House of Fame*, ed. Havely, 205, note to lines 1961–76).

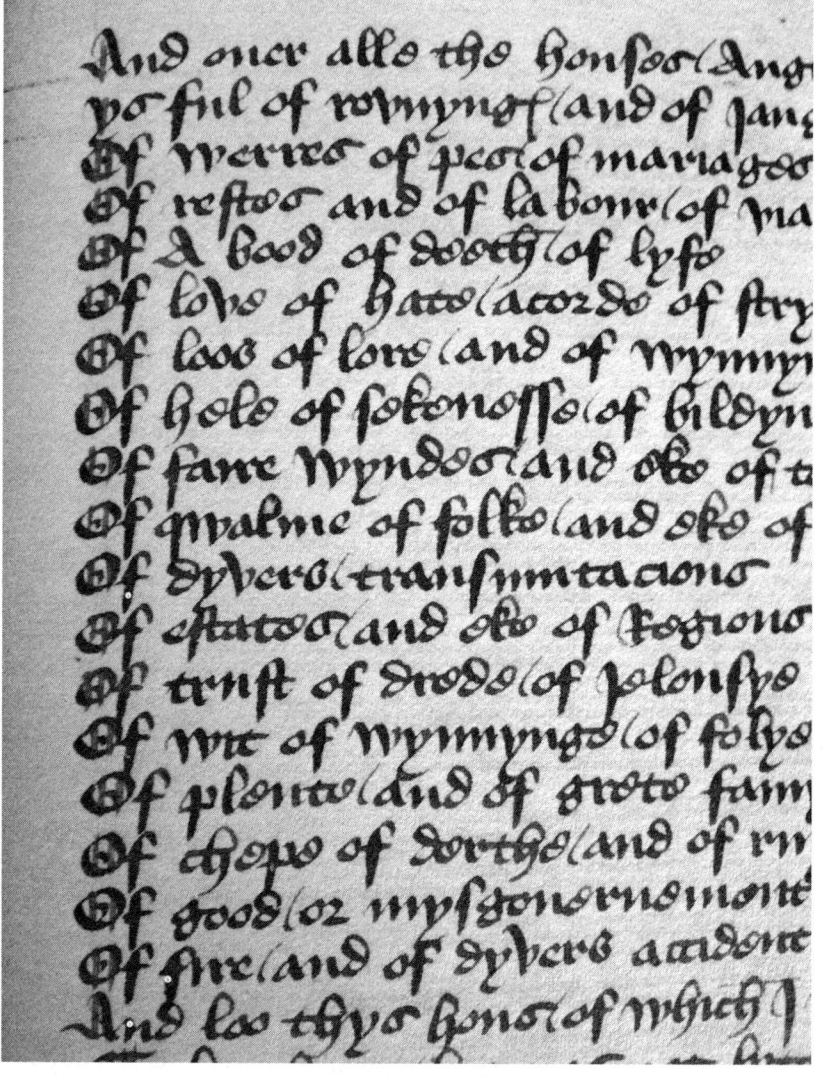

Fig. 5. Detail of the anaphora in the Fairfax manuscript (Oxford, Bodleian Library, MS Fairfax 16, fol. 181r). Courtesy of the Bodleian Library.

> Throwe on water now a stoon,
> Wel wost thou hyt wol make anoon
> A litel roundell as a sercle,
> Paraunter brod as a covercle.
>
> (789–92)

The eagle's everyday illustration of "multiplicacioun" (820) anticipates the poem's final lines, which similarly ask readers to visualize agitated water, roiled not by a stone, but by the rhythms of feet. The eagle's example itself produces a proliferation of circles, as the initial analogy of the concentric effect of waves on water gives way to a second analogy that compares the first "roundell" made by the stone to a "covercle," or pot lid.[65] Some see humor in the eagle's reference to the medieval kitchen, an intrusion of mundane imagery into philosophical discourse. But we might rather interpret the "covercle" as belonging to the poem's catalogue of workaday vessels, the "panyers," "boystes," "dossers," and eel traps to which I have called attention. A lid, moreover, evokes a very particular function with respect to containment: out of its context, this lid suggests a pot whose contents have spilled over. Indeed, as the eagle's explanation continues, the native motion of water does just that: once roused, it continues opening ever broader circles:

> That whel wol cause another whel,
> And that the thridde, and so forth, brother,
> Every sercle causynge other
> Wydder than hymselve was;
> And thus fro roundel to compas,
> Ech aboute other goynge
> Causeth of othres sterynge
> And multiplyinge ever moo,
> Til that hyt be so fer ygoo
> That hyt at bothe brynkes bee.
>
> (794–803)

---

[65] Boethius also uses the example of concentric circles to illustrate the movement of sound in *De musica*, I.14. Bennett, *Chaucer's Book of Fame*, 79, cites the association of sound and circular waves in Vitruvius's *De architectura*, 5.3.6; and Irvine, "Medieval Grammatical Theory," 866–67, locates these analogies in medieval commentaries on Priscian's *Institutiones grammaticae*. Both the "covercle" and the continuity of waves under water, however, appear to be Chaucer's own embellishments to the analogy.

This generative circularity does finally expire, but only when its "sterynge" energy extends to the full capacity of its container or medium, touching both "brynkes" (shores or banks). And in the two lines that follow this description, the eagle reanimates the vanished circles, adding, "Although thou mowe hyt not ysee / Above, hyt gooth yet alway under" (804–5). This is not to suggest that the waves extend beyond the boundaries of the water; rather, the final couplet extends the life of the analogy by returning to dwell a bit longer on the persistent motion of the waves. A purveyor of excess and ornament, the loquacious eagle suggests that the effects of an original event continue in their course even in unseen and unexpected ways.

In thinking about the function of formal circles, *The House of Fame* can be profitably compared to *Pearl*, a poem whose taut organization and closed structure produce a formal vision nearly opposite to that of Chaucer's frenetic and notionally unfinished poem. Nevertheless, both poems play with the concept of a structural circle to produce two different sorts of perpetuity. Using *Pearl* as a test case, Christopher Cannon proposes "a comprehensive theory of form" that takes into account not only those salient features of a work, but also (and especially) its anomalies and "most recalcitrant aspects," those instances that seem not to fit the "governing logic" of the work as a whole.[66] Pointing to the discrepancy between *Pearl*'s elaborately structured formal circularity and the dreamer's desire to move forward—physically across the river that separates him from the Pearl-Maiden, and emotionally beyond the trauma of her loss—Cannon characterizes this incommensurability as the "flaw in the pearl that actually constitutes its larger and more complex symbolic function."[67] In circling back to its beginning, *Pearl* traces an image of unity, purity, and wholeness that aptly characterizes the maiden who motivates the vision, but it also evokes her absence at its center. The greater meaning conveyed by the "flaw" in its form, Cannon argues, is the truth that "consolation and understanding are processes without destination."[68] Perpetually chasing its own tail, as it were, the form of *Pearl* embraces failure as part of its meaning.

[66] Christopher Cannon, "Form," in *Oxford Twenty-First Century Approaches to Literature: Middle English*, ed. Paul Strohm (Oxford: Oxford University Press, 2007), 177–90 (188, 190). Cannon's rationale depends on his observation of the formal reticence of Middle English poetry, which "usually employ[s] governing logics so unusual that they have remained virtually invisible to critical analysis, often appearing to such analysis in the guise of their opposite, as the very absence of structure" (184).
[67] Ibid., 188.
[68] Ibid., 189.

Whether *The House of Fame* is unfinished by chance or by design may be impossible to determine. Its fugitive poetics nevertheless assumes a form almost the opposite of *Pearl*'s concatenated return, ending instead with a headlong thrust into empty space.[69] Unlike *Pearl*'s narrator, Geffrey never wakes from his dream. In *Pearl*, a river forms an impenetrable barrier between the narrator and his desire; in *The House of Fame*, as I have suggested throughout this essay, waterways facilitate and emblematize forward motion rather than impeding it. Indeed, as we have seen, the poem's underlying fluid dynamics surface once again in its conclusion, and it leaves its readers, with the thronging crowd, stamping on the "brynke," at a boundary, to be sure, but not at a barrier. If *Pearl*'s circularity dances round an aporia, in *The House of Fame*, circularity becomes a loophole, not to aestheticize (and theologize) loss, but through which to "leten" its fugitive matter "out goo" (1950).

Recent scholarship has challenged the way we understand the unfinished nature of the *Canterbury Tales*, especially its received form in *The Riverside Chaucer*. Robert J. Meyer-Lee raises doubts about whether the editorial term "fragment" accurately represents the textual history of the work at all, characterizing the *Tales* as a "dynamic, unpredictable, open-ended structure."[70] Taking a similar approach, Arthur Bahr proposes that the *Canterbury Tales* invites us to play a "compilational game" by encouraging "active, restless, creative forms of reading" its sundry and moveable parts.[71] These exchanges shed new light on the formal grounds of the work's ambitious thematization of harmony, the relationship of parts to wholes, or, as Bahr puts it, "how literary, social, and physical constructions . . . interrelate and either cohere or collapse."[72] This essay argues that Chaucer begins that project in *The House of Fame* by examining how to gather parts together in the first place. The answer

---

[69] The poem ends mid-folio in its two best manuscripts—Oxford, Bodleian Library, MS Fairfax 16 and Oxford, Bodleian Library, MS Bodley 638—and in both manuscripts an extra leaf (three in Fairfax) awaits further material. The copyists of these manuscripts, like generations of later readers, evidently surmised something was missing. In the third extant manuscript, Cambridge, Magdalene College, MS Pepys 2006, the poem breaks off at line 1843, prior to the description of the house made of "twigges." See John Burrow, "Poems without Endings," *SAC* 13 (1991): 17–37; and A. S. G. Edwards, "The Text of Chaucer's *House of Fame*: Editing and Authority," *Poetica* 29–30 (1989): 80–92. Minnis, *Oxford Guides to Chaucer*, summarizes the state of the manuscripts and scholarly views toward the unfinished nature of the poem (167–72).

[70] See Robert J. Meyer-Lee, "Abandon the Fragments," *SAC* 35 (2013): 47–83 (71).

[71] Arthur Bahr, *Fragments and Assemblages: Forming Compilations of Medieval London* (Chicago: University of Chicago Press, 2013), 168, 257.

[72] Ibid., 169.

that emerges is to let matter make its own way to form, which is not quite to say that poets are just mouthpieces of stories that "mot out" (2139). Porous forms do imagine a passive model of art, deemphasizing authorial agency, much as the pilgrim narrator will claim in *The General Prologue* that he does no more than "reherce" the other pilgrims' tales, relaying them "pleynly," or "ful brode" (732, 727, 739, and cf. *MilP*, 3173–74). Chaucer's obfuscations of authorial agency, which frequently take the form of disavowals such as these, explore serious questions about literary authority, the claims of audiences, and the vagaries of transmission. But in confronting the problem of fugitivity, what I have described as the "kynde" tendency of things to "out goo" (1950), *The House of Fame* finally secures the place of the author by endorsing the value of a good design. Chaucer's fugitive poetics discovers in motion not an antithesis to form but its condition of possibility. Formal structures designed to take advantage of material agency use motion as a principle of collection. As the eel trap exploits the river's current, so a "hostelrye" along the road to Canterbury exploits every pilgrim's need for a temporary stopping place, gathering in "sondry folk" with "chambres" and "stables . . . wyde" (*GP*, 23, 28). Keeping these companies together is another story.

The Place of the Bedchamber in Chaucer's *Book of the Duchess*

Sarah Stanbury
College of the Holy Cross

CHAUCER'S *Book of the Duchess*, a dream-vision, begins and ends in a bedroom. A point of departure for the dream that forms the poem's central narrative, the bedroom also comes stunningly outfitted with luxury goods. Opening with a long insomniac meditation in which the narrator strategizes about ways to get to sleep, *The Book of the Duchess* invokes increasingly lush imaginary interiors in which the bedroom becomes a scene of invention, not just for the dream but for the poem as well. Unable to sleep, the narrator starts his story with himself sitting in bed late at night, eschewing the sociable activities of chess and backgammon for romance reading. Then, having read a story—Ovid's tale of Ceyx and Alcyone, which involves Morpheus, the god of sleep—he concocts a plan for bribing Morpheus, first by offering him a featherbed of pure white doves' down, striped with gold and covered in black satin from abroad, and many pillows, with every pillowcase made from "cloth of Reynes," or fine linen from Reims in France:

> Yif he wol make me slepe a lyte,
> Of down of pure dowves white
> I wil yive hym a fether-bed,
> Rayed with gold and ryght wel cled
> In fyn blak satyn doutremer,
> And many a pilowe, and every ber
> Of cloth of Reynes, to slepe softe—
> (249–55)[1]

I thank Theresa Coletti and Michelle Warren for helpful comments on earlier versions of this essay, which was first presented as a talk at the New England Medieval Conference in 2012.

[1] Citations from Chaucer refer to *The Riverside Chaucer*, gen. ed. Larry D. Benson, 3rd ed. (Boston: Houghton Mifflin, 1987).

The narrator then ups the ante by including other furnishings—"al that falles [belongs] to a chambre"—and offering to paint Morpheus's halls with gold and to cover the walls with tapestries:

> And I wol yive hym al that falles
> To a chambre, and al hys halles
> I wol do peynte with pure gold
> And tapite hem ful many fold
> Of oo sute; this shal he have
> (Yf I wiste where were hys cave),
> Yf he can make me slepe sone.
> (257–63)

The imaginary bribe works. Immediately the narrator falls asleep, and in his ensuing dream he even seems to be living in the elegant house he promised to Morpheus, or at least one of equivalent style. In his dream he awakens to the sound of birds singing from their perches on the tiles of his bedroom roof, and to his room filled with sunlight. The walls of his room are painted with scenes and gloss from *The Romance of the Rose*, and his windows are not only fully glazed but also painted with the entire Troy story.

What, for Chaucer, is the value of a bedroom? As readers have long recognized, *The Book of the Duchess*, Chaucer's first long poem in English, is a *bricolage* of echoes from Ovid—the *Metamorphoses* and the French *Ovide moralisé*—and from courtly *dits amoureuses* by Machaut, Froissart, Guillaume de Lorris, and others.[2] A public poem, *The Book of the Duchess*

---

[2] Sources from the *dits* include Machaut's *Le jugement dou roy de Behaigne, Le dit de la fonteinne amoureuse, Remede de fortune*, and *Le dit dou Lyon*; and Froissart's *Le paradys d'amours*; as well as Guillaume de Lorris's *Roman de la rose*. On the poem's French sources see especially James Wimsatt, *Chaucer and the French Love Poets* (Chapel Hill: University of North Carolina Press, 1968); B. A. Windeatt, ed., *Chaucer's Dream Poetry: Sources and Analogues* (Cambridge: D. S. Brewer, 1982); Alistair Minnis, with V. J. Scattergood and J. J. Smith, *Oxford Guides to Chaucer: The Shorter Poems* (Oxford: Clarendon Press, 1995), 83–97; Geoffrey Chaucer, *The Book of the Duchess*, ed. Helen Phillips, Durham and St. Andrews Medieval Texts 3 (Durham: University of Durham, 1982), 19–27, 168–88; Barbara Nolan, "The Art of Expropriation: Chaucer's Narrator in *The Book of the Duchess*," in *New Perspectives in Chaucer Criticism*, ed. Donald M. Rose (Norman: Pilgrim Books, 1981), 203–22; A. C. Spearing, "Dream Poems," in *Chaucer: Contemporary Approaches*, ed. Susanna Fein and David Raybin (University Park: Pennsylvania State University Press, 2009), 159–78, esp. 162–63. According to Wimsatt, while the prologue of *The Book of the Duchess* is indebted to a range of other French poets, "every facet of the elegy proper—mode, form, and detail—is permeated with the influence of Machaut's *dits*. The connection is so strong as to make it remarkable that Chaucer's originality shows through as it does"; Wimsatt, *Chaucer and the French Love Poets*, 70.

was almost certainly written for an occasion commemorating the 1368 death of Blanche, first wife of John of Gaunt, and would have been presented to a London court audience versed in French love poetry and accustomed to hearing occasional poetry read in French, not in English.[3] Chaucer's choice to write in English measures an important step in his own growth as a writer as well as a milestone in the history of English.[4] As Ardis Butterfield has noted, Chaucer's choice to write the *Duchess* in English articulates the increasing acceptance of English, which had achieved sufficient stature to legitimize a translation project: French poetry *can* be reworked in English.[5] Taking pieces of well-known French verse, translating some of them and reworking others in an English-language occasional poem that will then be read before an audience versed in the French poetry of Guillaume de Lorris and Machaut, Chaucer offers in the *Duchess* a public performance of English as well as a strategic act of language promotion. Do it once and you can do it again.

The *Duchess*'s vernacular reprisal of French love poetry may also involve the promotion of a certain vision of Englishness, other readers have suggested. Lexical analysis of the poem's opening lines, a paraphrase of Froissart's *Paradys d'amours*, suggests that Chaucer repeatedly chooses from an Anglo-Saxon rather than a Romance lexicon, peppering his complaint about insomnia with native colloquialisms and words.[6] According to Barbara Nolan, the opening of the *Duchess* is a "poetic manifesto" for *simplicitas*; in the prologue Chaucer parodically reworks familiar French courtly love poetry through the vision of a narrator absorbed not in the rituals of *fin amors* but in "the accidents of daily life."[7] More recently Deanne Williams has also read the *Duchess* as a

---

[3] In the *Retraction* to the *Canterbury Tales*, Chaucer names "the Book of the Duchesse" (X.1085), and in the *Prologue to the Legend of Good Women* the narrator includes among his compositions the "Deeth of Blaunche the Duchesse" (*LGW*, F 418); on the poem's audience see Paul Strohm, *Social Chaucer* (Cambridge, Mass.: Harvard University Press, 1989), 51–55.

[4] D. W. Robertson, Jr., "The Historical Setting of Chaucer's *Book of the Duchess*," in *Mediaeval Studies in Honor of Urban Tigner Holmes, Jr.*, ed. John Mahoney and John Esten Keller (Chapel Hill: University of North Carolina Press, 1965): 169–95 (171–72).

[5] Ardis Butterfield, *The Familiar Enemy: Chaucer, Language, and Nation in the Hundred Years War* (Oxford: Oxford University Press, 2009), 292.

[6] Derek Brewer, "The Relationship of Chaucer to the English and European Traditions," in *Chaucer and Chaucerians: Critical Studies in Middle English Literature*, ed. Brewer (London: Nelson, 1966), 1–38 (3); cited by Michael Hanly, "France," in *A Companion to Chaucer*, ed. Peter Brown (Oxford: Blackwell, 2000), 149–66 (160–61). See also Arthur W. Bahr, "The Rhetorical Construction of Narrator and Narrative in Chaucer's *Book of the Duchess*," *ChauR* 35 (2000): 43–59 (43–47).

[7] Nolan, "Art of Expropriation," 218. See also Butterfield, *The Familiar Enemy*, 290.

"manifesto for English poetry," whose plain speaking, voiced by a comically literal-minded narrator, takes the floor against the formal artifice and allegorizing of French prosody.[8]

The bedroom that stages Chaucer's first foray into English translation and prosody also localizes the act of writing, I argue in this essay. Furnished with deluxe objects that are freighted with desire and tagged with exchange values, the bedroom in *The Book of the Duchess* offers an "ethnography of things" that links the poem's work of elegy and commemoration with place and patronage as well as language.[9] The bed linens that the narrator offers Morpheus have values that derive partly from their promise of bodily pleasure, or their worldliness, and also from an international marketplace. Performers in the poem's dream-work, they are objects of desire networked through the textile trade and endowed with substantial cash values, a sense of which can be gleaned from contemporary inventories and wills. In the poem's ending, bilingual language-play explicitly locates the place of composition in England—with spatial nomenclature that even partners with the material world of John of Gaunt, Chaucer's benefactor and one of the poem's commemorative subjects. The bedroom, I will argue, isn't just a point of departure for the dream-vision, but bricks and mortar that conjoin with language to build a story on English ground.

I

That work of construction in the *Duchess* begins with the translation of narrative fragments as well as objects. Many elements of *The Book of the Duchess*, including the general structure of the dream-vision as well as narrative elements and plot points, draw heavily on popular French courtly love poems by Machaut, Froissart, and Guillaume de Lorris that readers in Chaucer's literary cohort would likely have known. For the

---

[8] Deanne Williams, *The French Fetish from Chaucer to Shakespeare* (Cambridge: Cambridge University Press, 2004), 30.

[9] I take the term "ethnography of things" from Sara Ahmed, *Queer Phenomenology: Orientations, Objects, Others* (Durham, N.C.: Duke University Press, 2006), 39. For an argument that the bedroom in *The Book of the Duchess* is an "anti-primitive" description that contrasts with an idealized vision of the primitive in Guillaume de Lorris's *Romance of the Rose*, see Lorraine Kochanske Stock, "'Peynted . . . text and [visual] glose': Primitivism, Ekphrasis, and Pictorial Intertextuality in the Dreamers' Bedrooms of *Roman de la rose* and *Book of the Duchess*," in *"Seyd in Forme and Reverence": Essays on Chaucer and Chaucerians in Memory of Emerson Brown, Jr.*, ed. T. L. Burton and John F. Plummer (Provo: Brigham Young University, 2005), 133–50.

story of Ceyx and Alcyone, Chaucer draws on Machaut's *Dit de la fonteinne amoureuse* as well as Ovid. The motifs of the narrator's sleeplessness and appeal to Morpheus for sleep appear in *Le paradys d'amours* by Froissart, who was in attendance at the English court until the death of Queen Philippa of Hainault in 1369, the year after Blanche of Lancaster died. Chaucer borrows elements of the Black Knight's lament in the wood from Machaut's *Le jugement dou roy de Behaigne*, conflating the *Jugement*'s debate over which loss is more devastating—the loss of love or the death of the beloved—into a single catastrophe: the once fey, then true, lover who dies. The long introduction is closely indebted to Guillaume de Lorris's *Rose*, according to James Wimsatt, who notes that the *Rose* also serves as a model for other sections of the *Duchess*, such as the animal-filled park through which the narrator follows the puppy.[10] Bribes, some of them involving textiles, also appear in his sources. In the *Dit de la fonteinne* the lamenting lover tells the story of Ceyx and Alcyone as a death at sea that parallels his own love-sickness, and has Alcyone offer Juno sacrifices and gifts if she will locate Ceyx's body. He himself then promises Morpheus ".i. chapiau de pavaut," or one poppy hat, and ".i. mol lit de plume de gerfaut" (lines 807–9), or one soft bed of gyrefalcon feathers, if the sleep god can plead his case to his beloved, itemizing his offerings like a writ.[11] Sleep barters, indeed, are almost a convention. *Le paradys d'amours* opens with the insomniac narrator winning sleep by offering Juno a golden ring.[12]

In *The Book of the Duchess* Chaucer elaborates on the skimpy bribes in Froissart and Machaut and fills out details of the room, turning furnishings and chamber into a stage set, with the narrator's bed a key point of orientation in an imaginative landscape with multiple coordinates. Guillaume de Lorris's *Rose*, and the courtly *dits* by Machaut and Froissart on which Chaucer draws, offer notably few details of household furnishings and nothing that compares with the ekphrastic interior that opens

---

[10] Wimsatt, *Chaucer and the French Love Poets*, 21, 24.

[11] Guillaume de Machaut, *"The Fountain of Love" ("La fonteinne amoureuse") and Two Other Love Vision Poems*, ed. and trans. R. Barton Palmer (New York: Garland, 1993), 133. Windeatt, *Chaucer's Dream Poetry*, 33, translates the lines as "a cap and a soft feather-bed," and Palmer as a "nightcap and a soft bed filled with feathers." Neither includes "gerfaut" nor "pavaut" (probably "poppy," or "poppy-colored," from French *pavot*). The fanciful "gerfaut" has a correlate in *The Book of the Duchess*'s bed of doves' down, an equally unlikely source for feathers.

[12] Jean Froissart, *Le paradis d'amour; L'orloge amoureus*, ed. Peter F. Dembowski (Geneva: Droz, 1986), 42, lines 15–18.

The Book of the Duchess. While both the *Duchess* and Froissart's *Paradys* begin with a narrator suffering from sleeplessness, in Froissart the malady is resolved after 32 lines with the gift to Juno. In *The Book of the Duchess*, however, the narrator's sleeplessness lasts for 269 lines. A major section of Machaut's *Behaigne* takes place in the king's bedroom in Durbuy Castle, "beaus et jolis," yet the only furnishings named are two rugs, one of silk, another from Norway (lines 1473, 1970) used for seating.[13]

The *Duchess* also spiffs up the interior decorating. In another departure from his sources, Chaucer appropriates Morpheus's bed for his narrator while rusticating the god of sleep's cave. In the *Fonteinne*, Morpheus's house is "bele a merveille" (line 595), marvelously beautiful, and furnished with "un lit trop riche et une couche" (604), a rich bed and couch. In Book XI of Ovid's *Metamorphoses* and in the *Ovide moralisé*, even more direct sources for this part of the *Duchess*, Morpheus lives in a fertile valley and sleeps luxuriously on a bed draped in black satin. The *Ovide moralisé* raises the comfort level with an ebony bed:[14]

> Ou mi leu d'une cave obscure
> Ot un mol lit de riche atour,
> Couvert d'un bel noir couvertour.
> Li challis ne fu pas de tramble,
> Ains fu d'ebenus, ce me samble.
>
> [Near the middle of a dark cave
> Was a soft bed of rich appearance,
> Covered with a beautiful black coverlet.
> The bedstead wasn't made of aspen,
> But was made of ebony, it seemed to me.]

In *The Book of the Duchess*, however, Morpheus inhabits a stripped-down landscape, living (or rather sleeping) in a cave "as derk as helle-pit" (170–71), in a rocky wasteland. A bed is mentioned—"And somme lay naked in her bed / And slepe whiles the dayes laste" (176–77)—but no

---

[13] Citations are from *"Le jugement du roy de Behaigne" and "Remede de fortune,"* ed. James I. Wimsatt and William W. Kibler (Athens: University of Georgia Press, 1988).

[14] Ovid, *The Metamorphoses*, trans. Horace Gregory (New York: Viking, 1958), 316; *Ovide moralisé*, ed. C. de Boer, 5 vols. (Wiesbaden: Martin Sändig, 1966–68), Vol. 4, lines 3465–69.

linens and less luxury: the bed (or beds) is a tumble of snorers in awkward positions.

And in the *Duchess* the black satin coverlet belongs to the narrator, not to Morpheus, an act of textual (and textile) appropriation that also serves as a geographic orientation. The story of Ceyx and Alcyone, with its long account of the visit from Juno's messenger to Morpheus's cave—under a distant classical rock in a "derke valeye" (155)—orients the point of narrative back to the one who is reading the story about those faraway places: that is, to the narrator in his English bedroom.[15] When the narrator promises Morpheus to trade beds, linens, and gilded and tapestried halls in exchange for sleep, he is really offering to renovate Morpheus's cave as a prosperous fourteenth-century urban home—and inasmuch as you can only barter what you have, one just like his own house. *There* (an Ovidian wilderness of rocks) stands in stark contrast to *here*, the at-home comforts of pillows, down, and a black silk coverlet.

It is also a home grounded in England, however paradoxically, by the use of French words—"Reynes" and "doutremer"—to name bed linens. As E. Jane Burns notes, textiles in Old French literature work as "visual maps," marking elite status through their connections to global trade.[16] Textiles and other objects in English texts do similar cartographic work. Throughout his writings Chaucer employs a versatile craft and trade vocabulary to indicate foreign origins, qualifying objects, especially textiles, with place markers to indicate sites of production, often in ways that also annotate those points of origin through their exoticism or reputation. To name a few: In *The Squire's Tale*, the mechanical horse is compared to steeds of Lombardy and an Apulian courser (V.193, 195). In *The Knight's Tale*, Emetreus, the king of India, rides in procession wearing glittering regalia that include a pearl-bedecked tunic made of "cloth of Tars," cloth from Tarsia, in Turkestan (I.2160). In *The General Prologue* the Merchant's "Flaundryssh bever hat" (I.272) identifies its wearer's prosperity and fashion sense, but more important, maps him, as a merchant, on trans-channel trade routes of his profession.

---

[15] For the use of the description to give "spatial specificity," see Peter Brown, *Chaucer and the Making of Optical Space* (Oxford: Peter Lang, 2007), 183.

[16] *Courtly Love Undressed: Reading through Clothes in Medieval French Culture* (Philadelphia: University of Pennsylvania Press, 2002), 182–97; cited in Sharon Kinoshita, "Almería Silk and the French Feudal Imaginary," in *Medieval Fabrications: Dress, Textiles, Clothwork, and Other Cultural Imaginings*, ed. E. Jane Burns (New York: Palgrave Macmillan, 2004), 165–76 (167).

In a discussion of French/English language play in Chaucer's *Shipman's Tale*, Ardis Butterfield comments that the tale uses double-sided language terms to "trade between plural cultures" in a narrative that is itself about trade and exchange.[17] In *The Book of the Duchess*, textiles similarly trade between cultures and annotate location. The pillowcases are French imports, "cloth of Reynes." Precisely which French town "Reynes" refers to is uncertain. Editors of *The Book of the Duchess* have glossed "Reynes" as Rennes, a town in Brittany, apparently following the lead of Skeat.[18] More likely, however, "Reynes" should be understood as Reims. In his study of the phrase "tele [linen] de Reyns," which appears frequently in Middle English romances and account books, including the household register of Edward III, Arthur Christopher Moule argues that "Reyns" (spelled variously as "Reyns," "Rayns," "Rennes," or "Raynes") most likely points to Reims, a city near the Champagne trading fairs and known for linen production.[19] As either Rennes or Reims, the term would resonate with the poem's own cosmopolitanism. Blanche's father, Henry of Grosmont, duke of Lancaster, led a year-long siege of Rennes that ended in 1357; and John of Gaunt accompanied his father Edward III on the siege of Reims in 1359, where Chaucer himself was captured by the French and ransomed for £16.[20] In the poem, the textile reference is a material, geographic pin to mark where we are not: not in Reynes, where the cloth comes from, but here.

Another place marker is the word "doutremer" or, in two manuscripts, "de owter mere."[21] The fine black satin covering for the featherbed comes from "doutremer," usually glossed in the *Duchess* as meaning foreign, or from across the seas. "Doutremer" in *The Book of the Duchess* is the word's one recorded appearance in Middle English, which suggests it is a nonce-term or phrase imported for the occasion. *Doutremer*, or

---

[17] Butterfield, *Familiar Enemy*, 222.

[18] In *Chaucer's Dream Poetry*, ed. Helen Phillips and Nick Havely (London: Longman, 1997); *The Riverside Chaucer*; and Geoffrey Chaucer, *Dream Visions and Other Poems*, ed. Kathryn Lynch (New York: Norton, 2007) the location is translated as Rennes.

[19] Arthur Christopher Moule, "Linen of Rens," in *Quinsai: With Other Notes on Marco Polo* (Cambridge: Cambridge University Press, 1957), 67–69. See also Sir J. Nicolas, "Expenses of the Great Wardrobe of Edward III," *Archaeologia* 31 (1845): 1–163 (37, 51, 57, 77–79); as noted in Phillips and Havely, *Chaucer's Dream Poetry*, 62n. For Reims as a site of linen production see also E. Jane Burns, *Sea of Silk: A Textile Geography of Medieval French Literature* (Philadelphia: University of Pennsylvania Press, 2009), 116.

[20] Anthony Goodman, *John of Gaunt: The Exercise of Princely Power in Fourteenth-Century Europe* (New York: St. Martin's Press, 1992), 35–36.

[21] Oxford, Bodleian Library, MSS Fairfax 16 and Bodley 638; see *The Riverside Chaucer*, 1137, note to *BD*, 253.

outremer, does not resurface again in English, according to the *Oxford English Dictionary*, until the early nineteenth century, when Longfellow describes himself as having in his youth been a pilgrim to "Outre-Mer" as an imaginative voyager to the Holy Land or exotic East. Longfellow's sense of the word is certainly present in medieval French; *outremer* was commonly used to refer to the Holy Land or French territories in the East, a meaning that appears in at least one manuscript that may have been circulating in English court circles in Chaucer's time: Jean de Vignay's 1331–33 translation of Odoric da Pordenone's well-known travel narrative, *Les merveilles de la terre d'Outremer*.[22] Signaling what Burns calls the "textile geography" of Old French romances, *outremer* means the East, rich in association with silk and luxury fabrics: "Lors veïssiez genz acesmer: / de samiz, de dras d'outremer, / de baudequins d'or a oiseaus / orent et cotes et manteaus." ("There you would see people adorned in heavy silk and cloth from across the sea. They had tunics and cloaks made of gold-infused Baghdad-style silks with bird motifs.")[23]

Outremer could also serve more literal and mundane language purposes, denoting a location across a body of water that could be the Channel as well as the Mediterranean. In Anglo-French documents *outremer* appears commonly in the context of cross-Channel and Mediterranean trade and simply means "overseas": casks can't be shipped "devers outremer" until they're weighed according to English measure; silk and brocade come from "d'Outremer" for the making of paltoks, or short coats.[24] Froissart's journey "oultre la mer" in *Espinette amoureuse*

---

[22] Odoric's text, housed in the British Library, is in a mid-fourteenth-century compendium on the wonders of the East, and may have been commissioned by Philip VI of France. The title in the BL manuscript is *La division frere Odoric des merveilles de la terre sainte*, as noted in the edition by D. A. Trotter, *Les merveilles de la terre d'Outremer* (Exeter: University of Exeter Press, 1990), v. For the earlier French uses of "Outre mer" as the Holy Land and overseas Latin kingdoms, see D. A. Trotter, *Medieval French Literature and the Crusades (1100–1300)* (Geneva: Droz, 1988), 41–43. For notes on the manuscript see the British Library's online record: http://www.bl.uk/catalogues/illuminatedmanuscripts/record.asp?MSID=8467&CollID=16&NStart=190401 (accessed March 17, 2015).

[23] Jean Renart, *Le roman de la rose ou de Guillaume de Dole*, ed. Félix Lecoy (Paris: Champion, 1962), vv. 233–36; cited and translated in Burns, *Sea of Silk*, 86; on oriental fabric and desire for the East, see also Geraldine Heng, *Empire of Magic: Medieval Romance and the Politics of Cultural Fantasy* (New York: Columbia University Press, 2003), 194–95.

[24] *The Anglo-Norman Dictionary*, http://www.anglo-norman.net/cgi-bin/form-s1 (accessed April 23, 2015), s.v. "outremer" (overseas): "Trespassant sui estrange ki m'en veng d'utre mer *S Aub* 27; Qe nul tonel . . . ne soit eskippez [shipped, embarked] devers outre meer *Rot Parl* ii 172.61." In the Old French *Dit des marchéans*, merchants to England, Spain, and Brittany travel "outremer"; see Burns, *Sea of Silk*, 181.

141

may refer autobiographically to his own crossing to England in 1361.[25] A notably politically nuanced use of *outremer* to reference English–French relations appears in Machaut's *La fonteinne amoureuse*, one of Chaucer's principal sources for *The Book of the Duchess*. The grieving lover, identified in Machaut's anagram as Jean, duke of Berry, despairs of hope coming "d'outre mer" to find him in his place of exile (line 479). His suffering also comes "d'outre la mer" (493)—locus of an ambiguous malady comprising separation from his beloved as well, perhaps, as the toxic political will of England.[26] The occasion for Machaut's *dit* is generally understood to have been the duke's departure in 1360 for England, where under terms of the Treaty of Brétigny he was to serve a sentence as hostage. He remained in England as a hostage until 1369. The duke was newly married, and hence the beloved evoked in the poem likely refers to Jeanne d'Armagnac, his new wife.[27] Throughout his lament, the lover uses terms of imprisonment to pun on a lover's torment and literal forced exile: he is "en cage," "en servage" (402), and "en ostage" (hostage; 398) as both a lover and as political prisoner. His land of exile—perhaps comically, for Machaut's readers—is a "païs sauvage" (2248): England, where people speak an "estrange langage" (2249). When he speaks of suffering coming "d'outre mer," then, the phrase carries a charged geographic specificity. For Machaut's court audience and English readers, that *mer* or sea would clearly be the Channel: a boundary, during the Hundred Years War, marking politics, affinities, and conflict.

Describing a satin coverlet in *The Book of the Duchess*, "doutremer" thus rings the changes twice on the otherness of French and of France: it is a word from elsewhere that also *means* elsewhere. Being from overseas in an English text, and in an English chamber, becomes part of the condition of fine black satin furnishings. When the narrator of the *Duchess* offers the house, he is not just buying sleep with all the gold in the world or all the tea in China but with the material and economic ground of English household economics, including luxury goods marking international trade. "Doutremer" and "Reynes" thus place the poem, and its

---

[25] "Or me prist voloirs d'aler fors / Dou pays et oultre la mer, / Pour moi un petit refremer / En santé et pour mieuls valoir"; lines 2383–86. Jean Froissart, *L'espinette amoureuse*, ed. Anthime Fourrier (Paris: Klincksieck, 1963), 117. For the autobiographical speculation see Wimsatt, *Chaucer and the French Love Poets*, 118 and 175n.

[26] Guillaume de Machaut, *The Fountain of Love*, ed. R. Barton Palmer (New York: Garland, 1993), 114, 116. Citations from the text refer to this edition.

[27] Windeatt, *Chaucer's Dream Poetry*, 26; Wimsatt, *Chaucer and the French Love Poets*, 112.

place of production, on a global or at least continental map. In an English poem presented to an audience accustomed to hearing poetry in French, the migratory geography of its French bed linens marks both proximity and difference. Morpheus's black bed has been brought into Channel trade. Textiles as well as words have come *doutremer*, and now are here.

II

The ekphrastic work of naming also tags these textiles with readable, if not exact, values as household goods. Constructions of the narrator's imaginary bribe, these objects are themselves poised on the border between the real and the fantastic: featherbeds, in late medieval Europe, were filled with goose and duck down, not dove down. As objects that serve the body at its most intimate moments—birth, sex, death—bed linens, such as those in *The Book of the Duchess*, no doubt invite readings as signs or metaphors. It is primarily as signs, indeed, that the textile references in Chaucer's poem have been understood by the few readers who have paid any attention to them. The white doves' down and the black bed covering introduce a pattern of white and black imagery that recurs throughout the dream-vision in the form of Lady White and the Man in Black, who seem themselves to be signs for real people.[28] Through the language-crossing play on her name, White is almost certainly meant to invoke the Duchess Blanche of Lancaster, and the Man in Black to suggest John of Gaunt.[29] Beds are also apt images for the poignant stories of love and death in the legend of Ceyx and Alcyone and in the Man in Black's lament in the dream; the bed, bartered for sleep, recalls other uses for beds, and in this elegy for a long-wooed lady named White, stand-in for Blanche, dead wife of John of Gaunt (the Man in Black), those associations include both sex and death—where you make love, where you die.[30] And the bed barter works as a characterizing signal or alert for the narrator's literal-mindedness and self-absorption, obsessed with sleep fantasies and conjuring home-decorating

---

[28] Whiteness, a familiar term in medieval philosophical discourse, evokes both absence and cognition, and hence sharpens this elegy's epistemological edge; see Peter Travis, "White," *SAC* 22 (2000): 1–66. See also Kathryn L. Lynch, *Chaucer's Philosophical Visions* (Cambridge: D. S. Brewer, 2000), 51.

[29] See *The Riverside Chaucer*, 976, note to *BD*, 1314–29.

[30] In practical terms, the association of death with the family bed seems to have been problematic, at least in twelfth-century England. According to Benedict of Canterbury in *The Miracles of St. Thomas Becket* (1171–late 1170s), ritually sanctioned bed-taboo proscribed the family bed for the dying. In describing a woman on the point of death

schemes when he might well be reflecting on the darker aspects of the tragic story of Ceyx and Alcyone he has just read.

However, tied to an imaginary trade register, the poem's bedroom textiles are expressly described in terms of cash and barter exchanges. After naming his textile gifts to Morpheus, the narrator reckons that the god of sleep will be better remunerated with these "feës" than he has ever been before, and that Juno, his queen, will consider herself rewarded, or "payd."

> And thus this ylke god, Morpheus,
> May wynne of me moo feës thus
> Than ever he wan; and to Juno,
> That ys hys goddesse, I shal soo do,
> I trow, that she shal holde her payd.
> (265–69)

Then, after 269 lines of sleeplessness, he finally falls asleep. The word "payd," which can mean rewarded or pleased, seems to work as a kind of sleeping-pill or magic spell:

> I hadde unneth that word ysayd
> Ryght thus as I have told hyt yow,
> That sodeynly, I nyste how,
> Such a lust anoon me took
> To slepe that right upon my book
> Y fil aslepe.
> (270–75)

The narrator says the word "payd" and then gets what he wants. Even if the bed barter itself is an act of whimsy, "fees" and "payments" bespeak exchanges of objects that carry value not just as metaphors but also as material goods, with purchase powers on the imagination that calibrate with their circulation in the household economy. In the later Middle Ages, beds, particularly canopied ones, were prestige items, objects of value that also served as symbols of political and social authority. Beds

---

Benedict writes, "By the third day she had weakened to the point of death, so much so that she was taken out of her bed lest, contrary to the custom of the Christian religion, she lie dying in a comfortable feather bed." Cited in John Shinners, *Medieval Popular Religion: A Reader* (Peterborough, Ont.: Broadview Press, 1997), 161.

of state were not intended for sleeping at all, but rather for royal display.[31] In his account of the revolt of 1381, Froissart describes rebels breaking the bed of the king's mother, Joan of Kent, an act that no doubt references the association of the royal bed with affairs of state: "Encore entrèrent cil glouton en la chambre de la princesse et despécièrent tout son lit, dont elle fu si eshidée que elle s'en pasma." ("Also these gluttons entered into the chamber of the princess and broke her bed, whereupon she was so afraid that she swooned.")[32] Over-the-top textile decadence is targeted in Christine de Pizan's critique of a bedroom in *The Treasury of the City of Ladies*. A "truly outrageous woman," a merchant's wife with delusions of royalty, uses her lying-in as an occasion to display her bedding and textile wealth for all comers:

Et puis de celle on entroit en la chambre de la gisant, laquelle esoit grant et belle, toute encourtinee de tapisserie faicte a la devise d'elle ouvree tres richement de fin or de Chipre, le lit grant et bel encourtiné tout d'un parement et les tapis d'entour le lit mis par terre sur quoy on marchoit, tous pereilz a or ouvréz, les grant draps de parement qui passsoient plus d'un espan par soubz la couverture de si fine toile de Raims que ilz estoient prisiéz a .ccc. frans . . . En ce lit estoit la gisant, vestue le drap de soye taint en cramesy, appuiee de grans oreilliers de pareille soye a gros boutons de perles, atournee comme une demoiselle.

[This particular woman made a huge display at her lying-in for her recently-born child. Before entering her room, one passed through two other very fine chambers; in each one was a large ornamental bed, richly curtained; in the second was a large dresser decorated like an altar, all covered with silver vessels. Only then did one enter the woman's own bedchamber. Large and handsome, it was hung all round with tapestries marked with her coat-of-arms richly worked in fine gold thread from Cyprus. The bed, large and beautifully curtained with a single hanging, and the rug surrounding the bed, on which one

---

[31] Penelope Eames, "Furniture in England, France and the Netherlands from the Twelfth to the Fifteenth Century," *Furniture History: The Journal of the Furniture History Society* 13 (1977): 1–303 (85–86); W. M. Ormrod, "In Bed with Joan of Kent: The King's Mother and the Peasants' Revolt," in *Medieval Women: Texts and Contexts in Late Medieval Britain; Essays for Felicity Riddy*, ed. Jocelyn Wogan-Browne, Rosalynn Voaden, Arlyn Diamond, Ann Hutchison, Carol Meale, and Lesley Johnson (Turnhout: Brepols, 2000), 277–92 (280).

[32] Jean Froissart, *Oeuvres*, ed. J. B. M. C. Kervyn de Lettenhove, 25 vols. (Brussels: Victor Devaux, 1870–77), 9:404; trans. R. B. Dobson, *The Peasants' Revolt of 1381*, 2nd ed. (London: Macmillan, 1983), 191; and cited in Ormrod, "In Bed with Joan of Kent," 278.

could walk, were likewise embroidered with gold. The great, wide display sheets beneath the coverlet were of such fine toile from Rheims that they were valued at three hundred francs . . . . Sitting in the bed was the woman herself, dressed in crimson silk, propped up against large pillows covered in the same silk and decorated with pearl buttons, wearing the headdress of a lady.]³³

Fabrics like these also would have come with hefty price tags. Along with kitchen utensils, beds and bedding comprised much of the value of the late fourteenth-century household, and hence the narrator's offer to trade a bed and bed textiles is hardly just a flippant gesture.³⁴ Textiles of all sorts, as well as references to textile commerce, appear throughout records of London debt recovery, with beds and bedding often commanding top values. In the 1376 inventory of goods of the wealthy London merchant Richard Lyons, furniture, books, and ornamental objects are strikingly overshadowed by textiles. There are bedding and hangings for the five bedrooms; a vast garderobe of furred and brocaded gowns; and towels and tablecloths, as well as—in a chest next to the chapel—a tent for the bathtub. Similarly, the 1391 inventory of Richard Toky's London house shows an important part of the household value as tied up in chamber textiles: a bed with a tester (brocade headboard and canopy), sheets, quilts, and mattresses as well as a long inventory of gowns, cloaks, caps, and hats.³⁵ At over £13, or $13,000 in today's equivalent, the value ascribed to items in Toky's bedchamber exceeds the total annual income of many London merchant traders in the late

---

³³ Christine de Pizan, *Le livre des trois vertus*, ed. Charity Cannon Willard and Eric Hicks (Paris: Champion, 1989), 185, lines 51–69. English translation: *A Medieval Woman's Mirror of Honor: The Treasury of the City of Ladies*, trans. Charity Cannon Willard, ed. Madeleine Pelner Cosman (New York: Persea Books, 1980), 194–95. For other examples of bedclothes in estate commentary, see Laura F. Hodges, *Chaucer and Clothing: Clerical and Academic Costume in the General Prologue to the "Canterbury Tales"* (Cambridge: D. S. Brewer, 2005), 22n, 70.
³⁴ P. J. P. Goldberg, "The Fashioning of Bourgeois Domesticity in Later Medieval England: A Material Culture Perspective," in *Medieval Domesticity: Home, Housing and Household in Medieval England*, ed. Maryanne Kowaleski and Goldberg (Cambridge: Cambridge University Press, 2008), 127, 131.
³⁵ The next most valuable objects in the Toky inventory are the "jewels in the chamber" at £11 12 s. 7d., and then a significant drop to the other rooms: hall, pantry and buttery, kitchen, counting house, and storehouse. Assessment for the counting house, which includes a large box bound with iron, a book of the statutes, a quire of paper, a brass balance, an inkhorn, miscellaneous pieces of armor, and even alabaster tablets of the Virgin and of John the Baptist plus much else, comes to only £4 12s. 4d.; and hall, kitchen, pantry and buttery, and storehouse total less than £4 for each room. In A. H. Thomas, ed., *Calendar of Select Pleas and Memoranda of the City of London, 1381–1412* (Cambridge: Cambridge University Press, 1932), 209–10.

fourteenth and fifteenth centuries, which has been estimated at £10 or less,³⁶ and stands in dramatic contrast to the total value of goods—27 s.—inventoried for a mid-fourteenth-century peasant household in Oxford.³⁷

Bedding and beds also appear routinely in late medieval wills, detailed down to pattern, fabrics, and condition. In the context of *The Book of the Duchess*, John of Gaunt's will offers a particularly resonant testimonial. Even though the will's composition in 1398 postdates *The Book of the Duchess* by many years, the listing of fabrics and beds bespeaks Gaunt's famous penchant for fine design and expensive objects, and no doubt includes objects that were part of his estate when Blanche was alive. To Katherine, his third wife, Gaunt bequeaths a wealth of bed linens and other objects, including—in an intriguing echo of the "fyn blak satyn" covering the featherbed in *The Book of the Duchess*—a black bed:

jeo devise mon grant lit de noir velvet enbroude d'un compasse de ferures, et gartiers, et un turturell en mylieu de les compasses avecq' trestout les tapites et tapicerie et cuissins a ycelle lit ov chambres appurtenantes et a cella jeo le devise trestouts mes autres lits faitz pur mon corps, appelles en Engleterre trussyng beddes [a bed that can be packed up for traveling], ove les tapites et autres appurtenances, et mon meillour cerf ov le bonne rubie, et mon meillour coler ovecq' touts les diamandes ensemble, et mon second covertur d'ermyn.

[To her I will my large bed of black velvet embroidered with a design of furs, garters, and a turtle dove in the middle of the designs, with all the hangings and tapestries and the cushions of that bed or subsidiary rooms, and to her I will all my other beds made for my own use, called in England trussing beds, with hangings and other appurtenances, and my best drinking horn with the good ruby, and my best collar with all the diamonds together, and my second ermine cloak.]³⁸

---

³⁶ Richard Dyer, *Standards of Living in the Middle Ages: Social Change in England c. 1200–1520* (Cambridge: Cambridge University Press, 1989), 194; the annual income of masons and carpenters was around £5, according to Dyer (196). Dollar equivalents with today's currency are based on Jeffrey L. Forgeng and Will McClean, *Daily Life in Chaucer's England* (Westport: Greenwood Press, 2009), 35.

³⁷ Dyer, *Standards of Living*, 170.

³⁸ Sydney Armitage-Smith, *John of Gaunt: King of Castile and Leon, Duke of Aquitaine and Lancaster, Earl of Derby, Lincoln and Leicester, Seneschal of England* (Westminster: Archibald Constable, 1904), 420–36 (426). The echo of royal textile inventories is noted in Phillips and Havely, *Chaucer's Dream Poetry*, 148n.

To his king and nephew (Richard II):

et a cella xii. draps d'or donc la champ rouge satyn raye d'or, les quelx draps j'avoye ordenuz d'en faire un lit, lequel n'est uncore comencez, et un covertur d'ermyn le meillour qu j'ay ovecq' la coverchief de la suyte ensembler, et la piece d'arras la quelle le Duc de Burgoyn me donna.

[And to him 12 gold bed cloths with a satin red background striped in gold, the same bed cloths I ordered to have made into a bed that hasn't been started yet, and my best ermine coverlet with a matching kerchief, and the piece of tapestry given to me by the Duke of Burgundy.][39]

To his daughter Elizabeth:

Item jeo devise a ma treschere fille Elizabeth Duchesse d'Excestre mon blank lit de soi overez des egles bloyes displaies, les curteins de taffeta blank batuz de la suyte, xiiii. tapitz de tapiterie, et mon meillour nouch qu j'ay apres ceulx qu sont devisez.

[I will to my dear daughter Elizabeth Duchess of Exeter my white silk bed covered with blue eagles with outstretched wings, matching white taffeta curtains, 14 tapestry hangings, and my best brooch left after those which are willed.][40]

Even Saint Paul's gets a bed:

Item jeo devise a la suisdit aultier du Seynt Poule mon graunt lyt de drap d'ore, le champ piers poudres des roses d'or myses sur pipes d'or, et en chescun pipe deux plums d'ostrich blankes, les curteines de taffeta piers batuz de sembleable ovrage.

[I will to the aforesaid altar of St. Paul's my large bed of gold cloth, the blue background powdered with gold roses on gold piping, and in the same piping two white ostrich feathers, the blue taffeta curtain decorated with similar work.][41]

[39] Armitage-Smith, *John of Gaunt*, 426.
[40] Ibid., 427.
[41] Ibid., 422–23.

In Gaunt's bequest to Katherine, beds and linens are followed by drinking horns and gem-encrusted clothing, the logic of the list suggesting that beds and gems are items of comparable value.

Pillows, also named in the poem's bed barter, also circulated as important luxury goods in addition to serving as functional furniture. In fourteenth- and fifteenth-century houses, pillows and cushions were not the accessories for improving the comfort or enlivening the look of a chair that they are in western homes today, but often as not the seats themselves.[42] We can see this in numerous accounts of pillows in late medieval narratives. In Book II of *Troilus and Criseyde*, Criseyde emerges from her private closet, where she has gone to write a letter to Troilus, to sit next to Pandarus on such a cushion, a "quysshyn gold-ybete," (II.1229), its deluxe quality marked by gold embroidery. In *The Book of Margery Kempe*, Jesus describes the chamber of Margery's soul as furnished with "a cuschyn of gold, an other of red velvet, the thryd of white sylke."[43] And in Christine's arch domestic ekphrasis in the *Livre des trois vertus*, the pillows propping up the merchant's wife in bed are luxury items worthy of particular attention. The importance of pillows is also underscored in household records. The inventory of the vast array of goods in Richard Lyons's London house in 1376 lists only two chairs (settles), ten bench covers, and seven stools, but it includes a staggering thirty-nine cushions.[44] As P. J. P. Goldberg has observed, pillows are found almost exclusively in the wills and inventories of bourgeois, urban families, a fact that suggests that they were costly.[45] In *The Book of the Duchess*, the extravagance of the narrator's offer is indicated by multiples; he doesn't just offer Morpheus one pillow, but many pillows, all with linen cases: "many a pilowe, and every ber / Of cloth of Reynes."

The prominence of bed linens in wills and in debt-recovery records,

---

[42] For the importance of pillows in late medieval English houses and imagery, see my essay, "The Bourgeois Bedroom in Alabaster Adorations of the Kings," forthcoming in *Alabaster Sculpture in Medieval England: A Reassessment*, ed. Jessica Brantley, Stephen Perkinson, and Elizabeth Teviotdale.

[43] *The Book of Margery Kempe*, ed. Lynn Staley, TEAMS (Kalamazoo: Medieval Institute Publications, 1996), Chap. 86, line 5007. For the importance of textiles in the *Book* see Gabrielle Parkin, "Objects and Anxiety in Late Medieval English Writing," Ph.D. diss. (University of Delaware, 2014).

[44] The inventory is printed in A. R. Myers, "The Wealth of Richard Lyons," in *Essays in Medieval History Presented to Bertie Wilkinson*, ed. T. A. Sandquist and M. R. Powicke (Toronto: University of Toronto Press, 1969), 301–29. On Lyons's household goods see D. Vance Smith, *Arts of Possession: The Middle English Household Imaginary* (Minneapolis: University of Minnesota Press, 2003), 53.

[45] Goldberg, "The Fashioning of Bourgeois Domesticity," 132.

and attention to bed textiles in poetry and social critique, all point to the social significance of late medieval London's textile economy: fabrics of the bedroom are both ledger and software, core components of a household's wealth, comfort, and aesthetics. In *The Book of the Duchess*, the bed and linens that the narrator offers to Morpheus gesture to economic surplus and bourgeois and gentry power, essential components of what D. Vance Smith calls the urban "household imaginary."[46] By doing so, they help situate the bedroom and place of composition locally by enumerating the material occupation of space. Little in the description of the *Duchess*'s phantasmatic house would have been out of place in gentry houses of Paris, Bruges, Florence, or Prague, of course. Itinerant artisans, vigorous Mediterranean and Channel trade, and design-conscious merchants and members of the gentry conspired to generate shared international tastes in elite domestic furnishings. The fourteenth-century frescoes of the *Chastelaine de Vergy*, a French romance, decorating the chamber walls in the *palazzo* of the Davizzi, a family of merchants and bankers in Florence, would have looked at home on the walls of a London palace.[47] Nevertheless, the ekphrastic description of textiles is an act of grounding through concrete particulars. Indeed, *The Book of the Duchess* turns the bedroom into the locus of art and imagination. While the Troy story in Machaut's *Fonteinne amoureuse* unspools from an inscription on a marble fountain outdoors (1313ff.), for example, in the *Duchess* the same Troy story appears in the bedroom's stained glass.[48] The bedroom in *The Book of the Duchess* may be like deluxe interiors elsewhere, but as the imagined chamber of an insomniac narrator lying in bed, about to have a dream that he will recount in English, it is graphically *here*.

III

What does the bed buy him, then? The narrator succeeds in trading the household for sleep, which in this text enables states of aliveness and

---

[46] Smith, *Arts of Possession*, subtitle.

[47] The Davizzi house is now a museum, the Palazzo Davanzati. For the frescoes see Rosanna Caterina Proto Pisani and Maria Grazia Vaccari, eds., *Museo di Palazzo Davanzati: Guida alla visita del museo* (Florence: Polistampa, 2011), 200–202.

[48] In Machaut's *Le jugement du roy de Behaigne*, line 1473, the king of Bohemia listens to the Troy story being read to him while he is seated on a silk rug in his bedroom. According to Wimsatt, *Chaucer and the French Love Poets*, 63–64, the closest analogue for the story inscribed in glass is Watriquet de Couvin's *Tournois des dames*, in which the narrator finds himself in bed in a tower trying to decipher the meaning of a stained-glass joust between knights and ladies.

productivity: empathy with the bereaved; writing poetry.[49] It also buys him English ground. If the center section of the poem is driven by a search for a "phantasmatic object" in the figure of White, as Peter Travis argues, then its opening and closing sections ground that search in notably material- and place-based language.[50] At the end of the poem, *The Book of the Duchess* returns both the narrator and the Man in Black to their homes, with home even more explicitly situated than in the opening section of the poem. Immediately after the narrator acknowledges that White is dead, a hunting horn sounds that it is time to end the chase and turn around:

> With that me thoghte that this kyng
> Gan homwarde for to ryde
> Unto a place, was there besyde,
> Which was from us but a lyte—
> A long castel with walles white,
> Be Seynt Johan, on a ryche hil,
> As me mette; but thus hyt fil.
> (1314–20)

A castle bell then strikes twelve, and the narrator wakes up to find himself lying in his own bed, his book still in his hand.

This double return home—for both the narrator and the Man in Black—uses French language sources and conventions to locate home now literally in England. As readers have long noted, the poem now identifies John of Gaunt through language puzzles. "Long castle" is almost certainly a play on Lancaster; "Seynt Johan" most likely points to John of Gaunt; the "ryche hil" identifies Richmond Castle, whose earldom was granted to Gaunt in 1342;[51] and the castle's white walls suggest the Duchess Blanche. The parsing of these words not only identifies players and places but also strips place names to their geological foundations and English language roots. "Rich Hill" transforms the French of *Richmond* Castle into an English hill. "Long Castle" renders Gaunt's marital affiliation with Blanche's House of Lancaster as literal bricks and mortar. It also exposes English language origins. "Long"

---

[49] For sleeplessness in the poem as a metaphor for writer's block, see Lisa J. Kiser, "Sleep, Dreams, and Poetry in Chaucer's *Book of the Duchess*," *PLL* 19 (1983): 3–12.
[50] Travis, "White," 53.
[51] See *The Riverside Chaucer*, 976, note to *BD*, 1314–29; also Phillips and Havely, *Chaucer's Dream Poetry*, 29.

derives from Old English; and though "castle" derives from Latin *castellum*, the word had been in English since before the Conquest. This play with language at the end of the poem is a further echo of the elegy's French sources, in which identifying anagrams were commonplace.[52] Machaut opens the *Dit de la fonteinne* with an anagram of his name and the name of his dedicatee—Jean, duke of Berry—and ends the *Dit dou Lyon* and the *Jugement du roy de Behaigne* with anagrams on his own name. In *The Book of the Duchess* the place names play bilingually with French and English origins; and unlike Chaucer's sources, where anagrams hide names of persons, his point also to places and buildings. As a set of clues, they tell us that, if we've had any doubts, we have been in England all along.

Where we are precisely is an amalgamated virtual or dream location that reaches from London to Gaunt's northern holdings. The poem's opening call to a bedroom imagines it in a prosperous urban home—perhaps conjuring London, which has been called a "virtual presence" in much of Chaucer's writing.[53] With far more geographic specificity, the ending appears to name Richmond Castle in Yorkshire, which was John of Gaunt's principal castle as a young man. Gaunt was presented with the earldom of Richmond in 1342 when he was two years old, a grant that was confirmed by Edward III in 1351 and that Gaunt held until 1372.[54] Language also marks the local through its express invitation to read the poem biographically as a memorial to Blanche of Lancaster, her name Englished as White and inscribed as the castle's limewashed walls: the "long castel with walles white" (1318). The geographic references at the end of the poem may even return recursively to the imagined chamber and hall conjured at the beginning of the poem in an insider nod to Gaunt's tastes for good living.[55] Such tastes seem to have been in evidence early on with ongoing building projects at his various estates, among them Richmond Castle, which his father,

---

[52] Wimsatt, *Chaucer and the French Love Poets*, 12.

[53] Ruth Evans, "The Production of Space in Chaucer's London," in *Chaucer and the City*, ed. Ardis Butterfield (Cambridge: D. S. Brewer, 2006), 41–56 (56).

[54] Goodman, *John of Gaunt*, 30–31.

[55] For Gaunt's taste for good living see ibid., 358. For arguments that the wall paintings may have been influenced by Westminster see Michael Norman Salda, "Pages from History: The Medieval Palace of Westminster as a Source for the Dreamer's Chamber in *The Book of the Duchess*," *ChauR* 27 (1992): 111–25, and Stock, "Primitivism, Ekphrasis," 147; and for the poem as an exploration of Chaucer's relationship with Gaunt, see Strohm, *Social Chaucer*, 51–55.

Edward III, gave him a grant to refurbish in 1358. In 1360 Gaunt was granted Hertford Castle, closer to London, in part because it was felt that he did not yet possess a place of residence "as befits his estate."[56] Gaunt's biographers have remarked not only on his expensive, ongoing building and renovation projects but also on his tastes for "conspicuous consumption," and in particular for "draps d'Arras": sets of French tapestries.[57] If we want to tease out an echo between the black bed in Gaunt's will and the black satin bed covering in the narrator's offer to Morpheus, we might even hear in the bedroom bribe not just a reference to Ovid but also to Gaunt's own bedroom, an echo made all the more tantalizing by the fact that black bedspreads seem to have been unusual; they rarely appear in genre scenes in contemporary English manuscript painting and are seldom found in English inventories. Coverlets are green, red, gold, blue, and white, but rarely are they black.[58] A black coverlet was perhaps a Lancastrian bedroom fashion accessory of note. This taste for luxury appointments continued throughout Gaunt's life with his ongoing renovations of Hertford Castle. In later years he made elaborate renovations to his castle at Kenilworth to reflect the latest in architectural design. Its triple-bay fireplace (now destroyed) echoed the triple fireplace of the duke of Berry in Poitiers, and its great hall was modeled on Edward III's new hall at Windsor.[59] The Savoy in London, Gaunt's principal London home from the 1360s to 1381, was described by Thomas Walsingham as "unrivalled in splendour and nobility within England."[60] When the Savoy was destroyed in the revolt of 1381 the rebels targeted among other items the bedroom textiles: "They took all the torches they could find, and lit them, and burnt all the clothes, coverlets and beds, as well as all the very valuable testers, of which one, decorated with heraldic shields, was said to be worth a thousand marks."[61]

One final if metaphoric bed that may give the poem distinctive London grounding is the double tomb, an elaborate bed in alabaster, for

---

[56] Goodman, *John of Gaunt*, 302.

[57] Ibid., 358. According to Nancy Ciccone, the story of Troy told in the painted glass may reference the duke's interest in empire building; "The Chamber, the Man in Black, and the Structure of Chaucer's *Book of the Duchess*," *ChauR* 44 (2009): 205–23.

[58] See the accounts printed in Eames, "Furniture in England," 73–93.

[59] Richard K. Morris, *Kenilworth Castle* (London: English Heritage, 2010), 14–15; for Gaunt's rebuilding of Kenilworth see Goodman, *John of Gaunt*, 305–6 and 311.

[60] Thomas Walsingham, cited in Goodman, *John of Gaunt*, 8; for the Savoy's grandeur, 304.

[61] *Anonimalle Chronicle*, cited in Ormrod, "In Bed with Joan of Kent," 281.

Blanche and Gaunt in Saint Paul's Cathedral. The poem's date of composition has been the subject of a long scholarly debate, with many readers placing it between Blanche's death, in 1368, and 1372, when Gaunt forfeited Richmond Castle.[62] Other readers, less convinced that the reference to Richmond would necessarily allude to Gaunt's holdings at the time of the poem's composition, have dated the poem in or after 1374, the year in which Gaunt began his annual annuities to Chaucer and also the year of the erection of Blanche and Lancaster's magnificent double tomb in Saint Paul's Cathedral. Phillipa Hardman has suggested that *The Book of the Duchess* may have been occasioned by Gaunt's tomb commission, with the poem presented either at a memorial service in 1374, or even 1375 or 1376, when the tomb was mostly completed—though work continued at least until 1380.[63] Other readers have also pointed to the likelihood that the *Duchess* is a public poem whose occasion was not so much consolation as commemoration and even petition; and while the poem's ostensible subject is an elegy for Blanche, it also references Chaucer's relationship with Gaunt.[64] According to Paul Strohm, "the dream is not only a consolation to John of Gaunt for his loss of Duchess Blanche, but an exploration of Chaucer's own existing and potential relations with Gaunt, in a form at once tactful and quietly self-promotional."[65] Indeed, bids for patronage appear throughout Chaucer's French sources, with Machaut's petitionary plea to the duke of Berry in the *Dit de la fonteinne* a particularly vivid example.[66] D. W. Robertson suggests a date in 1374, on the basis of the duke's annuity that year to Chaucer of £10 a year for life, a reward "pur la bone etc. [i.e. la bone et agreable service] que nostre bien ame Geffray Chaucer

---

[62] For a review of the debate on dating see Michael Foster, "On Dating the *Duchess*: The Personal and Social Context of *The Book of the Duchess*," *RES* 59 (2007): 185–96 (196).

[63] Phillipa Hardman, "*The Book of the Duchess* as a Memorial Monument," *ChauR* 28 (1994): 205–15 (206–7); Goodman, *John of Gaunt*, 257–58.

[64] For the poem as a memorial see Mary Carruthers, " 'The Mystery of the Bed Chamber': Mnemotechnique and Vision in Chaucer's *The Book of the Duchess*," in *The Rhetorical Poetics of the Middle Ages: Reconstructive Polyphony; Essays in Honor of Robert O. Payne*, ed. John M. Hill and Deborah M. Sinnreich-Levi (Teaneck, N.J.: Fairleigh Dickinson University Press, 2000), 67–87.

[65] Strohm, *Social Chaucer*, 52.

[66] See Stephanie Gibbs Kamath and Rita Copeland, "Medieval Secular Allegory: French and English," in *The Cambridge Companion to Allegory*, ed. Rita Copeland and Peter T. Struck (Cambridge: Cambridge University Press, 2010), 136–147; and J. A. Burrow, "The Poet as Petitioner," in his *Essays on Medieval Literature* (Oxford: Clarendon Press, 1984), 161–76.

nous ad fait" (for the good, and so on, that our good friend Geoffrey Chaucer has done for us).⁶⁷ The exact service Chaucer performed isn't specified, though Robertson argues it may well have been the presentation of *The Book of the Duchess*.⁶⁸ Although the tomb had not been fully finished in 1374, an altar had already been erected next to it. It may be more than just coincidence that Gaunt ordered six cartloads of alabaster for an "ymage" for the tomb in June of that year, the same month he made his life annuity to Chaucer. Although surviving records show Gaunt contracting for memorial services from 1370, he himself may have been present at the September 12 memorial for the first time in 1374.⁶⁹ Records show expenditures of £45 for the memorial that year, the largest amount on record.⁷⁰ In other words, 1374 marks several significant gestures of commemoration from Gaunt to Blanche as well as his first payment to Chaucer for services rendered. Read this way, we might surmise that what the bed buys is an annuity for Chaucer. That is, the imaginary barter of elite household goods—luxury items appropriate for a duke's bedroom—for sleep, a condition necessary for poetic creation, may be a wry aside to Gaunt's patronal relationship with the poet.

And perhaps the poem's memorial work also doubled as a bid by Gaunt for public rehabilitation of his reputation. Michael Foster, who also suggests a later dating, has recently argued that the poem needs to be considered in the context of Gaunt's relationship not just with Blanche but also with Chaucer; Chaucer's wife Philippa; and Chaucer's sister-in-law Katherine, Gaunt's mistress from shortly after Blanche's death. Chaucer's relationship with Gaunt, through the marital connection, dated from approximately 1371, or three years following Blanche's death in 1368.⁷¹ The poem, Foster proposes, was a bid for patronage at a time when Gaunt faced public hostility for his military failures and for his Castilian marriage to Constance in 1371. In picturing Gaunt as the grieving widower of the *Duchess*, Chaucer's poem was

---

⁶⁷ Martin M. Crow and Clair C. Olson, eds., *Chaucer Life Records* (Oxford: Clarendon Press, 1966), 271.

⁶⁸ Robertson, "Historical Setting," 178, 173; Robertson also calls the poem "a literary counterpart of Henry Yevele's alabaster tomb" (171). Based on contracts and payments to artisans, Goodman, *John of Gaunt*, 257–58, gives dates of the tomb's construction and elaboration over the next six years.

⁶⁹ N. B. Lewis, "The Anniversary Service for Blanche, Duchess of Lancaster, 12th September 1374," *BJRL* 21 (1937): 176–92 (182).

⁷⁰ Records for the anniversary service begin in 1371 and end in 1394; see ibid., 178.

⁷¹ Foster, "On Dating the *Duchess*," 188.

a strategic work of political theater, a patronal poem aimed toward public rehabilitation of Gaunt's reputation.[72] In the context of public animus against Gaunt, I might add, the duke's energetic tomb building and commission of a poetic memorial for his deceased and publicly venerated first wife could be understood as gestures of both atonement and public appeasement.

Although the tomb itself was destroyed when Saint Paul's burned, a Wenceslas Hollar engraving in antiquarian William Dugdale's 1658 *History of St. Paul's* (Fig. 1) indicates it fully merited the praise of contemporary viewers such as the Monk of Saint-Denys, who called it "in sepultura incomparabili."[73] The tomb was partly the work of Henry Yevele, master mason of some of the most important late Gothic commissions in London, including the 1362 nave of Westminster Abbey. Indeed, the tomb can be seen as one more kind of bed, whose white alabaster effigies, supporting stone pillows, and perpendicular spires may themselves offer a stone housing for the poem's play with whiteness. Or for white and black. For the 1374 solemn high mass, Blanche's tomb was draped with black cloths brought over from Gaunt's palace, the Savoy. The practice of draping the church in black appears to have been customary at Saint Paul's for distinguished memorials and funerals.[74] House, bed, tomb, and castle are all metamorphic, even interchangeable substances that tie the elegy to English places, people, and affairs: to Blanche the duchess, to the white walls of Richmond Castle that the narrator sees at the end of Chaucer's poem, and even to her white alabaster tomb in Saint Paul's.

IV

Where *The Book of the Duchess* also returns us, at the end, is to a bedroom as a scene of imagination, an amalgam between public audience hall and place for private retreat. The narrator wakes up with Ovid in his hand and, of course, a story to write. Felicity Riddy has coined the term "bourgeois domesticity" or "burgessry" to describe a changing ideology, marked by "a subtle vocabulary of privacy and intimacy," of urban

---

[72] Ibid., 191. For Gaunt's unpopularity see Armitage-Smith, *John of Gaunt*, 124; see also David K. Coley, "'Withyn a temple ymad of glas': Glazing, Glossing, and Patronage in Chaucer's *House of Fame*," *ChauR* 45, no. 1 (2010): 58–84 (75).

[73] *Chronique du religieux de Saint-Denys*, ed. M. L. Bellaguet, Vol. 1 (Paris, 1839–40), 448–49, in Goodman, *John of Gaunt*, 361, 256.

[74] Lewis, "Anniversary Service," 179.

THE PLACE OF THE BEDCHAMBER IN *BOOK OF THE DUCHESS*

Fig. 1. Tomb of Blanche of Lancaster and John of Gaunt in Old Saint Paul's Cathedral. Wenceslas Hollar engraving from William Dugdale, *The History of St. Paul's Cathedral in London* (1658; London: George James, 1716). By kind permission of the Thomas Fisher Rare Book Library, University of Toronto.

households in late fourteenth-century England.[75] Houses of merchants and prosperous craftspeople—freemen such as Chaucer's five guildsmen, who were allowed to buy and sell retail, trade in other towns, and train apprentices—were now larger, comprising four or five rooms, as opposed to single-room houses referred to as *cotagium* or *shopa*.[76] Medieval houses, it has often been remarked, were notable for their lack of privacy, with many people crowded into a few sparsely furnished rooms. "Burgeis" houses, with multiple rooms as well as separate spaces for living and labor, allowed for clearer distinctions between spaces dedicated for work (brewhouses, shops, and workshops) and those for living (halls, chambers, pantries, butteries).[77] As Langland notes, these changes in home design and use had consequences for social life. Both parlors and chambers feature in Dame Study's complaint in *Piers Plowman* about the abandonment of the great hall by the gentry, who now choose to dine instead in private parlors or chambers:

> Elenge is the halle, ech day in the wike
> Ther the lord ne the lady liketh noght to sitte.
> Now hath ech riche a rule—to eten by hymselve
> In a pryvee parlour for povre mennes sake,
> Or in a chambre with a chymenee, and leve the chief halle
> That was maad for meles, men to eten inne.[78]

This apparent elegy for the old order, when everyone in the household dined together in one room, bespeaks a changing practice; how we live

---

[75] Felicity Riddy, "'Burgeis' Domesticity in Late Medieval England," in Kowalewski and Goldbert, *Medieval Domesticity*, 14–36 (17). For bedrooms and privacy see Glenn Burger, "In the Merchant's Bedchamber," in *Thresholds of Medieval Visual Culture: Liminal Spaces*, ed. Elina Gertsman and Jill Stevenson (Woodbridge and Rochester, N.Y.: Boydell, 2012), 239–59.

[76] Ibid., 9, 22.

[77] Ibid., 25.

[78] William Langland, *The Vision of Piers Plowman: A Critical Edition of the B-Text*, ed. A. V. C. Schmidt, 2nd ed. (London: Everyman, 1995), X.96–101. Also noted by John Schofield, *Medieval London Houses* (New Haven: Yale University Press, 1994), 66, with H. M. Smyser, "The Domestic Background of *Troilus and Criseyde*," *Speculum* 31 (1956): 297–315; and D. Vance Smith, "The Silence of Langland's Study: Matter, Invisibility, Instruction," in *Answerable Style: The Idea of the Literary in Medieval England*, ed. Frank Grady and Andrew Galloway (Columbus: Ohio State University Press, 2013), 263–83 (272, 280). On the division of larger spaces into smaller rooms see also Schofield, *Medieval London Houses*, 115. Among the Benedictines there was also concern that monks were retreating from public dining halls to eat alone; see Diana Webb, *Privacy and Solitude in the Middle Ages* (London and New York: Hambledon, 2007), 205.

now, the "rule" by which the rich now organize their mealtimes, Dame Study says, has changed, and not for the good. Langland's primary concern with the proliferation of parlors and chambers is not nostalgia for the old ways, however, but to do with the negative effects of new dining practices on social relations within the household. When the household elite retreat to dine in their private parlor or cozy chimneyed chamber, it comes with a cost to a blended community. As the lord and lady retreat to dine alone, the household's poor—presumably the servants—then have to dine alone as well.

Few of Langland's qualms are present, though, in the narrator's claim of the bedroom in *The Book of the Duchess* as a place for reading and imagining. Indeed, the exuberant bed barter that opens the *Duchess*, and the return at the end to the narrator in bed with his book, may offer a glimpse of a novel household commodity: the private room as a place where one can practice vernacular composition. Writing in bed is not itself new; as Mary Carruthers notes, lying prostrate—lying in bed—is the *locus classicus* for writing and remembering.[79] Quintilian describes someone trying to write "[lying] back with eyes turned to the ceiling, trying to fire [his] imagination by muttering ... in the hope that something will present itself."[80] The trope persists through late Antiquity and the Middle Ages—and even today the image of the writer composing in bed, with paper or laptop, does not surprise: Edith Wharton famously wrote in bed. When Boethius sees Lady Philosophy towering over him, he is in his bed composing. In the French *dits*, a bedroom is conventionally the point of departure for imagination or an eavesdropping excursion. When the narrator in the *Fonteinne* rises from bed to document the complaint of the lover he's hearing outside his window, he takes up his ivory-inscribed "escriptoire," or writing desk (1229–31). In Froissart's *Paradys d'amours*, the narrator touches his bed when he awakens from his dream—with the bed as literal touchstone for his dream-inspired writing (1689) where he learns the art and practice of singing "balade et rondiel / et virelay" (1713–14).[81] For Froissart, beds and bedrooms were also real places for public presentation of his writing; as he recounts for 1395, when he presented Richard II with a volume of his poems, he left the book on the king's bed. The king, pleased

---

[79] Carruthers, "Mystery of the Bed Chamber," 73.
[80] Ibid., 75.
[81] As noted in Phillips and Havely, *Chaucer's Dream Poetry*, 107n. Froissart, *Le paradis d'amour*, ed. Dembowski.

with the gift, handed it to a chamber knight to take to his private bedroom ("chambre de retraite").[82]

V

Writing about a table belonging to Edmund Husserl, Sara Ahmed likens her desire to peer into the "domesticity of his world" as a wish "to imagine philosophy as beginning here, with the pen and the paper, and with the body of the philosopher, who writes insofar as he is 'at home' and insofar as home provides a space in which he does his work."[83] I too admit to the pleasures of looking into spaces of others—at the diorama, the miniature, the garden, living rooms through windows at night. My curiosity about the lived spaces of others includes a hope that peering in will give me insight, through the tools, furniture, design, or beauty, into the mind or even soul of their occupants. Space, Ahmed writes, is a kind of second skin, and the places of writing—the writer's bed or desk—are extensions of the body that provide orientations from which the writer observes the real or imagined world. Ahmed's approach to phenomenological places is an act of grounding, an "ethno-phenomenology" that supplements the generalized spatial poetics of Gaston Bachelard with an "ethnography of things." She cites Ann Banfield: "Tables and chairs, things nearest to hand for the sedentary philosopher, who comes to occupy chairs of philosophy, are the furniture of 'that room of one's own' from which the real world is observed."[84] And imagined, known, and recorded. To visit Emily Dickinson's bedroom on a tour of her house in Amherst is to glimpse her orientation, the space from which she looked out.[85] Seeing the real

---

[82] Andrew Taylor, "Into His Secret Chamber: Reading and Privacy in Late Medieval England," in *The Practice and Representation of Reading in England*, ed. James Raven, Helen Small, and Naomi Tadmor (Cambridge: Cambridge University Press, 1996), 41–61 (41).

[83] Ahmed, *Queer Phenomenology*, 29.

[84] Ibid., 3; Ann Banfield, *The Phantom Table*: *Woolf, Fry, Russell, and the Epistemology of Modernism* (Cambridge: Cambridge University Press, 2000), 66.

[85] Or, as Diana Fuss sees it, a domestic ethnography that graphs the architectural coordinates of writers' mental landscapes—a poetics of interiority. In *The Sense of an Interior* Fuss maps the houses of Emily Dickinson, Sigmund Freud, Marcel Proust, and Helen Keller as keys to those writers' figurations of mental life. Combining close reading with site-specific architectural history, Fuss's interest lies in the "theater of composition" as a "place animated by the artifacts, mementoes, machines, books, and furniture that frame any intellectual labor." To know the design, location in the house, and furnishings of a writer's workplace is to "attempt to encounter these writers where they

thing, the bed or the desk, holds out a promise of insight into the scene of writing—even if we might find ourselves disappointed, when we see it, by the recalcitrance of furniture to give up any real secrets.

The Book of the Duchess makes the bed, furniture of desire for the insomniac poet, visible as an object that links writing to the household economy and to newly available bourgeois house design. The bed also gives material weight to the possibility that writing in English can proceed not from a French but from an English bedroom, and from patronage enacted through exchanges of goods, marked through their continental sourcing, on home turf. In this sense it offers what Ahmed might describe as a reorientation or even a disorientation. Although bedchamber reading and dream composition in the *Duchess* may follow conventions from the French *dits*, Chaucer transforms them with a close-up view on composition's locally available decorative objects. As this poem with its allusions to people and places invites readers into the bedroom, it also makes visible the networks linking patronage and poetic production to castles, houses, and private chambers. In particular the poem underscores the potent work of material objects in grounding poetry in place and in language. In her recent book, *The Island Garden*, Lynn Staley writes of the ways fourteenth-century English writers created a language of place for England, often using metaphors of enclosure that reference England's special status as an island nation.[86] *The Book of the Duchess* may be understood as participating in this process, I've argued in this essay, through a locational poetics not of gardens or islands but of the home, conveyed through ekphrastic enumeration, topographic language play, and a bilingual textile geography. Furnished with deluxe objects that are freighted with desire and tagged with exchange values, the bedroom offers an ethnography of things that reorients the poem's work of elegy and memory through politics, language, and place. The concluding wordplay identifies where that place is. The poem marks a milestone in English literature through its language; and through named objects tied to the body and to the act of writing, it sets the act of composition on English ground.

---

live, to meet them, to whatever extent possible, on their own ground and on their own terms." Diana Fuss, *The Sense of an Interior: Four Writers and the Rooms that Shaped Them* (New York and London: Routledge, 2004), 1, 5.

[86] Lynn Staley, *The Island Garden: England's Language of Nation from Gildas to Marvell* (Notre Dame: University of Notre Dame Press, 2012).

Beaten for a Book: Domestic and Pedagogic Violence in *The Wife of Bath's Prologue*

Ben Parsons
University of Leicester

WHILE EDUCATION IS A RECURRENT THEME across Chaucer's work, *The Wife of Bath's Prologue* contains perhaps his fullest engagement with the subject.[1] His portrayal of Alisoun's fifth husband Jankyn not only provides an important focus for pedagogic concerns, but develops into a complex interrogation of the larger implications of study. Jankyn himself is a virtual personification of formal instruction: as well as being characterized as "clerk of Oxenford" from the moment he appears in the text (III.527), his emphatic youthfulness at "twenty wynter oold" suggests he has little knowledge beyond the classroom (III.600), painting him as "all 'auctoritee' and no 'experience.'"[2] But what complicates Chaucer's portrayal in particular is the way that learning infuses Jankyn's behavior as a husband. Not only does the *Prologue* conflate wedlock with instruction at several points, most tellingly in Alisoun's boast "five husbands scoleiying am I," but Jankyn seems to call on the schoolroom to sustain dominance over the Wife (III.45f.). His interactions with Alisoun invariably position him as teacher and her as pupil: his harangues from the book of "wykked wyves" are specifically intended to "teche" her, and he is evidently responsible for the detailed knowledge of classical and patristic material she displays

---

An early version of this paper was given at the International Medieval Congress, University of Leeds, July 10, 2014. The author would like to thank the AHRC for funding the research on which the paper is based.
[1] Nicholas Orme, "Chaucer and Education," *ChauR* 16 (1981): 38–59 (55–56).
[2] Citations from Chaucer refer to *The Riverside Chaucer*, 3rd ed., gen. ed. Larry D. Benson (Boston: Houghton Mifflin, 1987). Mary Carruthers, "The Wife of Bath and the Painting of Lions," *PMLA* 94 (1979): 209–22 (219).

(III.642).³ Even the term Chaucer uses to denote supremacy in the household recalls education. Alisoun's desired "maistrie" evokes both *magister* and the specialist learning of clerks: hence it is used in *The Seven Sages of Rome* (c. 1275) to describe "twei clerkes" who have "maistri on honde," and in *Kyng Alisaunder* (c. 1300) to refer to "clerkes wel ylerede . . . in her maistre."⁴ Schooling is therefore at the center of Jankyn's marriage, both cementing and conceptualizing his authority in the household.

Much of this is of course widely recognized in existing criticism, as Jankyn's reliance on pedagogy has been frequently discussed.⁵ However, less often appreciated is the way that Jankyn's clerkliness affects the most active manifestation of his power, his use of violence. In fact, most interpretations of his beating tend to turn away from education altogether, instead regarding aggression as a product of marital norms. Elisabeth Biebel, for instance, argues that he is driven to beat Alisoun as part of his role as "breadwinner" and "head of household," while Angela Jane Weisl situates the *Prologue* within a "history of normalized violence against women" that sees "battery" as "a kind of duty for leaders of households."⁶ Eve Salisbury likewise treats Jankyn's behavior as an extension of "accepted disciplinary practices reflecting 'natural' social relations," and even Sara Butler's careful analysis sets his behavior against a wider acceptance of "physical violence as a remedy" for "the dangers of giving a wife too free a rein."⁷ Such a line of reasoning therefore swerves away from the classroom in which Jankyn grounds his

---

³ W. A. Davenport, "*Fabliau*, Confession, Satire," in *Chaucer*, ed. Corinne Saunders (Oxford: Basil Blackwell, 2001), 250–69 (265); Stephen A. Barney, "Chaucer's Lists," in *The Wisdom of Poetry: Essays in Early English Literature in Honor of Morton W. Bloomfield*, ed. Larry D. Benson and Siegfried Wenzel (Kalamazoo: Medieval Institute Publications, 1982), 189–223.

⁴ *The Seven Sages of Rome*, ed. Karl Brunner, EETS o.s. 191 (London: Oxford University Press, 1933), 90, lines 2021–22; *Kyng Alisaunder*, ed. G. V. Smithers, 2 vols., EETS o.s. 227, 237 (London: Oxford University Press, 1952–57), 1:5, lines 41–43.

⁵ Carolyn Dinshaw, *Chaucer's Sexual Poetics* (Madison: University of Wisconsin Press, 1989), 113–31; Marilynn Desmond, *Ovid's Art and the Wife of Bath: The Ethics of Eroticized Violence* (Ithaca, N.Y.: Cornell University Press, 2006), 116–43.

⁶ Angela Jane Weisl, "Quiting Eve: Violence against Women in the *Canterbury Tales*," in *Violence against Women in Medieval Texts*, ed. Anna Roberts (Gainesville: University Press of Florida, 1998), 115–36 (116–17); Elizabeth M. Biebel, "A Wife, a Batterer, a Rapist: Representations of 'Masculinity' in *The Wife of Bath's Prologue* and *Tale*," in *Masculinities in Chaucer: Approaches to Maleness in the "Canterbury Tales" and "Troilus and Criseyde*," ed. Peter G. Beidler (Woodbridge: D. S. Brewer, 1998), 63–76 (71).

⁷ Eve Salisbury, "Chaucer's Wife, the Law and Middle English Breton Lays," in *Domestic Violence in Medieval Texts*, ed. Eve Salisbury, Georgiana Donavin, and Merrall Llewelyn Price (Gainesville: University Press of Florida, 2002), 71–93 (74); Sara M.

authority, looking to a different discourse altogether to make sense of his assaults. For all four commentators, Jankyn's use of discipline is treated in purely matrimonial terms, as a direct outgrowth of the "violence that accompanies medieval marriage," arising out of the implicit rules and hierarchies of the medieval home.[8] In short, "Jankyn oure clerk" tends to be eclipsed by "Jankyn . . . oure sire" in most discussions of his beating (III.595, 713).

Nevertheless, these conclusions only succeed in giving a partial account of the forms violence assumes in the text. As this essay will argue, Jankyn's aggression is more complex in its underlying imperatives than such judgments can allow. Just as the medieval classroom penetrates the space of the household via Jankyn, so it penetrates his use of corporal discipline against the Wife. Pedagogy in fact proves to be a vital component of the beating he inflicts on Alisoun, coloring its execution, guiding the forms that it takes, and conditioning the type of authority he is able to claim over her. It is not the only mode of violence the text evokes: marital discourse is clearly at work in the *Prologue*, as the domestic setting of the piece and its focus on "wo that is in mariage" obviously place Jankyn's actions in such a framework (III.3). Yet insisting on this discourse alone not only neglects a significant range of meanings in his violence, but also fails to identify an important conflict within the text, overlooking a tension at work in his beating. As a consequence, it is only by recognizing the points at which pedagogy is evoked, and the points at which it generates friction with other disciplinary practices, that Chaucer's understanding of physical correction can be fully drawn out.

"Nat of hym corrected": Pedagogic Violence and Its Problems

Chaucer aligns Jankyn's violence with the schoolroom at a number of levels. Most obvious is the simple fact that his aggression is part and parcel of his general identity. Alisoun describes it as both habitual and idiosyncratic to him: she depicts regular beating "on every bon" and "on my ribbes al by rewe" rather than isolated attacks, and suggests

---

Butler, *The Language of Abuse: Marital Violence in Later Medieval England* (Leiden: Brill, 2007), 228, 254. See also John Davenant, "Chaucer's View of the Proper Treatment of Women," *Maledicta* 5 (1981): 153–61.

[8] Mikee C. Delony, "Weaving the Sermon: The Wife of Bath's Preaching Body in the *Canterbury Tales*," in *Sex, Gender, and Christianity*, ed. Priscilla Pope-Levison and John R. Levison (Eugene: Cascade Books, 2012), 33–57 (52).

that he is the only man to treat her in this way, being "mooste shrewe" of all her spouses (III.511, 505–6). Given the lack of similar mistreatment by her previous husbands, and given Jankyn's emphatic status as "clerk of Oxenford," there is already a hint here that violence stems more from the world of learning Jankyn represents than from matrimony and its structures. At a lexical level too Jankyn's violence often recalls the classroom. The same pattern of terms that identifies household authority with "maistrie" and marriage itself as "scoleiyng" also yokes together study and beating. This process is perhaps most visible in the loaded term "glose," which is treated as a complement to Jankyn's blows: Alisoun presents both as part of a single pincer-movement manipulating her, reflecting that "so wel koude he me glose . . . thogh he hadde me bete . . . he koude wynne agayn my love" (III.509–12). As Peggy Knapp's careful unpicking of these lines has shown, the "glosing" that accompanies Jankyn's violence is as academic as it is rhetorical, encompassing the sense of "interpretive commentary" as well as "beguile and cajole."[9] A similar case is presented by "correct," which Alisoun uses when describing her defiance of his regime: as she says, "I sette noght an hawe / Of his proverbs . . . Ne I wolde nat of hym corrected be" (III.659–61). The Middle English "correcten" carries strong connotations of literacy, as it is often used to describe accuracy of transcription or translation: hence Caxton in *The Four Sons of Aymon* (c. 1489) asks readers "that vnderstande the cronycle" to "correcte & amende there as they shall fynde faute," while the General Prologue of the Wycliffite Bible declares "Latyn biblis han more nede to be corrected . . . than hath the English bible late translatid."[10] But the term also has connections to beating as well as writing. Under the influence of Ephesians 6:4, which advises that fathers educate their sons "in disciplina et correptione," "correccion" also comes to signify the physical reprimand of children. Thus Henry Watson asks that "chyldren in theyr florysshynge youthe" receive "veretably swete correccyon and dyscyplyne," while Lydgate's version of the *Pèlerinage de vie humaine* directs Pylgrym to treat his body as though he were "a mayster" and to "bete, / And

---

[9] Peggy Knapp, *Chaucer and the Social Contest* (London: Routledge, 1990), 115–16. See also Dinshaw, *Chaucer's Sexual Poetics*, 120–26.

[10] William Caxton, *The Foure Sonnes of Aymon*, ed. Octavia Richardson, 2 vols., EETS e.s. 64, 65 (London: Kegan Paul, Trench, Trübner, 1884–85), 1:4; *The Holy Bible, Containing the Old and New Testaments*, ed. Josiah Forshall and Frederic Madden (Oxford: Oxford University Press, 1850), 58.

correcte" it.[11] When Chaucer himself uses "correcten," the term often drifts between these literary and punitive senses. On the one hand, he complains to Adam Scriveyn that he must regularly "correcte" his sloppy work; on the other, he depicts a schoolmaster in *The Parson's Tale* threatening to "bete" a pupil "for thy correccioun" (X.671). There is even some suggestion that "debaat," Alisoun's final euphemism for her running battle with Jankyn, might also recall formal classroom disputation (III.822). At least Gower may be using it in this sense when he refers to pedantic clerks staging a "gret debat" in which "this clerk seith yee, that other nay, / And thus thei dryve forth the day."[12] The vocabulary surrounding Jankyn's violence mirrors the schoolmasterly posture he assumes in his household, reflecting his campaign to "teche" the Wife "of olde Romayn geestes" (III.642).

However, perhaps more striking is the way in which Chaucer evokes the established imagery of schooling through Jankyn. The two main activities Jankyn is shown to perform, reading and beating, have clear resonances with the standard iconography of instruction. The two objects invariably linked with tuition in medieval visual culture are the book and the ferula or birch, no doubt representing the two alternatives of careful study and swift retribution.[13] The *locus classicus* of these images is probably the south portal of Chartres Cathedral, with its complex sequence of carvings depicting the liberal arts and the ancient authorities associated with them. Executed in around 1150 under the direction of Thierry of Chartres, this shows Grammatica standing over two students, one diligent and the other inattentive, with an open book in her left hand and an upright birch in her right.[14] While this symbolism may owe something to Martianus Capella's *De nuptiis* (c. 420), which gives Grammatica a "teres quoddam ex compactis annexionibus ferculum" (smooth chest built of interlocking parts) that contains several allegorical implements, the portal's choice of equipment sets the pace for later

---

[11] Henry Watson, *The Shyppe of Fooles* (London: Wynkyn de Worde, 1509) (*STC*, 517), fol. 9v; John Lydgate, *The Pilgrimage of the Life of Man*, ed. F. J. Furnivall and Katharine B. Locock, 3 vols., EETS e.s. 77, 83, 92 (London: Kegan Paul, Trench, Trübner, 1899–1904), 2:254, lines 9208–9.

[12] John Gower, *Confessio Amantis*, in *Complete Works of John Gower*, ed. G. C. Macauley, 4 vols. (Oxford: Clarendon Press, 1899–1902), 1:15, Prol.372–74.

[13] Suzanne Reynolds, *Medieval Reading: Grammar, Rhetoric, and the Classical Text* (Cambridge: Cambridge University Press, 1996), 18.

[14] Adolf Katzenellenbogen, *The Sculptural Programs of Chartres Cathedral: Christ, Mary, Ecclesia* (Baltimore: Johns Hopkins University Press, 1959), 20–25.

depictions.¹⁵ The same pairing occurs in the illustrations for Herrad of Landsberg's *Hortus deliciarum* (c. 1180), the ceiling of the west nave in Peterborough Cathedral (c. 1220), and the Palazzo Trinci frescoes at Foligno (c. 1420), among other sources.¹⁶ In fact, by the time that Chaucer was writing, the same pair of symbols had crossed from allegory to actuality, as the book and birch collectively stand as the teacher's "badge of office."¹⁷ There are portrayals of masters bearing these two instruments in several manuscript illustrations, including those accompanying the copy of the *Roman d'Alexandre* in MS Bodley 264 (c. 1330) and James le Palmer's *Omne bonum* in MS Royal 6 E.VII (c. 1370).¹⁸ The same symbolism finds its way on to the frontispieces of early printed schoolbooks: woodcuts of teachers carrying books and birches introduce Synthen's *Composita verborum* (1485), Niger's *Ars epistolam* (1477), Rodericus's *Speculum humane vite* (1488), and Hilarius's *Exposicio himnorum* (1496).¹⁹ Even the official seals of schools use the same iconography, such as those founded at Höxter in 1365 and Macclesfield in 1502.²⁰ By dividing Jankyn's activity between beating and reading "gladly, nyght and day" (III.669), Chaucer aligns him decisively with these conventions, importing his main activities within the household from the classroom and its attendant imagery.

---

¹⁵ *Martianus Capella*, ed. James Willis, Bibliothecae Teubnerianae (Berlin: De Gruyter, 1983), 60. See Adolf Katzenellenbogen, "The Representation of the Seven Liberal Arts," in *Twelfth Century Europe and the Foundations of Modern Society*, ed. Marshall Clagett, Gaines Post, and Robert Reynolds (Madison: University of Wisconsin Press, 1961), 39–55; Rudolf Wittkower, "'Grammatica': From Martianus Capella to Hogarth," *Journal of the Warburg and Courtauld Institutes* 2 (1938): 82–84; John A. Alford, "The Grammatical Metaphor: A Survey of Its Use in the Middle Ages," *Speculum* 57 (1982): 728–60.

¹⁶ Herrad of Hohenburg, *Hortus deliciarum*, ed. Rosalie Green, T. Julian Brown, and Kenneth Levy, 2 vols., Studies of the Warburg Institute 36 (Leiden: Brill, 1979), 2:104; C. J. P. Cave and Tancred Borenius, "The Painted Ceiling in the Nave of Peterborough Cathedral," *Archaeologia* 87 (1938): 297–309; Laura Laureati and Lorenza Mochi Onori, *Gentile da Fabriano and the Other Renaissance* (Milan: Electra, 2006), 118.

¹⁷ Nicholas Orme, *Medieval Schools: From Roman Britain to Renaissance England* (New Haven: Yale University Press, 2006), 144.

¹⁸ Mark Cruse, *Illuminating the "Roman d'Alexandre": Oxford, Bodleian Library, MS Bodley 264; Manuscript as Monument* (Cambridge: D. S. Brewer, 2011), 186–87; Lucy Freeman Sandler, *Omne bonum: Fourteenth-Century Encyclopedia of Universal Knowledge*, 2 vols., Studies in Medieval and Early Renaissance Art History 18 (London: Miller, 1996), 2:80.

¹⁹ These and other images are reproduced in Wilhelm Ludwig Schreiber, *Die deutschen "Accipies" und Magister cum Discipulis-Holzschnitte als Hilfsmittel zur Inkunabel-Bestimmung* (Strasburg: J. H. E. Heitz, 1908).

²⁰ Evamaria Engel and Frank-Dietrich Jacob, *Städtisches Leben im Mittelalter: Schriftquellen und Bildzeugnisse* (Cologne: Böhlau Verlag, 2006), 105; Nicholas Carlisle, *The Concise Description of the Endowed Grammar Schools in England*, 2 vols. (London: Baldwin, Cradock, and Joy, 1818), 1:117.

Jankyn's use of punishment is therefore redolent of the schoolroom, much like his conduct as a whole. His violence shares in the general "associations of teaching and preaching" that come from his position as "the man with the book," engaged in an "intellectual force-feeding" of the Wife.[21] What Chaucer presents through him, in other words, is a portrait of a man trying to impose his accustomed power structures on to a space outside their usual compass. Jankyn functions as a conduit through which the discipline of the classroom enters into the space of the household. This might be seen as a joke on the part of Chaucer, as the inexperienced clerk attempts to deploy the rules of the school in a wholly inappropriate context: indeed, Jankyn may be designed to recall the comic stereotype of the bad-tempered schoolmaster, a stock figure already crystallizing in the late Middle Ages, as "Sire Grumbald the grammier" in *Mum and the Sothsegger* (c. 1409) and "mastyr grett Morell" in the *Digby Magdalen* (c. 1490) can attest.[22] Jankyn's attempts to govern his household as though it is a classroom might be a further level at which Chaucer ridicules his misguided performance as a husband.[23] But the key point here is that his violence becomes the site of a crucial discontinuity in the text. The two strands of meaning at work in his beating, the domestic and the pedagogic, are not merely comically incongruous but are in direct conflict with one another. Jankyn is in effect trying to employ one set of disciplinary practices in the territory of another, and this mismatch ultimately and fatally compromises his position.

These problems become most visible at the end of the *Prologue*, in the aftermath of Alisoun's final beating. At this point it becomes clear that Jankyn's violence cannot achieve domestic "maistrie," as it signally fails to sustain his authority as a husband. There are of course grounds for seeing this final fight purely as an extension of his dominance and a "capitulation" on the part of the Wife.[24] Her final admission, "I was to

---

[21] Priscilla Martin, *Chaucer's Women: Nuns, Wives and Amazons* (Iowa City: University of Iowa Press, 1990), 6–7.

[22] *Mum and the Sothsegger*, ed. Mabel Day and Robert Steele, EETS o.s. 199 (London: Oxford University Press, 1936), 37, line 330; *Mary Magdalen; Digby Mysteries*, ed. Frederick Furnivall, Shakespeare Society Series 8 (London: Trübner, 1882), 99, line 1157.

[23] Kathryn Jacobs, *Marriage Contracts from Chaucer to the Renaissance Stage* (Gainesville: University Press of Florida, 2001), 42–43.

[24] Sheila Delany, "Sexual Economics, Chaucer's Wife of Bath and *The Book of Margery Kempe*," in *Feminist Readings in Middle English Literature: The Wife of Bath and All Her Sect*, ed. Ruth Evans and Lesley Johnson (London: Routledge, 1994), 78–87 (85); Alcuin Blamires, *The Canterbury Tales* (Atlantic Highlands: Humanities Press International, 1987), 33.

hym as kynde / As any wyf from Denmark unto Ynde" (III.823–24), has struck some readers as an abandonment of the resistant position staked out in the rest of the text, a moment in which her rebellion is "feebly extinguished" or she has "merely transferred her cell."[25] Nevertheless, the fact remains that Jankyn's own power is also rendered visibly less secure by this last "strook." In its wake, the bases on which masculine authority rests are methodically taken from him: he is compelled to relinquish economic authority, the "hous and lond" the Wife signed over to him at the point of wedlock (III.814); he loses discursive authority, as his arsenal of language and ability to deploy it are equally renounced, his book burned, and Alisoun given "governaunce . . . of his tong" (III.815); even his physical advantage dissipates, as he awards Alisoun power "of his hand," and ends the narrative in a posture of supplication, kneeling "faire adoun" over the stricken woman (III.803). Over and above these forfeitures, however, there is also a sense that Jankyn has lost any wider social sanction for his behavior. Any notional support he might possess from his wider community is effectively canceled at the moment of his aggression, a point highlighted by his craven response when he believes he has killed the Wife: "whan he saugh how stille that I lay, / He was agast and wolde han fled his way" (III.797–98). Evidently he fears retribution from his community rather than its approval, anticipating only expulsion from its bounds. In short, far from continuing to enjoy precedence through violence, Jankyn's standing is systematically demolished once he has carried out the assault.

What makes this slippage all the more significant is that these effects have not been brought about by any response to his aggression, but from the exercise of aggression itself. It is clearly the fact that Jankyn is "aghast at the effects of his own violence" that obliges him to make the wider concessions demanded of him, not resistance he has met from any external force.[26] Rather than amplifying or entrenching his authority as a husband, therefore, violence has rendered it forfeit, depriving his stance of its legitimacy: as a fifteenth-century reworking of the *Prologue* puts it, "on his cheke he ys chekmate."[27] Precisely why Jankyn's authority should collapse under its own weight has proven difficult to explain

---

[25] Stephen Knight, "Chaucer and the Sociology of Literature," *SAC* 2 (1980): 15–51 (34); Hope Phyllis Weissman, "Antifeminism and Chaucer's Characterization of Women," in *Geoffrey Chaucer: A Collection of Original Essays*, ed. George D. Economou (New York: McGraw-Hill, 1975), 93–110 (110).

[26] Jill Mann, *Feminizing Chaucer* (Cambridge: D. S. Brewer, 2002), 68.

[27] Roman Dyboski, ed., *Songs, Carols, and Other Miscellaneous Poems*, EETS e.s. 101 (London: Kegan Paul, Trench, Trübner, 1907), 110–11.

using the standard interpretation of his behavior. Readings that see his beatings as straightforward expressions of marital norms have often struggled to recognize this problem at all, preferring to see his violence as shoring up his position. For Biebel, for instance, while Jankyn is "a victim of his culture's construction of manliness" his violence is indeed "able to maintain power and control over his wife"; likewise for Weisl, his actions only buttress his authority, as the validity of his "abuse . . . goes primarily unquestioned" by the text.[28] Assuming that Jankyn's behavior arises directly from marital discourse, in other words, fails to acknowledge any drawbacks to his violence at all, let alone account for them.

However, recognizing the disparity between Jankyn's violence and the context in which it is deployed allows his failures to be understood more fully. Both of the discourses Jankyn recalls, pedagogy and matrimony, are of course bound up with the exercise of violence: his status as husband and his status as schoolmaster license him equally to use physical discipline against his wife-cum-pupil. Both therefore share a common foundation in castigation, using it to implement and support their hierarchies. Yet closer study reveals that the classroom and household only travel together so far before parting ways. The two discourses diverge sharply in their approaches to violence, configuring it in highly distinctive ways: each makes different demands of beating, places it in the service of differing needs, and surrounds it with specific limits and functions. By tracing out the contours of these departures, a range of valuable details come into view. Most immediately, these points of separation highlight why Jankyn is ultimately unsuccessful in using pedagogic violence within the household, why his chosen mode of violence should prove so literally misplaced. But at the same time they also allow larger questions to emerge, exposing the codes and constraints medieval culture used to render violence licit, and the procedures by which discipline was keyed to particular contexts. Ultimately, the complexities within Jankyn's violence shed clear light on the cultural uses of discipline in the fourteenth century, both as a whole and within the specific discourses Chaucer evokes.

"Myself have been the whippe": Punishment and Subjectivity

One of the clearest differences between the two discourses is the way in which they connect beating with agency. This is a concern at the center

---

[28] Biebel, "A Wife, a Batterer, a Rapist," 70–71; Weisl, "Quiting Eve," 117.

of both uses of violence. In the case of marital discipline, subjectivity is frequently evoked by texts portraying and discussing wife-beating, as the practice is usually presented as an antidote to the reckless voices of women: as Butler writes, aggressive measures are frequently justified as means of subduing "an overly vocal wife."[29] One tradition in which such a view can be observed, albeit in caricatured form, is the popular antifeminist lyric. General hostility to female speech is of course crucial to this group of texts as a whole. As a string of commentators has made clear, satirical verse routinely targets "women's tongues," blaming them for using language for seditious ends, for forming speech-communities "antipathetic to men," and even for destabilizing linguistic meaning itself.[30] Accordingly, when violence features in misogynous lyrics it is generally colored by this preoccupation, as the "countless wife-beating scenes" offered by the literature show a strong link between beating and silencing women.[31] A clear example of this pattern emerges in one of the many lyrics claiming to give access to a secret subculture of "gossipis," preserved in the commonplace book of Richard Hill.[32] In the piece, one of the assembled women recounts how pitilessly her husband thrashes her:

> For my husbond is so fell,
> He betith me lyke þe devill of hell,
> And þe more' I crye,
> Þe lesse mercy.[33]

The function of beating here is unambiguous. With its description of a husband's violence increasing in proportion to his wife's "crye," multiplying as her vocalization escalates, beating is clearly presented as a

---

[29] Butler, *Language of Abuse*, 254.

[30] See, among other sources, Henrietta Leyser, *Medieval Women: A Social History of Women in England 450–1500*, 2nd ed. (New York: St. Martin's Press, 1995), 152; Patricia Meyer Spacks, *Gossip* (New York: Knopf, 1985), 35; Sarah Kay, "Women's Body of Knowledge: Epistemology and Misogyny in the *Romance de la rose*," in *Framing Medieval Bodies*, ed. Sarah Kay and Miri Rubin (Manchester: Manchester University Press, 1994), 211–35 (219); R. Howard Bloch, "Medieval Misogyny," *Representations* 20 (1987): 1–24.

[31] Jody Enders, *The Medieval Theatre of Cruelty: Rhetoric, Memory, Violence* (Ithaca, N.Y.: Cornell University Press, 1999), 19.

[32] See Karma Lochrie, *Covert Operations: The Medieval Uses of Secrecy* (Philadelphia: University of Pennsylvania Press, 1999), 45–57; W. P. Hills, "Richard Hill of Hillend," *N&Q* 111 (1939): 452–56.

[33] Dyboski, *Songs, Carols, and Other Miscellaneous Poems*, 108.

means of blotting out woman's speech: the more the wife verbalizes her resistance to the husband, the more needful his beating becomes. Comparable sentiments can be found at least two centuries earlier, as a thirteenth-century lyric included in a preaching compendium also regards beating in the same terms. In this brief dialogue, a woman asks a *sortilege* or "wist y þe brom" how to end her husband's mistreatment of her, only to be told: "Þyf þy bonde ys ylle / Held þy tonge stille."[34] Again, cruelty serves to disable the woman's speech: the lyric's general message is that silence can fend off further abuse because it is the objective of that abuse. A further witness is the Towneley *Play of the Flood* (c. 1460). While this text is more self-conscious in its treatment of beating, it attributes much the same intent to its operation.[35] When Noah throws his first punch at his wife, his stated purpose is to keep her from speaking, as he vows "hold thi tong, ram-skyt / or I shall the still"; later on, he threatens to "make the still as stone, begynnar of blunder."[36] The understanding of chastisement running through these texts is much as Butler writes, with beating being seen as a reliable method of canceling women's troublesome speech.

The other side of the same coin is represented by a unique piece in Bodleian Library, MS Engl. Poet. e.1 (c. 1480). In the course of its wider complaints against women, this delivers the following pronouncement:

> An adamant stone it is not frangebyll
> With no thyng but with mylke of a gett;
> So a woman to refrayne it is not posybyll
> With wordes, except with a staffe þou hyr intrett.[37]

Just as the other verses conceive beating as an antidote to female speech, this quatrain sees it increasing women's receptivity to male language,

---

[34] Carleton Brown, ed., *English Lyrics of the XIIIth Century* (Oxford: Clarendon Press, 1932), 21. On the text and its variants, see Karin Boklund-Lagopoulou, "Popular Song and the Middle English Lyric," in *Medieval Oral Literature*, ed. Karl Reichl (Berlin: De Gruyter, 2011), 555–80 (565–66).

[35] Mary P. Freier, "Woman as Termagant in the Towneley Cycle," *EMSt* 2 (1985): 154–67; Martin Stevens, "Language as Theme in the Wakefield Plays," *Speculum* 52 (1977): 100–117; Martin Stevens, *Four Middle English Mystery Cycles: Textual, Contextual, and Critical Interpretations* (Princeton: Princeton University Press, 1987), 170–71.

[36] *Noah and the Ark*, lines 217, 406–7; *Towneley: The Towneley Plays*, ed. George England and Arthur Pollard, EETS e.s. 71 (London: Oxford University Press, 1897), 29.

[37] Richard Leighton Greene, ed., *Early English Carols*, 2nd ed. (Oxford: Clarendon Press, 1977), 241.

metaphorically "softening" wives in order that they might better absorb male instruction. Indeed, there is a careful alignment of beating with male speech throughout the stanza: in the final line, the use of the word "intrett" to describe the blows of a staff renders speech and beating not merely parallel but directly interchangeable, underscoring their movement toward a common end. This affinity also appears in similar pieces. It can be seen in one of the snippets of proverbial advice collected in the English version of *Salomon and Marcolphus* (c. 1492): this argues that "a rybaude she is lost / If she be nat well beate and tost."[38] Again, what is at stake is the receptivity of women to male language, as without violence women are simply "lost" in the natural unruliness and indecency of their voices. What runs through these verses, therefore, is a sense that beating is a means of disabling a woman's language on the one hand, and of rendering her more amenable to male language on the other. In their underlying logic, these texts might be compared to Elaine Scarry's observations on pain, as they seem to rest on the conviction that "physical pain does not simply resist language but actively destroys it," silencing the sufferer by replacing her words with inarticulate yells.[39] Beating as they see it reduces women to silent, passive objects that can be accommodated into masculine language. Ultimately, wife-beating is presented in the lyrics as an assault on female subjectivity itself, a means of transforming a potentially disobedient agent into a compliant object.

Of course, such statements cannot be taken entirely at their word, as they have passed through the exaggerating prism of comedy. Whatever expectations surrounded wives in the medieval period, they did not demand the absolute passivity and silence propounded by the lyrics. Wives were charged with authority over children and servants as a matter of course, and their role in the household asked them to implement discipline as well as receive it.[40] As a deportment text such as "How the Good Wiff tauȝte Hir Douȝtir" (c. 1430) makes clear, wives may have been required to be "fair of speche" and "trewe in worde," and even "meekely . . . answere" their husbands, but they should also "wijsli gouerne" their children and "þi meyne," and not hesitate to "take a

---

[38] *The sayinges or proverbes of King Salomon/ with the answers of Marcolphus* (London: Richard Pynson, n.d.) (*STC*, 22899), fol. 3.

[39] Elaine Scarry, *The Body in Pain: The Making and Unmaking of the World* (Oxford: Oxford University Press, 1985), 4.

[40] See Barbara Hanawalt, *The Wealth of Wives: Women, Law, and Economy in Late Medieval London* (Oxford: Oxford University Press, 2007), 116–34, 185–207.

smert rodde, & bete hem on a rowe" when necessary.[41] Indeed, the satiric discourse from which the lyrics arise often acknowledges this duty, as the stereotype of the bloodthirsty wife is as pervasive as the garrulous or unruly woman. A case in point is the widely read *Quinze ioyes de mariage* (c. 1380): in De Worde's version, this features a wife who takes a rod to her "lytell chylde that can not go but crepe" and "upon the buttockes . . . dooth it bete and dynge," purely for spite.[42] Chaucer himself provides another example of this commonplace, as Harry Bailly's wife Goodelief has a stated fondness for "grete clobbed staves" when overseeing the punishment of her "knaves" (VII.1897–98).[43]

The antifeminist lyrics cannot therefore be considered as straightforward witnesses to domestic norms. Not only did wives hold authority in the household rather than being objects to be defined and directed, but they were often called on to perform much the same formalized aggression as their husbands. Yet these texts also remind us that the agency of the wife was always provisional or contingent in nature. The position of wife was after all an intermediate one in the domestic hierarchy. Wives were equally subject and subaltern, and they usually functioned more as transmitters than possessors of power: even in "the Good Wiff" it is clear that the wife is only ever deputizing for her husband rather than acting entirely on her own initiative, as the duty to "lete not þi meyne goon ydil" comes into force when "þin husbonde be from hoome."[44] This is also the larger point that the *Quinze ioyes* raises, as its implicit claim is that wives need a male arbiter to keep their actions from giving way to sheer vindictiveness. The wife's authority was then clearly not autonomy, as she should ideally be a vehicle for her husband's will. The lyrics should be read in this light. Although they overstate the power of violence, as the outright cancellation of a wife's agency was not desirable in reality, their depiction of beating as a reduction of subjectivity seems to have at least a grain of truth. Despite the hyperbole, their characterization of beating suggests its importance in maintaining the secondary role demanded of wives, in reinforcing the cap on their

---

[41] *The Babees Book*, ed. Frederick J. Furnivall, EETS o.s. 32 (London: N. Trübner, 1869), 36–47.

[42] *The fyftene joyes of maryage* (London: Wynkyn de Worde, 1509), sig. Ei–Ei[v] (*STC*, 15258).

[43] See Laura Kendrick, *Chaucerian Play: Comedy and Control in the "Canterbury Tales"* (Berkeley: University of California Press, 1988), 111.

[44] *Babees Book*, 41.

subjectivity; although it might not neutralize a wife's authority altogether, beating would still ensure that she remained beneath the husband's command, counteracting any excessive willfulness. In short, the husband's violence is best seen as repressive in its overall purpose, keeping action and speech within designated limits, even if it cannot be quite as dictatorial as the lyrics suggest.

Returning to the *Prologue*, one thing immediately apparent is the outright lack of these results. Despite having been beaten extensively by her husband, the Wife is clearly not conceived as a dependent or second-tier subject: in fact a central maneuver of the *Prologue*, whether the reader is asked to endorse it or not, is to grant this female speaker the "male prerogative" of "public speech," as she is allowed to address the pilgrims in the same terms as men.[45] Furthermore, she hardly suffers the restriction on language that the lyrics associate with violence. She is after all the most voluble and uncontainable of Chaucer's speakers: indeed, as one early reader states, she seems to possess a "Tongue . . . like a River,/ Set it once going, it will go for ever."[46] What makes this all the more striking is that Alisoun's agency does not seem to develop out of her status as wife, and the limited subjectivity it allows. There is a remarkable absence in the *Prologue* of any figures over whom a wife's power might be exerted. Despite her appeal to the directive "wexe and multiplye," no reference is made to any children, and she is similarly silent on the issue of servants (III.28).[47] Chaucer therefore does not equip Alisoun with any of the bases of authority ordinarily granted to wives, suggesting that her agency is founded elsewhere.

Where it seems to be located is in the violence that Jankyn employs against her. The text makes clear that Jankyn has not merely been unsuccessful in containing the Wife's subjectivity, but has actively contributed to its development. His influence can be seen most directly in the traces his beating leaves on her body. As becomes explicit at the end of the Wife's account, the deafness that opens her portrait in *The General Prologue* is the result of Jankyn striking her: the fact that she was "somdel deef, and that was scathe" (I.446) is the outcome of the blow that

---

[45] Margaret Hallissy, *Clean Maids, True Wives, and Steadfast Widows: Chaucer's Women and Medieval Codes of Conduct* (Westport: Greenwood Press, 1993), 173.

[46] Richard Brathwait, *A Comment upon the Two Tales of our Ancient, Renovvned, and Ever Living Poet Sr Jeffray Chaucer, Knight* (London: W. Godbid, 1665) (*STC*, B4260), 140.

[47] See for instance E. Talbot Donaldson, "Designing a Camel; or, Generalizing the Middle Ages," *Tennessee Studies in Literature* 22 (1977): 1–16 (8); Bernard Huppé, *A Reading of the "Canterbury Tales"* (Albany: State University Press of New York, 1964), 110.

concludes the *Prologue*, as this final "strook" is responsible for making "myn ere wax al deef" (III.636). That the main result of this blow is the first detail reported about Alisoun, even preceding her "cloothmakyng" and number of "housbondes at chirche dore," is extremely telling (I.447, 460). Through being assigned this privileged place, it effectively becomes the platform on which Alisoun's entire performance is played out, serving to introduce the prolonged act of self-assertion that constitutes the *Prologue*. This point is further borne out by the role her deafness plays in her performance. Since at least the work of John Alford on Alisoun's use of rhetoric, the centrality of deafness to her peculiar voice has been clear.[48] More recently Edna Sayers has given a detailed account of the role her deafness plays in her speech, noting that it not only causes her "to pursue a monologue from which she cannot be budged," but becomes an inbuilt means of resisting masculine control and the discourses that support it: the fact she cannot hear what men say to or about her becomes a wholesale "resistance to antifeminism" in practice.[49] Deafness, by sealing her off from the language of others, is the wellspring of the eccentricity and resistance to prescriptive discourses Chaucer places at the center of her voice. In the course of the *Prologue*, therefore, violence becomes nothing short of an enabling rather than suppressive factor. The Wife's entire performance as a speaker is facilitated and informed by the violence she has undergone: this experience, and the physical stamp it has left on her, have led directly to the transference of Jankyn's "heigh maistrie" to her (IV.1172). The end result of the violence Alisoun undergoes is not subservience but subjectivity, as its effects do not limit her activity, but carve out a space from which her linguistic agency can be displayed in its own right.

That Jankyn's blows produce such results can be attributed to their strongly educational inflection. When medieval sources engage with the beating carried out in instruction, they often present it as a necessary step in the formation of adult subjectivity. This tendency is already in evidence among the monastic and cathedral schools of the early medieval period. Hence in a letter to his former community at York, Alcuin discusses punishment as an entry-point into maturity and the full level

---

[48] John A. Alford, "The Wife of Bath versus the Clerk of Oxford: What Their Rivalry Means," *ChauR* 21 (1986): 108–32 (110).

[49] Edna Edith Sayers, "Experience, Authority and the Mediation of Deafness: Chaucer's Wife of Bath," in *Disability in the Middle Ages: Reconsiderations and Reverberations*, ed. Joshua R. Eyler (Farnham: Ashgate, 2010), 81–104 (88–89).

of agency it entails, commending the monks for helping him transcend "lascivum pueritae tempus" (the frivolous time of childhood) and reach "perfectam viri . . . aetatem" (the perfect age of manhood) by means of their "paternae castigationis" (fatherly chastisement).[50] Sigebert of Gembloux presents discipline in similar terms in his *vita* of Saint Lambert of Maastricht, describing how his subject "fieri uir perfectus . . . sub ferula . . . magistri" (became a perfect man under the rod of the master).[51] More pointed still is another letter written by Everaclus of Liège to his former master Ratherius of Verona: for Everaclus, discipline becomes not only the key to manhood but a necessary admission into literate culture itself. As part of his tribute to the older man, Everaclus tells him that "Omnia nostra erunt in manu vestra, secundum quod animo vestro insederit, o dilecte Ratheri. Cuncta praevidete, disponite, constituite, et ut libuerit, in omnibus agite. Sub vestro pollice docto et artifice manum ferulae non erubescam subducere" (Everything of ours is in your hands, according to what your intellect decided, dear Ratherius. You have conducted all, foreseen, arranged, established, as it pleases you. Under your thumb, learned and skillful, I do not blush to flinch my hand from the rod).[52] Since Everaclus is in fact quoting Juvenal here, adapting lines from the first and seventh *Satires*, beating represents not merely his debt to the master but his own Latinity, marking his ability to access ancient texts.[53] Indeed, the Juvenalian phrase "flinch my hand from the rod" almost becomes a shibboleth when referring to formal instruction. Writers such as Alan of Lille, Heriger of Lobbes, and others frequently use it to signal membership of the educated elite, commemorating literacy in both the author it echoes and the experience it reflects.[54]

[50] Alcuin, *B. Flacci Albini seu Alcuini: Opera omnia*, Epistola VI, in *Patrologia cursus completus*, ed. J.-P. Migne, series secunda 100 (Paris: J.-P. Migne, 1851), col. 145.

[51] Sigebertus Gemblacensis, *Vita prior Sancti Lamberti Episcopi Trajectensis et Martyris Leodii in Belgio*, III, in *Patrologiae cursus completus*, series secunda 160 (Paris: J.-P. Migne, 1854), col. 762.

[52] H. Silvestre, Comment on rédigeait une lettre au Xe siècle: L'épître dÉracle de Liège à Rathier de Vérone, *MA* 58 (1952): 130 (8).

[53] "Nos ergo manum ferulae subduximus; ceu pollice ducat / ut si quis cera uoltum facit." Juvenal, *Satires*, ed. J .D. Duff (Cambridge: Cambridge University Press, 1932), I.15, VII.237–38, 1, 53.

[54] See Alanus ab Insulis, *De planctu naturae*, *Opera omnia*, I, in *Patrologiae cursus completus*, ed. J. P. Migne, series secunda 210 (Paris: J.-P. Migne, 1855), col. 452; Herigerus Lobiensis, *Gesta pontificum Tungrensium et Leodiensium*, ed. R. Koepke, Monumenta Germaniae Historica s.s. 7 (Hanover: Impensis Bibliopolii Avlici Hahniani, 1846), 178; Petrus Cellensis, *Commentaria in Ruth: Tractatus de tabernaculo*, ed. Gerard de Martel (Turnhout: Brepols, 1990), 137.

These attitudes toward beating not only persist into the fourteenth and fifteenth centuries but grow increasingly institutionalized. In his own remarks on education, Froissart likewise sees punishment at school as a factor increasing agency rather than reducing it. In the quasi-autobiographical segments of *L'espinette amoureuse* (c. 1372), Froissart's narrator describes the salutary effect of the beatings he received for "varioie au rendre / Mes liçons" (deviating when making my lessons). On the one hand they improved his general sophistication and disposition, "se chagierent moult mi meur" (changing me much for the better) and rendering him "plus assagis" (more reasonable) and "plus sougis" (more restrained). But at the same time he also uses beating to symbolize his growing subjectivity: when outlining his education, his relationship with *batus* fluctuates continually from recipient to performer, as he describes himself treating the other children as his master treats him, stating "J'ère batus et je batoie" (I took beatings, and so I beat).[55] Beating at school is also seen in similar, fluctuating terms by Christan of Lilienfeld, writing in the Cistercian abbey of Basse-Autriche in the first quarter of the fourteenth century.[56] As well as arguing that the rod is a necessary means of "taming" children, Christan argues that it serves to increase their own will and discretion: he specifically argues that "ne ignescens eorum spiritus socie carnis incendio suffocaretur, verum pocius eius assidua mortificacione fortificaretur, ipsam proiecta castrimargia nexibus parsymonie, ferula discipline, vigiliarum calcaribus domuerunt" (their flaming spirit is not suffocated by mingling with the fire of the flesh; rather their constancy is strengthened by mortification, as they subdue abject gluttony with the bonds of temperance, the rod of discipline, the spurs of vigilance taming them).[57] The same appreciation may also underpin Dante's meeting with Brunetto Latini in hell, as he tells his old teacher that their lessons together "la mente m'è fitta" (are stamped into my mind).[58]

However, perhaps the most powerful witness to these sentiments is

---

[55] Jean Froissart, *L'espinette amoureuse*, ed. Anthime Fourrier (Paris: Librairie Klincksieck, 1963), 54–55, lines 249–67.

[56] Myriam Despineux, "Les miracles mariaux de Christan de Lilienfeld d'après la *Légende dorée*: Procédés et finalités d'un abréviateur," *Revue belge de philologie et d'histoire* 67 (1989): 257–71.

[57] Christanus Campililiensis, "Officia officium," X.34, in *Opera poetica*, ed. Walter Zechmeister, Corpus Christianorum 72 (Turnhout: Brepols, 1992), 62.

[58] Dante Alighieri, *Inferno*, XV.82, in *La divina commedia*, ed. Tommaso Casini (Florence: G. C. Sansoni, 1888), 112.

the medieval classroom itself, and the texts generated out of its activities. Such thinking is especially visible in the *latinitates* or *vulgaria*, collections of brief translation exercises that begin to appear in the middle of the fourteenth century.[59] The surviving texts refer to flogging liberally: they include such phrases as "some children will be well ruled for loue: some for fere/ some nat without bettynge or correction," "Do not so that thou be betyne," "thou arte worthy to be bette," and "what meanys shall I use to lurne withoute betynge."[60] While these statements might at first glance seem to serve a repressive function, reminding pupils of the master's authority over them and his right to chastise them, this is not always the case. In a number of instances the *latinitates* encourage students to regard themselves as potential performers of violence as well as its targets. For example, in a collection compiled by the London schoolmaster Robert Whittinton, there are several sentences that position the translator as the subject rather than object of blows: Whittinton asks his students to render such phrases as "If euer I be a man/ I wyll revenge his malyce," "wordes I may suffre/ but strypes I may not withall," and simply "I bete or punysshe."[61] What is more, these particular exercises were evidently used by at least one early educator: a copy of Whittinton's text once belonging to Sion College, and now held at the British Library, singles out these particular sentences with marginal notations.[62] Nor is Whittinton the only teacher to take such an approach. An anonymous collection of exercises compiled at Magdalen School in the late fifteenth century goes even further, asking students to assume the voice of the chastising master himself: it includes such statements as "now, sithe the mater lieth all in my handes, aske me mercy and take it," and "there is nothynge that I desire more than to use softe and easy correccioun unto the scolars . . . but sum wolde

---

[59] The surviving texts have been recently edited in Nicholas Orme, *English School Exercises, c. 1420–c. 1530* (Turnhout: Brepols, 2013). On the texts and their purpose, see Nicholas Orme, *Education and Society in Medieval and Renaissance England* (London: Hambledon, 1989), 76–98; David William Sylvester, *Educational Documents, England and Wales 800 to 1816* (London: Methuen, 1970), 91–94.

[60] William Horman, *Vulgaria uiri doctissimi* (London: Richard Pynson, 1519) (*STC*, 13811), fols. 84v–85; John Anwykyll, *Vulgaria quedam abs Terencio in anglicam linguam traducta: Compendium totius grammaticae* (Oxford: Theodoric Rood and Thomas Hunte, 1483) (*STC*, 696), fol. 65; Beatrice White, *The Vulgaria of John Stanbridge and the Vulgaria of Robert Whittinton*, EETS o.s. 187 (London: Oxford University Press, 1932), 28.

[61] Stanbridge, *Vulgaria*, 102, 107.

[62] Robert Whittinton, *Vulgaria Roberti VVhitintoni Lichfeldiensis, et de institutione grammaticulorum opusculum: Libello suo de concinnitate grammatices accommodatum. Et in quattuor partes digestum* (London: Wynkyn de Worde, 1529), fols. 32v, 34v.

never lurne yf thei wer sure thei sholde never be bett."[63] Through these sentences, students are invited to regard themselves as prospective performers of violence in the course of performing literacy. As they draw such statements into their own written language, they insert themselves into the subject position each text sketches out for them, becoming the beating "I" as they acquire command over letters. In effect, discipline in the schoolroom becomes a symbolic pivot around which pupils shift from object to subject, moving from the recipient to agent of learning. Put simply, it serves as an initiation into the community of the educated: in the words of Anthony Burgess, "to have beaten, been beaten, witnessed the same beatings" serves as "a red badge of something" shared by members of this elite.[64]

The constructive effects of Jankyn's violence can be attributed to this function, as his abuse also gives Alisoun passage into literate culture, even despite his own intentions. Although his beating and reading might be designed to disenfranchise the Wife, placing her in the role of submissive pupil, they succeed in creating an agent capable of contending with his authority and authorities, who uses her voice to dispute with him and the texts on which his power rests. In other words, the resistance Jankyn encounters directly emerges out of the form of violence he has chosen to deploy, as its results inevitably turn against him by the end of the *Prologue*. While Alisoun's deafness is the clearest symbol of this process, it leaves other traces within the narrative. For instance, it might also account for the puzzling ambivalence Alisoun expresses toward her beatings, as her accounts of Jankyn's mistreatment often seem to hover "between pleasure and danger" to a degree little short of "masochistic."[65] Such uncertainty might again reflect the role violence plays in instructing her. Chaucer makes her both value and resent Jankyn's blows because they perform a dual role, simultaneously victimizing the Wife and empowering her to speak in the terms she does: in effect, Alisoun's combination of affection and impatience toward Jankyn is the mixture of indebtedness and rivalry implicit in every teacher–pupil relationship, as tutelage raises the student to the

---

[63] William Nelson, *A Fifteenth Century School Book* (Oxford: Clarendon Press, 1956), 34–35.
[64] Anthony Burgess, "The Whip," in *Homage to Qwert Yuiop* (London: Hutchinson, 1986), 109–11 (111).
[65] Elaine Tuttle Hansen, "'Of his love daungerous to me': Liberation, Subversion, and Domestic Violence in *The Wife of Bath's Prologue and Tale*," in *The Wife of Bath*, ed. Peter G. Beidler (Bedford: St. Martin's, 1996), 273–89 (278).

level of the master. The same conditions also color the vocabulary Alisoun uses to reflect on her own subjectivity. As she boasts at the beginning of the text, she has both been whipped and "myself have been the whippe," undergoing the same movement from object to subject that didactic violence is intended to produce, and describing her transition in the same terms used by the *latinitates* (III.175). At the very least, these factors signal why Jankyn's violence should prove resoundingly ineffective within the immediate context of the household. It cannot subordinate the Wife to his command, being designed to promote the very subjectivity domestic discipline should restrict.

"Wood al outrely": Reason and the Limits of Punishment

Agency is not the only point at which pedagogy intrudes into the *Prologue*, or the only distinction between the two types of violence Chaucer's text serves to highlight. Closely related to the functions pedagogic and marital discipline perform are the limits they are compelled to observe. The notion that violence occupies implicit parameters again arises at the climax of the *Prologue*. In the lines immediately following his final assault, there is a clear sense that Jankyn has overstepped some unspoken limit, that his violence has broken free of the confines that ought to govern it. His breach can be seen in the care Chaucer takes to differentiate this blow from the regular abuse Jankyn inflicts on Alisoun: she specifies "he smoot me ones on the lyst," expressly describing this assault and the form it takes as something that happened only on a single occasion, as a departure from her husband's usual habits (III.634). While the final attack is therefore an extension of Jankyn's established conduct, it also seems to possess a new and unprecedented element, setting it apart from the routine violence to which he subjects the Wife when beating her "on my ribbes al by rewe" (III.506). Violence of this particular variety occurs only "ones" and not in the daily course of things, as it has in some way slipped free of conventional patterns.

The question this detail provokes, however, is exactly what form of limit Jankyn has transgressed here. In terms of their broader social currency, each of the discourses evoked by the *Prologue* places firm boundaries around beating, having a particular set of standards to determine acceptability and excess. Both subscribe to "a rhetoric of rationality," using "the concept of reason . . . to proscribe excessive violence," even if their sense of "reasonableness" differs in fundamental ways.[66] It is clear, for instance, that violence in the household was made to operate within specific channels. Although some commentators have argued that husbands could injure or kill their wives with impunity, a position that authors such as Geoffroy de la Tour Landry or Boccaccio appear to voice, in practice wife-beating was tightly regulated.[67] The pressure on husbands to limit their violence emanated from several centers. Thus Barbara Hanawalt has found evidence of "social norms . . . calling attention to responsibility, restraint, and good judgment" in forensic and folkloric sources, while Martha Brozyna and Larissa Taylor identify similar proscriptions in canon law and popular preaching.[68] What is more, husbands faced material as well as social disincentives, as improper levels of violence might be penalized by fines, the pillory, or enforced separation.[69] Nevertheless, despite these wide calls for moderation, the parameters around matrimonial discipline tended to be fluid and even negotiable: often "the limits are difficult to define" in general terms, beyond a loose intolerance for "murder[ing] or maiming" women.[70] Such limits were also inconsistently applied, as they tended to vary substantially from region to region, and even differed widely within single communities at different points in time. The standards Robin Stacy

---

[66] Emma Hawkes, "The 'Reasonable' Laws of Domestic Violence in Late Medieval England," in Salisbury, Donavin, and Price, *Domestic Violence in Medieval Texts*, 57–70 (57–58).

[67] See Georges Duby, "The Aristocratic Households of Feudal France," in *A History of Private Life*, ed. Phillippe Ariès, Georges Duby, Paul Veyne, Arthur Goldhammer, Michelle Perrot, Antoine Prost, and Gerard Vincent, 5 vols. (Cambridge, Mass.: Belknap Press, 1987–98), Vol. 2, ed. Goldhammer, 35–155 (77); Del Martin, *Battered Wives* (San Francisco: Glide, 1976), 29; Frances Gies and Joseph Gies, *Marriage and the Family in the Middle Ages* (New York: Harper and Row, 1987), 155; Marilyn Migiel, *A Rhetoric of the Decameron* (Toronto: Toronto University Press, 2003), 147–59; Tory Vandeventer Pearman, *Women and Disability in Medieval Literature* (Basingstoke: Palgrave Macmillan, 2010), 45–72.

[68] Barbara A. Hanawalt, "Violence in the Domestic Milieu of Late Medieval England," in *Violence in Medieval Society*, ed. Richard W. Kaeuper (Woodbridge: Boydell, 2000), 197–214 (214); Martha A. Brozyna, "Not Just a Family Affair: Domestic Violence and the Ecclesiastical Courts in Late Medieval Poland," in *Love, Marriage, and Family Ties in the Later Middle Ages*, ed. Isabel Davis, Miriam Müller, and Sarah Rees Jones (Turnhout: Brepols, 2003), 299–311 (301); Larissa Taylor, *Soldiers of Christ: Preaching in Late Medieval and Reformation France* (Oxford: Oxford University Press, 1992), 169.

[69] See Andrew Finch, "Women and Violence in the Later Middle Ages: The Evidence of the Officiality of Cerisy," *Continuity and Change* 7 (1992): 23–45 (31).

[70] Derek G. Neal, *The Masculine Self in Late Medieval England* (Chicago: University of Chicago Press, 2008), 80.

identifies in Wales, for instance, differ considerably from those Hannah Skoda sees at work in Paris and S. D. Goitein sees among Jewish communities in the Mediterranean.[71] Likewise, the materials examined by Karen Jones from the Church courts at Kent suggest that willingness to prosecute ill-treatment of wives was at best sporadic, appearing "on the agenda of the court" at certain times "and only then," rather than being a pervasive or ongoing concern.[72]

Nonetheless, despite such mutability, what does emerge is a sense that wife-beating is to be judged by its effects on the woman's body above all. Death, miscarriage, broken bones, attempted murder, bloodshed, and assault on sacred ground usually mark the end-points of its legitimacy, opening up the husband to prosecution or at least intervention by community and court.[73] In effect, inappropriate wife-beating seems to be conceptualized along the same lines as sexual assault, as an offence that needs to be provably "written on the body," requiring the traces of "visible injuries . . . bleeding wounds and torn clothing" to be identified and condemned.[74] Thus in legal discourse, there is often a high degree of emphasis on physical damage when wives plead against their husbands. A vivid illustration of this tendency is a plea brought before the Star Chamber by Agnes Lewys of Ospringe against her husband Thomas, a "servyngman" in the royal garrison at Calais. The appeal can be dated tentatively to 1532, as Lewys appears on a register of soldiery drawn up in this year; it may however date from up to nine

---

[71] Robin Chapman Stacy, "Wales," in *Women and Gender in Medieval Europe*, ed. Margaret Schaus (London: Routledge, 2006), 825–26; Hannah Skoda, *Medieval Violence: Physical Brutality in Northern France, 1270–1330* (Oxford: Oxford University Press, 2013), 193–231; S. D. Goitein, *A Mediterranean Society: The Jewish Communities of the Arab World*, 6 vols. (Berkeley: University of California Press, 1967–99), 3:184–89.

[72] Karen Jones, *Gender and Petty Crime in Late Medieval England: The Local Courts in Kent 1460–1560* (Woodbridge: Boydell, 2006), 87.

[73] See Wolfgang Müller, *The Criminalization of Abortion in the West: Its Origins in Medieval Law* (Ithaca, N.Y.: Cornell University Press, 2012), 45–76; Roderick Phillips, *Untying the Knot: A Short History of Divorce* (Cambridge: Cambridge University Press, 1991), 97–98. See also the cases discussed in Sara M. Butler, "The Law as a Weapon in Marital Disputes: Evidence from the Late Medieval Court of Chancery, 1424–1529," *JBSt* 43 (2004): 291–316 (291–92); Susan Stewart, "Outlawry as an Instrument of Justice in the Thirteenth Century," in *Outlaws in Medieval and Early Modern England: Crime, Government and Society c. 1066–c. 1600*, ed. Paul Dalton and John C. Appleby (Farnham: Ashgate, 2009), 37–54 (51); Peter Coss, *The Lady in Medieval England, 1000–1500* (Stroud: Sutton, 1998), 160.

[74] Kim M. Philips, "Written on the Body: Reading Rape from the Twelfth to Fifteenth Centuries," in *Medieval Women and the Law*, ed. Noël James Menuge (Woodbridge: Boydell, 2000), 125–44 (129).

years later, as Agnes places Sir John Wallop at the "Castell of Guysnes" or Guînes, where he was made lieutenant in April 1541.[75] However, what makes the complaint important is the long, highly specific catalogue of injuries Agnes feels obliged to recount. She describes Lewys not only "drawing of wepons, thretenyng, and beating contynually" but periodically assaulting her so severely that she was "constrayned monthely and quarterly to kepe her bedde," being "so brosyd and sore with beatyng and treading upon her leggs and armes, wherby she ys skant able to move." The plea goes on to claim that Thomas had also "givon unto your sayd Oratrice poyson" and still "intendyth utterly to distroy" her, although it dwells most extensively on an episode before his departure for France: immediately before leaving, Lewys apparently

thretened to slay her and drewe his wepon, ranne at her, and so if she hadde not made the better shifte she hadde bene slayne, and then and ther he toke a pewter potte and toke your sayd Oratryce withe the same potte under the lyst of the eare that she fell downe ... and wast nye ded onlesse the socour wast nyghe hand of good ffrendes and neyghbores.[76]

This vivid account of a married life "as hevy ... as curseth any honest poor woman" encapsulates a common rhetorical strategy in legal discourse. Other records also appeal to the wounded body of the woman in order to signal when husbands have departed from the bounds of reason. Hence in a petition made to parliament sometime between 1366 and 1382, Thomasina de Fornivall pleads for financial recompense from her estranged husband William on precisely these grounds: she notes the "cruelte et duresce de son dit mariage" (cruelty and harshness of her said marriage), the "tote humilitee ne so grevouses censures" (total humiliation and grievous censures) she has suffered at his hands, and the impossibility of "cohabiter ad luy pur doute de on mort on ele" (living with him for fear of her life).[77] This last phrase is also echoed in a petition to the Common Bench of approximately 1533–38, in which Margaret Robens of Cromer is said to have gone in "ffering of her lyff" after rumors of infidelity sparked "stryff debatte and variaunce"

---

[75] See P. T. J. Morgan, "The Welsh at Calais," *Welsh History Review/Cylchgrawn hanes Cymru* 2 (1964–65): 181–85 (183); David Grummitt, *The Calais Garrison: War and Military Service in England, 1436–1558* (Woodbridge: Boydell, 2008), 108–10.
[76] The National Archives, STAC 2/21/62, fol. 1.
[77] The National Archives, SC 8/46/2291.

between herself and her husband Stephen Sheppard.[78] These two cases are particularly interesting because the reported cruelty is incidental to the main objective of each suit. Thomasina is actually seeking "suffisante suretee de la pees et covenable susteintuer ses" (sufficient guarantee of peace and suitable income to sustain herself), while Margaret is only mentioned in the course of a larger complaint against Sheppard and his rumor-mongering.[79] The inclusion of such details therefore seems designed to discredit the husband in the eyes of the court, again underscoring how reports or threats of injury are indicators of a lack of reason. That plaintiffs were driven to such measures is perhaps due to the problems legal discourse faced when confronted with female deponents and witnesses: when dealing with violence against women medieval law tended to operate on the assumption "that men were inherently rational and women naturally less rational," which not merely "contributed to the alienation of women from the courts" but enabled men to be the final arbiters of "the boundaries of reasonable chastisement."[80] Appealing to the body could be seen as a response to these beliefs by the courts and women alike, a means of circumventing the supposed faultiness of female testimony by looking to the more objective record provided by their flesh. At any rate, whatever the mechanics underpinning it, the point remains that domestic violence is directly tied to its effects on the wife's body: the standards separating reasonable from unreasonable force are emphatically corporeal.

Pedagogic discourse, on the other hand, functions along different lines and within different limits. Here the emphasis falls more on the psychological motivation driving the teacher to punish rather than the outcome of that punishment, physical or otherwise. Writers on education repeatedly stress that, since his role is to cultivate systematic thought in his charges, the teacher should not step beyond these bounds himself in implementing beating; he certainly should not allow irrationality to intrude into the classroom by striking out rashly or furiously. One of the most striking illustrations of this conviction is the elaborate set of provisions laid down in Vincent of Beauvais's *De eruditione filiorum nobilium* (c. 1261), a handbook written at the request of Marguerite of Provence for the tutors of her son, the future Philip the Bold.[81] While

[78] The National Archives, C1/845/38.
[79] The National Archives, SC 8/46/2291.
[80] Hawkes, "'Reasonable' Laws of Domestic Violence," 66.
[81] See Robert J. Schneider, "Vincent of Beauvais' *Opus universale de statu principis*: A Reconstruction of Its History and Contents," in *Vincent de Beauvais: Intentions et réceptions*

Vincent makes discipline one of his central concerns, dedicating no fewer than three full chapters to the questions surrounding punishment and the circumstances that make it necessary, his emphasis throughout is on subordinating punishment to balance and calculation. As he explicitly states in the course of his discussion, "In disciplina cohercionis requiruntur tria, sc. austeritas et mansuetudo et discrecio siue modestia . . . austeritas ergo uel asperitas esse debet in disciplina, ne sit ultra modum remissa" (in the practice of coercion three things are required: rigor, gentleness, and discretion or self-control . . . the harshness or severity obliged by teaching should not exceed correct measure in form).[82] In his comments, Vincent not only seeks to ensure that *discretio* governs the teacher's blows in principle, but even attempts to embed calm reflection in their actual execution. In particular, he advises waiting to inflict any punishment rather than lashing out immediately, urging that "Obseruandum est eciam tempus, ut non statim quasi cum furore correptio delinquenti adhibeatur, sed usque ad tempus oportunum aliquando differatur" (time is to be observed, so you do not bring about disgrace by attacking as though with fury straightaway, but always wait at length for an opportune time).[83] Such circumspection enables a series of further checks to be performed. With such a delay observed, the "uirge disciplinam" (discipline of the rod) can be accompanied by "conminacio, sicut excommunicacionis sentenciam admonicio" (a denunciation much like the admonishment in the sentence of excommunication).[84] It can also be varied in accordance with the offence, since "Si uero sit manifesta et correpcio in manifesto est facienda" (if the sin in truth is open then correction should be made openly), and allow time for the character of the offender to be considered, so that "Per disciplinam occurrere . . . diuersimode secundum disposicionem uel habilitatem uniuscuiusque" (discipline can occur . . . in different ways according to the disposition or ability of each pupil).[85] The *tempus* Vincent places between offense and beating therefore allows a whole raft of further refinements to be put into place. Above all, violence in the classroom

---

d'une œuvre encyclopédique au Moyen Âge, ed. Monique Paulmier-Foucart, Serge Lusignan, and Alain Nadeau (Montreal: Bellarmin, 1990), 285–300 (289–98).

[82] Vincent of Beauvais, *De eruditione filiorum nobilium*, ed. Arpad Steiner (Menasha: Medieval Academy of North America, 1938), 92.
[83] Ibid., 95.
[84] Ibid., 91.
[85] Ibid., 95, 89.

must be stringently calibrated, requiring the master to banish emotion and impetuosity alike in favor of sober *discretio*.

While Vincent's thinking is unique in some respects, his proposals are echoed by a range of further commentators. In the fourteenth century, the English Dominican John Bromyard reiterates many of his key ideas in the mammoth preaching compendium *Summa praedicantium* (c. 1352). Although Bromyard also believes that discipline is essential during education, observing that attaining "scientia Dei" (knowledge of God) requires "disciplina delinquentis" (the physical correction of error) as much as any other factor, he maintains that all penalties must be governed exactly.[86] In his eyes "proportionalitatem" (proportionality) is a key feature in the just execution of punishment, as he asks that "ubi maior est culpae deformitas, durior poenae infligatur acerbitas, pensatis circumstantiis et conditionibus" (where the impropriety of the offense is great, then the severity of the punishment inflicted should be bitter, with the circumstances and conditions weighed up).[87] In the 1430s the Beccles schoolmaster John Drury lays out similar provisions in his rule for teachers. Although he also confesses that "Necessarium est discolum verberari" (it is necessary that irregularity be flogged), he adds the stipulation that only substantial offenses or those born out of bodily appetite should receive such treatment, urging that masters always be attentive to the difference between major and trivial lapses.[88] As well as echoing his abstract standards for punishment, pedagogy also follows Vincent in insisting that its exercise be divorced from unruly emotion. Such a sentiment appears in the work of Dirck Valcooch, a schoolmaster in North Holland in the mid-sixteenth century.[89] Valcooch echoes Vincent's counsel that discipline should be implemented with caution and calculation rather than impulsive passion: he specifically advises that the "Schoolmeester" should "houdt maet in slaen en stuypen, / Weest coel ghesint, niet hittigh van gemoeden" (take care when slapping and

---

[86] John Bromyard, *Summa praedicantium*, 2 vols. (Venice: Dominicum Nicolinum, 1586), 2:347.

[87] Ibid., 232.

[88] Johannes Drury, "Regula date per magistrum," Cambridge University Library, Add. MS 2830, fol. 6.

[89] See G. Stuiveling and P. J. Verkruijsse, "Valcoogh, Dirk Adriaensz," in *De Nederlandse en Vlaamse auteurs van middeleeuwen tot heden met inbegrip van de Friese auteurs*, ed. G. J. van Bork and Verkruijsse (The Hague: Weesp, 1985), 577–78.

punching; be cool in mind, not heated in temperament).[90] Again the foundation of proper violence in the classroom is psychological, as medieval pedagogues not only seek to contain and systematize its forms, but demand that it be implemented with the correct *gemoeden* or level of *discretio*.

This more internalized means of judging violence and its propriety is not confined to prescriptive handbooks and manuals. In poetic discourse, the same attitudes toward beating often emerge. One example is Henry Bradshaw's life of Saint Ermengild, told as part of his *Holy Lyfe and History of Saynt Werburge* (c. 1513). Among Ermengild's miracles, Bradshaw includes an episode relating to a "scole-mayster of Innocentes" who is crippled by the saint after mistreating his pupils. Bradshaw presents this offense as a transgression against balanced thought above all, as he refers to the teacher acting with "hastynes and enuy," and striking out "without dyscrecyon."[91] Langland also seems to share in the same logic, pointedly placing the imperative "to chastisen . . . children" in the mouth of Reson.[92] Likewise when questions arise over teachers' use of discipline in the field of law, they are usually conceptualized along similar lines, with calm rationality providing the benchmark of permissibility. One example is a dispute over fees in 1485 between Thomas Fosse, "Scholemaster of Bristoll," and John Peers, father to one of his pupils. While Fosse argued that he ought to receive his "competent rewarde" for having taught Peers's son "perfecte congruete" in grammar, Peers maintained that he "unressenable shuld bete and intrete his seid sone," and as a result merited punishment rather than payment.[93] Comparable charges appear at Nottingham a few decades later, where John Depupp was dismissed from his post at the Free School for having "abused his skollers with suche unressonable correccion."[94] In both of these cases, the same focus on motivation is in evidence, as the teacher's ability to exercise reason when carrying out

---

[90] Dirck Adriaensz Valcooch, *Den reghel der Duytsche schoolmeesters*, ed. G. D. J. Schotel (The Hague: Ykema, 1875), 10.
[91] Henry Bradshaw, *The Life of Saint Werburge of Chester*, ed. Carl Horstmann, EETS o.s. 88 (London: Trübner, 1887), 83–84, lines 2241–43.
[92] William Langland, *The Vision of Piers Plowman: A Complete Edition of the B-Text*, ed. A. V. C. Schmidt (London: Dent, 1978), V.34–40.
[93] The National Archives, C1/61/390.
[94] A. F. Leach and F. Fletcher, "Schools," in *Victoria History of the County of Nottingham*, ed. William Page, 2 vols. (London: Constable, 1906–10), 2:179–264 (225).

punishment is the only guarantee of its legitimacy. Therefore, in sum, the cluster of terms around pedagogic violence directs attention inwards: *discretio, modestia, gemoeden,* "dyscrecyon," and above all "resson" all situate its proper origin within the mental processes of the master, rather than looking to its results on the student's body.

Most importantly, these convictions extend directly into the work of Chaucer himself. They receive their most explicit articulation in the section of *The Parson's Tale* dealing with patience. When outlining the "remedium contra peccatum Ire," the Parson includes a brief exemplum that directly addresses schooling: although lacking an identifiable source, his narrative has clear resonances with the proposals of Vincent of Beauvais and the other authorities.[95] In the course of this episode, the Parson recounts how "a philosophre upon a tyme" was provoked into beating a young pupil. The man, it is reported, "wolde have beten his disciple for his grete trespas, for which he was greetly amoeved, and broghte a yerde to scoure with the child" (X.670). His threats and anger dissipate, however, when he is rebuked by the boy: "For sothe, quod the child, ye oghten first correcte yourself, that han lost al youre pacience for the gilt of a child./ For sothe, quod the maister al wepynge, thow seyst sooth. Have thow the yerde, my deere sone, and correcte me for myn inpacience" (X.672–73). Although the story ends with a larger moral generalization, as the Parson comments "of pacience comth obedience, thurgh which a man is obedient to Crist," it remains grounded in the specific requirements of the classroom (X.674). Like pedagogic discourse in general, the focus falls squarely on the impulses underlying the desire to punish. Chaucer leaves the reader in no doubt that the philosopher was fundamentally right to chastise the child, describing his pupil as committing a "grete trespas," which self-evidently warrants correction. Where the philosopher appears to be at fault is his abandonment of sober calculation in favor of emotion, the fact that he is "greetly amoeved" and "han lost al . . . pacience": he is directly comparable, in effect, to Fosse, Depupp, or Bradshaw's "scole-mayster of Innocentes." But the Parson's exemplum also goes further than these sources, as it shows a keener sense of the dangers of unreasoning violence. Unlike the hagiographic and legal records, Chaucer shows the master's transgressions being answered within the framework of the school itself, rather

---

[95] See Siegfried Wenzel's discussion in his edition of the *Summa virtutum de remediis anime* (Athens: University of Georgia Press, 1984), 28.

than by outside intervention from supernatural or legal agency. In his account, the master's wish to "scoure" the child in anger is enough to invert the proper hierarchy of the classroom. After giving way to unthinking rage, the master becomes the receiver rather than performer of lesson and punishment alike, not only taking instruction from his "disciple" but authorizing him to "correcte me." He is effectively demoted to the level of an unreasoning child through his exhibition of immoderate anger, as losing his grip on cool reasoning costs him his status as master. Ultimately, the exemplum sees heedless correction as contravening the rules of the classroom so completely that it disrupts the structures of learning: a teacher acting in such a way can simply no longer be thought a teacher.

These differing standards are clearly tied to the functions described earlier, as the distinct methods of calculating reason that emerge from the school and the household reflect the different demands that the two contexts make on violence. The emphasis on the teacher's mentality when carrying out punishment, for instance, can be linked to the sense that he is transmitting his own mature subject-position to the pupil, a project that calls for him to uphold the adult values of self-restraint while doing so; by contrast, the fact that marital discipline seeks to make an abstract hierarchy material obliges it to take a more concrete form when reckoning its own legitimacy.[96] Such specific concerns also feed into the conclusion of the *Prologue*, as they explain many of the details Chaucer includes in its final sequence. After the climactic beating of Alisoun and the fatal collapse of authority it precipitates, both benchmarks for measuring violence are clearly brought into play. The marital system of measuring violence is of course a significant element in this collapse, as Chaucer specifically acknowledges the effects of Jankyn's blow on Alisoun's body. By detailing her wounds, and even raising the possibility that Jankyn has "mordred" her, Chaucer makes clear that the Wife's body has contributed toward the husband's loss of standing. However, alongside these corporeal traces, this moment in the text also veers more decisively toward pedagogic discourse and its ideas on the proper deployment of violence. Chaucer takes care to show that Jankyn is driven by the same emotive, impulsive stimulus that pedagogues

---

[96] On this point, see for instance Ruth Mazo Karras, *From Boys to Men: Formation of Masculinity in Late Medieval Europe* (Philadelphia: University of Pennsylvania Press, 2003), 67–108; Walter J. Ong, "Latin Language Study as a Renaissance Puberty Rite," *SP* 56 (1959): 103–24.

repeatedly warn against. In the first place, the final blow is presented as a kneejerk response lacking in any form of consideration or meditation. Jankyn is shown to "up stirt" directly after Alisoun shreds "three leves" out of his book, delivering his blow immediately after the offense, without any pause for reflection of the kind advocated by Vincent of Beauvais (III.794, 790). But more importantly, Jankyn is emphatically placed beyond reason during the attack. His stated resemblance to "a wood leoun" not only identifies him with insanity but animalizes him, situating him beyond the compass of human rationality (III.794). Indeed, this simile connects his assault to other outbursts of temporary mania in Chaucer's work, as the same idiom is used to denote Palamon's frenzied struggle against Arcite in *The Knight's Tale* (I.1656), and the friar's wrathful response after his humiliation in *The Summoner's Tale* (III.2152). To press home the point still further, Chaucer describes Jankyn leaping from "oure fyr" in order to lash out at Alisoun, a detail with obvious connotations of rage and ferocity (III.793). The fact that these details receive such attention in the *Prologue* can again be attributed to the presence of pedagogic discourse in the text. Since Jankyn founds his authority on education, using his knowledge to cement his standing in the household, he is also compelled to adhere to the implicit standards schooling carries with it. When he acts without the thoughtful deliberation this position requires, he immediately sacrifices that position, ending the text in much the same position as the Parson's "philosophre upon a tyme." In other words, pedagogy supplies him not merely with power but also a threshold beyond which he and his violence will cease to enjoy the mandate of authority. The tipping-point Jankyn and the text recognize, in short, comes from the clerkliness he wields over the Wife, as he is undone by an intrinsic part of his chosen basis of authority.

"Diverse practyk": Conclusions

The *Prologue* is a record of Jankyn's failure to reconcile the two models of violence he uses against the Wife. His is a failure occurring at two levels. On the one hand, it is caused by overstepping the implicit limits of his violence, by an incorrect performance of aggression; on the other it stems from the nature of that violence itself, its eventual production of an educated and fully authoritative subject. Trying to play at both husband and teacher, drawing one disciplinary mode into the domain of another, Jankyn ends up being and exploiting neither role. The two modes may converge to a certain extent, allowing him to govern his Wife by these means for a time: indeed, the distance between the two forms of violence is perhaps not as acute as Chaucer makes it appear, as both household and school would ordinarily be venues for training children. But they inevitably part ways at a certain reach, and in so doing pull the legs from beneath his "maistrie," as Jankyn's chosen form of punishment cannot sustain his position in this foreign framework. Nevertheless, Jankyn's failures are our gain. Through them, the *Prologue* shines revealing light on the mechanics of sanctioned violence in the fourteenth century. In the first place, it serves as a reminder not merely of the regulation of violence in medieval culture but of the rigor with which such codification took place. As a host of recent commentators has made clear, far from promoting an unthinkingly "violent tenor of life," medieval institutions tended to situate violence within strictly regimented channels, with full awareness of its disruptive effects if left unchecked.[97] Such management has been discussed across a range of discourses: in the field of chivalry by Richard Kaeuper and Peter Haidu, in the application of judicial torture by Steve Guthrie and Larissa Tracy, in the doctrine of just war by Philippe Contamine and Jenny Benham, and in ascetic practice by Linda Georgianna and Mari Hughes-Edwards, to name but a few examples.[98] Chaucer's treatment of Jankyn not only confirms that violence was tailored to specific institutional needs, but suggests that he was fully conscious of its resulting division into numerous disjunctive patterns. By bringing two disciplinary modes into close proximity, the *Prologue* sees violence as specialized to the point of fragmentation. Jankyn's behavior indicates that one set of punitive measures

---

[97] Johan Huizinga, *The Waning of the Middle Ages*, trans. Frederick Jan Hopman (London: Edward Arnold, 1924), 1–21.
[98] Richard W. Kaeuper, *Chivalry and Violence in Medieval Europe* (Oxford: Oxford University Press, 1999); Richard W. Kaeuper, "Chivalry and the 'Civilising Process,'" in *Violence in Medieval Society*, 21–38; Peter Haidu, *The Subject of Violence* (Bloomington: Indiana University Press, 1993); Steve Guthrie, "Torture, Inquisition, Medievalism, Reality, TV," in *Cultural Studies of the Modern Middle Ages*, ed. Eileen A. Joy, Myra J. Seaman, Kimberly K. Bell, and Mary K. Ramsey (New York: Palgrave Macmillan, 2007), 189–216; Larissa Tracy, *Torture and Brutality in Medieval Literature* (Cambridge: Boydell and Brewer, 2012); Jenny Benham, *Peacemaking in the Middle Ages: Principles and Practice* (Manchester: Manchester University Press, 2011); Philippe Contamine, *War in the Middle Ages*, trans. M. Jones (Oxford: Blackwell, 1984), 279–301; Linda Georgianna, *The Solitary Self* (Cambridge, Mass.: Harvard University Press, 1981); Mari Hughes-Edwards, *Reading Medieval Anchoritism: Ideology and Spiritual Practices* (Cardiff: University of Wales Press, 2012).

cannot simply be transplanted into the territory of another; each is so firmly anchored to a particular set of conditions that uprooting it strips away its meaning and efficacy. Chaucer therefore sees licit violence in much the same terms that modern scholarship presents it when taken as a whole, regarding it as discontinuous and localized. He does not understand violence in general, indiscriminate terms, as something that is everywhere and always the same: since his culture demands that discipline submit to a host of specific channels in order to gain sanction, its performance is for him scattered into several mutually incompatible forms.

But alongside this general point, the *Prologue* also allows us to mark out some of the specific points at which these disparate systems of violence might diverge. The inability of didactic violence to support a marital hierarchy shows exactly how two discourses can differ in the demands they make on beating. Perhaps most obvious is their discrete methods of reckoning legitimacy. While each calls for the moderation of violence, the ways in which they separate moderate from immoderate activity is markedly different, with one appealing to the body and the other to the mind to determine acceptability. The metric by which reasonable punishment is calculated is clearly different in either case. Along the same lines, each differs in the type of subjectivity it seeks to construct. One attempts to fix its sufferer to a limited and dependent position, while the other serves to create a fully literate and autonomous subject. Each in effect serves to accommodate its recipient into a particular type of hierarchy: discipline in the household seeks to maintain a subordinate in her secondary position, ensuring that the allocation of power between beater and beaten remain stable, while school punishment assumes a more dynamic framework, one in which the beaten party will in time move into the position of beater. Ultimately, therefore, the contradictory nature of violence in the *Prologue* traces out some of the larger frontiers that stand between forms of sanctioned violence, as it contrasts two criteria of acceptability and two sets of subject-positions. The collapse of Jankyn's authority does not merely highlight the profound division of medieval violence into plural, irreconcilable practices, but flags up some of the points of departure between forms of discipline, mapping the points at which they part company.

"Now y lowve God": The Process of Conversion in *Sir Gowther*

Alan S. Ambrisco
The University of Akron

OSTENSIBLY A TRIUMPHALIST NARRATIVE recounting both the possibilities of Christian redemption and the surety of Christian military endeavors, the late Middle English poem *Sir Gowther* is at times a shocking text, even by the standards of medieval romance. Childless after ten years of marriage to the duke of Austria, a duchess encounters a man "as lyke hur lorde as he myght be" and the two have sex, after which the man stands up as "A felturd [hairy] fende" and announces he has "geyton a chylde on [her] / That in is yothe full wylde schall bee" (74, 76–77).[1] The demon's words prove true, and the duchess delivers a child

---

[1] *Sir Gowther* (c. 1400) exists in two late fifteenth-century manuscripts, British Library (BL), MS Royal 17 B.XLIII and National Library of Scotland, MS Advocates 19.3.1. The Royal MS, which identifies Gowther as Saint Guthlac, is generally taken to be a revision of the Advocates MS, the subject of this study. Unless otherwise noted, all references to *Sir Gowther* are to line numbers in Anne Laskaya and Eve Salisbury's edition of the Advocates MS in *The Middle English Breton Lays* (Kalamazoo: Medieval Institute Publications, 1995), 263–307. While the main contours of my argument hold for the Royal MS as well, enough of its lines are distinctly different from the Advocates MS that considerations of space preclude all but a few references to it. Any references here to the Royal MS are to line numbers in *Sir Gowther*, ed. Thomas C. Rumble, in *The Breton Lays in Middle English* (Detroit: Wayne State University Press, 1965), 179–204. The poem has additionally been edited by Karl Breul (*Sir Gowther* [Oppeln: E. Franck, 1886]), whose edition usefully surveys the poem's analogues and its main source, which he identifies as an early text of *Robert le diable*. Cornelius Novelli's unpublished Ph.D. dissertation, *"Sir Gowther"* (University of Notre Dame, 1963) helpfully has facing-page editions of both the Royal and Advocates MSS. In general, the Royal version is viewed as the more courtly version of the two, with some of the more shocking and graphic material of the Advocates version absent. For discussions of manuscript differences, see Henry Vandelinde, "*Sir Gowther*: Saintly Knight and Knightly Saint," *Neophil* 80 (1996): 139–47; and Andrea Hopkins, *Sinful Knights: A Study of Middle English Penitential Romance* (Oxford: Clarendon Press, 1990), 144–45. For a full discussion of the manuscript context arguing the Advocates MS was intended for instructing children, see Anna Chen, "Consuming Childhood: *Sir Gowther* and National Library of Scotland MS Advocates 19.3.1," *JEGP* 111 (2012): 360–83. The precise generic identification of the poem, which has been labeled a Breton lay, a hagiographical romance, a romance of identity, a secular hagiography, and a penitential romance, among other things, has been well studied. See Hopkins, *Sinful Knights*, 144–78; Vandelinde, "Saintly Knight

who, within the first year, prodigiously grows to the size others reach in seven years, slays nine nursemaids through monstrously gluttonous nursing, and even bites off his own mother's nipple. When grown, Gowther rampages through the duchy, committing rape, arson, and other heinous crimes, and he ceases only when he learns of his demonic parentage and converts to a life of Christian penitence and humility. Battling his own pride and an army of Saracens, Gowther eventually becomes both emperor and saint, the once notorious sinner explicitly identified in one manuscript as Saint Guthlac. Drawn to the text by Gowther's demonic actions and pedigree, critics have debated whether Gowther should be considered an Everyman figure or an atypical, even monstrous, sinner, thereby examining the romance as a commentary on chivalric identity, penitence, the mechanics of salvation, and the psychological and cultural processes at work in the text's monstrous construction of alterity.[2] This essay focuses not on the representativeness of Gowther's sins or what his penitence says about the possibilities for spiritual transcendence, but rather on the pattern of his conversion and the representation of the post-conversion self, demonstrating how both are

---

and Knightly Saint," 139–47; E. M. Bradstock, "*Sir Gowther*: Secular Hagiography or Hagiographical Romance or Neither?," *AUMLA* 59 (1983): 26–47; and Jeffrey Jerome Cohen, "Gowther among the Dogs: Becoming Human c. 1400," in *Becoming Male in the Middle Ages*, ed. Cohen and Bonnie Wheeler (New York: Garland, 1997), 219–44.

[2] Despite Gowther's demonic parentage, one scholar claims "he is also Everyman, who has inherited Original Sin, and seeks to escape from the burden of his naturally sinful flesh." Hopkins, *Sinful Knights*, 170. Similarly, Jane Gilbert writes that Gowther's monstrousness is representative of all humans who have not "come to personal realization . . . of God." "Unnatural Mothers and Monstrous Children in *The King of Tars* and *Sir Gowther*," in *Medieval Women: Text and Contexts in Late Medieval Britain; Essays for Felicity Riddy*, ed. Jocelyn Wogan-Browne, Rosalynn Voaden, Arlyn Diamond, Ann Hutchison, Carol Meale, and Lesley Johnson (Turnhout: Brepols, 2000), 329–44 (343). Gowther's identification as an Everyman figure is rejected by Joanne A. Charbonneau, "From Devil to Saint: Transformations in *Sir Gowther*," in *The Matter of Identity in Medieval Romance*, ed. Phillipa Hardman (Cambridge: D. S. Brewer, 2002), 21–28 (27).

For essays stressing Gowther's pursuit of a proper chivalric identity, see Alcuin Blamires, "The Twin Demons of Aristocratic Society in *Sir Gowther*," in *Pulp Fictions of Medieval England: Essays in Popular Romance*, ed. Nicola McDonald (Manchester: Manchester University Press, 2004), 45–62; and Ilan Mitchell-Smith, "Defining Violence in Middle English Romances: *Sir Gowther* and *Libeaus Desconus*," *FCS* 34 (2009): 148–61. For the claim that the romance's "message" is that "even the most grievous sinner can be saved," see Hopkins, *Sinful Knights*, 146. See also E. M. Bradstock, who argues that "The greater the sin, the more significant the regeneration and God's granting of His mercy." "The Penitential Pattern in *Sir Gowther*," *Parergon* 20 (1978): 3–11 (3). For discussions of Gowther's monstrosity, see Cohen, "Gowther among the Dogs"; and Dana Oswald, *Monsters, Gender, and Sexuality in Medieval Literature* (Woodbridge: D. S. Brewer, 2010), 159–95.

deeply implicated in social attitudes toward conversion in the fifteenth century. Specifically, I claim this text fully participates in the fifteenth century's sense of the problematics of conversion, a process referring both to the adoption of a previously unheld religion and the process undertaken by those who were already Christian but, in John Van Engen's words, "voluntarily took up more intense forms of religious life."[3] Both senses of conversion are invoked in *Sir Gowther*, which constructs for the convert a space of radical indeterminacy in which his identity is never fully fixed, even after he has given up his sins and turned to God.

Demonic Conduct and Religious Conversion in *Sir Gowther*

From its very start, the poem emphasizes not just Gowther's supernatural conception and infantile appetites but also the outrage subsequently engendered by this "warlocke greytt" and "his warcus wylde" once he embarks on a life of willful sin (22, 24). At the age of fifteen, Gowther fashions his own sword, a falchion, with which he terrorizes the duchy, and the duke knights him in an effort to curb his crimes. Like the baptism ceremony conducted at his birth, this knighting ceremony is meant to regulate identity by conferring inclusion in a larger community defined by ideology and proper conduct. Knighting, however, proves ineffective, and because of Gowther's excessive actions his purported father dies "for sorro" (154). The duke's death, moreover, further destabilizes the duchy, promoting Gowther to the rank of duke and endangering its people until, having learned of his demonic heritage, Gowther journeys to Rome to seek penance from the pope.

Noting how the new duke and his men rape an entire nunnery, after which Gowther sets fire to it and kills the inhabitants, scholars have identified Gowther's focused persecution of the clergy, but the poem specifies he also attacks those who have not taken holy orders but who "on Cryst con lefe" (193).[4] The list of atrocities committed against all Christians, professed and unprofessed, is substantial:

---

[3] John Van Engen, "Conversion and Conformity in the Early Fifteenth Century," in *Conversion: Old Worlds and New*, ed. Kenneth Mills and Anthony Grafton (Rochester, N.Y.: University of Rochester Press, 2003), 30–65 (30–31).
[4] See David Salter, *Holy and Noble Beasts: Encounters with Animals in Medieval Literature* (Cambridge: D. S. Brewer, 2001), 72; and Hopkins, *Sinful Knights*, 151.

> Meydyns maryage wolde he spyll
> And take wyffus ageyn hor wyll,
> And sley hor husbondus too,
> And make frerus to leype at kraggus
> And parsons for to heng on knaggus,
> And odur prestys sloo;
> To bren armettys was is dyssyre,
> A powre wedow to syt on fyre,
> And werke hom mykyll woo.
> (196–204)

This passage reminds us that Gowther is antagonistic not only to the institution of the Church and its representatives but also to lay Christians living in his realm. Gowther's antagonism to the Christian community and pre-conversion identity as an enemy of Christ are further emphasized once he arrives in Rome and the pope tellingly mentions he was planning to wage war on Gowther had he not come himself. Not merely depicted as an exceptionally sinful Christian, Gowther in fact is pointedly framed as a non-Christian at odds with the very community to which he nominally belongs.

An unnamed earl in the poem voices this idea when, immediately after the passage describing Gowther's rampage against his own people, he approaches Gowther and says, "We howpe thu come never of Cryston stryn [descent], / Bot art sum fendys son" (208–9). These telling lines frame Christianity as a kind of ethnicity and suggest Gowther, despite his baptism, is not Christian because his true father, a demon, was not himself Christian. It is, however, not merely the earl's speculation that Gowther is not Christian; he is explicitly speaking for a larger religious community that fails to regard Gowther, despite his baptism, as belonging to it, thus questioning Gowther's religious conviction and affiliation. When the earl suggests Christianity is a matter of ethnicity more than belief, the text problematically implies lineage and public opinion impinge as much upon Christian identity as does participation in the sacraments themselves.[5]

---

[5] For a discussion of how the "discourse of religious alterity and the discourse of ethnic alterity are aligned," see Suzanne Conklin Akbari, *Idols in the East: European Representations of Islam and the Orient, 1100–1450* (Ithaca, N.Y.: Cornell University Press, 2009), 157. Lisa Lampert-Weissig, *Medieval Literature and Postcolonial Studies* (Edinburgh: Edinburgh University Press, 2010), 73–86 similarly discusses how *Parzival* and *The King of Tars* "focus on whiteness as the normative marker of Christian identity" (80).

Hearing these public suspicions, Gowther seeks the truth from his mother, who confirms his demonic descent. Gowther then declares, "Y wyll to Rome or that y rest / To lerne anodur lare," an intention the text stresses "come on hym sodenly" (236–37, 238). A pivotal point in the romance, this passage shows Gowther's determination not only to avoid sin but also to learn a different spiritual lore or teaching, thereby changing his conduct, his religious inclinations, and his physical location. Indeed, Gowther's conversionary turn here is presented as a turn to Rome, and the metaphysical act of conversion is framed as a physical change in direction, one overtly emphasized in the text. In the space of twenty-six lines, the poet twice discloses Gowther's intent to travel to Rome (236, 250) and additionally describes the journey, mentioning that "Toward Rome he radly ranne" and "Toward Rome cety con he seche" (256, 262). This journey, moreover, is undertaken alone, with neither companion nor horse, and the text shifts in two lines from Austria to Rome with breakneck speed, mentioning only in passing that "Or he come to tho Powpe speche / Full long he con abyde" (263–64). These emphatic repetitions occur in a compressed space in the narrative, and Gowther's arrival at Rome follows so quickly on the heels of his "sudden" conversion as to elide the difference between them, the lengthy process of a hard physical and spiritual journey being reduced to no more than the length of time taken to contemplate it. This is not what Karl F. Morrison calls the "hard road of conversion" but the fantasy of an easy road wholly traveled in the blink of an eye and the turn of a foot.[6]

Nearly all critics discussing Gowther's sudden decision and its coincident change of direction refer to it as Gowther's moment of conversion, one processed as a change of heart and subsequently reinforced by acts of spiritual rehabilitation. Aside from labeling this, as does David Salter, a "sudden act of conversion,"[7] most critics say little about the conversion itself, preferring to analyze instead the penitential acts that follow it. One of the few scholars who discuss Gowther's conversion in any detail, E. M. Bradstock notes Gowther's transformation is "reminiscent, in its suddenness and its finality, of the conversion of St. Paul."[8] Instead of pursuing the text as dramatizing conversion itself, however, Bradstock

---

[6] Karl F. Morrison, *Understanding Conversion* (Charlottesville: University Press of Virginia, 1992), 77.
[7] Salter, *Holy and Noble Beasts*, 73.
[8] Bradstock, "The Penitential Pattern," 4.

reads the romance as a commentary on "the nature of original sin and redemption."⁹ In its suddenness and its construction as a revelation, Gowther's conversion does, as Bradstock claims, invoke the Pauline model of conversion.¹⁰ Moreover, the pre-conversion Gowther, like Saul of Tarsus prior to his conversion on the road to Damascus and his adoption of the name Paul, was an enemy of the Church and a persecutor of Christians. Saul is traveling to Damascus to arrest and persecute Christians prior to his conversion experience, and like Saul, Gowther transforms from victimizer of Christians into Christian adherent and eventual saint, the pre- and post-conversion selves standing in stark contrast to one another and thus underscoring the radical reversal wrought in each convert.

Paul's conversion narrative, presented in Acts 9:1–18, 22:3–16, and 26:9–18, became for medieval Christians the idealized paradigm for a sudden, intense, and irreversible conversion experience. Accounts of Paul's conversion circulated in the fourteenth and fifteenth centuries in such Middle English texts as the *South English Legendary*, John Mirk's *Festial*, the *Speculum sacerdotale*, the *Gilte Legende*, and *Cursor mundi*.¹¹ Following the biblical account and Jacobus de Voragine's *Legenda aurea*, each narrative details the sudden and radical reversal wrought by Saul's conversion into Paul. For example, the *Gilte Legende* uses the word "sodeyn" or a form of it no fewer than four times to describe the divine light prompting Saul's conversion or his life-changing response to it.¹² Mirk's *Festial*, composed in the late 1380s and widely disseminated in

---

⁹ Ibid., 3.

¹⁰ Louis R. Rambo identifies Paul as the paradigmatic example of a "mystical conversion," which he defines as "a sudden and traumatic burst of insight, induced by visions, voices, or other paranormal experiences." *Understanding Religious Conversion* (New Haven: Yale University Press, 1993), 15. While the impetus for Gowther's conversion is the earl's voice, not the voice of God or an angel, his conversion is framed by his sudden awareness of his own paranormal parentage, and the trauma of that revelatory knowledge propels his conversion.

¹¹ *The South English Legendary*, ed. Charlotte D' Evelyn and Anna J. Mill, Vol. 1, EETS o.s. 235 (London: Oxford University Press, 1967), 264–74; *John Mirk's Festial*, ed. Susan Powell, Vol. 1, EETS o.s. 334 (Oxford: Oxford University Press, 2009), 51–55; *Speculum sacerdotale*, ed. Edward H. Weatherly, EETS o.s. 200 (New York: Kraus, 1971), 21–23; *Gilte Legende*, ed. Richard Hamer and Vida Russell, Vol. 1, EETS o.s. 327 (Oxford: Oxford University Press, 2006), 131–34; and *Cursor mundi: A Northumbrian Poem of the XIVth Century*, ed. Richard Morris, Part 4, EETS o.s. 66 (London: Oxford University Press, 1966), 1116–30.

¹² *Gilte Legende*, 1:132, 133.

England, explicitly states that men "wondred of [Paul's] sodeyn conuercyon."[13] The *Festial*, then, registers the doubt potentially caused by such sudden change, but it defensively disallows the possibility that this change is anything but genuine, adding that "Holy Chyrch halweth [Paul's] conuersyon, and so heo doth of non oþur seynt" in part because of the "hegh ensampul of amendyng" he provides in his turn from "cursed tyrand into Goddes seruand."[14] As recounted in the *Festial*, then, Paul's conversion is the preeminent conversion in Christian history, but in so emphatically insisting on its validity, I argue, the text registers suspicion about the possible inconstancy of that conversion.[15]

Paul's sudden transformation was not, however, the only conversion model operative within medieval Christian cultures and texts. In his landmark study of conversion, Morrison notes that conceiving of conversion as a sudden "cataclysmic change" frames it as "an irreversible peripety and therefore leaves aside the whole range of systemic doubt that made fear of apostasy a great element in the concept of conversion,"[16] and he demonstrates that Saint Augustine's conversion, as recounted in his *Confessiones*, was a "long, pedagogical process" entertaining the very doubts belied by the Pauline paradigm and presenting the conversion process as "lasting until death, full of pitfalls and reversals, and by no means assured of attaining its goal, no matter what its beginning."[17] Lacking a single moment that constitutes a sharp, dramatic reversal in the life of the convert, the Augustinian paradigm instead amounts to

---

[13] Mirk, *Festial*, 1:53, line 71.

[14] Ibid., 1:51, lines 8–9, 11–12, 4–5.

[15] Sarah Salih, "Staging Conversion: The Digby Saint Plays and *The Book of Margery Kempe*," in *Gender and Holiness: Men, Women, and Saints in Late Medieval Europe*, ed. Samantha J. E. Riches and Salih (London: Routledge, 2002), 121–34 makes a similar point about the late fifteenth-century Digby *Conversion of Saint Paul*. The play places weight on Paul's status as an enemy of the Church and on his sudden, wholesale conversion, and a figure called *Poeta* twice appears onstage to emphasize the irreversible nature of the changes wrought in Paul. Salih suggests this overt emphasis on Paul's constancy may end up "raising the question of whether conversion really is, as [the play] claims, irreversible and perfect, or whether it might produce unpredictable excess" (126). For *The Conversion of Saint Paul*, see David Bevington, ed., *Medieval Drama* (Boston, Mass.: Houghton Mifflin, 1975), 665–86.

[16] Morrison, *Understanding Conversion*, 23, 24.

[17] Ibid., 24. For one fourteenth-century reader's understanding of Augustine's conversion as "an ongoing process," see Linda Olson, "Reading Augustine's *Confessiones* in Fourteenth-Century England: John de Grandisson's Fashioning of Text and Self," *Traditio* 52 (1997): 201–50 (228). See as well Appendix B to her essay, which lists known English manuscripts of the *Confessiones* (251–57).

conceiving of conversion as a sequence of stages, none of which can properly be identified as *the* moment of conversion. Augustine's conversion experience, as recounted in *Confessiones*, was relatively well known in the Middle Ages,[18] and Ryan Szpiech, who notes the differences between "the Augustinian and Pauline paradigms as they were understood in later medieval sources," claims the former became "the dominant medieval counterpoint to Saul/Paul's story in Acts."[19] The spread of the Augustinian paradigm, moreover, was largely due to its influence on the Benedictine Rule, which "assimilated Augustine's notion of conversion as a gradual process, one accompanied by asceticism, self-doubting criticism, and the terror of apostasy."[20]

If hagiographical texts such as Mirk's *Festial* prioritize the Pauline paradigm, vernacular lives of Augustine in the late Middle Ages likewise spread the Augustinian paradigm of prolonged conversion, and these two models were not limited to hagiography but were also employed by romances.[21] Suzanne Conklin Akbari has shown how the various medieval versions of *Fierabras* present two models of conversion from Islam to Christianity: the instantaneous conversion of the easily assimilable Fierabras, and the more difficult, protracted conversion of his sister, Floripas. In the case of Fierabras, who takes the name Florien at his baptism, "Both his name and his body are changed by the act of conversion," while Floripas is not renamed and her "aggressive behavior remains unchanged up until the poem's last lines."[22] While Akbari

---

[18] See E. Ann Matter, "Conversion(s) in the *Confessiones*," in *Collectanea Augustiniana*, ed. Joseph C. Schnaubelt and Frederick Van Fleteren (New York: Peter Lang, 1990), 25; Teresa Webber, "The Diffusion of Augustine's *Confessiones* in England during the Eleventh and Twelfth Centuries," in *The Cloister and the World: Essays in Medieval History in Honour of Barbara Harvey*, ed. John Blair and Brian Golding (Oxford: Clarendon, 1996), 29–45; and Olson, "Reading Augustine's *Confessiones*," 201–57.

[19] Ryan Szpiech, *Conversion and Narrative: Reading and Religious Authority in Medieval Polemic* (Philadelphia: University of Pennsylvania Press, 2013), 51.

[20] Frederick H. Russell, "Augustine: Conversion by the Book," in *Varieties of Religious Conversion in the Middle Ages*, ed. James Muldoon (Gainesville: University of Florida Press, 1997), 13–30 (27).

[21] The earliest extant Middle English life of Saint Augustine of Hippo is found in the Vernon manuscript (c. 1390–1400), Bodleian Library, MS Eng. Poet. a. 1, fols. 96r–100r. In the fifteenth century, lives of Augustine were included in the *Gilte Legende* (*Gilte Legende*, ed. Richard Hamer and Vida Russell, Vol. 2, EETS o.s. 328 [Oxford: Oxford University Press, 2007], 616–29) and written by John Capgrave ("Life of St. Augustine," in *John Capgrave's Lives of St. Augustine, St. Gilbert of Sempringham, and a Sermon*, ed. J. J. Munro, EETS o.s. 140 [London: Kegan Paul, Trench, Trübner, 1910], 1–60).

[22] Akbari, *Idols*, 171.

rightly shows how these two patterns of conversion are gendered in the *Fierabras* texts, the contrast, I argue, could also be framed in Pauline and Augustinian terms.[23] Furthermore, Dabney Anderson Bankert has explored how Chaucer's *Troilus and Criseyde* employs these contrasting paradigms of religious conversion to describe the secular experience of falling in love. Troilus shifts quickly from pride to humility, from persecuting lovers to becoming one of them, and his conversion is "abrupt, radical, and complete."[24] Criseyde's conversion, however, involves "a protracted interior struggle" that is "paradigmatically Augustinian," replete with self-doubt and recidivism.[25]

Sir Gowther, I argue, likewise uses both the Pauline and Augustinian models of conversion, but unlike their appearance in *Troilus and Criseyde* or the *Fierabras* texts, in *Sir Gowther* both the Augustinian and Pauline models are mapped onto a single convert. By so clearly invoking the Pauline model, *Sir Gowther* initially presents Gowther's conversion as genuine, efficacious, and instantaneous, and critics have seized on this, framing Gowther's subsequent penance as indicative of a state of conversion fully achieved. Morrison, however, claims redemption is part of conversion itself and warns against seeing it as a "sequel to conversion," figured as a single "incandescent moment."[26] I suggest that Gowther's conversion—despite the text's overt description of it as sudden, Pauline transformation—is not isolated to a single epiphanic moment in the narrative but is concurrently and paradoxically constructed as a process of unfolding that occurs in definite stages. The Pauline paradigm then functions as a convenient narrative model foregrounding a particular

---

[23] The type of conversion that takes a prolonged period of time has often been identified as feminine. The Augustinian model employed in *Sir Gowther* perhaps presents a challenge to customary gender roles, but the romance addresses this by emphasizing Gowther's masculinity on the battlefield even as it identifies him closely with the silent woman of the narrative. Moreover, the Augustinian model, like the Pauline one, does posit change in the convert rather than the consistency seen in female hagiographies, which tend to exhibit continuity between pre- and post-conversion selves. For a discussion of this latter point, see Caroline Walker Bynum, *Holy Feast and Holy Fast: The Religious Significance of Food to Medieval Women* (Berkeley: University of California Press, 1987), 25.

[24] Dabney Anderson Bankert, "Secularizing the Word: Conversion Models in Chaucer's *Troilus and Criseyde*," *ChauR* 37, no. 3 (2003): 196–218 (197). The transformation from pride to humility was expressly identified as integral to Paul's conversion in Bede's commentary on the Acts of the Apostles. See The Venerable Bede, *Commentary on the Acts of the Apostles*, ed. and trans. Lawrence T. Martin (Kalamazoo: Cistercian Publications, 1989), 87.

[25] Bankert, "Secularizing the Word," 211.

[26] Morrison, *Understanding Conversion*, 23.

idealized view of conversion's efficacy,[27] but it is belied by the subsequent division of Gowther's conversion into multiple stages.

The first narrative moment questioning the efficacy and finality of Gowther's sudden, Pauline conversion occurs when Gowther tells the pope of his demonic pedigree and the pope asks if he is christened. Gowther responds affirmatively but adds, "My name it is Gwother; / Now y lowve God" (279–80). Gowther's response acknowledges that his earlier baptism is not enough to indicate his commitment to God. His proclamation that he now loves God signals a new intent that was lacking before and identifies a new stage in Gowther's transformation. When, prior to absolution, the pope tells Gowther that until he receives a sign from God he should not speak or eat food that has not first been in the mouth of a dog, he links spiritual transformation to a protracted period of penance and a future mark of divine favor. The romance thus supplants the Pauline model of immediate and wholesale conversion, replacing it with an understanding of conversion as a process, an inward turning achieved by degrees and manifested in a series of partial movements over time.

Even after his meeting with the pope, the text insists on multiple identities for Gowther, each marking a processual stage in his spiritual conversion and implicating the romance in an Augustinian paradigm. After leaving the pope, Gowther wanders into "anodur far cuntré" and remains there for three days, sustained by the bread mysteriously brought by a white greyhound (308). As Michael Uebel says, Gowther here "base[s] his interactions with this gentle other . . . upon restraint and receptivity," and this encounter returns him to "an early state of non-aggressivity."[28] This period of internal examination is an important stage in Gowther's humbling and spiritual rehabilitation, allowing him to confront his aggressive instincts without the demands of human society and interaction.

When the greyhound fails to appear, Gowther reenters the inhabited world, arriving at the court of an unnamed emperor and reengaging

[27] James Muldoon notes the propagandist appeal of "a story of sudden, dramatic conversions," claiming it "was no doubt more attractive than the reality of a process that took decades, even generations, before true Christian conversion of the sort that Augustine experienced could occur." See "Introduction: The Conversion of Europe," in Muldoon, *Varieties of Religious Conversion*, 7.

[28] Michael Uebel, "The Foreigner Within: The Subject of Abjection in *Sir Gowther*," in *Meeting the Foreign in the Middle Ages*, ed. Albrecht Classen (New York: Routledge, 2002), 96–118 (106).

human society. As part of his humiliation, Gowther voluntarily adopts the posture of a dog by taking a seat under the high table. Gowther suffers the steward's efforts to chase him away, learning to endure aggression from others and accept a diminished social standing. While his earlier actions involved private asceticism, this public humiliation places him at the feet of a court similar to the one he once ruled tyrannically.

The final stages of Gowther's conversion occur when he combats the enemies of the Church. A sultan demands the emperor's mute daughter as a bride, a proposition that sets up a military confrontation with the sultan's Saracen army. Desperate to help the emperor, Gowther prays to God and miraculously receives, over the space of three days, three different horses, shields, and suits of armor. Each day he performs great military feats, but only the mute maiden recognizes these three different knights are in fact one man, Gowther. When the emperor himself regards Gowther as a different knight on each day, he is essentially correct, for each day marks a stage in Gowther's conversion.

The romance indeed signals Gowther's presumed assumption of his most refined spiritual state by having him dispatch the sultan himself, but when this defeat does happen, it is so sudden as to be easily missed, and it is followed by an entire series of equally sudden plot developments. The emperor has been taken by the sultan, and a line later we are told the unspeaking Gowther "gard hym ley a wed, / Stroke of his hed anon," best translated as "made him [the sultan] leave his hostage [the emperor], struck off his head at once" (629–30).[29] The only subsequent stroke of the battle follows immediately when an unnamed Saracen strikes Gowther on the shoulder, a blow that is not returned. In fact, no further mention of the Saracen forces or the larger battle is made at all, the thousands of remaining enemies seemingly dissipating with the sultan's death as the poem focuses not on the battle's aftermath but on Gowther's condition. Gowther's injury, itself nearly simultaneous with the sultan's decapitation, is quickly followed by the fall from a tower of the mute maiden, who apparently dies. When, a few lines and two days later, the pope arrives to give her last rites, she lifts her head

---

[29] Line 629 is troublesome, and my translation takes its cue from a suggestion in Laskaya and Salisbury's explanatory notes, wherein they suggest "ley a wed" is to be understood, along the lines of the Royal MS, as "leve his wedde" or "leave his hostage" (305–6).

and miraculously tells Gowther to speak and eat freely, as God has forgiven him. The pope then proclaims "Now art thu Goddus chyld," suggesting Gowther has at last discerned his true paternity in God (673).

The quick succession of these events, matched only by the suddenness of Gowther's earlier epiphany and conversionary turn to Rome, should draw our attention to the Pauline model, and indeed Bradstock sees in the maiden's fall a direct allusion to a miracle achieved by Paul, who reanimates a young man who died falling from a third-story window.[30] Cohen, in discussing this rapid pacing, says "The sequence of events . . . is extraordinary in its toppling domino effect. Gowther strikes off the head of his enemy, overcoming and vanquishing the very thing he once was, renouncing monstrousness forever."[31] Gowther's defeat of the sultan is written, in short, as another conversionary moment, and his battlefield heroics are not a demonstration of a state of piety achieved much earlier in the romance but a significant stage in his conversion, figured as Augustinian process. By constructing Gowther's conversion as a process, moreover, the poem consistently undercuts the Pauline model's portrayal of an efficacious and immediate conversion with the Augustinian model's implications that any such spiritual transformation is piecemeal, prolonged, and contingent.

Alterity and the Authenticity of Conversion in *Sir Gowther*

Failing to perceive the poem's use of the Augustinian model of conversion, as well as this model's role in undercutting the Pauline model, critics have simplified the poem, viewing Gowther's success against an acknowledged enemy of the faith as proof of his successful conversion. Donna Crawford, for example, claims "the injuries that Gowther inflicts on the Saracens" serve "to substantiate Gowther's own rehabilitation," and she avers "Gowther's quest for righteousness has been achieved."[32] Bradstock likewise sees the poem's ending as an endorsement of Gowther's rehabilitation, claiming Gowther's "rise in . . . heroic status is dependent upon the improved state of his soul and is thus a symbolic statement of it."[33] Typical of what I call redemptive readings, these

---

[30] Bradstock, "The Penitential Pattern," 9. The biblical passage is Acts 20:7–12.
[31] Cohen, "Gowther among the Dogs," 235.
[32] Donna Crawford, "'Gronyng wyth grysly wounde': Injury in Five Middle English Breton Lays," in *Readings in Medieval English Romance*, ed. Carol M. Meale (Cambridge: D. S. Brewer, 1994), 35–52 (44).
[33] Bradstock, "The Penitential Pattern," 9.

essays accept the sincerity of Gowther's conversion and consider his victories on the battlefield as "proof" of his salvation. I would argue, however, that the text does not substantiate such readings, that at key moments it questions the identity of the post-conversion self and fully participates in wider late medieval suspicions about the authenticity of conversion. Despite the poem's invocation of a Pauline model, then, Gowther's "conversion" early in the romance does *not* amount to a wholesale and irreversible character change, and disturbing traces of the pre-conversion self actually remain to plague the text's overt endorsement of the conversion process and the redemptive reading adopted by most critics.

Chief among these traces is Gowther's falchion, the sword Gowther himself fashions early in the romance and uses both to terrorize his people and, after his conversion, to achieve distinction fighting for the emperor. Gowther's falchion is mentioned ten times in the romance, and he is not once but twice presented as unwilling to relinquish it, even when instructed to do so by the pope. Gowther's retention of the falchion has been noted but often dismissed by critics. Salter, for example, observes that "after his conversion, the sword is the one possession that Gowther refuses to abandon, in spite of its association with his evil past," but he fails to see this as a troubling trace of the pre-converted self, arguing instead that "God grants him a place in heaven as a reward for so conscientiously discharging the morally burdensome obligations expected of a knight."[34] A few critics, however, have made much of the falchion, labeling it a weapon of eastern origin and, because of its resemblance to the scimitar, linking it and Gowther to Saracens. Jesus Montaño, for example, cites Bradstock in noting the sword is an "Arabic falchion" of "oriental origin" and calls the falchion "the very image that Christian Europe held of Islam and Saracens."[35] While the falchion was likely influenced by contact with the weapons of the Muslim world, it did not originate outside Europe and was not wielded by Muslims,[36] and it is an exaggeration to claim that the falchion, one of the most common European swords in the Middle Ages, is a "representative weapon and

---

[34] Salter, *Holy and Noble Beasts*, 75, 76.

[35] Jesus Montaño, "*Sir Gowther*: Imagining Race in Late Medieval England," in Classen, *Meeting the Foreign*, 118–32 (123). See as well Bradstock, "The Penitential Pattern," 7; Uebel, "The Foreigner Within," 103; and Cohen, "Gowther among the Dogs," 225.

[36] I would like to thank the anonymous reviewer for *SAC* who drew my attention to this point and encouraged me to conduct further research into falchions.

symbol of Saracens."[37] Montaño's larger point, however, still stands. Gowther's sword, emphatically and repeatedly identified by its specific subtype of falchion rather than by more general terms, is a key marker of alterity in the poem. While it does link Gowther with Saracens, the linkage is nonetheless more complex than critics claim, and the falchion's use in western Europe as well as its representation in western literary manuscripts are worth discussing at some length.

The falchion is by all accounts an exceedingly powerful weapon, a single-edged sword that, unlike most swords, widens rather than tapers from the hilt, making it heaviest at the point of impact nearer the end of the sword than at its base. R. Ewart Oakeshott discusses two basic kinds of falchions, one of which he calls the Durham type (after the Conyers Falchion in the library at Durham Cathedral). The other was used throughout the fourteenth century and until the mid-eighteenth century, a surviving specimen of which comes from Thorpe and is housed in the Castle Museum of Norwich.[38] What Oakeshott calls the Durham type ceased to be used after 1300, and thus the Thorpe type, appearing around 1290, is the falchion regularly depicted in manuscript illustrations of the fourteenth and fifteenth centuries and the type used commonly in Europe during the period of the poem's composition around 1400.[39]

Saracens and converted Saracens use falchions in many fourteenth-century Middle English romances. The Saracen knight Otuel carries one in *Otuel a Knyght*, and Roland is attacked by a Saracen knight wielding a falchion in *Roland and Vernagu*.[40] A Saracen called Lucafer uses one against the hero of *Sir Ferumbras*, the sultan of Damas carries a falchion in *The King of Tars*, and Saladin himself wields a falchion against King Richard in *Richard Coer de Lyon*.[41] Such figures are, of course, not the only combatants to use this common European sword, but the frequency of the falchion's association with despised, non-European, and

---

[37] Montaño, "*Sir Gowther*: Imagining Race," 123.

[38] R. Ewart Oakeshott, *The Archaeology of Weapons: Arms and Armor from Prehistory to the Age of Chivalry* (New York: Frederick A. Praeger, 1960), 237–38.

[39] Ibid., 238.

[40] *Otuel*, in *The English Charlemagne Romances*, Part 6, ed. Sidney J. H. Herrtage, EETS e.s. 39 (London: N. Trübner, 1882), 98, line 1119; *Roland and Vernagu*, in *The English Charlemagne Romances*, 6:60, line 831.

[41] *Sir Ferumbras*, ed. Sidney J. Herrtage, in *The English Charlemagne Romances*, Part 1, EETS e.s. 34 (London: Oxford University Press, 1966), line 2244; *The King of Tars*, ed. Judith Perryman (Heidelberg: Winter, 1980), line 1114; *Der mittelenglische Versroman über Richard Löwenherz*, ed. Karl Brunner, Wiener Beiträge zur englischen Philologie 42 (Vienna: Wilhelm Braumüller, 1913), line 5759.

especially non-Christian groups is noteworthy, so much that experts in military weaponry Kelly DeVries and Robert Douglas Smith have noted, but not explored, how in western manuscript illuminations "the falchion was often depicted as the sword of Muslim and Mongol warriors, or the sword used for executions."[42]

As DeVries and Smith suggest, manuscript illustrations and other visual arts from the fourteenth and fifteenth centuries associate falchions with Saracens. In her book-length study of alterity in medieval art, Debra Higgs Strickland includes a number of such images.[43] Strickland regularly misidentifies falchions as scimitars, but as falchions are broader near the point than at the hilt—a key feature distinguishing the falchion from the curved scimitar to which it bears a resemblance—these are clearly falchions.[44] That such a connection between falchions and Saracens is not simply the result of placing any sword in the hands of a non-Christian enemy is made by an illumination from William of Tyre's *History of Outremer*, which shows an impending battle between two groups of cavalry, mounted Christians on the left side of the image and Saracens with falchions on the right.[45] Saracen rulers are also depicted on the Catalan Atlas (c. 1400) as wielding falchions,[46] and Saladin wields one in the fifteenth-century *Six Ages of the World*.[47] In particular, Saladin's use of a falchion seems to have a long history. I have already mentioned the fourteenth-century Middle English *Richard Coer de Lyon*, which describes Saladin as wielding one against Richard I in a fictional

---

[42] Kelly DeVries and Robert Douglas Smith, *Medieval Military Technology*, 2nd ed. (Toronto: University of Toronto Press, 2012), 23. See as well Anthony North, "Barbarians and Christians," in Michael D. Coe, Peter Connolly, Anthony Harding, Victor Harris, Donald J. LaRocca, Anthony North, Thom Richardson, Christopher Spring, and Frederick Wilkinson, *Swords and Hilt Weapons* (New York: Weidenfeld and Nicolson, 1989), 30–43 (38).

[43] Debra Higgs Strickland, *Saracens, Demons, and Jews: Making Monsters in Medieval Art* (Princeton: Princeton University Press, 2003), 176, Fig. 85; 181, Fig. 89; and 185, figs. 93 and 94. See as well the image of a child being sacrificed to Muhammad in the duke of Berry's *Livre des merveilles du monde*, Bibliothèque nationale de France (BNF), Fr. 2810, fol. 185r. Reproduced in Michael Camille, *The Gothic Idol: Ideology and Image-Making in Medieval Art* (Cambridge: Cambridge University Press, 1989), 159, Fig. 88.

[44] Stephen N. Fliegel, the curator of medieval art at the Cleveland Museum of Art and an expert on medieval European arms and armor, generously provided technical assistance to verify this point, and I thank him for his help throughout this section of the article.

[45] BNF, Fr. 22495, fol. 154v, reproduced in Strickland, *Saracens, Demons, and Jews*, 181, Fig. 89.

[46] Cited by Montaño, "*Sir Gowther*: Imagining Race," 131 n. 22.

[47] BL, Add. MS 30359, no. 86.

duel, and a depiction of this same fictional encounter in the English Chertsey tiles of the late thirteenth century likewise shows Saladin holding a European falchion rather than a scimitar.[48] Roger Sherman Loomis has convincingly argued that Saladin's use of a falchion here is indebted to an "artistic tradition for representing the overthrow of pagan warriors by Christian champions," and among the evidence he cites for the currency of this tradition in fourteenth-century England is fol. 184r of the *Queen Mary Psalter*, British Library, MS Royal 2.B.VII, which depicts a mounted duel between a Christian and Saracen knight that closely resembles the depiction of the falchion-wielding Saladin's fight with Richard the Lionheart in both *Richard Coer de Lyon* and the Chertsey tiles.[49]

In addition to actual Saracens, various non-Christian or monstrous figures iconographically associated with Saracens wield falchions in the leaves of illuminated manuscripts. At least two among a group of Cyclopes depicted with Saracen attributes brandish falchions in the *Romance of Alexander*.[50] Similarly, the English Luttrell Psalter of the fourteenth century and British Library, MS Harley 2278's *Lives of Saints Edmund and Fremund*, written by John Lydgate somewhat later than *Sir Gowther* in the fifteenth century, each superimpose Saracen iconographic details onto Scots and Danes, respectively, and these hybrid figures are notably wielding falchions.[51] A fifteenth-century bench-end in East Harling (Norfolk) likewise depicts a wildman with numerous Saracen attributes, and this pseudo-Saracen hybrid holds what appears to be a falchion.[52] What I am suggesting here is that the falchion, a common European weapon noted for its striking force, became a marker of alterity in medieval European manuscript illuminations—one often, if not exclusively, associated with non-Christian or non-European groups. While

---

[48] See Roger Sherman Loomis, "*Richard Coeur de Lion* and the *Pas Saladin* in Medieval Art," *PMLA* 30 (1915): 509–28; see http://www.britishmuseum.org/explore/highlights/highlight_objects/pe_mla/c/chertsey_tiles.aspx (accessed March 9, 2015) for an image of the tile.

[49] Loomis, "*Pas Saladin*," 515, 517–18. For the image from the Queen Mary Psalter, see the British Library's online digital version of the text, http://www.bl.uk/manuscripts/FullDisplay.aspx?ref=Royal_MS_2_b_vii (accessed July 29, 2014).

[50] BL, MS Royal 20.B.XX, fol. 79v. See Strickland, *Saracens, Demons, and Jews*, 185, Fig. 94.

[51] See Michael Camille, *Mirror in Parchment: The Luttrell Psalter and the Making of Medieval England* (Chicago: University of Chicago Press, 1998), 287; and Robyn Malo, *Relics and Writing in Late Medieval England* (Toronto: University of Toronto Press, 2013), 77–79.

[52] See Strickland, *Saracens, Demons, and Jews*, 184, Fig. 92. The falchion is misidentified as a scimitar.

falchions are carried by some romance heroes, in many medieval European manuscripts they are exclusively weapons used by Saracens and other denigrated groups, and Gowther's emphatic retention of his falchion after his so-called rehabilitation casts suspicion on the efficacy of his conversion, a suspicion that is underscored in the text by other means.[53]

A number of scholars have suggested Gowther's affiliation with dogs and his resemblance to the sultan identify him with Muslims, so often disparaged as "hounds" by Christians in the Middle Ages,[54] and this constitutes another feature of the text complicating Gowther's conversion and questioning its finality. Noting, for example, that both Gowther and the sultan are rivals for the emperor's daughter, and claiming the sultan's violence toward Christian society recapitulates Gowther's early crimes, Ilan Mitchell-Smith argues that the sultan is a "double of the pre-redemptive Gowther" and that Gowther's "becoming a dog . . . increases the symbolic link between Gowther and the Sultan, as Saracens were often associated with dogs."[55] This connection between Saracens and hounds,[56] it should be stressed, is one made within the text of *Sir Gowther* itself, as the emperor, in rejecting the sultan's demands for his daughter, states he "wyll not, be Cryst wonde, / Gyffe hor to no hethon hownde" (391–92). In his attack on the sultan, then, Gowther, himself one of the text's "heathen hounds," essentially attacks himself, and he bears the wound to prove it, a wound that has proved hard for critics to explain.[57] In my reading, Gowther is both aggressor and victim, attacking Christian as well as attacked Muslim: a

---

[53] While he does not discuss falchions or conversion in any detail, Uebel has made a similar claim, arguing "the falchion is a permanent marker of [Gowther's] abjection," and that it "always undermin[es] the authenticity of Gowther's purported salvation" ("The Foreigner Within," 104).

[54] Uebel claims Gowther's efforts toward asceticism, achieved by adopting the position of a dog, fail, and that Gowther becomes "another version of the 'hethon hownde' . . . he will eventually fight in the emperor's name." Ibid., 107. See as well Montaño, "*Sir Gowther*: Imagining Race," 124–26; and Cohen, "Gowther among the Dogs," 230–33.

[55] Mitchell-Smith, "Defining Violence," 158.

[56] Such connections were fairly widespread, involving not just the figurative use of "hound" as an epithet but also the literal representation of Muslims as dog-headed *cynocephali*. For a discussion of both uses, see John Block Friedman, *The Monstrous Races in Medieval Art and Thought* (Cambridge, Mass.: Harvard University Press, 1989), 67–75.

[57] Crawford, for example, all but ignores the wound, saying it "has no consequence" aside from precipitating the princess's fall and setting the stage for yet another miracle; "Gronyng wyth grysly wounde," 45.

hybrid figure[58] who must defeat the pagan within before becoming "Goddus chyld," a process not achieved in a single moment of revelation earlier in the romance.

Further evidence undercutting the purported effectiveness of Gowther's conversion is offered by the pope himself when, after proclaiming Gowther to be God's child, the pope says to the convert, "the thar not dowt tho warlocke wyld / Ther waryd mot he bee" (674–75). Laskaya and Salisbury gloss the phrase "warlocke wyld" as referring to Satan and the word "waryd" as "vanquished," and the proclamation thereby becomes a comforting assertion of Gowther's safety from the devil. But the word "warlocke" had been used in the very beginning of the romance to refer to Gowther himself when the poet proclaimed

> [Y] schall tell yow of a warlocke greytt,
> What sorow at his modur hart he seyt
> With his warcus wylde.
>
> (22–24)

The word "waryd," as Dana Oswald has shown, derives from *varien*, a verb the *Middle English Dictionary* defines in part as "to undergo a change in form, attribute, status, etc., be altered; undergo successive or

---

[58] Similar arguments have been made for the depiction of King Richard in *Richard Coer de Lyon*, a Middle English romance with similarities to *Sir Gowther*. Like Gowther, Richard has a demonic heritage and participates in a three-day tournament with changes in armor. Moreover, *Richard Coer de Lyon* repeatedly makes use of the epithet "hound" to refer to Saracens even as it articulates the French claim that the English are "tailed" like hounds; see Lynn Shutters, "Lion Hearts, Saracen Heads, Dog Tails: The Body of the Conqueror in *Richard Coer de Lyon*," in *Masculinities and Femininities in the Middle Ages and Renaissance*, ed. Frederick Kiefer (Turnhout: Brepols, 2009), 71–100 (89). Given that the romance's most notorious episodes depict Richard as consuming Saracens in acts of cannibalism, a number of scholars have suggested a dual or hybrid identity for Richard. Suzanne Conklin Akbari says Richard "displays a bloodthirstiness and abandon more typical of a Saracen than a Christian knight" and refers to a "Saracen identity already latent in Richard" that "becomes heightened" once he engages in cannibalism; "The Hunger for National Identity in *Richard Coer de Lion*," in *Reading Medieval Culture: Essays in Honor of Robert W. Hanning*, ed. Robert M. Stein and Sandra Pierson Prior (Notre Dame: University of Notre Dame Press, 2005), 198–227 (216, 209). Noting Richard's similarity to Saracen depictions, I have argued in "Cannibalism and Cultural Encounters in *Richard Coeur de Lion*," *JMEMSt* 29, no. 3 (1999): 499–528 that Richard is "both 'other' and 'same' " (521) and that the text "hovers on the brink of a dangerous hybridity" (522); and Suzanne M. Yeager discusses Richard's "associations with Muslim bodies" through cannibalizing them: *Jerusalem in Medieval Narrative* (Cambridge: Cambridge University Press, 2008), 58. Cohen, moreover, discusses the canine qualities of Gowther's and Richard's hybridity. See Jeffrey Jerome Cohen, *Of Giants: Sex, Monsters, and the Middle Ages* (Minneapolis: University of Minnesota Press, 1999), 131–41.

alternate changes," and it here functions as a past participle designating Gowther's changed condition.[59] The pope's reference to the "warlocke wyld" invokes Gowther's pre-conversion self, whom Gowther need not fear because he is "waryd"—changed or converted.[60] Despite the pope's appraisal, however, the poem's ending serves simultaneously to question the finality of Gowther's conversion. The very word used to designate Gowther's having converted, "waryd" can not only point to a fixed change in status but also radically undermine such notions of fixity so that the individual who has "waryd" or converted is thereby "inconsistent," "inconstant," "erratic," even "unstable."[61] Like Gowther's retention of the falchion and his association with hounds, the text's verbal ambiguity here undercuts its efforts to stabilize Gowther's identity. Most importantly, these textual complexities follow rather than precede Gowther's Pauline conversion early in the text, the effect being that the poem problematically undermines Gowther's Christian identity and portrays him as a potential enemy of God after his supposed conversion.

Suspect Conversions in Medieval Europe

The text's only convert, Gowther is a site of radical indeterminacy, and by eroding the line between post- and pre-conversion selves, *Sir Gowther* reminds us forcefully how late medieval Christian converts, far from being greeted with unqualified enthusiasm, provoked anxiety, ambivalence, and suspicion, a state of affairs largely resulting from Christianity's changing sense of its role in the world. In the thirteenth century, as scholars have shown, Europe was essentially optimistic about the eventual Christian control of the world, whether through conversion, conquest, or both.[62] Some Europeans in the thirteenth century considered

---

[59] *MED*, s.v. *varien*; Oswald, *Monsters, Gender, and Sexuality*, 187. While Oswald argues for physical changes to Gowther designating a shift from demonic to human form, my argument is that "waryd" here draws attention to a change in status, specifically Gowther's religious classification.

[60] The Royal MS here makes a similar point. In place of lines 668–69 it reads, "The dare not dred of thi workys wyld; / Forsoothe, I tell it the" (*Sir Gowther*, ed. Rumble, 626–7). Both manuscripts, then, present the pope as expressing the idea that Gowther is protected, not from the devil, but from his former self.

[61] *MED*, s.v. *varien*; Oswald, *Monsters, Gender, and Sexuality*, 192.

[62] See Robert I. Burns, "Christian–Islamic Confrontation in the West: The Thirteenth-Century Dream of Conversion," *American Historical Review* 76, no. 5 (1971): 1386–1434; and John V. Tolan, *Saracens: Islam in the Medieval European Imagination* (New York: Columbia University Press, 2002), 171–274.

Islam as having relatively minor differences from Christianity, and missionary efforts were undertaken by mendicant orders because prospects for conversion through preaching were deemed good. The author of *De statu Saracenorum*, written in 1273, for example, waxed exceedingly optimistic about the possibilities of converting Muslims through preaching because Muslims "are close to the Christian faith and close to the way of salvation."[63] Others, like Ramon Llull, felt barriers to the conversion of Muslims were more substantial but could be overcome through dialogue and intellectual exchange.[64]

Any exuberance about the possibilities of worldwide conversion to Christianity diminished quickly in the late thirteenth and fourteenth centuries as a sober assessment of geopolitical realities began to replace the fantasies the West constructed for itself. The Fifth Crusade's hopes to capture Egypt, and eventually all of the Holy Land, were inflamed by an early victory at the key port of Damietta but dowsed by subsequent losses as crusaders were defeated en route to Cairo in 1221.[65] By the end of the fourteenth century, Ottoman Turks pushed into Europe, having secured victories in Bulgaria and Hungary, and of course the Muslim presence in Spain was considerable. Chief among the long list of political events causing hopes for "mass conversions of Muslims" to be "regularly dashed," as John Victor Tolan puts it, was the loss in 1291 of Acre, the final European crusader colony.[66] Europeans, who had long treasured the dream of converting the Mongol Empire to Christianity, watched instead as various Mongol factions converted to Islam,[67] and

---

[63] Quoted in Tolan, *Saracens*, 204. Benjamin Z. Kedar, *Crusade and Mission: European Approaches toward the Muslims* (Princeton: Princeton University Press, 1984) emphasizes this text's influence on the popular *Mandeville's Travels*, but he notes that Mandeville also endorses military action, suggesting a perception that doctrinal similarities and preaching alone could not achieve conversion (180–82). Many chansons de geste in the thirteenth century, however, clearly reject the idea of doctrinal similarities between Christianity and Islam, routinely representing Saracens as polytheistic idolators, an accusation found in non-literary texts as well and not merely part of a "fanciful" view of Muslims found in literary culture. See Akbari, *Idols*, 200–247.

[64] E. Randolph Daniel, *The Franciscan Concept of Mission in the High Middle Ages* (Lexington: University Press of Kentucky, 1975), 55–75. For specific discussions of Llull, see Tolan, *Saracens*, 256–74; and Burns, "Christian–Islamic Confrontation," 1398–1400. Llull's optimism about dialogue and intellectual conversion was modified later in his life as he came to endorse some military action.

[65] James M. Powell, *Anatomy of a Crusade 1213–1221* (Philadelphia: University of Pennsylvania Press, 1986), 175–93.

[66] Tolan, *Saracens*, 195.

[67] Denis Sinor, "The Mongols and Western Europe," in *A History of the Crusades*, Vol. 3, ed. Harry W. Hazard (Madison: University of Wisconsin Press, 1975), 513–44.

views toward the practicality of efforts to convert Muslims were affected to the degree that "Europeans in the early fourteenth century have a darker, more pessimistic view of Islam."[68]

Western Europeans not only feared the encroachments of Muslim cultures; they actively worried about conversion from Christianity to Islam, especially when the thirteenth century's fantasies of Christian domination dissipated. Benjamin Z. Kedar tells how in 1255 Humbert of Romans, then serving as the Dominicans' master general, promoted knowledge of Arabic as a means of converting Muslims to Christianity but abandoned such a view twenty years later when he realized few Muslims converted to Christianity but many Christians converted to Islam.[69] The difficulty involved in converting Muslims was apparent in western Europe and attributed to various causes,[70] and while rates of conversion are difficult to assess, some conversions from Christianity to Islam undoubtedly occurred.[71] Some of these may have been a consequence of Muslim military success,[72] and some

---

[68] Tolan, *Saracens*, 173.

[69] Kedar, *Crusade and Mission*, 155.

[70] Kedar, for example, discusses both the Islamic prohibition against the preaching of Christian doctrine, punishable by death, and also "Islam's positive hold over its believers." Ibid., 156. See also R. N. Swanson, *Religion and Devotion in Europe, c. 1215–1515* (Cambridge: Cambridge University Press, 1995), 261–62. Both Ricoldo of Monte Croce and Fidenzio of Padua saw economic advantages from conversion to Islam as a motivation for Christians abandoning their faith. See Sylvia Schein, *Fideles crucis: The Papacy, the West, and the Recovery of the Holy Land, 1274–1314* (Oxford: Clarendon Press, 1991), 97.

[71] For an attempt at such a study of an earlier period in medieval history, see Richard W. Bulliet, *Conversion to Islam in the Medieval Period: An Essay in Quantitative History* (Cambridge, Mass.: Harvard, 1979). For responses to Bulliet's methods, see Ragnhild Johnsrud Zorgati, *Pluralism in the Middle Ages: Hybrid Identities, Conversion, and Mixed Marriages in Medieval Iberia* (New York: Routledge, 2012), 26–31; and Michael G. Morony, "The Age of Conversions: A Reassessment," in *Conversion and Continuity: Indigenous Christian Communities in Islamic Lands, Eighth to Eighteenth Centuries*, ed. Michael Gervers and Ramzi Jibran Bikhazi (Toronto: Pontifical Institute of Mediaeval Studies, 1990), 135–50. For an essay arguing that in Crusader states conversions between Christianity and Islam were far from rare, see Benjamin Z. Kedar, "Multidirectional Conversion in the Frankish Levant," in Muldoon, *Varieties of Religious Conversion*, 190–99. See as well T. W. Arnold, *The Preaching of Islam: A History of the Propagation of the Muslim Faith* (London: Constable, 1913), 88–95.

[72] Jean de Joinville, for example, records forced conversions to Islam during Louis IX's crusade. See Swanson, *Religion and Devotion*, 263. Of course, conversions of Christians to Islam following Muslim military successes need not have been directly coerced but could have been deemed a sensible act, as seems to have been the case following the Christian loss of Acre. Witnessing such conversions to the victorious faith, Ricoldo of Monte Croce despairingly inquired whether "God wants the whole world to become Saracen?" Schein, *Fideles crucis*, 125–26.

occurred through intellectual and philosophic engagement with Islam.[73] Others, of course, constituted sincere religious change following exposure to another religion. Predictably enough, in Spain conversion to Islam caused particular concern, as seen, for example, in Pedro Pascual's concerted efforts through his writing to guard Christians living in Muslim territories from conversion and apostasy.[74]

While late medieval European concerns about Muslims were understandably greatest in Spain, the English nobility consistently returned to thoughts of crusade in the Holy Land and against the Ottoman Empire even as English society entertained widespread fears of imagined Saracen agents surreptitiously lurking in the realm. Both Edward I and Edward II took the cross, and while neither actually went on crusade, for the former at least the focus on Jerusalem's recovery in the 1280s and 1290s was more than political posturing.[75] Even when actual crusade planning took a back seat to the more local and nationalistic struggles engendered by the Hundred Years War, emotional investment in the Holy Land's recovery was strong. In the 1380s and 1390s, many English nobles, including John of Gaunt and Henry Bolingbroke, were deeply invested in crusade planning. In 1390, Bolingbroke assembled men to participate in a crusade to Tunis, and he abandoned participation in the crusade when, waiting in Calais, his requests for pledges of safe conduct from the French were rejected. Significant numbers of English noblemen nonetheless participated in the campaign, which "returned crusading against Islam to the agenda of practical politics after a generation's absence."[76] No later than 1392, John of Gaunt became interested

---

[73] The intellectual culture of Islam held great attraction for western scholars, an allure felt by some to be spiritually dangerous. John Tolan, for example, has discussed Peter the Venerable's efforts to chastise those Europeans who, drawn by the achievements of Muslim scholars in science and philosophy, may be swayed toward their religion. See John Tolan, "Saracen Philosophers Secretly Deride Islam," in *Travellers, Intellectuals, and the World beyond Medieval Europe*, ed. James Muldoon (Farnham: Ashgate, 2010), 145–69 (153). An example of one such convert prompted by intellectual reflection is the Franciscan Anselm Turmeda, who converted to Islam in the late fourteenth century after determining Muhammad to be a manifestation of the Holy Spirit. See Swanson, *Religion and Devotion*, 263.

[74] Kedar, *Crusade and Mission*, 155–56 and n. 60.

[75] Simon Lloyd argues that Edward I's failure actually to embark on crusade as king stemmed less from any personal disinclination and more from domestic pressures. See Simon Lloyd, *English Society and the Crusade 1216–1307* (Oxford: Clarendon Press, 1988), 233–39. See as well Christopher Tyerman, *England and the Crusades, 1095–1588* (Chicago: University of Chicago Press, 1988), 230–46; and Michael Prestwich, *Edward I* (London: Methuen, 1988), 326–33.

[76] Tyerman, *England and the Crusades*, 280. For evidence among the "true gentility" that "crusading enthusiasm [was] alive" in the late fourteenth century, see Maurice Keen, "Chaucer's Knight, the English Aristocracy, and the Crusade," in *English Court*

in plans long envisioned by Philippe de Mézières for a joint crusade with France, one that, as Tyerman explains, linked the "extravagantly emotional incentive" of the Holy Land's recovery with "a severely practical objective, the defeat of Islam."[77] Many of the most powerful men in England, moreover, had significant interactions with Muslims themselves or those fleeing Ottoman advances,[78] and Londoners too may have had some exposure to converts from Islam. Henry Ansgar Kelly catalogues a small number of likely Muslim converts living in London in the late fourteenth century, and he speculates that the *Domus conversorum*, or House of Converts, established in London for the purpose of facilitating Jewish conversion to Christianity, may have contained a number of former Muslims.[79] More significant than the actual number of converts, however, was the widespread belief in a Muslim presence in England, attested to, for example, by the popular belief that no less a figure than Saint Thomas Becket was half Saracen.[80] Even more telling is a decree by the "Good Parliament" of 1376, which notes with alarm that "Jews and Saracens and secret spies" were living in England, masquerading as Lombards and spreading "a horrible vice."[81]

In its poetry, too, late medieval England continued to engage Islam, and English literary texts tended to hold on to dreams of conversion and Christian ascendency long after they vanished in the political realm. Indeed, many romance narratives all the more vividly depict Christian power and prominence over Europe's non-Christian neighbors when such hopes are revealed as little more than medieval pipe dreams. Geraldine Heng captures the spirit of much of medieval European romance's treatment of Muslims when she writes "Saracens in romance are . . . neatly managed and contained by the military and conversionist strengths of triumphal Christianity."[82] *The King of Tars*, to which *Sir*

Culture in the Later Middle Ages, ed. V. J. Scattergood and J. W. Sherborne (London: Duckworth, 1988), 45–61 (58, 60).

[77] Tyerman, *England and the Crusades*, 297.

[78] Sheila Delany argues both points and notes John of Gaunt's protracted contact with Muhammad V of Granada. See "Chaucer's Prioress, the Jews, and the Muslims," in *Chaucer and the Jews: Sources, Contexts, Meanings*, ed. Sheila Delany (New York: Routledge, 2002), 43–57 (45–46).

[79] Henry Ansgar Kelly, "Jews and Saracens in Chaucer's England: A Review of the Evidence," *SAC* 27 (2005): 129–69, esp. 130–41.

[80] Ibid., 169.

[81] Ibid., 145. As Kelly says, "it is beyond a doubt that there was a suspicion that Saracens as well as Jews were living in England under false pretenses" (145).

[82] Geraldine Heng, "Jews, Saracens, 'Black Men,' Tartars: England in a World of Racial Difference," in *A Companion to Medieval English Literature and Culture, 1350–1500*, ed. Peter Brown (Malden: Blackwell, 2007), 247–70 (260).

Gowther has been compared, neatly exemplifies her point.[83] When a Muslim sultan and a Christian princess wed, a child described as a lump is born, and the child only transforms into a recognizable human infant in the baptismal font. Seeing this miracle, the sultan himself converts to Christianity and experiences an emphatic whitening of his skin. He is, moreover, a zealous convert and wages war on those of his own people who will not convert to Christianity. In the end, the sultan gives 30,000 people in his realm a choice between conversion or extermination, and the poem, written in the early fourteenth century, not only portrays an optimism about military conquests but also, by linking religious conversion to dramatic physical changes, underscores the genre's hopes that religious conversion to Christianity is both effective and permanent.[84]

Medieval Europeans may have desired and even idealized the conversion of Muslims to Christianity, in both life and literature, but it does not follow that such conversions were deemed wholly successful or lasting. Conversion requires a turning to something and a turning away from something else—what Robert Markus calls "disenchantment."[85] This process of distancing and disowning, however, is never complete or absolute for, in Frederick H. Russell's words, "In conversion there is always something left behind."[86] Medieval Europeans certainly felt the force of this theoretical point. In speaking of "Christian anxieties about Jewish and Muslim bodies," for example, Steven F. Kruger has examined the "uncertainty about whether religious conversion truly transformed those bodies, cleansing them of their impurities, repairing their imperfections, and removing the tinges of animality that clung to them in Christian fantasies."[87] The result is that "Conversion to Christianity leads to a kind of inclusion in Christian society, but that inclusion is by no means complete or unambivalent."[88] Indeed, in an essay focused on

---

[83] Gilbert refers to each as a story of "monstrous birth," and her Lacanian reading of these two texts charts the process by which "conversion is effected" and examines "the ideological move which identifies the Father with the Christian God." "Unnatural Mothers," 329, 342, 344. See as well Montaño, "*Sir Gowther*: Imagining Race," 125–27.

[84] See Akbari's discussion of *The King of Tars* (*Idols*, 189–98), which emphasizes "the transformative power of the Christian community" (158).

[85] R. A. Markus, *Conversion and Disenchantment in Augustine's Spiritual Career* (Villanova: Villanova University Press, 1989).

[86] Russell, "Augustine: Conversion by the Book," 13.

[87] Steven F. Kruger, "Conversion and Medieval Sexual, Religious, and Racial Categories," in *Constructing Medieval Sexuality*, ed. Karma Lochrie, Peggy McCracken, and James A. Schultz (Minneapolis: University of Minnesota Press, 1997), 158–79 (167).

[88] Ibid., 171.

the perceived "inefficacy of conversion" from Judaism to Christianity, Jonathan M. Elukin refers to likely "doubts in the minds of Christians about the fixity of baptism."[89] While such questions about baptism's efficacy as a tool of conversion demonstrably interested medieval Spain to a much greater degree than medieval England, *The King of Tars* and other English romances invest a great deal of interest in converting Muslims to Christianity and many dramatically underscore the role of the baptismal font in doing so.[90]

While *Sir Gowther* and *The King of Tars* have much in common, however, they differ in their assessment of the baptismal font's efficacy, for, unlike the miraculous baptism in *The King of Tars*, baptism in *Sir Gowther* effects no apparent change in the youthful Gowther. One might, of course, rightly contend that both texts reveal the same historical anxiety about baptism's efficacy but process those anxieties in different ways. This explanation, while true, does not delve deep enough, as it overlooks an even more perplexing aspect of the romance. Thus far, I have been discussing Gowther's conversion as though it were his adhering to a religion not previously held, a perspective the text underscores when the unnamed earl suggests Gowther is not of Christian "stryn." But Gowther was born of one Christian parent, fostered by a second, and baptized. When the pope, desirous of learning Gowther's identity, asks him if he has been baptized, Gowther answers affirmatively. In this sense, if the poem is about conversion, it is not about the conversion of non-Christians. Indeed, unlike *The King of Tars*, *Sir Gowther* evinces no effort toward or interest in converting the sultan or his Saracen forces. Instead, the conversionary impulse is focused on the conversion of an already baptized individual, on his turning more radically to the Christian God so that inner conviction mirrors outer conformity.

Much more common in late medieval England than converts from other religions, this kind of convert likewise drew suspicion from the larger Christian community. Lewis R. Rambo labels this form of religious conversion "intensification," defined as a "revitalized commitment to a faith with which the convert has had previous affiliation, formal or

---

[89] Jonathan M. Elukin, "From Jew to Christian? Conversion and Immutability in Medieval Europe," in Muldoon, *Varieties of Religious Conversion*, 171–89 (178).

[90] Siobhain Bly Calkin argues *Sir Ferumbras* and *The King of Tars* both underscore baptism's efficacy as an instrument of conversion by manifesting religious change on the body itself. "Romance Baptisms and Theological Contexts in *The King of Tars* and *Sir Ferumbras*," in *Medieval Romance, Medieval Contexts*, ed. Rhiannon Purdie and Michael Cichon (Cambridge: D. S. Brewer, 2011), 105–19.

informal."⁹¹ As John Van Engen explains, this kind of convert "turned away from ordinary Christian life . . . to pursue more intense forms of religiosity, freely chosen."⁹² Medieval society exhibited a great deal of anxiety over those who converted without attaching themselves to religious houses where they were subject to both a rule and superiors able to govern their conduct. Even when deemed to be sincere, lay converts posed problems for the larger Christian community. Van Engen notes that while converts "might elicit admiration," they nonetheless "generated tension" because "each act of conversion was an act of repudiation, a rejection, implicit or explicit, of surrounding society, meaning, the christened, the already converted,"⁹³ and he argues that such "'self-converts' lived in a precarious space, subject to suspicion and reprisal, with acceptance of their way of life ad hoc and tenuous."⁹⁴ This precarious space, I suggest, is the space Gowther inhabits.

Van Engen's essay posits that while suspicions and tensions always existed between such converts and the larger Christian community, "the strains around the year 1400 nearly shattered all the working systems for accommodating converts" seeking a deeper adherence to their faith.⁹⁵ As already shown, these same troublesome years around 1400 were also marked by growing skepticism about the likelihood and sincerity of conversion of non-Christians to Christianity, the result being that conversion in both forms was both ardently desired and consistently questioned.⁹⁶ Of course, the two types of conversion were not fully separate, either in theory or in practice. Bert Roest has shown how Franciscans in the thirteenth and fourteenth centuries adopted attitudes of

---

⁹¹ Rambo, *Understanding Religious Conversion*, 13.
⁹² Van Engen, "Conversion and Conformity," 31.
⁹³ Ibid., 35.
⁹⁴ Ibid., 32–33. Van Engen describes how the suspicion surrounding unprofessed converts was such that one medieval clergyman claims only two "long-term options" existed for the individual undergoing conversion: "professed religion or persecuted heresy" (32). While many such conversions resulted from sincere religious inclinations, it was felt that, in converting, many "acted more as tax dodgers, claiming the status but hardly altering their lifestyle" (33). Moreover, the Dominican Friar and famous convert Henry Suso, in his fourteenth-century *Horologium sapientiae*, warns "against routine or late conversions," which were seen as "attempts to circumvent judgment" (32).
⁹⁵ Ibid., 34. Van Engen argues that, because of sharp declines in population from plague in 1348–49, as well as the 1370s and 1390s, monastic houses experienced difficulty in maintaining both sufficient recruits and quality of life. The result was a decline in "mood"; a lessened tendency within monastic houses to observe the rule; increased suspicion toward those within monastic orders; and a loss to the orders of "serious" converts, many of whom sought their own way without the structure of a rule at all (40).
⁹⁶ In an article focused on converted Jews in Spain following the mass conversions of 1391, David Nirenberg asks, "why do societies that struggle sincerely and mightily to

earlier theologians about the importance of personal conversion, but since they "could not afford to concentrate only on their own spiritual welfare," Franciscans welded their personal intensification to the equally important goals of "converting the infidel to the Christian faith and of converting the ordinary believers to a real life of evangelical perfection."[97] Thus, among Franciscans at least, "Although the balance was not always found, the conversion of the self and the conversion of the other were often seen to be concomitant activities that should reinforce one another."[98] Lynn Shutters, moreover, sees a causal relationship between the self-doubt the already-converted reserved for themselves and the suspicions directed toward converts from Judaism and Islam. Noting that "doubts, fears, and suspicions of one's own motives . . . [were] part of the conversion experience," she reminds us that "Christians were particularly suspicious regarding converts to Christianity from other religions . . . because such suspicions allowed Christians to displace concerns regarding . . . their own progress toward God."[99]

In conflating the convert from a former religion with the already Christian convert seeking a deeper adherence to the faith, *Sir Gowther* underscores the structural and cultural connections among both forms of conversion and attempts to validate each. But this conflation is deeply problematic, and Shutters is right to see a link in the suspicions each type of conversion engenders. Disavowing conversion from without in its depiction of a sultan who evinces no desire to convert to Christianity, *Sir Gowther* likewise indicts intensification, conversion from within, by awkwardly linking the two. Moreover, in foregrounding the convert's Pauline moment of conversion, *Sir Gowther* holds out the hope of an immediate and irreversible conversion, but its subsequent employment of an Augustinian paradigm undermines the validity of that same Pauline moment, and the result is that, as in late medieval Europe, conversion is ardently desired and deeply distrusted.

---

assimilate their minorities ferociously resist that assimilation once they have succeeded?" "Enmity and Assimilation: Jews, Christians, and Converts in Medieval Spain," *Common Knowledge* 9, no. 1 (2003): 137–55 (138).

[97] Bert Roest, "Converting the Other and Converting the Self: Double Objectives in Franciscan Educational Writings," in *Christianizing Peoples and Converting Individuals*, ed. Guyda Armstrong and Ian N. Wood (Turnhout: Brepols, 2000), 295–301 (300, 297–98).

[98] Ibid., 301.

[99] Lynn Shutters, " 'Christian Love or Pagan Transgression': Marriage and Conversion in *Floire et Blancheflor*," in *Discourses on Love, Marriage, and Transgression in Medieval and Early Modern Literature*, ed. Albrecht Classen (Tempe: Arizona Center for Medieval and Renaissance Studies, 2004), 87.

Ambivalence and the Romance Ending

The ambivalence surrounding Gowther and his conversion is perhaps nowhere so pronounced as at the very end of the romance. The poem's last stanza states that "Syr Gwother coverys is care," recovers his estate, but on returning to his lands at the end of the romance, Gowther voluntarily gives them up (745). Having married the emperor's daughter with the pope's blessing, Gowther returns home and bestows his inheritance on the old earl who figured so importantly in his initial conversion moment. As the text says, he

> gaff tho old erle all;
> Made hym Duke of that cuntré,
> And lett hym wed his modur fre.
> (687–89)

Interestingly, both the character of the earl himself and Gowther's bestowal of the duchy on him are unique to *Sir Gowther*, inventions of the English text rather than a borrowing from its sources or a parallel to its analogues.[100] The peculiar ending thus aligns with neither its sources nor the generic expectations of romance, a genre that often signals the resolution of conflict and tension through the successful restoration of the protagonist's inheritance and the settlement of his succession.

Most critics overlook Gowther's disinheritance or ignore the implication of leaving the duchy to a very old man and a woman who sixteen years earlier was unable to conceive without demonic intervention. Crawford, for example, argues, "this marriage restores the social order in the country that Gowther has earlier terrorized."[101] Arguing "Gowther needs to restore, not claim, the paternal position," Alcuin Blamires states the romance "articulate[s] a trajectory of profound

---

[100] See Shirley Marchalonis, "*Sir Gowther*: The Process of a Romance," *ChauR* 6 (1971): 14–29 (28); and Dorothy S. McCoy, "From Celibacy to Sexuality: An Examination of Some Medieval and Early Renaissance Versions of the Story of Robert the Devil," in *Human Sexuality in the Middle Ages and Renaissance*, ed. Douglas Radcliffe-Umstead (Pittsburgh: Center for Medieval and Renaissance Studies of the University of Pittsburgh, 1978), 29–39 (37).

[101] Crawford, "Gronyng wyth grysly wounde," 45. Similarly, Dinah Hazell claims that "rather than disrupting social stability by ruining marriages, [Gowther] enters into his own union, and weds his mother to the earl who has ruled Estryke for him." Dinah Hazell, *Poverty in Late Middle English Literature: The Meene and the Riche* (Dublin: Four Courts Press, 2009), 168.

recovery."[102] Each of these readings neglects the problems implicit in Gowther's bestowal of the duchy on an elderly stepfather, a situation Patricia Parker calls a "preposterous generational ordering," one "in which son precedes father rather than the other way around."[103] Even if we see Gowther's relinquishing the duchy as a form of asceticism, the convert to God giving up the world, we are nonetheless left to conclude Gowther's conversion leaves the unsettled duchy worse than it was at the romance's beginning.

Gowther does, finally, return to Austria at the end of the romance, but he does so as a body ready for burial. Among the good deeds Gowther enacts following his marriage is the building of an abbey as reparation for the rape and murder of nuns, which he cannot forget. When he dies as emperor and "a varré corsent parfett" (a truly pious person), Gowther is buried at the abbey (727). At that same site, moreover, miracles occur to those who "sechys hym with hart fre" (733), for Gowther "was inspyryd with tho Holy Gost / That was tho cursod knyght" (737–8). While the Advocates MS refers to him as truly pious, the Royal MS specifically identifies him as "Seynt Gotlake."[104] The tension between Gowther's transformation to sainthood and his earlier role as chivalric, falchion-wielding knight has long been noted by critics, but by and large it has resulted in a substantial amount of scholarship geared toward examining the generic classification of the tale rather than prompting scholars to scrutinize the larger issues surrounding the text's treatment of Gowther's sainthood and conversion.[105] Indeed, for those willing to take the text at face value, Gowther's final transformation to sainthood is perhaps the best evidence of true rehabilitation and conversion,[106] his miraculous achievements both at the end of his life and

---

[102] Blamires, "Twin Demons," 56.

[103] Patricia Parker, "Preposterous Events," *Shakespeare Quarterly* 43, no. 2 (1992): 186–213 (188).

[104] *Sir Gowther*, ed. Rumble, 681. Citing in particular Guthlac's youthful violence, Vandelinde has argued that the identification of Gowther as Guthlac is "far from spurious." "Saintly Knight and Knightly Saint," 144.

[105] For discussions of the poem's genre, see note 1, above. The poem in the Royal MS actually ends with "Explicit Vita Sancti," and this Latin explicit alone has provoked much discussion among scholars. For an essay that ascribes credibility to the Royal MS's claim to be a *vita*, see Jane Zatta, "*Sir Gowther*: The Marriage of Romance and Hagiography," *Mediaevalia* 22 (1998): 175–98.

[106] Mitchell-Smith, for example, claims that the romance grants to Gowther "Christ-like redemptive power" with which he "heals the body that he once threatened." Mitchell-Smith, "Defining Violence," 159. Corinne Saunders likewise writes that "The violation and death of the first part of the narrative are replaced by miracle and healing: rape is reversed, rewritten in penance, love, and divine approval." Corinne J. Saunders,

in his death seemingly balancing and redressing the youthful Gowther's monstrous proclivities and sins.

This reading is widely embraced, and only a few critics have rejected it. Uebel disbelieves "Gowther's hygienic transformation," arguing instead that Gowther "remains fully the son of a demon, a perpetual foreigner, and unassimilable outsider."[107] Similarly, while Dana Oswald charts the transformation of what she considers Gowther's monstrous body into "something recognizable, understandable, and not only safe, but saintly,"[108] she nonetheless argues Gowther "retains a trace of the monster" and the poem "resolves this dilemma . . . by removing Gowther from reproductive circulation."[109] While these critics do see real complexity in Gowther's "transformations," they fail to connect that complexity, that excess, to social attitudes surrounding conversion at the time of the poem's composition. In my reading, Gowther's sainthood is not, as Oswald claims, a mechanism for assuaging fears about potentially monstrous progeny but a potent fantasy framing conversion as authentic, complete, and irreversible. Moreover, Gowther's sanctity does not so much repair his demonic sins as much as recapitulate, even resurrect, them. The final stage of Gowther's conversion, sainthood renders him able to cure the ills of the earthly realm, but in doing so it reminds each reader how Gowther once committed such ills against that same community. The monastery he founds, after all, is not merely a marker of his spiritual progress; it also serves as permanent reminder of Gowther's rape and murder of the land's former inhabitants. Although he earlier burned both nuns and church and thus "made hor plasse so bare" (702), the new construction stands on that previously evacuated space, a resurrected monument to sins that can be forgiven but not forgotten. The crowds gathered to Gowther's burial site are drawn, then, not just to a holy place where Gowther's remains hold healing power but also to the very site of the saint's most unholy actions. If, as René Girard claims, "All sacred creatures partake of monstrosity, whether overtly or covertly," then Gowther's sanctity is a powerful marker and reminder of the monstrosity it is meant to supplant.[110] Far

---

"'Symtyme the fende': Questions of Rape in *Sir Gowther*," in *Studies in English Language and Literature: "Doubt Wisely"; Papers in Honour of E. G. Stanley*, ed. M. J. Toswell and E. M. Tyler (London: Routledge, 1996), 286–303 (299).

[107] Uebel, "The Foreigner Within," 96, 97.

[108] Oswald, *Monsters, Gender, and Sexuality*, 180.

[109] Ibid., 194.

[110] René Girard, *Violence and the Sacred* (Baltimore: Johns Hopkins University Press, 1972), 251.

from being its polar opposite, Gowther's post-conversion self is stunningly like his pre-conversion self, the residue of which never fully leaves him and remains to trouble both text and careful reader.

In *Sir Gowther*'s depiction of a conversion that is both sudden and prolonged, the poem anxiously returns to and attempts to validate the process of conversion, which is never finished or complete. We may be tempted to see this merely as couching a larger theoretical point about conversion. Elukin, for example, writes that "Christianity was . . . a religious culture built upon the idea of incremental and imperfect conversion" and that "conversion promoted suspicion of converts."[111] As I have shown, however, *Sir Gowther* manifests no hope for the conversion of non-Christians to the Christian fold as do so many romances, and the conversion experience that is offered—the intensification of a Christian faith already formally adhered to—is problematized, revealing the deep distrust of any conversion efforts. Gowther becomes more, rather than less, like a Saracen after his supposed conversion early in the romance, and this peculiar identification serves to question the legitimacy of his religious commitments. Occupying the position of both Saracen and Christian, Gowther's post-conversion self is as much a hybrid figure as his pre-conversion, demonic self, and this unstable identity casts aspersion on the work of conversion, on its ability to effect lasting change. Having mobilized, from without and within, extreme challenges to the idea of a stabilized and stabilizing Christian identity, the romance resorts to the extraordinary measure of sanctifying Gowther in order to repair the ruptures to its representation of conversion and Christian community. The saving power of sainthood, however, never fully repairs the abject, sin-stained Gowther, and the poem thereby reveals deep suspicions about the same spiritual process it overtly embraces. Far from reveling in the hopes of an enlarged Christendom, *Sir Gowther* settles for indulging in a fantasy about its repair, but in the process it anxiously replicates late medieval European concerns about the power, potential, and practicality of conversion in all its cultural forms.

---

[111] Elukin, "Conversion and Immutability," 180.

The Poetics of Time Management from the *Metamorphoses* to *Il filocolo* and *The Franklin's Tale*

Kara Gaston
University of Toronto

Dorigen's rash oath in *The Franklin's Tale* exerts a claim both on her body and on her time.[1] She agrees not only to love Aurelius for removing the rocks from the coast of Brittany, but also to do so punctually: "Looke what day that endelong Britayne / Ye remoeve alle the rokkes, stoon by stoon, / . . . / Thanne wol I love yow best of any man" (*FT*, V.992–93, 997).[2] Dorigen's bargain represents a departure from Chaucer's presumed source, Boccaccio's *Filocolo*.[3] In the Italian text, a woman asks her unwanted suitor not for the removal of rocks, but rather for a May garden in January.[4] Yet I will argue that even as

---

My deepest thanks to William Robins and David Wallace for helping to inspire this article, to Jessica Lockhart for her assistance with Latin translation, and to Matthew Sergi and Leah Schwebel for their thoughtful readings.

[1] I must thank one of the anonymous readers from *Studies in the Age of Chaucer* for suggesting the extremely useful expression "poetics of time management."

[2] All citations of Chaucerian texts are from Larry D. Benson, gen. ed., *The Riverside Chaucer*, 3rd ed. (Boston: Houghton Mifflin, 1987). Line numbers are given parenthetically in the text. On the complex and unstable legal basis for the oath, see Richard Firth Green, *A Crisis of Truth: Literature and Law in Ricardian England* (Philadelphia: University of Pennsylvania Press, 2002), 293–335.

[3] Pio Rajna, "Le origini della novella narrata del 'Frankeleyn' nei *Canterbury Tales* del Chaucer," *Romania* 32 (1903): 204–67; and N. R. Havely, *Chaucer's Boccaccio: Sources of "Troilus" and the "Knight's" and "Franklin's Tales"* (Woodbridge: D. S. Brewer, 1980), 1–12, 154–61. See also Helen Cooper, *The Canterbury Tales* (Oxford: Clarendon Press, 1989), 233, for the argument that the two texts differ so extensively that Chaucer may be adapting Boccaccio from memory; and John Finlayson, "Invention and Disjunction: Chaucer's Rewriting of Boccaccio in the *Franklin's Tale*," *ES* 89 (2008): 385–402, for the suggestion that Chaucer used a second Boccaccian source, *Decameron*, X.5, to simplify and streamline his adaptation of Menedon's question.

[4] See David Wallace's account of the wisdom of this substitution, *Chaucer and the Early Writings of Boccaccio* (Woodbridge: D. S. Brewer, 1985), 67.

Chaucer replaces the garden, he retains its formal and thematic implications. Boccaccio's May garden episode carries out an exploration of literary time management: that is, of the way that literature divides up time, locates events within it, and assigns meaning to time's overarching structure. The May garden thematizes such efforts. An anachronistic pocket of springtime, it offers an escape from the cyclical time of the passing seasons. Chaucer's Dorigen, too, resists the regular passage of time. Her lengthy complaint attempts to "buy time" and postpone the fulfillment of her oath.[5] Chaucer, then, asks the same question as Boccaccio does in the *Filocolo*: Is it possible to create extra time within the schedules laid out by the seasons, the sun, and the moon? For Dorigen, this question has pressing stakes: as long as she "buy[s] time," she retains power over her body.

In coordinating an exploration of literary time management against issues of gender and power relations, Chaucer not only responds to Boccaccio, but also resurrects a central theme of Boccaccio's own source text, Book VII of Ovid's *Metamorphoses*.[6] The *Filocolo* derives the story of the May garden's creation from Ovid's description of an even more impressive manipulation of time: Medea's rejuvenation of her aged father-in-law, Aeson. The first part of this article reads the Medea episode in the context of the *Metamorphoses*' extended exploration of the various ways in which men and women, politicians and poets, attempt to manage one another's time. Time in the *Metamorphoses* emerges as contested territory, with powerful figures competing to interpret it and articulate its underlying structure. Ovid, paralleling his poetic *carmen* (song) with Medea's magical *carmina* (spells), presents his own poetry as a challenge to imperial timing. Yet he also recognizes his limitations. The *Metamorphoses* cannot transcend time, and ultimately presents its perspective on time as limited and transient.

The second section of this article turns to Boccaccio's adaptation of the *Metamorphoses* in the *Filocolo*. There, too, literature plays an important role in measuring time and articulating its underlying structure.

---

[5] Susan Crane, "The Franklin as Dorigen," *ChauR* 24, no. 3 (Winter 1990): 236–52 (248).

[6] Nicola Zingarelli, "La fonte classica di un episodio del *Filocolo*," *Romania* 14 (1885): 28–441 (438). Dorigen has previously been read in comparison with various female speakers in Boccaccio's works: see Michael Calabrese, "Chaucer's Dorigen and Boccaccio's Female Voices," *SAC* 29 (2007): 259–92. Here, I propose that her complaint should be instead placed in an aesthetic tradition that includes both male and female participants.

However, Boccaccio, writing from a Christian perspective, takes a more assured approach to the overarching structure of time than does Ovid. The *Filocolo* advances an interpretation of time in which Christ's advent allows for the reinterpretation and fulfillment of everything that came before it. Boccaccio parallels this Christian time management with the way that he manages the expansive, seemingly unregulated form of his own text. The *Filocolo* layers digression upon digression, challenging efforts to describe the text as part of a single, coherent plan. Yet Boccaccio ultimately provides a redemptive conclusion that allows for the reinterpretation of everything that preceded it.

The Franklin's Tale disavows the redemptive, Christian timing of the *Filocolo*, instead focusing on earthly attempts to manage and regulate time.[7] Although Chaucer does not directly draw on Ovid when adapting Boccaccio's text, his changes to the *Filocolo* resurrect the *Metamorphoses'* sense that time is contested territory and its manipulation an important source of power.[8] The third section of this article describes the various ways in which Dorigen attempts to manage her own time—or failing that, to forestall the efforts of other characters to manage it for her. Dorigen's complaint, in particular, defies measurement and assessment. I propose that the qualities readers often critique in the complaint (irrelevance, excess, disorganization) should be read as Chaucer's version of the powerful, disruptive *carmina* of the *Metamorphoses*. The complaint's resistance to measurement, moderation, and integration into the *Tale*'s larger narrative is also Dorigen's resistance to the management of her time by others. And as I illustrate in a brief coda to this article, the unruly timing of this collection of exempla may provide insight into the way that Chaucer represents the time of the *Canterbury Tales* themselves.

I. Managing Time in Ovid's *Metamorphoses*

The Aeson episode in Book VII of the *Metamorphoses* connects spellcasting with poetic composition in order to explore the boundaries of

[7] There is no direct evidence that Chaucer knew the entire *Filocolo*. Robert Edwards explains that the *Questioni d'amore* often circulated independently and that Chaucer may have used one such manuscript: see Robert R. Edwards, "Source, Context, and Cultural Translation in the *Franklin's Tale*," MP 94 (1996–97): 141–62. However, for readings that emphasize affinities between Chaucer's writing and the *Filocolo* as a whole see Wallace, *Chaucer and the Early Writings*; and Dominique Battles, "Chaucer's 'Franklin's Tale' and Boccaccio's 'Filocolo' Reconsidered," ChauR 34, no. 1 (1999): 38–59.

[8] I do not propose that Chaucer actually used the Medea episode in his response to Boccaccio. However, Kenneth Bleeth does suggest that Medea's claim to be able to root up rocks inspired Chaucer's adaptation of the rash oath: see Kenneth A. Bleeth, "The

both. The episode begins when Jason and Medea return from Colchis with the Golden Fleece. Jason, alarmed at how old his father Aeson suddenly seems, begs his new wife for help. With characteristic guile, he exclaims: "si tamen hoc possunt (quid enim non carmina possunt?) / deme meis annis et demptos adde parenti!" (VII.166–67)[9] (If your spells can do it—and what can they not?—subtract a few of my years to add to the years of my father.)[10] Even as Jason flatters Medea, this request challenges her to prove the efficacy of her spells. If she is really as powerful as she seems, she ought to be able to manipulate time. And when the power of magic comes under scrutiny, so too does the power of poetry, since the term *carmen* can mean both "spell," and "song" or "poem." The *Metamorphoses* itself is, in Ovid's words, a "perpetuum . . . carmen," an "unbroken poem" or "unbroken spell" (I.4). Medea's response rejects Jason's temporal mathematics but confirms this relationship between spell and poem. She asks, "ergo ego cuiquam / posse tuae videor spatium transcribere vitae? / nec sinat hoc Hecate" (VII.172–74) (Do you truly think that I could ever transfer a part of your life to another? Hecate wouldn't allow it.) Medea spurns the notion of merely transferring or copying (*transcribere*) the years from one location to another with her spell. She accepts Jason's challenge, but positions herself as poet rather than copyist. Her *carmen* begins with an outsized imitation of poetic conventions, invoking the night, Hecate, earth, the winds, mountains, rivers, the gods of the forest and of the night.

Medea continues by reciting her previous achievements, a résumé that evokes the ambitions of Ovid's own poetic past.[11] She boasts of having "turned rivers back to their fountain-heads" and made mountains tremble (VII.199–200), imagery that recalls the chaos wreaked by her own relative, Phaëthon, in *Metamorphoses*, II.[12] There, Helios's chariot scorches the mountains and turns the Nile back to its source. Phaëthon's chariot ride not only throws the landscape into chaos, but also

---

Rocks in *The Franklin's Tale* and Ovid's Medea," *American Notes and Queries* 20 (1982): 130–31.

[9] All quotations of the *Metamorphoses* are from *P. Ovidii Nasonis Metamorphoses*, ed. William S. Anderson (Leipzig: BSB Teubner, 1977).

[10] Translations based on *Ovid: Metamorphoses*, trans. David Raeburn (London: Penguin, 2004). I have frequently modified Raeburn's translation for clarity.

[11] For a different approach to parallels between Ovid and Medea, see Barbara Pavlock, *The Image of the Poet in Ovid's "Metamorphoses"* (Madison: University of Wisconsin Press, 2009), 41–42.

[12] On Medea's genealogical association with cycles of the days, nights, and seasons, see Alain Moreau, *Le mythe de Jason et Médée: La va-nu-pied et la sorcière* (Paris: Belles Lettres, 1994), 111.

disrupts the passage of time. When the bereaved sun hides his face in sorrow, days and nights are on the verge of losing their meaning. Ovid writes, "si modo credimus, unum / isse diem sine sole ferunt" (II.330–31) (if we can believe what is said, one day passed without the sun). Andrew Zissos and Ingo Gildenhard observe that "this sly reference to the sun's role as guarantor of temporal regularity problematizes linear chronology . . . *one* day went by without the sun—but how?"[13] Ovid's poem, audaciously measuring off days without the sun, offers instead its own mode of regulating the passage of time. When Phaëthon arrives at the court of the Sun, he is amazed to see assembled there the Days, Months, Years, and Centuries. Denis Feeney points out that these figures are novel, recent innovations with respect to the originary chaos with which the *Metamorphoses* begins. Ovid's *carmen perpetuum* contains and exceeds them.[14] Its poetic timing absorbs and manages solar time. Similarly, Zissos and Gildenhard observe that events in Book II diverge from a "'natural' temporal sequence," a narrative analogue to Phaëthon's wild chariot ride. Ovid rewrites time so that "narrative 'reality' seems to be torn between competing variants, creating an obvious disruption of continuity and linear progress."[15] In the very act of matching chaotic narrative time to the account of Phaëthon's flight, Ovid implicitly demonstrates his own virtuosic control over the poem's form and content. Unlike Phaëthon, the poet need not stick to the tracks of the sun in order to trace out the path of time.

Ovid's challenge to solar time anticipates his challenge to imperial time, a project in which Medea plays an important role. The management of time represented both a key element of Augustan politics and a defining characteristic of much of Ovid's pre-exilic poetry.[16] Andrew Wallace-Hadrill observes that Augustus's public calendars "turn[ed] all

---

[13] Andrew Zissos and Ingo Gildenhard, "Problems of Time in *Metamorphoses* 2," in *Ovidian Transformations: Essays on the "Metamorphoses" and Its Reception*, ed. Philip Hardie, Alessandro Barchiesi, and Stephen Hinds (Cambridge: Cambridge Philological Society, 1999), 31–47 (38).
[14] Denis Feeney, "*Mea tempora*: Patterning of Time in the *Metamorphoses*," in Hardie, Barchiesi, and Hinds, *Ovidian Transformations*, 13–30 (25).
[15] Zissos and Gildenhard, "Problems of Time," 39.
[16] See Mary Beard, "A Complex of Times: No More Sheep on Romulus' Birthday," *Proceedings of the Cambridge Philological Society* 33 (1987): 1–15; Andrew Wallace-Hadrill, "Time for Augustus: Ovid, Augustus, and the *Fasti*," in *Homo Viator: Classical Essays for John Bramble*, ed. Michael Whitby, Philip Hardie, and Mary Whitby (Bristol: Bristol Classical Press, 1987), 221–41; Alessandro Barchiesi, *Il poeta e il principe: Ovidio e il discorso augusteo* (Rome: Laterza, 1994); Stephen Hinds, "After Exile: Time and Teleology from *Metamorphoses* to *Ibis*," in Hardie, Barchiesi, and Hinds, *Ovidian Transformations*, 48–67.

Roman time into Augustan time," defining history, the daily calendar, and even the cosmic passage of time through Augustus's advent.[17] Ovid's poetic almanac, *Fasti*, brings the Roman calendar into conversation with—and, potentially, into competition with—the governing structures of poetry.[18] The *Metamorphoses* also treats the measurement of time as contested territory, beginning with a promise to describe history from before the creation to "mea . . . tempora"—"my time" (I.4). With these words, the poet claims as his own the era of Augustus. Feeney argues that Ovid's "mea tempora" represents a redefinition not only of the time of Augustan Rome, but also of imperial temporality, explaining, "the patterning of time [in the *Metamorphoses*] is *his* [Ovid's], and not anyone else's."[19] Part of this patterning involves rearticulating Rome's cultural debt to Greece. As Feeney shows, Ovid rewrites elements of his chronology in order to eliminate the possibility of a "time of pristine Romanness before foreign influence."[20] Building on Feeney's argument, I would add that in the Medea episode, Ovid binds his poem to the Greek past by conflating his process of invention with Medea's. Having finished her invocation, the sorceress embarks on a nine-day chariot ride across the Greek mainland that takes her to the mountains Ossa, Pelion, Othrys, Pindus, and Olympus, then to the rivers Apidanus, Amphrysus, Enipeus, Peneus, Sperchios, Boebe, and Anthedon. By sending his surrogate within the poem gathering herbs for her *carmen* within Greece, Ovid implicitly acknowledges his own debt to Greek culture. But here spell and poem do not merely resemble one another; rather, they work in concert, for with every site Medea visits, Ovid gathers more material into his poem, expanding his catalogues of mountains and rivers. The sheer excess of each of these catalogues is suggestive of the extra time Medea aims to create for Aeson. Meanwhile, as it dwells on the spell, Ovid's poem pulls more and more of Medea's story and the Greek past into its own time of composition, rather than confining the *Metamorphoses* to a Roman moment that would leave such material behind.

---

[17] Wallace-Hadrill, "Time for Augustus," 226.

[18] Along with the secondary sources cited in note 16 above, see Molly Pasco-Pranger, *Founding the Year: Ovid's "Fasti" and the Poetics of the Roman Calendar* (Leiden: Brill, 2006), which focuses explicitly on the interaction between "poetic didactic structures and . . . calendrical structures" (16).

[19] Feeney, "*Mea tempora*," 13.

[20] Ibid., 24.

THE POETICS OF TIME MANAGEMENT

The Aeson episode concludes by taking its ambitions one step further, not merely disrupting imperial historiographical narratives, but advancing poetry as a means of creating unexpected time. As Medea herself emphasizes, the powers of her spell extend beyond copying and adding years onto what already exists. In order to create more years for Aeson, Medea first brings his life to an end. She drains his blood, then pours her own potion into his veins. The old man wakes up one part at a time:

> stricto Medea recludit
> ense senis iugulum veteremque exire cruorem
> passa replet sucis; quos postquam conbibit Aeson
> aut ore acceptos aut vulnere, barba comaeque
> canitie posita nigrum rapuere colorem,
> pulsa fugit macies, abeunt pallorque situsque,
> adiectoque cavae supplentur corpore rugae,
> membraque luxuriant: Aeson miratur et olim
> ante quater denos hunc se reminiscitur annos.
> (VII.285–93)

[Medea unsheathed her sword and drew a cut in the old man's throat, so letting the blood drain out of his body. She replaced it with juice from the pot. When Aeson had fully absorbed this, either by mouth or by way of the wound, his hair and his beard lost all of their whiteness and quickly turned to a lustrous black. His leanness, pallor, and withered features all disappeared; those wrinkled and creased old cheeks filled out with their firm new flesh; his limbs grew supple and strong. In utter amazement and wonder, Aeson remembered that this was he forty years ago.]

Different fragments of Aeson's identity are gathered together as he awakens. Imitating this coming-together of parts, Ovid places different aspects of Aeson into the subject position of each sentence as his body returns to life. The old man's frailty flees; his pallor vanishes; his beard and hair change color. Only at the end of this series of transformations does Aeson himself occupy the subject position. Yet, at the very moment that his different parts cohere, Aeson's identity emerges as fragmented across time. This passage modifies Ovid's common technique of describing a metamorphosis from the perspective of astonished onlookers, instead positioning the old man as an onlooker to himself as he used to be.²¹ Aeson's rejuvenation comes as an encounter with an earlier version of himself. Such alienation might be compared to that of the time traveler: as Carolyn Dinshaw explains, when the Rip Van Winkle-style sleeper awakens and "confronts others around him, two different temporalities are manifest simultaneously; the present moment is multiple, the fact of temporal heterogeneity revealed."²² For Aeson, temporal heterogeneity appears not in his contact with others, but in his apprehension of himself. Constructing an identity in this context demands yet another type of collection: Aeson's self emerges as an assembly of heterogeneous fragments spread out across time. In granting Aeson this perspective, Medea's *carmen* transforms his relationship to time. Rather than simply adding more moments onto his life, the spell creates time in which Aeson looks back over his past. He occupies a coda to his own life—from within which he might gather the scattered moments of his life and achieve a representation of his own lifetime.²³

The reader of Ovid's poetry similarly occupies a coda: a time where the poem's own rhythms are gathered up and rendered comprehensible. Line 293 of the passage quoted above, "ante quater denos hunc se reminiscitur annos," describes Aeson's sudden, disconcerting, glimpse of his own past self. His dividedness is reflected in the line's two pronouns: "hunc," "this," describing the self that Aeson sees; and "se," the self with which he identifies. The line's scansion emphasizes the complex relationship between these two pronouns: "āntĕ quătēr dēnōs hūnc ‖ sē rĕmĭnīscĭtŭr ānnōs." "Hunc" and "se" are divided by a bucolic dieresis (here marked by double bars): that is, a pause created by an alignment between the ending of a word and the ending of a foot. The pause is indicative of the gap of years across which Aeson sees himself, as well as the shock involved in associating the "hunc" that he sees with the "se"

---

²¹ See *Ovid's Metamorphoses: Books 6–10*, ed. William S. Anderson (Norman: University of Oklahoma Press, 1972), 275.

²² Carolyn Dinshaw, *How Soon Is Now? Medieval Texts, Amateur Readers, and the Queerness of Time* (Durham, N.C.: Duke University Press, 2012), 41–42.

²³ This reading is strongly influenced by the account of "messianic time" as "an operational time in which we take hold of and achieve our representation of time" in Giorgio Agamben, *The Time that Remains: A Commentary on the Letter to the Romans*, trans. Patricia Dailey (Stanford: Stanford University Press, 2005), 68. Compare the similarly Christological interpretation of this passage in the *Ovide moralisé*, which reads Aeson's death as a figure for baptism and redemption through Christ. See Joel N. Feimer, "Medea in Ovid's *Metamorphoses* and the *Ovide moralisé*: Translation as Transmission," *Florilegium* 8 (1986): 40–55. Cf. *"Ovide moralisé": Poème du commencement du quatorzième siècle*, Vol. III, ed. Cornelis de Boer, Martina G. de Boer, and Jeannette Th. M. Van't Sant (Amsterdam: J. Müller, 1931), VII.1081–1246.

THE POETICS OF TIME MANAGEMENT

that he knows so well. But the two pronouns are also bound together by the same meter that performs this division. Metrics thus articulate the time that divides and connects different moments in Aeson's life, just as each they divide and connect the different parts of the poem.[24] Their hidden presence, moreover, comes abruptly into view as the alignment between meter and content, emphasized by the dieresis, creates a jangling overemphasis on the beginnings and endings of feet. Just as Aeson sees, from within time, his own identity unfolded over the years, so Ovid turns the binding numbers of his own poem into an object of representation.[25]

Such a perspective is only provisional. Even as Ovid uses poetic numbers to order and arrange time, he himself is subject to the passage of days and years. Susan Stewart, focusing on the Pythagoras monologue in Book XV, argues, "Ovid realizes that his own account is taking place in time and that, as he has seemed to embrace time in his writing, so will time eventually overcome that inscription."[26] However, the lines that she cites—a recognition that "desinet ante dies, et in alto Phoebus anhelos / aequore tinguet equos, quam consequar omnia verbis / in species translata novas" (XV.418–20) (the day will end, and Phoebus will plunge his panting steeds in the ocean deep before I complete my recital of change to new forms)—are not in the poet's own voice: they are uttered by Pythagoras. Indeed, for Ovid, part of the problem of speaking within time is the inability to represent himself fully. Instead, his voice is fragmented between different speakers. And moreover, as long as Ovid continues to write, he pushes the destination of his poem—*mea tempora*, "my time"—into the future. His own voice and his own lifetime evade representation.[27] The Aeson episode thus represents only one

---

[24] Compare Alessandro Barchiesi's comments on temporal discontinuity and poetic continuity in the *Fasti*: "Giorni, mesi e festi sono un invito alla separazione culturale del tempo vissuto, ma la separazione si percepisce solo su una continuità di fondo"; Barchiesi, *Il poeta e il principe*, 75.

[25] Agamben himself identifies messianic time with the rhythms of poetry, but focuses on lyric: he closely reads an Arnaut Daniel sestina, with its coda-like concluding *tornada*. As he argues, "the *tornada* returns to and recapitulates the rhyming end words [from the rest of the sestina] in a new sequence, simultaneously exposing their singularity along with their secret connectedness." *The Time that Remains*, 82.

[26] Susan Stewart, *Poetry and the Fate of the Senses* (Chicago: University of Chicago Press, 2002), 201.

[27] Helga Nowotny's account of "the longing for the moment" provides an evocative and relevant account of identity fragmented across time: "the search for the moment can . . . point inwards, to the unfolding of one's own, temporal self, to the development of an identity repeatedly reassembled from fragments." See Helga Nowotny, *Time: The*

experiment with poetic time management within the poem's longer movement. Similarly, for Medea herself, the coda that she adds to Aeson's life emerges less as a stable stopping point than as another weapon in a complex arsenal. Her success with Aeson lays the groundwork for her murder of Pelias, one of her many challenges to genealogical succession. In the *Metamorphoses*, even the act of interpreting time is contained within time, emerging as one among the many ways that people attempt to gain power over one another.

II. Managing Digression in Boccaccio's *Filocolo*

Boccaccio's *Filocolo* also uses interpretive codas as sites of enclosure, assembly, and interpretation. However, Boccaccio digresses even more egregiously than Ovid, and his codas, when they arrive, are correspondingly more definitive. The thirteen *Questioni d'amore* that make up the text's central digression exemplify this productive tension between closure and expansion. Queen Fiammetta proposes the question exchange to her "court," a group of young nobles gathered in a garden, promising that the questions will let the group forget the passage of time. As she says, "secondo il mio avviso, noi non avremo le nostre quistioni poste, che il caldo sarà, sanza che noi il sentiamo, passato" (IV.17.6) ("in my opinion, we shall no sooner have asked our questions than the heat will have passed without our noticing it").[28] Fiammetta presents as a virtue the distracting impulses that early readers of the *Filocolo* often saw as a vice. As Victoria Kirkham notes, early critics of the *Filocolo* identified quite a bit of material that "did not seem to 'belong'" to Boccaccio's text, of which the *Questioni d'amore* are only the most egregious.[29] Kirkham shows, in contrast to such readings, that the *Questioni* follow a pattern that repeats throughout the *Filocolo*: enthusiastic digression followed by retraction and conversion. Indeed, Fiammetta does not depict the question exchange as an escape or avoidance of the coming evening. Rather, she situates the *Questioni* in the context of an end point that is,

---

Modern and Postmodern Experience, trans. Neville Plaice (Cambridge: Polity Press, 1994), 152.

[28] All quotations from *Il filocolo* refer to *Tutte le opere di Giovanni Boccaccio*, Vol. I, *Caccia di Diana, Filocolo*, ed. Vittore Branca (Milan: Mondadori, 1967). Translations are from *Giovanni Boccaccio: Il filocolo*, trans. Donald Cheney with Thomas G. Bergin (New York: Garland, 1985).

[29] Victoria Kirkham, *Fabulous Vernacular: Boccaccio's "Filocolo" and the Art of Medieval Fiction* (Ann Arbor: University of Michigan Press, 2001), 187.

ultimately, to be desired. Boccaccio's digression does not contest solar time, as Ovid's does, but rather exploits its internal spaces.

This same structure is writ large across the lifetimes of the questioners. At the center of the *Questioni d'amore*, Caleon, overcome with love for Fiammetta, asks whether one ought to fall in love at all. Fiammetta responds by admitting that the group has been discussing love for pleasure to which, "niuno, che virtuosa vita disideri di seguire, si dovria sommettere" (IV.44.8) ("nobody who wants to lead a virtuous life ought to submit"). With the game's founding assumptions destroyed, the action can only resume when Pola, the next questioner, argues, "impossibile mi pare che la giovane età degli uomini e delle donne, sanza questo amore sentire, trapassare possa" (IV.47.2) ("it seems impossible to me that men and women should pass through their youthful years without experiencing this love"). She will therefore set aside Fiammetta's words "for now," "al presente," and proceed as if such love were acceptable (IV.47.2). As Pola's words show, the young people have a carefully plotted understanding of the shape their own lives take, locating their youth on a developmental timeline that leads inevitably to wisdom and recantation. They already have the perspective that Ovid's Aeson achieves at the conclusion of Medea's spell: they can see their own present moment as one within a series of moments gathered into a lifetime. This preemptive sense of closure facilitates the question exchange, for without the expectation that the young people are in a temporary state, its subject matter could not be justified.

Menedon's is the longest of the *Questioni d'amore*, a digression within a digression that scrutinizes the relationship between expansion and closure at the level of Boccaccio's language. Here, as elsewhere in the *Questioni d'amore*, an anticipated end point impinges upon the action from the outset. Menedon begins by explaining that he will use "una novella, che non fia forse brieve" (IV.31.1–2) ("a story which perhaps cannot be shortened") to explain his question. He argues that this narrative will be necessary for the group to come to a decision, a questionable argument that would, decades later, be belied by Boccaccio's stripped-down revision of Menedon's question for *Decameron*, X.5. There, Boccaccio eliminates the lengthy Ovidian borrowing that describes the magician Tebano creating the garden. Yet Menedon's egregious, seemingly unnecessary magical narrative has a parallel in the May garden itself: a garden within a garden ostensibly set apart from the normal flow of time. Precisely because they are out of place, the garden and its creation may be central to understanding the digressive, discursive form of the *Filocolo* as a whole. Lucia Battaglia Ricci argues that gardens such as Fiammetta's constitute part of a "gioco di specchi" (game of mirrors) that connects the storytellers at the heart of the *Filocolo* with the storytelling *persona* carefully developed in its opening section—and with Boccaccio himself.[30] Similarly, Menedon's May garden, along with the digression that describes its creation, is the central term within an interlocking series of digressive forms and *loci amoeni* in the *Filocolo*. As such, they anchor the romance's aesthetics. Indeed, as Warren Ginsberg observes, Boccaccio's description of Tebano's magic "revels in its eye-catching virtuosity," incorporating exotic details in a tour-de-force performance of literary prowess.[31] Tebano's magic thus offers both an analogue for and an embodiment of Boccaccio's literary art, just as Medea's *carmen* does for Ovid's.

Boccaccio's most virtuosic moments in this passage do not, as the *Metamorphoses* does, use literary form to challenge authoritative measures of time. Rather, the passage's brilliance derives from its ability simultaneously to evoke familiar forms of grammar and syntax—what might also be described as familiar patternings of time—and to put off bringing them to completion. One of Boccaccio's key transformations of Ovid is the encapsulation of Medea's entire invocation within a single grammatical unit. Ovid's Medea begins with a seven-line call to Hecate and various gods of the natural world, concluding with the vocative "adeste" (VII.198) (be present). She then recounts previous miracles accomplished with the aid of the gods, concluding with her recent exploits in Colchis. Only then does she get to the point: "nunc opis est sucis, per quos renovata senectus / in florem redeat primosque recolligat annos" (VII.215–17) (now I have need of the juices to make an old man in his weakness recover his youthful strength and return to the bloom of his prime). Boccaccio's translation preserves the content of the invocation with only slight alterations.[32] However, Boccaccio changes the placement of the vocative relative to the rest of the invocation. Rather than

---

[30] Lucia Battaglia Ricci, *Boccaccio* (Rome: Salerno, 2000), 85.

[31] Warren Ginsberg, "'Gli scogli neri e il niente che c'è': Dorigen's Black Rocks and Chaucer's Transformation of Italy," in *Reading Medieval Culture: Essays in Honor of Robert W. Hanning*, ed. Robert M. Stein and Sandra Pierson Prior (Notre Dame: University of Notre Dame Press, 2005), 387–408 (398).

[32] These changes remove explicit connections with the Medea story and soften the passage's darkest pagan connotations: Tebano invokes Ceres rather than Tellus and leaves out some direct references to events in Colchis.

THE POETICS OF TIME MANAGEMENT

wrapping up the first part of the invocation by calling on the gods to "be present," Tebano proceeds directly, by way of a relative pronoun, from the opening call to the gods to a recitation of his own past. Only after he recites his previous triumphs does he reach the vocative, delivering it with almost the same breath as he announces his new project:

siate presenti, e 'l vostro aiuto mi porgete. Io ho al presente mestiere di sughi e d'erbe, per li quali l'arida terra, prima d'autunno, ora dal freddissimo verno, de' suoi fiori, frutti e erbe spogliata, faccia in parte ritornare fiorita, mostrando, avanti il dovuto termine, primavera.

(IV.31.26–27)

[be present, and give me your aid. I have the need now for juices and herbs through which to make the arid land, which has been despoiled of its flowers, fruits, and herbs, first by autumn and now by coldest winter, return in part to flower, and to make a show of springtime before its proper season.]

Delaying the invocation's grammatical resolution, Boccaccio amplifies the passage's suspense. In the process, he displays his own control over grammar and syntax. And by combining the arrival of the vocative with the announcement of Tebano's new project, he pairs grammatical closure with interpretive clarity. The auxiliary, second sentence of the invocation assembles and makes sense of everything that has come before, subordinating it to a single purpose even as Boccaccio has enclosed it within a single sentence.

There are suggestions within Menedon's question that a similarly overarching structure lies, half-hidden, behind time itself. The question's pagan protagonists each propose different ways of managing time, both of which emerge as merely provisional.[33] When the story's would-be lover, Taralfo, encounters the magician Tebano, the latter is wandering the plains of Pharsalia, "lo misero piano che già tinto fu del romano

---

[33] Boccaccio's later interpretation of the Aeson episode in his *Genealogie deorum gentilium* emphasizes the subjectivity of time. There, he proposes that Aeson's rejuvenation is a matter of perspective: from Aeson's point of view, upon seeing Jason, "tam grandis letitia addita est, ut etas, que tendebat in mortem, in etatem retrocessisse floridam videretur" (such a great joy was added, that his age, which was drawing toward death, seemed to have reversed into a flowering youth). See Boccaccio, *Tutte le opere*, Vol. VIII, 13.xxv.2. A similar sense that this episode is an important locus for thinking about the experience of time emerges in Giovanni del Virgilio's commentary on Ovid (1322–23), which explains, "nam dum Eson uideret filium uenisse cum tam magnis diuitiis et tam pulcra uxore ita gauisus est quod uidebatur iuuenis esse. Quod Medea quia magica erat

239

sangue" (IV.31.10) ("that wretched plain which had once been stained with Roman blood"). The blood that once soaked the ground is useful fertilizer from Tebano's perspective, for he spends his time gathering herbs growing there ("cogliendo erbe") (IV.31.11). The image of Tebano literally gathering up the legacy of the dead has its figurative parallel in the magician's warning to Taralfo: "non sai tu la qualità del luogo come ella è? Perché inanzi d'altra parte non pigliavi la via? Tu potresti di leggieri qui da furiosi spiriti essere vituperato" (IV.31.15) ("don't you know what kind of place this is? Why didn't you choose some other place to wander? Here you could easily be attacked by angry ghosts"). Tebano, whose very name evokes the recursive disasters of Thebes, sees a landscape organized and interpreted by the events of history. The extreme violence that took place at Pharsalia transforms the battlefield into a space where the past threatens to repeat itself. Gathering herbs from the field, Tebano seems willing to take advantage of such an inheritance even as he fears its implications.

Taralfo, however, responds by articulating a perspective that homogenizes time and space. He argues, "in ogni parte puote Iddio igualmente: così qui come altrove gli è la mia vita e 'l mio onore in mano" (IV.31.15) ("God is equally powerful everywhere; here as elsewhere my life and honor are in His hands"). Taralfo refuses to allow the events of human history to create divisions within the landscape, insisting instead upon a divine perspective that is indifferent to the changeable events of the sublunary world. Nevertheless, his response creates its own problems. Taralfo leaves the battle of Pharsalia wholly in the past, as if it had no relevance at all for his own time and place. His words might be read as a refusal to gather, assemble, or interpret history at all. Later in the question, this attitude leaves Taralfo struggling to anticipate an end

---

sciebat facere aliquas medicinas cum quibus ipse Eson manebat in bona etate. Nam hoc sciunt facere medici. Vnde dictum est, arte nurus magice uixit yocundior Eson. Et redit in iuuenem prosperitate senex" (for while Aeson saw his son had come with such great riches and such a beautiful wife he rejoiced so much that he seemed to be a young man. And Medea [since she was magical] knew how to make certain medications with which Aeson himself remained in thriving age. For doctors know how to do this. Hence it is said that Aeson lived to be happier through the magical art of his daughter-in-law. And as an old man, he returned to youth through prosperity). My transcription, based on Florence, Biblioteca Medicea Laurenziana, Plut. 36 16, fo. 81r. I have modernized capitalization and punctuation and expanded abbreviations silently. On the composition and dating of Giovanni's commentary, cf. A. J. Minnis and A. B. Scott, with David Wallace, *Medieval Literary Theory and Criticism, c. 1100–1375*, rev. ed. (Oxford: Clarendon Press, 1988), 316–17, 360–66.

THE POETICS OF TIME MANAGEMENT

point for Tebano's spell. As he waits for the magician to finish his journey, he fears that he may have been made a fool of ("beffato") (IV.31.36). (Boccaccio's reader, caught within an extended digression, might share his concerns.) Yet if Taralfo had a Christian perspective from which to measure and read the spell's timing he might arrive at a different conclusion, for Boccaccio transforms the nine days and nights of Medea's spell into a three-day journey. This new timespan anticipates not only the resurrection of spring, but also the conversionary trajectory of the *Filocolo* as a whole.[34] As a corrective to Tebano and Taralfo's efforts to read time, the three-day spell hints that both Boccaccio's text and time itself have meaningful structures and impending conclusions—that they are as sure to arrive at an ending as are Boccaccio's sentences—even when they seem interminable.

When perspective on time finally arrives in the *Filocolo*, it comes to the characters as a sudden, divinely granted insight. In the same instant, Boccaccio provides the reader with a similar insight: a system for assembling and managing the text that has come before, generated through imagery of gathering itself. Steven Grossvogel observes that the meeting between Tebano and Taralfo evokes Lucan's *De bello civili* not only in being staged on the plains of Pharsalia, but also through specific allusions to the meeting of Sextus and the witch Erichtho, as well as to Cato's sacrifice of his wife Marcia.[35] Lucan also plays an important role earlier in the *Filocolo*. Boccaccio's early description of the slaughter of the Romans by Marmorino's pagan troops includes a description of a battlefield stained with blood ("tinta terra"—"discolored earth") that is based on lines from the *Pharsalia* (I.32.8).[36] When Tebano comes across such a field, he uses it to gather herbs for his spells. At the end of the *Filocolo*, however, the scene of gathering material from a battlefield is replayed to different effect. After their conversion, Florio and Biancifiore return to the site of the Romans' defeat and discover the bleached bones of the dead. They decide to gather up the scattered bones ("recogliere . . . le sparte ossa") but despair of separating the human bones from those of animals until a divinely provided vision conveniently color-codes them (V.89.1). The lovers collect the proper bones and return

---

[34] For the Christological allusions of the May garden spell, see Steven Grossvogel, *Ambiguity and Allusion in Boccaccio's "Filocolo"* (Florence: L. S. Olschki, 1992), 218–19.
[35] Ibid., 212.
[36] James H. McGregor, *The Image of Antiquity in Boccaccio's "Filocolo," "Filostrato," and "Teseida"* (New York: P. Lang, 1991), 130–31.

them to Rome. Very soon after this, the *Filocolo* itself comes to an end. Post-conversion, Florio and Biancifiore operate from a perspective that makes the past legible and interpretable. Collecting these bones and putting them into their places, Florio and Biancifiore assemble and interpret the fragments of past events. But for Boccaccio, this interpretive perspective is not a possibility offered up in the context of an ongoing struggle over chronology. Rather, it comes as the fulfillment of a long-deferred, half-forgotten promise. These final scenes allow the reader, too, to gather and assemble the events of the romance. For example, the contrast between the Christian lovers' burial of the dead and Tebano's herb-gathering retroactively uncovers significance in the magician's act. His name ties him to the city that famously forbade the burial of the Greek dead, and his magic similarly relies on keeping the dead unsettled: on extracting herbs from a plain that, from his perspective, is still haunted by unsatisfied ghosts. The conclusion to the *Filocolo* both puts the dead to rest and, figuratively, inters Tebano himself. He is fixed in place as a figure that foreshadows the romance's concluding scenes and yet never achieves the insight that comes with Christian conversion.

The *Filocolo*'s concluding interpretive coda comes with the force of a sudden, surprising insight, offering more finality than do Ovid's multiple, provisional patternings of time precisely because it has been so often deferred. Indeed, rather than setting the romance's concluding coda in rhetorical context, as Ovid does, Boccaccio associates it with the definitive perspective on time gained through Christian conversion. The end of the *Filocolo* brings not only a reinterpretation of the events of the romance, but also a reinterpretation of history. The priest Ilario explains at length to Florio that time is transformed by Christ's birth at the beginning of the sixth age, "piena di grazia, nella quale dimoriamo" (V.54.1) ("full of grace, in which we live"). Christ's birth turns the sixth age into the age of grace, in which history itself can be reinterpreted and redeemed such that it becomes possible "a salire a quella gloria donde ne cacciò disubidendo il primo padre" (V.54.6) ("to rise to that glory from which our first father exiled us through his disobedience"). But what happens when an interpretive coda, with all of its power to manage the significance of both the past and even individual lives, becomes a platform for rhetorical and political gain? This appears to be the case in *The Franklin's Tale*. Chaucer's poem, perhaps unwittingly, resurrects Ovid's strong sense of the politics of time management. In the *Tale*, efforts to define the shape of time are associated not with divine intervention, but with earthly claims of political and sexual power. In the third section of this article, I will argue that Chaucer counters such efforts by writing poetry that does not allow for the representation of its own timing or its own form. He removes the promised ending that underpins Boccaccio's entire enterprise. Instead, Dorigen's lament reorganizes itself with each new line, deferring indefinitely the time of assembly, assessment, and interpretation.

III. Managing Dorigen in *The Franklin's Tale*

In adapting Menedon's question for *The Franklin's Tale*, Chaucer eliminates both the request for the May garden and the magical interlude describing its creation. Nevertheless, both elements of Boccaccio's text are refracted across the *Tale*. Dorigen and Aurelius make their deal while in a "gardyn of swich prys / but if it were the verray paradys" (V.911–12).[37] Aurelius's prayer to Apollo proposes that the sun and moon remain in opposition for "thise yeres two," thus creating an extended high tide, a request that recalls Tebano's magical disruption of natural cycles (V.1068).[38] Tebano's magic has a further counterpart in the clerk of Orléans's careful observations of lunar motion, a magical performance that is also matched by literary ostentation: Chaucer replaces Boccaccio's Ovidian borrowing with a proliferation of technical, astrological language.[39] However, whereas Tebano's magic works upon time itself, the clerk works within time. His magic is only a temporary illusion: "for a wyke or tweye / it semed that alle the rokkes were aweye" (V.1295–96). Indeed if, as Karla Taylor argues, his trick is simply the product of the careful observation of the tides, he has done nothing more than

---

[37] See Linda Charnes, "'This Werk Unresonable': Narrative Frustration and Generic Redistribution in Chaucer's 'Franklin's Tale,'" *ChauR* 23 (1989): 300–15, 308, for the argument that the garden embodies a movement into new generic expectations.

[38] See Jamie Fumo, "Aurelius's Prayer, *Franklin's Tale* 1031–79: Sources and Analogues," *Neophilologus* 88 (2004): 623–35. Fumo proposes that the prayer that begins Tebano's spell may actually be a source for Aurelius's prayer. Cf. Richard L. Hoffman, *Ovid and the "Canterbury Tales"* (London: Oxford University Press, 1966), 170–71 (cited in Fumo, "Aurelius's Prayer," 628–31) on the role of Apollo as regulator of the seasons.

[39] As David Wallace observes, whereas Boccaccio enacts an "exotic *imitatio*," Chaucer "dazzles with a virtuoso display of technical vocabulary"; *Chaucer and the Early Writings*, 67.

recognize the right time to act.[40] A creative figure who produces illusory images of knights, ladies, and courtly life, the clerk of Orléans represents a possible counterpart for Chaucer himself, just as Medea does for Ovid. However, in contrast to his precursors, the clerk is caught within time. Unlike the spells of Medea and Tebano, his *carmina* cannot alter natural cycles; he must, instead, use those cycles to his advantage.

Having downplayed associations between literary timing and any overarching, definitive perspective on time, Chaucer instead depicts his characters using interpretations of time to exert power over one another. For example, Aurelius, for all of his professions of haplessness, is a canny reader and manager of social timing. In contrast to a lover such as *The Book of the Duchess*'s Black Knight, who simply realizes "upon a day" that he must speak to White or burst, Aurelius bides his time in order to strike at the right moment (*BD*, 1182). He steers his conversation with Dorigen in the right direction before recognizing the best time to speak: "forth, moore and moore, / Unto his purpos drough Aurelius, / And whan he saugh his tyme, he seyde thus" (V.964–66). Aurelius's ability to think on his feet, recognizing when to speak and when to be silent, embodies what David Wallace describes as "*kairos*: the timeliness of an utterance and its appropriateness to the particular circumstances obtaining at the moment of speaking."[41] Aurelius is equally strategic when he breaks the news of his success to Dorigen. He knows Dorigen's schedule well enough to anticipate her arrival: "to the temple his wey forth hath he holde, / Where as he knew he sholde his lady see" (1306–7). He addresses her, once again, with perfect timing that belies his fear:

> And whan he saugh his tyme, anon-right hee,
> With dredful herte and with ful humble cheere,
> Salewed hath his sovereyn lady deere.
> (V.1308–10)

---

[40] Karla Taylor, "Chaucer's Uncommon Voice: Some Contexts for Influence," in *"The Decameron" and "The Canterbury Tales": New Essays on an Old Question*, ed. Leonard Michael Koff and Brenda Deen Schildgen (London: Associated University Presses, 2000), 47–82 (73).

[41] David Wallace, *Chaucerian Polity: Absolutist Lineages and Associational Forms in England and Italy* (Stanford: Stanford University Press, 1997), 233. Compare the treatment of *kairos* in Robert W. Hanning, *The Individual in Twelfth-Century Romance* (New Haven: Yale University Press, 1977), 5–6 and 53–104. Hanning also explains that the term refers to a "subjective" and social sense of timing, but places more emphasis than does Wallace on the "far-reaching consequences" of particular "critical moments" of action (61).

Aurelius is as observant a reader of social cycles as the clerk is of the tides, and both are able to choose the right moment to turn time to their advantage.

In contrast to Aurelius's strategic manipulations of social timing, Dorigen, who attempts a leap in perspective comparable to that achieved by Boccaccio's lovers, finds that her own language is inexorably caught up within time. In questioning the "purveiaunce" of a perfect God, she inquires into the organizing structure behind time itself (V.865). Yet even as she reflects on how the rocks off the coast of Brittany threaten mankind, she struggles to define "mankynde" in stable terms:

> Se ye nat, Lord, how mankynde it destroyeth?
> An hundred thousand bodyes of mankynde
> Han rokkes sleyn, al be they nat in mynde,
> Which mankynde is so fair part of thy werk
> That thou it madest lyk to thyn owene merk.
> (V.876–80)

In order to argue that the rocks destroy "mankynde"—and that this is a bad thing—this passage must oscillate between different interpretations of the word. The *Middle English Dictionary* gives three definitions for the noun "mankynde," of which the first, "the human race, people in general," is most immediately relevant for Dorigen's argument.[42] This definition is itself subdivided into two specific meanings, one collective ("the human race") and the other referring to individual examples of the human race ("an individual human being"). Dorigen's first use of the term "mankynde" rests uncomfortably between these two meanings: is all of "mankynde" really threatened by the rocks? Or do the rocks represent a threat to any one member of the human race unlucky enough to encounter them? The following line clarifies: the rocks have destroyed 100,000 individuals: "bodyes of mankynde." Even as this phrase focuses in upon individual experience, however, it fixes "mankynde" in its collective meaning, for "mankynde" is the whole in which individual "bodyes" participate. This redefinition proves fatal to Dorigen's argument as it continues, for mankind, as an idea, will persist without Arveragus or the other hundreds of thousands who have died.

---

[42] *MED*, s.v. *man-kind(e)* (n.), available at http://quod.lib.umich.edu/m/med/ (accessed January 21, 2014).

Dorigen argues that God made "mankynde . . . lyk to thyn owene merk." Yet as she herself has shown, the rocks do not destroy the formal cause or the divine idea of "mankynde," but rather individual "bodyes" of it. In the very act of imagining a divine perspective capable of assembling, interpreting, and managing human history, Dorigen's language reveals its temporality, shifting beneath her.[43] Her lexicon is, itself, heterogeneous and divided across time, its meanings changing from moment to moment.

Accordingly, in her complaint, Dorigen changes tactics: rather than attempting to achieve an overarching insight into the world's governance, she reacts against forms of time management that are political, rhetorical, and gendered. These efforts to shape time are located firmly within history and constitute sites of conflict rather than of coherence. The complaint's first series of exempla begins, "whan thritty tirauntz, ful of cursednesse, / Hadde slayn Phidon in Atthenes atte feste" (V.1368–69). Chaucer's translation of the *Adversus Jovinianum* here closely follows Jerome, who writes, "Triginta Atheniensium tiranni, cum Phidonem [necassent in convivio]" (when the thirty tyrants of Athens had killed Phidon at a banquet).[44] In switching from inflected syntax to uninflected, Chaucer moves the relative adverb "when" to the beginning of the sentence, adding emphasis to the moment of action. Still translating Jerome closely, Chaucer reiterates the language of time throughout the opening six exempla.[45] The maiden Stymphalides installs herself in Diana's temple "whan that hir fader slayn was on a nyght" (1391). Hasdrubales' wife slays herself and her children "whan she saugh that Romayns wan the toun" (V.1401). Each of these exempla

---

[43] Compare the comments on the rocks in Kellie Robertson, "Exemplary Rocks," in *Animal, Vegetable, Mineral: Ethics and Objects*, ed. Jeffrey Jerome Cohen (Washington, D.C.: Oliphaunt Books, 2012), 91–122 (106). As Robertson argues, the rocks organize people, exposing their ideas and investments: whereas Dorigen sees danger, Aurelius sees opportunity. The rocks might also be read as introducing yet another form of measuring time—the geological scale—into the poem. Cf. Jeffrey J. Cohen, "Time out of Memory," in *The Post-Historical Middle Ages*, ed. Elizabeth Scala and Sylvia Federico (New York: Palgrave Macmillan, 2009), 37–61.

[44] *Adversus Jovinianum*, I.41, all texts and translations from *Jankyn's Book of Wikked Wyves*, Vol. II, ed. Ralph Hanna III and Traugott Lawler (Athens: University of Georgia Press, 1997).

[45] Donald C. Baker has suggested that the timing of suicide is a central concern throughout these examples. Noting that, unlike most of the other women, Lucrece commits suicide after rape, he proposes that Dorigen "is not wondering *whether* to commit suicide, but . . . asking herself *when*." See "A Crux in Chaucer's 'Franklin's Tale': Dorigen's Complaint," *JEGP* 60, no. 1 (1961): 56–64 (62).

derives the word "when" from Jerome. But elsewhere Chaucer adds the term. Jerome introduces Lucretia by referencing his own rhetorical timing and moral hierarchy: "ad Romanas feminas transeam; et primam ponam Lucretiam, que violate pudicitie nolens supervivere, maculam corporis cruore delevit" (let me now move to Roman women; and I put Lucretia first, who, not wishing to outlive her violated chastity, removed the spot from her body with her own blood).[46] Chaucer, however, locates Lucretia within the "when" of Tarquin's attack: she slays herself "whan that she oppressed was / Of Tarquyn" (V.1406–7). The *Adversus Jovinianum* includes many different kinds of "when," including social occasions such as the moment that Porcia the younger overheard praise for a remarried woman ("Porcia minor, cum laudaretur apud eam quedam bene morata que secundum habebat maritum respondit" [Porcia the younger, when a certain upright woman who had a second husband was praised in her hearing, answered]).[47] In collecting and assembling a series of exempla in which the "when" is that of imperial violence, Chaucer transforms Jerome's rhetorical "when" into a historiographical one, in which each moment in the complaint emerges as contested time.[48] The "when" of masculine, imperial force provides the coordinates for making sense of female suicide. But at the same time, the suicides transform each "when" into the occasion of resistance, putting a stop to the smooth forward movement of empire.[49]

In the very process of describing this decisive action, Dorigen uses language to avoid coming to terms with her own lifetime. Dorigen appears to sense herself being written into a predetermined narrative: evoking Boethian terminology more often associated with divine providence than with Fortune's wheel, she laments that Fortune has wrapped her in a "cheyne / fro which t'escape woot I no socour, / Save oonly deeth or elles dishonour" (V.1356–58). Her complaint responds to this limited future not by creating a contesting account of her timeline, but by resisting occupying any one time at all. As she transitions between

[46] *Adversus Jovinianum*, I.46.
[47] Ibid.
[48] See Warren Smith, "Dorigen's Lament and the Resolution of the 'Franklin's Tale,'" *ChauR* 36 (2002): 374–390 (382), which argues that Chaucer alters the tone of the material that he takes from Jerome, substituting "grief for the suffering maidens" and "contempt for their barbarous torturers" for Jerome's praise of chastity.
[49] See David Raybin, "'Wommen, of kynde, desiren libertee': Rereading Dorigen, Rereading Marriage," *ChauR* 27 (1992): 65–86 (72–74), for a reading that also emphasizes the power dynamics at work in Dorigen's complaint.

exempla and her own situation, her grammar moves dexterously from past to future, avoiding the present tense:

> What sholde I mo ensamples heerof sayn,
> . . .
> I wol conclude that it is bet for me
> To sleen myself than been defouled thus.
> I wol be trewe unto Arveragus.
> (V.1419, 1422–24)

Wan-Chuan Kao compares such language to "Pierre Bourdieu's notion of emotion as 'a (hallucinatory) "presenting" of the impending future, which . . . leads a person to live a still suspended future as already present, or even already past, and therefore necessary and inevitable— "I'm a dead man," "I'm done for."'" As Kao observes, even as Dorigen articulates her future, she holds it off, remaining in "a temporal nowhere, tiptoeing around other people's death wishes without an unequivocal course of action or guidance."[50] Such inaction might be read as comparing unfavorably with the women of the first six exempla, but it also suggests an alternative means of resisting the "deeth or dishonour" imposed upon Dorigen.[51] As long as Dorigen continues to speak, she moves forward in time, avoiding any one decisive moment.

The opposition between imperial time and the time of Dorigen's complaint recalls Ovid's positioning of "mea . . . tempora" against Augustus's time. Both Chaucer and Ovid consider how empire constructs particular narratives for itself, and both use digressive, expansive language in exploring how such narratives might be disrupted. For Ovid, this means inscribing his own poetry into a close relationship with its Greek origins as well as using poetic form to articulate the rhythm binding the poem together. Chaucer, in contrast, focuses on a different kind of origin for his poetry and different connections within it. As Dorigen's complaint continues, it performs its own provisionality, inventing each new example from the ephemera of the last. The seventh to tenth exempla use the resources of grammar, rhyme, and meter to propel themselves from line to line:

---

[50] Wan-Chuan Kao, "Conduct Shameful and Unshameful in *The Franklin's Tale*," *SAC* 34 (2012): 99–139 (135).

[51] The complaint is often read as an expression of confusion or distress: see for example James Sledd, "Dorigen's Complaint," *MP* 45 (1947): 36–45.

> I wol be trewe unto Arveragus,
> Or rather sleen myself in som manere,
> As dide Demociones doghter deere
> By cause that she wolde nat defouled be.
> O Cedasus, it is ful greet pitee
> To reden how thy doghtren deyde, allas,
> That slowe hemself for swich manere cas.
> As greet a pitee was it, or wel moore,
> The Theban mayden that for Nichanore
> Hirselven slow, right for swich manere wo.
> Another Theban mayden dide right so;
> For oon of Macidonye hadde hire oppressed,
> She with hire deeth hir maydenhede redressed.
>
> (V.1424–36)

The series of exempla begins as part of one long either–or sentence. But in a recapitulation of the overall digressive structure of the complaint, the seemingly unavoidable choice outlined in its first two lines quickly gives way to an analogy, beginning "As dide Demociones doghter." Here Chaucer's use of digression differs significantly from Boccaccio's. Whereas in Menedon's question, grammatical closure is deferred only to arrive all the more emphatically, Chaucer abandons anticipated end points altogether. Nor do the connections binding his verse together have the consistency of Ovid's dactyls. The story of Demotion's daughter extends two lines, leaving "be" in line 1427 unrhymed and setting the stage for another story. The account of Cedasus's (Scedasus's) daughters ends with a complete couplet, but connects with the next example through comparison. Chaucer highlights this incessant forward movement with the internal rhyme in line 1433. The rhyme on "slow . . . wo" simultaneously encapsulates the exemplum and propels the complaint into the next line, which completes the couplet with a third rhyme introducing another Theban maiden. Rather than calling attention to the overarching structure of a meter such as dactylic hexameter, Chaucer discovers within the ephemera of each exemplum the resources to keep writing. Thus even when this series concludes with the *rime riche* on "oppressed . . . redressed," an ostensibly satisfying stopping point, Chaucer uses the very notion of performing rhetorical prowess to move forward. The lament continues with a flourish of *occupatio*: "What shal I seye of Nicerates wyf, / That for swich cas birafte hirself hir lyf?" (1437–38).

This sense of productive contingency becomes increasingly significant as the lament's concluding lines each grow out of what are, seemingly, the least relevant aspects of the line before. The lament concludes by developing not content but names:

> The parfit wyfhod of Arthemesie
> Honured is thurgh al the Barbarie.
> O Teuta, queene, thy wyfly chastitee
> To alle wyves may a mirour bee.
> The same thyng I seye of Bilyea,
> Of Rodogone, and eek Valeria.
> (V.1451–56)

The exempla become increasingly compressed until the complaint concludes with "Bilyea, / . . . Rodogone, and eek Valeria," none of whom receives any description at all. Rhyme scheme and meter emerge as the only visible motivation for including these women's names, for the content of these exempla, even were Chaucer to include it, is often irrelevant. Bilyea, for example, is famous only for enduring her husband's bad breath. Yet her name becomes the starting point for a gratifyingly tripartite list of names that finally lands on Valeria, echoing the trisyllabic conclusion of the line before. Chaucer builds the complaint line-by-line, seizing upon whatever detail of form or grammar allows for its perpetuation, never gathering exempla according to a single, stable standard.

Critics making their own attempts to assemble and organize the complaint differ on its governing structure. Donald Baker identifies a three-part movement, from unmarried suicides, to wives who commit suicide, to good wives who survive.[52] Gerald Morgan assimilates the three parts of the complaint to the veneration of classical values—"chastity, fidelity, and honor."[53] In contrast, Warren Smith proposes breaking the lament into two sections of eleven exempla each, one consisting of women who commit suicide, the other of outstanding wives.[54] That multiple systems of assembling and arranging Dorigen's exempla are possible suggests that such acts of organization are themselves provisional. Nevertheless, measurement and division, including that of the complaint, have often

---

[52] Baker, "A Crux."
[53] Gerald Morgan, *The Shaping of English Poetry* (Oxford: Peter Lang, 2010), 166–67.
[54] Smith, "Dorigen's Lament," 386.

served as a basis for interpretations of *The Franklin's Tale*. Steele Nowlin remarks that the proliferation of units of almost-three throughout the poem "suggest[s] the imposition of a Christian time frame onto the pagan world of the tale."[55] Susanna Fein, meanwhile, cites Smith's reading of the complaint in support of "an underlying imagery of duality" associated with Boethian harmony between elements.[56] She is, however, careful to note that division into two is only one possible approach to the complaint.

I would argue that Chaucer resists representing the complaint as complete in order to render provisional any effort to gather, assemble, or organize its parts. Boccaccio digresses only to conclude with a conversionary coda, using the end of the *Filocolo* to expose the entire text as part of a coherent picture. But Chaucer does not provide the recapitulation of a coda so much as an extension of Dorigen's exemplary language. He writes,

> Thus pleyned Dorigen a day or tweye,
> Purposynge evere that she wolde deye.
> But nathelees, upon the thridde nyght,
> Hoom cam Arveragus, this worthy knyght.
> (V.1457–60)

The complaint itself becomes an exemplum: it stands in for a particular way of using time. And in the process, it resists the impulse of masculine readers (and rulers) to put events in their place. Chaucer transforms the "when" of events such as the rape of Lucrece into the "thus" of Dorigen, who passes time without ever staking a claim to be within a particular moment.[57] Ovid also uses poetic time to resist imperial efforts to define the shape of history. However, whereas Ovid opposes the rhythmic numbers of his poem to imperial measures of time, Chaucer leaves even the structure of his own poem partially obscure. The time of Dorigen's complaint cannot even be identified with the time of the written lament,

---

[55] Steele Nowlin, "Between Precedent and Possibility: Liminality, Historicity, and Narrative in Chaucer's *The Franklin's Tale*," *SP* 103, no. 1 (2006): 47–67 (62).
[56] Susanna Fein, "Boethian Boundaries: Compassion and Constraint in the *Franklin's Tale*," in *Drama, Narrative, and Poetry in the "Canterbury Tales,"* ed. Wendy Harding (Toulouse: Presses Universitaires du Mirail, 2003), 195–212 (206).
[57] Compare the comments on temporality and poetics in Eleanor Johnson, *Practicing Literary Theory in the Middle Ages: Ethics and the Mixed Form in Chaucer, Gower, Usk, and Hoccleve* (Chicago: University of Chicago Press, 2013), 144–45.

which acts as a metonymic stand-in for a longer period of speech.[58] Indeed, multiple manuscripts of the complaint include a gloss referring the reader to Jerome for more exempla: "Singulas has historias et plures hanc materiam concernentes recitat beatus Ieronimus contra Iouinianum in primo suo libro capitulo 39" (Blessed Jerome recites each of these stories and more concerning this material in *Contra Jovinianum*, in Book I, Chapter 39).[59] This gloss appears on line 1462, the end of Dorigen's complaint as printed, in Ellesmere and Additional 35286, but earlier in the complaint in other manuscripts. In some manuscripts, it appears immediately after the first exemplum; in others, after the initial list of unmarried suicides. According to Manly and Rickert, this suggests that the complaint may have "once ended earlier."[60] The complaint's ending appears almost accidental, a precarious point that disallows any effort to gather, assemble, or define its parts.[61] Such grounds for interpretation are as provisional as Dorigen's sense of "mankynde," a concept that relies on experience that is, necessarily, incomplete.[62]

Coda: Managing Story Collections from *The Legend of Good Women* to the *Canterbury Tales*

The *Filocolo* does not completely reveal the significance of Tebano's journey until it evokes the scene in its concluding section. Might the underlying structure of Dorigen's complaint also emerge retroactively?

---

[58] As Emma Lipton observes, throughout the *Tale*, Chaucer manipulates the relationship between "the duration of the purported events of the narrative" ("story-time") and "the time that it takes to read the tale" ("discourse-time"), sometimes setting the two into opposition and at other points allowing them to coincide. See *Affections of the Mind: The Politics of Sacramental Marriage in Late Medieval English Literature* (Notre Dame: University of Notre Dame Press, 2007), 33.

[59] John M. Manly and Edith Rickert, *The Text of the Canterbury Tales, Studied on the Basis of All Known Manuscripts*, Vol. III (Chicago: University of Chicago Press, 1940), 513 (my translation).

[60] Ibid.

[61] As Stephen Knight puts it, the exempla "seem to tail off into *etcetera, etcetera.*" See "Rhetoric and Poetry in the 'Franklin's Tale,'" *ChauR* 4 (1969): 14–30 (27).

[62] Although Dorigen's complaint does not retain the explicitly magical content of its digressive analogues in the *Metamorphoses* and the *Filocolo*, it nevertheless presents a suggestive analogue to the "feminine magic" of romance as Susan Crane defines it. As Crane observes, in both Chaucer's *Wife of Bath's Tale* and other English vernacular romances, feminine magic is associated with a resistance to completeness, encapsulation, and interpretation: "woman's uncanniness lies in her difference from men, but also in an inner differing that defies understanding." See Susan Crane, *Gender and Romance in Chaucer's "Canterbury Tales"* (Princeton: Princeton University Press, 1994), 157.

Whereas Boccaccio closely aligns the structure of Menedon's question with the structure of the *Filocolo*'s framing narratives, Dorigen's complaint does not evoke the frame narrative of the *Canterbury Tales* so much as it does that of *The Legend of Good Women*. The *Legend* resembles Dorigen's complaint at a basic level—both list famous women—but it also shares with *The Franklin's Tale* a tendency to approach storytelling as a way of using time. And in the *Legend*, as in the *Tale*, time is subject to regulation by powerful men. Alceste, mitigating the God of Love's anger, commands the poem's narrator,

> Thow shalt, while that thou lyvest, yer be yere,
> The moste partye of thy tyme spende
> In makyng of a glorious legende
> Of goode wymmen, maydenes, and wyves.
> (*LGW*, F 481–84)

As punishment for his representation of Criseyde, the *Legend*'s narrator is asked to give over the "moste partye" of his time. As critics including John Fyler and Rita Copeland have observed, the prologues to *The Legend of Good Women* position the text as a potential analogue to Ovidian palinode.[63] Although such readings rarely focus on the *Metamorphoses*, the *Legend* narrator's situation might be read as a reversal of the bravado of Ovid's claim to narrate world history up to "mea . . . tempora." For the narrator of the *Legend*, "thy tyme" is time measured out and allotted to the poet by a political power. The God of Love himself dictates the starting point of the narrator's catalogue of good women, insisting "at Cleopatre I wol that thou begynne / And so forth, and my love so shal thou wynne" (*LGW*, F 566–67). Cleopatra's story begins with a rhetorical gesture similar to those that pervade Dorigen's complaint, locating the action "after the deth of Tholome the kyng" (*LGW*, 580). With both his time and his historical perspective commandeered by the God

---

[63] See Rita Copeland, *Rhetoric, Hermeneutics, and Translation in the Middle Ages: Academic Traditions and Vernacular Texts* (Cambridge: Cambridge University Press, 1991), 186–202. See also John Fyler, *Chaucer and Ovid* (New Haven: Yale University Press, 1979), 115, on *The Legend of Good Women* as an Ovidian palinode that explores what happens when "art becomes propaganda." See also Wallace, *Chaucerian Polity*, 337–78, on the God of Love as absolutist monarch. Cf. Alessandro Barchiesi, "Voci e istanze narrative nelle *Metamorfosi* di Ovidio," *Materiali e discussioni per l'analisi dei testi classici* 23 (1989): 55–97 (91), which notes that the post-exilic *Tristia* rewrite the *Metamorphoses*' "mea . . . tempora," claiming instead, "in tua deduxi tempora, Cesar, opus" (II.560).

of Love, the *Legend of Good Women* narrator begins, appropriately, in time counted off in terms of imperial succession.[64]

Yet for all this, the *Legend* provides a cautionary example against the assumption that digression can be put in its place: that it derives from, and can be reintegrated into, a single overarching plan. In both *The Franklin's Tale* and the *Legend*, what remains unsaid—or what is about to be said—is of as much importance as the material on the page. In the F version of the *Legend*'s prologue, Chaucer's God of Love proves himself a poor reader of silence when he condemns the *balade* "Hyd, Absolon, thy gilte tresses clere" for failing to mention Alceste. In fact, the *balade* invokes various beautiful figures only to argue that they cannot compare with a lady who is about to arrive, presumably Alceste herself.[65] The *balade*'s refrain locates it in a moment of anticipation: "my lady cometh, that al this may dysteyne" (*LGW*, F 269). The God of Love assumes that a text fully signifies, and only signifies, those things that it names as part of its present moment. Yet the *balade*'s rejection of various beauties paves the way for a new possibility: a beauty imagined and anticipated, but never named.[66] Cupid's confidence that the names called out as part of the past can be left in the past—that their articulation has no bearing on possible futures—has a surprising analogue in Arveragus's response to his wife's confessions: "is ther oght elles, Dorigen, but this?" (V.1469). Dorigen's condition is inevitably more than what she says it is, for in the very saying, it changes. She has spent her time evoking different modes of knowing herself and her situation (whether as part of "mankynde" or in terms of ancient exempla) only to find, in each word and each exemplum, yet further expressive possibilities. Her complaint might therefore be read as a hinge between the homogeneous *Legend* and the *Canterbury Tales*, where new tales often develop as responses to accidental qualities of the previous tale. Even as the complaint reiterates its overarching theme, it discovers new expressive potential within each new rearticulation. As a result, even its

---

[64] See Laura J. Getty, "'Other Smale Ymaad Before': Chaucer as Historiographer in the *Legend of Good Women*," *ChauR* 42 (2007): 48–75.

[65] In the G version of the prologue, the *balade* explicitly names Alceste. Accordingly, the God of Love's protest has been altered: he argues that Chaucer should write about Alceste instead of Criseyde.

[66] The individual legends may have a closer relationship with the future than the prologue does. See L. O. Aranye Fradenburg, "Beauty and Boredom in *The Legend of Good Women*," *Exemplaria* 22 (2010): 65–83 (79), who argues that the legends deny the possibility of "imaginative metamorphosis, which transforms the signifiers of the past into something that has not been before."

subtlest interpretations are merely provisional. From this perspective, the *Canterbury Tales* does not delimit and interpret the complaint so much as the complaint models the contingent, opportunistic poetics of the *Tales*. Not "when" but "thus": the complaint does not delineate an extent of time, but rather enacts a way of being within time. As a result, neither the complaint nor the *Canterbury Tales* itself coincides precisely with chronologies that attempt to delineate them, whether the "thridde nyght" return of Arveragus or the arrival at Canterbury (V.1459).[67]

In this regard, Dorigen's complaint might be read as a process that unfolds unpredictably from word to word and line to line. It creates for itself an imperfection or infinitude that resists the claims that the various men surrounding Dorigen place upon her time. The patterns discovered within such a structure depend on how the interpreter establishes its beginning and ending—points that Chaucer leaves ambiguous at best. Similarly, the political stakes of Dorigen's complaint change depending upon how readers gather up and partition off its source texts. With the *Metamorphoses*' Medea established as the point of origin for Boccaccio's May garden, *The Franklin's Tale* can be read as Chaucer's return, via Boccaccio, to Ovidian concerns about literature and imperialism—concerns themselves familiar from *The Legend of Good Women*. The Ovidianism of Dorigen's complaint seems almost accidental, developing as Chaucer casts off elements of the *Filocolo*. Nevertheless, the surfacing of the *Metamorphoses* as part of the intertextual background for *The Franklin's Tale* corresponds with Chaucer's sensitivity to how readers' perspectives change over time and between contexts. This is apparent, for example, in his tendency to pick arguments with Italian sources that were unknown to virtually any of his early English readers. The result is poetry that, both in its internal structures and in its evocation of literary history, resists an Ovidian assembly of times or Boccaccio's interpretive coda. More precisely, it treats the establishment of interpretive perspective as, itself, an event that takes place within time. Chaucer preemptively evokes and rejects the powers of Walter Benjamin's historical materialist who "cannot do without the notion of a present which

---

[67] See Bonnie Wheeler, "*Trouthe* without Consequences: Rhetoric and Gender in Chaucer's *Franklin's Tale*," in *Representations of the Feminine in the Middle Ages*, ed. Wheeler (Cambridge: Academia, 1993), 91–116 (99), for the suggestion that the Franklin offers Dorigen and Arveragus's relationship as a "coda to *The Canterbury Tales*' previously voiced views of love and marriage." As Wheeler shows, this coda is ultimately unsatisfactory, potentially opening up new lines of consideration rather than closing down the old.

is not a transition, but in which time stands still and has come to a stop."⁶⁸ Such interpretive perspective is achieved through a claim to power over time that is gendered for Benjamin as it is for Chaucer: the historical materialist must be "man enough ('Manns genug') to blast open the continuum of history."⁶⁹ To the extent that Dorigen's complaint remains susceptible to changing modes of gathering and assembly throughout its afterlife, Chaucer turns the tables on readers, putting them into context and leaving the text open to the sudden, revelatory reassessment of the shape and significance of its contents.

---

⁶⁸ Walter Benjamin, "Theses on the Philosophy of History," in *Illuminations*, trans. Harry Zohn (New York: Schocken Books, 1968), 262. Compare Dinshaw, *How Soon Is Now?*, 16–24. Dinshaw turns to amateur readers as a means of unmooring textual interpretation from the measurement and assessment of time that underpin professional literary study. I propose that Chaucer's poetic form carries out a related move on even its most professional readers, destabilizing (and thus rendering contingent, ephemeral, and even personal) modes of division, analysis, and interpretation.

⁶⁹ Ibid. German text from Walter Benjamin, *Gesammelte Schriften*, I.2 (Frankfurt: Suhrkamp Verlag, 1974), 702.

"The writyng of this tretys":
Margery Kempe's Son and the
Authorship of Her Book

Sebastian Sobecki
University of Groningen

THE AUTHORSHIP OF *The Book of Margery Kempe* (henceforth *The Book*) has been the subject of much debate ever since the sole manuscript copy of the text was identified by Hope Emily Allen in 1934.[1] This

---

I am deeply grateful to Lena Wahlgren-Smith for transcribing and translating Gdańsk, Archiwum Państwowe, APG 300, 27/3, fol. 12r (printed in the appendix), without which this article would not have been possible. An early version of this article was first presented at the New Chaucer Society Congress in Reykjavík, in July 2014. I would like to thank Amy Appleford and Cathy Sanok for inviting me to give the paper. This article has greatly benefited from my exchanges with Anthony Bale, Stephen Alsford, Nicholas Watson, Rory Critten, and David Wallace. My Groningen colleagues Kees Dekker, John Flood, and Alasdair MacDonald generously gave their time to discuss the Gdańsk letter with me. I am also grateful to the Editor, Sarah Salih, and the two anonymous readers for *Studies in the Age of Chaucer* for making a series of valuable suggestions. I have modernized the letter thorn in the title quotation.

[1] All references to and citations from *The Book* are, unless otherwise stated, to *The Book of Margery Kempe*, ed. Sanford Brown Meech and Hope Emily Allen, EETS o.s. 212 (London: Oxford University Press, 1940). The complete text survives only in London, British Library, MS Additional 61823 (also known as the Salthows manuscript). Wynkyn de Worde printed extracts from the text in 1501 as *Here Begynneth a Shorte Treatyse of Contemplacyon Taught by Our Lorde Jhesu Cryste, or Taken out of the Boke of Margerie Kempe of Lyn{n}* (STC, 14924). On de Worde's printing, see Sue Ellen Holbrook, "Margery Kempe and Wynkyn de Worde," in *The Medieval Mystical Tradition in England: 4th Exeter Symposium: Papers*, ed. Marion Glasscoe (Cambridge: D. S. Brewer, 1987), 27–46; Jennifer Summit, *Lost Property: The Woman Writer and English Literary History, 1380–1589* (Chicago: University of Chicago Press, 2000), 126–38; and Allyson Foster, "A Shorte Treatyse of Contemplacyon: The Book of Margery Kempe in Its Early Print Contexts," in *A Companion to "The Book of Margery Kempe,"* ed. John H. Arnold and Katherine J. Lewis (Cambridge: D. S. Brewer, 2004), 95–112. The most important recent editions of *The Book* are *The Book of Margery Kempe*, ed. Lynn Staley (Kalamazoo: Medieval Institute Publications, 1996); and *The Book of Margery Kempe*, ed. Barry Windeatt (Cambridge: D. S. Brewer, 2004). The essays gathered by Arnold and Lewis in *A Companion to "The Book of Margery Kempe"* offer a good overview of the critical reception of the work since the discovery of the Salthows manuscript in 1934. In following Lynn Staley I use "Margery" when referring to the literary persona but "Kempe" when talking about the historical person; Lynn Staley, *Margery Kempe's Dissenting Fictions* (University Park: Pennsylvania State University Press, 1994). On the question of authorship, see my discussion below.

article presents two pieces of new evidence relating to Margery Kempe's son and to Robert Spryngolde, her confessor. The first item, a letter prepared for her son in Danzig (modern Gdańsk) in 1431, discloses the son's name and the reasons for his journey to Lynn.[2] This information, in turn, sheds new light on the account of *The Book*'s production as given in the proem. As a result, the discovery of the letter corroborates the theory that the son was Kempe's first scribe. A second previously overlooked document shows the extent of Robert Spryngolde's ties to Margery Kempe's family, strengthening the case for his role as the clerical scribe behind much of *The Book*. Both findings help to anchor the supposedly autobiographical narrative in its immediate historical situation. Finally, I offer a revised explanation for the collaborative model behind the production of this text.

I. Margery Kempe's Son in Danzig

At the beginning of the second part of *The Book* the text introduces Margery's son, who had been working for a prominent Lynn merchant.[3] The son's personal conduct appears to have fallen short of Margery's exacting standards, and she yearns for him to be "drawyn owt of þe perellys of this wretchyd & vnstabyl worlde."[4] Her subsequent insistence that her son "leeuyn þe worlde" produces the undesired effect of his fleeing her company so that he "wolde not gladlych metyn wyth hir."[5] A time of misrule for the son follows: he goes abroad, falls into the "synne of letchery," contracts what may be a sexually transmitted disease, returns home, loses his job, and in turn earns a humiliating rebuke from his mother.[6] Eventually, however, he abandons his "mysgouernawnce," and, after seeking and receiving his mother's blessings, moves to Danzig, where he marries a German-speaking woman, with whom he has a daughter.[7] Years later, he pays a visit to his parents as a man transformed both in appearance and demeanour. Even Margery, at first suspicious of his new "gouernawns," gradually realizes that her son's conversion is genuine, to the extent that she "openyd hir hert to

---

[2] I refer to the modern city by its Polish name, *Gdańsk*, but denote the fifteenth-century city as *Danzig*.
[3] *The Book of Margery Kempe*, 221.
[4] Ibid.
[5] Ibid.
[6] Ibid., 222.
[7] Ibid., 222–23.

hym, shewyng hym & enformyng how owr Lord had drawyn hir thorw hys mercy & be what menys, also how meche grace he had shewyd for hir."[8] The text states that his mother's infectious devotion inspires in the son spontaneous bouts of piety: he goes on "many pilgrimagys to Rome & to many oþer holy placys" before returning to his wife and child as "he was boundyn to do."[9] Back in Danzig, the son's reports stir in his wife an unstoppable wish to visit her mother-in-law, and the couple resolve to travel to Lynn with their daughter. Plans for a sea-journey are thwarted by inclement weather, and they leave their child behind with friends and end up traveling to England by land. On the day following their arrival, the son is suddenly taken ill. He remains bed-ridden for about a month before he dies.[10]

It has been noted before that the literary relationship between Margery and her wayward son is loosely modeled on that of Bridget of Sweden and her son Charles.[11] And it could certainly be argued that the persona of Margery's son serves as an exemplum to showcase her religious talents and, perhaps, advertise her inspirational brand of spirituality, for, after all, she predicts the punishment for the son's promiscuous youth; she brings about his conversion to a settled, Christian life; and she makes him go on not one but a series of pilgrimages. Crucially, the son's sudden passing is a catalyst for Book 2 itself, since it is Margery's self-imposed mission from God of escorting her daughter-in-law to Danzig that lends sense and structure to this part of the narrative.[12] The description of her sea-voyage, with a vivid account of the shipping of the oars during a violent storm, shows the writer's familiarity with accounts of Brendan's journey and other hagiographical texts.[13] But

---

[8] Ibid., 224.
[9] Ibid.
[10] Ibid., 225.
[11] The parallels are explored by David Wallace, *Margery in Dansk (David Matthews Lecture 2005)* (London: Birkbeck College, 2005), 3–5.
[12] David Wallace and Jonathan Hsy have written illuminatingly on her stay in Danzig in, respectively, *Margery in Dansk*, and "Lingua Franca: Overseas Travel and Language Contact in *The Book of Margery Kempe*," in *The Sea and Englishness in the Middle Ages: Maritime Narratives, Identity, and Culture*, ed. Sebastian Sobecki (Cambridge: D. S. Brewer, 2011), 159–78. Hsy's chapter has been reprinted, with modifications, in Jonathan Hsy, *Trading Tongues: Merchants, Multilingualism, and Medieval Literature* (Columbus: Ohio State University Press, 2013).
[13] Sebastian Sobecki, "Margery's Flight to Dansk," in *The Sea and Medieval English Literature* (Cambridge: D. S. Brewer, 2008), 135–39; and Wallace, *Margery in Dansk*, 9. See also Hsy, *Trading Tongues*, 146. The travelers ship their oars: "þei left her craft & her cunnyng & leet owr Lord dryuyn hem where he wolde"; *The Book of Margery Kempe*, 229.

Margery's Baltic voyage also serves to prove a much more fundamental point. When she first hears of her son's marriage and the birth of his daughter, the demands of the spiritual life clash with a personal desire to see him and his family: "Hys modyr being in a chapel of owr Lady thankyng God of þe grace & goodnes þat he schewyd to hir sone & hauyng desyr to sen hem ȝyf sche myth, a-non it was answeryd to mende þat sche xulde seen hem alle er þan sche deyid."[14] Characteristically, her instinctive response to an inconvenient answer from God is sceptical: "Sche had *wondyr* of þis felynge how it xulde be so as sche felt, in-as-meche as þei weryn be-ȝondyn þe see & sche on þis halfe þe see, neuyr purposyng to passyn þe see whil sche leuyd."[15] Her sense of *wondyr* articulates the miraculous magnitude of the challenge of moving against her resolve. God says it will happen, but Margery says it cannot be done. "Neuyr-þe-lesse," she concedes that "she wiste well to God was nothyng impossibyl."[16] Structurally speaking, therefore, the son's death enables one of the greatest miracles of *The Book*: that of God changing Margery's mind.

Although the text at the beginning of Book 2 states that this part of the work was begun in 1438, the son's death is believed to have taken place in 1431.[17] It is now possible to confirm the historicity of the son's visit to Lynn, in addition to providing further details on his voyage as well as on the son himself. Among the collections of medieval and early modern missives produced for the senate of Danzig, the National Archives in Gdańsk hold the contemporary transcript of a letter furnished for one John Kempe on June 12, 1431, bearing the shelf-mark APG 300, 27/3 (fol. 12r) (Fig. 1).[18] According to this letter, the city of Danzig requested the English authorities to assist John Kempe in recovering a security of 15 Prussian mark he had paid on behalf of Robert

---

[14] *The Book of Margery Kempe*, 223.
[15] Ibid. (my emphasis).
[16] Ibid.
[17] Ibid., 225. Barry Windeatt states that the son's death occurred "probably in the summer of 1431" (*The Book of Margery Kempe*, ed. Windeatt, 5). Allen and Meech give the year as "in or before 1432" (vii). On the date, see also Kim M. Phillips, "Margery Kempe and the Ages of Woman," in Arnold and Lewis, *A Companion to "The Book of Margery Kempe*," 17–34 (19).
[18] The appendix to this article gives a full transcription and translation of the letter, kindly furnished by Lena Wahlgren-Smith. All references to and quotations from this letter are to the text printed in the appendix. On this collection of letters, see Maria Slawoszewska, "Gdańskie missiva," *Archeion* 29 (1958): 199–207.

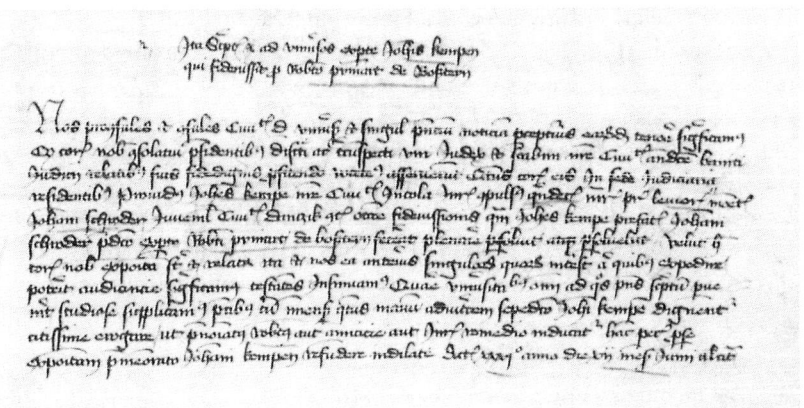

Fig. 1. Gdańsk, Archiwum Państwowe, APG 300, 27/3, fol. 12r. *Akta miasta Gdańska—Missiva*, June 12, 1431. By kind permission of the Archiwum Państwowe in Gdańsk.

Prinart of Boston to one Johannes Schroder.[19] Kempe bears the same first name as Margery Kempe's husband and her father-in-law.[20] Furthermore, Kempe is described as an inhabitant (*incola*) of Danzig in contrast to Schroder of the *Jungstadt* (an administrative division of the city), who is called "fellow burgess," or *concives* in Latin: "Johann*i* Schroder Iuueni*li* Ciui*tatis* Danczik *concivi*."[21] Despite the intimate and extensive

[19] In addition to local authorities requiring non-resident merchants to obtain securities, it was common practice in the various European maritime codes to secure capital and cargo. Robin Ward, *The World of the Medieval Shipmaster: Law, Business, and the Sea, c. 1350–1450* (Woodbridge: Boydell, 2009), 70–78; Edda Frankot, *"Of Laws of Ships and Shipmen": Medieval Maritime Law and Its Practice in Urban Northern Europe* (Edinburgh: Edinburgh University Press, 2012), 13–15; and Edwin S. Hunt and James Murray, *A History of Business in Medieval Europe, 1200–1550* (Cambridge: Cambridge University Press, 1999), passim.

[20] On the Kempes and Brunhams of Lynn, see Anthony Goodman, *Margery Kempe and Her World* (London: Longman, 2002), in particular chapters 1 and 2.

[21] The distinction between the rights and privileges of an inhabitant (*incola*) and a citizen (*cives*) was considerable both in the customary Hanseatic code of Lübeck and in the Teutonic Order's proprietary Kulm law. The Order gradually replaced Danzig's Lübeck law with its own code after it had gained possession of the city in 1308. See Andrzej Januszajtis, "Aus der Geschichte der Selbstverwaltung Danzigs," in *Deutsch–polnische Begegnung zu Wissenschaft und Kultur*, ed. Gilbert H. Gornig (Marburg: Danziger Naturforschende Gesellschaft, 2004), 144–67; and Sebastian Sobecki, "Danzig," in *Europe: A Literary History, 1348–1418*, ed. David Wallace (Oxford: Oxford University Press, 2015). Ulrich Meier discusses the legal meaning of "burgess" in medieval German cities (*Mensch und Bürger: Die Stadt im Denken spätmittelalterlicher Theologen, Philosophen*

Hanseatic relationships between Lynn and Danzig, full burgess rights were difficult to obtain for Englishmen, even for established members of the considerable colony of Lynn merchants who lived in Danzig. Marriage to a local woman would not have given Kempe burgess rights by default—hence the term *incola*.[22] One reason for such difficulties was the number of spats and retaliatory measures exchanged between England and the monastic state of the Teutonic Order, which ruled Danzig at the time.[23] "Robert Prinart," against whom this letter is directed, cannot be securely identified, but he may be a relation of the Lynn mayor John Parmonter.[24] The letter is issued in Latin, usually

---

und Juristen [Munich: Oldenbourg, 1994], 127–212). For the distinction between *incola* and *cives* in Lübeck law, see David Mevius, *Commentarii in Ius Lubecense* (Frankfurt: Wohler, 1744), Book 1, Section 28, Chapter 2, "Ad municipales et de incolis."

[22] Lynn merchants and their families constituted a sizeable community in Danzig, and there were also Danzigers living permanently in Lynn. Lynn's role in the Hanseatic network that connected the town with Danzig is treated by Dorothy Mary Owen, *The Making of King's Lynn: A Documentary Survey* (London: Oxford University Press for the British Academy, 1984), 278–82, 285–95; T. H. Lloyd, *England and the German Hanse, 1157–1611: A Study of Their Trade and Commercial Diplomacy* (Cambridge: Cambridge University Press, 1991), 91–94; Kate Parker, "Lynn and the Making of a Mystic," in Arnold and Lewis, *A Companion to "The Book of Margery Kempe,"* 55–73 (57–61); Goodman, *Margery Kempe and Her World*, 15–21; and, in particular, Stuart Jenks in a series of publications: "Der *Liber Lynne* und die Besitzgeschichte des hansischen Stalhofs zu Lynn," *Zeitschrift des Vereins für Lübeckische Geschichte und Altertumskunde* 68 (1988): 21–81; *England, die Hanse und Preußen: Handel und Diplomatie, 1377–1474*, 3 vols. (Cologne: Böhlau for the Hansischer Geschichtsverein, 1992), esp. 1:276–79, 417–23; 3:1017–24, 1116–25, and 1215–26; and "King's Lynn and the Hanse: Trade and Relations in the Middle Ages," in *Essays in Hanseatic History: The King's Lynn Symposium*, ed. Paul Richards and Klaus Friedland (Dereham: Larks Press, 2005), 94–114.

[23] Restrictions and expulsions were common during the trade disputes between England and the Teutonic Order in the fifteenth century. In 1402, for instance, only those Englishmen who were unmarried or married to "Prussian women . . . were allowed to remain," whereas in 1405 the Grand Master ordered "all Englishmen without burgess rights in Prussia" to leave the country; Lloyd, *England and the German Hanse*, 114, 115. The 1420s and 1430s saw renewed disputes between the two parties, resulting in various curtailments of rights for non-burgesses; ibid., 136–37. For the contemporary poundage crisis of 1431–34, see Jenks, *England, die Hanse und Preußen*, 2:575–88. An added layer of conflict was provided by the continued internal tensions between the city and the Order that led to the decision of Danzig and its fellow Prussian cities to join Poland in 1454; Sobecki, "Danzig."

[24] I have not been able to locate Robert Prinart or individuals with similar-sounding names in the Boston area. Since English names were entered in such documents by Prussian clerks, a considerable amount of phonetic corruption is common. One possibility is that Robert Prinart is Robert Parmenter (also spelled Permenter; Parmenter; Parmontier; Permontere; and, after 1500, Parmyter), the son of the then mayor of Lynn, John Parmonter. Robert only appears in one notorious document (dating from between 1430 and 1432) in which he and his father are accused of assaulting the gauger of the town's port at night (*Calendars of Proceedings in Chancery*, C1/26/290). The vintner John Parmonter was a prominent citizen of Lynn and six-time mayor between 1423 and

reserved for communication between Danzig and particularly England, Denmark, and Poland-Lithuania. Documents addressed to other Hanseatic member cities or to Dutch-speaking towns are composed in Low German, the language of the League and Danzig's town administration.[25] This letter, therefore, is clearly directed at the English authorities, asking them to induce Prinart "through the means either of friendship or of justice" to reimburse Kempe for the security the latter had paid to Schroder. At the same time, the validity of the letter is fixed at "three months [from] my putting my hand to this."

Given the date, contents, and address of the letter, I believe it safe to identify John Kempe with Margery Kempe's son, not least because the name "John" appears to have been a naming tradition in the Kempe family for at least two generations.[26] The three months' validity of the letter did not provide John with a great deal of flexibility in the first place, but it would have given him sufficient time to sail from Danzig to England to pursue this particular request, in addition to conducting other pressing business he may have had in Lincolnshire and East Anglia. This letter, therefore, must have been issued around the time of

---

1437, including 1431; L. S. Woodger, "Parmenter, John (d. 1437), of Bishop's Lynn, Norf.," in *The History of Parliament: The House of Commons 1386–1421*, ed. John Smith Roskell, L. Clark, and Carole Rawcliffe, 4 vols. (Stroud: Alan Sutton for History of Parliament Trust, 1992), available at http://www.historyofparliamentonline.org/volume/1386-1421/member/parmenter-john-1437. In March 1406 he entered into a partnership with Robert Brunham, Margery Kempe's probable brother, to import wine from Gascony (Woodger, "Parmenter, John"), perhaps through Boston, a major import hub for Gascon wine responsible for almost all the region's trade in wine; E. M. Carus-Wilson, "The Medieval Trade of the Ports of the Wash," *Medieval Archaeology* 11 (1962): 182–201 (190). Parmenter certainly had business dealings with Boston wine merchants: D. M. Owen, ed., *William Ashbourne's Book*, Norfolk Record Society 48 (Norwich: Norfolk Record Society, 1981), 71. It is not inconceivable that Robert was based in Boston to oversee his father's interests in the wine trade. The family connections with the Brunhams may have helped facilitate the financial arrangements for the security paid by John Kempe in Danzig.

[25] Outside the cities, Prussia's spoken language of administration was the Teutonic Order's East Middle German (written communication was conducted in Latin); see Sobecki, "Danzig"; Freimut Löser, "Literatur im deutschen Orden: Vorüberlegungen zu ihrer Geschichte," in *Mittelalterliche Kultur und Literatur im Deutschordensstaat in Preussen: Leben und Nachleben*, ed. Sieglinde Hartmann, Jarosław Wenta, and Gisela Vollmann-Profe (Toruń: Wydawnictwo Naukowe Uniwersytetu Mikołaja Kopernika, 2008), 331–54 (336); and Christopher Young and Thomas Gloning, *A History of the German Language through Texts* (London: Routledge, 2004), 175–84.

[26] Both Margery Kempe's husband and her father-in-law were called John; Felicity Riddy, "Kempe (née Brunham), Margery," in *The Oxford Dictionary of National Biography*, ed. H. C. G. Matthew and B. Harrison (Oxford: Oxford University Press, 2004), available at http://www.oxforddnb.com.

his planned departure. *The Book* notes that bad weather prevents Margery's son from leaving Danzig by ship, and, after making arrangements for their daughter, he and his Prussian wife depart for England by land. The delay caused by the weather may have cost John and his wife a few days, perhaps up to a week. Therefore, his departure probably took place a few days after June 12, 1431 at the earliest. Traveling from Danzig to Lynn by land via northern France amounts to just over 1,000 miles, or 1,600 km. Given an average of 50 km per day, the Kempes would have required about 32 days to complete the journey.[27] At the earliest, therefore, they would have reached Lynn at the end of July 1431, but because the letter would have been valid for only some six more weeks at this stage, presumably John traveled first to Boston to present the letter to the town authorities. It is safe to assume, therefore, that John Kempe visited his mother in Lynn between the end of July and the beginning of August 1431, and that he therefore died either in late August or early September. His motivation for undertaking such a journey need not have been restricted to his wife's fervent desire to meet her mother-in-law (if this was indeed the case): it is difficult to establish the precise value of the security John was trying to recover given the many problems of calculating exchange rates for the middle of the fifteenth century, but 15 Prussian mark in the 1430s amounted to almost £4.[28] This was not a negligible sum, and it may have justified the outlay

---

[27] For travel times, see Michael McCormick, "Time under Way," in *Origins of the European Economy: Communications and Commerce AD 300–900* (Cambridge: Cambridge University Press, 2001), Chap. 16, 469–500. McCormick calculates the average speed of overland travel in early medieval Europe as ranging between 25 and 50 km per day (479). The higher figure is for journeys on horseback and depends on such factors as weather, season, and terrain. The Kempes traveled during the summer months over flat terrain with no mountain ranges or even hills to speak of. It is of course possible that they boarded a ship in northern Germany or the Low Countries. This would have accelerated their journey.

[28] This figure is based on recent research by Oliver Volckart on fourteenth-to-sixteenth-century exchange rates (http://www.lse.ac.uk/economicHistory/Research/Late%20Medieval%20Financial%20Market/datasheets/datasheetindex.aspx). I have used the data on the Prussian mark and pound sterling (The "Mark of Prussia" datasheet gives the value of the Prussian mark in 1431 as £0.25). Volckart's method uses the fine silver equivalent of each coin and is therefore more precise for this purpose than Peter Spufford's model, which relies on the Florentine florin as an index currency; Peter Spufford, Wendy Wilkinson, and Sarah Tolley, *Handbook of Medieval Exchange* (London: Boydell and Brewer, 1986). For an earlier approach, see Emil Waschinski, *Die Münz- und Währungspolitik des deutschen Ordens in Preussen, ihre historischen Probleme und seltenen Gepräge* (Göttingen: Göttinger Arbeitskreis, 1952), 248. Volckart discusses the fate of the Prussian mark (and its relatively low value in the 1430s) in *Die Münzpolitik im Ordensland und Herzogtum Preußen von 1370 bis 1550* (Wiesbaden: Otto Harrassowitz, 1996).

of expenses that was required to finance a round-trip journey to Lynn.²⁹ Therefore, the discovery of this letter assigns a name to Margery Kempe's son and validates some of the historical information provided in the book, while showing the reason for their journey to have been at least partly commercial.

II. The Writing Process

The Gdańsk letter has the potential profoundly to modify our understanding of *The Book* and the process by which the work was composed and copied. The idea that Margery Kempe's son was the original scribe was first suggested by Joan Wake to Hope Emily Allen in the 1930s.³⁰ This theory is based on the description of the transmission process in the opening folios of the Salthows manuscript. Accordingly, for some twenty years Margery resists repeated invitations to write her life, but when she finally decides to record her experiences, she finds no "wryter þat wold fulfyllyn hyr desyr ne ʒeue credens to hir felingys."³¹ The writer who eventually takes up the task exactly matches the account given of her son in Book 2:

a man dwellyng in Dewchlond which was an Englyschman in hys byrth & sythen weddyd in Dewchland & had þer boþe a wyf & a chyld, hauyng good knowlach of þis creatur & of hir desyr, meued I trost thorw þe Holy Gost, cam in-to Yngland wyth hys wyfe & hys goodys & dwellyd wyth þe forseyd creatur tyl he had wretyn as mech as sche wold tellyn hym for þe tym þat þei wer togydder. And sythen he deyd.³²

Not only does this description correspond to what can be gleaned about John from the surviving letter, but the circumstances are identical to what we know of his visit to Lynn in 1431 as narrated in Book 2: both

---

²⁹ In the late fourteenth century the purchasing power of £4 was equal to two years' tuition and board at one of the two English universities, or the annual salary of a chantry priest (Kenneth Hodges, *List of Price of Medieval Items*, http://medieval.ucdavis.edu /120D/Money.html). For another comparison, this amount would have covered the complete production costs of a late fourteenth-century *Evangeliarium* commissioned for the Collegiate Church of Saint George, Windsor, including the materials and the labor of scribes, limners, and binders; Joanne Filippone Overty, "The Cost of Doing Scribal Business: Prices of Manuscript Books in England, 1300–1483," *Book History* 11 (2008): 1–32 (8).
³⁰ *The Book of Margery Kempe*, vii.
³¹ Ibid., 3–4.
³² Ibid., 4.

he and the scribe are accompanied only by their wives, both stay with Margery, and both die shortly afterwards.³³ Margery then approaches a priest to furnish a clean copy. Claiming the original work to be illegible, the priest initially refuses Margery's invitation, and a third scribe is hired but struggles to produce more than one leaf.³⁴ However, some "iiij ʒer or ellys mor" after the first scribe's death, the priest is troubled by his conscience and eventually consents to this task.³⁵ He gives 1436 as the year when he first began to work on the clean copy of *The Book*.³⁶ Thus, the deaths of the son and the first scribe took place at the same time.³⁷

Critical attention has traditionally concentrated on the second scribe, the priest. In 1975, John Hirsh argued that this priest should be considered the co-author of the book because he gave the narrative its current shape.³⁸ This approach appeared to deny a considerable literary achievement to a medieval woman, and scholarship has struggled with Hirsh's theory over the years.³⁹ By contrast, in a series of important readings, Lynn Staley began to shift the attention away from a historical to a literary understanding of the second scribe as a trope, devised by Kempe to give credence to her tale.⁴⁰ Subsequently, Staley went on to establish an influential separation between the author Kempe and her literary avatar, the persona Margery.⁴¹ However, Nicholas Watson opened a significant new angle to this debate by suggesting that the "narrative bears a real relation to history" while maintaining that Margery Kempe is the

---

³³ Cf. the account in Book 2, ibid., 225.

³⁴ Ibid., 4. On the brief stint of the third scribe, see Diane Watt, *Medieval Women's Writing* (Cambridge: Polity, 2007), 122. Watt refers to this third scribe as "second secretary" and to the priest as "clerical secretary."

³⁵ *The Book of Margery Kempe*, 4–5. See also *The Book of Margery Kempe*, ed. Windeatt, 5.

³⁶ *The Book of Margery Kempe*, 5.

³⁷ Given the close mercantile and personal networks that connected Lynn and Danzig it is theoretically possible if highly unlikely that two men fitting this description and these circumstances stayed with Margery Kempe, unless we imagine her to have been not only a brewer and a miller but also an inn-keeper.

³⁸ John C. Hirsh, "Author and Scribe in *The Book of Margery Kempe*," *MÆ* 44 (1975): 145–50.

³⁹ Nicholas Watson gives a detailed overview of this debate in "The Making of *The Book of Margery Kempe*," in *Voices in Dialogue: Reading Women in the Middle Ages*, ed. Linda Olson and Kathryn Kerby-Fulton (Notre Dame: University of Notre Dame Press, 2005), 395–434 (396–98).

⁴⁰ Lynn Staley Johnson, "The Trope of the Scribe and the Question of Literary Authority in the Works of Julian of Norwich and Margery Kempe," *Speculum* 66 (1991): 820–38. See also Diana R. Uhlman, "The Comfort of Voice, the Solace of Script: Orality and Literacy in *The Book of Margery Kempe*," *SP* 91 (1994): 50–69.

⁴¹ Staley, *Margery Kempe's Dissenting Fictions*.

book's author.[42] Rather than seeing the second scribe as a trope or as the shaping writer behind *The Book*, Watson empowers Kempe with a form of literacy that does not require written fluency by arguing that Kempe remains in control of her material, which she first dictated to her son before the priest began working on the book.[43] Watson's identification of the first scribe with the son is persuasive; any other theory surely requires multiple additional layers of assumption. This second scribe or priest, Watson maintains, did little to modify Kempe's account. Watson doubts, though, that the son could have written such a substantial text during his second stay, when he was dying, so he must have produced the first draft during his visit a year earlier.[44] However, this initial visit does not match the account of the first scribe given above because John came to stay on his own, without his wife, at the time when his mother encouraged him to go on pilgrimage. In fact, according to *The Book*, the wife's desire to meet her mother-in-law provides the very rationale for the second trip, in 1431.[45] Watson assumes that the priest made a mistake and collapsed or confused the two visits, but it is hard to believe that a matter of underlying causality, which separates the two visits, could have been overlooked by the priest who produced the clean copy. Furthermore, *The Book* suggests that the original dictation took place under time constraints, for the scribe wrote as much as Margery was able to tell him during the time that they spent together.[46] Finally, the Danzig letter reveals that John's reasons for traveling to Lynn were at least partly commercial. This is relevant new evidence because *The Book* specifies that the first scribe came to Lynn with his wife and with his goods—evidently to engage in mercantile activity.[47] In other words, the correspondence between what *The Book* tells us about the first scribe and what we now know of John Kempe makes the identification of the one with the other compelling.

When the text gives the priest's reasons for rejecting the project of copying the book, we read that the text was "euel wretyn" and that it was "neiþyr good Englysch ne Dewch."[48] Furthermore, he adds that "þe

---

[42] Watson, "The Making of *The Book of Margery Kempe*," 397.
[43] Ibid., 398–415.
[44] Ibid., 399.
[45] *The Book of Margery Kempe*, 224.
[46] "[H]e had wretyn as mech as sche wold tellyn hym for þe tym þat þei wer togydder"; ibid., 4.
[47] "[He] cam in-to Yngland wyth hys wife & hys goodys"; ibid.
[48] Ibid. The point is repeated at the end of the preface, 6.

lettyr was not schapyn ne formyd as oþer letters ben."⁴⁹ "Þerfor," the text continues, "þer schuld neuyr man redyn it, but it wer special grace."⁵⁰ A few years later, however, the same priest found that it was "mych more esy . . . þan it was be-forn-tym."⁵¹ There is no explanation for this sudden change, other than that the priest now trusts in Margery's prayers. However, once the project is under way, the process actually turns out to rely on such mundane tasks as the priest reading out every word to Margery, who provides explanations and corrections.⁵² This sudden ability to read a text that was not readable before is therefore explained in terms that are not spiritual but thoroughly practical. Yet here, as in the account of the anonymous first scribe, there is now good reason not to trust the priest's narrative. Why should we accept the priest's assumption that the text was foreign and therefore illegible? Sarah Beckwith states that "the second scribe who attempts to transcribe the foreign, badly written text of the first scribe is suddenly granted clarity of understanding."⁵³ Kate Parker adds that even though the letters were "oddly shaped and formed, . . . the initial difficulties . . . disappeared the second time he tried, when perhaps he had simply 'got his eye in,' as palaeographers would say."⁵⁴ Watson characterizes the first scribe's text as written "in an unfamiliar spelling system, in a merchant's script that to the priest who became her second scribe" appeared an "unorthodox production."⁵⁵ He adds that the difficulties ("þe lettyr was not schapyn ne formyd as oþer letters ben") indicate not a morphological or lexical but an orthographical and paleographical problem.⁵⁶

Yet as the letter furnished for John Kempe in June 1431 shows, contemporary writing from Danzig and East Anglian administrative and literary handwriting were certainly not worlds apart.⁵⁷ This point can

---

⁴⁹ Ibid.
⁵⁰ Ibid.
⁵¹ Ibid., 5.
⁵² "[H]e red it ouyr be-forn þis creatur euery word, sche sum-tym hylpyng where ony diffculte was"; ibid.
⁵³ Sarah Beckwith, "Problems of Authority in Late Medieval English Mysticism: Language, Agency, and Authority in *The Book of Margery Kempe*," *Exemplaria* 4 (1992): 171–99 (190).
⁵⁴ Parker, "Lynn and the Making of a Mystic," 65.
⁵⁵ Watson, "The Making of *The Book of Margery Kempe*," 398.
⁵⁶ Ibid., 429 n. 16.
⁵⁷ On *The Book of Margery Kempe* and linguistic contact between Lynn and Danzig, see the chapter on Margery Kempe in Jonathan Hsy's *Trading Tongues*, 131–56.

be made more clearly when comparing the Salthows manuscript of *The Book of Margery Kempe*, which is believed to have been written by a Norfolk scribe, not with Latin but with vernacular Low German handwriting from Danzig (figs. 2 and 3).[58] The vernacular letter is dated 1437 and comes from the same collection of missives as the letter issued for John Kempe.[59] The cursive hand of the Danzig scribe shows considerable similarities with the mixed letter forms used in the anglicana script underlying Salthows's hand. For instance, both scribes employ an almost identical *w*, one of the more complex letters in anglicana hands. Similarly, both hands feature a two-compartment *d* with a forward-sloping ascender as well as a two-compartment *b* with a significantly larger

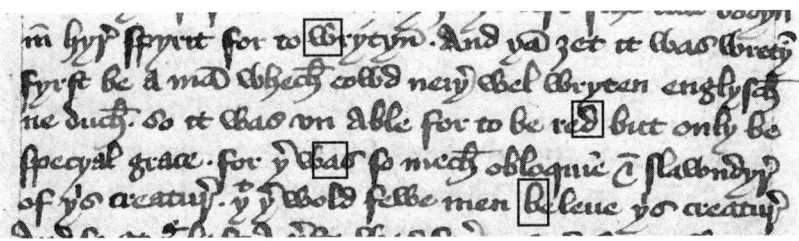

Fig. 2. *The Book of Margery Kempe*, London, British Library, Add. MS 61823, fol. 3v. © The British Library Board.

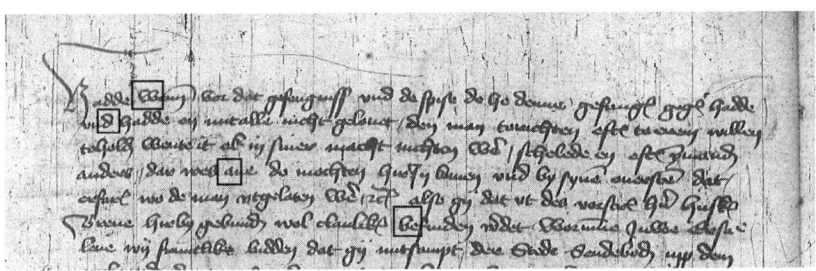

Fig. 3. Gdańsk, Archiwum Państwowe, APG 300, 27/2, fol. 176v. *Akta miasta Gdańska—Missiva*, July 1437. By kind permission of the Archiwum Państwowe in Gdańsk.

[58] The name of the manuscript's scribe, Salthaws or Salthouse, is common to Norfolk and Lincolnshire. Salthouse was a village in Norfolk, and one Edward Salthous was common serjeant in Lynn in 1477 (*The Book of Margery Kempe*, xxxiii). I have also been able to locate a Boston wool merchant named Robert Salthouse, who appeared twice as a plaintiff for debt in 1430 (CP40/677).

[59] Gdańsk, Archiwum Państwowe, APG 300, 27/2, fol. 176v (for the 1437 letter).

upper lobe. A final example of the similarities between the two hands, and the scripts on which they are modeled, is the single-compartment, characteristically angular secretary *a* employed by both scribes. The Danzig hand is a typical cursive business hand of the time, and such hands are usually more difficult to read than book hands or textura-based presentation scripts. Thus, it is difficult to see how mid-fifteenth-century Low German handwriting—even informal cursive scripts—that originated in Danzig could have presented problems for an educated reader from Lynn, a town that had seen a considerable volume of correspondence from Danzig since the early fourteenth century. This paleographical example further corroborates what Jonathan Hsy identifies as a "trans-lingual network of creation" behind *The Book of Margery Kempe*.[60] In fact, the similarities between a number of letter forms in these two examples is so striking that further research would be required to establish a possible mutual influence of English and Hanseatic business hands.

I would therefore suggest another explanation why the priest's account states that the handwriting of the son was not legible and that "þe lettyr was not schapyn ne formyd as oþer letters ben."[61] There is no reason why John could not have written a first draft during his final month in Lynn, when lying on what would become his deathbed.[62] I do not necessarily agree with the assumption that John must have been in agony or in a delirium for all of this time. Depending on his condition, there could have been better days during which writing would have progressed at a reasonable pace. John Audelay, if he is to be believed, claims to have written a whole book while being blind, deaf, and dying.[63] The colophon to Book 1 certainly suggests that John produced a more or less complete copy:

Her endith þis tretys, for God toke hym to hys mercy þat wrot þe copy of þis boke, &, þow þat he wrot not clerly ne opynly to owr maner of spekyng, he in hys maner of wrytyng & spellyng mad trewe sentens þe whech, thorw þe help

---

[60] Hsy, *Trading Tongues*, 133.

[61] *The Book of Margery Kempe*, 4.

[62] Windeatt suggests the possibility that the son's illness may have caused the poor condition of the text, though he speaks of the handwriting as "idiosyncratic" and prefers to view the son and the first scribe as two persons (*The Book of Margery Kempe*, ed. Windeatt, 5).

[63] On Audelay's deathbed composition, see Susanna Fein, "Good Ends in the Audelay Manuscript," *YES* 33 (2003): 97–119. I am grateful to Rory Critten for this point.

of God & of hir-selfe þat had al þis tretys in felyng & werkyng, is trewly drawyn out of þe copy in-to þis lityl boke.[64]

John could have produced a very rough draft, certainly with gaps—as the later addition of chapters 24 and 25 suggests.[65] If he was sick, would he not have accepted his mother's request to take her dictation precisely *because* he knew that he might not live long? He could write, of course, as his letters document, and Margery certainly had no difficulty reading them or having them read to her.[66] The supposedly poorly formed letters could have been caused by the fact that the son was unwell for much of the month. Yet it seems that the priest is deliberately forgetful about the first scribe: in an attempt to erase John's name and his own, the priest writes his identity and that of Kempe's son out of the book. This is distancing by design, a purposeful removal of named individuals from a little book that was to go its way and prove comforting to sinful wretches.[67] To my mind, the literary trope at work is not the existence of a second clerical, authorizing scribe but the desire, shared with so many vernacular religious works, to universalize Kempe's experience and maximize her readership. A closer look at the priest sheds light on the reasons behind this scribal decision.

III. Robert Spryngolde and the Brunhams

Sue Ellen Holbrook has formalized the surmise, shared by many readers, that Robert Spryngolde, Margery's priest-confessor, is the second scribe

---

[64] *The Book of Margery Kempe*, 220.
[65] On those chapters, see Watson, "The Making of *The Book of Margery Kempe*," 405–7; and Diane Watt, "Political Prophecy in *The Book of Margery Kempe*," in Arnold and Lewis, *A Companion to "The Book of Margery Kempe*," 145–60 (148–52).
[66] *The Book of Margery Kempe*, 224. A merchant in his situation would have been literate, certainly beyond what M. B. Parkes calls "pragmatic literacy" ("The Literacy of the Laity," in *Literacy and Western Civilisation: The Medieval World*, ed. David Daiches and Anthony Thorlby [London: Aldus, 1973], 555–77). On literacy among merchants in England and the Hanseatic League, see Debbie Cannon, "London Pride: Citizenship and the Fourteenth-Century Custumals of the City of London," in *Learning and Literacy in Medieval England and Abroad*, ed. Sarah Rees Jones (Turnhout: Brepols, 2003), 179–98; and Stuart Jenks, "Werkzeug des spätmittelalterlichen Kaufmanns: Hansen und Engländer im Wandel von Memoria zur Akte (mit einer Edition von *The Noumbre of Weyghtys*)," *Jahrbuch für fränkische Landesforschung* 52 (1992): 283–319.
[67] The work is introduced as "a schort tretys and a comfortabyl for synful wrecchys"; *The Book of Margery Kempe*, 1.

or at least the sponsor of the work.⁶⁸ A. C. Spearing has even gone as far as to suggest that "our understanding would surely be improved by an experimental envisaging of *The Book of Margery Kempe* as *The Book of Robert Spryngolde about Margery Kempe*."⁶⁹ Spearing makes the crucial point that "events are included at which she was not present but Spryngolde was."⁷⁰ Spryngolde is certainly known to have been alive in November 1436, when the clean copy was begun.⁷¹ He was, in all likelihood, the same "sharp confessor" who provided guidance to Kempe over a span of forty years.⁷² An overview of the many terms by which Spryngolde is referred to, gathered by Janette Dillon, gives a good sense of the degree to which his persona has been woven into the fabric of *The Book*: "'Sharp confessor' may be one more way of designating the man elsewhere referred to variously as Master Robert Spryngolde, Master Robert, Master R., (unnamed) bachelor of canon law, ghostly father, principal confessor or simply confessor."⁷³ Dillon closes her analysis with the estimation that "the book is the product of a more sceptical scribe, whose scanty profile accords with the little we know of her sharp confessor, Master Robert Spryngolde."⁷⁴

But Spryngolde was even closer to Kempe and her family than has been previously assumed. In a celebrated passage in *The Book*, Margery singles him out in a literary will. Before going on pilgrimage, she decides to name Christ

> myn executor of alle þe god werkys þat þow werkyst in me. In praying, in thynkyng, in wepyng, in pylgrimage goyng, in fastyng, er in any good word spekyng, it is fully my wyl þat þow ӡeue Maystyr R. halfyndel to encres of hys meryte as yf he dede hem hys owyn self. And þe oþer heluendel, Lord sprede on þi frendys & þi enmys & mi frendys & mi enmys.⁷⁵

---

⁶⁸ Holbrook, "Margery Kempe and Wynkyn de Worde." On Spryngolde, see also Watt, "Political Prophecy in *The Book of Margery Kempe*," 149–51. Goodman is hesitant on this identification; *Margery Kempe and Her World*, 90–91.

⁶⁹ A. C. Spearing, "Margery Kempe," in *A Companion to Middle English Prose*, ed. A. S. G. Edwards (Cambridge: D. S. Brewer, 2004), 83–97 (93). Watt considers Spearing's argument to be contentious; *Medieval Women's Writing*, 128–29.

⁷⁰ For compelling examples from chapters 57, 61, and 69, see Spearing, "Margery Kempe," 92.

⁷¹ *The Book of Margery Kempe*, ed. Windeatt, 7.

⁷² Ibid., 7.

⁷³ Janette Dillon, "Margery Kempe's Sharp Confessor/s: 1314," *LeedsSE* 27 (1996): 131–38 (135).

⁷⁴ Ibid., 138.

⁷⁵ *The Book of Margery Kempe*, 20–21. On this passage, see also Charity Scott Stokes, "Margery Kempe: Her Life and the Early History of Her Book," *Mystics Quarterly* 25 (1999): 9–68 (27).

We could brush this aside as a literary device, a spiritual mock-document embedded in a devotional narrative, but in 1430 Spryngolde was one of the executors of the will of Robert Brunham, who died before August 11, 1424.[76] This previously unnoticed document is a Common Pleas roll, CP40/677, Norwich, 1430 (Fig. 4). Spryngolde, together with two associates of Margery Kempe's father, John Wesynham and John Parmonter, appears as the executor of the will of Robert Brunham of Bishop's Lynn, submitting a plea for debt against John Grigges, a sheerman of Bishop's Lynn (the same roll also contains a previously unknown plea for debt by Margery Kempe's younger brother, John Brunham, Jr., against one William Kyverton of Lynn). In connection with another document, Anthony Goodman states that "the mayor [John Parmonter], John Wesenham, and Robert Springwell, executors of Robert Brunham, declared how Edmund Benet had injuriously arrested the mayor's goods for a debt owed to him by Brunham," but Goodman (or his source, H. Ingleby) must have misread "Spryngolde" as "Springwell," otherwise we would have known about the even deeper ties Spryngolde enjoyed with the Brunhams.[77]

Barry Windeatt and Clarissa Atkinson state that Robert Brunham was Margery Kempe's older brother.[78] While John Brunham's documented son, John Brunham, Jr., failed to make an impression on public

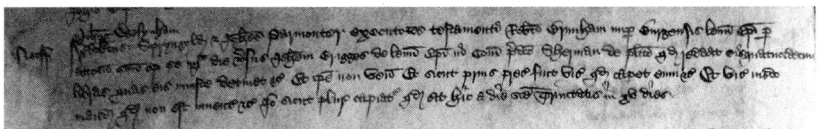

Fig. 4. Common Pleas, CP40/677, Norwich, 1430. John Wesynham, Robert Spryngolde, and John Parmonter, executors of Robert Brunham of Bishop's Lynn, submit a plea for debt against John Grigges, a sheerman of Bishop's Lynn. By kind permission of The National Archives.

[76] For the date of Robert's death, see Goodman, *Margery Kempe and Her World*, 51. This could be the same Robert Brunham who is said to have had a daughter called Alice and a granddaughter with the name of Margaret (Francis Blomefield, *An Essay towards a Topographical History of the County of Norfolk*, 5 vols. [Fersfield: 1739–75], 3:345).
[77] Goodman, *Margery Kempe and Her World*, 34.
[78] *The Book of Margery Kempe*, ed. Windeatt, 57–58, note to line 266; and Clarissa W. Atkinson, *Mystic and Pilgrim: The Book and the World of Margery Kempe* (Ithaca, N.Y.: Cornell University Press, 1985), 76 and 213. See also L. S. Woodger, "Brunham, Robert, of Bishop's Lynn, Norf.," in Roskell, Clark, and Rawcliffe, *The History of Parliament*, available at http://www.historyofparliamentonline.org/volume/1386-1421/member/brunham-robert (Woodger states that Robert may have been her brother or uncle). Goodman believes Robert to have been Margery Kempe's uncle (*Margery Kempe and Her World*, 50–51), but he is generally very cautious and does not necessarily accept as

life in Lynn, Robert Brunham "emulated the career of John Sr. [Margery's father]," collecting many of the distinctions previously amassed by John, Sr.[79] Furthermore, as Robert was older than John, Jr., it would make good sense to picture the former as John, Sr.'s eldest son, not least because he appears to have benefited from family ties by entering into business ventures with associates of John, Sr., such as William Herford (the executors of Robert's will, Wesynham and Parmonter, were also former associates of John, Sr.).[80] Robert was also a feoffee of Edmund Belleyettere, a former apprentice of John, Sr.[81] The life dates for John, Sr. and Robert point to different generations, whereas the continued business links and the fact that both John, Sr. and Robert were successful entrepreneurs suggest inherited capital and commercial influence.[82] In addition, Robert also inherited the family's reputation and political influence. He was a leading member of Lynn's elite during his lifetime, being twice elected mayor before becoming *jurat*—an uncommon sequence; and both he and John, Sr. were aldermen of the Holy Trinity Gild and repeatedly mayors of Lynn: the only family member from whom Robert could have inherited such a reputation and status was the elder John Brunham.[83] That the Brunhams passed on their prestige across generations is not a speculation: even John, Jr. was admitted to the Holy Trinity Gild "by virtue of birth," and when Margery Kempe was introduced into the Holy Trinity Gild in 1437/8 this was surely not because of her mercantile accomplishments.[84]

At the time at which both Margery Kempe's son and her husband died, Spryngolde was busy enforcing debts owed to the estate of the man who was in all likelihood her older brother. As I have shown above, civic handwriting produced in Danzig in the 1430s was not at all difficult to read for an Englishman, not to mention a trained canon lawyer with exposure to secular and religious legal documents who also happened to enjoy a regional reputation: in 1424 the monks of Norwich

---

proven the identification of the prominent John Brunham, Sr. as Margery's father in the first place (48), despite this being explicitly stated in the text in Chapter 45 ("I knowe wel j-now þu art Iohn of Burnamys dowtyr of Lynne"; *The Book of Margery Kempe*, 109). It is highly improbable that there was a second prominent John Brunham of Lynn who was old enough to be Margery Kempe's father.

[79] Goodman, *Margery Kempe and Her World*, 50.
[80] *The Book of Margery Kempe*, 361; Goodman, *Margery Kempe and Her World*, 38, 51.
[81] Goodman, *Margery Kempe and Her World*, 38.
[82] I am grateful to Stephen Alsford for this observation.
[83] I thank Stephen Alsford for this point. For details of the Brunhams' roles, see Goodman, *Margery Kempe and Her World*, Chap. 2.
[84] For John, Jr., see Stokes, "Margery Kempe," 19; and for Margery, see Goodman, *Margery Kempe and Her World*, 105.

appointed him as one of their proctors in a legal dispute.[85] Spryngolde was parish priest of Saint Margaret's, Margery Kempe's parish, and the church staffed two detached chapels that were contracted to the Holy Trinity Gild—the same organization of which John, Sr., Robert, John, Jr., and Margery became successive members.[86] Now that we know that Spryngolde was also the executor of Robert's will, it is highly probable that as parish priest he oversaw the chaplains to the Holy Trinity Gild and that he was responsible for liaising with the Gild.[87] In Lynn, as in *The Book of Margery Kempe*, spirituality and merchant money were woven into a tightly knit social fabric. If Spryngolde was not also the executor of the wills of John Kempe, Jr. and Sr., then he must have had regular matter-of-fact dealings with Margery Kempe that included the settling of Robert's estate—we know she had money to buy herself out of her marriage in around 1413, at the time when her father died, so she may have inherited a portion of his estate.[88]

Spryngolde's proximity not just to Kempe but also to the Brunhams draws attention away from her saintly life, instead embedding the protagonist in a specific local history that enhances the visibility of one of Lynn's most prominent families. If Kempe's book was to extend its reach beyond Norfolk, her written life had to be her own. Her actions are certainly situated in the microcosm of Lynn, but *The Book* never shares more than it needs to about Kempe's social context. What is revealed is almost always functional, so much so that the book only contains snippets of information about the Kempes and the Brunhams: her father's impressive local standing and his name are separated from one another in the text, the important Robert Brunham is not mentioned, we never learn the names of Margery Kempe's fourteen children, and the protagonist herself is consistently referred to as "creatur" by the narrator.[89] This tendency to distance and, hence, universalize the work has been articulated by Felicity Riddy, even though her own reading of *The Book* argues vehemently against a historicizing approach:

---

[85] Goodman, *Margery Kempe and Her World*, 84.
[86] Dillon, "Margery Kempe's Sharp Confessor/s," 131; and Goodman, *Margery Kempe and Her World*, 89. On the Holy Trinity Gild, see Owen, *The Making of King's Lynn*, 61.
[87] Some of the higher-level administration may have been shared with the prior of Lynn under whose jurisdiction Saint Margaret's fell.
[88] Barry Windeatt suggests that Kempe may have used (a part of) her inheritance for this purpose; *The Book of Margery Kempe*, ed. Windeatt, 89, note to line 780. John, Sr. died before October 16, 1413; Goodman, *Margery Kempe and Her World*, 50.
[89] When John Brunham's mayoral elections or his function as alderman are mentioned, his name is not (*The Book of Margery Kempe*, 9 and 111). His name only appears once (ibid., 109), not in connection with his status.

She is addressed as "Margery" by other characters within the text, but not until chapter 17 do we learn, almost by chance, it seems, that "worschepful burgeys" to whom she is married is called "John" . . . ; not until chapter 45 do we learn from a remark attributed to the bishop of Worcester that she is "John of Burnamys dowtyr of Lynne" . . . ; and not till very near the end of the second book do we discover that her married name is "Kempe."[90]

Riddy attributes all of these instances and measures to the "indirect narrative strategies" of *The Book* in an anachronistic reading that foists the conventions of the postmedieval genre of autobiography on a multivocal, unsubdued text.[91] In her formalist argument—at odds with three decades of criticism that negotiated texts with their contexts—Riddy posits that, in the case of *The Book*, the narrative reality of current autobiographical conventions is the only reality we should care about. Riddy's Barthesian objection to the intentional fallacy leads her to sever any ties between a historical and a narrative Margery Kempe, so much so that the historical situation surrounding the text is reduced to a set of unproveable hypotheses: "we have 'Mar. Kempe of Lynne' in the text, but no evidence at all for an author of this name outside it."[92] And what evidence there is for a contemporaneous person of this name in Lynn, such as the admission of a Margery Kempe to the Holy Trinity Gild, Riddy dismisses as insufficient proof for this individual to be the real-world alter ego of Margery's literary persona.[93] But by corroborating specific information given in *The Book* about the son and his visit, the Gdańsk letter changes the relationship between text and context because it links the historical reality surrounding the work to the narrative reality governing it. Furthermore, the closer ties enjoyed by the *historical* alter ego of Margery Kempe's *textual* confessor Robert Spryngolde with the *historical* Brunhams permit a more nuanced relationship

---

[90] Felicity Riddy, "Text and Self in *The Book of Margery Kempe*," in Olson and Kerby-Fulton, *Voices in Dialogue*, 435–53 (441).

[91] While Riddy characterizes Watson's approach to autobiography—by collapsing author with protagonist—as "old-fashioned," Watson considers Riddy's reading as marked by "presentism"; Riddy, "Text and Self in *The Book of Margery Kempe*," 436; and Nicholas Watson and Felicity Riddy, "Afterwords," in Olson and Kerby-Fulton, *Voices in Dialogue*, 454–57 (456). Although Watson and Riddy's joint "Afterwords" to their essays in *Voices in Dialogue* appear to establish the terms for their widely different readings, the fundamental variance appears to lie in the clash between Watson's historicist and Riddy's formalist approach.

[92] Riddy, "Text and Self in *The Book of Margery Kempe*," 436.

[93] Ibid., 448–49 n. 4.

between author and persona. Unless we wish to claim that a second Robert Spryngolde was a priest in Lynn shadowing the ecclesiastical functions of his literary *Doppelgänger*, then we have further evidence for the historicity of *The Book*.

The anonymizing tendency is therefore not a function of the narrative strategies of the autobiographical genre—of which *The Book* can be considered a premodern vernacular English prototype at best—but must serve a different purpose. The case of a spiritually gifted woman's life might have been overshadowed by the fact it was first written by her son and edited by the Brunhams' priest and notary. Scribal anonymity surely helped to distance the Brunham dynasty from the subject of this book and foreground not only Kempe's independence but also the universality of her experience. The same distancing, after all, stands behind the term "creatur," which, as Riddy grants, "seems to have been a slightly formal or distancing word."[94] But this distancing need not be a narrative device or Shklovsky's остранение (defamiliarization); rather, it articulates the text's attempted (though never fully completed) work of universalization. After all, the distancing does not only apply to Margery, her father, the scribes, and the scribal process, but also to Lynn itself. For the same reason the text initially conceals the name of the town of Lynn as "N" (*nomen*) in a pattern familiar from the *N-Town Plays*, where "N"—as a placeholder for the town currently hosting the performances—suggests touring and geographical mobility.[95] The same mobility, though not of performance but of experience, is sought by *The Book*: the attempt to distance Margery Kempe, the Brunhams, John Kempe, Robert Spryngolde, and Lynn focuses attention on Kempe as a spiritual "N," whose life is expressed in the universalizing vernacular idiom common to many religious works written in English.[96] As with

---

[94] Ibid., 441.
[95] Hardin Craig, *English Religious Drama in the Middle Ages* (Oxford: Clarendon Press, 1955), 279. See also John Thomas Sebastian, "Lewd Imaginings: Pedagogy, Piety, and Performance in Late Medieval East Anglia," Ph.D. diss. (Cornell University, 2004), 109.
[96] For the associations of vernacularity with writing in English, see Nicholas Watson, "Visions of Inclusion: Universal Salvation and Vernacular Theology in Pre-Reformation England," *JMEMSt* 27 (1997): 145–88; and Jocelyn Wogan-Browne, Nicholas Watson, Andrew Taylor, and Ruth Evans, eds., *The Idea of the Vernacular: An Anthology of Middle English Literary Theory, 1280–1520* (University Park: Pennsylvania State University Press, 1999), 325. I show that these associations endured into the sixteenth century, where they characterize the work of John Rastell (*Unwritten Verities: The Making of England's Vernacular Legal Culture* [Notre Dame: University of Notre Dame Press, 2015], 11–12 and 128–52).

the text's other attempts to distance the narrative from its specific historical context, "Lynn" replaces "N" as late as Chapter 16. In other words, not only is "N" an instance of the same distancing and concealing of identities as "creatur" and the other examples given above, but it follows the same chronological pattern. The fact that other characters refer to Margery by her first name is not an exception to this pattern but its confirmation: "Margery" was a common name that, unaccompanied by a localized surname, could contribute to the geographical mobility of *The Book*.

IV. The Authorship of *The Book of Margery Kempe*

Perhaps the greatest challenge for modern critical responses to *The Book* lies precisely in the unfinished nature of this project of distancing and universalizing Margery Kempe's experience. It is conceivable that the distancing features were provided by John Kempe during his stint, as an expression of Margery Kempe's wish to conceal herself. But it is also possible that Spryngolde tried to anonymize certain aspects of the text without having been able to complete the task. Finally, a later scribe—perhaps Salthows—may have tried to anonymize the text, never following through. It strikes me as improbable that either John Kempe or his mother were familiar, for instance, with the literary and ecclesiastical conventions of "creatur" and the use of "N." Spryngolde, on the other hand, was a parish priest trained in canon law: the practice of inserting "N," or *nomen*, for a name was found in the templates for baptismal services, wedding banns, and marriage vows, all of which belonged to the regular rituals performed by parish priests.[97] And the name of the *N-Town Plays* stems "from the fact that the writer of the banns declares that the play will begin at six of the bell 'in N. town.' "[98] "N," therefore, belongs to the liturgical and administrative register of English parish priests such as Spryngolde.

As for the pattern of the inconsistency of applying the distancing layer to places and characters: since "Lynn" is first mentioned in Chapter 16, Margery's husband is first named "John" in Chapter 17, her father's surname is first given in Chapter 45, and her own surname only

---

[97] For an example of "N" in a marriage context, see Barbara Hanawalt, *Growing Up in Medieval London: The Experience of Childhood in History* (Oxford: Oxford University Press, 1993), 215.
[98] Craig, *English Religious Drama in the Middle Ages*, 279.

appears toward the end of the work, it is possible that Spryngolde may not have been able to complete the narrative. His extant life records do not extend beyond 1436, when the clean copy of *The Book* was first begun, and the comparatively brief second book, begun in 1438, is different in character and length, leaving also a gap between the dateable events in the two books covering much of the period between 1421 and 1431. Furthermore, there is no attempt to conceal names or places, other than that Margery is referred to as "creatur." A further highly relevant inconsistency is noted, in passing, by John Erskine: "the second scribe says of Book One that his intention was to have 'wrytyn it betyr' [4/20], yet he then begins the second book, by stating that he 'copijd' [221/4] the first."[99] Whereas the first instance suggests an attempt to improve the spelling and language, the second states that the text was merely copied. It is not inconceivable, therefore, that the second book was written not by Spryngolde but by another local scribe, perhaps even Salthows, who assumed the priest's authorizing voice. The fact that the only surviving manuscript is written in the same hand throughout suggests that this scribe, Salthows, inherited these distancing features. Unlike the proem and colophon to Book 1 and the opening of Book 2, the colophon to the second book does not have the priest pray for divine grace. Instead, *The Book* ends rather surprisingly with a long, unpolished trademark prayer used by Margery on various occasions. This ending might suggest that Kempe enjoyed greater control over the narrative during the dictation process for Book 2, another reason to suggest the writer might not have been Spryngolde but someone else. Finally, the last folio of the Salthows manuscript, fol. 123r, has "Jhesu mercy quod Salthows" just below the ruled area, leaving some seven-to-eight lines' respectful distance between the scribal signature and the end of the text. If Salthows took Kempe's dictation for Book 2, this might explain why he thought it appropriate to include his name in the manuscript.[100]

The entanglement of the original text produced by Margery Kempe and her son John on the one hand and Spryngolde on the other finds an echo, some 500 years later, in the enmeshing of Sanford Meech and Hope Emily Allen in their 1940 EETS edition of *The Book of Margery Kempe*: here, the work of an independent female editor, sitting on scraps

---

[99] John A. Erskine, "Margery Kempe and Her Models: The Role of the Authorial Voice," *Mystics Quarterly* 15 (1989): 75–85 (81).

[100] On a possible Norfolk or Lynn background for Salthows, see my above comparison of his hand with those of Danzig scribes.

of notes, competes with that of an established male editor with the "right" institutional credentials; apparently, what was required to satisfy the (male) standards of the academy in twentieth-century England and America was not that different from the (male) standards of parish priests, abbots, and bishops in fifteenth-century England. Separated by more than half a millennium, two highly educated men, vetted and trained by the institutions whose approval the book sought, entered into competition with the raw work of two women who found themselves in unorthodox roles, both of whom were outside these institutions—Kempe and Allen. Many of the difficulties of answering the question of authorship are restated in the challenge of definitively establishing the editorship of the 1940 EETS volume.[101]

So whose book is it, Kempe's or Spryngolde's? Perhaps the debate about the book's authorship only serves to illustrate that the work was not written with our modern sensitivities in mind. I suggest that we transcend the limitations of such terms as "author," "scribe," or "secretary" by embracing the collaborative model of authorship commonly practiced in comparable situations, where a medieval religious woman is forced to rely on the written mediation of a man.[102] It seems to me that the experiential, local aspects of *The Book* are Kempe's, reflecting the microcosm in which she was embedded, whereas the distancing strategy has been attempted by Spryngolde to open the work up to a wider regional audience.[103] Our wish to see the authority of the female

---

[101] On Hope Emily Allen and Sanford Meech, see Frederic G. Cassidy, "Hope Emily Allen—A Personal Reminiscence," *Dictionaries: Journal of the Dictionary Society of North America* 11 (1989): 149–51; Deanne Williams, "Hope Emily Allen Speaks with the Dead," *LeedsSE* 35 (2004): 137–60; David Wallace, *Strong Women: Life, Text, and Territory 1347–1645* (Oxford: Oxford University Press, 2011), 61–132; Carolyn Dinshaw, *How Soon Is Now? Medieval Texts, Amateur Readers, and the Queerness of Time* (Durham, N.C.: Duke University Press, 2012), 105–28; and the work of John C. Hirsh: *Hope Emily Allen: Medieval Scholarship and Feminism* (Norman: Pilgrim Books, 1988); "Hope Emily Allen and the Limitations of Academic Discourse," *Mystics Quarterly* 18 (1992): 94–102; "Hope Emily Allen, the Second Volume of the *Book of Margery Kempe*, and an Adversary," *Medieval Feminist Forum* 31 (2001): 11–17; and "Hope Emily Allen (1883–1960): An Independent Scholar," in *Women Medievalists and the Academy*, ed. Jane Chance (Madison: University of Wisconsin Press, 2005), 227–38.

[102] See Laurie Finke, *Women's Writing in English: Medieval England* (London: Longman, 1999), 73; Watt, *Medieval Women's Writing*, 2; and Liz Herbert McAvoy and Diane Watt, eds., *The History of British Women's Writing, 1100–1500* (London: Palgrave Macmillan, 2012), 3.

[103] Rory Critten reads *The Book* in the same mould as Thomas Hoccleve's *Series*, seeing both works as attempts to regain control of their authors' reputations; Rory Critten,

voice restored should not silence the authentic participation of the male writer: after all, the porousness of premodern textual production encourages us to study all contributors to the development of a text, no matter how marginal, hostile, or eccentric their position may be. But this does not mean that the collaborative arrangement is democratic. Modern authors also collaborate with their copy-editors in a process that cleans up and polishes a raw product. And even when a copy-editor makes stylistic changes, alters sentences, or even decides to rewrite or excise an entire passage, the proprietorship of the work is never shared between the two collaborators. In the case of *The Book*, the terms against which Spryngolde's labors must be judged are the mandate given to him by Kempe, who was initially looking for a "wryter þat wold fulfyllyn hyr desyr" and "ȝeue credens to hir felingys."[104] And this mandate is actually not very different from the expectations of many modern authors, who wish for their works to have their impact and reach maximized. Kempe required a writer who could lend credibility to her story, and although such a brief may not permit Spryngolde to be considered a ghost writer or even to share the role of *auctor* or *compilour* with her, this particular collaboration turns him into an interventionist copy-editor of Margery Kempe's *Book*: Kempe dictates her localized and historicized experience to an intimate audience; Spryngolde's attempted yet never completed distancing opens up this experience for readers far beyond Lynn.[105] This is not to say that the voices can be neatly separated from one another in the work. Instead, I believe that *The Book*'s two narrative tendencies, the historicizing and the distancing, can be ascribed respectively to Kempe and to Spryngolde. But it is *The Book* itself that ascribes authorship to Margery Kempe in an often overlooked passage. The very brief colophon to Book 1 turns her lived memory and experience into an unwritten *Book of Margery Kempe*, anterior to the dictation process: "thorw þe help of God & of hir-selfe þat *had* al þis tretys in felyng & werkyng."[106] Margery Kempe *had* the book in her before anyone wrote it down.

"The Uses of Self-Publication in Late Medieval England," Ph.D. diss. (University of Groningen, 2013), 89–104.

[104] *The Book of Margery Kempe*, 3–4.

[105] The possible third voice, the amanuensis behind Book 2 (perhaps Salthows), does not significantly interfere with the historicity of the narrative and therefore with Kempe's dictation.

[106] Ibid., 220 (my emphasis).

Appendix

Gdańsk, Archiwum Państwowe, APG 300, 27/3, fol. 12r, transcribed and translated by Lena Wahlgren-Smith

Ita scriptum est ad vniuersos ex parte Johannis Kempen qui fideiussit pro Roberto primart de Boszteyn.

Nos proconsules et consules Ciuitatis Danczik vniuersis et singulis presencium noticiam percepturis earundem tenorem significamus Quod[107] coram nobis consolatui presidentibus discreti ac circumspecti viri Iudex et scabini nostre Ciuitatis antedicte baniti Iudicii relationibus suis fidedignis profitendo vocetenus asseruerunt Quatenus coram eis In sede iudiciaria residentibus Prouidus Iohannes Kempe nostre Ciuitatis Incola Iuris[108] compulsus quindecim marcas prusiensium leuiores monetas Johanni Schroder Iuuenili Ciuitatis Danczik conciui occasione fideiussionis quem Iohannes Kempe prefatus Iohanni Schroder predicto ex parte Roberti primart de Boszteyn fecerat plenarie persoluit atque persoluebat velut haec coram nobis exposita sunt et relata ita et nos ea anterius singulorum quorum interest ac quibus expedire poterit audiencie significamus testantes Infirmamus Quare vniuersitatibus omnibus ad quos presens scriptum peruenerit studiose supplicamus presentibus[109] trium mensium quatenus manum admitterem[110] sepedicto Johanni Kempen dignentur citissime erogare ut prenominatus robertus aut amicicie aut Iuris remedio inducatur hanc petitionem pro se expositam prememorato Iohanni Kempen refundere indilate Actum xxxi anno die xii mensis Iunii celeriter[111]

[Thus it is written to all on the behalf of John Kempe who [has made a pledge] on behalf of Robert Prinart of Boston.

We senators and aldermen of the city of Danzig to all those who will receive notice of the present letter indicate the tenor of it: We affirm testifying that before us, as we presided over our council, the discreet and circumspect men the judge and scabins of our aforesaid city in their trustworthy account of sworn

---

[107] "Testantes Infirmamus" is taken to be the predicate verb of "Quod."

[108] The abbreviation suggests "Iuris" but "compulsus" with a genitive is rare. It may be that it should be expanded as "Iure."

[109] Since the abbreviation sign is clearly above the "p," this has to be either "pnbus" (*presentibus*) or "pcibus" (*precibus*).

[110] The sudden first-person singular here is surprising but the ending confirms this form.

[111] The fourth letter could be an *a* rather than an *i*, yielding the reading "celeratur" or possibly "celeranter" without affecting the sense.

judgment[112] assured us viva voce, that the prudent John Kempe inhabitant of our city summoned by law has fully paid and paid out 15 marks of ready Prussian coin to Johannes Schroder, of the *Jungstadt*, fellow burgess of the city of Danzig on the occasion of a security that the aforementioned John Kempe had made to the aforesaid Johannes Schroder on behalf of Robert Primart of Boston before them[113] as they resided in the judicial court, just as these have been set out and related before us and (as) we indicate above to the hearing of those whom it concerns and to whom it can be of use. Wherefore we earnestly pray in this letter all those communities whom the present writing reaches, that they may deign to speedily pay out to the oft-mentioned John Kempe within three months of my putting my hand to this, in such a way that the before-named Robert through the means either of friendship or of justice may be induced to reimburse without delay this claim spent/set out on his behalf to the aforementioned John Kempe. Carried out in the 31st year[114] on the 12th day of the month of June. Expedited.]

---

[112] It is assumed that "baniti" (sworn, summoned) corresponds to "iudicii," though it could also be taken to accompany "iudex et scabini." Furthermore, "baniti iudicii" is taken to be a genitive attribute to "relationibus."

[113] The "judge and scabins" above.

[114] 1431.

REVIEWS

Dallas D. Denery II, Kantik Ghosh, and Nicolette Zeeman, eds. *Uncertain Knowledge: Scepticism, Relativism, and Doubt in the Middle Ages*. Turnhout, Belgium: Brepols, 2014. Pp. viii, 345. €90.00.

The thirteen essays in this excellent volume consider a range of medieval texts in which what is at stake, explicitly or implicitly, is some variety of epistemological "uncertainty": skepticism, relativism, or doubt, as the subtitle indicates; but also opinion, error, or *bêtise*. What emerges from the collection as a whole is a strong sense that these "varieties of uncertainty" played a crucial role in medieval intellectual and imaginative life, and indeed that it might not be inaccurate to speak of a "sceptical undercurrent that runs throughout the Middle Ages" (9). That the suggestion is a surprising one is a testament to the strength of the grip that the notion of the period as an "age of faith" maintains, rightly or wrongly, on the imagination not only of the public but also of medievalists themselves. The contributors to the volume complicate and disturb this notion, although (or perhaps because) the uncertainties in which they are interested are not religious but philosophical, or, more to the point, not pistological but epistemological. Rather than focusing on devotional or theological works, the authors dwell for the most part on "philosophical . . . historical, political, polemical, and literary texts" (1)—perhaps an arbitrary distinction, but one that acts as a generative constraint, allowing new patterns and contiguities to become visible.

One of the virtues of the collection is its spirit of interdisciplinarity, apparent not only in the fact that it is the record of a collaboration among scholars of varying methodological allegiances but also in the way that these scholars consider medieval texts that are themselves of quite different kinds and provenances. Indeed, what the editors identify as the ultimate goal of their project is "to understand more about how institutionally produced philosophy in Latin, itself polyvocal and conflict-ridden, might have interacted with the wider range of discourse produced outside these institutions" (2). In pursuing this goal, which the volume certainly achieves, the contributors thankfully make no recourse to "the tired binaries whereby the institutions of scholasticism are imagined to be a site of hegemony and the monologic, in contrast to a version of 'popular' culture constructed as diverse, critical, and iconoclastic" (5). Instead, what attracts their attention are the ways that different institutional, generic, and linguistic zones "situate" modes of uncertainty, and thereby situate themselves with respect to each other.

Another of the collection's virtues is that it will suggest, no doubt differently to each reader, additional lines of inquiry to be pursued. This particular reader found himself wondering about the place of madness and stupidity, literary or otherwise, in the constellation identified here; about the possibility of understanding apophaticism generally, and the *Cloud of Unknowing* particularly, along the lines provided by this project: the work of unknowing being "religious," to be sure, but not for that pistological; and, most of all, about what would happen if the question of the interimplication of literature and philosophy, one of the most frequently posed here, were formulated in less strictly medievalist terms: that is, whether there would be anything to be gained by consultation with certain works of continental philosophy, of which there would be worse definitions than that it is that tradition of philosophizing in the West that has proposed just such an interimplication.

The essays can be roughly sorted into three groups. Those in the first group address instances in which medieval academic institutions made room for, or were forced to confront, varieties of uncertainty. Those in the second consider texts in which the porosity of discourses to each other, and to broader social and political developments, comes into view. Those in the third treat literary works as fields across which academic ideas can migrate, and tend to suggest that the space of literature itself destabilizes whatever epistemological categories enter into it.

It remains to summarize the essays individually, following the order of the groups just enumerated. In "New Standards for Certainty: Early Receptions of Aristotle's *Posterior Analytics*," Eileen Sweeney argues that the "dialectic of certainty and uncertainty" that is taken to be characteristic of modernity is anticipated in thirteenth-century responses to the *Posterior Analytics*, in which "Aristotle's standards for science when applied to different speculative disciplines result in degrees of uncertainty, rather than what Aristotle wanted to distinguish, truth from seeming truth" (58). In "Can We Trust Our Senses? Fourteenth-Century Debates on Sensory Illusions," Dominik Perler, by contrast, identifies what he calls the "strict limits to the cogency of sceptical thoughts in the fourteenth century" (87), focusing on William Ockham and Walter Chatton to show that late medieval accounts of deception by the senses emerge within a reliabilist worldview and should not be read as foretastes of Cartesianism. In "How Is It Possible to Believe Falsely? John Buridan, the Vetula, and the Psychology of Error," Christophe Grellard investigates how someone with this kind of "naturalized epistemology" (92) might account for cognitive failure by examining how Buridan employs the figure of the "little old woman" to point to the cultural and social context that produces belief and thus error. In "Living with Uncertainty: Reactions to Aristotle's *Rhetoric* in the Later Middle Ages," Rita Copeland explores how the introduction of the *Rhetoric* to the Latin West—unassimilable as it is to the Ciceronian-Boethian tradition—resulted in the "unsettling of conventional conceptions of the rhetorical art" (118), which in turn resulted in a situation of taxonomic indeterminacy wherein rhetoric was classified, incoherently, as a "logic attached to civil affairs" (131). Finally, in "Uncertainty in the Study of the Bible," Lesley Smith identifies several registers in which interpreters of biblical texts in the new secular schools that emerged at the end of the eleventh century encountered the uncertainty of scripture, from the establishment of texts to their historical reference to exegetical authority, concluding that the very fact that "the credal certainties set the boundaries of debate" (154) allowed uncertainties to circulate surprisingly freely in the classroom.

Moving now to the second group, which (it should be said) in fact comprises those essays that are least easily grouped together with any others. In "Uncertainty and Deception in the Medieval and Early Modern Court," Dallas Denery demonstrates that the prevalent argument that modern doubt and skepticism arise with a new "crisis of confidence" in early modern institutions depends on a false comparison of humanist with Scholastic texts. Denery focuses on John of Salisbury as a *medieval* humanist, notable for his seemingly (but only seemingly) proleptic interests in prudence, the instability of life at court, and rhetorical rather than logical modes of analysis. In "Vernacular Opinions," Mishtooni Bose considers "opinion" in Christine de Pizan and Reginald Pecock as an ambiguous category, one that provides these authors with profitable "discursive opportunities" even as they argue in favor of more certain forms of knowledge, and serves as a hinge between institutional and popular debate. In "Logic, Scepticism, and 'Heresy' in Early Fifteenth-Century Europe: Oxford, Vienna, Constance," Kantik Ghosh shows the violent results of the encroachment of forensic discourses of heresy on academic discourses of debate, in which long-permissible modes of uncertainty "assume an entirely new kind of sceptical valence" (278) when understood apart from scholarly convention.

And now for the final group, the essays on literature. In "On Recognizing the Limits of Our Understanding: Medieval Debates about Merlin and Marvels," Karen Sullivan argues that, in the person of Merlin, romances offer a figure of the marvelous as neither divine nor diabolical but rather as the inassimilable site of a kind of non-understandable understanding. In "The Merits of Not Knowing: The Paradox of 'Espoir certain' in Late Medieval French Narrative Poetry," Helen Swift shows how poets used complex narrative structures to figure the desiring lover as a vehicle for "psychological probing," and focuses on their experiments with uncertainty. In "Philosophy in Parts: Jean de Meun, Chaucer, and Lydgate," Nicolette Zeeman locates an ironizing "anti-systematizing gesture" (217) in her authors, by which they exaggerate a marginal element in a philosophical system and thus take a skeptical stance with respect to that system. In "Laughter and Deception: Holcot and Chaucer Remain Cheerful," Hester Gelber shows how the narratorial strategies of the *Canterbury Tales* produce a situation of indeterminacy in which shifting fourteenth-century attitudes toward uncertainty, exemplarily in the case of divine contingency, find expression at once distinct from and continuous with their development in Scholastic contexts. In the volume's final essay, "Medieval Bêtise: Internal Senses and Second Skins in Richard de Fournival's *Bestiaire d'amours*," Sarah Kay describes Richard's text as an "experiment in trying to capture something of mental life below the level of thought" (329), one that enacts, if only partially, a kind of Derridean critique of the efforts to distinguish the human from the animal.

Uncertain Knowledge, immaculately edited and situated at the forefront of scholarship, constitutes an original and exciting contribution to medieval studies, and will prove essential reading.

JORDAN KIRK
Pomona College

ELIZABETH ELLIOTT. *Remembering Boethius: Writing Aristocratic Identity in Late Medieval French and English Literatures*. Farnham: Ashgate, 2012. Pp. 170. £63.00.

Elizabeth Elliott's book presents a study of late medieval Boethian narratives in the vernacular—French, English, and Scots. Elliott leaves aside more obvious and more frequently studied translations and adaptations of Boethius's *Consolation of Philosophy*, and concentrates on literary works that are less self-evidently Boethian, by authors such as Guillaume de Machaut, Jean Froissart, Thomas Usk, and King James I of Scotland. She identifies a particular concern with what she calls the "Boethian discipline of memory" (146) across her corpus, and argues that the texts examined "take the *Consolation* as a model for narratives that address similar, contemporary experiences of the political misfortunes of exile and imprisonment" (13).

The introduction begins by providing a broader overview of the cultural resonance of Boethius's *Consolation*, its translations, and adaptations in late medieval vernacular culture, with particular emphasis on its popularity with aristocratic readers. Chapter 1 focuses on Machaut's *Confort d'ami*, read not only as a piece of consolation addressed to Machaut's patron, Charles of Navarre, but also as a work that fulfills an ethical purpose by providing what Elliott calls "Boethian political counsel." Chapter 2 continues this exploration by turning to Machaut's *Remède de Fortune*, and examines its discourses on love and desire as a means of Boethian consolation. Chapter 3, the final one on Machaut, turns to the *Fonteinne amoureuse*, and focuses on motifs of imprisonment as tropes for the Christian, post-lapsarian existential condition. The chapter explores the use of such images as a means of consolation addressed to Machaut's patron-prisoner, Jean, duke of Berry. Chapter 4 is on Froissart's *Prison amoureuse*, and examines how the experience of captivity of another patron, Wenceslas, "is imaginatively recast as a Boethian education, through which he develops the ability to imprison himself through the pleasant exercise of discipline" (94). Chapter 5 turns to Thomas Usk's *Testament of Love*, proposing a transcendentalizing reading that departs from recent interpretations to argue that "Usk's *Testament* presents a powerful image of the completion of a visionary process of self-development that leaves its subject endowed with the internal stability that characterises the subject able to work towards the establishment of a social justice that prefigures the divine" (122). Chapter 6 turns to James I's *Kingis Quair*, arguing that the poem's "evocation of mnemonic practices of invention is in sympathy with the conception of the *Consolation* as depicting a process of therapeutic meditation that entails the exercise of the faculty of memory" (126).

A number of interesting points are made in this book, but there are numerous problems at the level of argument, conceptualization, focus, and style. While the study promises to explore the relevance of Boethius for the construction of aristocratic identity, much of the book reads like an extended series of observations on the theme of memory in medieval culture, with special attention given to Boethius and the texts that comprise the study's corpus. It would have been helpful to provide a separate chapter defining what the "Boethian discipline of memory" really is—i.e., how it differs from mnemonic traditions more broadly and how it is specifically relevant to the construction of aristocratic and political identity—before moving on to the discussion of the actual texts. More seriously, the question of literary self-representation or self-fashioning does not receive the attention it needs: the introduction duly acknowledges that the term pseudo-autobiography "superimposes an anachronistic horizon of generic expectations on texts whose indistinct and mobile forms evince a fluid sense of self" (2), but the question is evoked only in order to be evacuated. No alternative terminology is proposed, and no sustained theoretical discussion of subjectivity, self-representation, or identity construction is provided anywhere in this book. Here, too, a chapter or an extended section would have provided a far more solid basis for subsequent chapters to rest on.

Given that the book lacks such theoretical grounding, all six chapters are forced to shuttle back and forth among discussions of the actual texts, their contexts, theoretical or conceptual developments, Boethius, "Boethian memory," and a wide range of other subjects, in a nervous and distracting manner. This makes for a rather digressive structure within chapters, which is exacerbated by the tendency to favor unnecessarily obscure conceptual formulations. More explicit declarations of purpose, structure, and argument would have been helpful throughout, since without such guidance the reader is continually forced to infer the logic underpinning the author's progression through a wide range of rather tenuously related subjects. Elliott of course touches on many interesting issues, but it is often unclear how exactly such discussions contribute to the question in hand. Machaut's *Confort*, for instance, is read as warning about the dangers of unbridled imagination, easily seduced by *curiositas* and prone to a form of imaginative wandering (24–38)—themes that resurface in nearly all later chapters. While such discussions of cognition, imaginative idolatry, and mental wandering or *fornicatio* are interesting in themselves, it is simply not clear how such lengthy digressions through familiar territory contribute to our understanding of Machaut's poetry in particular, let alone its concern with constructing a specifically *aristocratic* identity. The chapter on the *Confort* simply ends by affirming that "the nobility have a duty to behave in a manner appropriate to their rank," and that the *Confort* seeks "to address the threat failure to conform to standards of noble behaviour poses to the social order" (39). But the chapter has, quite simply, provided no discussion of questions such as "social order," focusing exclusively on psychological matters. Like the book as a whole, the chapter does not, in fact, tell us much about the specifically *aristocratic* identity constructed in such texts, and never clarifies how the latter differs from the identity of a generic Christian (or Boethian?) Everyman, or indeed from the identity produced by monastic meditation—which is, it must be emphasized, the primary context for the development of the mnemonic traditions Elliott evokes throughout this study. Rather than clarifying such questions, Elliott merely assumes that a re-balancing of cognitive faculties through memory work leads to virtuous behavior in an aristocratic patron/reader, which in turn automatically leads to political regeneration. The conclusions of this chapter are accordingly vague and ultimately evasive: "The *Confort*'s adaptation of Boethius suggests that the *Consolation* was perceived as a text that shares its own concern with the art of memory as means to the achievement of a stable identity, of becoming good. Machaut's poem provides a suggestive indication of an idea of the *Consolation* current in the later Middle Ages" (40).

Such statements finally imply that, for the author, any kind of ethical or didactic poetry in the vernacular automatically contributes to the construction of "aristocratic" identity and is therefore "political"—even if according to this logic the terms themselves are increasingly emptied of their precise meanings, and indeed "aristocratic" becomes loosely synonymous with "Boethian." This is a particularly problematic point of this study, which ultimately refrains from reading the texts as historically situated, contextualized pieces. When discussion of political and historical context is provided, this merely serves as a backdrop for an analysis that does not take into account the text's active interventions into this context, but limits itself to discussing matters of faculty psychology, cognition, and memory. This has the inevitable effect of highlighting broad similarities and flattening specific differences, and thus necessarily works against Elliott's declared interest in throwing light on the creative use of Boethian narrative to construct specific, historically situated, individual aristocratic identities. This also evacuates the most interesting and most problematic question that this book promises to address, and really ought to address much more directly: how do these different texts negotiate, in subtly different and distinctive ways, the dialectic construction of a paradoxical subjectivity that is simultaneously individual and paradigmatic, historically contingent and yet "Boethian," oriented toward a transcendental self-sufficiency yet solidly rooted in the here and now of the active life and its vicissitudes?

Elliott finally addresses this question directly in the conclusion, and here the answer is disappointingly brief and monolithic: these later Boethian texts supposedly "enlarge the meaning of the *Consolation*" because they are engaged in "[c]onstructing a homology in which Latin author and contemporary subject coincide" (145). But how can this "homology" possibly "enlarge" the meaning of the *Consolation?* "Homology" and "coincidence" can only ever "restrict" the relevance of Boethius's work, and indeed Elliott identifies in these texts "a dynamic by which particular and local attachments become a foundation for universalism" (146). This universalist reading essentially works to short-circuit texts rather than allowing them to keep their tensions in play, and dissolves their historical and literary specificity, their distinctive "identity" together with that of the subjects they construct. And indeed—despite the declaration that these texts "evince a fluid sense of self" (2)—the poems themselves are read almost invariably as producing a "stable identity" (40), or a "subject endowed with the internal stability" (122). This insistence on a rather simplistic version of universalism and transcendentalism supposedly at work in these texts is difficult to reconcile with the aristocratic emphasis Elliott nominally attributes to the texts in her corpus, and in this sense it appears facile and ultimately mystifying to claim that "the fantasy of transcendence contributes to the production of practical strategies, facilitating agency within a mutable world" (145). Speaking of "politicised practices of artificial memory" (146), "the production of practical strategies," and "agency within a mutable world" is one thing; it is quite another to show the reader what such concepts might actually look like in poetic and historical practice.

The book as a whole is thus marred by its reliance on loose, imperfectly defined terms and concepts, which creates endless problems and raises a number of troublesome questions: is the memory work evoked by Elliott throughout this study specifically Boethian? Is there really something like a "Boethian discipline of memory"? Is the reliance on such a "Boethian discipline of memory" really a sufficiently prominent, defining characteristic of these later vernacular texts to allow us to speak of them as a coherent "corpus"? In what sense is such discipline of memory not only loosely Boethian but specifically and directly relevant to constructions of aristocratic and political identity in the texts of this corpus, as the book's title implies? More attention to such matters at an earlier stage would have produced a genuine, nuanced argument, and made this a far more authoritative study. Still, there is a wealth of material covered here, much of it interesting, albeit loosely organized, and the study proposes some novel readings of Thomas Usk's *Testament* and James I's *Kingis Quair*.

Marco Nievergelt
Université de Lausanne

Matthew Fisher. *Scribal Authorship and the Writing of History in Medieval England*. Columbus: Ohio State University Press, 2012. Pp. ix, 221. $54.95.

Matthew Fisher's study "rejects the axiomatic division of scribes and authors by assessing the evidence from history writing in later medieval England" (1). As this opening salvo would indicate, Fisher's book contains a bold, revisionary thesis. By focusing on the work of scribes copying out vernacular histories, he aims to show that such a scribal act was not limited by a desire to reproduce the text slavishly from the exemplar. Rather, scribes participated in the composition of their histories, thereby muddying our all-too-comfortable scholarly divisions between authors and textual producers. Instead of the standard model of authors who compose and scribes who copy, Fisher proposes what he calls, from the words of the book's title, "scribal authorship," which "may be the product of composition, emendation, compilation, and various nontransparent forms of copying" (7).

The first two chapters establish the historical foundation for the close readings that will form the final two chapters. In Chapter 1, "The Medieval Scribe," Fisher contends that modern editorial practice has falsely dichotomized the act of writing into two discrete activities—the authorial and the scribal. Instead, Fisher argues, we need a suppler hermeneutic, one that can encompass the various ways scribes author their texts. To make this case, he surveys medieval writings about scribes, by both scribes themselves (from colophons) and authors (e.g., the *Fasciculus morum*, Aelfric, Richard of Bury, Chaucer, and Lydgate). These analyses reveal a tension at the heart of medieval textual culture: people wanted scribes who replicated texts faithfully, yet they simultaneously recognized that scribes inherited texts full of errors and thus relied upon scribes' perspicacity to catch and to correct those errors. In Chapter 2, "Authority, Quotation, and English Historiography," Fisher argues that medieval historians often engaged in what he terms "derivative textuality": they "assembled the words of numerous source texts, typically without acknowledging their textual indebtedness" (60). Thus, the very act of writing a history was, in the Middle Ages, a bit like copying a text, in that one duplicated the text of others, while fashioning it to one's own ends. Fisher proposes a radical change in attitudes toward historiography around the thirteenth century, at the time when vernacular histories (first in Anglo-Norman and then in Middle English) were emerging in England. The majority of this chapter takes up an earlier period of history writing, with a particular focus on the way Bede's *auctoritas* was reconfigured by twelfth-century Latin historians. By the thirteenth century, vernacular historians had moved away from the acceptance of textual *auctoritas* as a given. Instead, we now meet with text as a rhetorically contested ground in which the new vernacular histories foregrounded textual conflicts much more openly.

The final two chapters turn to close readings of particular historical writings from the fourteenth century. Chapter 3, "The Harley Scribe," looks at this famous literary scribe's less well known efforts at composing historical texts in London, British Library, MS Royal 12 C.XII, ultimately arguing that the Harley Scribe was largely responsible for "authoring" some of the historical texts in this manuscript. Fisher begins by discussing the scribe's inclusion of an Office for Thomas of Lancaster, the magnate executed under Edward II in 1322. Fisher then turns to *The Short Metrical Chronicle*, a Middle English historical text providing a cursory survey of the reigns of English monarchs from the

Anglo-Saxon period up to the fourteenth century. By meticulous attention to textual variation across copies, Fisher is able to argue, quite convincingly, that the Harley Scribe freely adapted the text to suit his own local, Herefordshire interests, while also correcting errors based on his own personal knowledge. By analyzing textual emendations made by the Harley Scribe, Fisher convincingly demonstrates that the scribe had first-hand knowledge of intricate details regarding Thomas of Lancaster's dispute with Edward II. Ultimately, Fisher is able to argue that the Harley Scribe wrote (copied, to some degree, but also authored) both *The Short Metrical Chronicle* and the Office for Thomas of Lancaster shortly after Lancaster's demise.

The final chapter, "The Auchinleck Manuscript and the Writing of History," likewise engages in a close reading of one particular copy of *The Short Metrical Chronicle* surviving in one celebrity Middle English manuscript—in this case, the Auchinleck Manuscript (Edinburgh, National Library of Scotland, MS Advocates 19.2.1). Like the Harley Scribe, Scribe 1 of the Auchinleck Manuscript, when copying *The Short Metrical Chronicle*, used materials to hand to edit, alter, and adapt it. In particular, Fisher shows that Scribe 1 had access to very *au courant* narratives about Albina, which he incorporated into *The Chronicle*. Moreover, Fisher shows that Scribe 1 incorporated bits of the romance *Richard Couer de Lyon*, which this scribe also copied into Auchinleck, into *The Short Metrical Chronicle*. He is, like the Harley Scribe, a good example of a "scribal author" who straddles the boundaries between copying and authoring historical texts.

Fisher is at his best and most convincing when close-reading particular manuscripts, for in chapters 3 and 4 he quite adroitly pivots between small-grain details and the "big picture," so that the reader does not lose sight of the argument. His analyses of the Harley and Auchinleck scribes' acts of historiographical creation were, to this reader, quite convincing. I have but two criticisms of this book. First, section divisions within the chapters would have helped. Fisher's prose is clear and jargon-free, and he does not hesitate to tell the reader what his argument is, yet the book traverses a lot of terrain, and thus I often found myself circling back to remind myself of where the argument had shifted gears. (I felt this need particularly acutely in Chapter 2, which cycles back and forth between the early and late Middle Ages.) Second, and more substantially, I think this book would have benefited from a tightening of its focus. Is it about vernacular historiography in late medieval England, as the final two chapters would suggest? If that's the case, then half the book (chapters 1 and 2) is spent setting the groundwork, which seems out of proportion. Or is the book about history writing in late medieval England writ large, as the title would suggest? If that's the case, then half of it (chapters 3 and 4) is focused on single manuscripts in a minority language, which likewise seems out of proportion. Ultimately, I found myself wishing Fisher had deployed his very considerable analytical skills toward a host of other late medieval historical texts. What, for example, would Fisher make of those seemingly ubiquitous Middle English histories, the prose *Brut* and Lydgate's "Verses on the Kings of England"? Or what about the numerous chronicles of London that survive in commonplace books copied out by Londoners? Such books are likely candidates for the sort of scribe-cum-author function Fisher sees the Harley Scribe and Auchinleck Scribe 1 playing. But, in the end, I do not mean this criticism as an indictment of Fisher's work, but rather as a wish that he would have shown us more. Fisher's study has some provocative implications for how we understand both the activities of late medieval scribes and late medieval attitudes to history. It is to be hoped that he will return to this topic and bring yet further insight into the complex, and fascinating, ways our medieval forebears wrestled with the past.

MICHAEL JOHNSTON
Purdue University

ELEANOR JOHNSON. *Practicing Literary Theory in the Middle Ages: Ethics and the Mixed Form in Chaucer, Gower, Usk, and Hoccleve*. Chicago: University of Chicago Press, 2013. Pp. 264. $40.00.

This book is the first extended consideration of a hitherto underappreciated tradition in late medieval English literature: the mixing of prose and verse, on the model of Boethius's *Consolation of Philosophy*—a formal technique that aims at the transformation of readers' interior and social dispositions. Eleanor Johnson's study shows that major and minor authors of the age of Chaucer manipulated form in decidedly Boethian ways in order to develop and define literature's ethical and public uses.

Johnson has written a literary history driven by the formalist concerns of the writers she studies. The *Consolation of Philosophy* became for late medieval writers a model of the powerful combination of prosimetrum and protreptic—a genre that "teaches ethical transformation to a reader by modeling an ethical transformation in its own narrator" (9). According to Boethius's Lady Philosophy, the sensual properties of language arranged in prose or meter prepare the soul to receive and to be reoriented toward truth and goodness. Her song pierces Boethius's soul and prepares it to be reordered by the rationality of her prose. Ethical transformation thus comes to the narrator in a medium also available to the reader: literary form. In this theory of literary ethics, literature transforms readers through its aesthetic properties—"the literary devices, forms, topoi, tropes, and styles by which a work engages its readers' sense perceptions" (3).

However, the Boethian theory of moral transformation by way of aesthetics underwent a number of permutations as later writers reconfigured the relationships among prose, meter, and ethical function. Chapter 1 shows how continental writers including Alain de Lille, Dante Alighieri, and Guillaume de Machaut made different forms of prose or verse achieve the effects Boethius had assigned strictly to one or the other. Chapters 2 through 4 treat Chaucer's own experiments with the ethical affordances of prose and verse in the *Boece*, *Troilus and Criseyde*, and the *Canterbury Tales*. In chapters 5 and 6, John Gower and Thomas Hoccleve are shown to hack traditional prosimetrum as they abandon the protreptic goal of personal ethical transformation in favor of literary experimentation and theorizing *about* the possibility of protrepsis. The book thus treats two kinds of works: those that want to use literary form to convert readers, and those that prefer to dwell theoretically on the artificial and merely conventional relationship between form and ethics.

To the former belong the disciples of Boethius—Alain de Lille, Machaut, the Chaucer of the *Boece* and *Troilus*, and Thomas Usk. These writers maintain Boethius's confidence in form and the example of a transformed narrator to accomplish protrepsis, but they play with the affordances of prose and meter. Usk's *Testament of Love*, for example, eschews verse in favor of a prose that embodies simplicity and forthrightness "to curry affective identification between narrator and reader by creating architectures of sonic and rhythmical likeness in its songful prose" (178). In the *Canterbury Tales*, Chaucer stages a theoretical debate between pilgrim narrators who undertake protrepsis in good faith and those who consider poetry a waste of time. With *The Parson's Tale* and the *Retractions*, Chaucer "forcefully and permanently eject[s] poetry from the *Canterbury Tales*," while prose remains to effect an ethical conversion in Chaucer the narrator and author, albeit without any "unified didactic goal or message that emerges for a reader" (165).

Of the eleven works Johnson studies in detail, only four fit the standard definition of prosimetrum in exhibiting a regular, proportioned mixture of prose and verse: the *Consolation*; its model, Martianus Capella's *De nuptiis Philologiae et Mercurii*; Alain's *De planctu naturae*; and Dante's *Vita nuova*, which, Johnson argues, is not a standard protreptic. The rest mix forms, to be sure, but usually different versions of the same form. Machaut's *Remède de Fortune*, for example, "recreates the mixed form of prosimetrum specifically as a mixing of different *verse* forms [and thereby] indicates its will to explore the possibility of producing a verse-only protreptic" (50).

In other cases, prosimetrum emerges from Johnson's critical framing, most compellingly in her conjoint reading of the *Boece* (prose) and the *Troilus* (verse) as "a single, unified stylistic project, in which Chaucer reinvents how Boethius's prosimetric *Consolation* renders meaning aesthetically available" (91). The *Canterbury Tales* intriguingly functions for Johnson as both conventional and unconventional prosimetrum. Conventionally, she finds in the Chaucer pilgrim's *Tale of Sir Thopas* (verse) and *Tale of Melibee* (prose) a "miniature prosimetrum" (127). Unconventionally, *The Second Nun's Tale*, with its syntax carefully measured to fit each line, "functions much like Boethius's prose, claiming psychological renewal as a function of the sense of order and temporality and as the product of a series of rational, dialogic encounters—in this case, with Cecile" (144). The counterpart to the Second Nun's "bisy rhyme," which orders and rationalizes time, is *The Canon's Yeoman's Tale*—a "haphazard," heavily enjambed, temporally ambiguous verse that "enacts the same kind of rupture that Boethius produces whenever he introduces a meter into the supervening temporal order of his prose dialogue" (152). Although this pair of tales does not display a mixture of prose and verse, its "poetry of order paired with a poetry of disorder" preserves a Boethian investment in form "as a vehicle of protrepsis" (153, 154).

On the whole, the "poetry of order" and "poetry of disorder" seem more fundamental categories for the works Johnson studies than prosimetrum. Through close readings of formal features such as cursus, alliteration, enjambment, and stanza form, Johnson convincingly demonstrates that her writers are deliberately crafting their prose and verse to body forth order and disorder, as well as other metaphysical, cosmological, and ethical themes. Both prose and verse, and sometimes their mixture, are used to manipulate order as well as disorder. Applied so inventively and dexterously, the theory of prosimetrum allows Johnson to fine-tune her readings by articulating the relative affordances of various forms of prose and verse.

Beyond her own application of the theory of mixed form, Johnson pursues the bolder thesis that the authors she studies are deliberately manipulating a highly refined theory—or "topos," as she sometimes puts it—of Boethian prosimetrum. This is often convincing, even revelatory. Johnson's explanation of why Chaucer translated the *Consolation* in prose—an apparent stumbling block for her argument—offers the most satisfying account of Chaucer's purposes that I have encountered. (It was an intervention in the emergent theory of vernacular prose as the vehicle of clarity and accuracy, as well as a bravura experiment in whether prose could do what verse was known to do: Chaucer's "aesthetic sentence" carries over Boethius's cursus and alliterative patterns.) However, when Johnson presents Gower's *Confessio Amantis* and Hoccleve's *Series* as avant-garde deconstructions of mixed-form protreptic, we must hypothetically grant that the authors deliberately deployed prosimetric theory because there is too little evidence to demonstrate that the tradition of prosimetrum was a determining factor in their inventive choices. In Gower's case, it is certainly plausible that the Latin glosses function like Boethian prose while the English functions like Boethian verse, but it is not clear to me that we need the theory of prosimetrum to grasp how the two languages are "marshaled and deployed for their syntactic renderings of nonlinearity and linear order" (189).

Moments like this would not present a methodological problem were it not for Johnson's insistence that all the works she studies are engaged in literary-theoretical reflection and inquiry. Johnson does not just argue that the *Confessio*'s ultimate identification of Amans as the aged and erotically spent Gower provides an occasion "to think more deeply about how and whether literature can—or even needs to—embody ethical learning" (199), but she also claims further that the work itself "deploys Boethian literary practice and theory as topoi of spiritually transformative, didactic literature, and it uses them as a springboard for a comical revision and reinterrogation of philosophical protrepsis" (199). The first claim offers a plausible reading while the second assumes that Gower's own dominant theoretical framework was that of Boethian mixed-form protreptic. Imputing this theory to Gower identifies his character as the Boethian counterpart to the reader, leading to the conclusion that the ethical literature that comprises most of the *Confessio* is impotent to effect ethical transformation, while only old age and diminished desire do the trick in the end. More convincing to my mind is Matthew Irvin's recent argument that, unconstrained by the Boethian model, is able to recognize how Gower's "experience (in the fiction) has come through long pain and suffering, but the art of the poem transfers that experience to readers in the real world without aging them; they are *iuvenes* provided with *experientia*."[1]

However, if Johnson occasionally overreaches, her ambition does not detract from the many other virtues and delights of this rigorously and lucidly argued book. She has identified a major literary tradition of the late Middle Ages that unites formal tactics with ethical strategy. Rarely does a single book venture profound reappraisals of the meaning and purpose of so many major and minor bodies of work. While Chaucer's debts to Boethius have long been studied, *Practicing Literary Theory* completely refreshes and reconfigures the Boethian Chaucer and will send many readers and teachers of Chaucer back to the *Consolation* with a renewed attention to form. The bold interpretation of the *Canterbury Tales* as a mixed-form protreptic and "a vernacular response to Boethius" will surely provoke fresh discussion of the work's unity and ethical purposes (163). The chapter on Hoccleve also presents a novel unity to the *Series* and constitutes a major reinterpretation not only of the poet but also of what Anne Middleton identified as "the idea of public poetry." The major thesis about mixed-form protreptics yields numerous, independently significant insights, including a fascinating argument that the *Troilus* defies Boethius's rejection of tragedy in order to "demonstrate that Philosophy's twin consolation can inhere as readily in tragic fiction as in philosophical allegory" (117). If there was ever any doubt that formalism and literary history belong together, this exemplary study lays it to rest.

RYAN MCDERMOTT
University of Pittsburgh

[1] Matthew W. Irvin, *The Poetic Voices of John Gower: Politics and Personae in the "Confessio Amantis"* (Suffolk: D. S. Brewer, 2014), 286–87.

DAVID MATTHEWS. *Medievalism: A Critical History*. Cambridge: Boydell and Brewer, 2015. Pp. 229. $90.00.

David Matthews's *Medievalism: A Critical History* is a stimulating and authoritative analysis not just of medievalism as a cultural phenomenon, but also of medievalism studies as an intellectual and disciplinary endeavor. Through examining where the study of medievalism has been, and where it is now, Matthews offers suggestions about where it could go in the future.

Matthews is recognized as a knowledgeable and articulate commentator on both the creative and scholarly practices of medievalism. He has unsettled the self-evidence of many of the field's key terms by engaging in meticulous yet lively excavations of their emergence and development. Those familiar with his published work on the history of medievalism will have encountered his genealogies of the key anglophone terms "medieval" and "medievalism."

These genealogical analyses are reprised and further developed throughout this book (which is predominantly anglophone in emphasis with some well-chosen European examples), as Matthews demonstrates how "medieval" and "medievalism" came respectively to refer to a particular time in the past and to a range of dispositions toward that past and the practices aimed at reviving it. A critical point on which Matthews's account turns is the evaluative discrepancy between the two terms: while "medieval" was initially coined as a neutral replacement for the more tarnished term "Gothic" (this neutrality has, of course, long since been lost in everyday parlance), "medievalism" was, from the outset, a pejorative term that marked a predilection for the medieval past that was not only untimely, but also unsavory in its flight from modernity. By carefully tracking the differing careers of these two terms, Matthews offers an illuminating historical explanation for the ambivalence that medievalism attracts, including within the modern academy.

Matthews proposes that medievalism's two dominant and opposing Middle Ages are the "grotesque" and the "romantic." This opposition will perhaps not surprise those familiar with the dominant tropes of medievalism. However, as a heuristic, the grotesque–romantic pairing is supple and serviceable; it is stark enough in its oppositions to draw attention to the contradictory valencies of the modern medieval, yet capacious enough to enable nuanced discussion of phenomena that are not easily reduced to either category. Matthews points out the way these two Middle Ages mutually implicate one another, illustrating this through numerous readings, including one of John Everett Millais's 1870 painting *The Knight Errant*, which also features on the book's striking cover. In this painting, Matthews points out, the knight's chivalrous (or "romantic") unbinding of a naked kidnapped maiden takes place against the shadowy background of the grotesque Middle Ages that has brought her there.

Matthews's other key taxonomic constellation—which distinguishes among medievalisms that offer a Middle Ages "as it was," a middle Ages "as it might have been," and a Middle Ages "as it never was"—is similarly serviceable, and is explored throughout the book in a range of analyses of literature, reenactment practices, artworks, and architecture. Some of the study's most accomplished readings are of architecture as the expression of spatial medievalism—historical time's transmutation into spatial dimensions. Exploring the reach of medievalism as well as its limits, Matthews uses (mostly nineteenth-century) medievalist utopianism to ask how the Middle Ages has been mobilized as social critique and as reenactment—to ask, among other things, what practices of the self are implicated in the physical embodiments of the medieval past.

The book is studded with nuanced and sometimes arresting interpretations that illustrate Matthews's key theses. Highlights include: a deft reading of the layered temporality of Proust's Combray Cathedral, in order to query how the deep multi-temporality of architectural spaces comes to be compressed under the sign of the "medieval"; an elegant tracing of Alan Hollinghurst's intertwining of the Gothic and the queer in the 2011 novel *The Stranger's Child*; and a compelling account of the modernist Gothicism, both latent and obvious, of the Sydney Opera House. As a life-long resident of Sydney and a long-term student of medievalism, I confess I had never noticed it; thanks to Matthews's account, it's now something I happily can't unsee. Matthews offers the last two examples as illustrations of medievalism's successful intersection with other discourses and visual idioms. The depth of his erudition allows him to move with grace among these close analyses and his assured synoptic commentaries, in which he traces the lineaments of medievalism's development as a cultural phenomenon.

The argumentative precision of Matthews's synoptic commentaries is undeniable. That said, some are more clearly provocative than others, and hence invite some contestation. For instance, even if one accepts his persuasive account that medievalism's cultural dominance in the 1840s was exceptional rather than paradigmatic, and that its subsequent status is better described by Raymond Williams's term "residual," it is less clear why this needs to be described by Matthews as a "decline." If one believes that medievalism's multi-temporality makes it inherently impure, syncretic, and under perpetual discursive strain, then its proliferation and absorption into other discursive frames is equally legible as an inevitable narrative of dissemination – a term that need not imply entropy or decline. One might also ask whether a fuller consideration of the emergence of international mass culture in the nineteenth century, and its vital role as a proliferative vehicle of "residual" medievalism, might have mitigated Matthews's slightly dualistic argument that cultural medievalism's decline was tied up with the rise of academic medieval studies.

The book's aesthetic and cultural allegiances are complex. On the one hand Matthews's accounts of reenactment societies and of Michael Crichton's fiction demonstrate the significance and sophistication of popular, non-professional forms of medievalism. On the other hand, the majority of the book's examples are high-art and/or canonical (Matthews's argument that Scott's *Ivanhoe* isn't canonical might—in the strictest sense—be correct, but a book that has streets, suburbs, and towns named after it comes about as close to canonicity as a non-canonical text can get). Moreover, the narrative of decline that frames the book continues to rest at some level on a distinction between texts that have achieved canonicity and cultural capital and those that haven't, even though in some cases they have achieved mass popularity.

These aesthetic allegiances are arguably visible in Matthews's assessment of anglophone cinematic medievalism, which he argues reflects a longer anglophone tradition of infantilizing the Middle Ages. While agreeing with his assessment that such cinema is more fantastic and mythic in its tenor than its European counterparts, one can supplement (or even challenge) his argument by offering an "industrial" explanation, which again brings us back to a consideration of the forces of mass culture. Unlike the auteurist undertakings of much European cinema, anglophone cinematic medievalism has more commonly been made with a global audience in mind. It has been, therefore, arguably less invested in preserving what could be construed as select (or even national) cultural legacies, and more committed to creating a shareable past that is more mythic in its complexion. A comparably broad (though still unmistakeably French) Middle Ages can incidentally be found in Jean-Marie Poire's *Les visiteurs* (1993), the European medievalist film most commonly cited for its box-office success and crossover appeal.

The argument advanced by Matthews in his conclusion—that medieval studies is in fact a species of medievalism—might not be entirely new, but it is wholly persuasive. In another apt example, Matthews queries the scholarly prejudices underlying the modern acceptance of Tyrwhitt's edition of the *Canterbury Tales* as nascent medieval studies and the relegation of Percy's *Reliques of Ancient English Poetry* to medievalism. Furthermore, his concluding call for "productive uncertainty" as medievalism studies' mode of inquiry is especially welcome, and I would suggest this process is already under way. A number of recent studies and journal issues engaged in reflexive examinations of medievalism speak against his suggestion that the field is afflicted by a "paralysing lack of self-definition." Also welcome is Matthews's suggestion that Robin Hood studies provides a sound model for the future of medievalism studies. For Matthews, Robin Hood furnishes a field of inquiry whose object is nominally located in the Middle Ages, but that greatly exceeds the boundaries of that period, and is hence unhampered by the tendency to separate its medieval and postmedieval sources from one another, or to privilege the former over the latter. Since the coherence of Robin Hood studies arguably emerges from its single focus as much as from any shared disciplinary practices, it would have been helpful to be given a sense of how such coherence could be maintained across a field such as medievalism studies, whose objects of study range far and wide. But this is a truly thought-provoking suggestion, and I would be keen to see what conversations might develop from it.

Finally, this is a truly pleasurable book to read, not least because it is written in polished prose that always manages to be stylish yet plainspeaking, garnished just often enough with Matthews's characteristic flashes of wry humor. This, together with the book's keen observations, reflective acuity, and sincere provocations, reflects a writer who doesn't just understand medievalism but *enjoys* it, and is determined that we will, too. I look forward to engaging further with Matthews's book in my own work, and to seeing its theses taken up and tested widely within the field.

LOUISE D'ARCENS
University of Wollongong

ALASTAIR MINNIS. *The Cambridge Introduction to Chaucer*. Cambridge: Cambridge University Press, 2014. Pp. ix, 167. $19.95.

Throughout *The Cambridge Introduction to Chaucer*, Alastair Minnis strives to capture Chaucer's caginess. Minnis establishes the challenges of introducing the notoriously hard-to-pin-down poet early on by quoting "Geffrey," the narrator of *The House of Fame*: "I wot myself best how y stonde" (*HF*, 1878). To this Minnis responds, "That statement of extraordinary self-sufficiency and self-containment, which hides more than it reveals, is as close as we can get to Chaucer" (11). The book's "Introduction" quickly explicates Chaucer's life and historical context, paying special attention to the poet's political and religious connections. Subsequent chapters progress more or less chronologically through Chaucer's literary career, moving from the earlier dream-visions to the *roman antique* of *Troilus and Criseyde* and *The Legend of Good Women*, and finally transitioning to the *Canterbury Tales* via *The Knight's Tale*. The core of the book is the two chapters on the *Canterbury Tales*. The two chapters consider the individual tales along roughly generic and thematic lines. A brief afterword, notes section, and index complement Minnis's critical readings. In lieu of a bibliography, he provides an extensive, annotated "Further Reading" section divided into topics that range from book history and biography to animal studies and afterlives.

Chapter 1 offers extended treatments of each of Chaucer's dream-visions. In contrast to *The Book of the Duchess* and *The Parliament of Fowls*, *The House of Fame* demonstrates Chaucer's willingness to "admit, and indeed to create, *discordia*" (34). The artistically confident Chaucer of *The House of Fame*, though, is concerned with "textual authority rather than socio-political authority" (34). Minnis's enjoyment of *The House of Fame* shines through when he declares, "The English poet has caused the pillars of textual authority to tremble and invited us to enjoy the spectacle" (26). He concludes this chapter with the important point that "class distinctions and stereotypes have been made the object of mirth, but that does not make them any less stable" (34).

Chapter 2 examines *Troilus and Criseyde* and *The Legend of Good Women* as "fictions of antiquity." The pagan past gives Chaucer space to think about issues of salvation, desire, and the gendering of ethical action. Troy, a "world all its own" filled with the possibility of virtue and "intricate philosophical analysis," is also the world of "fearful Criseyde," who is subject to exchange at the hands of a patriarchal gift economy. In considering Chaucer's rather sympathetic portrait of Criseyde, Minnis establishes an important through-line first raised in the book's introduction: Chaucer's depictions of women. Indeed, if the "other worlds" of the *Troilus* and the *Legend* are sites to think of pagan otherness, that cultural and historical otherness is grounded in female otherness. In the *Legend* Minnis finds a Chaucer who "takes great pains to protect the reputations of the . . . good pagan women" (55). In counterpoint to the possible "proto-feminist gestures" of the *Legend*, Minnis nevertheless returns to the issue of textual authority raised in the first chapter, asking whether Chaucer's concerns were: "predominantly, inevitably, literary?" (57). He concludes that the tension between the depiction of good pagan women and the deployment of that depiction to demonstrate poetic facility and authority is one that Chaucer "left as a matter for debate. One that continues even now" (57).

Matters of making and interpretation are key to the following two chapters, in which Minnis discusses the *Canterbury Tales*. He carefully connects Chaucer's poetic work to philosophical questions about perception, knowledge, and the nature of things. Chapter 3, "*The Canterbury Tales*, I: War, Love, and Laughter," gives us sections on *The Knight's Tale*; the Squire, *Sir Thopas*, and the Franklin; the Shipman, Miller, Reeve, Cook, and Merchant; and *The Nun's Priest's Tale* and *The Manciple's Tale*. Minnis's reading of *The Manciple's Tale* concludes the first *Canterbury Tales* chapter, an appropriately mimetic choice too, considering that the Manciple offers his story in the spirit of a last word. The antique world of *The Knight's Tale*, the marvels and magic of the romances and Breton lais, the linguistic play of the *fabliaux*, and the beastly moralities of *The Nun's Priest's Tale* and *The Manciple's Tale*—these elements ultimately raise questions about "the status of that 'auctour newe' Geoffrey Chaucer" (96), and they "reveal an undiminished excitement in the possibilities for interaction between 'earnest' and 'game'" (97).

The complicated ethics and epistemologies of the pairing earnest–game give way to the classic and perennially collapsing binary at the center of Chapter 4, "*The Canterbury Tales*, II: Experience and Authority." Focusing on the bases, uses, and limits of knowledge, the concluding chapter has sections on the Friar and the Summoner; the Pardoner and the Canon's Yeoman; the question of *auctoritas* as it relates to Alisoun, Prudence, Cecile, and Eglentyne; patience and its manifestations in Custance, Griselda, and Virginia; and, finally, the problems raised by *The Monk's Tale* and *The Parson's Tale*, and the *Retraction*. If the Monk interminably grasps at a distilled formula for tragedy, suggesting the incompleteness of the *Canterbury Tales* as a whole, the Parson signals "an abandonment of the tale-telling competition . . . and/or a disruption of the framework of the fictional pilgrimage" (136). Indeed, the earlier chapters' self-sufficient Chaucer who reveled in making game of textual authority here gives way to a maker who "takes his leave, having humbled himself before his Maker" (138).

The "Afterword" surveys Chaucer's popular and critical reception, from fifteenth-century successors and Victorian admirers eager to establish "English Literature," to twentieth-century critical contests between New Criticism and Robertsonianism. Minnis also considers the twenty-first-century Global Chaucer project, which demonstrates the ways that "Chaucer is deeply embedded in the mashup, the meddle, the muddle, the mingle, of world language" (144). As Minnis points out, despite shifting priorities and configurations in higher education, Chaucer remains an institution, an author whose "canonical weight must inevitably be felt" (144). Indeed, Chaucer remains one of only two named authors to head divisions of the MLA—the other being, of course, Shakespeare. The retention of that honor required energetic efforts on the part of medievalists, efforts that Minnis helped lead. When Minnis is at his best in this book—tracing critical debates, inviting further interpretation, showing the ways Chaucer weaves together compelling literary and philosophical strands—he provides a forceful argument for why Chaucer continues to merit introduction to today's students and interested readers.

COREY SPARKS
California State University, Chico

TISON PUGH, *Chaucer's (Anti-)Eroticisms and the Queer Middle Ages.* Columbus: Ohio State University Press, 2014. Pp. 242. $64.95 cloth; $64.95 e-book; $14.95 CD.

Reconsidering the "queer paternalism" (29) of both Chaucer and the English literary tradition, Tison Pugh's latest monograph charts the contrapuntal traffic between medieval eroticism and what he calls "antieroticism." Specifically, Pugh aims to untangle "the privileges and privations of heterosexual desire in medieval culture" (4). He seeks out the queer potential of human sexuality at the nexus of the self and society and discovers queer narrative tension in Chaucer's contradictory treatments of what Pugh calls (anti-)eroticism. Dialogic in nature, (anti-)eroticism moves from surface to depth, and back again; Pugh defines it as "juncture where eroticisms and anti-eroticisms converge" (10). He identifies (anti-)eroticism as the primary site of queerness in the Middle Ages. What is anti-eroticism? For Pugh, anti-eroticism can take several forms: virginity, chastity, bachelorhood, widowhood, and commitment to a nonreproductive future.

Theoretically grounded in Freud, Lacan, and Lee Edelman—among others—Pugh tackles topics such as masochism, brotherhood, oaths, thanatos, the child, the divine, and the nonhuman. He explores these problems through a series of close readings from the Chaucerian canon. Pugh's engaging work provides both an introduction to and an in-depth inquiry into many of the core concerns of medieval studies and queer studies.

Medieval romance, especially Chaucer's treatments of matters of courtly love and chivalry, makes up the bulk of Pugh's analysis. In a chapter devoted to *The Franklin's Tale*, he argues that Arveragus and Dorigen use masochism to register "the anti-eroticism latent in relationships predicated upon hierarchy" (32). According to Pugh, courtly love, at its heart, concerns itself with male narcissism; in performing heterosexuality, the knight reveals its inherent queerness. Reading the Courtly Lady via Lacan and Žižek, Pugh contends that the Lady mirrors the failure of the lover. As a catalyst of courtly rituals, the Lady metamorphoses into *das Ding*, a "Queer Thing" (36) whose gender is ultimately irrelevant and unnecessary. Occupying the anti-erotic position, the Lady becomes a "potentially hermaphroditic figure capable of inhabiting masculine and feminine genders simultaneously" (40). Pugh leverages these insights to argue that Dorigen, after her marriage, becomes a narcissistic masochist who is in love with the pain and longing she feels for her husband. In essence, Arveragus assumes the role of the Courtly Lady, the desired Thing. Hermaphroditism is a tactic deployed by this lady/wife and her lover/husband in their attempt to fulfill their marital contract. When Aurelius disrupts the marriage, the resulting erotic triangle exposes masochism as a productive force in marital relationships. According to Pugh, *The Franklin's Tale* never reaches the climax toward which it seems to build, ending on a decidedly anti-erotic note.

Masculinities and their queer discontents are the focus of chapters 3 and 4. In the former, Pugh notes Chaucer's satire of the tradition of medieval brotherhood oaths. Whereas works such as *Amis and Amiloun* and *Eger and Grime* valorize fraternal bonds, *The Knight's Tale*, *The House of Fame*, and *The Pardoner's Tale* all mark the failure of brotherhood oaths. Latently queer and overtly normative, brotherhood dissolves rapidly in the face of competing erotic and financial rivalries.

In Chapter 4, Pugh returns to the problem of male narcissism in romance. If love for women were the outward erotic manifestation of male narcissism, thanatos would be its inner anti-erotic core. The male lover's professed willingness to die for love is simultaneously figurative and literal. *The Knight's Tale* and *Troilus and Criseyde*, Pugh suggests, are examples of Chaucer's necrotic romance, in which male desire is inherently fatal; Arcite and Troilus *must* die. Men in a necrotic romance are interchangeable, and they turn the Lady into an adversary, a *swete foe*, who must be conquered and subdued. Emelye and Criseyde, resisting male necrotic desires, align themselves with "anti-heteroerotic freedom of life without men" (101), whether that is virginity or widowhood. In so doing, they reject motherhood and reveal the queerness of female anti-eroticism.

Pugh next shifts attention to what he terms the "queer families" in the *Canterbury Tales* and to Chaucer's representations of a masculine, (anti-)erotic God. Though typically depicted as asexual and anti-erotic, children in some of the tales are "drafted into amatory rivalries centered on their fathers' attenuated masculinities" (25). Serving the father's desires, which drive the narrative, a child must sacrifice her erotic agency. In *The Clerk's Tale*, the fantasy of infanticide exists alongside the possibility of incest between Walter and his daughter. And in *The Physician's Tale*, Virginia plays the roles of daughter and erotic prey; her chastity obscures sexual mores and makes possible Virginius's public performance of fatherhood. But if Virginia dies to preserve her virginity and spiritual purity, the Godhead is not necessarily devoid of eroticism. Here, Pugh pivots to a consideration of the sexual poetics of Chaucer's depictions of the divine. As exemplified in *The Miller's Tale*, God's *pryvetee* is figured both as divine secrecy and as private parts. Possessing potential carnality, the explicitly male God is the center of mystery and pleasure. Divine law is established only to be ignored; anti-erotic prohibition solicits queer erotic transgression. In Pugh's words, the Wife of Bath portrays Jesus as "virtually a pimp" (191).

The epilogue, "Chaucer's Avian Amorousness," is the most provocative piece in the monograph. Arguing that *The Nun's Priest's Tale* is a parodic play on romance's eroticisms, Pugh reads Chauntecleer as an erotic role model who has successfully built "a sustainable culture" (209) that is free of the shame of polygamy or incest. The chickens' farmyard is a sexual utopia that is unregulated, yet enlightened. Like the Wife of Bath, Chauntecleer intentionally mistranslates the Bible in order to justify his access to erotic pleasure. However, masculine discontents and the pressures of courtly love ultimately undermine even this avian pastoral. Pertelote must both mirror Chauntecleer's beauty and challenge his identity as a proper lover; ironically, Chauntecleer outsmarts the fox but does not defeat him in battle. Pugh observes that if the rooster emerges as the erotic paradigm of the entire Chaucerian corpus, readers are challenged to sacrifice their "sense of the human as a constituent factor of human culture" (211). Building on Deleuze and Guattari's notion of "becoming-animal," Pugh speculates on the possibility of our "becoming-queer" and thereby becoming "fully human" (215). The brevity of the epilogue leaves one wishing for more, especially in light of recent work on posthumanism, cross-species queerness, and ecomaterialism.

In a sense, Pugh's present monograph returns to his earlier consideration of cultural genres. Like sexuality and gender, eroticism and anti-eroticism are normalizing genres with non-normative potential. In the manner of a fugue, Pugh's work charts the contrapuntal melodies of amatory strategies in the Chaucerian corpus. At times, one wishes for some lingering over the dissonance between the notes—for example, a longer consideration of Aurelius's nameless brother, or of Hippolyta's sacrificial masochism. Navigating Chaucerian surfaces and depths, Pugh shows us that eroticism is not necessarily love or carnality. He decisively proves that erotic pursuits can easily be disguised by anti-erotic tactics, and that latency and manifestation are not always mutually exclusive. Pugh begins his book by unmasking Chaucer's various ludic guises (as author, narrator, fabulist, and pilgrim). One of these alter egos is Ganymede, through whom Chaucer queers himself and embodies both erotic and anti-erotic impulses. Pugh concludes by considering Chaucer in the guise of *trede-foul*.

Over all, this book tackles many key debates in both medieval studies and queer studies. Its creative engagement with central works of the

Chaucerian canon makes it a volume of scholarly interest and a valuable resource in the classroom.

Wan-Chuan Kao
Washington and Lee University

Nicole Rice, ed. *Middle English Religious Writing in Practice: Texts, Readers, and Transformations*. Late Medieval and Early Modern Studies 21. Turnhout: Brepols, 2013. Pp. ix, 278. €75.00 cloth.

The essays in *Middle English Religious Writing in Practice: Texts, Readers, and Transformation* are based on the premise that texts are not stable things, and are, in fact, inherently unstable and variable. As one of the contributors to this collection puts it: "One of the most exciting or annoying aspects of books, depending on one's perspective, is their mobility: once written, they have lives of their own and their circulation is largely uncontrollable . . ." (239). The essays in this volume are concerned specifically with religious texts, and how these texts and their readers responded to cultural changes, how older works were encountered by new—and sometimes surprising—readers, and how these new readers sometimes altered older works to suit their own purposes. Rice's introduction claims that "several of the essays will add significantly to the growing picture of the fifteenth century as a period of continued, though perhaps differently expressed, 'theological aspirations' in the vernacular" (5). After reading the essays, it is clear to see that this is no idle boast; the quality of the individual contributions is generally very high, and the sheer breadth of texts and topics covered is evidence of the vitality and depth of vernacular religious writing in the later Middle Ages.

Middle English Religious Writing in Practice is also noteworthy for its discussion of texts that have been neglected in favor of "canonical" works. One will not find here a rehash of Dante or Langland. Instead, these essays offer lively and informative discussions that illustrate how lesser-known texts can broaden and deepen our understanding of late medieval devotion. As a whole, the volume yields numerous new insights into how religious literature was produced, used, and read; the essays' authors extend these findings to reflect on what they suggest about some of the more obscure aspects of lay piety and affective religious experience.

The collection consists of eight essays organized into three sections, bookended by an introduction and two extensive indices (an index of manuscripts and a general index). The first section deals with writings about and by continental women and how these were received in England. The second deals with the compilation of religious manuscripts in the later medieval period. The third deals with questions of orthodoxy, heresy, and popular devotion in relation to the revision, annotation, and circulation of texts.

Like any such collection, synthesis across the essays is not always achieved, though one does engage the arguments of others (see 219). Otherwise, each is written in such a way that it can be read independently of the collection as a whole. On the one hand, this leads to some repetition among the different essays, most notably those that deal with the same texts (as with Margaret Connolly and Moira Fitzgibbons on *Pore Caitif*), but on the other hand, this increases the volume's utility, as individual essays on an array of topics can be consulted easily without reference to any of the others.

I am only able to engage a few of these essays in any depth here, and my selection should not be taken as a judgment on the quality of those not addressed. Rather, I will discuss some things that struck me while reading the essays, and I would encourage others to read the collection for themselves, as just about anyone will find something of interest in it.

Martha Driver's "Poetry as Prayer: John Audelay's 'Salutation to St. Bridget'" looks at the poet's use of repetition in salutation poems, which form a type of verse prayer in a meditative mode. Repetition of a word or phrase was a popular form of meditative prayer, one that Audelay used to great effect, and one that he drew from the liturgical tradition of the Church (specifically the antiphon). While the literary value of such verse prayer might be called into question (see 91), there can be little doubt about the affective power of such prayers, which was certainly the reason for their popularity. (Moreover, it should be noted that repetition is used to comparably moving effect in many world religions.) That Audelay's verse prayers were also *spolia*—in this case, goods taken from the treasury of the liturgy—demonstrates how an institutional, communal form of devotion can be appropriated for personal, affective contemplation and worship.

The second essay of the second section, "Lay Spiritual Texts and Pastoral Care in Two Fifteenth-Century Priests' Collections," by the volume's editor, looks at the contents of two anthologies (Cambridge, Jesus College, MS Q.D.4; and Cambridge University Library, MS Ii.IV.9) in an attempt to discern why these manuscripts were compiled in the way they were, who their intended audiences were, and to what purpose the gathered texts might have been put. Rice's contention is that "in these two collections . . . Middle English works originally written to shape lay piety took on new relevance for the development of priestly spirituality and the practice of pastoral care" (149). On the whole, her arguments are thorough and convincing, as she carefully inventories and discusses the various works collected in both manuscripts, demonstrating their utility to both clerical and lay readers. Yet, part of me wonders why we should be surprised that clergymen would have wanted to read the same affective texts as laymen and -women. Rice's essay addresses the shared need for personal edification that unites clerics and laypeople, but it does not consider the idea that clerical and lay audiences might look to certain texts to fulfill pastoral purposes. When commenting upon *Erthe upon Erthe*, a devotional poem about preparing for death, Rice notes that it "envisions a frail human, whether farmer 'with his plowe' or knight 'on a palfreye'" (172). Regardless of their station, these figures must ensure that their spiritual affairs are in order before they die—a lesson particularly suited to the hospital where Rice argues that the compilation may have been used. But does this poem not also offer instruction germane to the priest, who will also inevitably die, and might thus be drawn to such a poem in contemplation of, and preparation for, his own death? The nearness of clerical and lay spirituality in the later Middle Ages is, however, implicit in Rice's concluding—and helpful—suggestion that these compilations offer evidence of clerical and lay cooperation in the spiritual life, evidence that the spiritual growth of priests and laypeople was understood as a two-way process, rather than as something dictated by a clerical elite.

The final essay in this collection, "Sixteenth-Century Readers Reading Fifteenth-Century Religious Books: The Roberts Family of Middlesex," by Margaret Connolly, looks at the reading practices of a gentry family through their annotation of a number of religious books they possessed. These annotations ranged from the recording of births and deaths of family members; to marginal notations marking a "vere good praer" (see 252); to the copying of prayers; to erasures and emendations motivated by the turbulent religious changes of Tudor England, such as the removal of the Feast of Thomas Becket from the calendar of a book of hours. That these annotations are used to demonstrate the malleable nature of the religious texts contained in the Roberts' books—which changed hands as the family's devotional practices changed along with the times—makes Connolly's essay a fitting conclusion to this fine collection.

Sean Otto
Wycliffe College, University of Toronto

Wolfgang Riehle. *The Secret Within: Hermits, Recluses and Spiritual Outsiders in Medieval England*. Trans. Charity Scott-Stokes. Ithaca, N.Y.: Cornell University Press, 2014. Pp. 448. $35.00.

More than thirty years after publishing a translation of *The Middle English Mystics* (Routledge and Kegan Paul, 1981), Wolfgang Riehle returns to offer "a new history of English mysticism" (135). Unlike his previous volume, this large and impressive monograph steps away from a tight focus on metaphorical mystical language to include a much broader cultural and historical approach to understanding important mystical, devotional, and visionary texts that circulated in medieval England. The title captures one of several concerns driving the book—the development and broader cultural influence of anchoritic spirituality. It soon becomes clear that there are several other prominent concerns: most importantly, the strong connections that existed between English audiences and continental authors and texts, and the specific influence of the Cistercian tradition on English mysticism.

This Cistercian agenda drives the first two chapters of the book. Starting with the earliest desert monks of late Antiquity, and following the growth of the eremetical life in the early medieval British Isles, Riehle builds up to what seem like the central claims of the entire book: first, "that the Cistercians of the twelfth century provide a necessary backdrop for the specific affectivity of mystical experience in England" (3), and second, that "the anchoritic idea exerted an exceptionally intense influence on England" (14). Englishman Stephen Harding's role in the foundation of the Cistercian order on the Continent is fascinating.

Bernard of Clairvaux and Aelred of Rievaulx receive due attention here; Riehle cites the impact of Aelred's *Rule for a Recluse* frequently throughout the rest of the book, starting with the Wooing group, which he argues "bears the stamp of Cistercian spirituality" (38). In the third chapter we read that the *Ancrene Wisse*, too, bears this stamp, and Riehle strongly argues that this text needs to be situated within twelfth-century monastic theology, specifically the new affective Cistercian spirituality based on exegesis of the Song of Songs.

In turn, we learn that *Ancrene Wisse* and the Wooing group directly impacted another anonymous prose work, *A Talking of the Love of God*, the focus of the fourth chapter. Here Riehle goes so far as to support the possibility of a female author of *Talking*. He compares the *Talking* to the Monk of Farne's meditations, in order to try to figure out how spirituality may or may not be gendered. The answer to this question seems to fall flat: "we do not find an answer to what constitutes specific feminine spirituality" (68). Fortunately, other scholars such as Carolyn Walker Bynum, Karma Lochrie, Lynn Staley, Liz Herbert McAvoy, Diane Watt, and Jeffrey Hamburger (to name but a few) have pursued this question fruitfully, if with other texts.

The "leading mystics" Richard Rolle, the *Cloud*-author, Walter Hilton, Julian of Norwich, and Margery Kempe are joined by Marguerite Porete in chapters 5 through 10. The Cistercian thread continues with Rolle, whose "language bears the stamp of the Cistercians down to the smallest detail, even if insufficient attention has been paid to this hitherto" (95). Riehle leads us through an astonishingly detailed examination of all Rolle's texts in order to recuperate him as a legitimate mystic, albeit one who is "constantly surprising—and therefore engaging" (86). Both *The Cloud of Unknowing* and Porete's *Mirror of Simple Souls* receive extensive theological analysis, as well as discussion of the milieu of the authors/translators and their reading publics. While I am not convinced by the argument that Porete's presence in England is due to the *Mirror* translator's desire to introduce her text into the English court (like the *Cloud*, the *Mirror* would be inappropriate for such a lay audience), others may find the connections to secular poetry and flower imagery intriguing.

Hilton's *Scale of Perfection* receives especially close attention, where again Riehle argues that the Cistercians (particularly Bernard) generally inspire its spirituality. Riehle delves into the *Scale*'s original interpretation of the *imago Dei* doctrine; its view on contemplation, prayer, and meditation; and its treatment of knowing and loving God. After a similarly detailed discussion of Julian's theology and its influences, Riehle proposes that she was entrusted to a monastery as a child and then became a recluse in adulthood—in other words, that no lay experience informs her texts. Authorial biography plays a much larger part in the chapter on Margery Kempe, somewhat challenging the chapter introduction's claim to contribute to the "theological underpinning of her spirituality" (247). In the sections tracing Kempe's female precursors, there is a misguided attempt to undo Elizabeth Barratt and Sarah McNamer's important work of untangling the two Elizabeth of Hungary figures. Dietrich of Apolda's biography of laywoman Elizabeth of Thuringia does not, to me, sufficiently refute the much more logical connection of the *Revelations* with nun Elizabeth of Töss (as proven several times over in Barratt's articles and McNamer's edition). Riehle also strikes an unhelpfully contrarian pose against Birgitta of Sweden's influence on Kempe.

However, one of the most compelling aspects of this entire monograph is the author's admission that his estimation of Margery Kempe has changed drastically since his earlier treatment of her. While at least one reviewer rightly noted that she had been "consistently denigrated" in Riehle's first book,[2] in *The Secret Within* he adopts a "far more positive view" of Kempe (xvi) as a result of new research by others and his own reconsideration of the theological background of her work. He even offers a poignant reflection on that development:

she knows very well that in distant times there will be people (whereby she means, of course, men) who will set out to slander and condemn her—but she forgives them. It is humbling to have to include myself in that number, suddenly brought into relationship with a woman who lived six hundred years ago, and it has sharpened my awareness of the obligations we have as modern readers of her work. (xvi)

Perhaps three decades of diligent feminist recuperation of Margery Kempe have made a difference.

Chapter 11 addresses aspects of popularizing mysticism. It comments on several interesting (though somewhat randomly selected) texts such

---

[2] Valerie M. Lagorio, review of Wolfgang Riehle, *The Middle English Mystics*, trans. Bernard Standring (London and Boston, Mass. Routledge and Kegan Paul, 1981), *Speculum* 57, no. 4 (1982): 930–32.

as *The Abbey of the Holy Ghost*, Love's *Mirror of the Blessed Life of Jesus Christ*, religious and morality plays, *The Castle of Perseverance*, and *Piers Plowman*. In the conclusion, Riehle reflects on how the "favorite Cistercian theme of the human soul's likeness to God" recurs with the English mystics because they are "preoccupied with human *dignity*" (299) and thus also a "strong affirmation of corporeality" (300). Likewise Cistercian sweetness (*dulcedo*) emerges as one specific quality that appears most strikingly in English mystical texts.

The translation of this long book from German stands as a great accomplishment on its own; Charity Scott-Stokes has rendered readable, impeccable English prose. Yet slightly inconsistent citation of original text and modern translation are somewhat distracting (sometimes no translation of Latin or other languages, sometimes only translation). For example, lack of citation of the original Middle English weakens the analysis of *Ancrene Wisse* and Julian's writing. The strong Cistercian agenda seems to come at the expense of the Carthusians and Franciscans, whose influence Riehle diminishes at several points, usually unconvincingly. Why can't a range of influences co-exist peacefully, in a nuanced symbiosis? Similarly, Riehle is unnecessarily dismissive of several feminist readings.

Deeply learned and exhaustively researched, this book makes many valuable contributions to ongoing debates about the nuances of medieval English spirituality – even if it will spark some disagreement. Perhaps the inadequacy of the English title points to the difficulty of describing such an ambitious project. Undoubtedly, scholars will find much to engage with in this book for many decades to come.

LAURA SAETVEIT MILES
University of Bergen, Norway

WENDY SCASE, ed. *The Making of the Vernon Manuscript: The Production and Contexts of Oxford, Bodleian Library, MS Eng. poet. a. 1*. Turnhout: Brepols, 2013. Pp. xl, 331. €110.00.

The volume under consideration grows out of the AHRC-funded Vernon Manuscript Project. It follows on the heels of the project's first publication: a high-resolution digital facsimile of the Vernon manuscript

(Oxford, Bodleian Library, MS Eng. poet. a. 1)—one of the largest surviving manuscripts of Middle English religious literature. The multimedia CD entitled *A Facsimile Edition of the Vernon Manuscript: Oxford, Bodleian Library, MS. Eng. poet. a. 1* (also edited by Scase) includes digital images of the complete manuscript, along with full, searchable transcriptions of its texts. The *Facsimile Edition* has greatly increased access to the largely restricted manuscript.

The Making of the Vernon Manuscript acts as a companion to that digital contribution, and—as Scase indicates in her preface (xxii)—is the first collection of essays based on research undertaken using the *Facsimile Edition*'s innovative digital format. Fittingly, the volume is generously illustrated with forty-one colour plates and over sixty black-and-white figures, which support the close, detailed analyses presented in each of the essays. The term "making" in the title provides a shared focus for the essays, which describe the production of the Vernon manuscript through a consideration of its paleographical, codicological, and decorative features. The volume thus expands upon previous work on the manuscript, especially A. I. Doyle, ed., *The Vernon Manuscript: A Facsimile of Bodleian Library, Oxford, MS Eng. poet. a. 1* (Cambridge: D. S. Brewer, 1987), and Derek Pearsall's *Studies in the Vernon Manuscript* (Cambridge: D. S. Brewer, 1990).

The Making of the Vernon Manuscript differs in its approach from previous work which, Scase states, "tended to focus on literary and textual aspects of the manuscript"; instead this current essay collection considers the manuscript from "a variety of disciplinary perspectives" (xxiv). The division of the volume into three parts offers a neat structure for this shift in approach. Five of the twelve essays are by Scase, who provides conclusions to each part, resulting in a volume that is both comprehensive and focused.

The first part of the volume—"Copying, Editing, and Assembly of the Vernon Manuscript"—opens with A. I. Doyle's essay "Codicology, Palaeography, and Provenance." Doyle offers a traditional outside-to-in examination of the manuscript, detailing its size, weight, cost; the preparation of the page; and the scripts. Doyle also considers scribal stints and decoration, as well as questions about the manuscript's audience, and its relationship to the Simeon manuscript. Simon Horobin's "The Scribes of the Vernon Manuscript" builds on Doyle's work to present significant new findings on the manuscript's scribes: John Scriveyn, Scribe B (the main scribe of the manuscript), and Scribe A. Horobin examines the settings in which the scribes worked as a way to "reconsider their value as evidence for the manuscript's provenance" (28). He identifies Scribe B as a member of the secular clergy (39) and hypothesizes that Scribe A and John Scriveyn were most likely professional or legal scriveners. Horobin's thorough research finds a number of other documents written in the three scribes' hands. In the process, he builds a picture of the networks that connect their scribal activity, allowing him to make a convincing case for Lichfield Cathedral as a possible center for the production of the Vernon manuscript. Jeremy J. Smith, "Mapping the Language of the Vernon Manuscript," then builds upon Horobin's work. His consideration of scribal networks leads him to localize scribes A and B in Worcestershire. Smith helpfully examines "complex and dynamic social networks reflecting a significant degree of scribal mobility" while recognizing that—despite scribes' opportunities to work in different geographical and institutional settings—a "regional distinctiveness in language" is still evident in their work (56). Smith's concluding remarks, that the manuscript is a "repository" for living texts (67, attributed to Vincent Gillespie), are immediately taken up by Ryan Perry's "Editorial Policies in the Vernon Manuscript." Perry engages the literary-interpretive analyses found in Pearsall's edited volume on the Vernon manuscript. He questions the extent to which Vernon can be seen as a "safe repository for orthodox materials" (72). In keeping with the volume's focus on production, Perry's literary analysis of "The Sacrament of the Altar"—a text interpolated into the *Northern Homily Cycle*—is animated by a consideration of the editorial practices that gave rise to the manuscript. Scase's "Rubrics, Opening Numbering and the Vernon *Table of Contents*" brings this first section to a close, focusing on the manuscript's innovative English titles and the first quire's table of contents, which, she argues, was not made for inclusion in the manuscript, but was rather meant to serve as a physically separate guide to its contents.

Where the contributions in the first part develop and expand upon one other, yielding insights across their individual findings, the second part, "Decoration and Illustration of the Vernon Manuscript," is less connected. The section addresses the decorative features of the manuscript from several angles, offering relatively isolated insights into the manuscript's production, rather than the clear image of the manuscript's production that emerges in Part 1. Both Rebecca Farnham's "Border Artists of the Vernon Manuscript" and Alison Stones's "The Miniatures in the Vernon Manuscript" seek to address previous work on the manuscript's decorative scheme. They both offer a catalogue of its decoration and miniatures, leaving limited space for any extended interpretation of these features. Lynda Dennison's "The Artistic Origins of the Vernon Manuscript" proceeds along lines comparable to the contributions of Horobin and Smith, attempting to establish "a date and possible location" for the manuscript's production (171), though in this case by characterizing the styles of its illuminators. Dennison argues that the illuminators were familiar with one other, but worked independently, so that "actual collaboration may not have occurred" (202). Although Dennison finds evidence for the manuscript's provenance in the west Midlands convincing, her study focuses on Westminster and East Anglia (specifically Norwich Cathedral Priory) because of the artists' "peripatetic [movement] within a monastic, largely Benedictine, circuit" (203). Scase's "The Artists of the Vernon Initials" concludes the section by examining the "graphemic profiles of the Vernon scribes" (208) to suggest a "metropolitan provenance for the decoration of the Vernon manuscript" (226). Scase's appendix to Part 2—which outlines the classification of the artists' hands as they emerge in the essays of Dennison, Scott, Doyle, and Farnham—is particularly useful.

The elements of the final section of the volume, authored entirely by Scase, are closely linked and could be read as a longer essay in three parts. Scase carefully builds the case for the patron of the manuscript, which is presented as the culmination of the findings of the entire volume. In the first of these essays, "Patronage Symbolism and *Sowlehele*," Scase analyzes the absence of symbolism, which she believes "may be, in fact, symbolic" (238) in order to "disclose something of the ideological affinities of the patrons of the manuscript" (232). Placing the manuscript in the context of its analogues, the second essay, "Some Vernon Analogues and Their Patrons," argues that the manuscript both engages and updates traditions of "massy" book production (248). Scase also maintains that, while the format of the Vernon manuscript suggests fashions dominant in luxury book production, its "compilation activity suggests common ground with [its patrons'] clerical servants" (268). Drawing these strands together, the final essay, "The Patronage of the Vernon Manuscript," offers a carefully wrought hypothesis that the patron of the manuscript was the brother of the earl of Warwick, William Beauchamp.

Scase opens the volume by outlining eleven questions (though listed as ten, with the number 9 repeated) with the caveat that the volume attempts to tackle only "some of these problems" (xxiii–xxiv). These questions are all addressed, though sometimes rather hesitantly, and with cautious remarks such as "of course, further work needs to be done to test this proposition more fully" (226). This is perhaps the result of the volume's focus, concentrating on the manufacture and production contexts of the manuscript rather than on its literary value (Pearsall's volume remains the last major publication on that topic). The larger claim of the volume is made in relation to the AHRC project's aims to open up the digital humanities: the collection is "motivated by the conviction that digital corpora such as that we now have for Vernon require and will reward the development of new research methodologies" (xxiv). Though the volume does build on the work of the project, there is scope to do more with the newly digitized material. The essays, which "largely [use] close examination of the digital images of the manuscript obtained for the Vernon Manuscript Project" (97), employ the facsimile as a digital surrogate for the manuscript itself rather than exploiting fully the facsimile's new and innovative format. As the first volume based on the new facsimile, the collection is a wide-ranging, thorough examination of the "making" of the manuscript presented in a traditional format, and the existence of the innovative digital facsimile offers a range of exciting possibilities for further work.

ADITI NAFDE
Newcastle University

FIONA SOMERSET and NICHOLAS WATSON, eds. *Truth and Tales: Cultural Mobility and Medieval Media*. Columbus: Ohio State University Press, 2015. Pp. xiv, 294. $69.95 cloth; $14.95 CD.

Medievalists consider ourselves experts in disruptive media technologies. One good reason for this self-assessment is our intimacy with a range of media particular to the period that we study: charms on the body, bills on cathedral doors, traveling holster books, household medical compilations, among so many others. Another reason is our struggle with medieval sources, which abound in textual instabilities, vestiges of orality, shifts in language, scribal *mouvance*. Print itself is a late transformer of manuscript culture, and a phenomenon that mediates how modern students encounter works that originally circulated in manuscript. At a global historical moment when the mobile device has evolved in the course of a few years from *Star Trek*-style communicator to magic book, medieval media beckon as possible analogues to the digital disruptions that are forcing scholars of later periods to reexamine the homogeneities of print-think. Fiona Somerset's ambitious introduction to *Truth and Tales* argues that this collection's essays show us "the interplay between media, the modes and truth-claims they deploy, and the social status of the speakers and writers of that media" (7). Not all the essays here boldly go where media theory rewrites cultural history, but a consistently high level of discussion offers many pleasurable recognitions.

Any multi-author anthology, print or digital, now offers scant hope that readers will encounter its chapters in dialogue rather than in pdfs of single chapters from interlibrary loan, much like the lamentable JSTOR effect on journal editors' attempts to create thematic clusters—how many students or scholars now read articles in their published contexts? The editors of this collection do strive successfully to create dialogue despite the double whammy that this book represents a conference (the fourth Canada Chaucer Seminar) and serves as a festschrift for the distinguished literary scholar Richard Firth Green.

Among the most interesting lines of inquiry that develop over this collection is the position of orality in an England that was becoming increasingly dependent on documentary traditions, a topic treated extensively in Green's important study, *A Crisis of Truth: Literature and Law in Ricardian England* (University of Pennsylvania Press, 1999). Indeed, *Crisis of Truth* has served as the inspiration for several of the authors included here, a fact acknowledged by the collection's title. The medieval interpenetrations of orality and literacy in their various forms do provide fascinating analogues to emergent problems of digital literacy. A charming feature of this volume is that Green, the honoree, begins the discussion with an essay that sees continuity between medieval and modern orality in the use of truth-claims. "'The Vanishing Leper' and 'The Murmuring Monk': Two Medieval Urban Legends" argues that authenticating details in storytelling, specifically the citation of "friend-of-a-friend" sources (or "FOAF" in current messaging parlance) remain to this day as oral strategies, and that no real difference exists between medieval and modern credulity as "true stories" circulate among social networks.

Orality's power as an authenticating medium echoes through many of the other contributions. Four contributors follow Green's *Crisis of Truth* directly in showing how medieval law intertwined oral and literate authorities in ways that exceed the rote formulae for oaths and vows with which many of us are familiar. English common law and cherished traditions of "ancient customs and liberties" were grounded in an oral memory that was suspicious of—yet dependent upon—written witness. Stephen Yeager, in "The New Plow and the Old: Law, Orality, and the Figure of Piers the Plowman in B 19," argues that Piers and his *plouȝ* of land symbolize a preliterate tradition of land tenure based on the Domesday Book and on oral transmissions of early English law. Barbara Hanawalt's "Toward the Common Good: Punishing Fraud among the Victualers of Medieval London" cites Green directly to show that the "interplay between oral and written, popular and high culture, official law and folk-law . . . all come into play" (169–70). Hanawalt's survey of the conception of "common good" in matters related to food supply uncovers the many forms of media that enabled this abstraction to live, prosper, and circulate within social networks, independently of its life as a documentary formula. In "A London Legal Miscellany, Popular Law, and Medieval Print Culture," Kathleen Kennedy looks at a law miscellany (known as "Arnold's Book") from the late fifteenth century that does not draw on standard London Guildhall records; this popular guide instead uses a variety of sources, including Magna Carta and the Charter of the Forest, to offer ready reference in a home library for conversation, debate, and other social performance outside institutional settings such as the courts.

Andrew Taylor's "Oral Performance and the Force of the Law: Taillefer at Hastings and Antgulilibix in Smithers" circles back to Green's essential point about orality and authenticating details. Taylor renders visible an underlying theme of the volume: that orality is a tradition that must resist the dominance of the written record. He argues that oral traditions can only exist in performance, comparing a grand (but mysterious) lyric sung by the Norman knight Taillefer before charging into the Battle of Hastings to a recent court battle between two Canadian First Nations peoples, in which both groups attempted to reconstruct the original terms of a non-written treaty by singing relevant episodes from their oral history.

Robyn Malo, in "York Merchants at Prayer: The Confessional Formula of the Bolton Hours," looks at another interpenetration of oral and literate traditions: confession formulae. The Bolton Hours contains some striking variations on the formulae used to render confession. These were probably inscribed by members of the family and were likely the product of discussions that they had among themselves and perhaps with intimate members of their social circle. Malo argues that these variants set boundaries for sinful behavior that define merchant-class assumptions about their rights. Also pervasive but often overlooked by scholars are the wall-texts discussed by Michael Van Dussen in "Tourists and Tabulae in Late-Medieval England." These forerunners to museum gallery texts mediated the lived experience of many public places and spaces, and surely prompted group readings, if not a tour-guide industry.

Two chapters take up the current interest in fictional animals as projections of a culture's social systems. In "Mingling with the English in Laȝamon's *Brut*," Fiona Somerset considers King Arthur's visit to the supposedly four-cornered Loch Lomond, with its segregated populations of fish. Somerset sees the episode as an allegory for questions about ethnic identity that pervaded twelfth-century England. As the title of Lisa Kiser's "Resident Aliens: The Literary Ecology of Medieval Mice" makes clear, Kiser uses the lens of ecology studies to examine cultural anxieties (here, the tension between rural and urban populations).

The remaining chapters are also consistently strong, and also populated by major voices in the field, even if they hew closely to more familiar critical strategies. Thomas Hahn, in "Don't Cry for Me Augustinus," discusses affective responses—especially erotic ones—to the Dido legend, from Augustine to Chaucer and beyond to the Percy Folio. Hahn demonstrates that across the medieval millennium and into the libraries of early modern antiquarians, Dido's tragic passion becomes a recurring site of heteronormative reading, in which higher love is predicated on a tragic metanarrative wherein man meets woman for a period of serial monogamy whose duration is dictated by masculine destiny.

In "The Exegesis of Tears in Lambeth Homily 17" M. J. Toswell establishes strong continuities between Anglo-Saxon and post-Conquest homiletic collections. Alastair Minnis magisterially addresses one more thing *Pearl*'s grieving Jeweler does not understand. In his contribution, "Unquiet Graves: *Pearl* and the Hope of Reunion," Minnis shows that late medieval resurrection theology preserves hierarchy as an essential feature of Christian cosmology, even after the Apocalypse. Concerns about the interpenetrating economies and social structures that connect the landed to the merchant gentry might seem like a Victorian preoccupation, but Michael Johnston finds a medieval case study of the problem in his "Mercantile Gentility in Cambridge, University Library MS Ff.2.38." In the fifteenth-century compilation that Johnston considers, one tale constructs franklins as the crucial social competitors for the merchant class that it celebrates. "The Ignorance of the Laity: *Twelve Tracts on Bible Translation*" offers Nicholas Watson's incisive commentary on an anxiety expressed by followers of Wyclif and the aggregation of heresies called Lollardy: the gap between rote learning for penitential formulae (on which so many of the later medieval laity depended) and the meaningful comprehension required for salvation.

All of these essays can claim to examine, as Somerset's introduction asserts, the "continuities, communities, communalities, and negotiations that linked" the disparate social networks and media of later medieval England (xii). It is rarely the case that diversity becomes a virtue and a strength, but the theoretical range and skilled presentation of this collection make it a decisive exception to that rule.

JOEL FREDELL
Southeastern University

PAUL STROHM. *Chaucer's Tale: 1386 and the Road to Canterbury*. New York: Viking, 2014. Pp. xv, 284. $28.95.

Paul Strohm's latest book is not just another biography of Chaucer. Ingeniously, *Chaucer's Tale* (published in the UK as *The Poet's Tale: Chaucer and the Year that Made the "Canterbury Tales"*) paints an enthralling portrait of the poet at the turn of the year 1386, when his public career as a controller of customs came to an abrupt end. The book's argument is simple: as Chaucer's faction in London (and at court) fell from grace, he lost his respectable city job and rent-free lodgings above Aldgate, prompting him to lie low in Kent for a while, where he diverted his energies to crafting the *Canterbury Tales*.

Along the way, *Chaucer's Tale* yields a string of new glimpses into the poet's private life and milieu: the fortunes of his wife Philippa at John of Gaunt's court have rarely been delineated with greater clarity, Chaucer's years over Aldgate will make readers reconsider the physical setting of the writing process, and his rustication in Kent and Christendom generates new points of departure for future studies of the *Canterbury Tales*. *Chaucer's Tale* is Strohm at his best. Most of the chapters are exercises in history writing, well beyond the literary histories charted by *England's Empty Throne* or *Politique*, whereas the last section gives itself over to theoretical and, ultimately, literary considerations of audience, poetic authority, and literary tradition. Just as the book brings to life vignettes of political intrigue, graft, and subterfuge, Strohm sets up *Chaucer's Tale* as the prequel to *Social Chaucer*, introducing an opportunistic and political Chaucer who is about to channel his real-life frustrations into a visionary literary experiment. To use Strohm's own term, this book presents Chaucer as a *situated* writer, both politically and socially. Yet perhaps the time server who happened to be well connected and landed the sought-after lease of Aldgate, and who was summoned to parliament despite his modest social status, ought to be credited with more than passivity and having been in the right place at the right time. Chaucer may not have been visible enough to face punishment when his civic patrons climbed to their gallows, but to swim with the tide of Nicholas Brembre's political machine without being sucked into the ensuing maelstrom may have been the result of a strategy of prudence on Chaucer's part. Strohm's Chaucer is political, but not too political.

For all its focus on the poet, *Chaucer's Tale* is as much about London as it is about Chaucer. James Joyce once noted that Dublin could be rebuilt using *Ulysses*, and he claimed that he wanted "to give a picture of Dublin so complete that if the city one day suddenly disappeared from the earth it could be reconstructed out of my book."[3] If Joyce's exploration of June 16, 1904 through the urban meanderings of the unremarkable Dubliner Leopold Bloom is the ultimate microbiography of Dublin, then Strohm's meticulous depiction of the civic backdrop for the equally unremarkable Londoner Chaucer does much the same for the London of 1386. Strohm presents a replica of late medieval London built to a human scale, where spiritual time is computed by the tolling of bells, and space is measured by the steps of the city walker

---

[3] Frank Budgen, *James Joyce and the Making of "Ulysses," and Other Writings* (Oxford: Oxford University Press, 1972), 67.

Chaucer—a practiced space firmly situated in the premodern rituals of a city unimagined by de Certeau.

Grounded in the erudition of a scholar who has helped to redefine the practice of literary history, *Chaucer's Tale* occasionally stops short of answering its own questions, or even asking questions that have been carefully set up: if Chaucer was Brembre's man at parliament, how exactly did he escape repercussions later? And if, during his exile in Kent, Chaucer first conjured up the idea of a wide literary audience—prefigured by the social diversity of the pilgrims in the *Canterbury Tales*—was this then the birth of the professional English author-writer (as opposed to 'compiler')? But, then again, this is a generous book, written as much to invite reflection as to enable new departures. Slips are rare, and only occur when Strohm is furthest away from his area of expertise—the person introduced on page 99 as "an eighteenth-century commentator named Matthew Hale" is of course the towering seventeenth-century lawyer and jurist Sir Matthew Hale.

History in *Chaucer's Tale* is a means to a literary end, and the historical reality selected here serves to pinpoint Chaucer in 1386. The genre Strohm has chosen—microbiography—allows him to offer a narrative of non-binding literary possibilities and trajectories, boldly laying out paths for others to pursue. None of the suggestions advanced here needs to have happened, but they might have occurred, to varying degrees of probability—some readers, for instance, may remain skeptical about the suitability of Aldgate for getting any serious writing done, others may wonder whether the pilgrim characters in the *Canterbury Tales* are indeed a psychologized ersatz audience for Chaucer's lost London readers. Surely, the rigors of scholarly documentation would have closed off some of these paths, bracketing off others as speculative for their lack of definitive evidence. But such books must be written, and they deserve to enjoy a firm place in our current academic culture in order to envision readings that inspire and insinuate, surprise and interrupt.

This is not a coffee-table book; although it wears its learning lightly, *Chaucer's Tale* is the result of painstaking research and a career of prising insights from the clutches of a past that rarely shares its secrets. The slight critical apparatus and popular appeal of *Chaucer's Tale* belie the fact that Strohm here accomplishes the rarest of feats: an ambitious and powerful intervention in existing scholarship that is leavened by a limpid prose, itself unencumbered by the burdens of academic debate. If the final chapters extol Chaucer's imagining of the unimaginable—a broad English-speaking audience for his future work—then Strohm has broken such new ground himself by reaching out with this unassuming yet erudite book to an audience few of us approach.

SEBASTIAN SOBECKI
University of Groningen

CONRAD VAN DIJK. *John Gower and the Limits of the Law*. Cambridge: D. S. Brewer, 2013. Pp. vii, 221. $99.00.

Conrad van Dijk's *John Gower and the Limits of the Law* demonstrates persuasively that law is at the heart of Gower's poetic undertaking and brings to John Gower's poetry an engagement with law that is historically and theoretically informed. This book explores how legal reasoning and discourse inform Gower's narrative art, particularly in the uneasy narrative form of the "judicial exemplum," which Gower uses to explore contemporary controversies about topics such as nascent international law, the relationship between royal and legal authority, and the connection between private vengeance and official legal process. Although it focuses on the *Confessio Amantis*, this book treats all of Gower's works, including the *Mirour de l'omme*, *Vox clamantis*, the *Balades*, the *Traitié*, and *Cronica tripertita*. Van Dijk finds in Gower's writings a prudentialist legal and political ethos that does not precisely fit with some of the prevailing judgments about Gower that have grown out of critical debates of his works. For Van Dijk, Gower was neither a rigoristic moralizer who refused to see the moral incoherence of his own stories, nor a ludic postmodern writer who sought to expose the rhetorical aporias of self-contradictory exempla. Van Dijk's diachronic methodology offers an approach that works beyond "the opposing poles of openness and dogmatism, or of imaginative freedom and didacticism" (69)—a refreshing move in historicist criticism about Gower. It is a method that yields clear and nuanced insights into the author's works.

So who is Van Dijk's Gower? Generally speaking, Van Dijk meticulously avoids speculative biography, but nevertheless reviews evidence of Gower's connections to the legal profession and his knowledge of its practices. In doing so, he observes that the question of whether or not

Gower was a lawyer is ultimately irrelevant when writing about the poet's engagement with the law, on the grounds that being a lawyer does not mean that one will write about law and not being a lawyer does not mean that one cannot.

Van Dijk understands Gower's primary vocation as being a poet and a storyteller, but one whose work depends on the law as an interstitial discourse, a "hinge" between political, ethical, moral, learned, amatory, and religious discourses. The very act of confession named in the title *Confessio Amantis* links all of these discourses through that of the law. Van Dijk's Gower is a storyteller before he is a lawyer, and as such, seeks out exempla that test the limits of straightforward legal reasoning. Chapter 1, "The Exemplum and the Legal Case," reevaluates the distinction between the genres of the exemplum and the case by considering foundational texts of the period, including rhetorical handbooks; exemplum collections; and major texts of canon, civil, and common law. The exemplum in rhetorical and legal texts is "not principally didactic or dogmatic" but part of a "larger culture of dialogue and dispute" (16). The exemplum posits a principle that motivates the narrative while the case raises difficult, even casuistical questions, but both narrative forms animate legal and literary texts, from the "love-questions" of romance to the difficult *causae* in Gratian's *Decretum*. In Van Dijk's view, the distinction between example and case is overdrawn. Cases take on an exemplary value insofar as they dramatize the power of the law in action and provide narrative closure. The authority of the law is therefore predicated on the constant exploration of its limits, the difficult cases that do not offer clear-cut solution, but that cast light on the good will that animates justice. Van Dijk argues that Gower's use of the judicial exemplum is intentionally indeterminate and unsettled precisely so that readers are required to exercise their own judgment. Establishing the parameters and capabilities of the judicial exemplum in this way, Van Dijk uses it to unravel the generic messiness of other works, such as *The Seven Sages of Rome*, the *Gesta Romanorum*, and Chaucer's *Summoner's Tale*, each of which features a "difficult case."

The second chapter shows how the judicial exemplum works in the *Confessio Amantis* by focusing on that collection's most direct and literal treatments of law and legal process. Compared with contemporary case records and juristic writing, Gower's poem progressively exploits figurative transplantations of legal discourse into the domains of ethical and amatory inquiry. The Latin gloss's abundant use of legal discourse and argument is, moreover, offered as evidence for the centrality of law to Gower's work (44). In the third chapter, Van Dijk investigates the relationships among power, law, and justice, focusing on concepts of sovereignty and jurisdiction as they pertain to the legal structure of empire, particularly in historical tales about Rome, that most exemplary of empires. Van Dijk's reading of Genius's commentary on Nebuchadnezzar's dream statue brings nuance to debates about Gower's own views about the temporal authority of the clergy, and showcases Van Dijk's proficiency at identifying precise and topical legal arguments in what might otherwise seem to be fabulous or theological material. These chapters also develop his argument that Gower's conception of justice is premised on will and intentionality, as demonstrated by exempla that show how recourse to the law may be formally correct, but at the same time self-serving and opportunistic.

Chapter 4 moves from supranational conflicts over sovereignty to the "specific sovereignty of the king in relation to his own law" (89). The legal controversy treated by this chapter is whether the law makes the king, as Bracton argued, or whether the king is above the law (89). Here, the debate over Gower's own politics and affiliations during Richard II's tumultuous reign come to the fore, and Van Dijk identifies a split among Gower scholars between those who see him as a kind of constitutionalist (Peck, Simpson) and those who see him as an absolutist (Scanlon, Eberle). Van Dijk leans toward the former group, but advocates resistance to such specific labels (91), exploring the contradictions among Gower's many aphorisms about political authority. Despite the contradictions, Van Dijk sees Gower as having a coherently "moderate position" that combines support for "strong personal kingship" with "independent sovereignty" for the law (92)—the king is above the law, but should voluntarily submit himself to the law. Again, law and justice are only brought into alignment through the exercise of will toward justice, and the possibilities and limitations of this fact are illustrated through troubling cases in which it is not easy to decide whether or not the king has turned into a tyrant (109).

The fifth chapter turns to vengeance, the ultimate test case for "the limits of the law." As an avowed critic of maintenance, Gower has been portrayed as championing the rule of law over private vengeance, but his exempla reveal how vengeance is intertwined with public and institutional justice and with broader social conceptions of morality and lawfulness. Gower explores the possibility that there is a continuum between law and vengeance, in which neither has an exclusive claim to justice. Again, he makes his point by using difficult cases. Van Dijk focuses specifically on the tale of Orestes, asking readers to decide as judge and jury if Orestes' vengeance is wrong or right. One of the most interesting parts of this chapter is a comparison between views on revenge found in Aquinas versus those of the Lollards, which serves to show how the views expressed in Gower's poetry seem to vacillate between the two. This chapter also treats the *Cronica tripertita*'s account of Richard II's deposition under the rubric of vengeance, elaborating a theological doctrine in the Middle Ages that vengeance is justified when it has a divine office. In concluding, Van Dijk argues that Gower's consistent attention to the reality of legal practice contradicts the idealistic mimesis of the exemplum, particularly the narrative closure made possible in tales of justice and revenge.

Van Dijk's sensibility is one that seeks to synthesize, organize, and clarify, but to do so in a way that is informed by a theoretical awareness of its own limitations. His method is critically responsive to and reflective of Gower's poetry, which is at once enlivened by the desire for systematicity and equity in law, and simultaneously alive to the continued need to decide and interpret with a will toward justice. In one sense, Van Dijk is recovering a traditional thesis about medieval art and its synthetic desire to make of multiple, and seemingly multiple, meanings a greater whole rather than a self-consuming artifact. But Van Dijk's Gower recognizes that this synthesis calls for justice, defined in Justinian's *Institutes* as "a constant and unremitting will to give to each his own right" (99). Through its attention to will in the law, this study also demonstrates how legal thought and discourse involve the reader as judge and jury. This offers a significant new perspective to existing scholarship on Gower's project of ethical formation, but this line of inquiry is left underdeveloped, as is the fascinating discussion of the shifting meaning of "equity" in Chapter 4. There are a number of sections in the book that deserve more space for argument and evidence, and at 190 pages before apparatus, this book is not meager. It is rare to wish a book longer; in doing so, I intend to praise with faint condemnation. This is an important book for scholars of Gower as well as for those interested in law and literature.

JONATHAN M. NEWMAN
Bishop's University

DANIEL WAKELIN, *Scribal Correction and Literary Craft: English Manuscripts 1375–1510*. Cambridge: Cambridge University Press, 2014. Pp. xviii, 345. $99.00.

Under the influence of scholars such as Jean Rychner, Paul Zumthor, and Bernard Cerquiglini, the closing decades of the twentieth century witnessed an important reevaluation of scribal labor. The inevitable points of difference among manuscript versions of a given work came to be seen not solely as the unfortunate products of human error but also, potentially, as evidence of scribes' critical engagement with the works that they were engaged in copying. The effects of this trend on Middle English Studies are often traced back to Barry Windeatt's seminal article on "The Scribes as Chaucer's Early Critics" (*SAC* 1 [1979]: 119–41), in which Windeatt read the slips and aberrations among the extant manuscripts of *Troilus and Criseyde* as evidence of their copyists' responses to Chaucer's poetry. Studies of the critical and editorial work of Middle English scribes have since proliferated, but their focus continues to fall on the elements of a piece of writing that a given scribe has changed. In response to this trend, Daniel Wakelin's new book makes a compelling case for rethinking the question of scribal agency, so that it also include a consideration of those moments in which scribes make clear their determination to reproduce their exemplars accurately. Just like aberrance, Wakelin argues, correctness can make scribal priorities visible; when scribes correct their own or their colleagues' work, they manifest a series of attitudes toward both their craft and the texts whose transmission they ensure. Indeed, their corrections can be viewed as an implicit form of literary criticism that anticipates the more overt theorizing of writing in English that begins to be produced in the early modern period.

In his introduction (Chapter 1), Wakelin explains that he has pursued his account of correction in English manuscripts from two angles. On the one hand, he has made a broad survey of the corrections in eighty manuscripts containing Middle English that are now in the Huntington Library in California; on the other, he has conducted a series of case studies of individual manuscripts kept in the Huntington collection and elsewhere. In combination with the survey, the case studies allow Wakelin to offer a series of observations that are at once broadly relevant and nuanced, as his individual chapters move from general discussion into the analysis of specific manuscripts. The book is divided into two halves. In the first, Wakelin outlines the pains that some scribes took in order to produce accurate versions of the works that they copied. Preliminary chapters cover the cultural influences that promoted this pursuit of accuracy (in the case of Chapter 2) and demonstrate the degree of fidelity that scribes frequently attained. If it is unsurprising that divergences are few between known direct copies and their exemplars, for example (how else would we be able to identify them as direct copies?), it is nevertheless noteworthy that the majority of the corrections made by scribes to a sample of such known direct copies further reduce those divergences (Chapter 3). Turning to his Huntington corpus, Wakelin goes on to demonstrate that most of the corrections made in these books are in the hand of their main scribes, further implicating individual copyists in the pursuit of accurate reproduction (Chapter 4).

Chapters 5 to 7 discuss correcting techniques, as well as the frequency and the nature of scribal corrections in the Huntington corpus and in the books selected for closer study. The result is a rich account of the intelligence and the resourcefulness of Middle English scribes, whose engagement in the process of correcting their work often appears to reflect a sense of responsibility toward the texts that they reproduce. One among several intriguing observations made at this stage is that the majority of corrections that Wakelin logs in a sample of the Huntington manuscripts bring the texts thus corrected closer into line with modern critical editions of those works. While the limitations of such comparisons are clear, as Wakelin is well aware, this observation points to an apparently instinctive tendency among some scribes toward standardization. In many of the manuscripts Wakelin considers, scribes seem to have been motivated by a desire to produce texts that would look like already extant copies of the same work, not productions that were refashioned in order to appeal to their own or to their patrons' idiosyncratic interests.

The book's second half considers how scribes' behavior as correctors was shaped by their exposure to the Middle English texts that they copied. When scribes make corrections to their work that are not mandated by the requirements of Middle English grammar, those modifications might be an attempt to rectify a belatedly observed discrepancy between the copy and its exemplar. Modifications of this kind might represent an autonomous alteration, designed to bring the copy closer into line with a theoretical notion of its "correct" form—a notion developed over the course of the scribe's reading and copying of the text. As

Wakelin observes in Chapter 9, corrections to rhyme patterns provide the clearest indication of Middle English scribes' sensitivity to the dictates of genre and form; however, corrections that introduce otherwise superfluous adjectives, adverbs, and intensifiers also display a sensitivity to poetic style. When these scribal corrections are viewed as a kind of literary-critical judgment, it becomes evident that a poet like Lydgate—whose verse has not typically attracted close attention from modern critics—was actually a figure whose works sparked careful critical interest during the Middle Ages (see Chapter 5). Finally, in places where scribes signal gaps in their own copying, they clearly demonstrate an awareness of the gulf that might exist between any material manifestation of a text and its fullest, most correct version. Indeed, as Wakelin points out, by calling attention to such gaps, scribes articulate a belief that the unity of any given work might exist somewhere beyond the manuscript page; in this sense, their theoretical assumptions about the nature of a literary work might be said to anticipate Formalist conceptions of the text and of reading (Chapter 10). Where recent studies on the independent creativity of Middle English copyists have encouraged a blurring of the distinction between authorship and scribal work, Wakelin thus reestablishes the scribe in a position of subservience to the text. This is not the subservience of a dullard, however, but of a skilled and dedicated craftsman. Authors themselves did not disregard this kind of work; consideration of autograph manuscripts suggests that author-scribes behaved similarly when they wrote out their own texts (Chapter 11).

Criticisms of *Scribal Correction* will likely focus on the composition of its manuscript sample, about whose deficiencies Wakelin is unswervingly upfront. One group of texts known to have attracted significant scribal tampering—Middle English romances—happens to be underrepresented in the Huntington Library's collection. Somewhat more problematic is the omission of Anglo-French and Anglo-Latin copying from consideration. Since many medieval scribes were engaged in bi- or trilingual copying, Wakelin's focus on Middle English skews his study more seriously than does the omission of one literary genre: it limits what he can say about the "English" manuscripts announced as the subject of his book in its title. It would be churlish to push such objections too far, however. As it is, the breadth of the corpus studied in *Scribal Correction* far exceeds that covered by most Anglo-Saxon publications on paleographic topics, which still typically take the form of articles addressing individual scribes and/or codices. At the same time, Wakelin's sensitivity to the uniqueness of each manuscript book demonstrates the attention to detail with which that scholarly tradition continues to be associated. By illuminating the craftsmanship and the careful thinking that often went into accurate copying, Wakelin has made a welcome contribution to our understanding of typical scribal behavior. Its importance will be felt in subsequent studies of Middle English editing and textual history, the standardization of English before print, the early history of literary criticism in England, and several other topics.

RORY G. CRITTEN
University of Bern, Switzerland

JON WHITMAN, ed. *Romance and History: Imagining Time from the Medieval to the Early Modern Period.* Cambridge: Cambridge University Press, 2015. Pp. 331. $99.00.

This ambitious volume considers the relationship between romance and history from Geoffrey of Monmouth to Cervantes. Its sixteen chapters give attention to medieval and early modern Latin, English, French, Italian, and Spanish texts, assembled under the guiding question of "what kinds of history . . . such texts evoke" (8). This organizing principle admits quite a bit of ambiguity. The idea of "history" not only varies within the romances under consideration, but also shifts across different critical approaches. Such methodological differences can make it difficult to track any one idea about history across the entire set of essays. But the variety is also valuable. History and historicism have often been invoked as shibboleths that separate medieval thought from that of the Renaissance or divide one critical approach from another. In using "history" instead as a unifying term, Whitman lends perspective on the relationship among the different "kinds of history" that emerge beneath different critical lenses.

To organize the volume, Whitman must invoke literary historical categories even as he brings preconceived models of history under scrutiny. Accordingly, he uses a self-consciously constructed scheme, borrowing Jehan Bodel's "three matters" of Rome, Britain, and France, while modifying and supplementing them to suit the material (8). After the editor's introduction (Part 1), Part 2 of the collection gathers two essays under the heading "The Matter of Rome (and Realms to the East): Approaches to Antiquity." The first of these, Christopher Baswell's "Fearful Histories," describes the fraught, often unsuccessful efforts of Alexander romances to use architectural structures to contain and control threats to linear history. The second, by Catherine Croizy-Naquet, considers how the prose *Roman de Troie* and the poetic *Faits des Romains* use literary techniques to establish their historical perspectives. She proposes that, whereas the former aims for "sober and unadorned prose," the latter uses imaginative techniques to access the difference of the past (41). Both essays maintain that literature takes it upon itself to conceal and reveal different aspects of history, but Baswell and Croizy-Naquet differ on the extent to which they show the past pushing back against its literary container.

Part 3, "The Matter of Britain: Social and Spiritual Drives," encompasses an extremely diverse range of texts and approaches. Robert W. Hanning's essay shows cultural history transforming into literary history, exploring how Geoffrey of Monmouth's account of King Arthur's reign influences the "representation of socio-political and personal reality" in Chrétien de Troyes's *Cliges*, Guillaume Le Clerc's *Fergus of Galloway*, and the *Mort le roi Artu* (56). Particularly helpful is Hanning's discussion of *juvenes*, young men driven by restless energy—and their literary evolution into *chevaliers*, motivated by love. Meanwhile, Adrian Stevens focuses on historical context: the political motivations of Gottfried von Strassburg's *Tristan* and Wolfram von Eschenbach's *Parzival*. The significance of "history" shifts as the volume continues. It emerges as an ideological construction in Friedrich Wolfzettel's account of Grail legends, and as a quality of a text's own aesthetics—its representation of character and causality—in Edward Donald Kennedy's exploration of the conclusions of the prose *Brut*, Hardyng's metrical *Chronicle*, and the *Alliterative Mort Arthure*. Helen Cooper concludes the section by considering the nature of an author's immersion within literary history. She proposes that Malory's *Morte Darthur* might be seen as the result of a deep, empathetic familiarity with Arthurian material that allowed Malory to "internaliz[e] it and recast it mentally" (132).

The second half of the volume focuses on questions of veracity, verisimilitude, and the creation of history. Part 4, entitled "The Matters of France and Italy: Acts of Recollection and Invention," begins with a piece by Jean-Pierre Martin on the construction and use of the past in the chansons de geste. This is one of only a few essays in the volume to address not just history but time itself. As Martin observes, "the gap between the epic period and the time of performance is . . . not only temporal, but also ontological" (139). The type of time described by the epic is different from that lived by the reader. Martin's essay concludes by describing how epic time migrates from the stuff of memory to fiction over the course of the fourteenth century. Despite the chronological gap between the chansons de geste and the Italian *Orlandi*, Martin's discussion sets the stage for the two chapters that follow. The first of these is Riccardo Bruscagli's essay on the making of Ruggiero in both Boiardo's *Orlando innamorato* and Tito Vespasiano Strozzi's Latin *Borsias*, which shows Boiardo and Tito constructing "incredible genealogies" for the Este family (167). The second is Marco Praloran's on the structure of narration in European romance, a broad survey that gives special attention to artificiality and narrative timing.

Questions of veracity and verisimilitude persist through the volume's final section, "Matters of Fabulation and Fact: Shifting Registers." A supplement to the "three matters" that structure the rest of the volume, this group of essays includes contributions on English, Italian, and Spanish literature. Daniel Javitch's essay on "The Disparagement of Chivalric Romance" considers Tasso's defense of poetry in the wake of Boiardo and Ariosto. As Javitch explains, Tasso "wanted what he deemed to be the truth of historical testimony to control the poet's imagination in ways in which it had never been properly regimented in the prior fantastic constructs of romance" (198). Conversely, David Quint's piece "Romance and History in Tasso's *Gerusalemme liberata*" focuses on the problem of history for Tasso—namely, the troubling "*shapelessness*" of chronicle history (201). Gordon Teskey's essay, "The Thinking of History in Spenserian Romance," queries the ambiguity of the volume's central term, "history." Teskey proposes that *The Faerie Queene* accounts for history as a lived thing, not only in the sense that the past is still "collapsing over our heads," but also in the sense that Spenser's poetry "allow[s] the pastness of the past to arise in the present" (224–25). Finally, Marina Brownlee's "La Cava: Romance and History in Corral and Cervantes" guides the conversation into hybrid notions of genre and identity. As Brownlee explains, Corral and Cervantes' attempts to describe the "formative epoch" of contact between Christianity and Islam during the Moorish invasion of 711 reveal irresolvable "inconsistencies" of character, motivation, race, and religion (229, 238). Here, the genres of history and romance are embedded within one another. The volume concludes with a transhistorical editor's overview in which Whitman traces romance, conceived as a "prolonged reflection *about* history," back through the "three matters" and then ahead into the eighteenth and nineteenth centuries (245). He concludes that romance, and those thinking about it, are always *in medias res*, reconstituting the past in order to think about the future.

With a volume this expansive, many readers will not have expertise in every field and text covered. However, the essays are welcoming to non-specialists, supplying introductory overviews of the material before narrowing in on close readings. Certainly these pieces have much to offer scholars working in each of the fields represented. However, particularly for graduate teaching or discussion, the volume might be especially generative when considered as a whole. The complexities that arise from its heterogeneous treatment of history might themselves serve as discussion topics. The connections to be drawn among essays are typically associative and/or comparative: there is little here about the circulation, adaptation, or translation of romances among the different areas covered. Yet, among these essays, the idea of history remains productively unsettled, still a source of restless critical activity.

KARA GASTON
University of Toronto

STEPHEN M. YEAGER. *From Lawmen to Plowmen: Anglo-Saxon Legal Tradition and the School of Langland*. Toronto: University of Toronto Press, 2014. Pp. 280. $65.00.

This book constructs a new genealogy for the *Piers Plowman* tradition of Middle English alliterative verse. Through a combination of discourse analysis and close reading, Stephen Yeager situates the *Piers Plowman* tradition in a literary and documentary *longue durée* extending back through twelfth- and thirteenth-century alliterative verse to the tenth-/eleventh-century homilist Wulfstan.

In the introduction, Yeager forswears belief in the continuity of alliterative meter and nominates "Anglo-Saxon legal-homiletic discourse" (4) as a pre-Conquest ancestor for "the school of Langland." Chapter 1 defines this discourse as a symptom of transitional literacy, expressed in a cluster of self-authorizing rhetorical strategies, such as proverbs and alliterating lists. Chapter 2 reads the rhetorical, generic, codicological, and cultural contexts of Wulfstan's writings as exemplary of this discourse. Chapters 3 and 4 take the recopying of Old English texts at Worcester as the occasion to explore the ideological functions of Anglo-Saxon discursive forms in three twelfth- and thirteenth-century alliterative poems: the *First Worcester Fragment*, the *Proverbs of Alfred*, and Lawman's *Brut*. Chapters 5 and 6 read similar discursive forms (now fraught with new ideological functions) in two post-Langlandian alliterative poems: *Richard the Redeless* and *Mum and the Sothsegger*. In the conclusion, Yeager indicates how his arguments recontextualize other canonical works of Middle English poetry.

This account of the evolution of a group of formal strategies from Old to Middle English succeeds on a number of fronts. First, the book succeeds as a local history: all of Yeager's featured texts have ties to Worcestershire or Gloucestershire, lending geographical, institutional, and sometimes even codicological specificity to his reconstructed literary-historical *longue durée*. Second, Yeager takes pains to show how rhetorical gestures cross formal and generic boundaries in English writing. One of his central claims is that the disciplinary protocols of literary studies and diplomatics simplify, in complementary ways, a multifarious medieval English textual culture. This broadly historicist study reads literary structures in Anglo-Saxon charters as readily as it reads forms of documentation in *Mum and the Sothsegger*. Third, this book recuperates Wulfstan as a mover and shaker in English literary history. Indeed, Wulfstan is the unlikely hero of *From Lawmen to Plowmen*. Chapter 2 is the most closely argued in the book, making a strong case for understanding Wulfstan's homiletic and legal writings as different expressions of a single response to developments in textual culture and ecclesiastical institutions. In the remainder of the book, Wulfstan continually reappears as a source, an inspiration, a precedent, or an adjacent manuscript item. Fourth, Yeager shakes up literary-historical commonplaces by positioning Langland at the center, rather than the periphery, of an English alliterative tradition. Finally, this book directly connects Old English and Middle English literature. Too often, these subfields are regarded as non-overlapping magisteria; Yeager traces continuities in "documentary poetics" (162, quoting Emily Steiner) across 1066, in part by emphasizing one point of contact between the two halves of medieval English literary history: the antiquarianism of the Tremulous Hand of Worcester in the thirteenth century.

If this book succeeds in showing what is lost when literary historians project 1066 as an end point or a zero point, its specific arguments nevertheless reinforce the Old/Middle divide. Throughout the book, "Anglo-Saxon legal-homiletic discourse" functions as a consolidated discursive formation, which appears first as a suite of literary and textual practices (for Wulfstan), then as an archive to be recopied (for twelfth-century scribes), a lost textual-institutional unity to be lamented (in the *First Worcester Fragment* and *Proverbs of Alfred*), a historiographical attitude to be redirected (for Lawman), a documentary form to be renovated (in the *Piers Plowman* tradition), and an ideological model to be rejected (for Chaucer and the *Gawain*-poet). Yeager's early chapters extrapolate an "Anglo-Saxon" discursive mode largely from Wulfstan's oeuvre: one would have appreciated more discussion of literary-institutional continuities and discontinuities between Wulfstan and earlier writing in English (including Old English poetry, almost completely absent here) and Latin (Alcuin, Aldhelm, and Bede only come up in chapters 1 and 2, when later texts mention or imitate them). By the same token, Yeager's arguments for continuity into the late medieval centuries would be strengthened by supplementing the focus on the Tremulous Hand with more discussion of how, by what means, Wulfstanian rhetoric endured in English (and Latin and Anglo-Norman?) writing after 1066.

One way to connect various proverbs, alliterating lists, etc., more specifically and dynamically would have been to disaggregate them by literary form and genre. Yeager's avoidance of metrics accentuates rather than solves "The Problem of Form" (72, a section heading). The past thirty years have witnessed breakthroughs in alliterative metrics that support but also complicate Yeager's historical conclusions. Recent work by Thomas Cable, Hoyt Duggan, Judith Jefferson, Ad Putter, Geoffrey Russom, Myra Stokes, et al. suggests precisely what Yeager disclaims, that Old English meter evolved directly into Middle English alliterative meter. Yeager cites only a sliver of this new scholarship. And yet his arguments do depend on definitions of literary form, as witness his numerous references to alliteration and "two-beat metre" (121) as formal criteria. But post-1985 metrical scholarship emphasizes patterns of stressed and unstressed syllables over the mere fact of alliteration, and much of it challenges the presumption that alliterative half-lines always contain two metrical stresses. How does Yeager scan half-lines with three content words, like *Richard*, 28a: "Whedir <u>God</u> wolde <u>geve</u> him <u>grace</u>"? *From Lawmen to Plowmen* never engages with verse at this level of metrical detail. The lack of attention to literary form affects interpretation: *Brut*, 36 ("Nv seið mid loft-songe | þe wes on leoden preost") does not mean "Now the priest says, with the *loft-songe* that was in the people/language" (148), but "Now he who was priest in the land says with a song of praise," with double poetic inversion of syntax.

In its formal and historical claims, this book is at once expansive ("four-beat lines are by nature sententious" [41], in a section connecting the Old English poem *An Exhortation to Christian Living* to all Old English wisdom poetry, to Wulfstanian law codes, to the *Piers Plowman* tradition, to the modern proverb "A bird in the hand is worth two in the bush") and narrow (*Crowned King* and *Pierce the Ploughman's Crede*, assigned to the *Piers Plowman* tradition by Helen Barr, are not mentioned once). The sociocultural argument of the book is rather dichotomized, with "the ongoing centralization of English bureaucratic practices around the royal court" (7) serving as an all-purpose foil to a quasi-oral "Anglo-Saxon legal-homiletic discourse." Yeager sometimes assumes too much knowledge of legal history in a literary audience: the point that "disputes over tenurial rights to 'park and plow' provided the occasion for most late medieval citations of Anglo-Saxon law and history" (167), seemingly of fundamental importance to the literary arguments of chapters 3, 4, 5, and 6, is tucked away in the second section of Chapter 5 and receives no further exposition. Probably the most provocative omission is the absence of any sustained reading of *Piers Plowman*: Yeager contends that *Mum* and *Richard* "are manifestly concerned with legal, documentary authority, and discuss these issues with a degree of specificity unmatched by the other texts of the *Piers Plowman* tradition, including those attributed to Langland himself" (152).

This book strikes a blow for the long view, for the interdependence of literary and legal history, and above all for Wulfstan. The English literary tradition adumbrated by Yeager functions as an engaging regional history and raises more questions about alliterative meter than the book is designed to answer.

Eric Weiskott
Boston College

Books Received

Appleford, Amy. *Learning to Die in London, 1380–1540*. Philadelphia: University of Pennsylvania Press, 2014. Pp. 336. £42.50; $65.00.

Arner, Lynn. *Chaucer, Gower and the Vernacular Rising: Poetry and the Problem of the Populace after 1381*. University Park: Penn State University Press, 2013. Pp. 208. $29.95.

Ingham, Patricia Clare. *The Medieval New: Ambivalence in an Age of Innovation*. Philadelphia: University of Pennsylvania Press, 2015. Pp. 288. £42.50; $65.00.

Johnston, Andrew James, Margitta Rouse, and Philipp Hinz, eds. *The Medieval Motion Picture: The Politics of Adaptation*. New York: Palgrave, 2014. Pp. 256. $95.00.

Johnston, Michael. *Romance and the Gentry in Late Medieval England*. Oxford: Oxford University Press, 2014. Pp. 320. £57.00; $85.00.

Khanmohamadi, Shirin A. *In Light of Another's Word: European Ethnography in the Middle Ages*. Philadelphia: University of Pennsylvania Press, 2014. Pp. 216. £31.00; $47.50.

Lawler, Traugott, and Ralph Hanna, eds. *Jankyn's Book of Wikked Wyves*, Vol. 2: *Seven Commentaries on Walter Map's "Dissuasio Valerii."* Athens, Ga. and London: University of Georgia Press, 2014. Pp. 624. $89.95.

Leitch, Megan. *Romancing Treason: The Literature of the Wars of the Roses*. Oxford: Oxford University Press, 2015. Pp. 240. £55.00; $90.00.

Malo, Robyn. *Relics and Writing in Late Medieval England*. Toronto: University of Toronto Press, 2013. Pp. 308. $75.00.

Mann, Jill. *Life in Words: Essays on Chaucer, the Gawain-Poet, and Malory.* Ed. Mark Rasmussen. Toronto: University of Toronto Press, 2014. $75.00.

Mills, Robert. *Seeing Sodomy in the Middle Ages.* Chicago: University of Chicago Press, 2015. Pp. 400. $55.00.

Minnis, Alastair, and Stephen Rigby, eds. *Historians on Chaucer: The "General Prologue" to the "Canterbury Tales."* Oxford: Oxford University Press, 2014. Pp. 528. £65.00; $99.00.

Patterson, Serina. *Games and Gaming in the Middle Ages.* New York: Palgrave, 2015. Pp. 256. $90.00.

Perkins, Nicholas, ed. *Medieval Romance and Material Culture.* Woodbridge and Rochester, N.Y.: Boydell and Brewer, 2015. Pp. 311. £60.00; $99.00.

Phillips, Kim M. *Before Orientalism: Asian Peoples and Cultures in European Travel Writing, 1245–1510.* Philadelphia: University of Pennsylvania Press, 2014. Pp. 328. £52.00; $79.95.

Rentz, Ellen K. *Imagining the Parish in Late Medieval England.* Columbus: Ohio State University Press, 2015. Pp. 224. $62.95.

Scala, Elizabeth. *Desire in the "Canterbury Tales."* Columbus: Ohio State University Press, 2015. Pp. 248. $62.95.

Schreyer, Kurt A. *Shakespeare's Medieval Craft: Remnants of the Mysteries on the London Stage.* Ithaca, N.Y.: Cornell University Press, 2014. Pp. 280. $49.95.

Schrock, Chad D. *Consolation in Medieval Narrative: Augustinian Authority and Open Form.* New York: Palgrave, 2015. Pp. 256. $90.00.

Somerset, Fiona. *Feeling like Saints: Lollard Writings after Wyclif.* Ithaca, N.Y.: Cornell University Press, 2014. Pp. 336. $65.00.

Sponsler, Claire. *The Queen's Dumbshows: John Lydgate and the Making of Early Theater*. Philadelphia: University of Pennsylvania Press, 2014. Pp. 320. £42.50; $65.00.

Truitt, E. R. *Medieval Robots: Mechanism, Magic, Nature, and Art*. Philadelphia: University of Pennsylvania Press, 2015. Pp. 312. £36.00; $55.00.

An Annotated Chaucer Bibliography, 2013

Compiled and edited by Stephanie Amsel and Mark Allen

Regular contributors:

Mark Allen, *University of Texas at San Antonio*
Michelle Allen, *Grand Rapids Community College* (Michigan)
Stephanie Amsel, *Southern Methodist University* (Texas)
Brother Anthony (Sonjae An), *Sogang University* (South Korea)
Tim Arner, *Grinnell College* (Iowa)
Rebecca Beal, *University of Scranton* (Pennsylvania)
Debra Best, *California State University at Dominguez Hills*
Thomas H. Blake, *University of Iowa*
Matthew Brumit, *Southern Methodist University* (Texas)
Margaret Connolly, *University of St. Andrews* (Scotland)
John Michael Crafton, *West Georgia College*
Stefania D'Agata D'Ottavi, *Università per Stranieri di Siena* (Italy)
Geoffrey B. Elliott, *Oklahoma State University*
Maggie Gilchrist, *University of Alabama*
Jon-Mark Grussenmeyer, *Rowan University* (New Jersey)
James B. Harr III, *Wake Technical Community College*
Douglas W. Hayes, *Lakehead University*
Ana Sáez Hidalgo, *Universidad de Valladolid* (Spain)
Andrew James Johnston, *Freie Universität Berlin* (Germany)
Yoshinobu Kudo, *Keio University* (Japan)
Wim Lindeboom, *Independent Scholar* (Netherlands)
Warren S. Moore III, *Newberry College* (South Carolina)
Daniel M. Murtaugh, *Florida Atlantic University*
Thomas J. Napierkowski, *University of Colorado at Colorado Springs*
Ashley R. Ott, *St. Louis University*
Teresa P. Reed, *Jacksonville State University* (Alabama)
Christopher Roman, *Kent State University at Tuscarawas* (Ohio)
Martha Rust, *New York University*

Gregory M. Sadlek, *Cleveland State University* (Ohio)
Thomas R. Schneider, *California Baptist University*
Gale Sigal, *Wake Forest University* (North Carolina)
David Sprunger, *Concordia College* (Minnesota)
Jeffery G. Stoyanoff, *Duquesne University* (Pennsylvania)
Anne Thornton, *Abbot Public Library* (Marblehead, Massachusetts)
Winthrop Wetherbee, *Cornell University* (New York)
Elaine Whitaker, *Georgia College & State University*
Susan Yager, *Iowa State University*
Martine Yvernault, *Université de Limoges* (France)

Ad hoc contributions were made by Joyce K. Coleman of the University of Oklahoma, Norman, Oklahoma; Michael Johnston of Purdue University, West Lafayette, Indiana; and Anna Narinsky. The bibliographers acknowledge with gratitude assistance from librarians at Southern Methodist University.

This bibliography continues the bibliographies published since 1975 in previous volumes of *Studies in the Age of Chaucer*. Bibliographic information up to 1975 can be found in Eleanor P. Hammond, *Chaucer: A Bibliographic Manual* (1908; reprint, New York: Peter Smith, 1933); D. D. Griffith, *Bibliography of Chaucer, 1908–1953* (Seattle: University of Washington Press, 1955); William R. Crawford, *Bibliography of Chaucer, 1954–63* (Seattle: University of Washington Press, 1967); and Lorrayne Y. Baird, *Bibliography of Chaucer, 1964–1973* (Boston, Mass.: G. K. Hall, 1977). See also Lorrayne Y. Baird-Lange and Hildegard Schnuttgen, *Bibliography of Chaucer, 1974–1985* (Hamden, Conn.: Shoe String Press, 1988); and Bege K. Bowers and Mark Allen, eds., *Annotated Chaucer Bibliography, 1986–1996* (Notre Dame, Ind.: University of Notre Dame Press, 2002).

Additions and corrections to this bibliography should be sent to Stephanie Amsel, Department of English, Southern Methodist University, GO2AB Clements Hall, P.O. Box 750283, Dallas, Texas 75275-0283. An electronic version of this bibliography (1975–2012) is available via the New Chaucer Society web page at http://artsci.wustl.edu/~chaucer/, or directly at http://uchaucer.utsa.edu. Authors are urged to send annotations for articles, reviews, and books that have been or might be overlooked to Stephanie Amsel, samsel@smu.edu.

Classifications

Bibliographies, Reports, and Reference 1–2
Recordings and Films
Chaucer's Life 3
Facsimiles, Editions, and Translations
Manuscripts and Textual Studies 4–16
Sources, Analogues, and Literary Relations 17–25
Chaucer's Influence and Later Allusion 26–37
Style and Versification 38–44
Language and Word Studies 45–57
Background and General Criticism 58–83

The Canterbury Tales—General 84–94

CT—The General Prologue
CT—The Knight and His Tale 95–101
CT—The Miller and His Tale 102–3
CT—The Reeve and His Tale 104
CT—The Cook and His Tale 105
CT—The Man of Law and His Tale 106–8
CT—The Wife of Bath and Her Tale 109–13
CT—The Friar and His Tale 114–15
CT—The Summoner and His Tale 116–17
CT—The Clerk and His Tale 118–23
CT—The Merchant and His Tale 124
CT—The Squire and His Tale 125–26
CT—The Franklin and His Tale 127–29
CT—The Physician and His Tale
CT—The Pardoner and His Tale 130–32
CT—The Shipman and His Tale
CT—The Prioress and Her Tale 133–39
CT—The Tale of Sir Thopas 140–42
CT—The Tale of Melibee
CT—The Monk and His Tale 143
CT—The Nun's Priest and His Tale 144
CT—The Second Nun and Her Tale 145

CT—The Canon's Yeoman and His Tale
CT—The Manciple and His Tale 146–47
CT—The Parson and His Tale 148–49
CT—Chaucer's Retraction

Anelida and Arcite
A Treatise on the Astrolabe 150
Boece
The Book of the Duchess 151–53
The Equatorie of the Planetis
The House of Fame 154
The Legend of Good Women 155–58
The Parliament of Fowls 159–60
The Romaunt of the Rose
Troilus and Criseyde 161–72

Lyrics and Short Poems
An ABC
Adam Scriveyn
The Complaint of Chaucer to His Purse
Former Age

Chaucerian Apocrypha
Book Reviews 173–201

Abbreviations of Chaucer's Works

ABC	An ABC
Adam	Adam Scriveyn
Anel	Anelida and Arcite
Astr	A Treatise on the Astrolabe
Bal Compl	A Balade of Complaint
BD	The Book of the Duchess
Bo	Boece
Buk	The Envoy to Bukton
CkT, CkP	The Cook's Tale, The Cook's Prologue
ClT, ClP, Cl–MerL	The Clerk's Tale, The Clerk's Prologue, Clerk–Merchant Link
Compl d'Am	Complaynt d'Amours
CT	The Canterbury Tales
CYT, CYP	The Canon's Yeoman's Tale, The Canon's Yeoman's Prologue
Equat	The Equatorie of the Planetis
For	Fortune
Form Age	The Former Age
FranT, FranP	The Franklin's Tale, The Franklin's Prologue
FrT, FrP, Fr–SumL	The Friar's Tale, The Friar's Prologue, Friar–Summoner Link
Gent	Gentilesse
GP	The General Prologue
HF	The House of Fame
KnT, Kn–MilL	The Knight's Tale, Knight–Miller Link
Lady	A Complaint to His Lady
LGW, LGWP	The Legend of Good Women, The Legend of Good Women Prologue
ManT, ManP	The Manciple's Tale, The Manciple's Prologue
Mars	The Complaint of Mars
Mel, Mel–MkL	The Tale of Melibee, Melibee–Monk Link
MercB	Merciles Beaute
MerT, MerE–SqH	The Merchant's Tale, Merchant Endlink–Squire Headlink

MilT, MilP, Mil–RvL	The Miller's Tale, The Miller's Prologue, Miller–Reeve Link
MkT, MkP, Mk–NPL	The Monk's Tale, The Monk's Prologue, Monk–Nun's Priest Link
MLT, MLH, MLP, MLE	The Man of Law's Tale, Man of Law Headlink, The Man of Law's Prologue, Man of Law Endlink
NPT, NPP, NPE	The Nun's Priest's Tale, The Nun's Priest's Prologue, Nun's Priest Endlink
PardT, PardP	The Pardoner's Tale, The Pardoner's Prologue
ParsT, ParsP	The Parson's Tale, The Parson's Prologue
PF	The Parliament of Fowls
PhyT, Phy–PardL	The Physician's Tale, Physician–Pardoner Link
Pity	The Complaint unto Pity
Prov	Proverbs
PrT, PrP, Pr–ThL	The Prioress's Tale, The Prioress's Prologue, Prioress–Thopas Link
Purse	The Complaint of Chaucer to His Purse
Ret	Chaucer's Retraction {Retractation}
Rom	The Romaunt of the Rose
Ros	To Rosemounde
RvT, RvP, Rv–CkL	The Reeve's Tale, The Reeve's Prologue, Reeve–Cook Link
Scog	The Envoy to Scogan
ShT, Sh–PrL	The Shipman's Tale, Shipman–Prioress Link
SNT, SNP, SN–CYL	The Second Nun's Tale, The Second Nun's Prologue, Second Nun–Canon's Yeoman Link
SqT, SqH, Sq–FranL	The Squire's Tale, Squire Headlink, Squire–Franklin Link
Sted	Lak of Stedfastnesse
SumT, SumP	The Summoner's Tale, The Summoner's Prologue
TC	Troilus and Criseyde
Th, Th–MelL	The Tale of Sir Thopas, Sir Thopas–Melibee Link

Truth	*Truth*
Ven	*The Complaint of Venus*
WBT, WBP, WB–FrL	*The Wife of Bath's Tale, The Wife of Bath's Prologue, Wife of Bath–Friar Link*
Wom Nob	*Womanly Noblesse*
Wom Unc	*Against Women Unconstant*

Periodical Abbreviations

Anglia	*Anglia: Zeitschrift für Englische Philologie*
Anglistik	*Anglistik: Mitteilungen des Verbandes deutscher Anglisten*
ANQ	*ANQ: A Quarterly Journal of Short Articles, Notes, and Reviews*
Archiv	*Archiv für das Studium der Neueren Sprachen und Literaturen*
Arthuriana	*Arthuriana*
Atlantis	*Atlantis: Revista de la Asociacion Española de Estudios Anglo-Norteamericanos*
AUMLA	*AUMLA: Journal of the Australasian Universities Language and Literature Association*
BAM	*Bulletin des Anglicistes Médiévistes*
BJRL	*Bulletin of the John Rylands University Library of Manchester*
C&L	*Christianity and Literature*
CarmP	*Carmina Philosophiae: Journal of the International Boethius Society*
CE	*College English*
ChauR	*Chaucer Review*
CL	*Comparative Literature* (Eugene, Ore.)
Clio	*CLIO: A Journal of Literature, History, and the Philosophy of History*
CLS	*Comparative Literature Studies*
CML	*Classical and Modern Literature: A Quarterly* (Columbia, Mo.)
CollL	*College Literature*
Comitatus	*Comitatus: A Journal of Medieval and Renaissance Studies*
CRCL	*Canadian Review of Comparative Literature/Revue Canadienne de Littérature Comparée*
DAI	*Dissertation Abstracts International*
DR	*Dalhousie Review*
EA	*Etudes Anglaises: Grand-Bretagne, Etats-Unis*
EHR	*English Historical Review*
EIC	*Essays in Criticism: A Quarterly Journal of Literary Criticism*

EJ	*English Journal*
ELH	*ELH: English Literary History*
ELN	*English Language Notes*
ELR	*English Literary Renaissance*
EMS	*English Manuscript Studies, 1100–1700*
EMSt	*Essays in Medieval Studies*
English	*English: The Journal of the English Association*
Envoi	*Envoi: A Review Journal of Medieval Literature*
ES	*English Studies*
Exemplaria	*Exemplaria: A Journal of Theory in Medieval and Renaissance Studies*
Expl	*Explicator*
FCS	*Fifteenth-Century Studies*
Florilegium	*Florilegium: Carleton University Papers on Late Antiquity and the Middle Ages*
Genre	*Genre: Forms of Discourse and Culture*
H-Albion	*H-Albion: The H-Net Discussion Network for British and Irish History, H-Net Reviews in the Humanities and Social Sciences* http://www.h-net.org/reviews/home.php
HLQ	*Huntington Library Quarterly: Studies in English and American History and Literature* (San Marino, Calif.)
Hortulus	*Hortulus: The Online Graduate Journal of Medieval Studies* http://www.hortulus.net/
IJES	*International Journal of English Studies*
JAIS	*Journal of Anglo-Italian Studies*
JBSt	*Journal of British Studies*
JEBS	*Journal of the Early Book Society*
JEGP	*Journal of English and Germanic Philology*
JELL	*Journal of English Language and Literature* (Korea)
JEngL	*Journal of English Linguistics*
JGN	*John Gower Newsletter*
JMEMSt	*Journal of Medieval and Early Modern Studies*
JML	*Journal of Modern Literature*
JNT	*Journal of Narrative Theory*
L&LC	*Literary and Linguistic Computing: Journal of the Association for Literary and Linguistic Computing*

L&P	*Literature and Psychology*
L&T	*Literature and Theology: An International Journal of Religion, Theory, and Culture*
Lang&Lit	*Language and Literature: Journal of the Poetics and Linguistics Association*
Lang&S	*Language and Style: An International Journal*
LeedsSE	*Leeds Studies in English*
Library	*The Library: The Transactions of the Bibliographical Society*
LitComp	*Literature Compass* http://www.literaturecompass.com/
MA	*Le Moyen Age: Revue d'Histoire et de Philologie* (Brussels, Belgium)
MÆ	*Medium Ævum*
M&H	*Medievalia et Humanistica: Studies in Medieval and Renaissance Culture*
Manuscripta	*Manuscripta: A Journal for Manuscript Research*
Marginalia	*Marginalia: The Journal of the Medieval Reading Group at the University of Cambridge* http://www.marginalia.co.uk/journal/
Mediaevalia	*Mediaevalia: An Interdisciplinary Journal of Medieval Studies Worldwide*
MedievalF	*Medieval Forum* http://www.sfsu.edu/~medieval/index.html
MedPers	*Medieval Perspectives*
MES	*Medieval and Early Modern English Studies*
MFF	*Medieval Feminist Forum*
MLN	*Modern Language Notes*
MLQ	*Modern Language Quarterly: A Journal of Literary History*
MP	*Modern Philology: A Journal Devoted to Research in Medieval and Modern Literature*
N&Q	*Notes and Queries*
Neophil	*Neophilologus* (Dordrecht, Netherlands)
NLH	*New Literary History: A Journal of Theory and Interpretation*
NM	*Neuphilologische Mitteilungen: Bulletin of the Modern Language Society*

NML	New Medieval Literatures
NMS	Nottingham Medieval Studies
NYRB	The New York Times Review of Books
Parergon	Parergon: Bulletin of the Australian and New Zealand Association for Medieval and Early Modern Studies
PBA	Proceedings of the British Academy
PBSA	Papers of the Bibliographical Society of America
PLL	Papers on Language and Literature: A Journal for Scholars and Critics of Language and Literature
PMAM	Publications of the Medieval Association of the Midwest
PMLA	Publications of the Modern Language Association of America
PoeticaT	Poetica: An International Journal of Linguistic Literary Studies
PQ	Philological Quarterly
Quidditas	Quidditas: Journal of the Rocky Mountain Medieval and Renaissance Association
RCEI	Revista Canaria de Estudios Ingleses
RenQ	Renaissance Quarterly
RES	Review of English Studies
RMSt	Reading Medieval Studies
SAC	Studies in the Age of Chaucer
SAP	Studia Anglica Posnaniensia: An International Review of English
SAQ	South Atlantic Quarterly
SB	Studies in Bibliography: Papers of the Bibliographical Society of the University of Virginia
SCJ	The Sixteenth-Century Journal: Journal of Early Modern Studies (Kirksville, Mo.)
SEL	SEL: Studies in English Literature, 1500–1900
SELIM	SELIM: Journal of the Spanish Society for Medieval English Language and Literature
ShakS	Shakespeare Studies
SIcon	Studies in Iconography
SiM	Studies in Medievalism
SIMELL	Studies in Medieval English Language and Literature
SMART	Studies in Medieval and Renaissance Teaching
SN	Studia Neophilologica: A Journal of Germanic and Romance Languages and Literatures

SoAR	*South Atlantic Review*
SP	*Studies in Philology*
Speculum	*Speculum: A Journal of Medieval Studies*
SSt	*Spenser Studies: A Renaissance Poetry Annual*
TCBS	*Transactions of the Cambridge Bibliographical Society*
Text	*Text: Transactions of the Society for Textual Scholarship*
TLS	*Times Literary Supplement* (London, England)
TMR	*The Medieval Review* https://scholarworks.iu.edu/dspace/handle/2022/3631
Tr&Lit	*Translation and Literature*
TSLL	*Texas Studies in Literature and Language*
UTQ	*University of Toronto Quarterly: A Canadian Journal of the Humanities*
Viator	*Viator: Medieval and Renaissance Studies*
YES	*Yearbook of English Studies*
YLS	*The Yearbook of Langland Studies*
YWES	*Year's Work in English Studies*

Bibliographical Citations and Annotations

Bibliographies, Reports, and Reference

1. Allen, Mark, and Bege K. Bowers. "An Annotated Chaucer Bibliography, 2011." *SAC* 35 (2013): 455–504. Continuation of *SAC* annual annotated bibliography (since 1975); based on contributions from an international bibliographic team, independent research, and *MLA Bibliography* listings. 166 items, plus listing of reviews for 42 books. Includes an author index.

2. Binski, Paul, and Patrick Zutshi, with the collaboration of Stella Panayotova. *Western Illuminated Manuscripts: A Catalogue of the Collection in Cambridge University Library*. Cambridge: Cambridge University Press, 2011. Comprehensive catalogue of western European illuminated manuscripts in the Cambridge University Library. Includes several indices of iconography, scribes, artists, binders, and authors (with Chaucer listed under "G" for Geoffrey), along with provenance, descriptions, and bibliographic information of early Chaucer manuscripts in the collection. Entries include *CT*, *Astr*, *LGW*, *PF*, *TC*, *ABC*, *For*, and *Form Age*.

Recordings and Films

See nos. 29, 38, 57, 83.

Chaucer's Life

3. Downes, Stephanie. "Chaucer and His French Readers: Eighteenth-Century Copies in the Bibliothèque Nationale de France." *N&Q* 258 (2013): 572–74. Rebinding and rearrangement of John Dart's biography of Chaucer in one of the six seventeenth- and eighteenth-century editions of his work held in Paris effectively reframe it as having been modeled "culturally and linguistically from French materials."

See also nos. 50, 77.

Facsimiles, Editions, and Translations

See nos. 3, 5, 89, 119.

Manuscripts and Textual Studies

4. Bahr, Arthur, and Alexandra Gillespie. "Medieval English Manuscripts: Form, Aesthetics, and the Literary Text." *ChauR* 47, no. 4 (2013): 346–60. Introduces a special issue on manuscript studies and the history of the book in relation to critical theory; also summarizes the issue's articles. Discusses *CT*, *TC*, and *Th*.

5. Caie, Graham D. "Two Revolutionary Periods for the Text: The Fifteenth and the Twenty-First Centuries." *SIMELL* 28 (2013): 1–16. Explores how the presentation of texts, as well as the reader's response to them, might be influenced by new textual forms, focusing on the manuscript (Glasgow University Library, MS Hunter 197), printed (William Thynne's edition), and electronic versions of *Rom*.

6. Cayley, Emma, and Susan Powell, eds. *Manuscripts and Printed Books in Europe 1350–1550: Packaging, Presentation, and Consumption*. Liverpool: Liverpool University Press, 2013. Foreword by Derek Pearsall. Essays address issues of packaging, presentation, and consumption of manuscripts. Also discusses producers, owners, and readers of manuscripts and early printed books. For essays pertaining to Chaucer, see nos. 9 and 102.

7. Coleman, Joyce. "The First Presentation Miniature in an English-Language Manuscript." In Joyce Coleman, Mark Cruse, and Kathryn A. Smith, eds. *The Social Life of Illumination: Manuscripts, Images, and Communities in the Late Middle Ages* (*SAC* 37 [2015], no. 8), pp. 403–37. Explores the argument that the lack of Chaucerian presentation miniatures suggests that Chaucer did not write for wealthy patrons. Identifies the first presentation miniature in an English-language manuscript as the 1409 incipit image in John Trevisa's *Governance of Kings and Princes*; reviews the history of presentation miniatures in French-language manuscripts; and shows that, in both languages, presentation miniatures seem to be reserved for "serious" literature, such as national chronicles and translations of learned Latin material.

8. Coleman, Joyce, Mark Cruse, and Kathryn A. Smith, eds. *The Social Life of Illumination: Manuscripts, Images, and Communities in the Late Middle Ages*. Turnhout: Brepols, 2013. xxiv, 552 pp. Interdisciplinary

anthology focusing on interplay of social and political interactions and medieval French and English illuminated manuscripts produced between the thirteenth and sixteenth centuries. For an essay pertaining to Chaucer, see no. 7.

9. Gellert, Anamaria. "Fools, 'Folye' and Caxton's Woodcut of the Pilgrims at the Table." In Emma Cayley and Susan Powell, eds. *Manuscripts and Printed Books in Europe 1350–1550: Packaging, Presentation, and Consumption* (*SAC* 37 [2015], no. 6), pp. 150–68. Analyzes woodcut of pilgrims seated at table in Caxton's second edition of *CT*. Argues that "early editors' interpretations of given literary works are thus reflected in their editorial choices."

10. Horobin, Simon. "Chaucer Manuscripts and the *Middle English Dictionary*." In Ana Laura Rodríguez Redondo and Eugenio Contreras Domingo, eds. *Focus on Old and Middle English Studies* (*SAC* 37 [2015], no. 79), pp. 11–23. Studies the treatment of manuscripts in the *MED*, especially those containing Chaucer's works. Detects potential for confusion in the use of the double-dating system (manuscript and composition dates, not always consistently cited), and in the combined use of manuscript sources and modern editions. Chaucer's works are treated differently from other authors', following the commonplace that Chaucer was crucial for the development of English.

11. ———. "Compiling the *Canterbury Tales* in Fifteenth-Century Manuscripts." *ChauR* 47, no. 4 (2013): 372–89. Focusing on the *MerE–SqH*, argues that what has been seen as evidence of authorial revision in the manuscripts may simply be reflecting problem areas encountered by the scribes, including problems in accessing exemplars and linking passages, which often circulated on single leaves.

12. Mooney, Linne R., and Estelle Stubbs. *Scribes and the City: Guildhall Clerks and the Dissemination of Middle English Literature, 1375–1425*. Rochester, N.Y.: Boydell Press, 2013. x, 155 pp. Comprehensive study of scribes from the London Guildhall responsible for copying Chaucer's earliest manuscripts, including Adam Pinkhurst, Guildhall scrivener from 1378 to 1410.

13. Nafde, Aditi. "Hoccleve's Hands: The *Mise-en-Page* of the Autograph and Non-Autograph Manuscripts." *JEBS* 16 (2013): 55–83. Compares Chaucer's and Hoccleve's manuscripts in terms of authorial control, contrasting the "muddle of disparate exemplars" of *CT* with Hoccleve's detailed attention to format. Specifically contrasts Hoccleve's

"mid-stanza paraph" in his autograph manuscripts with the mid-stanza paraph's complete absence from manuscripts of *TC* in the same period.

14. Nolan, Maura. "Medieval Habit, Modern Sensation: Reading Manuscripts in the Digital Age." *ChauR* 47, no. 4 (2013): 465–76. Examines what is lost when we look at a digitized manuscript instead of the material book, which invokes the senses of touch, smell, and taste and the habits of the medieval reader. Mentions the graphic tail-rhyme in *Th* as a type of habit that invokes particular perceptions.

15. Pearson, Richard. "William Morris Interrupted Interrupting Chaucer." In Clíodhna Carney and Frances McCormack, eds. *Chaucer's Poetry: Words, Authority and Ethics* (*SAC* 37 [2015], no. 61), pp. 158–84. Examines the significance of William Morris's direct engagement with Chaucer's works. The illustrations and intricate frames of his Kelmscott *CT* are complex and communicative, serving as creatively productive interruptions to the act of reading.

16. Thaisen, Jacob. "*Gamelyn*'s Place among the Early Exemplars for Chaucer's *Canterbury Tales*." *Neophil* 97, no. 2 (2013): 395–415. Applying ANOVA/Tukey's Range Test on nine early *CT* manuscripts, the author finds that none of them is based on exemplars written in more than three hands. Attributes the final ordering in the first manuscripts of *CT* to "the poem's first two scribes, probably working after Chaucer's death and spuriously adding the *Tale of Gamelyn*."

See also nos. 2, 89, 116, 119, 140, 168, 170.

Sources, Analogues, and Literary Relations

17. Bertolet, Craig E. *Chaucer, Gower, Hoccleve, and the Commercial Practices of Late Fourteenth-Century London*. Burlington, VT: Ashgate, 2013. ix, 168 pp. Examines influence of commerce and trade in *CT*, Gower's *Mirour de l'omme* and *Confessio Amantis*, and Hoccleve's *Male regle* and *Regiment of Princes*. Looks at social and cultural implications of how market economies affect literary narratives and the portrayal of Chaucer's pilgrims.

18. Fulton, Sharon. "Animal Speech and Political Utterance: Articulating the Controversies of Fourteenth-Century England in Non-Human Voices." *DAI* A73.08 (2013): n.p. Suggests that Langland, Chaucer, and Gower represent political speech with the speech of animals, and argues that this device was later appropriated in anti-Ricardian discourse.

19. Johnson, Valerie B. "Politicizing the Landscape: Ricardian Literary Languages of Power." *DAI* A74.03 (2013): n.p. Considers depictions of wilderness in *GP* and *ManT*, along with works by Gower and Langland, as metaphors for undisciplined rulers.

20. Lee, Jenny Victoria. "*Confessio auctoris*: Confessional Poetics and Authority in the Literature of Late Medieval England, 1350–1450." *DAI* A74.02 (2013): n.p. Looks at confessional elements in works by Chaucer, Langland, Gower, Usk, and Hoccleve, ultimately arguing that such practice is central to an understanding of early English vernacular literature.

21. Rodríguez Mesa, José Francisco. "Religious *in itinere* Frame Stories: Roles in Sercambi's *Novelle* and Chaucer's *Canterbury Tales*." In Ana Laura Rodríguez Redondo and Eugenio Contreras Domingo, eds. *Focus on Old and Middle English Studies* (*SAC* 37 [2015], no. 79), pp. 159–73. Studies Sercambi's *Novelle* and *CT* against the background of historical writing, and classical and medieval traditions of *narratio brevis*, including the oriental models, in particular the frame-stories *in itinere*. Analyzes features of short stories from the perspective of the Sociocritic School, which sees them as a subversion of the macro-story of religious pilgrimage and the morals and religion of the late fourteenth century.

22. Seyed-Gohrab, A. A. *Metaphor and Imagery in Persian Poetry*. Leiden: Brill, 2012. viii, 281 pp. Collection of essays on classical Persian literature. Includes article by F. D. Lewis, linking Arabic and Persian tales to Boccaccio and Chaucer. Item not seen; listed in WorldCat.

23. Staley, Lynn. *The Island Garden: England's Language of Nation from Gildas to Marvell*. Notre Dame: University of Notre Dame Press, 2012. x, 345 pp. Beginning with Gildas's depiction of England as a beautiful garden, explores metaphorical and physical gardens in medieval English cultural history, arguing that Chaucer indicates "awareness of nation as landscape" in *CT*. Chapters 2 and 3 emphasize that Chaucer employs Langland's peasant "*croft*, or half acre" as an image of nation in *NPT*, *ClT*, *KnT*, and *PF*. In Chapter 4, an analysis of the narrative of Susanna and the Elders (Daniel 13) cites *ClT*, *MLT*, and *ParsT*.

24. Warner, Lawrence. "The Vision of *Piers Plowman*, Said to Be Wrote by Chaucer: Leland's *Petri Aratoris fabula* and Its Descendants Revisited." *ChauR* 48, no. 1 (2013): 113–28. Addresses "existence of a tradition that attributes *Piers Plowman* to Chaucer." Surveys notes and items that contribute to Chaucer's and Langland's "reception histories."

25. Wiggin, Bethany. "World Literature and the Eighteenth-Century Novel: Amsterdam, Leipzig, 1701." *Seminar: A Journal of Germanic Studies* 49, no. 2 (2013): 112–31. Argues that the novel has a far-reaching international history, evident in early eighteenth-century works translated and published in Amsterdam and Leipzig such as *Les mémoires de Madame la Marquise de Frêne*, which shows not only proof of novel-writing/publishing in eighteenth-century Amsterdam and Leipzig, but also the influence of the East upon the European novel. The importance of the oriental frame-tale in western narratives can be seen as early as *CT*.

See also nos. 40, 48, 70, 72, 74, 91, 95–97, 99, 102–3, 106, 108, 117–18, 120, 127, 132, 134–35, 138, 143, 145–46, 149–50, 155–56, 162, 166, 172.

Chaucer's Influence and Later Allusion

26. Borges, Jorge Luis. *Professor Borges: A Course on English Literature*. Ed. Martín Arias and Martín Hadis. Trans. Katherine Silver. New York: New Directions, 2013. xiv, 306 pp. Based on student transcriptions of Borges' 1966 lectures. Chapters are divided into chronological class sessions; lecture topics begin with the fifth century and conclude with nineteenth-century writers. Describes the history of the English language and the British Empire to provide context for discussions of literary works, including Chaucer's influence on William Blake and William Morris. Notes Chaucer's appearance as a character in Morris's *The Earthly Paradise*.

27. D'Arcens, Louise, and Chris Jones. "Excavating the Borders of Literary Anglo-Saxonism in Nineteenth-Century Britain and Australia." *Representations* 121, no. 1 (2013): 85–106. Refers to P. R. Stephenson's deployment of Chaucer as a descriptor for early twentieth-century Australian poetry, noting his assertion of "Chaucerian" as shorthand for "a golden age of national self-confidence in which cosmopolitan sophistication combines with local pride to create a proud, distinctive literature and culture."

28. Forni, Kathleen. *Chaucer's Afterlife: Adaptations in Recent Popular Culture*. Jefferson, N.C.: McFarland, 2013. vii, 168 pp. Distinguishes between academic and popular versions of Chaucer, defining and discussing various categories of popular intertextuality: adaptations, appropriations, invocations, and citations—diminishing degrees of

engagement with original works. Also focuses on select popular materials produced since 1990: detective fiction, filmed adaptations, literature of the African diaspora, and market-driven capitalizing on Chaucer and his image. This popular tradition engages *CT* almost exclusively among Chaucer's works, particularly its satire, tale-telling, and pilgrimage motif.

29. ———. "Teaching Chaucer and Popular Culture: A Prolegomena." *ChauR* 48, no. 2 (2013): 190–204. Reflects on importance of incorporating the "professional and popular" representations of *CT* to enhance classroom teaching of Chaucer. Films, including Brian Helgeland's *A Knight's Tale*, Jonathan Myerson's animated *Canterbury Tales* trilogy, and contemporary murder mysteries, such as Paul C. Doherty's Canterbury Tales Murders series, can be used to "offer a fuller understanding of Chaucer's continuing canonicity and value in the larger cultural economy."

30. González Mínguez, M. Teresa. "Medievalism in E. E. Cummings' Works: Dante, Chaucer and the Troubadours among the Modern." In Ana Laura Rodríguez Redondo and Eugenio Contreras Domingo, eds. *Focus on Old and Middle English Studies* (*SAC* 37 [2015], no. 79), pp. 209–17. Analyzes E. E. Cummings's recovery and revision of medieval themes, models, and authors, including Chaucer, who inspired him to express the exaltation of beauty. Both authors' use of language is considered revolutionary for their times.

31. Haley, Gabriel Michael. "Niche Poetics: Institutional Solitude and the Lyric in Late Medieval England." *DAI* A73.12 (2013): n.p. Discusses the eremitical image of Chaucer promulgated by Shirley and Lydgate in the context of efforts to promote solitary, contemplative modes of life.

32. Harmoush, Mohammed Kasim. "Laureateship under the Reign of Queen Victoria." *English Language and Literature Studies* 3, no. 4 (2013): 68–77. Discusses Chaucer as the first English poet laureate in a larger argument for the political impetus behind the selection of Robert Southey, William Wordsworth, Samuel Rogers, and Alfred Tennyson as laureate poets of the Victorian period.

33. Lasa Álvarez, Begoña. "Los *Cuentos de Canterbury* revisitados: Versiones y traducciones de finales del siglo XVIII y principios del siglo XIX." *Oceánide* 5 (2013): n.p. (web publication). Considers Harriet and Sophia Lee's *Canterbury Tales* as an eighteenth-century rereading of *CT*. The moral and didactic character of the Lees' *Tales* made possible the

inclusion of three of them in Spanish anthologies of 1800 and 1808, providing Spanish readership a glimpse of British culture.

34. McAleavey, Maia. "The Plot of Bigamous Return." *Representations* 123, no. 1 (2013): 87–116. Refers to Elizabeth Gaskell's footnotes to *Mary Barton* that explain unfamiliar phrasing in terms of Chaucer and Langland, identifying them as evidence for the synchronic nature of the bigamous return plot in sensation novels.

35. Miller, T. S. "Flying Chaucers, Insectile Ecclesiasts, and Pilgrims through Space and Time: The Science Fiction Chaucer." *ChauR* 48, no. 2 (2013): 129–65. Focuses on how *CT* influences English science fiction authors such as Margaret Atwood, James Gunn, and Dan Simmons. Also analyzes "pilgrimage motif"; refers to *HF*, *LGW*, and *TC*; and discusses "Chaucerian science fiction" in South America.

36. Royle, Nicholas. "Quick Fiction: Some Remarks on Writing Today." *Mosaic* 47, no. 1 (2014): 23–39. Examines the history, purpose, and effects of "quick fiction." Royle draws examples from his own writings, as well as the works of past authors, noting how "quick fiction" explores themes of "lifedeath [*sic*], spectrality, and radical otherness," seeing this genre as "a sort of spectral writing: I think of fleeting appearances or apparitions in Chaucer, Shakespeare, Wordsworth . . . and so on."

37. Urban, Malte. "Chaucer in the Twenty-First Century: Some Thoughts on Digital Afterlives." In Clíodhna Carney and Frances McCormack, eds. *Chaucer's Poetry: Words, Authority and Ethics* (*SAC* 37 [2015], no. 61), pp. 146–57. Examines "afterlives" of Chaucer created by postmedieval scholars using digital tools. Argues for attention to digital engagements with Chaucer, such as *Geoffrey Chaucer Hath a Blog*, as having significant existences separate from a historical Chaucer.

See also nos. 18, 41, 43, 47, 74, 78, 95, 105, 112, 124, 131, 161.

Style and Versification

38. Baragona, Alan. "The Long and the Short of It: Teaching Chaucer's Verbal Music." In Susan Yager and Elise E. Morse-Gagné, eds. *Interpretation and Performance: Essays for Alan Gaylord* (*SAC* 37 [2015], no. 83), pp. 117–34. Students of Chaucer's poetry can easily appreciate its sounds and syntactical patterns, and should examine for themselves issues such as the pronunciation of final *-e*. Prosodic analysis can also be

applied to translated versions of Chaucer. Live performances and recordings as well as attentive readings can help to replicate the Chaucerian "soundscape."

39. Chickering, Howell. "Chaucer's Riding Rhyme." In Susan Yager and Elise E. Morse-Gagné, eds. *Interpretation and Performance: Essays for Alan Gaylord* (*SAC* 37 [2015], no. 83), pp. 49–63. Chaucer's poetry should be declaimed or at least heard with the "mind's ear." His decasyllabic couplets, once dismissed by critics as "riding rhyme" and even confused with the doggerel of *Th*, are "eminently playable," offering a variety of phonological and semantic possibilities. Rhyme, enjambment, and caesurae contribute to Chaucer's conversational style in *CT*.

40. Cole, Kristin Lynn. "Chaucer's Metrical Landscape." In Clíodhna Carney and Frances McCormack, eds. *Chaucer's Poetry: Words, Authority and Ethics* (*SAC* 37 [2015], no. 61), pp. 92–106. Questions idea that Chaucer's relationship with the alliterative verse of his contemporaries, such as the *Gawain*-poet and Langland, was antagonistic. Instead, suggests that the alliterative and the London poets participate in a shared metrical phonology and a range of metrical choices far more complex than a simple binary between long-line alliterative and decasyllabic verse.

41. Duffell, Martin J. "Tennyson's 'metre of Catullus': The Ambivalent Hendecasyllable." *Lang&Lit* 22, no. 1 (2013): 19–31. Argues that, "while Tennyson thought he was composing quantitative hendecasyllables, he was in fact producing accentual verse of a type that English poets had been studiously avoiding for 500 years." Traces the development of Chaucer's iambic pentameter, through its recovery in Spenser and Sydney.

42. Fenn, Jess R. "Aural Literacy: Rhetorical Community and Shared Sayings in Late Medieval England." *DAI* A73.09 (2013): n.p. Examines authorial use of commonly heard sayings (e.g., proverbs) as a means of incorporating listeners into the rhetorical community formed by the audience.

43. Nolan, Maura. "Performing Lydgate's Broken-Backed Meter." In Susan Yager and Elise E. Morse-Gagné, eds. *Interpretation and Performance: Essays for Alan Gaylord* (*SAC* 37 [2015], no. 83), pp. 97–114. Lydgate's meter differs from Chaucer's for several reasons, but their differences have been exaggerated by editorial practices. When performed, the "Lydgate" or "broken-backed" line emerges as an aesthetic choice. The broken-backed line characterizes Lydgate's Host as an

authoritative figure in the Prologue to the *Siege of Thebes*. The *Siege* is a literary experiment in imitation of Chaucer.

44. Yager, Susan. "Sounding Out the Host." In Susan Yager and Elise E. Morse-Gagné, eds. *Interpretation and Performance: Essays for Alan Gaylord* (*SAC* 37 [2015], no. 83), pp. 65–78. Addresses Chaucer's Host as both character and rhetorical device. The Host's speech is characterized, in *GP*, by pauses, asides, and delayed rhyme, creating Lydgate (or "broken-backed") lines and a prosaic tone. The Host's speech also displays his egotism and occasional mockery of the pilgrims.

See also nos. 14, 52, 66, 139, 144, 169.

Language and Word Studies

45. Asaka, Yoshiko. "Chaucer's *Natura naturans* and *Natura naturata*: Middle English *Nature* and *Kynde* to Signify '*Shizen.*'" *Comparative Civilization* (Japan Society for the Comparative Study of Civilizations) 29 (2013): 121–38. Elaborates on the distinction between *natura naturans* and *natura naturata* in relation to their Greek, Latin, and Germanic etymology, and examines uses of the words *nature* and *kynde* in *BD*, *HF*, *PF*, and *Rom* to show the tendency of each word's meaning according to that distinction. In Japanese.

46. Burrow, J. A. "Versions of 'Manliness' in the Poetry of Chaucer, Langland, and Hoccleve." *ChauR* 47, no. 3 (2013): 337–42. Examines the connotations of *man*, *manly*, and *manhood* and discusses concept of "real" manhood for these three authors.

47. Eads, Martha Greene. "Raising the Dead in Denise Giardina's Appalachian Fiction." *C&L* 63, no. 1 (2013): 75–87. In discussing Denise Giardina's novels set in Appalachia, offers observations regarding the effective portrayal of life in the mountains of the South, and compares this understanding to how original language of Chaucer enhances the reading and understanding of *CT*.

48. Hardy, Duncan. "The Hundred Years War and the 'Creation' of National Identity and the Written English Vernacular: A Reassessment." *Marginalia* 17 (2013): 18–31. Argues that the Hundred Years War has been overemphasized as a moment in which war, identity, and language coalesced to form distinct English and French nations and vernaculars. Portrayals of France in the works of Chaucer and others are not oppositional, and Chaucer's attitude toward French is self-deprecating.

49. Horobin, Simon. *Chaucer's Language*. 2nd ed. Basingstoke: Palgrave Macmillan, 2013. xii, 221 pp. Rev. 2nd ed. of 2007 publication focusing on Chaucer's dialect and language usage. Examines Middle English dialects and discusses Chaucer's word choice and grammatical structures. Points out how words that look identical in present-day English may have entirely different meanings in Middle English, and advocates that readers of Chaucer utilize the *MED* rather than rely on definitions of Middle English words provided by editors. Acknowledges the need for additional studies of Chaucer's language. Includes glossary of Chaucer's words and sample quotations.

50. Hsy, Jonathan. *Trading Tongues: Merchants, Multilingualism, and Medieval Literature*. Columbus: Ohio State University Press, 2013. xii, 237 pp. 6 figs. Examines multilingualism in the Middle Ages, in particular its role in medieval literature, and focuses on merchants and their transportation of language as well as goods. Chapters 1 and 2 deal extensively with Chaucer's exposure to "London's many tongues," through his roles as diplomatic envoy and customs official, analyzing Chaucer's uses of "mixed-language milieu" in *ShT* and *HF*.

51. Iyeiri, Yoko. "Cognitive Aspects of Negation in *The Tale of Melibee*, *The Parson's Tale*, and *A Treatise on the Astrolabe*." In Yoshiyuki Nakao and Yoko Iyeiri, eds. *Chaucer's Language: Cognitive Perspectives* (*SAC* 37 [2015], no. 54), pp. 5–25. Pointing out the co-existence of various forms of negation in the Middle English period, the author analyzes choices of negative forms in *Mel*, *ParsT*, and *Astr* from cognitive viewpoints. The analysis particularly focuses on elaboration of styles (in relation to use of multiple negation), the "weight of negation," and the subject of negative sentences as potentially relevant to the choice of negative forms.

52. Kumamoto, Sadahiro. "The Creation of 'Tone' in Chaucer's Poetic Lines: A Tentative Study on Chaucer's Emotive Language." *Kumamoto Journal of Culture and Humanities* (Kumamoto University) 104 (2013): 41–60. Contends that the uniqueness of Chaucer's poetry lies in the combination of emotive theme and manipulation of "tone." Classifies "tone-elevators" and compares their effects among different genres of Chaucerian texts as well as between Chaucerian and non-Chaucerian romances. In Japanese, with English abstract.

53. Miura, Ayumi. "*Namely* and Other Particularisers in Chaucer's English." In Yoshiyuki Nakao and Yoko Iyeiri, eds. *Chaucer's Language: Cognitive Perspectives* (*SAC* 37 [2015], no. 54), pp. 99–124. Examines

Chaucer's uses of the word *namely* and argues that, while it is widely assumed that the word functioned only as a particularizer in Chaucer's time, some cases do not exclude the possibility of another function as appositive marker.

54. Nakao, Yoshiyuki, and Yoko Iyeiri, eds. *Chaucer's Language: Cognitive Perspectives*. Studies in the History of the English Language. Suita: Osaka Books, 2013. iv, 152 pp. Includes six articles that pertain to specific aspects of Chaucer's language. See nos. 51, 53, 84, 116, 142, 163.

55. Proto, Teresa. "Correspondencia de prominencia en las canciones inglesas: Una perspectiva histórica." *Signa: Revista de la Asociación Española de Semiótica* 22 (2013): 81–104. Diachronic study of how the linguistic stress matches metrical strong positions in spoken poetry and songs of the Middle and early modern English periods, including discussion of Chaucer's works. Prominent mismatches are more frequent in earlier songs because of phonological, rather than metrical, factors.

56. Sasamoto, Hisayuki. "Chaucer's Onomatopoeias as Auditory Expressions." *Review of the Osaka University of Commerce* 9, no. 2 (2013): 19–37. Lists forty-eight onomatopoeic words used by Chaucer. Examines some of these words' auditory, as well as visual, effects within their literary context. In Japanese.

57. Stock, Lorraine K. "Costumes, Props, Role-Playing, Active Learning: Performative Pedagogy in the Medieval Studies Classroom." In Susan Yager and Elise E. Morse-Gagné, eds. *Interpretation and Performance: Essays for Alan Gaylord* (*SAC* 37 [2015], no. 83), pp. 135–47. Oral performance of ambiguous lines can illustrate their various possible meanings. Emphasizes how recordings and online materials can supplement student reading and performance, and how films can help readers visualize key moments. Costumes, props, and role-plays also enliven Chaucer and medieval literature for students.

See also nos. 18, 72, 114, 116, 142, 144, 146–47, 155, 168, 171.

Background and General Criticism

58. Beidler, Peter G. "Performing Academic Papers." In Susan Yager and Elise E. Morse-Gagné, eds. *Interpretation and Performance: Essays for Alan Gaylord* (*SAC* 37 [2015], no. 83), pp. 149–68. Demonstration and performance, accepted aspects of classroom practice, can make academic

conference presentations more memorable. Examples of performative practice include an enacted battle in *KnT*, created costumes illustrating the Wife of Bath's dress in *GP* and Griselda's dress in *ClT*, two models of the shot-window in *MilT* (photographs included), and a debate on the anatomical location of Absolon's kiss.

59. Bourgne, Florence. "The Innocence of Medieval Objects?" *EA* 66 (2013): 277–80. Reflects on the term "object" in relation to whether it means a manuscript, circulating text, or real object; includes recurrent references to Chaucer and Chaucer scholarship.

60. Boyarin, Adrienne Williams. *Miracles of the Virgin in Medieval England: Law and Jewishness in Marian Legends*. Cambridge: D. S. Brewer, 2010. xiii, 230 pp. Discusses Marian identification in *PrT*, in particular Marian miracles, as well as connections to the Virgin Mary in *SNT*, *Th*, and *WBPT*. Emphasizes development of Middle English Marian miracle texts, and Mary's "symbolic connection to Jews." Claims that Chaucer altered emphasis of these texts from "monastic-devotional to literary-secular realms."

61. Carney, Clíodhna, and Frances McCormack, eds. *Chaucer's Poetry: Words, Authority and Ethics*. Dublin: Four Courts Press, 2013. 203 pp. Eleven essays about Chaucer and his works that form, in the words of its editors, a "general" rather than a "thematically unified" collection. Threads that run through multiple chapters include rhetoric, ethics, and poetic form. See nos. 15, 37, 40, 76, 91–92, 114, 118, 137, 139, 160.

62. Chaganti, Seeta, and Penn R. Szittya, eds. *Medieval Poetics and Social Practice: Responding to the Work of Penn R. Szittya*. New York: Fordham University Press, 2012. vi, 256 pp. Essays emphasize the importance of poetry and poetics in the "formation of social structures, actions, and utterances" in this festschrift for Penn R. Szittya. For essays that pertain to Chaucer, see no. 159, and *SAC* 36 [2014], no. 210.

63. Cooper, Helen. "Literature Reformations of the Middle Ages." In Andrew Galloway, ed. *The Cambridge Companion to Medieval Culture* (*SAC* 37 [2015], no. 68), pp. 261–78. Surveys Chaucer's works and literary importance.

64. Crane, Susan. *Animal Encounters: Contacts and Concepts in Medieval Britain*. The Middle Ages Series. Philadelphia: University of Pennsylvania Press, 2013. vii, 270 pp. Deconstructs the human/animal binary once useful in the emerging field of animal studies by casting anew these relationships into a "multiplicity of intersecting and competing distinctions that better reflect medieval ways of thinking." Through

close literary analysis, explores how "bodies, minds, and affects interpenetrate within and across species." Included in this "multiplicity" are *ManT*, *PF*, *SNT*, and *Th*. Chapter 5, "Falcon and Princess," discusses the parallels between culture and species in *SqT*.

65. Dinshaw, Carolyn. "All Kinds of Time." The Presidential Address, The New Chaucer Society, Eighteenth International Congress, July 23–26, 2012. Portland State University, Portland, Oregon. *SAC* 35 (2013): 3–25. Contemplates the queer potential of parody and other forms of "engaging multiple temporalities," commenting on two nineteenth-century responses to the *Book of John Mandeville* and on a fictional incident posted on Brantley Bryant's *Geoffrey Chaucer Hath a Blog*. Discloses how awareness of asynchronicity can and should disturb boundaries that divide medieval studies and medievalism, academic study and pleasure, and other perceived binaries.

66. Douglass, Kurt E. "Who Rules the Waves? Reading the Sea in Late Medieval and Early Modern English Literature." *DAI* A73.10 (2013): n.p. Considers Chaucer's uses of seafaring imagery in the course of a larger discussion of the uses of the sea as religious metaphor.

67. Flannery, Mary C., and Katie L. Walter, eds. *The Culture of Inquisition in Medieval England*. Cambridge: D. S. Brewer, 2013. viii, 194 pp. A variety of essays seek to redefine the role of inquisition in medieval English culture and law. For an essay that pertains to Chaucer, see no. 158.

68. Galloway, Andrew, ed. *The Cambridge Companion to Medieval Culture*. Cambridge: Cambridge University Press, 2011. vii, 321 pp. Includes several essays on political, material, and legal medieval culture. For an essay that pertains to Chaucer, see no. 63.

69. Gillmeister, Heiner. "Chaucer's Monk and Sports and Games in Medieval Monasteries and Cathedral Churches." In Jörg Sonntag, ed. *Religiosus ludens: Das Spiel als kulturelles Phänomen in mittelalterlichen Klöstern und Orden* (Berlin: De Gruyter, 2013), pp. 149–70. Explores the impact of medieval monastic culture on the evolution of sports, such as hockey, football, and, in particular, tennis, including commentary on Chaucer's criticism of ecclesiastics engaged in sport. Argues that Chaucer's clerics reflect the contradictory nature of a supposedly sinful, yet popular monastic pastime.

70. Johnson, Eleanor. *Practicing Literary Theory in the Middle Ages*. Chicago: University of Chicago Press, 2013. ix, 254 pp. Examines fiction's role in shaping readers' ethics: the transformation of the narrator

encourages and mirrors the transformation of the reader (protrepsis). Discusses medieval texts that theorize themselves and teach the reader *how* to read, positing that Chaucer, Usk, Gower, Hoccleve, and Boethius experimented with literary form (prose poems) as a way to produce ethical transformation. Explores the intersection between ethics and aesthetics/form in *Bo, TC,* and *CT. CT* is the most transformative (for the narrator and the reader) and self-theorizing text ("literary theory in practice").

71. Kamath, Stephanie A. Viereck Gibbs. "A Cruel Spoon in Context: Cutlery and Conviviality in Late Medieval Literature." *EA* 66 (2013): 281–86. Exemplifies the symbolic and sociohistorical importance of cutlery in medieval literature, including discussion of instances from works by Chaucer.

72. Middleton, Anne. "Loose Talk from Langland to Chaucer." The Biennial Address, The New Chaucer Society, Eighteenth International Congress, July 23–26, 2012. Portland State University, Portland, Oregon. *SAC* 35 (2013): 29–46. Documents William Langland's use, in *Piers Plowman,* of sudden, irruptive, colloquial, and polysemous language, distinguishing it from so-called "real" speech and assessing its thematic, narratological, and ethical values. Gower found this device of "loose talk" to be disturbing, while Chaucer embraced it as a fundamental source of inspiration, underpinning a number of his innovations.

73. Morse-Gagné, Elise E. "Introduction." In Susan Yager and Elise E. Morse-Gagné, eds. *Interpretation and Performance: Essays for Alan Gaylord* (*SAC* 37 [2015], no. 83), pp. xix–xxxii. Includes brief biography of Alan Gaylord and summary of his teaching career at Michigan and Dartmouth. Among the hallmarks of Gaylord's work are interdisciplinarity, a sense of playfulness, and the value of performance both within and outside the traditional classroom.

74. Perkins, Nicholas, and Alison Wiggins. *The Romance of the Middle Ages*. Oxford: Bodleian Library, 2012. 176 pp. Examines the use of desire in stories of romances in Dante, Chaucer, and Malory. Traces development of the medieval romance genre in later periods, including novels of J. R. R. Tolkien and J. K. Rowling, and films, such as *Star Wars* and *Monty Python and the Holy Grail*.

75. Petitt, Thomas. "Approaching Medieval Disorder: Folk Routes." In Tatjana Silec, ed. *Voix (et voies) du désordre au Moyen Age: Volume issu du colloque du Centre d'Etudes Médiévales Anglaises de Paris-Sorbonne (22–23*

mars 2012). AMAES, no. 34. (*SAC* 37 [2015], no. 81), pp. 5–49. Refers to Chaucer in connection with rebellion and violence.

76. Phillips, Helen. "Chaucer and the Sun-God: King and Poet." In Clíodhna Carney and Frances McCormack, eds. *Chaucer's Poetry: Words, Authority and Ethics* (*SAC* 37 [2015], no. 61), pp. 75–91. Examines Chaucer's use of sun-king imagery and references to Apollo in a variety of works. Compiles historical connections among Chaucer's allusions and the iconography of Richard II and other political figures, suggesting a multivalent portrayal of kingship involving both "fear" and "splendour."

77. Powell, Jason E., and William T. Rossiter, eds. *Authority and Diplomacy from Dante to Shakespeare*. Farnham: Ashgate, 2013. ix, 256 pp. "Examines the duality of the roles of author and ambassador through a study of the connection between the discourses and practices of authority and diplomacy in the literature of the late medieval and early modern periods." Essays "argue that concepts of diplomacy and of the diplomatic are central in English literature and culture of the period under review." Chaucer is mentioned only occasionally.

78. Pugh, Tison. *An Introduction to Geoffrey Chaucer*. Gainesville: University of Florida Press, 2013. xviii, 251 pp. Includes biographical information, historical context, Chaucer's sources, a pronunciation guide, and glossary of common Middle English words. Chapter 2, "Chaucer's Literature," is a comprehensive guide for beginning readers, and covers Chaucer's works for students of all levels to use as reference. Explanations go beyond plot summaries. Also uses genre theory to contextualize each text and show how and when Chaucer subverts the reader's expectations. Rather than translate Chaucer's language, aims to help readers understand Chaucer's language for a greater appreciation of his writing. Includes overview of Chaucer's influences and adaptations of his work.

79. Rodríguez Redondo, Ana Laura, and Eugenio Contreras Domingo, eds. *Focus on Old and Middle English Studies*. Madrid: Universidad Complutense de Madrid, 2011. 217 pp. Includes four articles related to Middle English manuscripts, *CT*, and medievalisms. For essays pertaining to Chaucer, see nos. 10, 21, 30, 109.

80. Rust, Martha. "Blood and Tears as Ink: Writing the Pictorial Sense of the Text." *ChauR* 47, no. 4 (2013): 390–415. Looks at "late medieval texts in which writing functions both verbally and pictorially," such as texts of the Passion, in which red ink in the manuscript creates a picture of Christ's blood, mentioned in *ABC*. *TC* similarly describes

tearful verses, and Oxford, Bodleian Library, MS Arch. Selden B.24 reflects that weeping with eyes and faces. Also addresses the botanical metaphor in *The Four Leaves of the Truelove*.

81. Silec, Tatjana, ed. *Voix (et voies) du désordre au Moyen Age: Volume issu du colloque du Centre d'Etudes Médiévales Anglaises de Paris-Sorbonne (22–23 mars 2012)*. AMAES, no. 34. Paris: Association des Médiévistes Anglicistes de l'Enseignement Supérieur, 2013. 173 pp. Includes three essays that pertain to Chaucer; see nos. 75, 101, 131.

82. Strickland, Deborah Eileen. "Model Failures: Lost Women and the Scene of Writing, 1353–1603." *DAI* A73.10 (2013): n.p. Examines figures of women writers in the work of male authors from Chaucer to Marlowe, with the goal of recovering the woman writer's significance, even in the absence of female-authored direct texts.

83. Yager, Susan, and Elise E. Morse-Gagné, eds. *Interpretation and Performance: Essays for Alan Gaylord.* Provo, Utah: Chaucer Studio Press, 2013. xxxii, 214 pp. CD-ROM. Fourteen essays by various authors, plus an introduction, honoring the scholarship and teaching of Alan Gaylord. The essays mirror Gaylord's work and methods, including exegetical historicism, close reading, prosodic criticism, and pedagogy. The final item, a fairy tale parody, is written in Middle English; the CD-ROM provides examples for several essays. For individual essays pertaining to Chaucer, see nos. 38–39, 43–44, 57–58, 73, 95, 105, 126, 134, 141, 144, 171.

The Canterbury Tales—General

84. Asaka, Yoshiko. "A Model of the Ideal and Natural in Social Groups in *Mum and the Sothsegger*: A Metaphorical Analysis." In Yoshiyuki Nakao and Yoko Iyeiri, eds. *Chaucer's Language: Cognitive Perspectives* (*SAC* 37 [2015], no. 54), pp. 125–48. Interprets the ideological content of *Mum and the Sothsegger* metaphorically by viewing it as advice on kings' rule and social hierarchy. Refers to thematically relevant passages from *CT* and *TC*.

85. Bahr, Arthur. *Fragments and Assemblages: Forming Compilations of Medieval London*. Chicago: Chicago University Press, 2013. x, 285 pp. In a chapter entitled "Constructing Compilations of Chaucer's *Canterbury Tales*," considers *CT* through the lens of Walter Benjamin's historical materialism. Teases out three narrative threads by means of "compilational construction." The *KnT–MilT–RvT–CkT* and *KnT–SqT–Th*

threads dismantle the relevance of the courtly ideal as a relevant construct in the sociopolitical milieu of late fourteenth-century London. The *KnT–FranT* thread disrupts this pessimism with a partial reinstatement of courtly imitation as productive of social harmony, but fails to right the balance entirely.

86. Colley, Dawn Fleurette. "Reclaiming Reason: Chaucer's Prose and the Path to Autonomy." *DAI* A74.01 (2013): n.p. Examines how *Astr*, *Bo*, *Mel*, *ParsT*, and *Ret* can encourage readers to develop their own interpretive strategies and move toward autonomy.

87. Fletcher, Alan J. *The Presence of Medieval English Literature: Studies at the Interface of History, Author, and Text in a Selection of Middle English Literary Landmarks*. Turnhout: Brepols, 2012. ix, 294 pp. Series of essays focusing on medieval vernacular literature and "the presence of a text to its own age and the presence of that age within it." Special emphasis on Chaucer in Chapter 6, which examines *CT*, *ABC*, and *LGW*, to "restore the presence of the radical/heretical ferment in Chaucer's writing."

88. Maslanka, Christopher W. "Christening Women, Men and Monsters: Images of Baptism in Middle English Hagiography and Romance." *DAI* A73.10 (2013): n.p. Considers the use of baptism as a symbol and source of identity in *CT*.

89. Meyer-Lee, Robert J. "Abandon the Fragments." *SAC* 35 (2013): 47–83. Documents how editors' presentation of *CT* as a sequence of *fragments* is misguided, and encourages that the label be abandoned. The term misrepresents the evidence of the manuscripts, and is misleading because Chaucer's discontinuities are habitual. Encourages editors to follow the best "structural labeling" among the manuscripts, perhaps that of the Ellesmere manuscript.

90. Middleton, Anne. *Chaucer, Langland, and Fourteenth-Century Literary History*. Ed. Steven Justice. Farnham: Ashgate, 2013. xix, 279 pp. Introduction by Steven Justice. Collection of essays on a range of subjects, including Ricardian public poetry, form and authorship, and the role of the modern annotator. Includes three chapters primarily devoted to *CT*: "Chaucer's 'New Men' and the Good of Literature in the *Canterbury Tales*" (27–60); "The *Physician's Tale* and Love's Martyrs: 'Ensamples Mo than Ten' as a Method in the *Canterbury Tales*" (61–84); and "The Clerk and His Tale: Some Literary Contexts" (85–112).

91. Murton, Megan. "Chaucer's Ethical Poetic in the *Canterbury Tales*." In Clíodhna Carney and Frances McCormack, eds. *Chaucer's*

Poetry: Words, Authority and Ethics (*SAC* 37 [2015], no. 61), pp. 48–60. Argues for an "ethical" reading of Chaucer's view of poetry in *CT* distinct from didacticism, examining Chaucer's engagement with *sententiae* of Plato and Saint Paul and suggesting that, for Chaucer, poetry's value is in the process of interpretation it asks of the reader. Learning and "doctrine" arise from this activity, and so the aesthetic and instructive values of poetry are inseparable.

92. O'Connell, Brendan. "Chaucer's Counterfeit *Exempla*." In Clíodhna Carney and Frances McCormack, eds. *Chaucer's Poetry: Words, Authority and Ethics* (*SAC* 37 [2015], no. 61), pp. 134–57. Notes that counterfeit and forged documents appear frequently in *CT*, but most frequently in exemplary and ethical tales such as *MLT* and *ClT*. This suggests Chaucer's lack of trust in this kind of writing and his preference for an ethics based on imperfect, lived experience.

93. Seal, Samantha Lily Katz. "The Unnatural Womb: Anxieties of Sex and Authority in 'The Canterbury Tales.'" *DAI* A74.05 (2013): n.p. Argues that female bodies in *CT* represent texts that are unreadable by husbands, and suggests that ultimately, this is symptomatic of an impossibility of "cognitive seeking."

94. Smilie, Ethan Kobus. "Inquisityf of Goddes Pryvetee and a Wyf: Curiositas in the 'Canterbury Tales.'" *DAI* A73.10 (2013): n.p. Examines the vice of curiosity, arguing that Chaucer both expands its application from the realm of the intellectual to the realm of the physical, and suggests that poetry may be a cause and a remedy for the desire to inquire into private matters. Discusses *MilT*, *RvT*, *WBPT*, *FrT*, *SumT*, and *ClT*.

See also nos. 4, 16–17, 21, 23, 25, 28–29, 33, 44, 69–70, 105, 107.

CT—The General Prologue

See nos. 17, 19, 105.

CT—The Knight and His Tale

95. Bowden, Betsy. "What Spooks Arcite's Steed? According to Boccaccio, Chaucer, Dryden, and Shakespeare." In Susan Yager and Elise E. Morse-Gagné, eds. *Interpretation and Performance: Essays for Alan Gaylord* (*SAC* 37 [2015], no. 83), pp. 33–46. Discusses four versions of Arcite's

death and focuses on the actions of the horses in each: in Boccaccio, as in Statius, divine interventions frighten the horses; Chaucer's Arcite falls because of both a god's intervention and his own pride; in Dryden, pride is the primary cause; and in Shakespeare's offstage version, Arcite is thrown after a spark frightens his horse.

96. Fumo, Jamie C. "The Pestilential Gaze: From Epidemiology to Erotomania in *The Knight's Tale*." *SAC* 35 (2013): 85–136. Various associations of sight and death indicate that *KnT* is a "nightmare vision of vision itself" that, in comparison with Boccaccio's *Teseida*, flattens the character of Emelye, intensifies her agency, and indicts chivalry. In *KnT* the motifs of "perilous vision and toxic sexuality" that inhere in legends of Thebes and Amazonia combine with imagery of pestilential vision associated with plague in various treatises, emphasized by association with Saturn's malevolent gaze.

97. Rigby, S. H. "Worthy but Wise? Virtuous and Non-Virtuous Forms of Courage in the Later Middle Ages." *SAC* 35 (2013): 329–71. Surveys classical and medieval notions of courage (*fortitude*) with particular attention to Giles of Rome and chroniclers of the Battle of Agincourt, and recurrent comments on Chaucer's Knight and Squire, and Troilus. Describes the criteria and nuances of Giles's seven types of *fortitude*, noting parallels in Christian and pagan antecedents and in late medieval chronicles and romances.

98. Rigby, Steve. *Wisdom and Chivalry: Chaucer's "Knight's Tale" and Medieval Political Theory*. Brill: Leiden, 2013. xvi, 329 pp. Corrected reprint of 2009 edition.

99. Schildgen, Brenda Deen. "Reception, Elegy, and Eco-Awareness: Trees in Statius, Boccaccio, and Chaucer." *CL* 65, no. 1 (2013): 85–100. Focuses on the episode of "wood-stripping" that occurs in Statius's *Thebaid* (VI.84–117), Boccaccio's *Teseida* (11), and *KnT* (2919–62). While Statius's account is the major model for the others, all versions imply social-political criticism, express nostalgia for a localized landscape, and evoke an emotional response to natural phenomena.

100. Shimomura, Sachi. "The Walking Dead in Chaucer's 'Knight's Tale.'" *ChauR* 48, no. 2 (2013): 1–37. Addresses how "manipulations of time" affect the narrative structure of *KnT*, and "recreate instabilities inherent to fourteenth-century chivalric ideas." Views Theseus, Palamon, and Arcite as the "walking dead," since they only "exist in literature and imagination."

101. Yvernault, Martine. "Confusions dans la forêt: Ce que nous disent les arbres." In Tatjana Silec, ed. *Voix (et voies) du désordre au Moyen Age: Volume issu du colloque du Centre d'Etudes Médiévales Anglaises de Paris-Sorbonne (22–23 mars 2012)*. AMAES, no. 34. (*SAC* 37 [2015], no. 81), pp. 109–24. Explores the ambivalence of the forest in several examples, especially ones drawn from *KnT* and *BD*.

See also nos. 23, 58, 85, 103.

CT—The Miller and His Tale

102. Friedman, John Block. "Anxieties at Table: Food and Drink in Chaucer's Fabliaux Tales and Heinrich Wittenwiler's *Der Ring*." In Emma Cayley and Susan Powell, eds. *Manuscripts and Printed Books in Europe 1350–1550: Packaging, Presentation, and Consumption* (*SAC* 37 [2015], no. 6), pp. 169–86. Analyzes Chaucer and Wittenwiler from the "perspective of anxiety at the table." Explores how "food- and drink-conveyed class anxieties are used as plot devices" to develop action in *MlT*, *RvT*, and *Der Ring*. Also mentions possible connections between *MerT* and *Der Ring*.

103. Walker, Greg. *Reading Literature Historically: Drama and Poetry from Chaucer to the Reformation*. Edinburgh: Edinburgh University Press, 2013. 206 pp. Explores the "potential value and pitfalls of reading the literature and drama of this period 'historically.'" Chapter 6 addresses Chaucer and argues that Absolon "defies categorization," but seems to have origins in popular religion and medieval drama. Argues that, from a Freudian perspective, Absolon is obsessed with oral pleasure and compares *MilT* to *KnT*, comparing Absolon to Palamon and Arcite. Also compares Absolon to Gawain in *SGGK* and *Th*. Ultimately, reads *MilT* as critiquing medieval drama and its Mariolatry.

See also nos. 58, 85, 94.

CT—The Reeve and His Tale

104. King, Andy. "'Fer in the north, I kan nat telle where': Gentility and Provincialism in Chaucer's *Reeve's Tale*." *NMS* 57 (2013): 89–110. Argues that the name "Strother" in *RvT* is not a place name but a surname, and suggests a connection between the tale's fictional clerks,

John and Aleyn, and two junior members of the prominent Strother family of Northumberland.

See also nos. 85, 94, 102.

CT—The Cook and His Tale

105. Lee, Brian S. "Continuation of the Cokes Tale." In Susan Yager and Elise E. Morse-Gagné, eds. *Interpretation and Performance: Essays for Alan Gaylord* (*SAC* 37 [2015], no. 83), pp. 199–210. A comic completion, in mock Middle English, of *CkT* as a version of both Little Red Riding Hood and the parable of the Prodigal Son, with allusions to *TC*, *GP*, and several stories from *CT*.

See also no. 85.

CT—The Man of Law and His Tale

106. Legassie, Shayne Aaron. "Among Other Possible Things: The Cosmopolitanisms of Chaucer's 'Man of Law's Tale.'" In John M. Ganim and Shayne Aaron Legassie, eds. *Cosmopolitanism and the Middle Ages* (New York: Palgrave Macmillan, 2013), pp. 181–205. Compares cosmopolitanism in Trevet, Gower, and Chaucer's Constance legends. Establishes that Chaucer's sultan in *MLT* represents more of an aesthetic cosmopolitan than do his analogues in Trevet and Gower, who portray cosmopolitanism as a means of "advanc[ing] the universal expansion of orthodox Christian belief." Suggests that Chaucer questioned the success of a cosmopolitan world.

107. Nelson, Ingrid. "Premodern Media and Networks of Transmission in the *Man of Law's Tale*." *Exemplaria* 25 (2013): 211–30. Maintains that *MLT* represents cultural and textual transmission through a network of premodern media: voices, texts, bodies, culture, human actions, and nonhuman forces—media that represent an alternative to the hegemonic, institutional, and linear *translatio studii et imperii*. The Christian culture Custance transmits flickers from noise to signal, indicating medieval cultural mobility, and suggesting that "mediation" is a condition of life. Also suggests that transmission is a paradigm for the structure and poetic project of *CT*.

108. Stavsky, Jonathan. "'Gode in all thynge': The Erle of Tolous,

Susanna and the Elders, and Other Narratives of Righteous Women on Trial." *Anglia* 131 (2013): 538–61. Examines the righteous-woman-on-trial motif in *Earl*, and its relation to Susanna (Daniel 13) and to medieval romances involving the same motif. By exploiting narrative structure, shifting perspectives and the differing perceptions of characters and audience, *Earl* draws a more complex character of the heroine than its analogues and replaces their conception of virtue with a more pragmatic ethics.

See also nos. 23, 92, 150, 156.

CT—The Wife of Bath and Her Tale

109. Arboleda Guirao, Immaculada de Jesús. "Chaucer's *The Wife of Bath's Prologue* in *The Canterbury Tales*. The Wife's Personality, Language and Life: Revisiting Feminism." In Ana Laura Rodríguez Redondo and Eugenio Contreras Domingo, eds. *Focus on Old and Middle English Studies* (*SAC* 37 [2015], no. 79), pp. 149–57. A feminist reading of the Wife of Bath's personality and behavior, focusing on her married life, her sexual attitudes, and linguistic usage.

110. Arboleda Guirao, Immaculada de Jesús, and M. Esther Mediero Durán. "Alison, una figura femenina controvertia prólogo de las esposa de Bath en *Los cuentos de Canterbury*, de Geoffrey Chaucer." *Cartaphilus: Revista de investigación y crítica estética* 11 (2013): 8–15. Discusses the Wife of Bath's personality from feminist viewpoint. Spanish version of no. 109.

111. Houser, Richard McCormick. "Alisoun Takes Exception: Medieval Legal Pleading and the Wife of Bath." *ChauR* 48, no. 1 (2013): 66–90. Argues that the Wife of Bath "employs the courtroom pleading techniques of *excepcion* and *confession and avoidance* to challenge the misogynist teachings of clerical authority." Demonstrates how Alisoun's discourse in *WBP* reveals her familiarity with legal argument, and her understanding and use of "masculine language" enhance her authority within *WBT*.

112. Simons, Christopher E. J. "Idle and Extravagant Stories in Verse: 400 Years of Narrative Poetry from Sir Gawain to Wordsworth." *Humanities: Christianity and Culture* (International Christian University) 41 (2013): 31–70. Clarifies what kind of poems William Wordsworth criticized as "idle and extravagant stories in verse" and examines four

English narrative poems before Wordsworth, including *WBT*. All four turn out to be more or less "idle and extravagant" by Wordsworth's standards.

113. Spencer, Jaime. *Fictional Religion: Keeping the New Testament*. New Salem, Ore.: Polebridge Press, 2011. Argues how authors, from Chaucer to C. S. Lewis, are influenced by the "flexible tradition" of religious stories. Chapter 1 analyzes how Chaucer reveals understanding of Christian doctrine in *WBT*.

See also nos. 58, 60, 94, 118.

CT—The Friar and His Tale

114. Scattergood, John. "*Goodfellas*, Sir John Clanvowe and Chaucer's *Friar's Tale*: 'Occasions of sin.'" In Clíodhna Carney and Frances McCormack, eds. *Chaucer's Poetry: Words, Authority, and Ethics* (*SAC* 37 [2015], no. 61), pp. 15–36. Explores the use of the phrase "good fellow" as it is used in Martin Scorsese's film *Goodfellas*, Clanvowe's Lollard treatise *The Two Ways*, and *FrT*.

115. Weiskott, Eric. "Chaucer the Forester: The *Friar's Tale*, Forest History, and Officialdom." *ChauR* 47, no. 3 (2013): 323–36. In light of the abuses of power in the medieval forest industry, the forest as backdrop to romance tales, and the hunt as an aristocratic privilege, *FrT* critiques administrative bureaucracy through a reworking of the "devil-and-advocate" fable.

CT—The Summoner and His Tale

116. Ohno, Hideshi. "Variation in the Use of 'Think' in *The Summoner's Tale*, Line 2204." In Yoshiyuki Nakao and Yoko Iyeiri, eds. *Chaucer's Language: Cognitive Perspectives* (*SAC* 37 [2015], no. 54), pp. 79–98. Assesses the significance of variant readings of think (*thinken* or *thenken*) in *SumT*, line 2204, from several linguistic points of view, and emphasizes the semantic and syntactical differences between the impersonal and personal constructions.

117. Salter, David. "'He is ane Haly Freir': *The Freiris of Berwik*, *The Summoner's Tale*, and the Tradition of Anti-Fraternal Satire." *Scottish Literary Review* 5, no. 2 (2013): 23–40. Compares the fifteenth-century

Scottish fabliau *The Freiris of Berwik* to *SumT* and finds that the treatment of friars in the Scottish tale is more ironic than satirical, and is more concerned with eliciting laughter than with advancing an antifraternal agenda.

See also no. 94.

CT—The Clerk and His Tale

118. Carney, Clíodhna. "How to Say 'I': The Clerk, the Wife and Petrarch." In Clíodhna Carney and Frances McCormack, eds. *Chaucer's Poetry: Words, Authority and Ethics* (*SAC* 37 [2015], no. 61), pp. 61–74. Considers the relationship between the Wife of Bath and the Clerk, focusing on their shared approach to self-presentation through the words of other writers and their interrelationship as speakers. Highlights the Wife's use of clerical authority and the Clerk's sudden "verbal ingenuity" when speaking about marital issues in his Envoy, after he departs from his Petrarchan source material and speaks, in a sense, in his own voice.

119. Farrell, Thomas J. "Editors and Scribes in Two *Clerk's Tale* Cruxes." *ChauR* 47, no. 3 (2013): 300–22. Variant treatments of *ClT*, 507–8 reflect editorial practices as well as scribal power, specifically Adam Pinkhurst's, in shaping Chaucer's texts.

120. Harkins, Jessica. "Chaucer's *Clerk's Tale* and Boccaccio's *Decameron* X.10." *ChauR* 47, no. 3 (2013): 247–73. Chaucer's translations of key phrases in the Griselda story reveal his use of the Boccaccio source material as a way to underscore the "complexity" of the story and the varied authorial voices involved in translation.

121. Raby, Michael. "The *Clerk's Tale* and the Forces of Habit." *ChauR* 47, no. 3 (2013): 223–46. Aristotelian and Augustinian concepts of moral virtue illuminate Walter's and Griselda's behaviors in terms of habit and its relation to place.

122. Schwebel, Leah. "Redressing Griselda: Restoration through Translation in the *Clerk's Tale*." *ChauR* 47, no. 3 (2013): 274–99. Chaucer's modification of Petrarch's Griselda material returns *ClT* closer to Boccaccio's original version of the story. By working with multiple versions of the story, Chaucer places himself in the pantheon of Italian writers.

123. Stasik, Tamara L. "Forms of Living: Asceticism, Culture, and

Articulating the 'Medeled Liyf' in Late Medieval English Literature." *DAI* A74.01 (2013): n.p. Using *ClT* and other texts, looks at the intersection of asceticism and secular lifestyles.

See also nos. 23, 58, 90, 92, 94.

CT—The Merchant and His Tale

124. Brown, Peter. "Chaucer and Shakespeare: The *Merchant's Tale* Connection." *ChauR* 48, no. 2 (2013): 222–37. Examines scholarship that traces Chaucer's "subtle" influence on Shakespeare, by drawing connections between *MerT* and *A Midsummer Night's Dream*.

See also no. 102.

CT—The Squire and His Tale

125. Czarnowus, Anna. *Fantasies of the Other's Body in Middle English Oriental Romance*. Studies in English Medieval Language and Literature. Frankfurt: Peter Lang, 2013. 233 pp. Considers the body of the "Other" in various medieval romances. Chapter 1, "Ethnic Difference and Body Marvelous: The Case of Chaucer's *Squire's Tale* and Sir Ferumbras," focuses on how *SqT* highlights Canace's ethnicity as a space for fantasy. Canace represents an exotic other, symbolizing a "new world" in the East that is attractive to the West. *SqT* ties together the wonder inimical to the genre of romance with the fear of the eastern Other, revealing the competing ideologies at work in the text.

126. Quinn, William A. "Chaucer's Fancy Squire." In Susan Yager and Elise E. Morse-Gagné, eds. *Interpretation and Performance: Essays for Alan Gaylord* (*SAC* 37 [2015], no. 83), pp. 185–98. The Squire's digressive, complex tale may be understood as a reenactment of the creative process. Critics may be mistaken in trying to explain the significance of the four gifts, the falcon's distress, and other details, if the center of the tale is the extravagance of invention itself.

See also nos. 64, 85, 97, 150.

CT—The Franklin and His Tale

127. Carruthers, Leo. *Reading the Middle English Breton Lays and Chaucer's "Franklin's Tale."* Paris: Atlande (Collection Clefs Concours),

2013. 190 pp. Discusses the genre of "lay" as a subset of romance, and places individual lays in their historical and literary contexts, reexamining the meaning of "Breton" in relation to medieval Celtic literature more generally. Compares Chaucer's lays to earlier ones in Middle English, and observes connections with modern folk- and fairy tales.

128. Johnston, Michael. "Romance, Distraint, and the Gentry." *JEGP* 112 (2013): 433–60. Argues that many late Middle English romances appeal to the gentry by coded references to the practice of *distraint*, whereby gentry landowners were forced to take up knighthood or to pay fines. Concludes by comparing the attitudes expressed in these romances to those of Chaucer's Franklin, who desires a less elite status among landowning society.

129. Narinsky, Anna. "'The Road Not Taken': Virtual Narratives in *The Franklin's Tale*." *Poetics Today* 34, nos. 1–2 (2013): 53–118. Studies "virtual" narratives in *FranT*. Compares *FranT* to earlier lais of Marie de France and *Sir Orfeo*. Suggests that Chaucer's "unrealized possibilities" mark a moment in the history of genre development when medieval lais begin to resemble modern psychological narratives.

See also nos. 85, 94.

CT—The Physician and His Tale

See no. 90.

CT—The Pardoner and His Tale

130. Malo, Robyn. *Relics and Writing in Late Medieval England*. Toronto: University of Toronto Press, 2013. ix, 298 pp. Emphasizes "relic discourse" in England from the twelfth to sixteenth centuries. Chapter 4, "Relic Discourse in the *Pardoner's Prologue and Tale* and *Troilus and Criseyde*," discusses how the Pardoner's performance "reveals the workings of relic discourse," and how parody is revealed in *TC*.

131. Parsons, Ben. "The Pardoner's Two Bodies: Reading beyond Sexuality in the Prologue of the *Tale of Beryn*." In Tatjana Silec, ed. *Voix (et voies) du désordre au Moyen Age: Volume issu du colloque du Centre d'Etudes Médiévales Anglaises de Paris-Sorbonne (22–23 mars 2012)*. AMAES, no. 34. (*SAC* 37 [2015], no. 81), pp. 81–108. Focuses on the popularity of

the Pardoner's character and on the connection between Chaucer and the *Beryn*-poet.

132. Rollo, David. *Kiss My Relics: Hermaphroditic Fiction of the Middle Ages*. Chicago: University of Chicago Press, 2011. vii, 250 pp. Explores the relationship between textuality and sexuality in various texts, including Martianus Capella's *De nuptiis philologiae et mercurii*, Jean de Meun's *Roman de la rose*, and *PardT*, particularly the Pardoner's invitation to the Host to kiss his relics. Chaucer's Pardoner is a figurative hermaphrodite who resists gendered and sexual categorizations, comparable with *Roman de la rose*'s Bel Acueil, and sharing in a degree of creative and poetic freedom increasingly associated in literature with the hermaphrodite.

See also no. 137.

CT—The Shipman and His Tale

See no. 50.

CT—The Prioress and Her Tale

133. Albin, Andrew. "The 'Prioress's Tale,' Sonorous and Silent." *ChauR* 48, no. 1 (2013): 91–112. Examines how song and sound create narrative meaning within *PrT*. Chaucer's choice of using the antiphon *Alma redemptoris mater* reveals the "transformative force that sound bears." Discusses issues of performance, voice, and silences; aural reception and community; and societal conflicts between urban Jews and Christians.

134. Astell, Ann W. "The Prioress's Prologue to her Passionate Tale: Psalm 8:2, Matthew 21:16, and Jesus's Prophecy of Singing Stones." In Susan Yager and Elise E. Morse-Gagné, eds. *Interpretation and Performance: Essays for Alan Gaylord* (*SAC* 37 [2015], no. 83), pp. 3–11. The quotation of Psalm 8 in *PrP* would have reminded Chaucer's audience of two Gospel narratives of Jesus's entry into Jerusalem, one referring to singing children, the other to speaking stones. The power of this combined allusion links the *clergeoun* to Jesus, clarifying the semantic power of the singing body and the motivation for the tale's violent anti-Semitism.

135. Comber, Abigail Elizabeth. "The Cultural Construction of

Monsters: 'The Prioress's Tale' and *Song of Roland* in Analysis and Instruction." *DAI* A74.05 (2013): n.p. Suggests that texts like *PrT* might be taught by examining their presentation of non-followers of Christianity as monsters, an alternative to postcolonial approaches.

136. Jang, Sunghyan. "The Symbolism of the Pit in the Prioress's Tale: Jewish–Christian Disputes over the Virgin Mary." *MES* 21, no. 2 (2013): 173–91. Examines the symbolic role of the privy pit in *PrT*, arguing for analogy "between the pit in the Jewish ghetto and the womb of the Virgin Mary."

137. McCormack, Frances. "'By mouth of innocentz': Rhetoric and Relic in the *Prioress's Tale*." In Clíodhna Carney and Frances McCormack, eds. *Chaucer's Poetry: Words, Authority and Ethics* (*SAC* 37 [2015], no. 61), pp. 107–20. Discusses the relationship among the Prioress's "empty" rhetoric, audience reception, and emphatically feminine representation. The Prioress, in this reading, is a kind of false prophet, more dangerous than the Pardoner who plays a similar role.

138. Nolan, Maura. "Medieval Sensation and Modern Aesthetics: Aquinas, Adorno, Chaucer." *The Minnesota Review* 80 (2013): 145–58. Analyzes two medieval explorations of sensation—one by Thomas Aquinas, the other by Chaucer—and locates them within Theodor Adorno's account of aesthetics. Views Chaucer's poetry as a hinge between Aquinas's explanation of sensory perception and Adorno's formulation of aesthetic change over time, referring to Chaucer's portrayal of the Prioress in *GP*.

139. Pattwell, Niamh. "Patterns of disruption in the *Prioress's Tale*." In Clíodhna Carney and Frances McCormack, eds. *Chaucer's Poetry: Words, Authority, and Ethics* (*SAC* 37 [2015], no. 61), pp. 37–47. Looks at Chaucer's use of "two *sententiae*" to explore the interplay between Chaucer's use of silences and pauses in *PrT*, and the reader's engagement with the story.

See also nos. 60, 140, 153.

CT—The Tale of Sir Thopas

140. Brantley, Jessica. "Reading the Forms of *Sir Thopas*." *ChauR* 47, no. 4 (2013): 416–38. Observes that the tail-rhyme meter's layout on the manuscript page alludes not to romance but to a range of other

forms, including liturgical hymns, vernacular lyrics, and drama. Examining *Th* in these contexts suggests that the text perhaps parodies all kinds of oral performances, that the format indicates a particular type of dramatic reading, and that *Th* is "devotional" in the context of *PrT* and *Mel*.

141. Hodges, Laura F. "Costume Comedy: Sir Thopas's 'Courtly' Dress." In Susan Yager and Elise E. Morse-Gagné, eds. *Interpretation and Performance: Essays for Alan Gaylord* (*SAC* 37 [2015], no. 83), pp. 171–83. Alone among Chaucer's knights, Thopas receives a full costume description, but it defies readers' expectations of a top-to-toe *effictio*. *Th* also juxtaposes cheap and costly materials, mentions unattractive colors, and omits expected details, all for comic effect. These costume details would be emphasized in oral performance.

142. Nakao, Yoshiyuki. "Progressive Diminution in 'Sir Thopas.'" In Yoshiyuki Nakao and Yoko Iyeiri, eds. *Chaucer's Language: Cognitive Perspectives* (*SAC* 37 [2015], no. 54), pp. 47–77. Proposes that *Th* is not merely a parody of romance but is composed according to the principle of "progressive diminution," demonstrating its "prototype" and "extension" from geographical to temporal, social to linguistic "domains."

See also nos. 4, 14, 39, 60, 64, 85, 103.

CT—The Tale of Melibee

See nos. 51, 86, 140.

CT—The Monk and His Tale

143. Gerber, Amanda J. "'As olde bookes maken us memorie': Chaucer and the Clerical Commentary Tradition." *Florilegium* 29 (2013 for 2012): 171–200. Argues that the condensing and synthesizing of sources in *MkT* mirror the way in which clerical commentary changed in the fourteenth century to accommodate new readers uneducated in monastic tradition.

CT—The Nun's Priest and His Tale

144. Thomas, Paul R. "Transcribing and Analyzing the "Lerned" and "Lewed" Music of Chaucer's Chickens." In Susan Yager and Elise

E. Morse-Gagné, eds. *Interpretation and Performance: Essays for Alan Gaylord* (*SAC* 37 [2015], no. 83), pp. 79–96. In *NPT*, Chaucer combines a learned, polysyllabic vocabulary with Anglo-Saxon, monosyllabic words. Shifts in vocabulary create the tale's mock-heroic tone, as a "drop" from Latinate to English words at the end of a passage undercuts the preceding lines. Syllable length and stress play a part in the complex, musical aurality of the tale.

See also no. 23.

CT—The Second Nun and Her Tale

145. Dobbs, Elizabeth A. "The Canaanite Woman, the Second Nun, and St. Cecilia." *C&L* 62, no. 2 (2013): 203–22. Observes that Saint Matthew's account of the Canaanite's interaction with Christ is far more descriptively verbose than the version recorded by Saint Mark, and argues that in *SNP* Chaucer very purposefully chose Matthew's version in order to augment his portrayal of the rhetorical prowess and power of women, evident throughout *CT*.

See also nos. 60, 64.

CT—The Canon's Yeoman and His Tale

CT—The Manciple and His Tale

146. Coley, David K. *The Wheel of Language: Representing Speech in Middle English Poetry, 1377–1422*. Medieval Studies. Syracuse, N.Y.: Syracuse University Press, 2012. x, 258 pp. Discusses nominalism, speech, and power in *ManT*, along with speech and rhetoric in Gower's *Confessio Amantis*, Langland's *Piers Plowman*, and works of Hoccleve.

147. Lim, Hyunyang. "Transgression and Containment: Language, Defamation, and *The Manciple's Tale*." *MES* 21, no. 2 (2013): 193–214. Examines concern with slander and defamation during Richard II's reign as context for a reading of *ManT*, contending that *ManT* reveals Chaucer's skepticism toward the power of language as a method of political control.

See also nos. 19, 64.

CT—The Parson and His Tale

148. Price, Merrall. "The Caytif Body: Fiction and Flesh in the *Parson's Tale*." *MedPers* 28 (2013): 45–62. The Parson is exceptional among the Canterbury pilgrims for his corporeal invisibility; his *GP* portrait gives no corporeal details and *ParsPT* efface his body, along with fiction, verse, and the colors of rhetoric. Moreover, *ParsT* displays hostility to sexuality beyond its analogues and expresses a pathological vividness in its metaphors and similes for the flesh as a fetid captor of the soul. Only with difficulty does the Parson reconcile himself to a Redemption accomplished by Incarnation.

149. Smith, Nicole D. "Love, Peraldus, and the *Parson's Tale*." *N&Q* 258 (2013): 498–502. Echoes of Peraldus's notion of sin as "*amor inordinatus*" in the section of *ParsT* on contrition and confession, thought to have been adapted primarily from Pennaforte, suggest that the former's *Summa de vitiis* "exerts a more significant influence on a larger part of the *ParsT* than previously understood."

See also nos. 23, 51, 86.

CT—Chaucer's Retraction

See no. 86.

Anelida and Arcite

A Treatise on the Astrolabe

150. D'Agata D'Ottavi, Stefania. "Between Astronomy and Astrology: Chaucer's 'Treatise on the Astrolabe' and the Measurement of Time in Late-Medieval England." In Rachel Falconer and Denis Renevey, eds. *Medieval and Early Modern Literature, Science, and Medicine*. Swiss Papers in English Language and Literature, no. 28 (Tübingen: Narr Verlag, 2013), pp. 49–66. Referencing *SqT* and *MLT*, maintains that *Astr* was literally meant for a juvenile audience, adducing its concise language, repetition, exhaustive definitions, and liberal use of adjectival possessives as pedagogical tools fit for young readers. Posits Richard Billingham's

Speculum puerorum as a possible model for *Astr*'s analytical and pedagogical methodology.

See also nos. 51, 86.

Boece

See nos. 70, 86.

The Book of the Duchess

151. Davis, Nick. *Early Modern Writing and the Privatization of Experience*. London: Bloomsbury Academic, 2013. viii, 244 pp. Examines a diverse range of authors from the fourteenth to the early eighteenth centuries for their political, philosophical, and scientific perspectives in order to map a movement away from a trust in collective experience and toward a focus on the individual as the source of authentic perception, thought, and feeling. Chapter 5 refers to *BD*.

152. Lears, Adin Esther. "Something from Nothing: Melancholy, Gossip, and Chaucer's Poetics of Idling in the 'Book of the Duchess.'" *ChauR* 48, no. 2 (2013): 205–21. Focuses on themes of gender, sexuality, and melancholy, through analysis of "productive potential" of idleness in *BD*.

153. Rooney, Kenneth. *Mortality and Imagination: The Life of the Dead in Medieval English Literature*. Turnhout: Brepols, 2011. Explores the "literary negotiation of the macabre aesthetic in Middle English literature." Chapter 2, "The Progress of the Dead: From Body to Revenant," discusses "*physical* return of the dead" in *BD* and *PrT*.

See also nos. 45, 101.

The Equatorie of the Planetis

The House of Fame

154. Orlemanski, Julie. "Scales of Reading." *Exemplaria* 26 (2014): 215–33. Uses *HF*, which sets "archival totality" in an uncertain relation to the experience of reading, to introduce a discussion of how in our reading "discursive *systems*, rather than particular texts, become objects

of knowledge." Aims to theorize a strategy of reading that incorporates extrinsic as well as intrinsic sources of meaning, hermeneutics in collaboration with "close reading."

See also nos. 35, 45, 50.

The Legend of Good Women

155. Arner, Lynn. *Chaucer, Gower, and the Vernacular Rising: Poetry and the Problem of the Populace after 1381*. University Park: Pennsylvania State University Press, 2013. ix, 198 pp. Explains how the "vernacular rising" expanded Chaucer's and Gower's readership to include "lesser merchants and prosperous artisans" (introduction and Chapter 1). Chapters 4 and 5 emphasize *LGW*. In contrasting Gower and Chaucer, argues that in *LGW*, Chaucer "disarticulat[es] gender as a site of analysis" to "declare equity and social justice outside the domain of poetics" and "partition literature from political discourse." Concludes that "Chaucer helped found a bourgeois notion of the poet" and that English literature "represented a new means of constructing authority and imposing social control as a form of education."

156. Desmond, Marilynn R. "The *Translatio* of Memory and Desire in *The Legend of Good Women*: Chaucer and the Vernacular *Heroides*." *SAC* 35 (2013): 179–207. Explores the influence of Italian and French vernacular versions of Ovid's *Heroides* on the legends of *LGW*, where Chaucer engages and undermines the historical emphasis of these vernacular versions and reasserts the literary, rhetorical authority of the Ovidian originals. Also comments on the Ovidianism of letters in *TC* and on the presentation of *LGW* in *MLP*.

157. Nowlin, Steele. "The *Legend of Good Women* and the Affect of Invention." *Exemplaria* 25 (2013): 16–35. Analyzes *LGW* as "a narrative treatise on the 'affect of invention,'" linking the processes of emergence that precede the mind's conscious recognition of emotion with the inventional processes that culminate in poetic art. *LGWP* introduces a method for reconceptualizing invention, and the legends dramatize the process by which affect and invention collapse into emotion and poetry. The poem exposes the discourses that shape late medieval ideas of gender and the affect that infuses those discourses with power.

158. Steiner, Emily. "Response Essay: Chaucer's Inquisition." In Mary C. Flannery and Katie L. Walter, eds. *The Culture of Inquisition in*

Medieval England (*SAC* 37 [2015], no. 67), pp. 164–72. Examines Chaucer's use of inquisition in *LGWP*, where Chaucer "uses inquisition to rewrite *publica fama* as literary reputation."

See also nos. 35 and 87.

The Parliament of Fowls

159. Sebastian, John T. "The Idea of Public Poetry in Lydgatean Religious Verse: Authority and the Common Voice in Devotional Literature." In Seeta Chaganti and Penn R. Szittya, eds. *Medieval Poetics and Social Practice: Responding to the Work of Penn R. Szittya* (*SAC* 37 [2015], no. 62), pp. 95–108. Looks at the public aspect of devotional poetry, referencing Chaucer and *PF*.

160. Steenbrugge, Charlotte. "Time and Authority in Chaucer's *Parliament of Fowls*." In Clíodhna Carney and Frances McCormack, eds. *Chaucer's Poetry: Words, Authority and Ethics* (*SAC* 37 [2015], no. 61), pp. 121–33. Enters the discussion about apparent temporal discrepancies in *PF* and reframes it with a reminder that the poem occurs in a dream-vision, and need not correspond literally to English weather and bird behavior. Embraces contradictory references to time in the poem rather than seeking to resolve them. These contradictions are likely purposeful and part of the work's message about eternity and mutability.

See also nos. 23, 45, 64.

The Romaunt of the Rose

See nos. 5, 45.

Troilus and Criseyde

161. Crocker, Holly A. "'As false as Cressid': Virtue Trouble from Chaucer to Shakespeare." *JMEMSt* 43 (2013): 303–34. Looks at Shakespeare's *Troilus and Cressida* in the context of its medieval legacy, including works by Chaucer, Lydgate, and Henryson, to argue that Shakespeare "continues an important late medieval poetic tradition, which highlights the problematic consequences of virtue's performativity for idealized women in premodern England."

162. Federico, Sylvia. "Two Troy Books: The Political Classicism of Walsingham's *Ditis ditatus* and Chaucer's *Troilus and Criseyde*." *SAC* 35 (2013): 137–77. Treats *TC* and Thomas Walsingham's *Ditis ditatus* as the two major Troy narratives of late fourteenth-century England, considering the influences of Dictys and Dares (along with Boccaccio) on the two works, and focusing on their depictions of various secondary characters (Helen, Paris, Deiphebus, and Hector) as mirrors of late medieval political events and conditions.

163. Jimura, Akiyuki. "Chaucer's Imaginative and Metaphorical Description of Nature." In Yoshiyuki Nakao and Yoko Iyeiri, eds. *Chaucer's Language: Cognitive Perspectives* (*SAC* 37 [2015], no. 54), pp. 27–45. Illustrates how the descriptions of nature in *TC* reflect main characters' cognitive processes as well as the development of love.

164. Jost, Jean E. "Fortune or Free Will in Chaucer's *Troilus and Criseyde*: How Fortune 'Pleyeth with Free and Bonde.'" *MedPers* 28 (2013): 145–82. Though medieval orthodoxy insisted on the reality of free will, *TC* presents three characters subject to fortune at every turn, perhaps because they are pre-Christian pagans. Troilus is a victim of fortune from the moment he sees Criseyde. Pandarus is similarly enchained, but achieves a kind of agency by taking up Troilus's cause with Criseyde, whose compliant nature he manipulates shamelessly. History itself is another of Fortune's agents as the tragedy unwinds.

165. Judkins, Ryan Russell. "Noble Venery: Hunting and the Aristocratic Imagination in Late Medieval English Literature." *DAI* A74.02 (2013): n.p. Contends that metaphors of hunting in *TC* and the *Alliterative Morte Arthure* are intended for a noble audience, and in turn, they shape that audience's attention to ideas of love and chivalry.

166. Mann, Jill. "In Defence of Francesca: Human and Divine Love in Dante and Chaucer." *Strumenti critici* 131 (2013): 3–26. Argues that *Inferno*, V does not justify dismissing Francesca's love for Paolo as "lust," given the continuity between the *disiato riso* that leads them to kiss and the *santo riso* of Beatrice that draws Dante upward to paradise. Echoing Dante and Guinizelli, Chaucer shows Troilus discovering a divine dimension in human existence.

167. Moreno, Christine M. "Secrecy and Fear in Confessional Discourse: Subversive Strategies, Heretical Inquisition, and Shifting Subjectivities in Vernacular Middle English and Anglo-French Poetry."

DAI A74.05 (2013): n.p. Reflects on secrecy and fear in confessional moments in several works, including *TC*.

168. Nakao, Yoshiyuki. *The Structure of Chaucer's Ambiguity*. Frankfurt am Main: Peter Lang, 2013. 311 pp. Proposes a theoretical "double prism structure" framework to examine ambiguity attributable to textual, interpersonal, and linguistic "domains" in *TC*.

169. Quinn, William A. *Olde Clerkis Speche: Chaucer's "Troilus and Criseyde" and the Implications of Authorial Recital*. Washington, D.C.: Catholic University of America Press, 2013. x, 252 pp. Recovers clues to Chaucer's own authorial recital by searching for evidence of tonal intentions in *TC*. Provides a performance-based reading of the poem that begins with "the premise that Chaucer himself once recited *TC* aloud," thus allowing "evidence within the text to be read as historical evidence of its own prior enactment."

170. Vines, Amy N. *Women's Power in Late Medieval Romance*. Cambridge: D. S. Brewer, 2011. xi, 169 pp. Examines what "medieval romances convey about the possibilities for female social and cultural influence" during the Middle Ages. Chapter 1 analyzes how Chaucer's depictions of Cassandra and Criseyde were influenced by "representations of women's reading and interpretation" in the Corpus Christi MS of *TC*.

171. Wetherbee, Winthrop. "Grace and Place in *Troilus and Criseyde*." In Susan Yager and Elise E. Morse-Gagné, eds. *Interpretation and Performance: Essays for Alan Gaylord* (*SAC* 37 [2015], no. 83), pp. 13–22. The key rhyming pair *place* and *grace* appears several times in *TC*, notably at the center of the poem. Up to the moment of the lovers' consummation, both words have a positive, sometimes spiritual connotation and intensity, but after that passage each term becomes associated with materiality rather than the ideal.

172. Yasui, Michael. "Ambiguity and Disruption in Chaucer's *Troilus and Criseyde*: The Effects of Hermeneutic Mimetics." *Journal of Social Sciences and Humanities* (Tokyo Metropolitan University) 479 (2013): 1–10. Discusses how origins of the meaning of *TC* are "decentred" on different levels. Argues that complicated use of external sources obfuscates the meaning of the text and that the subject-positions of Pandarus and the narrator create a "disruption" in the text.

See also nos. 4, 35, 69–70, 80, 84, 97, 105, 130, 156.

Lyrics and Short Poems

An ABC

See nos. 80, 87.

Adam Scriveyn
The Complaint of Chaucer to His Purse
Former Age
Chaucerian Apocrypha

Book Reviews

173. Allen, Mark, and John H. Fisher, eds., with the assistance of Joseph Trahern. *A Variorum Edition of the Works of Geoffrey Chaucer Volume II. The Canterbury Tales: The Wife of Bath's Prologue and Tale.* Parts 5a and 5b (*SAC* 36 [2014], no. 12). Rev. Simon Horobin, *SAC* 35 (2013): 373–76.

174. Besserman, Lawrence. *Biblical Paradigms in Medieval English Literature: From Caedmon to Malory* (*SAC* 36 [2014], no. 82). Rev. William Marx, *SAC* 35 (2013): 379–82; Kevin R. West, *C&L* 63, no. 1 (2013): 121–23.

175. Binski, Paul, and Patrick Zutshi, with the collaboration of Stella Panayotova. *Western Illuminated Manuscripts: A Catalogue of the Collection in Cambridge University Library* (*SAC* 37 [2015], no. 2). Rev. Jessica Brantley, *SAC* 35 (2013): 382–84.

176. Boyarin, Adrienne Williams. *Miracles of the Virgin in Medieval England: Law and Jewishness in Marian Legends* (*SAC* 37 [2015], no. 60). Rev. Emily Leverett, *C&L* 62, no. 2 (2013): 296–99.

177. Bryant, Brantley L. *Geoffrey Chaucer Hath a Blog: Medieval Studies and New Media* (*SAC* 34 [2012], no. 117). Rev. Dylan Jones, *SIMELL* 28 (2013): 49–58.

178. Coley, David K. *The Wheel of Language: Representing Speech in Middle English, 1377–1422* (*SAC* 37 [2015], no. 146). Rev. Nicholas Perkins, *SAC* 35 (2013): 398–401.

179. Crane, Susan. *Animal Encounters: Contacts and Concepts in Medieval Britain* (*SAC* 37 [2015], no. 64). Rev. Marijane Osborn, *Comitatus* 44 (2013): 250–53.

180. Davidson, Mary Catherine. *Medievalism, Multilingualism, and*

Chaucer (*SAC* 34 [2012], no. 95). Rev. Hisato Ebi, *SEL* 54 (2013): 191–95.

181. Echard, Siân. *Printing the Middle Ages* (*SAC* 32 [2010], no. 20). Rev. Peter J. Lucas, *N&Q* 258 (2013): 118–19.

182. Flannery, Mary C., and Katie L. Walter, eds. *The Culture of Inquisition in Medieval England* (*SAC* 37 [2015], no. 67). Rev. Phil Robins, *Marginalia* 17 (2013): 48–51.

183. Fletcher, Alan J. *The Presence of Medieval English Literature: Studies at the Interface of History, Author, and Text in a Selection of Middle English Literary Landmarks* (*SAC* 37 [2015], no. 87). Rev. Hannah Zdansky, *Comitatus* 44 (2013): 267–70.

184. Galloway, Andrew, ed. *The Cambridge Companion to Medieval Culture* (*SAC* 37 [2015], no. 68). Rev. Jennifer S. Key, *N&Q* 258 (2013): 117–18.

185. Gillespie, Alexandra, and Daniel Wakelin, eds. *The Production of Books in England, 1350–1500* (*SAC* 35 [2013], no. 17). Rev. Marianne O'Doherty, *SAC* 35 (2013): 401–4.

186. Holley, Linda Tarte. *Reason and Imagination in Chaucer, the "Perle"-Poet, and the "Cloud"-Author: Seeing from the Center* (*SAC* 35 [2013], no. 61). Rev. Eleanor Johnson, *SAC* 35 (2013): 407–10; Kathyrn L. Lynch, *SP* 88, no. 1 (2013): 312–13.

187. Hume, Cathy. *Chaucer and the Cultures of Love and Marriage* (*SAC* 36 [2014], no. 95). Rev. Gillian Adler, *Comitatus* 44 (2013): 280–82; Emma Lipton, *SAC* 35 (2013): 410–13.

188. Jimura, Akiyuki. *The World of Chaucer's English* (Hiroshima: Keisuisha, 2011). Rev. Masatoshi Kawasaki, *SIMELL* 28 (2013): 71–79.

189. Kamath, Stephanie A. Viereck Gibbs. *Authorship and First-Person Allegory in Late Medieval France and England* (*SAC* 36 [2014], no. 96). Rev. Lisa H. Cooper, *SAC* 35 (2013): 413–16; Sarah Laseke, *Variants: The Journal of the European Society for Textual Studies* 10 (2013): 287; Erica R. Machulak, *Comitatus* 44 (2013): 284–86; Helen J. Swift, *French Studies* 67, no. 2 (2013): 246; Katie L. Walter, *MÆ* 82, no. 2 (2013): 341.

190. Kerby-Fulton, Kathryn, Maidie Hilmo, and Linda Olson. *Opening Up Middle English Manuscripts* (*SAC* 36 [2014], no. 33). Rev. Sarah Kathryn Moore, *Comitatus* 44 (2013): 288–89.

191. Mooney, Linne R., and Estelle Stubbs. *Scribes and the City: Guildhall Clerks and the Dissemination of Middle English Literature, 1375–*

1425 (*SAC* 37 [2015], no. 12). Rev. A. S. G. Edwards, *Library* 7, no. 15 (2013): 79–81.

192. Partridge, Stephen, and Eric Kwakkel, eds. *Author, Reader, Book: Medieval Authorship in Theory and Practice* (*SAC* 36 [2014], no. 106). Rev. Bryan P. Davis, *JEBS* 16 (2013): 300–302; Robert J. Meyer-Lee, *SAC* 35 (2013): 388–93.

193. Perkins, Nicholas, and Alison Wiggins. *The Romance of the Middle Ages* (*SAC* 37 [2015], no. 74). Rev. Marco Nievergelt, *N&Q* 258 (2013): 308–9.

194. Robinson, Carol L., and Pamela Clements, eds. *Neomedievalism in the Media: Essays on Film, Television and Electronic Games* (*SAC* 36 [2014], no. 107). Rev. Carole M. Cusack, *Parergon* 30, no. 1 (2013): 313–15.

195. Rollo, David. *Kiss My Relics: Hermaphroditic Fiction of the Middle Ages* (*SAC* 37 [2015], no. 132). Rev. Jessica Rosenfeld, *SAC* 35 (2013): 427–30.

196. Rooney, Kenneth. *Mortality and Imagination: The Life of the Dead in Medieval English Literature* (*SAC* 37 [2015], no. 153). Rev. Amy Appleford, *SAC* 35 (2013): 430–32.

197. Saunders, Corinne, ed. *A Companion to Medieval Poetry* (*SAC* 34 [2012], no. 157). Rev. Sarah Tolmie, *SAC* 35 (2013): 433–35.

198. Spencer, Jaime. *Fictional Religion: Keeping the New Testament New* (*SAC* 37 [2015], no. 113). Rev. Claudia M. Champagne, *C&L* 63, no. 2 (2014): 305–8.

199. Smith, Nicole D. *Sartorial Strategies: Outfitting Aristocrats and Fashioning Conduct in Late Medieval Literature* (*SAC* 36 [2014], no. 112). Rev. Susan Brooks, *Comitatus* 44 (2013): 339–41; Sarah-Grace Heller, *SAC* 35 (2013): 435–38.

200. Staley, Lynn. *The Island Garden: England's Language of Nation from Gildas to Marvell* (*SAC* 37 [2015], no. 23). Rev. Sebastian Sobecki, *SAC* 35 (2013): 438–42.

201. Vines, Amy N. *Women's Power in Late Medieval Romance* (*SAC* 37 [2015], no. 170). Rev. Hélène Dauby, *MA* 119 (2013): 481–82.

Author Index–Bibliography

Adler, Gillian 187
Albin, Andrew 133
Allen, Mark 1, 173
Appleford, Amy 196
Arboleda Guirao, Immaculada de Jesús 109–10
Arias, Martín 26
Arner, Lynn 155
Asaka, Yoshiko 45, 84
Astell, Ann W. 134

Bahr, Arthur 4, 85
Baragona, Alan 38
Beidler, Peter G. 58
Bertolet, Craig E. 17
Besserman, Lawrence 174
Binski, Paul 2, 175
Borges, Jorge Luis 26
Bourgne, Florence 59
Bowden, Betsy 95
Bowers, Bege K. 1
Boyarin, Adrienne Williams 60, 176
Brantley, Jessica 140, 175
Brooks, Susan 199
Brown, Peter 124
Bryant, Brantley L. 177
Burrow, J. A. 46

Caie, Graham D. 5
Carney, Clíodhna 61, 118
Carruthers, Leo 127
Cayley, Emma 6
Chaganti, Seeta 62
Champagne, Claudia M. 198
Chickering, Howell 39
Clements, Pamela 194
Cole, Kristin Lynn 40
Coleman, Joyce 7–8
Coley, David K. 146, 178
Colley, Dawn Fleurette 86
Comber, Abigail Elizabeth 135
Contreras Domingo, Eugenio 79
Cooper, Helen 63
Cooper, Lisa H. 189

Crane, Susan 64, 179
Crocker, Holly A. 161
Cruse, Mark 8
Cusack, Carole M. 194
Czarnowus, Anna 125

D'Agata D'Ottavi, Stefania 150
D'Arcens, Louise 27
Dauby, Hélène 201
Davidson, Mary Catherine 180
Davis, Bryan P. 192
Davis, Nick 151
Desmond, Marilynn R. 156
Dinshaw, Carolyn 65
Dobbs, Elizabeth A. 145
Douglass, Kurt E. 66
Downes, Stephanie 3
Duffell, Martin J. 41

Eads, Martha Greene 47
Ebi, Hisato 180
Echard, Siân 181
Edwards, A. S. G. 191

Falconer, Rachel 150
Farrell, Thomas J. 119
Federico, Sylvia 162
Fenn, Jess R. 42
Fisher, John H. 173
Flannery, Mary C. 67, 182
Fletcher, Alan J. 87, 183
Forni, Kathleen 28–29
Friedman, John Block 102
Fulton, Sharon 18
Fumo, Jamie C. 96

Galloway, Andrew 68, 184
Ganim, John M. 106
Gellert, Anamaria 9
Gerber, Amanda J. 143
Gillespie, Alexandra 4, 185
Gillmeister, Heiner 69
González Mínguez, M. Teresa 30

Hadis, Martín 26
Haley, Gabriel Michael 31
Hardy, Duncan 48
Harkins, Jessica 120
Harmoush, Mohammed Kasim 32
Heller, Sarah-Grace 199
Hilmo, Maidie 190
Hodges, Laura F. 141
Holley, Linda Tarte 186
Horobin, Simon 10–11, 49, 173
Houser, Richard McCormick 111
Hsy, Jonathan 50
Hume, Cathy 187

Iyeiri, Yoko 51, 54

Jang, Sunghyan 136
Jimura, Akiyuki 163, 188
Johnson, Eleanor 70, 186
Johnson, Valerie B. 19
Johnston, Michael 128
Jones, Chris 27
Jones, Dylan 177
Jost, Jean E. 164
Judkins, Ryan Russell 165
Justice, Steven 90

Kamath, Stephanie A. Viereck Gibbs 71, 189
Kawasaki, Masatoshi 188
Kerby-Fulton, Kathryn 190
Key, Jennifer S. 184
King, Andy 104
Kumamoto, Sadahiro 52
Kwakkel, Eric 192

Lasa Álvarez, Begoña 33
Laseke, Sarah 189
Lears, Adin Esther 152
Lee, Brian S. 105
Lee, Jenny Victoria 20
Legassie, Shayne Aaron 106
Leverett, Emily 176
Lim, Hyunyang 147
Lipton, Emma 187
Lucas, Peter J. 181
Lynch, Kathryn L. 186

Machulak, Erica R. 189
Malo, Robyn 130

Mann, Jill 166
Marx, William 174
Maslanka, Christopher W. 88
McAleavey, Maia 34
McCormack, Frances 61, 137
Mediero Durán, M. Esther 110
Meyer-Lee, Robert J. 89, 192
Middleton, Anne 72, 90
Miller, T. S. 35
Miura, Ayumi 53
Mooney, Linne R. 12, 191
Moore, Sarah Kathryn 190
Moreno, Christine M. 167
Morse-Gagné, Elise E. 73, 83
Murton, Megan 91

Nafde, Aditi 13
Nakao, Yoshiyuki 54, 142, 168
Narinsky, Anna 129
Nelson, Ingrid 107
Nievergelt, Marco 193
Nolan, Maura 14, 43, 138
Nowlin, Steele 157

O'Connell, Brendan 92
O'Doherty, Marianne 185
Ohno, Hideshi 116
Olson, Linda 190
Orlemanski, Julie 154
Osborn, Marijane 179

Panayotova, Stella 2
Parsons, Ben 131
Partridge, Stephen 192
Pattwell, Niamh 139
Pearsall, Derek 6
Pearson, Richard 15
Perkins, Nicholas 74, 178, 193
Petitt, Thomas 75
Phillips, Helen 76
Powell, Jason E. 77
Powell, Susan 6
Price, Merrall 148
Proto, Teresa 55
Pugh, Tison 78

Quinn, William A. 126, 169

Raby, Michael 121
Renevey, Denis 150

Rigby, S[teve] H. 97–98
Robins, Phil 182
Robinson, Carol L. 194
Rodríguez Mesa, José Francisco 21
Rodríguez Redondo, Ana Laura 79
Rollo, David 132, 195
Rooney, Kenneth 153, 196
Rosenfeld, Jessica 195
Rossiter, William T. 77
Royle, Nicholas 36
Rust, Martha 80

Salter, David 117
Sasamoto, Hisayuki 56
Saunders, Corinne 197
Scattergood, John 114
Schildgen, Brenda Deen 99
Schwebel, Leah 122
Seal, Samantha Lily Katz 93
Sebastian, John T. 159
Seyed-Gohrab, A. A. 22
Shimomura, Sachi 100
Silec, Tatjana 81
Silver, Katherine 26
Simons, Christopher E. J. 112
Smilie, Ethan Kobus 94
Smith, Kathryn A. 8
Smith, Nicole D. 149, 199
Sobecki, Sebastian 200
Sonntag, Jörg 69
Spencer, Jaime 113, 198
Staley, Lynn 23, 200
Stasik, Tamara L. 123
Stavsky, Jonathan 108

Steenbrugge, Charlotte 160
Steiner, Emily 158
Stock, Lorraine K. 57
Strickland, Deborah Eileen 82
Stubbs, Estelle 12, 191
Swift, Helen J. 189
Szittya, Penn R. 62

Thaisen, Jacob 16
Thomas, Paul R. 144
Tolmie, Sarah 197
Trahern, Joseph 173

Urban, Malte 37

Vines, Amy N. 170, 201

Wakelin, Daniel 185
Walker, Greg 103
Walter, Katie L. 67, 182, 189
Warner, Lawrence 24
Weiskott, Eric 115
West, Kevin R. 174
Wetherbee, Winthrop 171
Wiggin, Bethany 25
Wiggins, Alison 74, 193

Yager, Susan 44, 83
Yasui, Michael 172
Yvernault, Martine 101

Zdansky, Hannah 183
Zutshi, Patrick 2, 175

The New Chaucer Society
Nineteenth International Congress
July 15–20, 2014
University of Iceland, Reykjavík, Iceland

TUESDAY, JULY 15

9:30–4:45: Graduate Student Workshop (by application only) (Árnagarður 201)

11:00–6:00: Trustees' Meeting (Hannesarholt)

2:00–7:00: Early Registration (HT upper level)

2:00–5:00: Manuscript Exhibit (Þjóðarbókhlaðan, National Library/University Library)

5:00: Graduate Student Evening (open event) (Stúdentakjallarinn)

WEDNESDAY, JULY 16

8:00–4:30: Registration (HT upper level)

9:00–10:30: Concurrent Sessions, Group 1

Session 1A, Round Table: Ice (1) Theory (HT 103)
(Thread: North 1: Texts)
Session Organizer and Chair: Jeffrey Jerome Cohen
- "Like Ice/Ice-Like: Fluidity, Solidity, and Reading Metaphor Backwards," Timothy S. Miller, University of Notre Dame
- "Icespeak," Lowell Duckert, West Virginia University
- "Frost," Ethan Knapp, Ohio State University
- "Hugh Willougby Talks to the Seafarer about Ice," Steve Mentz, St. John's University

Session 1B, Round Table: Not Your Doktorvater's *General Prologue* (HT 104)
(Thread: The Ways We Read Now)
Session Organizer and Chair: Peter Travis
- "Reverse Prosopography," Monika Otter, Dartmouth College
- "Transition, Repetition, Substitution, Assimilation and Subversion in *The General Prologue*," Warren Ginsberg, University of Oregon

- "The Plowman's Creed: Commercial Ideology and Its Discontents in *The General Prologue*," Robert Epstein, Fairfield University
- "'Whan that they were seeke': Reading *The General Prologue* and Chaucer's Pilgrims through the Lens of Disability Studies," Samantha Seal, Weber State University
- "Framing Time in *The General Prologue*," Tim Asay, University of Oregon

Session 1C, Round Table: How to Do Things with Form (1) (HT 101)
(Thread: How to Do Things with Texts)
Session Organizers and Chairs: Elizabeth Robertson and Ad Putter
- "Literary Catalogues and Verse Units," Kara Gaston, University of Toronto
- "Rhyme Royal: Embodiment and Rhyme Royal in the Prologues to *The Prioress's Tale* and *The Second Nun's Tale*," Elizabeth Robertson, University of Glasgow
- "French Rhymes in the Chaucerian Stanza," Ad Putter, University of Bristol
- Respondents: Sarah Stanbury, College of the Holy Cross; and Jeffrey C. Robinson, University of Glasgow

Session 1D, Paper Panel: Chaucer's Life, Chaucer's Libraries (L 102)
Session Organizer and Chair: Orietta Da Rold
- "Books of Lives, Lives of Books in the *Canterbury Tales*," Elaine Treharne, Stanford University
- "A Reconsideration of Chaucer's Italian Books," Michael Hanly, Washington State University
- "Chaucer and the Private Libraries of Tuscany," William Robins, University of Toronto

Session 1E, Paper Panel: Edification of the Senses (1) (L 103)
(Thread: The Medieval Sensorium)
Session Organizers: Richard G. Newhauser and Larry Scanlon
Chair: Richard G. Newhauser
- "The Innovation of the Senses: Restored Receptivity in John of Morigny's *Book of the Flowers of Heavenly Teaching* (1301–1315)," Nicholas Watson, Harvard University

- "Sensory Perception and the Labour of Imagination in Fifteenth-Century Vernacular Theology," Katie L. Walter, University of Sussex
- "Water Gazing and Piss Prophets: An Analysis of the Senses and Uroscopy in the *Canterbury Tales* and Other 14th-Century Middle English Texts," Mary Rambaran-Olm, University of Glasgow
- "Erotic Edification: Henry Suso's *Life of the Servant* and Its Seduction of the Spirit," James Staples, University of Pittsburgh

Session 1F, Paper Panel: From Ash Clouds to Grisly Rokkes: Travel Disruptions in Medieval Literature (L 204)
(Thread: Movement, Networks, Economies)
Session Organizers and Chairs: Jessica Lockhart and Anna Wilson
- "Travel Disruption and Social Reorientation in Medieval Narratives," Elliot Kendall, University of Exeter
- "Bounty, Interrupted: Seashores, Shipwrecks, and the Costs of Investment Capital in Middle English Romance," Andrew Richmond, Ohio State University
- "The Man Out of Time: King Herla's Journey and Walter Map's *De nugis curialium*," Kaitlin Heller, University of Toronto
- "Figures of Geo-Political Spaces in *The Man of Law's Tale*," John F. Plummer, Vanderbilt University

Session 1G, Paper Panel: Inordinate Love (1) (L 205)
(Thread: Handling Sins)
Session Organizers: Robyn Malo and Nicole Smith
Chair: Sylvia Tomasch
- "Ordering Maternal Love in the *Legenda aurea*," Meg Cotter-Lynch, Southeastern Oklahoma State University
- "Radical Compassion: Restoring Love in *Cleanness*'s Flood," Erin Mann, Lindenwood University—Belleville
- "*Pleyndamour*: The Poetics of Middle English Romance," Nicola McDonald, University of York

Session 1H, Paper Panel: Erotic Flesh in Late Medieval Discourse (1) (L 201)
Session Organizers: Virginia Blanton and Mary Beth Long
Chair: Mary Beth Long
- "Tonguing the Text: Lingual Erotics in Late Medieval Discourse," Shari Horner, Shippensburg University

- "Enjoy Your Handlyng!" Lara Farina, West Virginia University
- "The Erotic Falconry Treatise: Training Wives and Training Readers," Sara Petrosillo, University of California, Davis

Session 1I, Paper Panel: Mathias of Linkoping: Poetics and Learned *Translatio* in Scandinavia (G 102)
(Thread: Scandinavia and Europe)
Session Organizers and Chairs: Karl-Gunnar Johansson and Rita Copeland
- "Mathias Lincopensis and the Vadstena Sermon," Roger Andersson, Stockholm University
- "Geoffrey of Vinsauf Reads Matthias of Linkoping," Martin Camargo, University of Illinois
- "An Unsuccessful Ascent: Birgitta's *Liber questionum* and the Critique of Matthias and Bonaventure," Unn Falkeid, University of Oslo

10:30–11:00: **Coffee Break**

11:00–12:30: **Plenary Session (HB Auditorium 1)**
Chair: Alastair Minnis
- "Manuscripts in Iceland in the Age of Chaucer: Production, Texts and Literary Culture," Gudrun Nordal, University of Iceland

12:30–1:30: **Lunch (HT upper level)**

1:30–2:30: **Business Meeting (HT 105)**

2:30–4:00: **Concurrent Sessions, Group 2**

Session 2A, Paper Panel: Writing Biography (HT 103)
(Thread: Chaucerian Biographies)
Session Organizer and Chair: Alastair Minnis
- "Writing Chaucer Biography: A Conversation," Ardis Butterfield, Yale University; and Paul Strohm, Columbia University

Session 2B, Round Table: Ice (2) Writing (HT 104)
(Thread: North 1: Texts)
Session Organizer and Chair: Jeffrey Jerome Cohen
- "Icerune," Dan Remein, New York University

- "Vanishing Ice and *The House of Fame*: An Ecocritical Interrogation," Leila K. Norako, Stanford University
- "Ice as Parchment, Ice as Pen," David Coley, Simon Fraser University
- "Ice as Social Signifier," Jeremy DeAngelo, University of Connecticut
- "Touch of Frost," James L. Smith, University of Western Australia
- Respondent: Oddur Sigurðsson, Icelandic Meteorological Office

Session 2C, Paper Panel: Adaptation and the *Gesta Romanorum* (HT 101)
Session Organizers: Glenn Burger and Holly Crocker
Chair: Glenn Burger
- "The Old-Norse Translation of the *Gesta Romanorum*," Hjalti Snær Ægisson, University of Iceland
- "Justice by Natural Causes: Etiological Imagination in the *Gesta Romanorum*," Julie Orlemanski, Boston College
- "*The Tale of Beryn*: Rome and the Mercers of London," Matthew W. Irvin, Sewanee: The University of the South
- "Boccaccio's Book of Wikkid Wives," Olivia Holmes, SUNY-Binghamton

Session 2D, Round Table: *The Prick of Conscience* (L 102)
Session Organizers and Chairs: Rosemary O'Neill and Ellen K. Rentz
- "*The Prick of Conscience*: Neighbors and Associates," Theresa Coletti, University of Maryland
- "*The Prick of Conscience* and the Poetics of Inertia," Moira Fitzgibbons, Marist College
- "That Disgusting Creature Called Man: Blood and Gore in HM. 128: The Southern Recension of *The Pricke of Conscience*," Jean E. Jost, Bradley University
- "Multiplying *The Prick of Conscience*: Scribes, Scribal Networks and the Rise of a Medieval Bestseller," Helen Marshall, University of Toronto
- "The Legacy of *The Prick of Conscience*: Re-Evaluating the 'Lollard Sub-Group,'" Ann Killian, Yale University
- "Manuscript Presentation and the Success of *The Prick of Conscience*," Daniel Sawyer, University of Oxford

Session 2E, Paper Panel: Mapping Narrative(s) in Medieval Literature (1) (L 103)
(Thread: Movement, Networks, Economies)

Organizer and Chair: Emily Lethbridge

- "By Sun and by Shadow: Narrative Mapping in the *Canterbury Tales*," Kristi J. Castleberry, University of Rochester
- "The Pilgrim's Path in the *Gesta Francorum*," Karen Elizabeth Gross, Lewis & Clark College
- "Falling off the Map: Towards a Medieval Digital Hermeneutics," T. S. Mendola, New York University
- "Space and Movement in the Houses of the Miller's and Reeve's Tales," Michael W. Twomey, Ithaca College; and Scott D. Stull, SUNY-Cortland

Session 2F, Paper Panel: Handling Secular Sins (L 204) (Thread: Handling Sins)

Session Organizer: Matthew McCabe
Chair: Laura Ashe

- "The 'Way of Curacion': Penitential Discourse in the Writings of John of Arderne," Mike Leahy, Birkbeck, University of London
- "Counseling Confession: Sinful Pagans and Christian Causality in Gower's *Traitié* and *Mirour de l'omme*," Stephanie L. Batkie, University of Montevallo
- "The Hagiographic Construction of Secular Sin in Chaucer's *Physician's Tale*," Jennifer L. Sisk, University of Vermont

Session 2G, Paper Panel: The Social Lives of Books (L 205) (Thread: The Book in Practice)

Session Organizers and Chairs: Heather Blatt, Janice McCoy, and Nicholas Perkins

- "Chaucer's Book in Antiquarian Hands: Re-Making the Medieval Past," Devani Singh, Emmanuel College, Cambridge
- "Catechetical Devotions in the Vernon Manuscript," Kathryn Vulic, Western Washington University
- "Addressing and Assessing the Reader in London, British Library, MS Additional 7970," Stephanie Morley, St. Mary's University

Session 2H, Paper Panel: Institutional Histories of Medieval English Literary Studies (L 201) (Thread: In Search of Things Past)

Session Organizer and Chair: Lynn Arner

- "The Two Chaucer Societies," Sylvia Tomasch, Hunter College, CUNY
- "Creating Alternative Communities: The Babel Working Group as a Response to the Adjunctification of the University," Mary Kate Hurley, Ohio University
- "The Society of Antiquaries and the Origin of Old English Literacy in Eighteenth-Century Britain," Justin Sevenker, University of Pittsburgh

Session 2I, Paper Panel: Erotic Flesh in Late Medieval Discourse (2) (G 102)
Session Organizers: Virginia Blanton and Mary Beth Long
Chair: Mary Beth Long
- "The Virgin Mary as Sanctified Transgressor in Ashmole MS 61," Wendy Matlock, Kansas State University
- "Masculinity, the Complexions and (Male) Sexual Anxieties," Elspeth Whitney, University of Nevada, Las Vegas
- "Chaucer's Queerly Erotic God," Tison Pugh, University of Central Florida
- "Desire across Worlds in *Melusine*," James F. Knapp, University of Pittsburgh

2:00–4:00: **Manuscript Exhibit (Þjóðarbókhlaðan, National Library/University Library)**

4:30–6:00: **Reception (City Hall)**

THURSDAY, JULY 17

8:00–4:30: **Registration (HT upper level)**

9:00–10:30: **Concurrent Sessions, Group 3**

Session 3A, Paper Panel: (Absent) Jews in the Middle (1) (HT 103) (Thread: In Search of Things Past)
Session Organizer and Chair: Kathy Lavezzo
- "Hugh of Lincoln, in and out of History," Miriamne Ara Krummel, University of Dayton

- "The Displacement of the Abject Womb in 'The Miracle of the Boy Singer,'" Thomas Blake, University of Iowa
- "England without Jews, Christian History without Judaism," Steven F. Kruger, Queens College, CUNY
- "'O cursed folk of Herodes al newe': *The Prioress's Tale* and the Jews of Prague," Alfred Thomas, University of Illinois at Chicago

Session 3B, Round Table: This World is But a Thurghfare: Transit, Transport, Scapes, and Flows (1) (HT 104)
(Thread: Movement, Networks, Economies)
Session Organizers and Chairs: Eileen Joy and James L. Smith
- "Foreign Objects: Adapting Greenblatt's Theory of Travel's Estrangement-Effect to Chaucer's *Troilus and Criseyde*," Jennie Friedrich, University of California, Riverside
- "Semiotic Flows," Gaelan Gilbert, University of Victoria
- "LeperNets," Sealy Gilles, Long Island University Brooklyn
- "Animal Transport," Carolynn Van Dyke, Lafayette College
- "Building Bridges to Canterbury," Sarah Breckenridge Wright, Duquesne University
- "Bios in *The Prick of Conscience*: The Apophatic Body and the Sensuous Soul," Christopher M. Roman, Kent State University, Tuscarawas
- "Poetic Footprints," Sarah Elliott Novacich, Rutgers University

Session 3C, Paper Panel: The Teller and the Tale: Life Writing and the *Canterbury Tales* (HT 101)
(Thread: Chaucerian Biographies)
Session Organizer and Chair: Robert Meyer-Lee
- "The (Unwritten) Life of Chaucer's Second Nun: Hagiography, Monastic Culture, and the Question of Chaucer's Religious Commitments," Nancy Bradley Warren, Texas A&M University
- "Tabloid Tales: Chaucer Exploits Pious Princesses," Pamela Troyer, Metropolitan State University of Denver

Session 3D, Paper Panel: Catechism, Confession, and Codicology (L 102)
(Thread: Handling Sins)
Session Organizer and Chair: Michael Johnston
- "Piercing the Gospel with a Paternoster: A Fragment of *La Somme le*

roi in British Library Additional 54325," Claire M. Waters, University of California, Davis
- "The Science of Confession in the Manuscripts of the *Mirour de Seinte Eglyse*," Anna Siebach Larsen, University of Notre Dame
- "Confession and Piers Plowman in British Library, MS Harley 6041," Robyn Malo, Purdue University
- "The Later Book History of *Dives and Pauper*," Kathleen Tonry, University of Connecticut

Session 3E, Paper Panel: Circulating Latinities between the North and Britain (L 103)
(Thread: Scandinavia and Europe)
Session Organizer: Dorothy Kim
Chair: Carissa Harris
- "Circulating Latinities: Thule and Iceland," Dale Kedwards, University of York
- "Networks of Ecclesiastical Influence," Margaret Cormack, College of Charleston
- "The Legend of Pallas's Tomb in Medieval Scandinavia," Ryder Patzuk-Russell, University of Birmingham
- Respondent: Sarah Baechle, University of Notre Dame

Session 3F, Round Table: Cambridge, Trinity College, MS R.3.20: Cultures of the Miscellany in Trilingual England (L 204)
(Thread: The Book in Practice)
Session Organizers and Chairs: Megan Cook and Elizaveta Strakhov
- "Shirley and Lydgate: *The Temple of Glass*," Julia Boffey, Queen Mary College, London
- "John Shirley and the Motives of Compilation," A. S. G. Edwards, University of Kent
- "John Shirley and Christine de Pizan," Stephanie Downes, University of Melbourne
- "John Shirley, Geoffrey Chaucer, and Women in Love," Kara Doyle, Union College
- "The Earl of Suffolk's French Poems and Lydgatian Coteries," R. D. Perry, University of California, Berkeley
- "TCC R.3.20, the Exchequer and Shirleian Literary Circles," Kathryn Veeman, Independent Scholar

Session 3G, Paper Panel: Medieval Soundscapes (1) (L 205)
(Thread: The Medieval Sensorium)
Session Organizers and Chairs: Hannah Johnson and Adin Lears
- "The Bark of the Dog," Susan Crane, Columbia University
- "'Oyez a Beaumont!' Sounding the Hounds," Emily Rebekah Huber, Franklin and Marshall College
- "'As Craft Contrefeteth Kynde': Geffrey's Eagle and the Poetics of Word Preservation," Megan Palmer-Browne, University of California, Santa Barbara
- "What is 'clothed red or blak' in *The House of Fame?*" Alexandra Gillespie, University of Toronto

Session 3H, Paper Panel: Skin Matters (L 201)
Session Organizer and Chair: Nicole Nyffenegger
- "Chaucer's Ethical Palimpsest: Dermal Reflexivity in the *General Prologue*," Catherine S. Cox, University of Pittsburgh
- "The Cook's Ulcer: Corrupted Flesh/Corrupting Flesh," Erin E. Sweany, Indiana University
- "Porous Surfaces and Queer Skin: Textual and Gender Boundaries in the Manuscript Glosses to the Wife of Bath's Prologue," Roberta Magnani, Swansea University
- "White, Brown, and Beautiful: The Color(s) of Christ's Skin," Mary Dzon, University of Tennessee

Session 3I, Paper Panel: Northern Arthurs (G 102)
(Thread: North 1: Texts)
Session Organizer and Chair: Leila K. Norako
- "Scottish Vikings and Norse Knights: The Orkneys as Palimpsest in Arthuriana," Leah Haught, Georgia Institute of Technology
- "'Ther com a schip of Norway': England, Norway, and the Case of *Sir Tristrem*," Ann Higgins, Westfield State University
- Respondent: Leila K. Norako, Stanford University

10:30–11:00: **Coffee Break**

11:00–12:30: **Presidential Address (HB Auditorium 1)**
Chair: Susan Crane
- "Fragmentations of Medieval Religion: Thomas More, Chaucer, and the Volcano Lover," Alastair Minnis, Yale University

12:30–2:00: **Lunch (HT upper level)**

2:00–3:30: **Concurrent Sessions, Group 4**

Session 4A, Roundtable: Global Chaucers (HT 103)
Session Organizer and Chair: Candace Barrington
- "Translating Chaucer's *Canterbury Tales* into Turkish," Nazmi Ağil, Koç University
- "Chaucer in Denmark since 1945: A Discussion of Some Adaptations and Translations, with a Focus on Illustrations," Ebbe Klitgård, Roskilde University
- "Reading Chaucer's *Canterbury Tales* in Spain," Alberto Lazaro, Universidad de Alcala
- "Tradition and Transition in the Translations of Chaucer's *Canterbury Tales* in Japan," Koichi Kano, Tohoku University of Community Service and Science
- "Pasolini, Chaucerian Irony, and the (Im)possibility of Revolutionary Politics in Italy's 'Years of Lead,'" Louise D'Arcens, University of Wollongong
- "Jorge Luis Borges and Chaucerian Novelty," Joseph Stadolnik, Yale University
- "Korean Translation of the *Canterbury Tales*: Variety and Limitation of Korean Equivalents," Professor Dongill Lee, Hankuk University of Foreign Studies

Session 4B, Round Table: The Sense of Emotion (1) (HT 104) (Thread: The Medieval Sensorium)
Session Organizers: Sarah Kelen, Rebecca F. McNamara, and Sarah McNamer
Chair: Rebecca F. McNamara
- "'As she that . . .': Displaced Affect in *Troilus and Criseyde*," Stephanie Trigg, University of Melbourne
- "Making Sense of Red, Green, and Pale: Hue and Its Metapoetic Function in *Troilus and Criseyde*," Nicole Nyffenegger, University of Bern
- "Heurodis 'crached hir visage,'" Elizabeth Allen, University of California, Irvine
- "*Pearl*'s Sensuous Surfaces," Sarah McNamer, Georgetown University
- "Lyrical Encyclopedias," Emily Steiner, University of Pennsylvania

- "'So ynly swete / So wonderful': Puzzling Sweetness in Chaucer's *Book of the Duchess*," Jessica Lockhart, University of Toronto

Session 4C, Paper Panel: (Absent) Jews in the Middle (2) (HT 101) (Thread: In Search of Things Past)
Session Organizer: Kathy Lavezzo
Chair: Anthony Bale
- "Coincident Departures: Mapping the Expulsion in the Hereford Mappamundi and Harley MS 2253," Daniel Birkholz, University of Texas at Austin
- "*The Prioress's Tale* at the Intersection of Antisemitism and Misogyny," Hannah Johnson, University of Pittsburgh; and Heather Blurton, University of California, Santa Barbara
- "Avenging Christ: The Absent Jew and *The Siege of Jerusalem*,'" Timothy L. Stinson, North Carolina State University

Session 4D, Paper Panel: The Ways We Read Now (L 102) (Thread: The Ways We Read Now)
Session Organizer and Chair: Thomas Prendergast
- "Chaucer and the Moving Image in Pre-WWII America," Lynn Arner, Brock University
- "Assembling the Pilgrims: Rereading the Ellesmere Illustrations," Disa Gambera, University of Utah
- "Alfred David and the Way We Read Now," John Ganim, University of California, Riverside

Session 4E, Paper Panel: Recovering the Middle Ages (1) (L 103)
Session Organizer and Chair: Tim W. Machan
- "John Urry and the 'Worst' Edition of Chaucer," Simon Horobin, Magdalen College, Oxford
- "Medieval Scandinavia in Early Canadian Literature," Laurel Ryan, University of Toronto
- "Romantic Past and Barbarian Frenzy: Allen French, J. R. R. Tolkien, Henry Treece, and Old Norse Literature," Jon Karl Helgason, University of Iceland

Session 4F, Paper Panel: Norse Elements in the Romances (L 204) (Thread: North 1: Texts)
Session Organizer and Chair: Helen Cooper

- "Fenland Romance and 'Fabula Danorum': Scandinavian Elements in *Le Roman de Waldef* and the *Gesta Herewardi*," Eleanor Parker, University of Oxford
- "*Sots*, *Kol-bitar* and *Gadelings*: Havelok as 'Male Cinderella': Norse Motif?" Ian Felce, University of Cambridge
- "Bleak Barrows and Haunted Howes," Will Biel, University of Iceland
- "The Middle English *Richard Coeur de Lion* and Old Norse Textual Networks," Marisa Libbon, Bard College

Session 4G, Round Table: How to Do Things with Form (2) (L 205)
(Thread: How to Do Things with Texts)
Session Organizers and Chairs: Elizabeth Robertson and Ad Putter
- "Presenting Chaucer's Rhyme," Aditi Nafde, Keble College, Oxford
- "Chaucer's Meter: Iambic Pentameter or Decasyllable?" Nicholas Myklebust, University of Texas at Austin
- "Problems of Scansion in Chaucerian Pentameter," Ad Putter, University of Bristol
- "*Rime Riche* and Gender in Chaucer," Kim Zarins, California State University, Sacramento
- "Chaucer's Bad Ear: A Study of Chaucer's More Questionable Lines of Poetry," Thomas Bourguignon, University of Montana

3:30–4:00: **Coffee Break**

4:00–5:30: **Concurrent Sessions, Group 5**

Session 5A, Round Table: The Sense of Emotion (2) (HT 103)
(Thread: The Medieval Sensorium)
Session Organizers: Sarah Kelen, Rebecca F. McNamara, and Sarah McNamer
Chair: Sarah McNamer
- "Two Bodies, One Flesh: The Skin of Marital Affection in *The Wife of Bath's Tale*," Glenn Burger, Queens College, CUNY
- "Multi-Sensory Allegory and the Embodiment of Medieval Emotion," Mary Flannery, University of Lausanne
- "The Thought and Feel of Virtuous Wifehood," Lynn Shutters, Colorado State University

- "Imagining Jewish Affect," Patricia DeMarco, Ohio Wesleyan University
- "The Neuro-Biology of Compunction," Mary Agnes Edsall, Independent Scholar

Session 5B, Round Table: This World Is But a Thurghfare: Transit, Transport, Scapes, and Flows (2) (HT 104)
(Thread: Movement, Networks, Economies)
Session Organizers and Chairs: Eileen Joy and James L. Smith
- "Moving with/in *The Book of Margery Kempe*," Robert Stanton, Boston College
- "Wormholes in Chaucer's Dreamscapes," Katherine Koppelman, Seattle University
- "'And in his swifte comynge brende': Chaucer's Aesthetics of Movement in *The House of Fame*," Thomas Schneider, University of California, Riverside
- "Sic transit gloria: *The Knight's Tale* and *The Two Noble Kinsmen*," Louise Bishop, University of Oregon
- "Inventional Movement," Steele Nowlin, Hampden-Sydney College
- "'That swerde shall be youre destruccion': Objects and Trajectories in Malory," Nicholas Perkins, St. Hugh's College, Oxford

Session 5C, Paper Panel: Inordinate Love (2) (HT 101)
(Thread: Handling Sins)
Session Organizers and Chairs: Robyn Malo and Nicole Smith
- "From the God of Love to the Love of God: 'Inordinate' Love in *Troilus and Criseyde*," Megan Murton, St. John's College, Cambridge
- "The Rhetoric of Inordinate Loves: Sinners' Voices in Pastoral Catechesis," Ed Craun, Washington and Lee University
- "Ordinate Love," Valerie Allen, John Jay College, CUNY

Session 5D, Paper Panel: Chaucer and the Autobiographical Fallacy (L 102)
(Thread: Chaucerian Biographies)
Session Organizer and Chair: Lynn Staley
- "Symkyn's Snub, Chaucer's Learning," Glending Olson, Cleveland State University
- "Consuming Chaucer," Marion Turner, Jesus College, Oxford

- "*Nom* and *Renom*: Conflicted Self-Naming in Machaut and Chaucer," Philip Knox, New College, Oxford

Session 5E, Paper Panel: Committing Poetry (1) (L 103)
(Thread: How to Do Things with Texts)
Organizer: Ingrid Nelson
Chair: Seeta Chaganti
- "The Commitments of the *Roman de Melusine*," Peggy Knapp, Carnegie Mellon University
- "The *Dietary* and Lydgate's Didactic Style," Spencer Strub, University of California, Berkeley
- "Thomas Hoccleve's Sovereign Commissions," Jenni Nuttall, Wolfson College and St. Edmund Hall, Oxford
- "'Som newe thing I scholde booke': Chaucer and Gower Doing Business(,) Doing Poetry," Brian W. Gastle, Western Carolina University

Session 5F, Paper Panel: Chaucerian Parchment (L 204)
(Thread: How to Do Things with Books)
Session Organizer: Bruce Holsinger
Chair: Myra J. Seaman
- "*Coactus tangere*: The Intra-Active Touch of Parchment," Angela Bennett Segler, New York University
- "Accursed Parchment: Opinions of Icelandic Scribes," Christine Schott, Erskine College
- Respondent: Orietta Da Rold, University of Leicester

Session 5G, Paper Panel: Anterior Motives: Chaucer and the Place of Early English Literature (L 205)
(Thread: In Search of Things Past)
Session Organizer and Chair: Jennifer Jahner
- "Back to the Future: The Importance of the Twelfth Century in the 'Golden Age of Chaucer,'" Venetia Bridges, University of York
- "The Thirteenth Century and Romance at the Borders of History," Marie Turner, University of Pennsylvania
- "Romancing Becket," Matthew Fisher, University of California, Los Angeles
- "After Petrarch? Periodization and Travel in Petrarch and Chaucer," Anna Wilson, University of Toronto

Session 5H, Paper Panel: The Ways We Might Read in the Future (L 201)
(Thread: The Ways We Read Now)
Session Organizer and Chair: Jessica Rosenfeld
- "Media Hermeneutics," Ingrid Nelson, Amherst College
- "Reading Chaucer's Game: Ludic Theory and the Medieval Text," Betsy McCormick, Mount San Antonio College
- "Cute Chaucer," Wan-Chuan Kao, Washington and Lee University
- "What Is the *Canterbury Tales*? A Meditation on Form and Medieval Literary Theory," Eleanor Johnson, Columbia University

Session 5I, Paper Panel: Norse by Way of Normandy (G 102)
(Thread: North 1: Texts)
Session Organizers and Chairs: Jeremy DeAngelo and Benjamin A. Saltzman
- "*Hic fides habetur regni sotiis*: Scandinavian Power in the *Encomium Emmae*," Emily Butler, John Carroll University
- "The Late Fourteenth-Century Literary Trickster in Iceland and England: *Kroka-Ref* (Ref the Sly) and Chaucer's Pardoner," Peter W. Travis, Dartmouth College
- "The Man in the Moon: A Survival of Germanic Mythology?" Juliette Dor, University of Liège

2:00–5:00: **Manuscript Exhibit** (Þjóðarbókhlaðan, National Library/University Library)

5:30–7:00: **Reception at the University of Iceland** (HT upper level)

7:30: **Polyglot Reading of Chaucer** (open event) (Stúdentakjallarinn)

FRIDAY, JULY 18

8:00–1:00: Registration (HT upper level)

9:00–10:30: Concurrent Sessions, Group 6

Session 6A, Paper Panel: Reassembling the Material Turn: Manuscript Texts as Vehicles in Network Formation (1) (HT 103)

(Thread: Movement, Networks, Economies 5.4.A)
Session Organizers and Chairs: Michael Van Dussen and Sebastian Sobecki
- "Gifts from Camelot: Networking with the Gruuthuse Froissart," Andrew Taylor, University of Ottawa
- "Material Possessions: How a Manuscript Imagines Its Audiences," Thomas Hahn, University of Rochester
- "From England to Eyjafjallajökull via Vercelli: The Curious Past of Vercelli MS 225," Zachary Stone, University of Virginia

Session 6B, Paper Panel: Thinking Chaucer (1) (HT 104)
(Thread: The Medieval Sensorium)
Session Organizer and Chair: Marion Turner
- "The Eyes Have It?" Sarah A. Kelen, Nebraska Wesleyan University
- "Thinking Voices: Mind, Affect and Imagination in Chaucer's Writing," Corinne Saunders, University of Durham

Session 6C, Paper Panel: (Absent) Jews in the Middle (3) (HT 101)
(Thread: In Search of Things Past)
Session Organizer: Kathy Lavezzo
Chair: David Raybin
- "Jews of the Past, Jews of the Future," Asa Simon Mittman, California State University, Chico
- "'A litel scole of Cristen folk': The Prioress's Jewish Lenders," Jenny Adams, University of Massachusets Amherst
- "Acoustic Alterity, *Alma Redemptoris Mater*, and the Nuneaton Book," Dorothy Kim, Vassar College
- "Gower's Jews," R. F. Yeager, University of West Florida

Session 6D, Paper Panel: *The House of Fame* as Hermeneutic Sound Garden (L 102)
(Thread: The Ways We Read Now)
Session Organizer and Chair: Tom Goodmann
- "'For al mot out': Form and Motion in Chaucer's *House of Fame*," Rebecca Davis, University of California, Irvine
- "Reading the Walls of *House of Fame*: Toward a Hermeneutics of Stained Glass," Boyda Johnstone, Fordham University
- "Sounds and Senses in *The House of Fame*," Tom Stillinger, University of Utah

Session 6E, Paper Panel: Late Medieval Speech Communities (1): Sound and Speech (L 103)
Session Organizer: Isabel Davis
Chair: Sarah Stanbury
- "'Folweth Ekko': Gossips and the Art of Listening," Christine Neufeld, Eastern Michigan University
- "Christ's Lyric Voice and the Community of Devotion," Barbara Zimbalist, University of Texas, El Paso
- "Kneeling and Naming: Speech Communities and the Late Medieval Subject," Isabel Davis, Birkbeck, University of London

Session 6F, Paper Panel: Masculinity and Fourteenth-Century Literature (L 204)
Session Organizer and Chair: Ásdís Egilsdóttir
- "'Open-Ers': The Femininized Voice of the Reeve's Old Age," Anna Waymack, Cornell University
- "Lovesickness and Masculinity: Literary Representations of a Medical Discourse from South to North," Marian Elizabeth Polhill, University of Puerto Rico, Río Piedras
- "'I have felled many men and made this poem about it': Violence and Masculinities in Late-Icelandic Literature and Chaucer," Angela Jane Weisl, Seton Hall University
- "'How do you know if it's Love or Lust?' On Male Emotions and Attitudes towards Women in Medieval Icelandic Literature," Aðalheiður Guðmundsdóttir, University of Iceland

Session 6G, Paper Panel: Committing Poetry (2) (L 205)
Thread: How to Do Things with Texts
Session Organizer and Chair: Ingrid Nelson
- "Do *Cleanness* and *Patience* Make Us Clean or Patient?" Arthur Bahr, MIT
- "Theologies of Alliteration, Theologies of Rhyme: Pastoral Poetry in North Yorkshire," Katherine Zieman, Independent Scholar
- "Henryson, Holland, and the Politics of Unnatural Form," Laura Wang, Harvard University

Session 6H, Paper Panel: Networks of Solitude (L 201)
Session Organizers and Chairs: Susannah Chewning and Liz Herbert McAvoy

- "Exiles or Diaspora? Eve of Wilton and Goscelin's *Liber confortatorius*," Diane Watt, University of Surrey
- "'For iþe ane mai ich alle frend finden": Notions of Networks and Anchoritic Friendship," Michelle M. Sauer, University of North Dakota
- "William Flete's *Remedies against Temptations* in the Context of Late Middle English Instructional Religious Literature," Gabriella Del Lungo Camiciotti, University of Florence
- "Audelay and Hoccleve," Sebastian Langdell, University of Oxford

Session 6I, Paper Panel: Views of the Scandinavian (Br)Other in Later Medieval England (G 102)
(Thread: North 2: Contexts)
Session Organizers: Molly Jacobs and Giselle Gos
Chair: Giselle Gos
- "Writing History on the Walls of Public Houses: A Fourteenth-Century Anglo-Scandinavian Encounter," Joanna Bellis, Pembroke College, Cambridge
- "Recuperating Cnut in the English Chronicles," Cynthia Turner Camp, University of Georgia
- "The Hermit and the Sailor: Readings of Scandinavia in North-Eastern Hagiography," Christiania Whitehead, University of Warwick
- "Danes, Tribute, Martyrs, and the Reeve's Rusty Blade," Stephen Yeager, Concordia University

10:30–11:00: **Coffee Break**

11:00–1:00: **Concurrent Sessions, Group 7**

Session 7A, Seminar: Ecomaterialism: Questions/Problems/Ideologies (HT 103)
Session Organizers: Myra Seaman and Kathleen Kelly
- "Ecoemotions: Nicole Oresme and the Kinematic World," Matthew Boyd Goldie, Rider University
- "The Resilience of Flowers: A Theorized Close Reading of *Book of the Duchess*, 397–427," Gillian Rudd, Liverpool University
- "The Matter of Medieval Newgate," Corey Sparks, Indiana University

- " 'By Chance' or 'in Itself': Spontaneous Generation and the Problem of Material Agency," Karl Steel, Brooklyn College, CUNY
- "Water's Love," Sharon O'Dair, University of Alabama
- "wordthing," Laurie Finke, Kenyon College

Session 7B, Seminar: Creatura (HT 104)
Session Organizers: George Edmondson and Robert Stein
- "Margery Kempe as a Twenty-First Century Creature," Tara Williams, Oregon State University
- " 'The ryche man hatz more nede thanne the pore': Creation and Dependence in *Dives and Pauper*," Elizabeth Harper, Mercer University
- "Creative Creatures," Patricia Clare Ingham, Indiana University
- "Sexing the Creatures of Anglo-Saxon Literature," Stacy S. Klein, Rutgers University

Session 7C, Seminar: Editing [for] the Future (HT 101)
Session Organizer: Vincent Gillespie
- "Rethinking Editing in the Digital Age," Wendy Scase, University of Birmingham
- "Nineteenth-Century Editing and the Poetical Works of Geoffrey Chaucer: How Society Influences Editorial Practices," Simone Celine Marshall, University of Otago
- "How Should We Approach Furnivall's Six-Text *Canterbury Tales*: With Incense or a Duster?" Helen Leith Spencer, Exeter College, Oxford
- "Editing Tolkien Editing Chaucer," John Bowers, University of Las Vegas
- "Toward a Queer Chaucer Edition," Robert Sturges, Arizona State University

Session 7D, Seminar: Re-Orienting Disability (L 102)
Session Organizers: Jonathan Hsy and Julie Orlemanski
- "Disability and Truth-Telling in Late Medieval England," Brantley Bryant, Sonoma State University
- "Attending to 'Beasts Irrational' in Gower's *Vox clamantis*," Haylie Swenson, George Washington University
- "Spiritual Prosthesis: Bodily Aberrance in Medieval Hagiographical Narrative," Leah Pope, University of Wisconsin-Madison

- "Mad for Margery," M. W. Bychowski, George Washington University
- "By Any Other Name: Negotiating Difference in Medieval Disability Studies," John P. Sexton, Bridgewater State University

Session 7E, Seminar: The Boundaries of Medieval Drama (L 103)
Session Organizers: John T. Sebastian and Christina M. Fitzgerald
- "Joyous Fruition: Vegetal Bodies and Virtual Hosts in the Croxton *Play of the Sacrament*," Robert W. Barrett, Jr., University of Illinois at Urbana-Champaign
- "*The Play of the Sacrament* as Tudor Drama," John T. Sebastian, Loyola University New Orleans
- "Histrionic and Historical Houses: Jewish Dwellings in Bury St. Edmunds and the Croxton *Play of the Sacrament*," Kathy Lavezzo, University of Iowa
- "Medieval Drama and Evidential Culture," Emma Lipton, University of Missouri
- "Multitemporal Objects and Spaces: The Abbey Gates in the Context of The Croxton *Play of the Sacrament*," Meisha Lohmann, SUNY-Binghamton
- "The Southern Banns: Croxton," Matthew Sergi, University of Toronto
- "Losses, Legendry, and the *Grocers' Pageant* in the Norwich Muniment Room," J. Case Tompkins, Purdue University

Session 7F, Seminar: Reading Chaucer (L 204)
Session Organizer: Helen Barr
- "Merchant–Squire: Love, Fiction, and Literary Value," Robert Meyer-Lee, Indiana University South Bend
- "Mother-Murder in *The Prioress's Tale* and *The Man of Law's Tale*," Karen Cherewatuk, St. Olaf College
- "When Chaucer's Women Talk about Themselves," Sheila Fisher, Trinity College, Hartford, Connecticut

Session 7G, Seminar: Extracurricular Chaucer: Creative Pedagogies (L 205)
Session Organizer: Ruth Evans
- "Chaucer, Vygotsky, and Wikipedia: New Ways of Reading," Amanda Bohne, University of Notre Dame

- "Chaucer's Wiki Speaks," Alex Mueller, University of Massachusetts Boston
- "Is Accessibility Simple? Is Simplicity Naive?" Susan Yager, Iowa State University
- "Participatory Pedagogy," Derrick Pitard, Slippery Rock University
- "Experiential Chaucer: Providing Tools to Make Meaning," Kara Crawford, The Bishop's School, La Jolla, California
- "Using Panopto and Dropbox to Enhance Students' Reading and Recitation," T. Ross Leasure, Salisbury University
- "Teaching Chaucer within the Framework of a Rhetoric and Composition Class," Stephanie Amsel, Southern Methodist University

Session 7H, Seminar: Digital Chaucer (L 201)
Session Organizer: Simon Horobin
- "A Computer-Assisted Textual Comparison among the Manuscripts and the Editions: With Special Reference to Caxton's Editions," Noriyuki Kawano, Yoshiyuki Nakao, Akiyuki Jimura, and Kenichi Satoh, Hiroshima University
- "Crowdsourcing the Medieval," Kathryn A. Lowe, University of Glasgow; and Benjamin Albritton, Stanford University
- "Digital Sagas and Saga Manuscripts," Emily Lethbridge, University of Iceland and Stofnun Árna Magnússonar
- "Ubiquitous *Canterbury Tales* MSS Archive and IT Scribes," Tomonori Matsushita, Senshu University
- "Scholarly Editing through Digital Pedagogy in the Hoccleve Archive," Robin Wharton, Georgia Regents University; and Elon Lang, University of Texas at Austin
- "Beyond the Body of the Book: The Future of Digital Materialities," Kathleen Ogden, University of Toronto
- "Global Chaucers: A New Digital Project," Candace Barrington, Central Connecticut State University
- "The *Canterbury Tales* as App," Richard North and Mari Volkosh, University College, London; Peter Robinson and Barbara Bordalejo, University of Saskatchewan and Scholarly Digital Editions; Terry Jones, Independent Scholar

Session 7I, Poster Session: How to Do Things with Books (walkway between HT and Gimli, directly facing HT 101)
(Thread: How to Do Things with Books)

Session Organizers: Anthony Bale and Alexandra Gillespie

- "Genealogies on the Page: Boccaccio, Dante, and the Chigiano Manuscript," Leah Schwebel, University of Connecticut
- "Translations of Form: Richard Rolle and the Development of Middle English Commentary," B. Kraebel, Yale University
- "Translating 'Skarsete' in Chaucer's *Complaint of Venus*,'" Elizaveta Strakhov, University of Pennsylvania
- "How to Read a Pseudotext: Recognizing and Reading the Texts of Pere Serra's *Altarpiece of the Virgin*," Chris Piuma, University of Toronto
- "*The Clensyng of Mannes Soule*: An Edition in the Making," Nicole Smith, University of North Texas
- "Identity and Difference: The Case of the 'Hooked-g' Scribe(s)," Daniel W. Mosser, Virginia Tech; and Holly James-Maddock, University of York
- "Imaginative Reading, Books of Hours, and the Late-Medieval Devotional Treatise *Of Three Workings in Man's Soul*," Laura Saetveit Miles, University of Bergen
- "Waste Not Want Not: Recycling and the Medieval Manuscript," Hannah Ryley, Worcester College, Oxford
- "Signs of Use in Fifteenth-Century Manuscripts," Thomas White, Birkbeck, University of London
- "The Augmented Palimpsest: From Chaucer to ChaucAR," Andrea R. Harbin, SUNY-Cortland; and Tamara F. O'Callaghan, Northern Kentucky University
- "Medical Manuscript as Practical Tool: Medical Illustrations in British Library, MS Harley 397 and Wellcome Library, MS 39," Jessica Henderson, University of Toronto

2:00: **Half-Day Excursion**

2:00–5:00: **Manuscript Exhibit** (Þjóðarbókhlaðan, National Library/University Library)

SATURDAY, JULY 19

9:00–10:30: Concurrent Sessions, Group 8

Session 8A, Paper Panel: Should We Believe in the Agential Object? (HT 103)

(Thread: How to Do Things with Books)
Session Organizer and Chair: Susan Crane
- "The Object of Failure," Andrew Cole, Princeton University
- "Agency and Instrumentality," Shannon Gayk, Indiana University
- "Magic Rocks," Jeffrey Jerome Cohen, George Washington University

Session 8B, Paper Panel: Cinematic Adaptations of Medieval Scandinavian Narratives and History (HT 104)
Session Organizer: Lorraine K. Stock
Chair: Martha Driver
- "*Outlaw*: The Icelandic Film of *Gisli's Saga*," James W. Earl, University of Oregon
- "Brutality and Bloodshed: Othering the Viking Age on Screen," Larissa Tracy, Longwood University

Session 8C, Paper Panel: Wycliffite Bible Networks: Makers, Patrons, and Users (HT 101)
Session Organizer and Chair: Kathleen E. Kennedy
- "Liturgical Paratexts: Old Testament Lectionaries in Middle English New Testaments," Matti Peikola, University of Helsinki
- "The Prioress's Bible? Evidence for Monastic Patronage and Ownership of the Manuscripts of the Wycliffite Bible," Elizabeth Solopova, Brasenose College, Oxford
- "The Chaucerian Wycliffite Bible," Kathleen E. Kennedy, Pennsylvania State University Brandywine

Session 8D, Paper Panel: Edification of the Senses (2) (L 102) (Thread: The Medieval Sensorium)
Session Organizers: Richard G. Newhauser and Larry Scanlon
Chair: Richard G. Newhauser
- "Learning to See by Being Seen: Optics and Counter-Experience in Eschatological Drama," Ryan McDermott, University of Pittsburgh
- "'So mery a belle': Wyclif, Chaucer, and the 'Voices of Words,'" Adin Lears, Cornell University
- "A Taste for Poetry," J. Allan Mitchell, University of Victoria
- "Investing the Senses in Late-Medieval England," Arthur J. Russell, Arizona State University

Session 8E, Paper Panel: Reassembling the Material Turn: Manuscript Texts as Vehicles in Network Formation (2) (L 103)
(Thread: Movement, Networks, Economies)
Session Organizers and Chairs: Michael Van Dussen and Sebastian Sobecki
- "A Token of Nobility: The Percys, the Tudors, and BL MS Royal 18 D II," Noelle Phillips, University of Toronto
- "English Presences in Manuscript Collections from the Medieval Low Countries," Dirk Schoenaers, University College London
- "Medieval Texts and Post-Medieval Materialities," Megan Cook, Colby College

Session 8F, Paper Panel: Poetics beyond Aureation (1) (L 204)
(Thread: How to Do Things with Texts)
Session Organizers: Anke Bernau and Sarah Salih
Chair: Anke Bernau
- "Laurence, Bochas, and the Metapoetics of Lydgate's *Fall of Princes*," Gania Barlow, Columbia University
- "Aureation, Doggie-Style: The Dissociative Poetics of Fifteenth-Century Doggerel Verse," Andrea Denny-Brown, University of California, Riverside
- "The Poetics of Scale," Catherine Sanok, University of Michigan
- "*Pearl* and the Arithmepoetics of Unknowing," Christopher Taylor, University of Texas at Austin

Session 8G, Round Table: Thinking Chaucer (2): Complaint, Memory, Gender (L 205)
(Thread: The Medieval Sensorium)
Session Organizer: Marion Turner
Chair: Carolyn Dinshaw
- "'To clerkes lete I al disputisoun': Patterns of Perception, Affect, Desire and Cognition in the *Franklin's Tale*," Darragh Greene, University College Dublin
- "The Fall of Sleep, or, Indifference: *The Book of the Duchess*," Elizabeth Edwards, University of King's College
- "'And every word [she] gan up and down to wynde': Cognition and the Female Reader in Chaucer's *Troilus and Criseyde*," Sarah W. Townsend, University of Pennsylvania
- "Chaucer's Fallen Language, the Grammar of Memory, and the Psychoanalytic Method," Reid Hardaway, Ohio State University

- "Forgetting Hoccleve: Memory and the Lost Self," Christopher J. Pugh, University of Toronto

Session 8H, Paper Panel: Recovering the Middle Ages (2) (L 201)
Session Organizer and Chair: Tim W. Machan
- "How Alliterative Verse Got Its Name (and Why It Matters)," Ian Cornelius, Yale University
- "'What Hath Speght Wrought?': Etymologies and Other Northernisms in the Three Eighteenth-Century Editions, Especially Morell's (1737)," Betsy Bowden, Rutgers University
- "Hilaire Belloc, Ancient Roads, and Mutual Culture," Melinda Nielsen, Baylor University
- "Edward Burne-Jones and the Kelmscott Chaucer," Paul Acker, Saint Louis University

Session 8I, Paper Panel: Linguistic Ideologies, Literary Form, and Poetics in Britain and the North (G 102)
(Thread: North 2: Contexts)
Session Organizer: Kristjan Arnason
Chair: Haraldur Bernharðsson
- "North Meets South: Vernacular versus Classical Poetics in Medieval Iceland," Kristján Árnason, University of Iceland
- "The Alliterating Harley Lyrics and Poetic Norms in Fourteenth-Century English Poetry," Kristin Lynn Cole, Pennsylvania State University
- "Germans to the Left, French to the Right: Mapping the Etymological Landscape of the *Canterbury Tales*," Heidi Kurtz, University of Oxford

10:30–11:00: **Coffee Break**

11:00–12:30: **Concurrent Sessions, Group 9**

Session 9A, Paper Panel: Poetics beyond Aureation (2) (HT 103)
(Thread: How to Do Things with Texts)
Session Organizers: Anke Bernau and Sarah Salih
Chair: Catherine Sanok
- "Monkeying Around: Towards a Curious Poetics," Anke Bernau, University of Manchester

- "The Wild Surmise of Medieval Poetic Form," Seeta Chaganti, University of California, Davis
- "Historical Fiction: *Exemplum*, *Integumentum*, and Fact in Lydgate's *Fall of Princes*," Taylor Cowdery, Harvard University
- "Ekphrasis as Poetics," Sarah Salih, King's College London

Session 9B, Paper Panel: Manuscripts, Texts and Traces of the Poet's Work (HT 104)
(Thread: Chaucerian Biographies)
Session Organizer: Linne Mooney
Chair: Daniel Mosser
- "The Authorship of the *Equatorie of the Planetis* Revisited," Kari Anne Rand, University of Oslo
- "Chaucer's Southwark Connections," Martha Carlin, University of Wisconsin-Milwaukee
- "Chaucer's London Networks," Caroline Barron, Emerita, Royal Holloway, University of London
- "Alleging Authors: The Glossing of Chaucer's *House of Fame*," Jane Griffiths, Wadham College, Oxford

Session 9C, Round Table: Teaching Things with Books (HT 101)
(Thread: How to Do Things with Books)
Session Organizer: Erick Keleman
Chair: Candace Barrington
- "Teaching Things with—and without—Books," David Watt, University of Manitoba
- "Publishing the Middle Ages," Krista Sue-Lo Twu, University of Minnesota Duluth
- "Book History and 'User-Created Content': Commonplace Books in the Medieval Literature Classroom," Christina Fitzgerald, University of Toledo
- "Teaching Textual Historicism; or, Getting Students to Care that the New Hoccleve Holograph Isn't," Lawrence Warner, King's College London
- "Teaching Frametale Collections and Codicologically-Organized Narratives," Karla Nielsen, Columbia University

Session 9D, Paper Panel: Mapping Narrative(s) in Medieval Literature (2) (L 102)

(Thread: Movement, Networks, Economies)
Session Organizer and Chair: Emily Lethbridge
- "Manuscripts, Metadata and (Tube) Maps: Mapping the European Breton Lai," Elizabeth Dearnley, University College London
- "Ambiguous Geographies and Kingship in the Alliterative *Morte Arthure*," Gina Hurley, Yale University
- "Navigating Peripheralization at the Edge of the World: Moving through Iceland's Narrative Topography," Amy C. Mulligan, University of Notre Dame

Session 9E, Paper Panel: Epochs and the Medieval Ecological Imagination (L 103)
(Thread: In Search of Things Past)
Session Organizers: Mary Kate Hurley and Ryan R. Judkins
Chair: Mary Kate Hurley
- "Hunger and Crisis on Either Side of the Fourteenth Century," Alexis Kellner Becker, Harvard University
- "Bring Out Your Dead: An Ecological Approach to Medieval Death and Dying," J. Justin Brent, Presbyterian College
- "Ecological Shift: The Rhetorical Object in Anglo-Saxon, Chaucerian, and Early Modern Poems," David Hadbawnik, SUNY-Buffalo
- "Mediation and Translation of Medieval Ecological Imaginations in *The House of Fame* and *Piers Plowman*," Jessica Rezunyk, Washington University in St. Louis

Session 9F, Paper Panel: The Work of Scribes (L 204)
Session Organizer: Stephen Partridge
Chair: Daniel Wakelin
- "Looking Again at Ricardus Franciscus: A Case Study in the History of the Book," Martha Driver, Pace University
- "The Harley 2253 Scribe's Datable Literate Activities and Library of Booklets," Susanna Fein, Kent State University
- "Manuscript Study and the Scale of Historical Inquiry: A Case Study of *Handlyng Synne*," Sarah Noonan, Lindenwood University

Session 9G, Round Table: Medieval Governmentalities (L 201)
Session Organizer and Chair: Ian Cornelius
- "Mortification and Secular Governance," Amy Appleford, Boston University

- "Governing without Reign: Medieval Governmentalities in the Anglo-French Conflict," Lee Manion, University of Missouri
- "The Gregorian Reform and the Integration of Sovereign and Pastoral Power," Suzanne Verderber, Pratt Institute
- "Governing and Emotions in Late Medieval Law," Rebecca F. McNamara, University of Sydney

Session 9H, Paper Panel: "Of Yseland to wryte is lytill nede . . .": Cultural and Literary Relations between England and Iceland in the Fourteenth and Fifteenth Centuries (G 102)
(Thread: North 2: Contexts)
Session Organizer and Chair: Gunnar Harðarson
- "*Enska vísan*: Literary Contact in the 'English Age' of Iceland," Martin Chase, Fordham University
- "The Icelandic Translations from Robert Mannyng's *Handlyng Synne*," Daniel Najork, Arizona State University
- "English Exempla in Iceland in the Fifteenth Century," Shaun F. D. Hughes, Purdue University
- "Chaucer, Langland, and Norse-Celtic Poetics," Rory McTurk, University of Leeds

12:30–1:30: **Lunch (HT upper level)**

1:30–3:00: **Concurrent Sessions, Group 10**

Session 10A, Round Table: Things Books Do (HT 103)
(Thread: The Book in Practice)
Session Organizers: Allan Mitchell and Alexandra Gillespie
Chair: Allan Mitchell
- "Can a Book Be Disabled?" Jonathan Hsy, George Washington University
- "Philobiblia, Then and Now," Kellie Robertson, University of Maryland
- "The Book as Eyewitness: Dares the Phrygian and the Trojan Network of the Latin West," Marilynn Desmond, SUNY-Binghamton
- "The Book Abides," Myra Seaman, College of Charleston
- "Ink Recipes and 'Adhocism,'" Michael Johnston, Purdue University
- "Nonreading Books," Heather Blatt, Florida International University

- "How to Do Wills with Things," Frank Grady, University of Missouri-St. Louis

Session 10B, Paper Panel: Between the Birgittines: Syon Abbey and Vadstena's Textual Exchanges (HT 104)
(Thread: Scandinavia and Europe)
Session Organizer and Chair: Laura Saetveit Miles
- "Understanding the Birgittine Idea: Exchange and Use of Birgittine Texts in Vadstena and Syon Abbey," Elin Andersson, Stockholm University
- "Walter Hilton in Vadstena: Two Trails of Transmission," Michael G. Sargent, Queens College, CUNY
- "*The Fifteen Oes* at Syon and Vadstena," Susan Powell, University of Salford
- "Life and Liturgy at Syon and Vadstena: The Evidence for the Brethren," Vincent Gillespie, University of Oxford

Session 10C, Paper Panel: Translation, *Mise-en-Page*, and Form (HT 101)
(Thread: How to Do Things with Texts)
Session Organizer and Chair: Sarah Noonan
- "Giving Form to Antagonisms? The Various Translations in *Sir Ferumbras*," Siobhain Bly Calkin, Carleton University
- "The Complaint of the Translator in the *Complaint of Venus*: Chaucer, Graunson, and French Vernacular Lyric Collections," Madeleine Elson, University of Toronto
- "Nativizing Iconography: Translation and the Material Illumination," Joyce Coleman, University of Oklahoma

Session 10D, Paper Panel: Monument, Edifice, Container: The Medieval Manuscript (L 102)
(Thread: How to Do Things with Books)
Session Organizers and Chairs: Elaine Treharne and Noelle Phillips
- "Treasure Trove to Drawer in Disarray: Newberry Library MS 33.5," Georgiana Donavin, Westminster College; and Eve Salisbury, Western Michigan University
- "Expandable Containers: Extra Bits of Book," Daniel Wakelin, St. Hilda's College, Oxford
- "The Book as Container, and Containing the Book; or . . . When Is

a Book Not a Book? When It's a Poppadum," Siân Echard, University of British Columbia
- "In Britain's Lyric Coronet: The Poems of MS Cotton Nero A.x. and the (Re)construction of the Manuscript," Zachary Hines, University of Texas

Session 10E, Paper Panel: Literature at Sea: Hanseatic Textual Networks (L 103)
(Thread: North 2: Contexts)
Session Organizers and Chairs: Amy Appleford and Catherine Sanok
- "'I xal go wyth þe in euery contre & ordeyn for þe': Women's Travelling Visions and the Transgressing of Boundaries," Liz Herbert McAvoy, Swansea University
- "A New Document on Margery Kempe: Gdansk, Lynn, and the Summer of 1431," Sebastian Sobecki, University of Groningen
- Respondent: David Wallace, University of Pennsylvania

Session 10F, Paper Panel: The Learning Space: How's It Done There (L 204)
Session Organizer and Chair: Sandy Feinstein
- "'Good Lond Wol Signifie': Poetry and Practice in *Palladius on Husbondrie*," Lisa H. Cooper, University of Wisconsin-Madison
- "Making a Good Horse and a Parfit Knight: Giordano Ruffo's *De medicina equorum*," Maud McInerney, Haverford College
- "The Alchemical Learning Space: Present and Absent Pedagogies," Cara Hersh, University of Portland
- "Exploring the 'Paleys Desolat': Translating the Limitations of Mnemonic in *Troilus and Criseyde*," Jenny Boyar, University of Rochester

Session 10G, Paper Panel: Late Medieval Speech Communities (2): Writing Speech (L 205)
Session Organizer: Isabel Davis
Chair: Katie Walter
- "Fantasies of Dialogue in *Alexander and Dindimus*," Kara L. McShane, University of Rochester
- "Capturing Speech in Writing: Social Networks and Communities of Practice in Late Medieval Manuscripts," Colette Moore, University of Washington

- "Translating the Talk of the (Late Medieval) Town," Susie Phillips, Northwestern University

Session 10H, Paper Panel: The Book in Pieces (L 201)
Session Organizers: Glenn Burger and Holly Crocker
Chair: Holly Crocker
- "Parting Words: The Holes in Chaucer's Wholes," William A. Quinn, University of Arkansas
- "Spectral Chaucer," Thomas Prendergast, College of Wooster
- "Genetic Evidence in *Piers* A and the *Canterbury Tales* Gamma Clade," Thomas J. Farrell, Stetson University

Session 10I, Paper Panel: Medieval Soundscapes (2) (G 102) (Thread: The Medieval Sensorium)
Session Organizers: Hannah Johnson and Adin Lears
Chair: Adin Lears
- "The Noise of Neighbors," George Edmondson, Dartmouth College
- "'An ydel man thou semest': Representation, Aesthetics, and Authorial Identity in *Piers Plowman*," Katharine Jager, University of Houston-Downtown
- "Letters that Fly: Bird Sound in Chaucer," Ashley Nolan, Saint Louis University
- "Soundscapes in Medieval Dream Poetry," Michael Raby, University of Toronto

3:00–3:30: **Coffee Break**

3:30–5:00: **Biennial Lecture (HB Auditorium 1)**
Chair: David Wallace, University of Pennsylvania
- "'Not Yet': Chaucer and Anagogy," James Simpson, Harvard University

7:00: **Congress Dinner**

SUNDAY, JULY 20

9:00: **Day tours** (Reykholt excursion departs at 10:00)

Index

Page numbers of illustrations are indicated in the index by *italics*.

Abbot, George 43, 47, 49
Ahmed, Sara 160
Akbari, Suzanne Conklin 202–3
Alan of Lille 178
Alcuin of York 177–78
Alford, John 177
Allen, Hope Emily 257, 265, 279–80
Anne of Bohemia 7
Aquinas, St. Thomas 35
Aristotle, *Physics* 106
Atkinson, Clarissa 273
Audelay, John 270
Augustine of Hippo, St. 39, 49, 108, 201; *Confessions* 106–8, 201–2
Augustus, Roman emperor 4, 231–32, 248

Bachelard, Gaston 160
Bahr, Arthur 131
Baker, Donald 250
Baker, Gary 97
Bale, John 9; *The Laboryouse Journey* 41, 44
Banfield, Ann 160
Bankert, Dabney Anderson 203
Banks, Joseph 11, 14
Baswell, Christopher 108
Becket, Thomas 4, 217
Beckwith, Sarah 268
Benet, Edmund 273
Benham, Jenny 193
Benjamin, Walter 255–56
Bennett, J. A. W. 112
Benson, Larry D., ed., *The Riverside Chaucer* 131
Bible: Ephesians 166; Jeremiah 49; John 39, 53; Wycliffite 166
Biebel, Elisabeth 164, 171
Birckbek, Simon 47; *The Protestants evidence taken out of good records* 43–44, 49
Blamires, Alcuin 222–23
Blanche of Lancaster 135, 143, 147, 151, 153, 154, 155, 156, *157*

Blyth, Charles 63
Boccaccio, Giovanni 183; *Decameron* 237–38; *Il filocolo* 227–29, 236–42, 243, 245, 249, 251, 252–53, 255
Boethius 49, 108, 110; *The Consolation of Philosophy* 101, 108, 109–11, 159
Bolingbroke, Henry *see* Henry IV, king of England
Book of the Knight of La Tour-Landry, The 18
Bourdieu, Pierre 248
Bradshaw, Henry 190; *The Holy Lyfe and History of Saynt Werburge* 189
Bradstock, E. M. 199–200, 206, 207
Bradwardine, Thomas 49; *De causa Dei contra Pelagium* 43
Brembre, Nicholas 77
Brendan, St. 259
Bridget of Sweden, St. 259
Bromyard, John, *Summa praedicantium* 188
Brozyna, Martha 183
Brunham, John, Jr. 273–77
Brunham, John, Sr. 273–77, 278
Brunham, Robert 273–77
Burgess, Anthony 181
Burns, E. Jane 139, 141
Burrow, John 64
Butler, Sara 164, 172, 173
Butterfield, Ardis 135, 140

Cannon, Christopher 130
Canterbury Interlude 26
Carabelli, Giancarlo 17, 19
Carpenter, John 56
Carruthers, Mary 120, 159
Catherine of Aragon 7
Caxton, William, *The Four Sons of Aymon* 166
Charles I, king of England 42
Chastelaine de Vergy 150
Chaucer, Geoffrey 24–25, 34–35, 41, 42, 50, 53, 55, 56, 57, 58, 59, 80, 84, 86,

INDEX

88, 92, 96, 99–100, 119, 136, 139, 140, 141, 154–55, 168, 190; *Adam* 167; *BD* 133–40, 142–44, 147, 149, 150–52, 153–56, 158, 159, 161, 244; *Bo* 55, 75, 96, 99, 108, 109–10; *CT* 19, 41, 43, 45–47, 49–50, 52, 56, 73, 86, 87, 88, 92, 93, 98, 103, 131, 229, 253, 254–55; *FranT* 227–28, 229, 242–56; *FrT* 103; *GP* 102, 103, 118, 132, 139; *HF* 101–23, 126–27, 129–30, 131–32; *KnT* 139, 192; *LGW* 253–54; *MilP* 132; *MkP* 175; *NPT* 43, 46, 49; *PardP* 44; *PardT* 21–23, 24, 25–26, 44, 49, 50, 51–53; *ParsT* 41, 49, 167, 190–91, 192; *Rom* 44; *ShT* 140; *SqT* 139; *SumT* 192; *TC* 46–47, 49, 55, 56, 85, 99, 149, 203; *WBP* 163–71, 176–77, 181–82, 191–94
Chaucer, Philippa 155
Christian of Lilienfeld 179
Christine de Pizan, *Livre des trois vertus* 149; *Treasury of the City of Ladies* 145–46
Cohen, Jeffrey Jerome 206
Colles, John 97
Constance of Castile 155, 156
Contamine, Philippe 193
Copeland, Rita 253
Cosmas, St. 12–14, 22, 25
Crawford, Donna 206, 222
Cursor mundi 200

d'Aubigné, Agrippa 9, 10, 14, 18, 21
Damian, St. 12, 13
Dante Alighieri 108; *La divina commedia* 40; *Inferno* 179; *Paradiso* 107
Dashwood, Francis, 15th Baron le Despencer 15–16
De Fornivall, Thomasina 185, 186
De Fornivall, William 185
De statu Saracenorum 214
De Worde, Wynkyn, *The fyftene joyes of maryage* 175
Delany, Sheila 112
Denery, Dallas D., II, Kantik Ghosh, and Nicolette Zeeman, eds., *Uncertain Knowledge: Scepticism, Relativism, and Doubt in the Middle Ages* 285–88
Depupp, John 189, 190
DeVries, Kelly 209

Dickinson, Emily 160
Digby Magdalen 169
Dillon, Janette 272
Dinshaw, Carolyn 234
Donaldson, E. Talbot 85
Doyle, A. I. 65–66, 67, 68–69, 84–85, 87, 88, 89, 91, 96
Drury, John 188
Dugdale, William, *The History of St. Paul's Cathedral in London* 156, *157*
Duggan, Hoyt 93, 94

Edward I, king of England 216
Edward II, king of England 77, 216
Edward III, king of England 55, 96, 97, 140, 152, 153
Edwards, Robert 117
Eliot, T. S. 17
Elizabeth, duchess of Exeter 148
Elliott, Elizabeth, *Remembering Boethius: Writing Aristocratic Identity in Late Medieval French and English Literatures* 289–93
Elukin, Jonathan M. 218–19, 225
Erasmus, Desiderius 24
Ermengild, St. 189
Erskine, John 279
Eutropius of Orange, St. 9
Evans, Ruth, "Chaucer in Cyberspace" 106
Evans, Walker 3, 7
Everaclus of Liège 178

Feeney, Denis 231, 232
Fein, Susanna 251
Fierabras 202–3
Fisher, Matthew, *Scribal Authorship and the Writing of History in Medieval England* 293–96
Forster, E. M., *A Passage to India* 33
Fosse, Thomas 189, 190
Foster, Michael 155
Foucault, Michel 37
Foutin, St. 9, 18, 22, 25
Frazer, James G., *The Golden Bough* 17
Freud, Sigmund 17
Froissart, Jean 134, 136, 137, 141, 145, 159; *L'espinette amoureuse* 141–42, 179; *Le paradys d'amours* 135, 137, 138, 159
Fyler, John 104, 112, 253

Gaimar, Geoffrey 18
Geoffroy de la Tour Landry 183
Georgianna, Linda 193
Gerald of Wales *see* Giraldus Cambrensis
Ghosh, Kantik *see under* Denery, Dallas D., II
Gibbon, Edward 18
Gildenhard, Ingo 231
Gilte Legende 200
Ginsberg, Warren 238
Giraldus Cambrensis 18
Girard, René 224
Gladiator (Ridley Scott) 34
Goldberg, P. J. P. 149
Good Morning Vietnam (Barry Levinson) 34
Goodman, Anthony 273
Gotein, S. D. 184
Gower, John 42, 56, 71, 99, 167; *Confessio Amantis* 56, 69, 85
Graves, Robert 17
Green, Richard Firth 97
Grigges, John 273
Grossvogel, Steven 241
Guillaume de Deguileville, *Le pèlerinage de vie humaine see* Lydgate, John, *The Pilgrimage of the Life of Man*
Gurevich, Aron 8
Guthlac, St. 196
Guthrie, Steve 193

Haidu, Peter 193
Hamilton, Lady Emma 10, 11
Hamilton, Sir William 10–13, 16, 17, 18, 19, 21, 26
Hanawalt, Barbara 183
Hanna, Ralph 86
Hardman, Phillipa 154
Havely, Nick 112
Heng, Geraldine 217
Henry IV, king of England 59, 216
Henry VIII, king of England 7
Henry of Derby *see* Henry IV, king of England
Henry of Grosmont, duke of Lancaster 140
Herford, William 274
Heriger of Lobbes 178
Herrad of Landsberg, *Hortus deliciarum* 168

Heywood, John 24; *The Foure PP* 25; *The Pardoner and the Friar* 25
Hilarius, *Exposicio himnorum* 168
Hill, Richard 172–73
Hirsh, John 266
History of Fulk FitzWarine, The 18
Hoccleve, Thomas 56, 58, 59, 60, 62, 63, 64–65, 66–71, 72, 74, 80, 96, 99, 100; *De regimine principum* 18; *Regiment of Princes* 56, 58, 59, 60, *61*, 63
Holbrook, Sue Ellen 271–72
Hollar, Wenceslas 156, *157*
Horobin, Simon 55, 57, 75–76, 86, 87, 88, 89, 92, 93, 94, 95, 98–99
Houwyk, John 97
"How the Good Wiff tauʒte Hir Douʒtir" 174–75
Hsy, Jonathan 270
Hugh of St. Victor 38–39
Hughes-Edwards, Marie 193
Humbert of Romans 215
Husserl 160

Ingleby, H. 273

Jack Upland 44
James, St. 4
Jean de Meun *see Roman de la rose, Le*
Jean de Vignay 141
Jean, duke of Berry 142, 152, 153, 154–55
Jeanne d'Armagnac 142
Jefferson, Judith 63–64
Jenkins, Ian and Kim Sloan, *Vases and Volcanoes: Sir William Hamilton and His Collection* 12
Jennings, Hargrave 16
Jerome, *Adversus Jovinianum* 246–47, 252; *Contra Jovinianum see* Jerome, *Adversus Jovinianum*
Joan of Kent 145
John of Gaunt 135, 136, 140, 143, 147–49, 151, 152–53, 154–56, *157*, 216–17
John of Lancaster, duke of Bedford 59
John of Northampton 55, 83, 98
Johns, Catherine 4–5, 7–8, 10, 21
Johnson, Eleanor, *Practicing Literary Theory in the Middle Ages: Ethics and the*

INDEX

Mixed Form in Chaucer, Gower, Usk, and Hoccleve 296–300
Jones, Karen 184
Joyce, James 17
Julian of Norwich 47, 48; *Revelation of Love* 40–41
Juvenal, *Satires* 178

Kaeuper, Richard 193
Kane, George 85
Kao, Wan-Chuan 248
Kedar, Benjamin Z. 215
Kelly, Henry Ansgar 217
Kelly, Jason M. 15
Kelom, Martin 77, 79
Kempe, John (father-in-law of Margery Kempe) 261
Kempe, John (husband of Margery Kempe) 261, 278
Kempe, John (son[?] of Margery Kempe) 260–62, 263–66, 267, 268–71, 277, 278, 279, 282–83
Kempe, Margery 261, 263, 264, 265–67, 274–77; *The Book of Margery Kempe* 149, 257–60, 265–72, 269, 275–79, 280–81
Kenne, John 97
Kerby-Fulton, Kathryn 57–58, 86
Killick, Helen 59
King of Tars, The 208, 217–18, 219
Kirkham, Victoria 236
Knapp, Peggy 166
Knapton, George 16
Knight, Richard Payne, 'The Worship of Priapus' 14, 16, 17, 18, 19; and Thomas Wright, *Sexual Symbolism: A History of Phallic Worship* 11, 12–13, 18, 20
Kolve, V. A. 103, 126
Kruger, Steven F. 218
Kynge Alisaunder 164
Kyverton, William 273

Lambert of Maastricht, St. 178
Langland, William 41, 56, 57, 87, 92, 95; *Piers Plowman* 18, 47–48, 50, 52, 55–56, 58, 75–76, 81–82, 83, 84–85, 87, 88, 90, 91, 92, 94, 98, 99, 111, 158–59, 189

Lantern of Light, The 50
Laskaya, Anne 212
Latini, Brunetto 179
Lawrence, D. H. 17
Le Palmer, James, *Omne bonum* 168
Levinson, Barry *see Good Morning Vietnam*
Lewys, Agnes 184–85
Lewys, Thomas 184–85
Lincoln, Abraham 32
Llull, Ramon 214
Longfellow, Henry Wadsworth 141
Loomis, Roger Sherman 210
Lorris, Guillaume de 134, 135, 136; *see also Roman de la rose, Le*
Lubac, Henri de, *Exégèse médiévale* 35
Lucan, *De bello civili* 241; *Pharsalia see* Lucan, *De bello civili*
Lucian 23
Luttrell Psalter *122, 123*
Lydgate, John 46; *Lives of Saints Edmund and Fremund* 210; *Pilgrimage of the Life of Man* 166–67
Lyons, Richard 146, 149

Machaut, Guillaume de 134, 135, 136, 137, 142; *Dit de la fonteinne amoureuse* 137, 142, 150, 152, 154, 159; *Dit dou Lyon* 152; *Le jugement dou roy de Behaigne* 137, 138, 152
Macrobius 53
Malory, Thomas, *Morte d'Arthur* 18
Manly, John M. 252
Marchaunt, John 56
Marguerite of Provence 186
Markus, Robert 218
Martianus Capella, *De nuptiis* 167
Marzec, Marcia Smith 59–62
Matthews, David, *Medievalism: A Critical History* 301–4
Maty, Paul Henry 14
Meech, Sanford 279–80
Meyer-Lee, Robert J. 131
Middle English Dictionary 212–13, 245
Middleton, Conyers 11; *Letter from Rome, shewing an exact conformity between popery and paganism* 12
Milton, John 46
Minney, Frank 19
Minnis, Alastair, *The Cambridge Introduction to Chaucer* 305–7

Mirk, John, *Festial* 200–202
Mitchell-Smith, Ilan 211
Monk of Saint-Denys 156
Montagu, Richard, *New Gag* 42
Montaño, Jesus 207–8
Mooney, Linne 55, 57–59, 60–63, 67–68, 69–71, 72, 73–79, 83, 84, 86, 87, 88, 89, 92, 93, 95, 97; "Chaucer's Scribe" 57; and Estelle Stubbs, *Scribes and the City: London Guildhall Clerks and the Dissemination of Middle English Literature, 1375–1425* 99
More, Sir Thomas 5, 6, 8, 10, 24, 25, 26; *The Confutation of Tyndale's Answer* 45; *Dialogue Concerning Heresies* 5, 6, 7, 8–9, 23–24; *Utopia* 23
Morgan, Gerald 250
Morrison, Karl F. 199, 201, 203
Moule, Arthur Christopher 140
Mum and the Sothsegger 169
Muskham, Robert 75–76

N-Town Plays 277, 278
Nafde, Aditi 72
Neckam, Alexander, *De naturis rerum* 18
Nelson, Horatio, 1st Viscount Nelson 10
Niger, *Ars epistolam* 168
Nolan, Barbara 135
Nowlin, Steele 251

Oakeshott, R. Ewart 208
Odoric da Pordenone, *Les merveilles de la terre d'Outremer* 141
Organ, John 83, 90
Oswald, Dana 212, 224
Otuel a Knyght 208
Ovid 133, 137, 153, 156; *Fasti* 232; *Heroides* 33; *Metamorphoses* 123, 134, 138, 228–37, 238, 242, 243, 248, 251, 253, 255
Ovide moralisé 134, 138
Owl and the Nightingale, The 18
Oxford Dictionary of National Biography 57
Oxford English Dictionary 141

Pardonneur, le triacleur et la tavernière, Le 25
Parker, Kate 268
Parker, Patricia 223
Parkes, M. B. 66, 68, 85, 86, 87, 96

Parmonter, John 262, 273, 274
Pascual, Pedro 216
Paul, St. 199–202
Pearl 48, 130–31
Peers, John 189
Philip the Bold, duke of Burgundy 186
Philippa of Hainault 137
Philippe de Mézières 217
Phillips, Noelle 88
Pinkhurst, Adam 55–58, 72–81, 83, 84, 86, 88, 89, 90, 91–92, 94–95, 96–99, 100
Pinkhurst, Joanna 96, 97
Play of the Flood (Towneley) 173
Ploughman's Tale, The 41, 44
Prinart, Robert 260–61, 262, 263, 282–83
Pugh, Tyson, *Chaucer's (Anti-)Eroticism and the Queer Middle Ages* 307–11

Queen Mary Psalter 210
Quintilian 159
Quinze ioyes de mariage see De Worde, Wynkyn, *The Fiftene joyes of maryage*

Rambo, Lewis R. 219–20
Ratherius of Verona 178
Redford, Bruce 18, 19
Ricci, Lucia Battaglia 238
Rice, Nicole, ed., *Middle English Religious Writing in Practice: Texts, Readers, and Transformations* 311–14
Richard II, king of England 7, 97, 159
Richard Coer de Lyon 208, 209–10
Richard of St. Victor, *Benjamin Minor* 38
Rickert, Edith 252
Riddy, Felicity 156, 275–77
Riehle, Wolfgang, *The Secret Within: Hermits, Recluses and Spiritual Outsiders in Medieval England* 314–17
Robens, Margaret 185–86
Roberts, Jane 57–58, 77, 79, 86, 87, 92, 95, 97–98
Robertson, D. W. 154–55
Robertson, Kellie 113
Rodericus, *Speculum humane vite* 168
Roest, Bert 220–21
Roland and Vernagu 208

INDEX

Roman d'Alexandre 168; see also *Romance of Alexander*
Roman de la rose, Le (Guillaume de Lorris and Jean de Meun) 24, 52, 134, 137
Romance of Alexander 219; see also *Roman d'Alexandre*
Romance of the Rose, The (Guillaume de Lorris and Jean de Meun) see *Roman de la rose, Le*
Russell, Frederick H. 218

Salisbury, Eve 164, 212
Salomon and Marcolphus 174
Salter, David 199, 207
Salthows 265, 269, 278, 279
Saul of Tarsus see Paul, St.
Sayers, Edna 177
Scarry, Elaine 174
Scase, Wendy, ed., *The Making of the Vernon Manuscript: The Production and Contexts of Oxford, Bodleian Library, MS Eng. poet. a. 1* 317–21
Schroder, Johannes 261, 263, 282–83
Schulz, H. C. 65, 66
Scott, Ridley see *Gladiator* (Ridley Scott)
Seven Sages of Rome, The 18, 164
Shakespeare, William, *King Lear* 33
Sheppard, Stephen 186
Shirley, John 73, 81
Shklovsky, Viktor 277
Shutters, Lynn 221
Sigebert of Gembloux 178
Sir Ferumbras 208
Sir Gowther 195–99, 203–7, 210, 211–13, 217–18, 219, 220, 221–25
Six Ages of the World 209
Skeat, W. W. 140
Skoda, Hannah 184
Sloan, Kim see under Jenkins, Ian
Smalley, Beryl, *Study of the Bible in the Middle Ages* 35
Smith, D. Vance 150
Smith, Robert Douglas 209
Smith, Warren 250
Somerset, Fiona and Nicholas Watson, eds., *Truth and Tales: Cultural Mobility and Medieval Media* 321–25
Sontag, Susan 11, 16
South English Legendary 200

Spearing, A. C. 272
Speculum sacerdotale 200
Speght, Thomas 43
Spenser, Edmund, *The Faerie Queene* 51
Springwell, Robert see Spryngolde, Robert
Spryngolde, Robert 258, 271–73, 274–77, 278–79, 280–81
Stacy, Robin 183–84
Staley, Lynn, *The Island Garden* 161, 266
Statius 46
Stevenson, Jane 80
Stewart, Susan 235
Stowe, Harriet Beecher 53; *Uncle Tom's Cabin* 31–33
Strickland, Debra Higgs 209
Strohm, Paul 154; *Chaucer's Tale: 1386 and the Road to Canterbury* 325–28
Stubbs, Estelle 55, 57, 58–59, 75, 78, 83, 84, 95, 97; see also under Mooney, Linne
Swynford, Katherine 147, 149, 155
Synthen, *Composita verborum* 168
Szpiech, Ryan 202

Tale of Beryn 26
Taylor, Karla 102, 243–44
Taylor, Larissa 183
Thaisen, Jacob 92
Thierry of Chartres 167
Toky, Richard 146–47
Tolan, John Victor 214–15
Tracy, Larissa 193
Travis, Peter 151
Turville-Petre, Thorlac 93, 94
Tyndale, William 6, 9, 23–24, 42, 45

Uebel, Michael 204, 224
Ulfsson, Charles 259

Valcooch, Dirk 188–89
Valéry, St. 5–6, 7, 8, 9, 25
Van Dijk, Conrad, *John Gower and the Limits of the Law* 328–31
Van Engen, John 197, 220
Van Winkle, Rip 234
Vincent of Beauvais 190, 193; *De eruditione filiorum nobilium* 186–88
Virgil 46, 115

Wake, Joan 265
Wakelin, Daniel 69–70; *Scribal Correction*

and the Literary Craft: English Manuscripts 1375–1510 332–35
Wallace, David 244
Wallace-Hadrill, Andrew 231–32
Wallop, Sir John 185
Walsingham, Thomas 153
Walston of Bawburgh, St. 9
Walter, Henry 6
Watson, Henry 166
Watson, Nicholas 266–67, 268; *see also under* Somerset, Fiona
Weisl, Angela Jane 164, 171
Welde, John 67
Wesenham, John *see* Wesynham, John
Weston, Jessie, *From Ritual to Romance* 17
Wesynham, John 273, 274
Wharton, Edith 159
Whitman, Jon, ed., *Romance and History: Imagining Time from the Medieval to the Early Modern Period* 335–38
Whittinton, Robert 180

William of Saint-Amour, *De periculis novissimorum temporum* 50
William of Tyre, *History of Outremer* 209
Williams, Deanne 135–36
Wimsatt, James 137
Windeatt, Barry 273
Wright, Thomas 16, 18; "The Worship of the Generative Powers during the Middle Ages of Western Europe" 18, 19; *see also under* Knight, Richard Payne

Yeager, Stephen M., *From Lawmen to Plowmen: Anglo-Saxon Legal Tradition and the School of Langland* 338–41
Yeats, W. B. 17
Yevele, Henry 156

Zeeman, Nicolette *see under* Denery, Dallas D., II
Zissos, Andrew 231